# BOB HOPE ON TV

# BOB HOPE ON TV

## Thanks for the Video Memories

by Wesley Hyatt

BearManor Media
2018

*Bob Hope on TV: Thanks for the Video Memories*

© 2018 Wesley Hyatt

All rights reserved.

No portion of this publication may be reproduced, stored, and/or copied electronically (except for academic use as a source), nor transmitted in any form or by any means without the prior written permission of the publisher and/or author.

Published in the United States of America by:

BearManor Media
P. O. Box 71426
Albany, GA 31708

BearManorMedia.com

Printed in the United States.

Typesetting and layout by John Teehan

Cover Photo: Bob Hope during a taping of a 1970 TV special. Courtesy of Getty Images.

ISBN—978-1-62933-217-8

*To Linda Hill Guzman, former neighbor, longtime friend, full-time mother, and forever a great human being in my eyes.*

# Table of Contents

Acknowledgments ............................................................... ix

Preface ........................................................................... xiii

1. Introduction: How Bob Became a TV Fixture ................. 1
2. Specials – 1950s ...................................................... 31
3. Specials – 1960s ...................................................... 85
4. Specials – 1970s .................................................... 145
5. Specials – 1980s .................................................... 203
6. Specials – 1990s .................................................... 257
7. Awards and Telethon Shows .................................... 283
8. Talk Shows ............................................................ 303
9. Game Shows and Sports ......................................... 323
10. Guest Shots—Variety Series and Specials ................ 335
11. Guest Shots—Sitcoms, Dramas, and One TV-Movie and One Cartoon ................................................. 425
12. News, Informational, Documentary, Retrospective and Archival Shows ............................................... 455

Epilogue ....................................................................... 477

Bibliography ................................................................. 481

Index ............................................................................ 485

# Acknowledgments

**I WILL TRY TO RESIST THE URGE** of hearing Les Brown and His Band of Renown striking up a peppy rendition of "Thanks for the Memory" in the background as I list the following notable names with dates of their interviews with me and thank them for their time in sharing recollections and opinions: Neile Adams (May 2, 2017); Bob Alberti (Feb. 21, 2017); Howard Albrecht (March 11, 2017); Cynthia Bell (May 3, 2017); Guion Bluford (May 11, 2017); Millicent Brower (May 1, 2017); Jerry Burgan (April 21, 2017); Harry Wayne Casey (April 15, 2017); Kevin Carlisle (May 8, 2017); Shirley Cothran (May 13, 2017); Cathy Lee Crosby (May 11, 2017); George Foreman (May 3, 2017); Doug Gamble (Feb. 18, 2017); Marianne Gordon (April 18, 2017); Leila Josefowicz (May 10, 2017); Melodie Johnson Howe (April 22, 2017); Bob Keane (March 11, 2017); Buz Kohan (May 10, 2017); Bo Kaprall (May 19, 2017); Wendy Liebman (May 8, 2017); Trini Lopez (May 30, 2017); Gloria Loring (May 12, 2017); Robert L. Mills (May 20, 2017); Don Mischer (May 10, 2017); Mark Nizer (May 5, 2017); Marie Osmond (May 17, 2017); Gene Perret (May 16, 2017); Pat Priest (April 18, 2017); Gerald Rafshoon (May 10, 2017); Carolyn Raskin (May 5, 2017); Vivian Reed (May 10, 2017); Carol Siskind (May 9, 2017); Andrew Solt (May 16, 2017); Dodie Stevens (April 3, 2017); Leona Toppel (May 2, 2017); Donn Trenner (May 5, 2017); and Jo Anne Worley (May 17, 2017).

Additionally, I am indebted thoroughly for receiving a wonderful amount of access to research Bob Hope's video career at three invaluable resources. First, thanks go out to Rosemary Hanes, reference librarian for the Moving Image Section at the Library of Congress in Washington, D.C. In Los Angeles, Mark Quigley, manager of the Research & Study Center for UCLA Film & Television Archive, was helpful as ever in setting up my visit. Last but never least, I received invaluable insights as well as assistance from Martin Gostanian, the knowledgeable supervisor for visitors services at the Paley Center for Media offices in Beverly Hills, and Mark Ekman and Jane Klein, manager of group visits and manager of research services respectively for the Paley Center for Media branch in New York City. Jane also was kind enough to introduce me to Carl Unegbu, Esq., an attorney who has a blog, O'Carl's Law, covering the intersection of comedy with law (strange but true!), and he shared some helpful material too.

I also need to thank the following websites and archivist who allowed me access to their collection of Bob Hope-related videos: Lighthouse Media and Entertainment; Aaron Mintz; Premiere Opera; Bruce Remy; Bruce Simon; and 70s-TV.com. A special shout out goes to Phil Gries of Archival Television Audio, Inc., who was able to get me two audio recordings of shows I needed at the last minute.

The wonderful photos in this book comes courtesy of the private collections of Gloria Loring and John Bernards (thank you both!) and Getty Images. Jill Jokisch, a customer service associate with the latter, helped me secure permission to use these pictures of Bob's TV career.

One of the benefits of being a regular interviewee on Stu's Show on the Internet for Stu Shostak (along with Professor Steve Beverly) has been developing great personal and professional relationships with other classic TV enthusiasts. These include Matt Ottinger, Rick Scheckman, and Randy West, all of whom helped me a lot in the seemingly never-ending research needed to make this book the best it can be. I thank all of those gentlemen.

When researching a performer with hundreds of TV performances by trying to watch as many as possible, confirm facts and figures and set up interviews for further verification, one has to sacrifice some quality time with others in his or her life in order to get the job done. So, with that noted, to Gayle Willard Hyatt, Art Callahan, LuAnn Hyatt Martinson, Skip Martinson, Bennett Martinson, Brynn Martinson, GerShun Avilez, John Bowser, Marion Carter, Todd Day, Renee Duncan, Julie Ellis, Ed Emory, Anthony Evans, Kevin Grady, David Guinnup, Linda Hill Guzman, Jeff Johnson, Jimmy Lancaster, Reggie Shuford, Desmond Sutton, Drew Trescone, and Joe Watkins, to paraphrase a certain tune, I thank you so much for understanding when work on this book took temporary priority over my abiding friendship and love for you all. I think when reading this, you will see the results of my labor.

I did try to interview Linda Hope, Bob's daughter, who runs her late father's charitable operations, but unfortunately, she was busy with handling his estate, a story that will be explained in more detail in the concluding chapter. I regret that we were unable to connect and hope that she will find this assessment of his considerable impact on TV faithfully reflects what he was trying to accomplish, as will other readers of this book.

# Preface

**THE NUMBERS STUNNED THE INDUSTRY.**

The 46.6 rating meant that nearly half of all homes in America with TV sets were watching. That's counting ones not using watching TV at the time too. And the 64 share meant that of all homes that did have their TVs on, nearly two-thirds of them were viewing this show.

The only shows that scored higher numbers than these were special events that aired on all the TV networks without commercials, like the assassination of President John F. Kennedy in 1963 and men walking on the moon in 1969. In contrast, this was just an entertainment program airing on one network on Jan. 15, 1970.

The show was *Chrysler Presents The Bob Hope Christmas Special: Around the World with the USO*, although most people including those in the industry referred to it as *The Bob Hope Christmas Special*. Its star had been a featured attraction for the NBC television network for twenty years and on NBC radio for more than ten years before that. And while Bob Hope certainly was well loved by the American public, no one had predicted this would be the highest-rated entertainment show in the medium's history up to that point.

One reason was competition. At the time, TV viewers could only choose between NBC, ABC and CBS in most markets (as well as noncommercial public television and a few independent stations in bigger markets, but the effects of those were negligible in the national ratings). On the night *The Bob Hope Christmas Special* aired, *Bewitched* on ABC was that network's top situation comedy, while *The Jim Nabors Hour* on CBS was a prime ratings contender as well, usually in the top thirty. This time slot looked like an imposing position for Bob to get a large audience.

Another was the show's content. This was the sixth annual visit Bob made to provide live entertainment via the United States Organizations, better known as the USO, to troops in the ongoing Vietnam War, which continued to be unpopular back home. There was every reason to suspect people were fatiguing of just the mention of the bloody conflict, which seemed to have no end in sight.

Then there was the guest list. Sure, Neil Armstrong was the first man on the moon just a few months earlier, but he had been interviewed and seen on TV previously. Teresa Graves was a regular on TV's number one series, *Rowan and Martin's Laugh-In*, but not its star attraction. It had been at least three years since singer/actress Connie Stevens had done a movie and longer than that for a regular TV series or hit record, while foreign actress Romy Schneider was largely unknown to most Americans. As for the Piero Brothers and Miss World Eva Rueber-Staier, they were as obscure then as they are now.

Yet Bob—who was executive producer as well as star of his show, a rarity among TV comedians—had crafted a show designed to attract eyeballs in spite of its perceived obstacles. He made a special performance before President Richard Nixon in December 1969 to kick off his overseas tour, which gained the project free advance publicity, and designed the trek to go throughout the world to glamour spots like Berlin and Rome, not just in Vietnam. Bob also did his customary promotion of the show in advance of its airing on TV talk and news shows. And he was on a roll too, as seven of his nine specials during the 1969-1970 television season, including this one, ranked among the top eleven specials of the year. He clearly was tapping into America's desire to laugh amid bad news with a familiar, comforting face.

For Bob, this ratings landmark was something of a bittersweet accomplishment. On the positive side, it confirmed his status as a leading entertainer as he was nearly in his seventies, an impressive accomplishment in the increasingly youth-obsessed world of show business. While most of his contemporaries were retired or scrambling for work, Bob was assured of his place in television.

It also showed that he remained popular with the younger generation of soldiers, even though many were the sons of men he had entertained first in World War II. Going to see Bob perform was a big deal to many of them, including future astronaut Guion Bluford. "I was in Cameron Bay in Vietnam in 1966, 1967," he says. "Bob did a Vietnam tour, he came on Cameron Bay there, and I saw him briefly in camp, but unfortunately I couldn't see his show because I was a fighter pilot on alert duty. I had to be ready to scramble F-4s if needed. I missed the program, which pissed me off, but that's life." He had no idea that he would later appear on one of Bob's specials as a guest in 1983.

The success also gave Bob favorable media coverage after months of unprecedented negative headlines for someone who consistently ranked as one of the most-loved entertainers in America. For one, reports came out that Bob had his regular stable of writers provide jokes for Vice President Spiro Agnew to bolster the latter's combative public image, calling into question Bob's proclaimed apolitical approach to comedy.

He also felt so upset for what he thought was inaccurate reporting of the Vietnam War that he took the unprecedented step of opening the gated doors to his home in Toluca Lake, California, on Nov. 12, 1969, to hold a press conference. Bob called out his home network's division of NBC News in particular to claim its stories about racial disparities in treatment of combat soldiers was wrong. Such defenses about what was occurring in Vietnam led some to label Bob a warmonger.

"There were some that say he was a hawk during the war, and I don't believe that," says Gene Perret, who wrote for Bob from the 1970s through 1990s. "His feeling was 'These guys are over there, fighting there for our country.' It was in support of people who were as much a victim as anyone else."

The ratings also were vindication for most of Hope's writers of the time, almost all of whom had been with him for at least a decade, usually more than that, and whose contributions Bob relied on extensively for the special. Lester White began writing for Hope when the latter was in vaudeville. When Bob went into radio full time in 1937, Norman Sullivan joined him and worked only on his monologues. Mort Lachman, who would direct the overseas Christmas specials as well as produce Bob's specials overall starting in 1964, started doing Bob's radio show in the 1940s.

Others joined Hope during the early 1950s on TV, including Lachman's writing partner Bill Larkin and British-born Charlie Lee, who wrote solo until paired in 1964 with occasional contributor turned regular writer Gig Henry. Lester White's writing partner had been Johnny Rapp for at least fifteen years until 1968, when Lester worked a year with Larry Rhine and then Mel Tolkin effective the fall of 1969.

Tolkin described his activities for Bob to Tom Stempel in *Storytellers to the Nation: A History of American Television Writing* thusly: "You work not only for his specials, you work for his gigs, his trips to Vietnam and Korea. You work on dinners, gigs in honor of somebody, charity gigs. Wherever he is, we get a poop sheet that we write jokes [from], who's on the dais, something about the man being honored, the occasion, areas for comedy... and of course the poop about the places, Vietnam and Korea, the temperature, the animals around, what the soldiers eat, where they hang out."

Despite having such insights provided, the writers' gag lines on the special did not always pan out. Bob found mixed reception at best to jokes about the new draft lottery system and the Paris peace talks. Clearly, the rank and file were sick of hearing about the progress of the war—or the lack of it—as much as being part of it.

In addition, Bob faced the toughest reception he ever encountered among usually friendly soldiers watching the performances before and during Christmas in 1969 (Bob and crew edited footage from several shows filmed along with visits with officials for use in the annual specials). The worst was in Lai Khe, where soldiers booed him heartily for saying President Nixon would bring them home soon and kept doing so as he brought out other performers on stage with him. It took Connie Stevens singing "Silent Night" to calm everyone down finally.

Indeed, for the performers joining Bob on his Vietnam shows, it was not a glamourous excursion. "It was very intense, because we went around the world in two weeks, and one woman came off the plane in a stretcher at the end," notes Gloria Loring, who toured with Bob in Christmas of 1970. She herself got so sick at one point that "In Thailand, when they were going to do a canal tour, I couldn't even raise my head off my pillow." Per Bob, they had to visit the wounded as part of their itinerary. "Going to the hospital ships, that was heartbreaking," Loring says.

Yet in spite of all the inconveniences—including having to ride in a cavernous C-130 aircraft she says troupe members nicknamed "the pregnant duck"—Loring was proud to do the show even for a war that was unpopular. She says her mindset was, "This is not about politics, this is about men and women who've served our country, and it's the least I can do. Being there was an extraordinary honor, and so memorable. It was an honor and a pleasure to be part of his special."

Bob also had faced personal tragedy prior to the 1969 trip. His oldest and youngest brother died within a week of each other in June 1969. The youngest, George Hope, had been production coordinator for Bob's specials until he died of cancer at age fifty-nine.

Indeed, it had been a tumultuous year for Bob prior to this show, starting with his previous Christmas special on Jan. 16, 1969, which had a very high rating itself (38.5) and featured a lot of famous names popping up announced during the trek to Vietnam. These included actor Roger

Smith (husband of Ann-Margret, the show's featured guest star); another USO entourage led by Johnny Grant with actresses Carolyn Devore, Sherry Alberoni, Monica Peterson, and Brenda Dickson; and most shockingly to modern viewers Adm. James S. McCain, whose son John McCain was a Naval flyer shot down over Hanoi and taken as a war prisoner. "Everybody pays in this conflict," Hope grimly states in recounting the facts on the special. John McCain would be released in 1973 and later become a U.S. Senator for Arizona and the 2008 Republican candidate for president.

Bob's son Kelly also appears when Bob entertains wounded warriors at the tour's start in Japan. When everyone returns, California Gov. Ronald Reagan and his wife, Nancy Reagan, greets them along with Bob's wife Delores. It is so star-studded one nearly forgets that the war remained very unpopular at home.

As for his part, Bob is in fine form and even able to ad-lib well. For example, when it rains heavily on one stage, he mockingly asks, "Where's Billy Graham when you need him?" Playing often on his cowardly image there, he notes, "I carry a cross, a St. Christopher medal and a Star of David. When I go, I'm gonna blame everybody!"

Bob got nearly as a high rating (34.9) for his next special on Feb. 17, 1969, but his performance was not as strong, as usually was the case with his shows taped in a studio. He does have a clever opening joke of "I think it's a big break for us following the program our president got his start on," referring to President Richard Nixon's cameo on *Rowan and Martin's Laugh-In*, which leads into this special. But the rest of his monologue was forgettable, and Bob used the vaudeville setup of program to let his guest carry more of the show than himself.

For example, Diana Ross and the Supremes get to sing not their usual one but two songs here, "Cornet Man" in shimmering gowns and "Sam You Made the Pants Too Long" in hobo outfits. Later Diana has a solo number, "My Man," which like the other two was first popularized by Barbra Streisand. To his credit, Bob comes out and wraps his arms around her to sing and dance with her, displaying a form of interracial affection previously taboo on television, but he undercuts the romantic mood by crooning several tunes about himself, like "I'm So Pretty."

His next special on March 19, 1969, is more typical of what was great about Hope on TV and what often disappointed. On the plus side was his annual grousing about not getting a nod for the Academy Awards. "The Oscar nominations are out, so I know what I'm giving up for Lent," he begins and adds, "I never thought the day would come that I would wish I was Rosemary's Baby." Bob humorously follows it up by comparing himself to Best Actress nominee Barbra Streisand in the proboscis department (his has been most often called "ski-sloped"): "Six nominations for *Funny Girl* and none for me—is it my fault because my nose took the wrong off ramp?"

On the downside, Bob makes a joke involving Phyllis Diller's looks that was one of his tired go-to ploys to imply ugliness. He also promoted another of his pictures (*How to Commit Marriage*), which is common practice for him, but what makes the plugging irritating this time is his moralizing joke of "It's a new concept in films. We all wear clothes."

Worst of all is his sexist jokes about a recent development at the Santa Anita Park racetrack in California: "A girl jockey won a race. Imagine that, girl jockeys! It'll certainly going to make the daily double a lot more interesting. I guess they've been accepted. The racing form now has a centerfold." He then implies that the horse thought the jockey was a man in drag and throws in another dated gender stereotype with "The other day at Santa Anita, the announcer yelled, 'They're off.' And the girl jockey wouldn't come out of the gate." This sort of material would peg Bob as old-fashioned and even reactionary among younger viewers, but nevertheless he kept doing material in the same vein for more than a decade afterward.

He got even more political on his season ender on April 17, 1969, only half-joking railing against certain members of the younger generation. "I was going to spend my vacation laying around Palm Springs, but it's going to pot ... Ten thousand hippies invaded the desert, and the gophers went crazy. The first time they ever smelled grass!" Once again, he came off as a little square by citing the permissiveness in films as part of his routine. "They were even dancing in the nude, but the cops didn't do anything. They thought it was just another movie company on location." He threw in a little xenophobia to conclude it with "The Indians got mad at the hippies because they couldn't tell which ones were the squaws. Until they took their clothes off. Still they weren't sure."

Later in that same show, Bob introduces Sergio Mendes by noting that "his unique and delightful sound is such a change, a pleasant change, from the dissonance that passes for music today." When did Bob become a music critic, and why should his opinion on it matter? He is not helping his case of a being a contemporary authority in the field by booking on the same show singer Patti Page, who had not had a hit in four years and would never make the pop charts again.

At the end of the show, Bob praises recently deceased former President Dwight Eisenhower and feels compelled to drop in the following: "In the last few years, our problems at home puzzled him a lot, because he was a man of discipline. And he couldn't understand citizens of this country who were reckless with their responsibilities." It was another swipe implied at those against the Establishment, and it was totally unnecessary.

Bob returns five months later and garners an impressive 31.9 rating, in part because it uses the format of *Rowan and Martin's Laugh-In* and even includes that show's stars in cameos. Clearly, and somewhat frustratingly, Bob was following trends on TV rather than setting them. He is both sentimental in a funny way about his long career ("When I started, NBC had a crystal set and a peacock egg. I sang on one and sat on the other.") while still being dismissive of the youth protest movement. Discussing the Woodstock rock concert, Bob quips, "When the cows got through eating the grass that was thrown away on the grass, they were so high, you had to climb a ladder to milk them… Some of the hippies tore off their clothes but they weren't arrested. They were still wearing a layer of dirt."

Still, Bob does try to keep things current and clever, so he employs Tom and Dick Smothers in inserts, watching the show and commenting on its theme of censorship. At one point, they wonder why they are no longer on network TV and muse maybe they'll be the summer replacement for *Hee Haw*, which actually was their summer replacement in 1969. It is smart comedy, but unfortunately it is paired with bits like Jack Carter and Soupy Sales playing astronauts about to stand on the moon. "It's not as bad as Burbank!" Jack exclaims before they find a 40-foot woman standing near them (amid bad special effects) who to their joy captures them. This stale stuff could have been done on TV twenty years earlier.

However, the 1970 Christmas special victory overshadowed all the shortcomings of the past months. Bob now held the record for the highest-rated TV show ever and went on emboldened with the triumph. His ratings stayed high the rest of the year, and when he did his next Christmas show on Jan. 14, 1971, he nearly matched what he did twelve months earlier with a 44.3 rating.

Those two shows held the record as the two highest-rated TV entertainment programs of all time until the network premiere of *Gone with the Wind* on NBC on Nov. 7, 1976 eclipsed them with a 47.7 rating. Coincidentally, Bob hosted the Oscars ceremony on radio in 1940 when *Gone with the Wind* won Best Picture.

Bob would continue to star on his own specials on television twenty years after *Gone with the Wind* set the new ratings record (a few other programs would later surpass it). By the time he retired in 1996, Bob had appeared in nearly 300 specials of his own, guest starred on nearly 200 other variety series and specials, shown up on hundreds of talk shows, hosted the Academy Awards thirteen times, acted in more than thirty TV sitcoms and dramas, and received more on-air tributes honoring his work than any other person.

Most impressively, Bob did all this while remaining an A-list star throughout his forty-six years on the medium. He entered TV as a superstar, and he left it as one too. It's a feat that has never been duplicated and most likely never will be. Cumulatively, Bob Hope set unprecedented accomplishments on television that have yet to be fully celebrated.

Until now.

# 1 Introduction: How Bob Became a TV Fixture

**WHILE HIS BIOGRAPHERS** have their disagreements, one thing they all agree on is this: Bob Hope made his television debut on April 9, 1950.

Unless one considers his appearance on *The Ed Sullivan Show* (then known as *The Toast of the Town*) on Sept. 27, 1948. That was on a network too, albeit just to a few cities in the Northeast. However, it was a guest shot, so it is not really a debut, right?

Oh wait, Bob did the opening ceremonies for the KTLA TV station in Los Angeles in 1947. Maybe that is the one that should count? After all, he did it for his movie studio, Paramount, and the occasion has been saved on film. Then again, it was only a local appearance, so maybe not?

There is one more claimant here. Sometime between August and November 1932, Bob joined his fellow vaudevillians Lulu McConnell and Willie Howard to appear before the experimental TV station W2AXB in New York City. Given the intense heating of the lighting and need to stand carefully to be seen with just one camera, it is no wonder that Bob delayed doing another appearance in the medium for fifteen years.

In any event, let's go with 1950. By then, Bob was feeling pressure to take part in the medium because Milton Berle, a comedian who never had success in radio, suddenly became TV's biggest superstar and began challenging Bob's status as America's favorite comedian. It is not like Bob needed the money to do television either—both *Time* and *Newsweek* labelled him a millionaire by 1949, the equivalent of more than $10 million in 2017.

The real reason was that it was virtually the only facet of the entertainment industry he had yet to conquer within his first fifty years of life. Born on May 29, 1903 in England, he was christened Leslie Townes Hope, the fifth of six sons born in his family. The brothers born immediately

Bob Hope talks casually to military officials between performances in Vietnam for troops in December 1970 as part of the filming for *The Bob Hope Christmas Special: Around the Globe with the USO*. Courtesy of Gloria Loring.

before and after him, Jack Hope and George Hope respectively, would later work for him on TV.

Bob moved with his family to Cleveland, Ohio, when he was four, as his father hoped to find more opportunity for them there. Growing up, he got tired of being teased for his name and adopted the more American-friendly moniker of Bob Hope by the time he was a teenager. After an abortive amateur boxing career calling himself "Packy West," Bob began dancing and singing for pennies on Cleveland street corners by the early 1920s. Intrigued by the stage, he finally made a go of it professionally there in 1923, teaming with Lloyd "Lefty" Durbin to do a comedy and dance act as part of the show for comedian Roscoe "Fatty" Arbuckle in Cleveland. Arbuckle liked what the duo did and recommended them to vaudeville producer Fred Hurley, who set them up as part of his Midwestern vaudevillian revue.

From there, Bob's career in show business progressed somewhat shakily, as Durbin died of tuberculosis and Bob got a new partner, George Byrne. They did well enough that by 1927, they broke into Broadway as a featured act as part of a musical called *Sidewalks of New York*. Near the end of that year, Bob went solo and had an increasingly successful career as a vaudeville emcee before winning a supporting role in a Broadway musical called *Roberta* in 1933, which contained a song that became a standard, "Smoke Gets in Your Eyes."

Bob got three more Broadway shows under his belt through *Ziegfeld Follies of 1936*, where he received praise as the comic highlight of the revue. After it ended in 1937, Bob became part of his first radio show, serving as host of *The Rippling Rhythm Revue*. Shortly after that began, he moved to Hollywood to appear in his first feature-length film, *The Big Broadcast of 1938*, where he starred opposite Shirley Ross. Playing a divorced couple, the two have a bittersweet love ballad expressing how much they still care for each other, "Thanks for the Memory."

"Thanks for the Memory" won the Oscar for Best Song and became Bob's theme for his radio series, *The Pepsodent Show*, which started in the fall of 1938 after his *The Rippling Rhythm Revue* (and another subsequent series, *Your Hollywood Parade*) went off the air after a few months in the preceding 1937-1938 season. *The Pepsodent Show* caught on well in part due to Jerry Colonna, a wild-eyed, manic comic and singer with a walrus mustache who would stay with Hope through TV until a stroke in 1966 and occasionally thereafter, always with the cameras avoiding his disabled left arm.

*The Pepsodent Show* was a bigger hit than *The Big Broadcast of 1938*, and Bob did not succeed in movies until the 1940s, particularly when teamed with Bing Crosby and Dorothy Lamour in the "Road" movies starting with *The Road to Singapore* in 1940. Crosby became a punchline for Hope for their work together for years afterward on TV, from his singing to his personal life.

All told, becoming an established entertainer was rockier for him than how George C. Scott blithely summarized Bob's achievements on the 1978 TV special *Happy Birthday Bob*: "He went into vaudeville in 1924, radio in 1937, films in 1938, television in 1950, and rose to the top of all of those fields." He had to fight to get into all of them except TV.

**Dipping Into the Boob Tube**

By the time 1950 rolled around, Bob ranked among the top ten movie actors in America and hosted a weekly radio show that was in the top ten as well. No one else ever held that distinction, so he was highly in demand to do television, where it was thought his talents would be a natural for the medium.

However, it took some coaxing to get Bob into TV. Hugh Davis, an executive vice president of the ad agency Foote, Cone and Belding, approached Bob in early 1950 with an offer from one of his clients, Frigidaire, an appliance manufacturer, to sponsor a comedy variety special on TV with him as host. Bob said he'd do it only for $50,000 for himself, an unprecedented sum at the time. He received a counteroffer a few days later from Davis to do one show for $40,000 and said yes. Bob eventually agreed to do four additional shows for Frigidaire a total of $150,000.

While there were mixed reviews for that first show, Jack Gould in *The New York Times* loved it, and his rave review was reprinted in trade publications. And it got lots of viewers too. Its full story will be told in the next chapter.

From that debut, the rush for Bob was on. He would appear on the medium as a headliner for an unprecedented forty-six years, despite some critical and popularity downturns. Much of it had to do with his reputation as being a top comedy monologist, a talent with which he used to launch almost all of his TV specials.

From left to right, Teresa Graves, Bobbi Martin, and Gloria Loring entertain the troops as part of *The Bob Hope Christmas Special: Around the Globe with the USO*, a show that aired Jan. 14, 1971 to one of the biggest TV audiences ever. Courtesy of Gloria Loring.

## The Master of the Monologue

How crucial was the monologue to Bob's success? Consider an unlikely and overlooked showcase of Bob in his element, the now virtually forgotten special *The 1974 Las Vegas Entertainment Awards*. Hope killed, as the saying goes when a comedian is on a roll with constant laughs in his set, even though he never starred in concert in Vegas (nobody was willing to pay his high requested fee, even given Hope's popularity). A little joke-by-joke analysis shows some of the basic principles Bob used to evoke howls.

It starts after some scantily clad female dancers finish their routines, then Bob strides onstage and quips, "Thank you, fellows." This slays the audience, as the contrast between what "fellows" normally do at work and how these ladies shimmy is very distinct.

Bob continues with "You know, Vegas started out as a watering hole. Now it's a milking station." Laughs ensue because those in attendance know how the gambling Mecca does a fine job of "milking" money from patrons who largely lose playing the games.

"This is one of the few places left where you can get three lemons for a nickel," he adds. The comedy here infers inflation while referencing a familiar result one sees when playing slot machines. It's timely as well as funny, a mark of many of Bob's best jokes.

The area's shady, go-for-broke atmosphere plays into Bob when he says, "So far, we've had to buy the [TV] cameras back five times." So does the town's reputation for sexual conquests by older men with younger women. He gets applause after noting, "We're coming to you from Caesars Palace. It's a family hotel. Every guy you meet here is with his niece."

Next comes one superbly constructed joke. "Around here, if you see a man naked running through the lobby, he's either a streaker, a loser or his wife arrived a day early." In one sentence, Bob gets in a reference to a current trend along with previous mentions of gambling and sexual misadventure. This is so tightly written and well-delivered by Bob that he even grins to bask in its strong reception.

More licentious behavior is implied by gags after that. "I think I have Caesar's suite. I found Cleopatra's girdle under the bed. The suites are really so luxurious. They have mirrors on the wall, mirrors on the ceiling, in case you've got a stiff neck." Delivering that last line, Bob gives a deadpan stare into the camera to indicate he really means something else he can't say, producing more audience hysteria.

Bob follows this with comments that draw truthful, relatable visuals—and therefore hearty chuckles—among the regulars in Vegas. "And a lot of women spend all day here playing the slot machines. They're easy to spot. They're four feet eleven with arms six feet long. And they're really weird. Where else do you see a woman slathered in diamonds and mink absolutely ecstatic because she just won twelve nickels?!"

He also references both the reputed mob influence and rich payouts to entertainers associated with Sin City. "They treat their stars like kings out here. When Tony Bennett left his heart in San Francisco, they sent a couple of boys to pick it up. And I don't know what they pay (Frank) Sinatra, but he just put a down payment on Australia."

Bob's rapturous reception continues as he discusses the competitive mood for the awards backstage and indicts himself as wanting a statuette too. "I've never seen so much swearing and scratching. I don't have a fingernail left." The desire for such public recognition is a staple of Bob's comedic repertoire.

He even gets off one joke mentioning the community's top grossing act along with inferring sexual lasciviousness once again. "Vegas has more beautiful girls than any other city in the world. At least that's what Elvis (Presley) told me when I stopped to see him in the rest home."

Even more material scores before the monologue ends. Bob jokes about his cheapness when gambling by saying, "When I'm down three dollars, I look like I'm in the middle of open heart surgery." A few other contemporary references occur too: "I use so much artificial sweetener, I now have artificial diabetes."

It's simply one of Bob's finest sets ever, and he follows it with great interplay in introducing the presenters. Bob counted on such monologues to set a jovial mood for what followed on his TV series, and they usually were the strongest and best parts of his shows (cynics might say the only good aspect of them).

Part of its appeal was Bob's rat-a-tat-tat delivery that gave him the nickname "Rapid Robert." Only a few other comics like Phyllis Diller, Rodney Dangerfield, Henny Youngman, and Milton Berle could match him, and there were substantial differences. Diller and Dangerfield's material sounded much more autobiographical than Bob's. Youngman relied on his screeching violin to punctuate his concise one liners. Berle had an aggressive approach to his audience in getting laughs. Bob almost always had the audience in the palm of his hand. He was one of a kind.

Steve Allen, in his 1982 critical assessment of comedians, *More Funny People*, credits Bob for knowing how to craft some of the best monologues ever. "Like Jack Benny, he has a superb editorial sense. He will sometimes take a dozen or more pages of jokes contributed by some of the best gag-writers in the business, read quickly through them, and, in just a few minutes, select those that are best for him. He would not argue that they are necessarily the best per se, merely that they are lines that he feels comfortable with, that he believes will make his audience laugh."

Sherwood Schwartz, who joined Bob's radio show in 1943 after writing jokes for his older brother Al Schwartz to share with Bob (Al would stay to do Bob's first TV shows), astutely recalled how to write for his boss to Jordan R. Young in *The Laugh Crafters: Comedy Writing in Radio and TV's Golden Age*. "Superfluous words were killed off, immediately—Hope had no use for them. He had a rhythm in his speech, and you learned that rhythm. An extra 'the' was cut out. You learned to write bare bones kind of dialogue. No fat."

Indeed, long before the *USA Today* newspaper set the standard in the 1980s of no more than twenty-five words in its articles' ledes (opening sentences), Bob followed that practice religiously. He sought the shortest time possible between the setup and the punchline for each joke. Writers who learned that trick would find themselves a steady employer with Bob.

**Writing for Bob**

From the start of his radio show in 1938, Bob depended on a larger staff of regular writers than other comedians to condense their work into what he thought was the best of each for him to use on air. One radio writer to make the transfer to TV was Larry Gelbart, who joined Hope's show in 1948 and worked together with Larry Marks as one of six staff writers.

"For Hope, this was almost a skeleton crew; in previous years, he had employed up to a dozen or so writers, all working at the same time turning out his material," Gelbart said in his autobiography, *Laughing Matters*. He learned that Hope expected to reach him 24/7 by telephone whenever he needed help and have as many jokes as possible for his boss.

The monologue process Gelbart outlined for Bob remained fairly consistent over the years. Howard Albrecht, who wrote for Bob in the

1970s, describes the process thusly: "A week before taping, we'd get a list of about ten topics he wanted to address for the monologue. You'd write two to four jokes for each topic. We would have thirty-five to forty jokes total. They'd have an entire script of all these jokes from the writers for Bob to review. He would read jokes three times to see if he liked them. He'd end up with thirty to forty jokes."

By the 1960s, Bob read those jokes before a studio audience for forty minutes. Typically these audiences were ones held over from a taping of *The Tonight Show Starring Johnny Carson* in Burbank, California, when Carson moved the show there permanently in 1972. "The folks in the audience were usually thrilled to get treated to an extra added attraction," says Gene Perret, a regular Hope writer in the 1980s and 1990s. "Carson would leave, and they would have the bonus of Bob Hope doing his opening gags."

The ones with the best reactions made the seven- to eight-minute set (on average) on the show that aired. Albrecht said he used a little secret when doing jokes for his boss: "Bob Hope liked to say the word 'mukluks,' so we would work that in when we could."

When it came to shows outside Los Angeles, Bob expected his writers to include plenty of jokes in his monologues about the area surrounding the venue he was playing, whether it was Phoenix or Fiji. "Hope had learned from the military shows to tailor his stuff for each ship or base we'd visit," says Robert L. "Bob" Mills, who wrote for Bob from 1977-1992. "We received filled out questionnaires that had been sent ahead in advance. So we had specific names, events, bars, etc., to make fun of."

"We had to research the old-fashioned way," adds Perret. "I might pick up a book on travel to Tahiti and see the local attraction, but also the color. What drink is big in Tahiti? Where are the hot spots?"

Perret says Bob's production company helped out too. "His PR team would call people and get input. They had newspaper connections, things happening in town." When performing before soldiers at a camp, "We'd get a lot of input from the military, loose-leaf books about an inch thick with background information."

It could tough for the writers to endure watching their efforts on their monologue during tapings. Mort Lachman, Bob's head writer and later producer from 1950-1975, commented in a 1961 documentary by NBC News on its *Project Twenty* series of specials titled "The World of Bob Hope" that he and his fellow scripters not only heard their jokes bomb, meaning they wouldn't appear on air, but also Bob coming with something off the cuff that did score with the studio audience. "The minute they know it's an ad lib, they fly off and all laugh and scream, and there we are, sitting in the booth, wondering what we're doing," Lachman said ruefully.

Generally though, the monologue jokes were strong. However, there were two repeated kinds of material submitted that Bob should have rejected. One was outdated references, particularly regarding TV. For example, even though the character of Chester had been off *Gunsmoke* since 1964, Bob resurrected him on his April 17, 1969, special on regarding the cancellation of *The Smothers Brothers Comedy Hour* with, "It's the biggest crisis at CBS since someone tried to fix Chester's leg." Two years later, his Sept. 13, 1971 show, Bob joked that injured football star Joe Namath would be showing up on *Gunsmoke* as Chester.

The other was sexist references. Consider what Bob said about one female astronaut in training on *The Bob Hope Buick Sports Awards Show* in 1961: "I tell you, women are better suited for the loneliness of space travel. Just give them a telephone and a hair dryer, and they're happy for years. Of course, there's bound to be a little trouble when blastoff time rolls around. Can't you see our seven male astronauts pointing at the dame and saying, 'Ladies first'? And you can't blame her for wanting to go. What woman could resist floating around in space and calling her best friend to say, 'Clara, guess what? I just lost 118 pounds!'? And she'll have on an anti-gravity garment. I don't know what to do about that, I know lots of women that wear them." It got laughs then, but it is painfully dated material today.

Other than those considerations, those monologues generally were strong, and Hope's team enjoyed the challenge of crafting them. "I prized the work on the opening monologue more than anything else," says Perret. "As a gag writer, that was where I wanted to shine. And of course, we did much more monologue writing than sketch writing."

**Sketchy Writing**

Most critics and fans agree that monologues on Bob's shows were much better than his sketches, and part of that can be blamed on the system established by Lachman. For each special, Lachman gave writers the sketch's subject, outline and, when known, guest stars. Each team of writers paired up would sit down and write their own sketch based on the idea and turn them into Lachman, who'd put the skit together using the best material from all submissions. "This is why the Hope sketches have always been more a collection of gags than a developed sketch, without the consistency, the narrative build, and the characterization of the best of the sketches on *Your Show of Shows* or later on *The Carol Burnett Show*," asserts Tom Stempel in *Storytellers to the Nation: A History of American Television Writing*.

Indeed, without a single writer or pair of writers serving as the original "voice" of a skit, Bob's comedy pieces on TV apart from the monologues typically came across as a bunch of asides being inconveniently interrupted by the thinnest of plot developments, with "funny" costumes, sets, and special effects taking precedence in the humor. Add to that editing for time and inserting reactions during post-production including a laugh track (by the 1960s, most sketches Bob performed before audiences were ones done on location—others generally occurred in NBC's Burbank studios over a two-week period), and the final product on air often emerged as childish or nonsensical to follow.

By the time Perret worked for Bob full time in 1981, he says the process had altered somewhat. "Writers could turn in completed sketches, and many of us did. I would venture to say that most of the sketches we did were fully written by one writer or one team of writers. It was rare that we got an outline and filled it in. That was a difficult way of writing.

"However, once a sketch was written, we might all be asked to contribute to it, or in a sense rewrite it. That's when some of the conflicts would arise—we'd do various rewrites, and Hope would select lines he liked, and often they weren't compatible. I do recall one sketch in which Brooke Shields had three entrances and only one exit. Difficult to do." The constant tampering with skits up to the last minute left no one feeling like he or she really created them, thus little to no emotional attachment came from writing them, and they suffered as a result.

Even Perret, who can easily and happily cite several skits he wrote for *The Carol Burnett Show* despite being on it earlier than Bob's shows and for a much shorter period (1973-1978), admits that "I can't recall off the top of my head a single sketch that I wrote for the Bob Hope specials that I was particularly proud of. And I never realized that until you asked this question."

Bob's sketches did have a reputation of being ribald and racy on the air, in part because he had been faded out a few times on his radio show by NBC censors and also because he appeared opposite a lot of beautiful women making suggestive comments. However, most stories about his ability to get dirty jokes through his specials are apocryphal.

Consider one reported incident in Kermit Schafer's *Blunderful World of Bloopers* that supposedly got Bob knocked off TV briefly. Jill St. John looks for Bob's car keys while the latter has his hands tied in a sketch. She tells him, "Gee Bob, going into your pocket like this, I feel a little silly." Bob responds with, "If you go a little lower, you'll feel a little nuts." It sounds believable, except Schafer reported this happened sometime in the early 1950s, when Jill St. John was barely a teenager. Bob was sly, sure, but not like this, and he was nowhere near as off color in his humor as most TV comedy is today.

Larry Gelbart admitted that Bob's writing system could be constricting. "We often didn't—we weren't allowed to do whatever might have been our best," he recalled to Jordan R. Young in *The Laugh Crafters: Comedy Writing in Radio and TV's Golden Age*. "We did our best for Bob Hope… but as I said, that was kind of writing for order."

Still, writers who adapted to the system stayed with Hope for years, often decades, even though they were at his beck and call to supply jokes at personal appearances as well as his TV work. Perret says that despite what some critics assert, Bob's extended work hours did not violate rules set by the Writers Guild of America.

He adds that "when there was a strike, Hope understood that if we couldn't legally work for him, we couldn't do it. However, after one strike, Hope decided to pay us for the variety shows, which were governed by the WGA, but also pay us as writers for his personal appearances. I—and I think most of the other writers—opted to accept that arrangement. That meant that we could write for his non-TV appearances and remain within the guild rules."

The process worked for them as well as for their boss. It all added up to Bob having enormous success that led to increased clout for controlling his shows, albeit not always for the better.

**Bob as Executive Producer**

After a few years on TV, Bob acted as his own executive producer, a title few other variety stars ever held on their shows, finding performing and sometimes writing for them a big enough chore. This title meant he had final edits on the shows too, so basically he could take the bulk of credit for them deservedly—as well as the criticism for it, which he hated and believed did not exist.

Talking on TV to Tom Snyder on *Tomorrow Coast to Coast* in early 1981, Bob said he thought each of his specials had had some element of quality to them. "I don't think your show is ever that bad to call it a clinker," he remarked.

Many critics and even some fans would disagree. For one thing, Bob favored using material "in the trunk"—that is, restaging some old skits that worked well in the past with slight modifications, which he did even early into his TV career in the 1950s. This indicates a laziness in putting together a show.

Also, while Bob demanded new jokes constantly from his writers, he was not above reusing some he liked in his shows' monologues or sketches. For example, when he enjoyed the reception for calling Bing Crosby "the one-man population explosion" on his Dec. 13, 1961, special (Bing had just become a father of several newborn children with his young wife), he decided to say it again just two months later on his Feb. 27, 1962 show.

He also had free range to engage in the occasionally irritating vernacular, such as referring to show business as "show bidness" and calling the cue cards he relied upon "idiot cards." Bob's use of the latter in skits as well as his monologue was obvious on every show.

The whole setup gave Bob's specials the reputation of not being as strong as they should be among many critics, and while he could handle not getting Emmy nominations in later years, criticism by trade papers in particular upset Bob, prompting his staff to write letters of protest and even pressure publishers to change their reviews. It was not becoming for a personality of his stature to stoop to such petty reactions, but he did it.

Bob also could be perturbed during the production of his shows, although he would try to hide it from his guests as best as possible. The 1961 *Project Twenty* documentary "The World of Bob Hope" noted that his staff knew that something was wrong with the show whenever Bob hummed and that he became angry when confronted with anyone being inefficient and prolonging the recording of a show. Bob truly took the adage "Time means money" to heart.

# Introduction: How Bob Became a TV Fixture • 13

**Bob the Hard Bargainer**

Off screen, Bob had a reputation of being fair but firm in what he wanted from the network in exchange for his services. Whenever his contract came up, Jimmy Saphier, Bob's agent from 1937 until his death in 1974, and thereafter Elliott Kozak, Saphier's former assistant, would start negotiations with NBC's president at the time, then Bob and that president would meet face to face to finalize the deal. Frequently, the contract called for more than just the standard perks.

"Every time we committed, it would be every four years … we had to commit to buy a piece of land Bob owned," former NBC President Herb Schlosser told the Archive of American Television. "And he owned a lot of land. Tom [Sarnoff, ex-NBC president] told me once that he owned more land than anybody but the state or federal government. He had a lot of land. And we'd buy it, and presumably he would get a capital gain." NBC also bought out Hope's production company, which was more successful getting motion pictures made than selling series beyond those involving Hope.

For the shows themselves, apart from working with the writers and directors on his vision, as executive producer, Bob went after many big names to appear as guests. Not surprisingly, he almost always got them too.

**The Big Guest Gets**

When Bob did his second TV special in 1950, he presented America's top crooner, Frank Sinatra, as his guest for the latter's first time on the medium. It was a big draw, and Bob now was competing with the likes of Ed Sullivan and Jack Benny to be the first to bring stars to his shows.

Among those big names for which Bob succeeded in obtaining their American TV debuts were Bob's frequent movie foil Bing Crosby (on a telethon he co-hosted with Bob), Fred MacMurray, Lana Turner, Maurice Chevalier, and Kathryn Grayson. Bob secured them largely due to his reputation for excellence as well as his popularity, and he leveraged that power to his advantage often.

One way was that Bob reportedly engaged in exclusivity contracts for some top talent requiring them not to do another TV series three weeks prior to and one week after the airing of his special with them. Only a few others like Ed Sullivan were able to get these demands of guests in writing.

Bob also allowed some input from his creative team regarding guests, says longtime writer Bob Mills. "We'd have one meeting when suggestions for guests could be made. We thought up sketch ideas first and tried to book guests who would be good in them. Bob always picked the guests. He'd take suggestions, but it was always his call, never the producer's."

Truth is, Bob had several sources from which he got his guests, beginning with those who were hot at the time his specials were recorded.

**The Newsmakers**

When astronaut Neil Armstrong joked on *Dean Martin's Celebrity Roast of Bob Hope* in 1974 that Bob's mantra in booking guests was "Exploit anybody in the news," there was a lot of truth to it. Bob had of course got Armstrong to tour with him on his USO Christmas tour shortly after Armstrong had walked on the moon, and he also convinced Olympic swimmer Mark Spitz to make his TV acting debut with him just a few months after the latter won multiple gold medals for a high rating. If you were an athlete who accomplished a big win recently, a call from Bob would be coming soon.

Such was the case for George Foreman, who heard from Bob's office about doing a guest shot almost immediately after he defeated Joe Frazier for the heavyweight championship in boxing on Jan. 22, 1973. "They told me, 'We can only pay you ten thousand dollars,'" he recalls. "I had never had anything like that!"

Bob had Foreman act as his bodyguard on a sketch as well as talk to him before the special ended. Foreman had a reputation of being surly to intimidate his opponents, but Bob told him, "I want you to be funny" and encouraged Foreman to show a lighter side of himself. It went so well that he came back after defending his title against Ken Norton in 1974.

"He opened up a whole new world for me in television to be more than a boxer," Foreman says. He also credits Bob for encouraging him to adopt a new public demeanor of being easygoing and playful in conversation to this day, noting that "I never had a serious conversation with him. He could actually pull funny out of anyone."

## The Up-and-Comers

Another type of guest Bob sought were promising young stars to book on his show. If they were attractive females, so much the better. Blonde Gloria Loring had been a frequent singer on TV variety and talk shows when Bob asked her to join his USO Christmas tour in 1970. He made her feel right at home as they appeared before several audiences of thousands of military men.

"Here I was, this young singer, I was probably in my late twenties, and I was waiting for one of us to go on, and he said, 'You look great! Have you had everything lifted?'" Loring laughs. She adds, "He was gracious to all of us, he was funny and lighthearted. I think you can always tell a lot by a person at the top by the atmosphere you are working, and the atmosphere was one of respect."

Bob adored working with Loring so much that he had her as his opening act on a few appearances plus as an occasional guest star on his shows into the 1990s. She credits him for giving her great advice on handling autographs requests as well: "He said, 'Always keep moving. If not, the crowds will get you.'"

A big hit record could also encourage Bob to book an act. Cynthia Bell of the Bell Sisters singing duo says she and her younger sister Kay got to sing their hit song "Bermuda" and do its B-side with Bob on his 1952 special because he and Bing Crosby were eager to showcase popular new young performers on their shows. As she recalls, "I was 16 years old at the time. It was a fluke. Whenever there was a new act that was talented, hot, they were very eager to have us." She says they enjoyed the experience, adding "They were very protective of us."

Dodie Stevens, who had a big hit in 1959 with "Pink Shoe Laces," says that while her memories of appearing on Bob's special to do that song are gone, "What I do remember is being invited to his home for dinner. That was special! He also asked me to be his opening act on some of his shows at colleges throughout the country."

An even younger musical performer did not even have management when she did Bob's show in 1988. Leila Josefowicz played classical pieces on the violin so well while was in elementary school that she secured several prestigious gigs in the Los Angeles as an amateur. She believes one of Bob's producers heard about her and booked her to as part of the entertainment for the Bob Hope Cultural Center in Palm Springs, California.

"This specific event was basically the catalyst for me getting management," Josefowicz recalls. "It was the first major step to turning what you would call being professional." The director of the IMG talent agency saw her performance, which earned a standing ovation at the show, and signed her immediately.

The prepubescent played a piece she had done for a year, but this time, the scale was much grander. Introduced by Lucille Ball ("She was such a delight and so sweet"), Josefowicz took the front of the stage following a short period for rehearsal and dazzled the crowd. She was intimidated on stage mostly by the space separating her from the rest of the orchestra—"I remember it was something like a 20-foot gap between me and the conductor"—while off stage, things were more chaotic for the big production.

"At that age, I was a little in awe of all the things I saw, from the decorations to the drug sniffing dog," Josefowicz says. "The security was so tight, and there was so much energy. So, I was pretty damn nervous." Nonetheless, she nailed it, shook hands with Bob and even President Ronald Reagan, which she thinks she took for granted ("I didn't understand the level this was at"), and developed a professional career as a result.

Other emerging music acts benefited from having a well-connected manager, such as Frank Werber with the We Five. "Werber was shaping us to be—even though they hadn't been in existence yet—the Carpenters," says Jerry Burgan, who started the folk vocal group with Michael Stewart in San Francisco as they eventually became a quintet. When "You Were on My Mind" became a hit in 1965, Werber worked with talent agent Jerry Perenchio to pitch the group to Hope.

The We Five secured a strong spot—the group even got to perform its flip side, "Small World," along with "You Were on My Mind"—but as with several musical acts at the time, Bob only introduced them by voice offstage, this time because he had to change into a 1920s football player outfit for a skit with Carol Lawrence. "He was physically there, because we met him, but because of the costume, he only shook our hands," notes Burgan.

Having the right connections to other guests never hurt either to get on Bob's shows. When Bob and his people secured Steve McQueen, then starring in the hit CBS western series *Wanted Dead or Alive*, to do their 1959 Christmas show, his actress/singer wife Neile Adams came along with him too, or as she puts it, "They approached Steve, and they just threw me in." She had just had a baby and "We'd never been to Alaska [where the show was filmed], so it was a fun time."

As a somewhat unplanned entertainer on the trip, Adams was left somewhat adrift to fend for herself initially. "I sang a couple of songs in Alaska in front of the troops, but I was rather stiff," she says. "I was not being choreographed as a singer, so Bob said, 'Move your hands a little bit!'" Apparently that worked, for when Bob asked Steve for a repeat visit in 1960, Neile joined him as well. Of Bob, she says, "He was a nice man. I liked him."

Beauty queens often popped up on Bob's specials, but Shirley Cothran, who did Bob's 1974 fall special freshly after winning the Miss America title for 1975, actually met him previously when she competed in a local contest at University of North Texas in Denton. "He liked pretty girls, and he had several queens there," she remembers. "I was beyond thrilled seeing Bob."

Cothran went on to compete on the state level, and Bob remembered here. "When I won Miss Texas, he sent me a telegram saying, 'Congratulations.' Which I thought was beyond the call of duty. Then when I won Miss America, he remembered me again. He sent me another telegram saying, 'See what my touch can do?'" While she barely encountered other guests on the show ("Carol Channing I met for a brief moment and Glen Campbell from a distance, but we didn't have any interaction"), she did tour with him some thereafter. He sent her Christmas cards for at least seven years thereafter plus gave her a telephone receiver where she could press down on a button to play "Thanks for the Memory." "He was a gem of a guy, so kind and gentle," she adds.

Speaking of beauty, that was the main criteria when Bob introduced the annual Hollywood Deb Stars from 1955-1963 and again in 1991, all showcasing up-and-coming starlets, some of whom later had some substantial acting success. He did a variation of this in 1966 with "The New Faces of Hollywood," which basically was an excuse by Universal Studios to promote young actresses it had under contract.

"We were just sent out to do things," recalls one of the participants, Melodie Johnson Howe, who later became a successful writer. "In fact, someone said to me, 'Now, you can get your SAG card,' because I had not done television before then. It was all inter-promotional. And I hated my hairdo. It was almost piled up." The beautiful gowns the women wore all came from the wardrobe department, she adds.

Another one of those featured, Marianne Gordon, says the studio set up a banquet hall with a stage so that people could sit in round tables and applaud them when introduced by Bob and his guest, Bing Crosby. It was loosely done and sometimes the mistakes were kept in during recording, as Gordon recalls. "They would take a girl out and interview her, and they were doing something before me, and there was a mess-up and they taped over it. But I remember Bing Crosby messed up and Bob Hope gave him this look and I laughed, but they went on."

Gordon enjoyed the experience with Bing and Bob even if it let her do little more than dress up and spout some scripted lines. "They were both very nice. There was something I thought that was a little warmer than Bob Hope. He was an incredible man."

Finally, some lucked out when other guests turned Bob down (yes, it did happen a few times). Bob wanted to have Sally Ride, the first female astronaut, on his 1983 special *Bob Hope Salutes NASA: 25 Years of Reaching for the Stars*, but she felt uncomfortable talking to him in front of a studio audience, so he replaced her with two men, astronauts Robert Crippen and Guion Bluford. "Bob was energetic, he was hard of hearing, and I was hard of hearing, but it was enjoyable," laughs Bluford, who adds that "For many years, I would get Christmas cards from Bob Hope."

**The Big Name Guests**

Often recognized names got a call to join Bob and show another side of themselves. Cathy Lee Crosby had established herself as a dramatic actress and hostess of *That's Incredible!* when she proved to have a previously hidden talent of great comic timing with Bob. She worked with him several times during the 1980s and credits him for unleashing her humorous skills on camera.

As Crosby acknowledges, "In my early acting training, I was always drawn to theatrical pieces that were more dramatic and 'meaty,' but at the same time, everyone seemed to love it when I did comedy! It might be the fact that in life, I tend to be pretty funny, albeit unintentionally. I can honestly say that Bob Hope encouraged that comedic side of my talent and made up many skits just to see how far he could push me. Yes, there was improvisation and 'winging it,' but as far as pure comedic talent goes, there was no one who could touch him. He was funny, but the perfect straight man all at the same time.

"And as for comedic timing, he was perfection. One of his looks could say it all. I will be forever grateful for all he taught me. I had the amazing opportunity to be able to perfect my comedic craft with one of the greatest of all time!"

Crosby notes it did take a little time for her to loosen up working with Bob. "Once I got the hang of his style and developed enough confidence to 'play' full out with him, it was a blast. We never knew what was going to happen or where the skit might go, which is the ultimate thrill for a performer .... the demand that one be absolutely 'in the moment' creating."

Bob impressed Crosby as well with his commitment to her pet cause in 1981, "Get High on Yourself," the first week of television ever dedicated to a charitable endeavor by a single network, in this case NBC. "Since Bob was a close friend of mine and was an NBC darling, I asked he and Bob Evans to join me in the effort to get my idea of a charitable week of prime time TV on the air. What's also amazing is that NBC agreed to our demand that no one, including them, Bob or myself, would own the rights to all the eventual footage, and that instead, all the film would be owned by 'The Kids of America in Perpetuity.' Can you imagine? ... As for Bob, he was a real trouper, being available to me whenever I needed him to film or anything else."

While she loved her time with Bob, Crosby also confirms that not every star meshed with him as well as she did. "Yes, it's true, some people didn't adapt well to Bob's timing and his preference for minimal rehearsal, but I'd rather not mention any names," she says with a smile.

Certain celebrities knew that they could use a boost to stand out when working with Bob. Carol Lawrence was smart enough on her guest shots with Bob in the 1960s and 1970s to insist that she use Kevin Carlisle, a choreographer she knew from her stage work. "I didn't have a contract with her, but she called me when something came up for her," Carlisle says. The singer/actress impressed him as a dancer. "She is spectacular. One of the best on the planet."

Working with Carlisle as a soloist or with chorus boys, Lawrence's routines are much athletic and graceful than most dance numbers appearing on Bob's specials. Especially stunning is her descending a staircase from high above the stage to the floor below in a 1965 special, not missing a beat as she goes down to the ground.

"It's my career to come up with things as unique as possible, so it's just something that gives me pleasure," Carlisle notes, adding "Most of the time they would ask me how I wanted it shot. I'm not ashamed to say that I'm very good." He took into account the show's limited budget and screen size when designing his routines.

Carlisle also recalls going over to Bob's house to rehearse anytime the comedian had a number with Carol. While Hope had been dancing since vaudeville, Carlisle dismisses the steps he learned and used on stage there, saying "Those are rather simplistic."

Actress Jo Anne Worley had the distinction of knowing Bob as a next-door neighbor as well as a fellow actor when she relocated to Toluca Lake, California. "I had just moved into a house right across the street from him, and he said, 'Tell her to come by and borrow a cup of money,'" giggles Worley. She says that contrary to some people's recollections that Bob was tight with a buck, his residence was a hit for children playing trick or treat on Halloween ("He would give away two full candy bars," she notes), and he personally once gave her a Tiffany clock that says "Thanks for the Memory" as a gift.

Regarding doing his show, Worley says coming from a theatrical background, she found the rehearsal and taping atmosphere easy and fun. "I would call it loosey-goosey," she says. Cathy Lee Crosby agrees with that assessment, saying that "Unless a song or dance routine was involved, the rehearsal time was next to nothing. It was just his style and I actually came to love doing things that way." So does another favorite of Bob's.

Marie Osmond was a frequent guest with Bob for two decades, and she says their relationship was more than just a professional one. "There was definitely love there, let me tell you," she says. "I think he had a real respect for my work ethic. He was kind of like a second father to me."

Bob first had her as a guest on his 1973 Christmas show. "It was the first time I sang 'Paper Roses' nationally," says Marie, referring to her first hit. Though she had worked on TV previously with Andy Williams and other stars, the instantaneous kinship with Bob was stronger than she had experienced.

"There was just something unique about Bob," Marie says. "He was so quick. He made me feel so welcome right off the bat. When I was able to give it back to him with the lines, he loved it, maybe because I had so many brothers. We loved to make each other laugh. He made me feel so easy."

Marie thinks Bob liked her because she listened to and followed through on his advice on how to deliver lines and wait for laughs. "I'm a little old school, and even though I was very young, I was vaudeville-ish. He'd give me tips on humor, and he loved doing that. He didn't do that for many people."

Her musical chops also impressed him. "He was so used to singing harmony [with other guests], so he loved that I could do that instead and let him handle the melody," she says. "I could sing a song really quick too, and he hated rehearsal. He also didn't like too many takes. So that's why he liked me too, because I was prepared."

Marie adds that besides caring about her personally ("When any of my children were born, he sent me flowers"), Bob extended a big help to her personal charity, Children's Miracle Network Hospitals, when she asked him to serve on its board of directors and he simply responded, "If you believe in it, I believe in it. You put my name on the board. Don't worry about my attorneys, I trust you." Marveling at the memory, Marie says, "He loved people with integrity and did things for the right reasons. He never acted like he was above anybody."

Indeed, several guests who worked with Bob echo his statement on the 1961 documentary "The World of Bob Hope" that "I don't like everybody, but I'm genuinely friendly." Harry Wayne Casey, lead singer of KC and the Sunshine Band, who appeared on Bob's seventy-fifth birthday special plus worked with him on *Donny & Marie*, says, "He was always very cordial to me."

"Bob was fun to work with, he was always cutting up. He was the way you saw him doing his act," says Pat Priest, who had a small part on one of his specials and an episode of Bob's 1960s anthology series before doing her best-remembered role as the daughter on *The Munsters*. "He was a lovely man, lovely to work with, no problems at all."

If Bob did enjoy seeing your act in person, that also translated into a guest shot. Trini Lopez performed his version of "Hello Dolly" in Spanish on Bob's November 1964 special at the host's request.

"I wrote the Spanish lyrics for the show," recalls Lopez. "He wanted me to do the song because he came to see me at Basin Street East in New York City, and I used to follow people like Ella Fitzgerald there. Every night, everybody came by. Even Ava Gardner came by one night."

The spot on Bob's special went over so well, according to Lopez, that "From then on, Mr. Hope wanted me to go on tour with him. We did college tours, the Garden Tour Center in New Jersey, and he wanted me to do all those Vietnam things, but I was so busy, I could never do one." He did get to do forty-five minutes as an opening act on the tours, an unusually long time for someone not billed as an attraction, which Lopez credits Bob for allowing him to do.

Actress/singer Vivian Reed had a similar experience when she followed her hit Broadway musical revue *Bubbling Brown Sugar* to the Pantages Theatre in Los Angeles and heard from Bob. "He probably called the show and asked about my availability," she says of her invitation to do his special in 1977. "It was great to be asked to be on Bob's special, because I had watched it so many times with my family, and I felt honored to do it and to be on the same stage with Lucille Ball." She had a substantial role in the show, singing "God Bless the Child," dancing in a medley with male dancers, and bantering with Bob.

Reed believes she got to sing her song before a studio audience while her other segments were taped separately. Rehearsing the dance, she recalled how its beauty and power stunned one notable onlooker who showed up. "Lucille Ball, she was a mess. When we finished, I heard her say, 'God, I'm glad I'm not following that!' Always loved her."

The biggest challenge to Reed was talking to Bob without an audience. "Applause must have been dubbed in, because when Bob made his jokes, I had to wait for his laughter. And when I messed it up the first time, he did not like it. I had to wait for laughter that would come in."

Like some other guests on Bob's specials, Reed learned it was a double-edged sword to be singled out for special attention from him in a supposedly ensemble production like *Bubbling Brown Sugar*. "In every cast, there were going to be haters, and *Bubbling* was no exception to the rule. Jealousy reared its head," she says. "When you have someone who comes out of the show and the critics say, 'OK, this is the one,' don't hate on the people who are doing what you'd like to do. Just do the work. Take the dance classes, learn to be a great performer. Success is how you set your own goals. Being jealous doesn't benefit anyone. Not at all."

Bob was able to massage such clashes of egos by his stars and their managers and agents to an extent on his own shows by using special designations in billing them. For example, on *Bob Hope's Bicentennial Star-Spangled Spectacular* in 1976, there was in order "Guest Star" Sammy Davis Jr.; "Bob's new friends" the Captain and Tennille; "Special Attraction" Debbie Reynolds; "Special Guest Stars" Donny and Marie Osmond; and "With Special Appearances By" listing ten acts. Such extravagant listings are artificial designations, so the guest lists in this book's entries carry no such divisions, even though the programs themselves ostentatiously gave them at the top of each special.

Arguably the only downside to the way Bob used guest stars was that he kept employing some personalities longer than he should have. He frequently included Danny Thomas, Milton Berle, Lucille Ball, Phyllis Diller, and Martha Raye into the 1980s, by which most show business leaders considered them has-beens. One could conceivably add Brooke Shields to this list, as her movie career sputtered in the middle of the decade, but she kept going strong in doing Bob's specials through 1990. Bob's defenders would counter that this was a sign of his loyalty to his peers in a business where professional relationship too often disappear once someone is no longer considered "hot."

**The Featured Players**

For some hardworking actors not yet household names who appeared on Bob's shows, they typically fell under the designation of featured players and were sometimes billed as "also appearing" on the specials at the credits at the end (or in a voiceover by the announcer or even not credited). Some would appear frequently, such as the tall and dignified Peter Leeds, who lent gravity to sketches as well as a sense of humor when working with Bob from the 1950s through 1990s.

Other supporting actors usually were hired for their physical characteristics as much as their line readings. Regarding her work with Bob, actress Millicent Brower says, "I think what intrigued Mr. Hope was I had a turned-up nose. So, when you put us together, it was funny. I think that was one of the reasons he engaged me, I believe."

Being billed as featured could be humbling if not humiliating to some who previously had higher profiles. For example, Donna Douglas fell into that designation on the Nov. 13, 1973 special, just two years after being a star on the CBS sitcom *The Beverly Hillbillies* from 1962-71. Also, while Nichelle Nichols attracted fans for reunions of the NBC sci-fi classic *Star Trek* after its run from 1966-69, she only merited an end credit for playing Redd Foxx's girlfriend on Bob's 1975 Christmas special. Still, it was work for them on a Bob Hope special, which was better than no job at all.

The featured actors also had to realize that unlike themselves, Bob would have the face of his orchestra conductor appear in opening titles through the 1970s. It was through such exposure that Les Brown and His Band of Renown remained one of the best recognized holdovers from the big band era for TV viewers.

**The Music Maker: Les Brown**

When Bob moved from radio to TV, he imported a big band that had been with his radio show since 1947 following a season with a band led by Desi Arnaz (yes, the same Desi who later starred in *I Love Lucy*) and before that by Skinnay Ennis, who was with Bob when the comedian's radio series started in 1938 until he was drafted in World War II (Skinnay would later do a few TV shows for Bob before his death in 1963). Les Brown and His Band of Renown formed in 1938, two years after Brown first conducted a group while attending Duke University in Durham, North Carolina, which is somewhat ironic given that his predecessor Skinnay Ennis attended nearby rival UNC in Chapel Hill, North Carolina.

Brown and his band racked up several hits during the early to mid-1940s, including "Sentimental Journey" with Doris Day as vocalist. When many other big bands fell apart after World War II in 1946, his ensemble stayed strong, and Bob appreciated the musicians' smooth backing as much as their ability to laugh loud at his jokes, even though several were directed at the band itself. Here are a sample of what Bob said of Les Brown and His Band of Renown in his monologues over the years:

"The only band that can play 'Sh-Boom' without instruments." (Oct. 12, 1954)

"They're so progressive, you have to call the auto club to find the melody." (Feb. 1, 1955)

"I'll never forget with Leopold Stokowski one said about Les Brown and his band. I can't repeat it, but I'll never forget it." (April 25, 1955)

"Right after the show tonight, Les and the boys open at the Hollywood Palladium. This isn't an invitation, it's a warning." (May 24, 1955)

"And of course, we have Les Brown and his band back with us with his new sound—music." (May 1, 1956, paraphrasing a joke he used previously on Oct. 4, 1955)

"That's the answer to the musical question, 'What became of the Brinks Mob?'" (May 22, 1956)

"For the orchestra, we have the California Grape Crushers headed by the Bad Seed himself." (Nov. 11, 1956)

"We've got a special treat for you music lovers. Les Brown isn't with us tonight!" (Jan. 10, 1957)

"Les Brown and his Seventeen Mouseketeers … The only thing they play is the horses." (April 8, 1957)

"And of course just back from a worldwide tour of the Pink Pussycat—Les Brown and his Tijuana Lead." (Nov. 29, 1967)

Bob even mocked them when they were not there. For his May 15, 1959 show, Bob cracked, "We're trying a daring experiment tonight in Les Brown's absence—music." Even as late as April 19, 1974, he thanked Les and his band for "Whatever they do."

Brown took all this in good stride, possibly because beyond truly beloved by Bob, he had other TV conducting gigs beside what Bob offered. One was on *The Hollywood Palace* in 1964-1965, where pianist/arranger Bob Alberti first met Brown while being part of the ABC staff orchestra. Brown's band normally did road tours during the summer hiatus of taping TV series, and he invited Alberti to join and do one new arrangement for the band through the 1960s.

"I became an arranger for the Bob Hope show in 1971, sharing the duties with J. Hill," Alberti says. "In 1973 Hope was asked to do a telethon in Baltimore for flood victims, and the Hope show producer, Mort Lachman, asked if I'd go and find a local orchestra for that event, since Les was otherwise occupied. I did so, and it became known at that time that I was a capable conductor as well as pianist and arranger.

"As time went on, NBC requested more shows be done on location than in the studio, but Les would only agree to do them if he could use his full ensemble. Logistics and finances often made that impossible, so I'd be tapped to do the musical director's job. I would be allowed to take five key members (usually a rhythm section and lead trumpet, plus lead woodwind), then have a contractor at the designated location fill in the other twenty chairs." This is why during the mid-1970s onward, viewers were less likely to hear Bob say at the end of his shows "Les?" to cue the bandleader to start "Thanks for the Memory," simply because it was Alberti conducting instead.

Traveling with the band could be pleasant or nerve-wracking, according to Alberti. "Often if it were a non-military show, we'd fly commercial first-class with the artists and the senior production staff. Those were fun. The military shows, however, would have us seated on pallets within a C-141 cargo plane—no heat, no air conditioning, no windows, no flight attendants, at least for us. Hope would have a complete mini-room for himself loaded on board with a couch, a bed, and plenty of goodies to snack on. We got blankets, since at high altitudes the cabin was rather frosty."

Alberti says he had a good rapport with his fellow musicians in Les Brown and His Band of Renown, and one stands out in particular to him, saxophonist Henry "Butch" Stone. "Although he had lived past his playing years with Les's band, he was the librarian on the Hope show," notes Alberti. "Butch was always like 'the mother hen' to the band members when they were on the road, as he was the road manager. He loved to keep busy, so even into his late seventies, he was always a welcome presence. He had boundless energy and was always ready to assist whenever and wherever needed."

As the years progressed, Alberti became the primary arranger and conductor for Les Brown and His Band of Renown. "Being musical director entails about six weeks from the first production meeting to the day of airing. Les Brown didn't really want to do all the meetings and logistics, so he appointed me to handle that. Being that I was paid hourly through NBC [he did other assignments such as play on *The Tonight Show with Johnny Carson*], I didn't mind putting in the time. Les preferred to play golf, which I guess he did while I did the orchestrations, worked rehearsals with the guest stars, and coordinated all the elements.

"If we were in Los Angeles, Les would come in the day of the show to conduct, and I'd run everything with him, then I'd retreat to the control booth with the audio engineer, where I'd supervise the pre-recording session. The day of the actual taping, I'd be under the center camera by the cue card guy, visually cuing Hope as to when to sing and when to stop. In his later years, his hearing failed and he had trouble hearing the audio playback, so I had hand signals for start and stop."

Alberti did not have to find what music to use for Hope's specials as part of his duties. "Rarely did I suggest songs or material. Whoever the producer was at the time would meet with the writers and Hope to come up with a theme for the particular show. Sometimes the writers would write some special material to which I would have to compose music for Hope (and a guest singer) to do as a duet."

Throughout his work on the specials, Alberti claims its star was the one who gave him the most grief during rehearsal and on-air performance. "Bob wasn't exactly one to 'button down' and learn anything seriously," he says. "As he aged, his retention ability became less, and he usually seemed preoccupied. We'd have to do numerous takes to get something decent, then I'd have to be in post-production and edit the best of them together to make a presentable version."

He also came to expect Bob making last-minute changes for music. "Many a night I'd sit up arranging something that he'd requested, only to find out the next day that he'd scrapped the idea and went on to something different. We used to joke that 'A Bob Hope show is like watching a dog walk on its hind legs; you know it won't be done well, but you're amazed that it gets done at all.'"

Not surprisingly, Alberti has a mixed opinion of his former employer. "Hope was an icon of generosity and patriotism to the world. For those of us on the inside, not quite so much. His notoriety for penny pinching was legendary, and his ego was there to match. I'll always remember a production meeting with the writers and myself at his house. He would not wear a hearing aid despite the fact that he had one. He claimed it made him appear old (he was in his eighties). The writers were becoming hoarse trying to speak loudly enough for Hope to get their input. One of them said it would help if he wore his hearing aid for the meeting. His reply, spoken in a very dry way, I'll never forget, was 'It's not important that I hear you; it's important that you hear me.' That says it all. His ego and sense of self-importance was as broad as I've ever seen, and I've been around a lot of stars in my career."

Despite his complaints, Alberti did work for Hope until 1992. Nick Perito took over the baton afterward, although Les Brown did continue to serve a figurehead for his band up to Bob's ninetieth birthday party in 1993, where he made a rare speech on camera to congratulate Bob. Brown would die in 2001, two years shy of Bob.

**The Criteria for Inclusion in This Book (Finally!)**

This book focuses on Bob's appearances on national television shows in the United States, principally on the networks (NBC, ABC, CBS, Fox, and public television), syndication (sold to individual stations or station groups across America), and cable/satellite channels. It is not a review of his life at the same time, although there will be references to a few incidences when they bear mentioning, such as his affair with actress Marilyn Maxwell because of her inordinately large guest shots on his early 1950s shows, and his daughter Linda Hope, one of his four adopted children, because she got involved in his production company.

Also excluded are Bob's innumerable guest shots on local and regional TV broadcasts, as well as closed circuit events such as the All Star Hollywood Celebrity USO special seen only on military television in 1958. Left out too are times when Bob showed up in commercials without being part of programs, such as pitching for the sponsor on ads between numbers in the special *Texaco Star Theater:* "Opening Night" on NBC on Sept. 11, 1982. All these occasions are too frequent and difficult to count and are of only trivial interest in terms of his impact on the medium.

Specials and series occur by category in chronological order in which they first aired. When possible, titles are the same as they appear on screen officially, and subtitles or episode titles in the case of series are included too, separated by a colon. Each entry lists days, dates, running times (Eastern Time zone) and network affiliation, with the exception of NBC. Bob appeared so overwhelmingly on the network where he did long-term business that any entry without a channel designation means that it was on NBC by default.

Included in each entry are the guests for Bob's specials or the cast list for other programs, plus the chief creative team of executive producers, producers, directors, writers, bandleaders and choreographers where known. To save space, abbreviations used are EP (executive producers), P (producers), D (directors), and W(writers), while Music indicates the name of the conductor. A summary covers the show's high and low points and other oddities of note.

An effort was made to view as many of Bob's specials and guest shots as possible. Some of his shows, like the ones from *The Colgate Comedy Hour* in 1952-1953, have no surviving copies. Regardless, most chapters have at least eighty percent of the content personally reviewed. For those seen, both Bob and show are graded on the following one- to five-star scale:

*****—This represents Bob/entertainment at his/its peak. Classic material worth viewing.

****—An almost perfect show and/or an above-average performance by Bob.

***—Roughly half of what Bob/the show offers works, the rest does not.

**—A lot more is wrong than right here. For Bob, this usually means he is disengaged or not working up to his potential or that of his cast mates.

*—A fiasco, something that Bob should be ashamed of if it applies to him (thankfully, this is rarely needed for his work, but unfortunately not the same for his shows).

While being critical about Bob's work, this is meant to be a celebration in general of what he accomplished in the medium. Carolyn Raskin, who worked with Bob on *Rowan and Martin's Laugh-In* and later produced some of his specials in the 1980s, declined a full interview about Bob, but her brief statements about him reflect in a nutshell what Bob did best on TV: "He is who he is, he's wonderful. He's a worker."

Indeed, he was all that and more. Let's review what he achieved starting with his first special.

Bob stands between the Bell Sisters on the bookends, Jane Russell and an unidentified uniformed man in an early 1950s appearance. Courtesy of John Bernards.

# 2  Specials – 1950s

"One thing about television—it's bringing back vaudeville to kill it at a more convenient time."
– Bob on his second TV special on May 27, 1950.

**CREDITS FOR THIS DECADE** are as follows (exceptions noted in individual shows when known): EP: Bob Hope. P: Al Capstaff (1951-1953), Jack Hope (1953-1959). D: Al Capstaff (1952), Jim Jordan (1952–1958), Jack Shea (occasional 1956-1958; regular 1958-1959). W: Mort Lachman, Norman Sullivan, Larry Gelbart (1950-1952), Larry Marks (1950-1951), Glen Wheaton (1950-1952), Marvin Fisher (1950-1952), Si Rose (1950), Al Schwartz (1950), Charles Lee (1952-1959), Jack Douglas (1952), John Rapp (1953-1959), Lester White (1953-1959), Bill Larkin (1953-1959), Gig Henry (occasional 1954-1959). Music: Les Brown and His Band of Renown. Announcer: Hy Averback (1951-1957), Frank Barton (1957-1959).

Bob arrived on TV in 1950 amid the possibility his show would not happen at all. His debut special aired barely live from New York City. The website EyesofaGeneration.com tells the full story, but basically after just three days of rehearsal, technicians for the show nearly walked off an hour before the show was to air due to disputes over lighting for the stage versus television.

The script also left something to be desired. Bob's writer Larry Gelbart admitted in his autobiography that "In terms of freshness the writing team came up empty, writing more a static radio show with cameras aimed at it rather than tapping into the potential of an exciting new medium. The humor, and it is an act of more imagination than the script contained to call it that, was almost entirely verbal. It was though we were trying to make words look funny."

The production cost an estimated total of $60,000 (more than $600,000 when adjusted for inflation in 2017 dollars), and it aired live to forty-five stations with another eighteen receiving it on kinescope (a filmed copy shot from a camera recording the live feed). While critical response was mixed, the public loved it. The Hooper rating service said the special averaged a 49.4 rating in New York, Chicago, Cleveland, and Washington, D.C., ranking it only behind *Texaco Star Theatre* featuring Milton Berle for that week.

After doing another special a month later, there were rumors Bob may be leaving NBC for CBS like many stars such as Jack Benny had done recently. However, by the time the latter network made moves for him, NBC executives had gotten wise on how to handle their talent, and they announced in June 1950 that Bob had signed a five-year radio and TV deal with NBC. The network offered him a high salary, a deal to lessen his capital gains taxes (which was the reason why most NBC stars had been defecting to CBS), and a minimum of $40,000 for talent for each of his TV specials, a huge amount for that time period.

**Bob the Occasional Guest Host**

Once Bob finished out his deal for specials with Frigidaire, the new sponsor for his radio show, Chesterfield cigarettes, decided to make the plunge into network TV series and scheduled a half hour variety series on NBC at the start of Sunday evenings in the fall of 1951. *Chesterfield Sound Off Time* officially listed Bob as an alternate host every week with Fred Allen and Jerry Lester, but Bob did the show much less than they did, only once a month.

When the pilot for the radio police drama *Dragnet* aired in the *Chesterfield Sound Off Time* slot Dec. 16, 1951, it attracted an audience bigger than what Allen and Lester had been generating, so Chesterfield decided to sponsor *Dragnet* as a series Thursday nights and have Bob's show alternate with it every other week. Bob rejected the offer, probably finding too hectic and not worth the effort for him to work so hard to do just a live thirty minutes of comedy rather than sixty. The sponsor had to cancel *Chesterfield Sound Off Time* in January and install as its alternate week offering *Chesterfield Presents*, a dramatic anthology that got nowhere near the audience of *Dragnet* and went off after two months.

Meanwhile, Bob finished out the 1951-1952 season with two other comedy variety series with alternating hosts, appearing once on *All Star*

*Revue* and twice on *The Colgate Comedy Hour*. *All Star Revue* employed a noisy filmed title sequence showing rather scary looking puppet heads of regular alternating hosts Jimmy Durante, [Ole] Olsen and [Chic] Johnson, Danny Thomas, and Ed Wynn parading by amid streamers, balloons, and confetti. Bob scored better there than most of the talent, and the series went off in 1953 after just two seasons as *The Jackie Gleason Show* on CBS opposite it began to make inroads.

Bob's stint on *The Colgate Comedy Hour* lasted longer, a year and a half, as he began appearing regularly every month in the 1952-1953 season. Making it appealing to him to do was that he no longer had to go to New York, as he did for his 1950-1951 Frigidaire specials, or do his shows in Hollywood at the El Capitan Theater or Radio City West. By the fall of 1952, NBC opened new TV studios in Burbank, California, with a steeped incline so all audience members could see the stage, and the drive was an easy one for Bob to make. Jo Anne Worley, Bob's future next-door neighbor, notes that it took her only ten minutes to get from her home in Toluca Lake to the studios without having to use Southern California's notoriously crowded freeways, which doubtlessly appealed to Bob as well. There were four studios in the building, and Bob used Studio One, naturally.

It is here where Bob began serving as executive producer of his shows—a role he retained for more than forty years—partly out of circumstance. The series' producer, Arthur Penn, told author Jeff Kisselhoff in *The Box: An Oral History of Television, 1920-1961* that unlike most other normal broadcasting protocol, the rotating star comedians received priority to oversee their programs on *The Colgate Comedy Hour*. "They would come in and do everything their own way, and there was nobody in control of the total show," he said. "As a result, perhaps with the exception of [Dean] Martin and [Jerry] Lewis, we never had the best of those people."

Judging how much of Penn's claims apply to Bob is hard to determine due to the scarcity of surviving Hope appearances on *The Colgate Comedy Hour*. Only three shows are in circulation, and Bob has claimed most copies for this period have been destroyed. Nevertheless, his monthly turns as host helped *The Colgate Comedy Hour* finish at number seven for the 1952-1953 season.

For the next season, he moved to Tuesday nights as the monthly fill-in for Milton Berle with General Foods as his sponsor. The Nielsen ratings ranked *The Bob Hope Show* starring Bob Hope as number five for the 1953-1954 and number seven for 1954-1955. Chevrolet took on sponsorship in the 1955-1956 season, and Nielsen counted *The Chevy Show* installments with and without Bob as one program, so the average ratings drooped to Twenty-Nine, but Bob's shows were all hits. The problem was that CBS had a hit opposite the time slot, *You'll Never Get Rich* starring Phil Silvers, and that was big enough to knock regular host Milton Berle off the air.

Bob did fewer specials thereafter the rest of the decade, and he pre-empted shows at different times as well. Around the same time in 1957, he secured a five-year deal worth twenty-five million dollars with NBC. It was retroactive to 1955, so it ran until 1960. That same year, *The Bob Hope Chevy Show* became history as Chevrolet invested its dollars elsewhere, but Bob finally found a new regular sponsor with Buick in 1958 that would last into 1961.

**Notable Shows and Guests**

A relatively unheralded part of Bob's mass appeal on television in the 1950s was his casual inclusion of minority talent on his shows from the start, like pianist Maurice Rocco (his first guest to appear on his TV debut), the Hi Hatters tap dancing duo in 1951, Pearl Bailey twice in 1956, and more. True, most shows tended to be lily white, but Bob offered more variety than what was available on video at the time.

As for women appearing as a comic foil for him, Marilyn Maxwell makes seven appearances from 1950-1956 in part because she was having an affair with Bob most of that period. A tall, curvaceous platinum blonde, she wore low-cut dresses on his show that showed a goodly bit of cleavage. Also of note was that Hy Averback went from announcing to guest starring (albeit in a featured role) on the specials by the end of the decade.

Bob also was a master of plugging his movies and other projects on his show in ways that were either clever or overkill, depending on one's opinion. For example, a poster from Bob's movie *Casanova's Big Night* appears prominently in his March 16, 1954 special, where he also announced a contest to find the Casanova from each college campus in America and unveiled the winner on his next show (April 13, 1954), adding that the gentleman will get a visit to the Mayo Clinic after dating some starlets. Such promotions did not make his movies hits—indeed, he fell out of the top ten box office stars listing after 1953—but they did make clear Bob spent as much time if not more promoting as well as performing on TV.

Specials – 1950s • 35

**The Special Specials**

Though he did a couple of shows on location during the early 1950s, Bob went beyond the usual scope outside the studios in 1954, when he informed NBC he would not be doing his November special in favor of a doing a Royal Command Performance at the Palladium. To appease network executives upset about losing the revenue, he promised to film a show there, and NBC promoted as the first international TV special—a somewhat dubious claim, given several TV news programs had shown films from abroad—when it aired on Dec. 7, 1954. It was a hit, and Bob felt less encumbered to do shows from just Los Angeles and New York.

Using the leverage of his star power, Bob began going overseas to film Christmas specials entertaining the military, starting when Gen. Rosie O'Donnell asked Bob to come to a Strategic Air Base in Greenland in December 1954. Airing every January after being edited to an hour, these shows usually were his highest-rated programs throughout the rest of the 1950s. When he filmed a movie like *The Iron Petticoat* in London in 1956, he made sure to squeeze out a couple of shows there for viewing at home too.

His most ambitious exercise was the first entertainment special filmed in Russia. His excursion behind the Iron Curtain had to pass through censors who cut out certain topics like the space race, but he still had enough comedy and music left to show with what was left to get a special that aired in April 1958 to high praise. It won a prestigious Peabody Award for Bob too, for Outstanding Contribution to International Understanding. Bob previously won a Peabody for his body of work in 1943. Nobody could come close to touching him in this regard.

**Let's Not Forget the Writers, Producers and Directors**

Although several critical fictional portrayals of TV comedians started appearing in the media in the mid-1950s, most notably the 1956 movie *A Face in the Crowd*, it was obvious that none were based on Bob, in part because of the generous ways he acknowledged his writers. In fact, Rod Serling's script for "The Comedian," a production on *Playhouse 90* on Feb. 14, 1957, underlined that when the show's head writer (Edmund O'Brien) wistfully recalled how better he might have been if he stopped working for his tyrannical star comic. "You know, Hope once offered me $300 a week. I should've grabbed it." ("You'd get $1,000 now," said Constance Ford as his assistant, emphasizing the point.)

By the time of that *Playhouse 90* show, Bob had established a basic team of seven writers upon which he regularly relied. Mort Lachman wrote with Bill Larkin, John Rapp with Lester White, and Charles Lee with Gig Henry. Norman Sullivan worked solo and handled just the monologue. Charles Lee and Gig Henry wrote separately at first, with Gig credited with special material, but by 1964 he and Charles were paired together, probably due to Screen Writers Guild payment policies that make it cheaper to have writers work as a team.

Bob also had a regular director for much of the 1950s with Jim Jordan, whose parents were Jim and Marian Jordan, better known as *Fibber McGee and Molly* on radio from 1935-1959. When Jordan left the job, his occasional replacement Jack Shea took over. On the production side, Bob eventually decided to keep it in the family and use his brother, Jack Hope.

With all this activity, Bob hoped to expand his TV presence the way stars like Lucille Ball did with her Desilu production company, but his Hope Enterprises had no luck in selling series to NBC or anyone else. In 1957 he filmed a pilot for a dramatic anthology series he would host, *The Police Hall of Fame*. NBC not only rejected it, they didn't even show it on the air as a special or part of a series collection of "unsold pilots" typically shown during the summers. This is odd, given that Hope was the network's top star. Undaunted, for the 1958-1959 season, Bob Hope Enterprises pitched two more potential series, *Jane Ahoy*, described by Lee Goldberg in *Unsold Television Pilots* as "A female 'Sgt. Bilko' in the Navy," and an adaptation of the newspaper daily comic strip *Prince Valiant*. Neither sold or were aired either. Bob just had to content himself with being the highest rated comedian on the air in the 1950s.

**Frisky in the Fifties**

For Bob Hope connoisseurs, the 1950s was where he was best on TV, with an assured, relaxed yet peppy delivery not just in his monologues but also in his sketches that no other personality was able to match. "Watching Hope function in front of a camera, one never feels the mixture of sympathy and concern that often wells up at the spectacle of other and newer TV comics plying their wares," noted Steve Allen in his book *More Funny People*. "Even when he has had a bad show, Bob personally is still in command. He's still moving at high speed, tossing off his lines with a remarkable facility and timing."

There's a looseness and irreverence on many of Bob's 1950s shows that sadly vanished in later decades too. Consider this freewheeling introduction he made on Nov. 11, 1956 of a guest who was the top regular series star on NBC at the time: "Ladies and gentlemen, it isn't often that we plug a record, but the young man who sings it now, though obscure, is most deserving. And it's a good record—it has a hole in the middle and it's round. So here it is, Perry Como attacking 'Chincherinchee,' which is Spanish for Dean Martin could do it better. Go!" Compare that to his stilted, often straightforward approach introducing singers in later years, and there's no contest.

Few of his later monologues were as consistent in getting belly laughs as the best ones he had in this period either. For example, in his March 13, 1959 special, the audience laps up his comments about concerns about his publicized recent eye appointments ("My X-rays have been seen by more people than my last pictures"), the Oscars ("Before I go any further, I just want to make one thing very clear: There was no connection between the Academy nominations and my going to the hospital") and once again easygoing Perry Como ("In other big news about robberies, Perry Como just got a twenty-five million-dollar contract with NBC. I want to tell you, if anyone deserves it, Perry does. He slept hard for this."). He even cleverly plugs his new movie, *Alias Jesse James*, with "I know we took a chance, but who knows? Maybe westerns will come back" and "I spent eight weeks in the saddle. You're looking at the oldest Dead End Kid in the business." Bob took such great material and delivered it better than about anyone else on TV.

Near the end of the decade, on May 6, 1959, Bob received the Trustees' Award from the Academy of Television Arts and Sciences, even though he had never been nominated for an Emmy previously. The inscription read, "Presented with appreciation and admiration for bringing the great gift of laughter to all peoples of all nations; for selflessly entertaining American troops throughout the world over many years; and for making television finer by these deeds and by the consistently high quality of his television programs throughout the years." He clearly had been a winner this decade, as the majority of the following summarizes will indicate.

***The Star Spangled Revue***
April 9, 1950, Sunday 5:30-7 p.m.

Beatrice Lillie, Douglas Fairbanks Jr., Dinah Shore. Featured: Hal LeRoy, Maurice Rocco, Walter Greaza, David Burns, Carl Reiner, Don Liberto & Gloria Patrice, The Look Magazine Cover Girls, The Mexico City Boys Choir. Announcer/Commercial Spokesman: Wendell Niles. P: Max Liebman. D: Hal Keith. Music and Lyrics: Mel Tolkin, Lucille Kallen, Irvin Graham, Jack Fascinato. Choral Director: Clay Warnick. Music: Charles Sanford. Choreographer: James Starbuck.

After a production number, Bob announces in top hat, tails and cane, "Television. Well, they finally got me!" He sports formal finery because "a lot of performers die on television, and if that happens to me, I want to be prepared for it!" Bob talks a lot to his cameraman and seems nervous as he cracks about New York Mayor William O'Dwyer and Congress. After Maurice Rocco plays his boogie woogie piano, Douglas Fairbanks tells Bob he is the real emcee for this special. The flaccid argument leads into Beatrice Lillie doing comic wordplay as a customer whose requests flummox those who serve her. This is better but labored. After a dance number, Bob awkwardly delivers lines before he gets a royal welcome to television by Carl Reiner, Walter Greaza (at the network president) and others on a cheap set. They patronize his every need, even providing him with the Look Magazine Cover Girls to pick a leading lady. Bob is more his wisecracking self here, but the skit drags. Dinah Shore sings and does a sketch with Bob as two Eskimos showing how "Baby It's Cold Outside" became a hit. "I'd like to see Milton Berle steal this!" as he and Dinah do pidgin English. Both act well amid so-so lines. Douglas introduces Beatrice singing and Hal LeRoy dancing, with Bob joining the latter in comic pantomiming. Beatrice reappears as a frontier gal at a saloon robbed by a proper British outlaw (Douglas) who seeks the help of Dragalong Cavendish (Bob), and her assured delivery and timing outshines Bob as the skit dies. The Mexico City Boys Choir perform Handel's "Messiah," then Bob, Beatrice, Douglas and Dinah sing a comic "Easter Parade" before Bob thanks everyone. It's a messy debut, but Bob is not solely responsible for this being a disappointment.

Bob and Show: **

Specials – 1950s • 39

*The Star Spangled Revue*
May 27, 1950, Saturday 9-10:30 p.m.

Frank Sinatra (TV debut), Beatrice Lillie, Peggy Lee, Michael Kidd and Janet Reed, Steve Condos and Jerry Brandow, Arnold Stang, David Burns, Louis Kirtland, Jack Russell, Tom Avera, Sylvia Miles. Announcer: Wendell Niles. Commercial Spokesman: Dennis James. Choreography: Michael Kidd. Music: Charles Sanford. P/D: Max Liebman.

Bob avoids looking directly into the camera during his monologue. He cracks about celebrities coming to TV ("I understand [Bing] Crosby is going to do it when they get a wider screen") and one appearing too much, Arthur Godfrey ("He's on eighteen hours a day, and now they got a new program for him from midnight to six a.m. It's called 'Arthur Godfrey Snores.'"). Frank Sinatra does "Come Rain or Come Shine" smoothly, then laughs as Bob calls him a "pooped out Pinza" and "a breadstick with lungs." Of skinny Sinatra's stint at the Copa, Bob says, "It's the first time in nightclub history that so many people paid a cover charge to see a minimum." Bob being harassed at an automat by a bad wannabe crooner (Arnold Stang) and more is very good, as is Beatrice Lillie bedeviling an actress backstage. Also fun is Bob and Frank as baseball players in a dugout who worry about being presentable on TV and are revealed to be on a ladies team. They will repeat this on Bob's April 8, 1957 special. The skit with Bob encountering four other suitors besides himself for the hand of Peggy Lee is sluggish, as are the songs and dances except for Bob's comic hoofing with Steve Condos and Jerry Brandow. Finally in "The Road to Frigidaire," Sinatra plays Crosby with big false ears and a pipe, and Milton Berle makes a cameo as the boyfriend of a Dorothy Lamour lookalike. Bob thanks everyone while sweating in a rushed curtain call.

Bob and Show: ***


*The Star-Spangled Revue*
Sept. 14, 1950, Thursday 8-9 p.m.

Dinah Shore, Lucille Ball, Bob Crosby, New York Mayor William O'Dwyer, Mary Wickes. The Jack Cole Dancers. P: Lee Morgan. D: Hal Keith. Music: Al Goodman.

Bob's third video effort teams him with the first of many times opposite Lucille Ball as a female mayor running the city while dealing with her henpecked husband (Bob). (William O'Dwyer, former mayor of New York turned ambassador to Mexico, also participates in the show.) It includes a final sketch with Bob as a surgeon, Dinah Shore as a nurse, and Bob Crosby as a suffering patient. This may have been remade on Bob's October 1954 special.

**The Comedy Hour: The Bob Hope Show**
Nov. 26, 1950, Sunday 8-9 p.m.

Marilyn Maxwell, Jimmy Wakely, The Taylor Maids, The Hi Hatters, Judy Kelly, Nelson Case. P/D: Danny Dare. W: Fred Williams.

Bob makes up for a lot of this being badly paced with weak gags. "I'm beginning to like it," Bob says of TV. He says not to put the camera on military members in the audience, as some may be AWOL. Getting claps after he jokes of being cowardly, he joshes, "Who cued that?" After the Taylor Maids female trio sing, Bob is a pilot whose duffel bag includes a woman who kisses him as he tells her to meet him at the officers club. Changing into a paratrooper outfit, he wears a helmet with a TV antenna on it in a failed visual gag before his plane flies and crashes offstage. Entering with a tire wrapped around him in full body underwear, he says he forgot to tie his shoelaces. After Judy Kelly dances, Bob is a soldier in a base so isolated that a bear enters to do the Charleston with him. It's intermittently funny. Marilyn Maxwell does a comic duet with Bob before the Hi Hatters superbly dance together and with Bob. Jimmy Wakely sings "Lonesome Train" and then does "Tumbling Tumbleweeds" with Bob's intentionally strained yodeling added. Next, Bob plays a sailor on shore leave told not disclose secrets as a spy (Marilyn) tries to get him drunk and seduce him. Too forced, slow, and awkward at parts, it ends weakly with Bob surrendering. Bob then struggles to get out through the curtains and quips of TV, "It's the only place where twenty million people can watch you have a nervous breakdown." He mentions freedom as an ideal being protected for Americans by military men at home and in Korea in a patriotic close for a rough show that nonetheless shows Bob is learning the medium pretty well.

Bob: **** Show: ***

*The Comedy Hour: The Bob Hope Show*
Dec. 24, 1950, Sunday 8-9 p.m.

Robert Cummings, New York Mayor Vincent R. Impellitteri, Lily Pons, Eleanor Roosevelt, The Choir of the Catholic Church of St. John the Devine. Featured: Betty Bruce, Robert Maxwell, B.S. Pully, Erik Rhodes, Jerry Bergen, Nelson Case. P/D: Danny Dare. Music: Charles Sanford. Special Musical Material: Edward Maxwell, Ben Oakland, Mike Stewart.

With two politicos as guests and three religious tunes, this special is more stuffy than comfy. As a woman shows title cards to young children, "O Come All Ye Faithful" plays in the background. Members of the Choir of the Catholic Church of St. John the Devine appear on screen to finish the song plus "Hark the Herald Angels Sing" before Bob appears. He is unsteady in his monologue, which is spotty, before he introduces the mayor of New York. The latter offers thanks to Bob for his work overseas and wishes everyone a merry Christmas. Bob remarks about the mayor cleverly before Lily Pons trills operatically. Bob's talk with Robert Cummings leads into a medley of "Beautiful Ohio/Carolina in the Morning," and little of either clicks. Harpist Robert Maxwell's number comes before Bob, Robert, B.S. Pully, Erik Rhodes and Jerry Bergen play commiserating department store Santas on the New York subway in a so-so skit. Betty Bruce's acrobatic dance routine precedes Lily, Robert, and Bob appearing in a genuinely funny operetta of three kids eager to open an oversized Christmas presents. They even do the Charleston at the end, which is delightful. The choir returns to do "It Came Upon the Midnight Clear" before Bob comes on stage to bring out former First Lady Eleanor Roosevelt, who obviously uses cue cards to deliver a 1776 address by George Washington. Given that only one skit really works and Bob still has trouble facing the camera at parts, this is disappointing.

Bob and Show: **

*The Comedy Hour: The Bob Hope Show*
April 8, 1951, Sunday 8-9 p.m.

Rex Harrison, Lilli Palmer, Janis Paige, Arthur Treacher, Frank "Sugar Chile" Robinson. P/D: Danny Dare. Choreography: James Starbuck.

Along with his writers, Bob is still getting adjusted to TV, not looking directly into the camera during his four-minute monologue in favor of side views. Some extraneous sounds destroy his jokes on Sen. McCarthy too. This rocky start segues to Bob visiting a dress shop run by a humorously snippy Arthur Treacher, who even infers Bob is gay. Reaching for laughs, Bob models a floppy Chinese housecoat and a Scottish kilt before donning a suit that promotes his new movie, *The Lemon Drop Kid*. Janis Paige sings a sultry tune before telling Bob he should see a worldwide talent agent in preparation for his trip to London. Carrying a seal with him on a leash, Bob mistakenly visits a psychiatrist's office instead, where people in the waiting room act bizarre. The writers of this setup fumble by thinking being loud and chaotic equals being funny. The show bounces back some with an energetic boogie woogie number by juvenile pianist Frank "Sugar Chile" Robinson, then deflates with a somewhat labored routine where Bob tried to convince Rex he's a better actor by romancing Rex's then-wife Lilli, prompting Rex to pretend to be Bob romancing Janis. It ends with Tex McCrary and Jinx Falkenburg, Ken Murray, Ed Wynn, Toots Shor, Faye Emerson, Sid Caesar, Imogene Coca, Eddie Cantor, Jimmy Durante and Frank Sinatra wishing Bob bon voyage as the latter head overseas, and everyone sings "Thanks for the Memory." Despite what some claim, Milton Berle wasn't among the well-wishers here.

Bob: *** Show: **


### *Chesterfield Sound Off Time*
Oct. 14, 1951, Sunday 7-7:30 p.m.

Dinah Shore, Jerry Colonna, Jack Dempsey. P: Glen Wheaton. D: Hal Keith.

At the start, one lady in a hair salon exclaims Bob Hope is on TV and the other says, "Oh, I like him much better on television than in the movies." "Why?" asks her friend. "On television you can turn him off!" Bob emerges from behind a magazine sitting between them and says, "That's the last time I'll come in this joint!" The credits roll and three men and two women sing an introduction to Bob, who comes out with "Well, here I am, doing my bit to increase movie attendance." There are jokes about the show going live to New York City and Bing Crosby coming to the medium ("He doesn't know whether to go with NBC or buy it"). Dinah Shore sings, then surprisingly Bob does too in a commercial for his sponsor along with the quintet seen earlier. Next, Dinah plays Cleopatra to Bob's Marc Antony in a skit that sputters until Jerry Colonna adds a wild twist to the proceedings as Julius

Caesar. Hy Averback does a commercial and introduces boxing champ Jack Dempsey, who says he'll give $500 to any competitor, so Bob shows up wearing oversized gloves and pulls his belt over his chest to gain an edge as Jerry plays the referee. Like the other skit, it's pretty amusing but silly, as Bob primps in the corner before dancing with Jack at the end. A clearly winded Bob sings "Thanks for the Memory" at the end joined by his guests.

Bob and Show: ***

## *Chesterfield Sound Off Time*
Nov. 25, 1951, Sunday 7-7:30 p.m.

William Bendix, Lina Romey. Cameo (unbilled): Red Skelton.

Bob spoofs movies with William Bendix and Lina Romey and follows it with Bob as a football player coached by William. Red Skelton appears toward the end as a water boy, and Bob makes a similarly unannounced appearance on Red's show later that same night.

## *The Colgate Comedy Hour*
Dec. 2, 1951, Sunday 8-9 p.m.

Eddie Bracken, Marilyn Maxwell, Bob Crosby, Georgie Price, Toni Arden, Frank Faylen, Billy Daniels and Lita Baron, The Skylarks, Wally Blair, Joe Mole, Pat Flick, The Rio Brothers. P/D: Ernest D. Glucksman. Script Supervision: Henry Taylor. Music: Al Goodman. Choreography: Larry Ceballos.

Presented in conjunction with the American Guild of Variety Artists (AGVA), this begins with a stagehand warning Bob Crosby, Marilyn Maxwell, Eddie Bracken, Toni Arden, and Bob Hope it's five minutes until curtain time. Then the Skylarks sing how vaudeville is back as dancing girls, juggler Wally Blair, comic cyclist Joe Mole, comedian Pat Flick, a male-female acrobatic dance duo, and the Rio Brothers trio appear. AGVA President Georgie Price speaks too before Bob finally comes out nearly twelve minutes into the show. Bob needles Georgie and begins a solid set about his supposed childhood and vaudeville experiences. For example, he says of his amorous first girlfriend, "She ran away and joined some of the Navy." After Toni sings, Eddie plays a vacuum cleaner salesman who destroys Frank Faylen's house for six minutes of labored slapstick. Afterward, Bob introduces Bob Crosby singing "Silver Bells," who mentions that his brother Bing recorded the tune and it isn't selling well, to Bob's delight. Bob then hams it up as a surgeon working on TV, getting nurses to kiss him and doing a mock cigarette testimonial. Patient Bob Crosby complains about his surgery while Bob makes moves on Marilyn. When Marilyn insists she is a nurse first and a woman second, Bob cracks "Well, let's get out of first and shift into second right now!" It is raucous good fun. Bob says this show will help the AGVA Welfare Fund before Georgie plays George M. Cohan with a medley of his hits. Apart from Bob, who's smooth throughout, the rest of this is pretty blah.

Bob: \*\*\*\*\* Show: \*\*\*


### *Chesterfield Sound Off Time*
Dec. 23, 1951, Sunday 7-7:30 p.m.

Constance Moore, The Nicholas Brothers.

From the USS Boxer aircraft carrier, Bob does an opening set that amuses the sailors greatly. "There was some discussion about where we should do the show. I wanted to do on the stern, but the captain thought it would be better in the head. Oh, for you civilians who don't understand Navy talk, the head of the ship means the reading room. Oh, it doesn't? Oh, I better get my luggage out of there!" He also says Bing Crosby could not attend because "He fell off his wallet." Constance Moore, who Bob calls "Connie," is a great foil comically for Bob and duets with him superbly singing and dancing to "I Wanna Go Home (With You)." Next, Bob is Ensign Broadside Hope promoted to be in charge of a carrier. Bob keeps grinning amid his rapid delivery of snappy lines even as his dubious activities leads him to be dishonorably discharged and stripped to his skivvies ("CBS had something to do with this!" he exclaims). The Nicholas Brothers nail a superb dancing number wearing white service uniforms, before the show turns serious as the sailors sing "Silent Night" and Bob narrates a note of thanks for what the crew has done during the Korea War under a shot of the Pacific Ocean. "Thank God for these lads who keep it a moat between your home and the hell of war." He energetically taps with the Nicholas Brothers before wrapping up a program nicely balancing patriotism with wild comedy.

Bob: \*\*\*\*\* Show: \*\*\*\*

## *The Colgate Comedy Hour*
March 9, 1952, Sunday 8-9 p.m.

Martha Stewart, Anna Maria Alberghetti, Georgie Tapps.

Entertaining female service members at Camp Elliott, California, Bob does his monologue before letting the musical talents of singers Martha Stewart and Anna Maria Alberghetti and dancer Georgie Tapps get a good chunk of time. Most of the sketches mocked the practices of military life.

## *All Star Revue: The Bob Hope Show*
April 26, 1952, Saturday 8-9 p.m.

Fred MacMurray (TV debut), The Bell Sisters, Gale Robbins, Alfred Apaka. W: Larry Klein.

From the Presidio of San Francisco, Bob says he would be in Alcatraz if he hadn't listened to his tax man. He says of the overcast weather, "This is where they come to make the kinescopes." Getting little laughter, he adds, "That's an inside joke. I should've left it outside." His fine monologue covers the queen of Holland, Nevada bomb tests, and more before he introduces Gale Robbins to sing. Les Brown complains about a new saxophonist, and Fred MacMurray emerges with fanfare. Fred and Bob discuss doing the musical *Roberta* on Broadway before Bob is Fred's son in a Little Lord Fauntleroy getup for "Small Fry," a routine where Bob does some comic dancing. Alfred Apaka plays the ukulele satisfactorily, then Bob and Fred unfortunately appear as clichéd Chinese coolies. Luckily, this is only three minutes. Bob and Fred next are Italian fishermen, with more stereotypes but more humor too. They change again into Alcatraz prisoners, with Gale assisting them in an escape. It is moderately funny. The Bell Sisters sing their hit song "Bermuda," and Bob joins them to do "Give Me a June Night" as the girls clown wonderfully with him. Then the world's richest man in the world (Bob) comes to the Barbary Coast. A saloon gal (Gale Robbins) and the bartender intend to find Bob's gold mine. A prospector (Fred) draws a map of the mine on Gale's back, but it is no help, as other saloon gals have similar maps on their backs too. This is mostly a hoot, although time expires for billed guest Matty King to do a dance routine.

Bob: \*\*\*\*\* Show: \*\*\*\*

*The Colgate Comedy Hour*
June 15, 1952, Sunday 8-9 p.m.

Paul Douglas, June Hutton, Johnny Mack. Cameos: Randy Merriman, Bess Myerson. Music: Harry Russell.

Having the honor of closing out this series' second season, Bob goes to the Douglas Aircraft Plant in Santa Monica, California, to feature the unrelated Paul Douglas along with notable guests like the Flying Tigers air patrol. "They finally found a plane big enough to carry all the presidential candidates," he cracks in a good monologue also touching on Howard Hughes and more. Paul walks behind Bob and mocks him before they talk about how Paul worked opposite Marilyn Monroe on *Clash By Night* and Bob opposite Jane Russell on *Son of Paleface*, both current pictures they are plugging. They enact a good skit where a psychiatrist (Bob) helps an upset umpire (Paul). One timely gag here has Paul weeping and Bob responding, "Definite Johnny Ray complex!" in reference to the latter singer and his hit "Cry." Randy Merriman and Bess Myerson interrupt the festivities to bring out prizes they carried with them from New York City to promote that their daytime game show, *The Big Payoff*, will have a nighttime run this summer replacing *The Colgate Comedy Hour*. After June Hutton sings, Bob and Paul do another skit that is noisier and less enjoyable than the first as cavemen who hit each other with clubs. Thereafter, the Paley Center for Media's copy of this show ends, so given only half is seen, no ratings are given for this. For a similar show, see June 15, 1953.


*The Colgate Comedy Hour*
Oct. 12, 1952, Sunday 8-9 p.m.

Fred MacMurray, Connie Haines, The Clark Brothers.

The presidential campaign forms the basis of Bob's monologue, which takes up nearly the first quarter of this show. Bob spoofs *Captain Video* as the hero opposite villain Fred MacMurray, and the two play French explorers going down the Mississippi as well.

*The Colgate Comedy Hour*
Nov. 9, 1952, Sunday 8-9 p.m.

Rosemary Clooney, Bill Goodwin, The Four Step Brothers.
Bob acts as a heroic football player, sings "Two Sleepy People" with Rosemary Clooney, plays famous brothers in history opposite Bill Goodwin, and imagines what private eye Sam Spade would do in the White House in this installment.

*The Colgate Comedy Hour*
Dec. 7, 1952, Sunday 8-9 p.m.

Tony Martin, Frances Langford, The Esquire Calendar Girls.
A sendup of mail delivery during the Christmas rush highlights this entry, where Bob works with his longtime radio vocalist Frances Langford for the first time on television. She and Tony Martin act as well as sing here, while the Esquire Calendar Girls appear in a skit set in Korea with the military.

*The Colgate Comedy Hour*
Jan. 4, 1953, Sunday 8-9 p.m.

Jack Buchanan, Don Cherry, Marilyn Maxwell. Cameo: Bing Crosby. Choreographer: Nick Castle.
To pitch his new movie *The Road to Bali* incessantly (*Daily Variety* counted twelve mentions of it during the show), Bob coerces co-star Bing Crosby to carry a neon sign with the film's name at one point in a surprise appearance. Don Cherry sings while Jack Buchanan and Marilyn Maxwell banter with Bob individually, appear in skits, and do a song and dance with Bob at the end.

*The Colgate Comedy Hour*
Feb. 1, 1953, Sunday 8-9 p.m.

Nelson Eddy, Margaret Whiting, Bob Sweeney, Monte Montana, The Blackburn Twins, Marian Colby.

Crooner Nelson Eddy shows his comic flair as both a be-bop hipster and a car driver who gets into a fight with Bob over a collision in this show. Margaret Whiting trades a few lines with Bob as well as sings, while the Blackburn Twins and Marion Colby sing and dance.

## *The Colgate Comedy Hour*
March 1, 1953, Sunday 8-9 p.m.

George Jessel, Constance Moore, Robert Alda.
Coming from New York City, this has Bob and Robert Alda playing gangsters and Constance Moore singing. Besides appearing live on the show, George Jessel also takes part in a filmed bit mocking Bob with Fred Allen, Milton Berle, and Danny Kaye.

## *The Colgate Comedy Hour*
March 22, 1953, Sunday 8-9 p.m.

Bud Abbott, Lou Costello, Eddie Cantor, Jerry Lewis, Dean Martin, Donald O'Connor. P/D: Ernest D. Glucksman.
As part of the series' 100$^{th}$ episode celebration, all of the main rotating stars of *The Colgate Comedy Hour* appear doing their individual routines. Bob opens it with an eight-minute monologue covering everything from the Oscars to his hit "Buttons and Bows."

## *The Colgate Comedy Hour*
March 29, 1953, Sunday 8-9 p.m.

Rosemary Clooney, Fred Clark, The Bell Sisters, Mickey Rooney (cameo). EP: Sam Fuller. W: Danny Shapiro (no Mort Lachman nor Bill Larkin). Choreographer: Billy Daniels.
Here's an extended commercial for Bob's new movie, *Off Limits*, before a military audience that laughs at anything. "I'm sort of a Judge Hardy without a sneer," Bob says of his film role, referencing his costar Mickey Rooney's past in Andy Hardy movies. *Off Limits* also has Marilyn Maxwell, "the type of girl soldiers go over the hill for. And Marjorie Main. She's the kind they find when they get there." Bob notes the recent 3-D

movie craze and says you don't need it with Maxwell. He drops jokes about his picture for the Bell Sisters to sing with and without him, then plays a man reacquainted with his wife (Rosemary Clooney) after being in the Navy for seven years. It's tepid, as is a supposedly cut bit from *Off Limits* where a technical advisor to the film (Fred Clark) critiques Bob's performance. Rosemary jokes with Bob and then sings before the last skit, a so-so remake from Nov. 26, 1950, of a woman spy trying to get secrets from Bob with Mickey as an MP who saves Bob. The rushed ending has Bob, Mickey and Rosemary sing "Easter Parade" as a bevy of beauties walk past them. Everybody seems livelier than the material given to them.
Bob: *** Show: **

*The Colgate Comedy Hour*
April 19, 1953, Sunday 8-9 p.m.

Phil Harris, Marilyn Maxwell, Bob Sweeney.
Bob plays a gambler as well as an escaping convict who finds more than he bargained for on his way out of the cell. Both Phil Harris and Marilyn Maxwell sing in addition to act opposite Bob in a drive-in restaurant sketch.

*The Colgate Comedy Hour*
May 24, 1953, Sunday 8-9 p.m.

Gloria DeHaven, Rocky Marciano, Don McNeill, The Castro Sisters.
Airing from Chicago, Bob appears as a conventioneer and acts opposite Gloria DeHaven in a sketch set in Paris. He also has separate comedy spots with Rocky Marciano and Don McNeill.

*The Colgate Comedy Hour*
June 15, 1953, Sunday 8-9 p.m.

Rosemary Clooney, Frankie Laine, Honey Boy Watson. Cameos: Randy Merriman, Bess Myerson.
Filmed at the USS Los Angeles docked in port, this is mostly a product of its time in jokes and subject matter. Bob's monologue touches on topics

like atomic bomb tests and 3-D movies ("You know how your eyes used to pop out when Jane Russell came on screen? Well, now she pops out and pushes them back in!") Young black dancer Honey Boy Watson works his tap shoes to "Tea for Two" before Rosemary Clooney struts into the audience to sing to a serviceman. The audience eats it up more than home viewers, and the same applies to a skit comparing the different experiences when a cocky ensign and a goony sailor (both played by Bob) return home after their military duties end. Frankie Laine croons his latest hit, "Your Cheatin' Heart," then a WAVE (Rosemary) encounters a nervous USO host (Bob) who she wins over so well that he dresses in drag to go along with her at the end. Like the previous sketch, it's just sporadically amusing. So is "Eye Witness," a parody of the anthology series of the same name with Rosemary enlisting Frankie to kill Bob, her husband. Bob will remake this on his May 1957 special. Frankie and Rosemary banter and sing with Bob before Bess Myerson and Randy Merriman tell viewers as they did last year that *The Big Payoff* will be the summer replacement for *The Colgate Comedy Hour.* Bess gives Bob a miniature mink coat for his Oscar, which like much of the show is cute but not much more than that.

Bob and Show: \*\*\*

### *The Bob Hope Show*
Oct. 20, 1953, Tuesday 8-9 p.m.

Phil Harris, Gloria DeHaven, Elvia Allman, Alan Reed, Ohio Gov. Frank Lausche. D: Jack Hope.

Celebrating Ohio's sesquicentennial, this broadcast from Cleveland has Bob joining Phil Harris as randy hotel guests and worrying about the activities at a butcher shop run by Alan Reed.

### *The Bob Hope Show*
Nov. 17, 1953, Tuesday 8-9 p.m.

Fred MacMurray, Janis Paige, Ben Grauer. Featured: Millicent Brower, Doug Rogers. Choreographer: Hal Belfer.

Following a mediocre opening number, Bob emerges in a tux, top hat and cane, and he gives the latter two to a dancer and quips, "Rush these back, we can save three dollars." He's live in New York City, having done an experimental color TV program the previous day. Regarding that innovation, he says, "They can tell how late you were out last night." It's a sprightly show thereafter, with Janis Paige presenting "New York, New York" well and later having good interplay with Bob prior to their energetic duet. "Did I throw you the wrong cue?" she asks at one point. "I'll work it out somehow," Bob answers. Between those moments, Ben Grauer introduces a rib-tickling send-up of making commercials with Fred MacMurray delivering goofy lines and Bob being an overeager actor. Janis, Fred and Bob participate in the final skit as college students, with Fred using Janis as a way to get his roommate Bob into becoming the school's new quarterback. Fred's bobbling of lines brings out hilarious ad libs from Bob, as does Fred strumming a banjo to serenade Janis as she reclines on a sofa with Bob underneath her. Somewhat winded after that, Bob nevertheless introduces a bevy of beauties with jokes about each and sings together with all ten of them before bringing out Fred and Janis for a final bow.

Bob and Show: \*\*\*\*

**The Bob Hope Show**
Dec. 3, 1953, Tuesday 8-9 p.m.

Gale Storm, Gene Nelson, Pat Horne, Maj. Gen. William F. Dean. Featured: Bill Goodwin (also announcer), Joan Shawlee, Jerry Desmond, Ray Kellogg, Jack Pepper.

Here Bob's monologue is packed with political and Yuletide jokes. Quipping that he was up all last night erasing his name from Christmas cards to reuse them, he gets in a risqué line by saying he asked a department store clerk where men's underwear was and "He said, 'Ours is on the eighth floor. Yours is on the third.'" Bob mentions Milton Berle ("He does a great job replacing us between shows") and adds of the recently remarried "Thief of Bad Gags," "He was his old self when his minister said, 'Repeat after me.'" After complimenting Les Brown's band for winning a *Down Beat* magazine music survey, Bob asks Gale Storm about working with an older man (Charlie Farrell on her series *My Little Margie*). "Oh, it's wonderful! I've loved every minute I've been here!" she shoots back. They play a couple ending a date who encounter actors playing their ex-flames. One is Joan Shawlee, who forgets a line, and Bob scores laughs ad libbing about it. When they get home, Charlie Farrell warns Bob not to kiss his daughter. Gale singing and Gene Nelson dancing with Pat Horne are blah numbers between Bob scoring as a beleaguered store clerk and a German scientist telling a Los Angeles committee he can end smog. Bob, Gene and Gale sing "Silver Bells" before stiff Maj. Gen. Dean tells viewers how to help recuperating soldiers from the Korean War, ending an up-and-down special.

Bob: **** Show: ***

*The Bob Hope Show*
Jan. 26, 1954, Tuesday 8-9 p.m.

Hillary Brooke, Cass Daley, Zsa Zsa Gabor, Tony Martin. Cameo: Milton Berle.

In the first of several pairings with Bob, Zsa Zsa Gabor talks with him briefly before playing lovers being watched in a Communist state. Besides singing, Tony Martin also appears in a spoof of *Studio One* with Hillary Brooke. Milton Berle's appearance toward the end is unannounced. Cass Daley's routine as a clowning waitress will reappear on the show two months later.

*The Bob Hope Show*
Feb. 16, 1954, Tuesday 8-9 p.m.

Gloria DeHaven, Nelson Eddy, Jerry Colonna, Norman Rockwell.

An extended commercial for Bob's memoirs written by Pete Martin and appearing as a series in *The Saturday Evening Post* magazine, this includes a split-screen interview with Norman Rockwell from New York talking about his cover painting of Bob while Bob is in Los Angeles. The show also has a fictional depiction of Bob's life, such as him living a crazy boarding house he plans to leave until he meets Gloria DeHaven. They overhear Jerry Colonna on the phone talking about his work at Paramount, and they plead with him to let them audition at the studio by enacting different genres. He responds with giving his card to them for a job at Paramount Car Wash. Jerry also sings "I Love Life." As this is a partial episode only for viewing, no ratings are given for this entry.

*The Bob Hope Show*
March 16, 1954, Tuesday 8-9 p.m.

David Niven, Cass Daley, Janis Paige, Verna Felton, Elvia Allman, Jack Benny (cameo). Featured: Hy Averback.

A little lumpy but pretty good overall, a Saint Patrick's Day opening number leads Bob to wish "a happy Pat O'Brien to you all." He has some Irish jokes plus gags on Jack Benny's cheapness at his daughter Joan's wedding and the upcoming Oscars. Bob promotes his autobiography in *The Saturday Evening Post* again before he recalls flopping with his vaudeville partner (Janis Paige). "Imagine them throwing tomatoes!" she exclaims of the audience. "The least they could've done was take them out of the cans," Bob adds. Her testy mom (Verna Felton) rescues her daughter amid barbs from Bob, but they unite before the skit ends. "Postcards to Priscilla" mocks Loretta Young's TV series as Elvia Allman pretentiously spins into her living room. She has a postcard from David Niven, a man addicted to women. David mistakes Bob, another patient, for the shrink, and they compare childhood stories before a doctor arrives with a bunk bed to hear both of them. The two learn they are dating the same girl (Janis), and in a good topper, the doctor says she is his wife! After Janis's dance routine, David introduces Cass Daley as a waitress and aspiring actress who mugs and flaunts so hard that she cracks up Bob, playing director Orson Von Hope. His prediction of stardom goes to her head, and she leaves him for Jack Benny. ("Since my daughter's wedding, I've had to pick up every dollar I can make!" he explains of his cameo.) Bob has prolonged goodbyes with his guests but rushes the ending without doing "Thanks for the Memory."

Bob and Show: ***

*The Bob Hope Show*
April 13, 1954, Tuesday 8-9 p.m.

Jack Benny, Rosemary Clooney. Featured: Margaret Dumont, Elvia Allman, John Gallaudet, Eddie Marr, Peter Leeds, Bob Jellison, Bob Bence. Choreography: Nick Castle. W: Larry Marks (no Bill Larkin or Charles Lee). Rosemary Clooney's Gown Designer: Edith Head.

There is lots of fun here as Bob ties an opening number set a baseball game into gags about President Dwight Eisenhower and Sen. Joseph

McCarthy (e.g., the Communist-accusing politico chased a vendor yelling "Get your red hots here!"). Regarding the latter demanding equal time for a scathing report on him on *Person to Person*, Hope quips, "You know, if McCarthy gets air time whenever someone takes a crack at him, he'll have more programs than Arthur Godfrey." Of Joe DiMaggio marrying Marilyn Monroe, Bob observes, "Yes sir, the old home run king has really got something to run home for now!" He even jokes about José Ferrer marrying Rosemary Clooney before playing a Lothario conned into marrying her. The hilarious, energetic sketch has good ad libs and bloopers (they nearly knock down a lamp!). Next, Hy Averback meeting Cleveland's rookie pitcher (Bob), who has a picture of Mom in his locker (Bing in drag), is okay enough, as is Rosemary's number with dancers. The show really sparkles as a jazz pianist (Bob) rubs his nose against an auditioning violinist (Jack Benny), who says, "He cut me!" Jack often mocks his lines and bobbles one to Bob's amusement. Rosemary loses her composure as she throws herself at Jack, who exclaims, "This is the lousiest thing I've ever been in!" cracking up everyone. Oddly but humorously, Bob and Jack kill each other and head to hell arm in arm at the end. Bob and Rosemary do "You Got Class," a tune from their new movie *Here Come the Girls*, then Bob "accidentally" destroys Benny's violin before this pleasant entry concludes.

Bob: \*\*\*\*\* Show: \*\*\*\*


**The Bob Hope Show**
May 11, 1954, Tuesday 8-9 p.m.

Dorothy Lamour, Edmond O'Brien. Featured: Hy Averback, Sheldon Leonard, Verna Felton, Peter Leeds, Bill Johnstone. Also: Jerry Hausner, Bob Jellison, Ray Kellogg, Mabel Mann, Ralph Montgomery, Jack Shea. W: Larry Masters (no Bill Larkin or Charles Lee). Choreography: Al White Jr.

Starting fine but sputtering at the end, this starts with Bob joking about Sen. Joseph McCarthy's hearing on supposed Communists in the Army. "Sen. McCarthy has certainly made a name for himself. I don't know what it is, but he's made it!" He hits a NBC hit drama's dry style too: "*Dragnet* is the only show I've heard of where a corpse is accused of overacting." Claps for mentioning again that Les Brown's band was voted Number One by *Down Beat* makes Bob crack about "shills in the audience" for the group before he does a solid skit as a seaman who mistakenly gets an eighty-six million-dollar check and lives it up. Also nice is the next spoof with Bob as Arthur Godfrey hosting a show in the South Sea islands with Dorothy Lamour as his sidekick in a colorful sarong ("I love that spangled teabag" he ad libs to her amusement). The fun continues with Dorothy doing a song and Bob doing a great bit as a boxer with Verna Felton as his mother, Edmond O'Brien as his manager and Sheldon Leonard as a gangster wanting him to throw the fight. Things slow though as Maj. Gen. John Selden delivers an Armed Forces Day message, Edmond O'Brien delivers a Shakespearean monologue and Randy Cardenas performs a long juggling routine. By the time Bob sings "Thanks for the Memory" and urges support for United Cerebral Palsy, a potential great show has become a routine one.

Bob: ***** Show: ***

**The Bob Hope Show**
June 1, 1954, Tuesday 8-9 p.m.

Marilyn Maxwell, Cass Daley, Jerry Colonna. Cameos: Zsa Zsa Gabor, Jack Benny. Featured: Elvia Allman, Peter Leeds.

It's the end of Bob's season, so after a June wedding theme opening number, he mocks how tired other TV stars are now, only he seems a little weary himself. "Mr. Peepers is pooped," goes one typical remark. Also mentioned are diets and the U.S. Army hearings by Sen. Joe McCarthy ("Most comedy shows go off for the summer—except for that one in Washington"). Bob then conducts a college course on love and marriage, and Marilyn Maxwell and the students do a number with him as Marilyn seduces Bob. It's a stupid timewaster. Cass Daley energetically sings a number after that, then Bob plays a pollster who talks with Peter Leeds (hysterical as a punch-drunk interviewee) and Jerry Colonna (intermittently amusing as a wacko). After Marilyn Maxwell's number with the dancers, Cass plays the ecstatic winner of "Princess for a Day" (a spoof of *Queen for a Day*). She gets a date with star Montgomery Hope, who's shocked by her looks and earthiness and refuses her. Lots of bloopers, the wildness of Cass, and a cameo by Zsa Zsa Gabor make this a winner. Bob then surprises the June bride winner of *Brides* magazine with her fiancé. After Bob, Marilyn, Cass, and Jerry sing goodbye to special comic lyrics to "Thanks to the Memory," Jack Benny brings out a birthday cake to Bob who accidentally drops it. Undaunted, he and Jack smash bits of it into each other's faces for a finish so raucous one wishes the rest of the show was as amusing.

Bob and Show: ***

**The Bob Hope Show**
Oct. 12, 1954, Tuesday 8-9 p.m.

David Niven, Marilyn Maxwell, Jose Greco. Featured: Peter Leeds, Charles Cooley, Jack Pepper, Alan Turner, Hy Averback, Sara Shane, The Jeff Tomlin Singers. W: Chet Castellaw, Martin Ragaway. Choreographer: Nick Castle.

Bob starts by needling entertainment trends from widescreen movies to TV "spectaculars" (specials 90 minutes or longer). For the latter, he claims NBC's owner "Gen." David Sarnoff gets dressed up as a little old lady to appear on the game show *Strike It Rich* to afford the high costs. He also jests about Joe DiMaggio leaving his wife, Marilyn Monroe. "I've heard of men giving up smoking, but this is ridiculous!" He's fitfully funny as a coach of David Niven, winner of running a four-minute mile (Niven carries Hope on his back to meet with reporters) and as a foil to Jose Greco after the latter performs a flamenco dance. Best of all is a wild spoof of the TV series *Medic* with Bob as a surgeon delivering snappy lines while trying to remove Niven's appendix and romance nurse Marilyn Maxwell at the same time. When Bob touches Niven's navel and ad libs, "I just pushed the button for room service, do you mind?" the actor loses his composure. The rest is good but anticlimactic, including Bob doing an odd presentation of honors to sixteen former American Olympians, Marilyn singing and Bob ending with a rendition of "Thanks for the Memory."

Bob: **** Show: ***

**The Bob Hope Show**
Dec. 7, 1954, Tuesday 8-9 p.m.

Beatrice Lillie, Maurice Chevalier (TV debut), Liane Dayde, Moira Lister, Jerry Desmond, The Cologne Male Voice Choir. Featured: Shirley Eaton, Victor Rietti, Doreen Dawn, Michael Hall. Music: Eric Robinson. W: Martin Ragaway, Gig Henry, Chet Castellaw.

Bob shows a fake newspaper with the headline "Bob Hope in London" as he strolls its streets before the credits. He gets rapturous applause before his monologue scores better there than for U.S. viewers due to obscure local references. The 182-member Cologne Male Voice Choir singing in German doesn't help, but Beatrice Lillie delights with a routine on how to seduce a man, even getting away with putting a fan in her cleavage at one point. She's also great as a raw cranky fan of Bob's whom he takes backstage and transforms to make her into a glamorous gal. Bob saw prima ballerina Liane Dayde at the Paris Opera and lets her do a rather static ballet number, then promotes his new book, *Have Tux, Will Travel*, with comic references to his roots in England ("After I was born, mother never spoke to father again"). Maurice Chevalier then plays the cousin of Moira Lister, who's on her honeymoon with Bob, and when Chevalier's Gallic glamor wows her, Bob brings out his sexy cousin in a so-so skit. Next, Maurice does funny impersonations of what people think foreign languages sound like to them, then sings "Louise" and gets a bear hug from Bob. The choir sings once more as Bob sermonizes about the need for peace in the world and concludes, "I wish we could all get together and sing in the harmony that most of the world is praying will be ours none too soon." He thanks the BBC crew and cast warmly before saying goodbye.

Bob and Show: ***

## *The Colgate Comedy Hour: The Bob Hope Show*
Jan. 9, 1955, Sunday 8-9 p.m.

William Holden, Hedda Hopper, Jerry Colonna, Anita Ekberg, Margaret Whiting, The Crew Chiefs (a U.S. Air Force band). Also: Brenda Marshall, Patty Thomas, Mara Lynn, Peter Leeds, Charles Cooley. W: Martin Ragaway, Chet Castellaw, Gig Henry. Choreographer: Nick Castle.

"Hello, fellow *Truth or Consequences* losers!" cracks Bob to the audience at Thule Air Force Base in Greenland in this excellent installment, Bob's first overseas military show to appear on TV. He jokes about the base's brutally cold weather ("four polar bears applied for a transfer") and isolation ("This guy here is so lonely, he's going steady with his tattoo"). It leads into a sketch where a colonel (Peter Leeds) complains about Hope's troupe being unreasonable and brings out Jerry Colonna and William Holden. The latter plans to add a gambling operation on the base that will be so big that "[President Dwight] Eisenhower will be pulling strings to get here!" Just as delightful is Bob attempting to romance Margaret Whiting with a threadbare set (e.g., William Holden ignites a lighter to represent a fireplace) and ending up inadvertently marrying her thanks to Jerry's shenanigans. Hedda Hopper gets some laughs before she introduces Margaret doing "We're Having a Heat Wave" with the Nick Castle Dancers. The final attraction is statuesque Anita Ekberg visiting three crazed soldiers (Bob, William and Robert Strauss, the latter aping his characterization from his *Stalag 17* movie with Holden). Their camp is so desolate that they end up dancing with each other (and Bob with a polar bear at one point) before Bob gets to leave by being declared insane. It's all swell until Secretary of the Air Force Harold Talbott insists on doing a boring five-minute speech at the end. Otherwise, this is top entertainment.

Bob: \*\*\*\*\* Show: \*\*\*\*


**The Bob Hope Show**
Feb. 1, 1955, Tuesday 8-9 p.m.

Line Renaud, Roy Rogers and Trigger, Dale Evans, Sons of the Pioneers, Shirley MacLaine. Featured: Peter Leeds, Sid Melton. Choreographer: Nick Castle.

Bob muses about the United Nations ("My brother has a job there. He's an interpreter in the washroom.") and Gen. Douglas MacArthur's recent visit to Los Angeles ("He just looked at Marilyn Monroe and said, 'I shall return!'") in his monologue. He also jokes that he thought Sons of the Pioneers referred to Crosby's brood in a smart set that is met equally well with most of the show's other content. Bob hilariously plays a cowboy with a broken-down filly named Zsa Zsa on a decrepit ranch who plays poker against Roy Rogers in an unsuccessful bid to win Trigger. Shirley MacLaine does a swell dance routine followed by Bob's sharp interplay with singer Line Renaud ("Why wouldn't they like your voice?" he tells the French native. "Look where it's been!") before they do a cute duet. Dale Evans finally shows up in a sketch as an unwitting assistant to Bob in a plot to drive the latter's brother (Roy) crazy, which is amusing if somewhat overlong. The Sons of the Pioneers present a song with Dale, then Bob has a wonderful soft-shoe routine with Shirley. "You sing?" he asks her. "No." "You tell jokes?" "No." Then she interjects, "You dance?"

to Bob's dismay. The rousing finale has Bob singing with the Sons of the Pioneers followed by an abrupt goodbye as time runs out.

Bob: \*\*\*\*\* Show: \*\*\*\*

*The Bob Hope Show*
March 1, 1955, Tuesday 8-9 p.m.

David Niven, Vivian Blaine, Quintetto Allegro. Featured: Peter Leeds, Sid Melton. W: Martin Ragaway, Chet Castellaw. Choreographer: Louis DaPron.

Flubs in this live show harm its comedy and irritate Bob. He has twelve bumpy minutes doing his monologue after pretending to be a chorus dancer. He tells a stagehand, "I can't see the words" and sings a little until the cue cards get in place. After a few more jokes, he stops and says, "Stay back, you're getting into the light, Jimmy" and looks peeved until the crew member adjusts his location. He then has good gags about politics and entertainment, such as his description of Russia: "Over there, 'Sh-Boom' isn't just a song, it's your life story." He also mocks the Oscar nominations ("I don't take the Academy Awards seriously—or any other way"), especially Bing Crosby for Best Actor ("I can't think of a more deserving actor. I guess they couldn't either."). The first skit is fitfully funny as a press agent (Bob) finds a female Marlon Brando equivalent (Vivian Blaine dressed in a motorcycle outfit) and promotes her with quick set and costume changes. It ends with a surprise cameo of Jimmy Durante as Brando. The rest stinks, from Quintetto Allegro, a five-man singing group from Italy, doing lame vocal parodies to David Niven playing a jeweler trying to make Bob buy a big diamond for Vivian, his girlfriend. At the end, Bob thanks the audience for joining them in "our dress rehearsal," exclaims "What the hell does that mean?" and leaves the stage disgusted before the credits run. He was right to do so.

Bob: \*\*\* Show: \*\*

*The Bob Hope Show*
April 26, 1955, Tuesday 8-9 p.m.

Lloyd Nolan, Line Renaud, Hans Conreid, Miss Malta and Company Dog Revue. Choreographer: Louis DaPron.

A sagging middle dampens an otherwise great show. Bob starts going after Arthur Godfrey's recent cast dismissals. He quips of Winston Churchill's retirement that "There no truth to the rumor Godfrey fired him." Saying the star's new show will be called "Arthur Godfrey and His Survivors," he adds, "The other day, he fired the network!" Bob then plays a tourist who interrupts Hans Conreid having a comic tiff on the Eiffel Tower with Line Renaud ("After I'm dead, you'll want me back. But I won't come!" says Hans). He gets lots of laughs as a rube Line tries to romance, as when she drops her handkerchief his way and he picks it up and says, "No, not mine!" The mirth droops as Bob and Lloyd play inmates in a fancy prison and earn chuckles only when Lloyd reprises his *Caine Mutiny* TV role and grouses, "Who stole the strawberries?" and Bob says of an empty TV screen, "Must be the Godfrey show. Nobody's left." Line's number with the dancers is similarly flat, but a *This is Your Life* parody afterward is hysterical, as Bob loses it as Miss Malta's dogs enter in costumes like a bebop singer and the honoree, Lassie, barks in response. *This is Your Life* host Ralph Edwards appears at the end to say, "Bob Hope, this is your lawsuit!" to laughter. It ends with another good guest cameo, Jerry Colonna, who stops pretending to be a cameraman to sing and play the trombone before Bob says good night.

Bob: ***** Show: ***


**The Bob Hope Show**
May 24, 1955, Tuesday 8-9 p.m.

Jane Russell, Bing Crosby, Don Hartman. Featured: Hy Averback. W: Martin Ragaway, Chet Castellaw (misspelled as Castalaw).

This is sheer promotional overkill starting with the monologue. Bob plugs his new book *Have Tux, Will Travel* before commenting on world affairs and the Davy Crockett craze sparked by the *Disneyland* TV series. "I didn't have to buy my kids any coonskin caps. We just stopped giving them haircuts in January," he says. He introduces Les Brown with a clip of Ed Sullivan's bandleader Ray Bloch, dissolving Brown and his band into hysterics. Bob then narrates an introduction for Paramount head of production Don Hartman, who tries to convince Hope to promote his latest production for the studio, *The Seven Little Foys*. Don shows Bob singing "Two Sleepy People" with Shirley Ross from *The Big Broadcast of 1938* and parts of *The Paleface, Monsieur Beaucaire* and *Son of Paleface* before he tells Bob that Jane Russell wants to escort him to a party Bing Crosby is throwing. Bob watches his love scene from *My Favorite Blonde* and Jane promotes her movies *The Tall Men* and *Underwater* before Bob plays more scenes from his movies. Bob arrives at Bing's house, learns that the party was thrown without him, and complains about how Bing treats him with clips from their Road pictures. Bing responds by putting a poster of his movie *The Country Girl* on Bob's back. Back on stage, Bob plays a clip of *Sorrowful Jones* before showing two long ones from *The Seven Little Foys*. Bob is chipper in the new parts, but this is a bad infomercial for all participants.

Bob: *** Show: **

**Bob Hope in *The Chevy Show***
Oct. 4, 1955, Tuesday 8-9 p.m.

Jane Russell, Wally Cox, Roy Rogers, Janis Paige, The Hollywood Deb Stars for 1955. Choreographer: Nick Castle.

A deadly filmed opener has Bob pulled over by two cops unimpressed until they want to escort him to the studio because he's in his sponsor's new car. Bob then delivers a lesser monologue with one good joke about Eddie Fisher and Debbie Reynolds going to a game during their honeymoon: "Now are you convinced that baseball is America's favorite sport?" Just as he did on last season's opener, Bob plugs his movie *The Seven Little Foys*, but here it's part of an elaborate spoof of the movie *The Desperate Hours* where Bob as a convict on the lam shocks the audience by "shooting" the camera lens while terrorizing Wally Cox and the latter's family watching a quiz show. As Bob threatens his family, Wally to tell his kids to go next door to watch Pinky Lee, "the world's greatest comedian," while Bob shoots the stereo system when it plays a Bing Crosby record in a funny sendup. Wally does good banter with Bob at the end of the show, as does Janis, but the rest is blah, although it is cute seeing Jane Russell introduce early appearances by "Hollywood Deb Stars" Gloria Talbot, Lori Nelson, Karen Sharpe and Cathy Crosby, Bing's niece ("What a beautiful first name!" jokes Bob when meeting her). Roy Rogers' appearance is a repeat from the Oct. 12, 1954 show.

Bob and Show: ***

***The Bob Hope Chevy Show***
Nov. 15, 1955, Tuesday 8-9 p.m.

Betty Hutton, Jeanne Crain. Featured: Hy Averback, Arthur Q. Bryan, Dick Elliot, Bob Jellison, Peter Leeds, Sid Melton, Almira Sessions. Choreographer: Nick Castle.

Betty Hutton comes off great but the rest of the show is a miss here. She delivers her tedious lines well in a filmed opening bit where Bob snares her as a guest on his show by showing her his sponsor's new car and telling her she can get one if she agrees to appear on it. After this forced shilling, Bob does a dated monologue with jokes about Prince Margaret and President Eisenhower in the hospital, then stars in a long and labored modern day version of "Romeo and Juliet" as an exterminator trying to win the hand of a rich janitor's daughter (Jeanne Crain). Next, Betty sings "The Little Rock Roll" in her exuberant brassy style, dancing with six men and looking great. A repeat of the Lassie skit from the April 26, 1955 show (but promoted as a new bit) pads out the middle before the show gains some life with "The Fink City Story," pitting a female district attorney (Betty) against a gangster (Bob). Betty lets him feel her up, prompting Bob and her to ad-lib and crack up so much that Bob exclaims, "Got to get back to the script sometime!" It ends as Bob's henchmen and Betty's policemen shoot at each other until Bob and Betty realize the gunfire is actually coming from the studio audience and they scram. Bob will remake this on his Oct. 24, 1962 special. Betty also sparkles in the final dance number with Bob and Jeanne, but it's too little too late.

Bob: \*\*\* Show: \*\*

***The Bob Hope Chevy Show***
Dec. 27, 1955, Tuesday 8-9 p.m.

Betty Grable, James Mason, Joan Rhodes. Choreographer: Nick Castle.

A Christmas show filmed in Iceland, this has the guest stars talk to Bob as well as participate in a couple of skits. The most memorable moment, however, comes from Joan Rhodes, a woman from England so strong that she is able to lift up Bob and carry him over her shoulder.

*The Chevy Show: The Bob Hope Show*
Feb. 7, 1956, Tuesday 8-9 p.m.

Fernandel, Diana Dors, Yana, Nancy Crompton, The Ballet Montmartre, Joan Rhodes, The George Mitchell Choir. Music: Ted Heath, Dennis Ringrowe.

As he films *The Iron Petticoat* in England, Bob tapes this show there and in Finland in fine form. "Thank you, relatives," he cracks in his opening monologue mocking British commercials, customs ("Every afternoon they stop for tea. Then at six, they serve."), fog ("I could finally make it out. It was the end of my cigarette."), and roads ("Over here, if you travel in a straight line, they arrest you for drunken driving."). He calls the film he's shooting *Not for Money* (an early title) and says costar Katharine Hepburn is doing it because "She needed the money." Bob adds, "Instead of dressing rooms, everybody sings a 'no peeking' pledge. I signed mine in invisible ink." He gets plenty of laughs about the recent wedding of the new princess of Monaco. "Only last year, Grace Kelly won the Oscar for *The Country Girl*. Today, the girl has her own country. Just shows you what one picture with Crosby can do for you—get you right out of the country!" Bob similarly shines in skits where a delivery man (Fernandel) shows excessive romantic interest to Bob's girlfriend and a bit in a makeup room where he plays himself opposite Diana Dors exaggerating her image as a ditzy dame. Too bad the rest is unexceptional music plus a presentation of the latest haute couture from Paris, which is not why people watch a Bob Hope show.

Bob: \*\*\*\*\* Show: \*\*\*


*The Bob Hope Chevy Show*
Feb. 28, 1956, Tuesday 8-9 p.m.

Douglas Fairbanks Jr., Cornel Wilde, Jean Wallace, Line Renaud, Tommy Trinder, The Bernard Brothers, Richard Wattis, Lucien Bob and Esther (dance duo), Elsa Martinelli, Melinda Lee, Maureen Swanson. Music: Dennis Ringrowe.

From London again, Bob mocks the country's transportation ("British roads are built on the system one bad turn deserves another") and recent cold spell. "British plumbing, you know, is pretty old. The hot water heater in my room has a sign—'For service, call Oliver Cromwell.'"

This launches into a sprightly spoof of the series *Foreign Intrigue* with Bob as a bumbling spy and Line as a seductress who attempts to kill him. Her numbers and Lucien Bob and Esther's are a bore, but the show recovers when Bob plays himself dealing with a wisecracking hotel clerk (Richard Wattis) and actor Cornel Wilde, who tells his real-life wife Jean Wallace how much he hates Bob. "Yesterday I almost forgot my name," says Bob. "Don't worry about it, I got one for you!" retorts Cornel. Douglas Fairbanks wants to avoid Bob too as the latter gets rejected for dates by Melinda, Maureen, Julia and Elsa. A funny monologue by Tommy Trinder helps this end strong, but it overall feels like a show better received by English audiences than American viewers.

Bob and Show: ***

**The Bob Hope Chevy Show: "The Awful Truth"**
March 20, 1956, Tuesday 8-9 p.m.

Bob Hope, Greer Garson, Dick Foran, Vivian Blaine, Hedda Hopper. Featured: Ray Walker, Peter Leeds, Eddie Marr, Dick Keane, Eleanor Audley, Pierre Watkins, Ken Christy, Margaret Dumont, Rex Evans, Howard Hoffman, Isobel Randolph. W: Arthur Richman (play), Vina Delmar (screenplay), adaptation by Hope's writers including Norman Sullivan.

Adapting the 1937 comedy movie classic by substituting Bob, Greer and Dick for Cary Grant, Irene Dunne and Ralph Bellamy, tailoring it to Bob, and cutting it to about 50 minutes is a risky proposition that pays off only occasionally. Following an introduction by Hedda Hopper, who later appears as Greer's mother, its pluses are Bob, doing his first straight acting role throughout a special splendidly, and a wonderfully trained dog, especially for a live show. Drawbacks are dead transitions of dark screen between scenes which should have had Les Brown scoring, some failed anticipated laugh lines, and a rather starchy performance by Greer. However, she does hold her own when Bob ad-libs following a phone call, "Honey, if that's the television survey, tell them I'm watching Bob Hope, will you?" and she responds "You tell them yourself!" She also gets to plug a charity at the curtain call.

Bob: ***** Show: ***

## *The Bob Hope Chevy Show*
May 1, 1956, Tuesday 8-9 p.m.

Kathryn Grayson (TV debut), George Sanders, Pearl Bailey. Featured: Hy Averback, Peter Leeds, Elvia Allman, Sid Tomack, Robert Carson, Jack Petruzzi, Adrienne D'Ambricourt, Ralph Sanford, Curley Clements. Choreographer: Nick Castle.

Bob opens ribbing Margaret Truman and Grace Kelly's weddings, Eisenhower's agricultural policies ("They pay the farmer not to farm. It's like hiring Marilyn Monroe to model sneakers.") and insomnia meds. "They have the new relaxing pills that come in four strengths: quiet, very quiet, rest in peace and Perry Como." His song-dance-and-patter routine with Pearl shines (Bob: "Maybe I should've stuck to dancing." Pearl: "You dance like you're stuck to something!"). George Sanders also sparkles playing himself being convinced to act opposite Bob (and Pearl) in their current film *That Certain Feeling*. Kathryn's two operatic solos hamper the fun, but she's okay as the love interest of hillbilly star Arkansas Bernie (Bob with a shaky Southern accent) in an intermittently funny skit. The show ends strongly as Bob is interrupted singing the theme for "That Certain Feeling" by surprise guest George Gobel, who sings the theme of his new movie, *The Birds and the Bees*.

Bob: \*\*\*\* Show: \*\*\*

## *The Bob Hope Show: The Chevy Show*
May 22, 1956, Tuesday 8-9 p.m.

Kim Novak, Pearl Bailey, Vic Damone, Ken Murray. Featured: Charlotte Atkins, Patricia Blake, Bart Bradley, Shari Clark, Billy Curtis, Steve Firstman, Marilyn Hanold, Tor Johnson, Danny Richards Jr., Mike Ross. W: Chet Castellaw (misspelled as Castalaw).

Screen goddess Kim Novak's only TV appearance with Bob is a flaccid filmed bit with canned laughter near the end of this show to promote her new film, *The Eddy Duchin Story*. It hurts a decent show spotlighting guests who somewhat overshadow Bob except for his monologue. There, he gets laughs starting with "This was the year Marilyn Monroe appeared on *Person to Person*. I hear Edward R. Murrow was so flustered, he forgot to light a cigarette." He also scores with a few about his new movie, *That Certain Feeling*, like claiming that he can't show a clip of it because Ed Sullivan has first rights, but two minutes discussing it is flogging the promotion to death. After Vic Damone sings "On the Street Where You Live," he and Bob are sailors on the prowl for women while singing "Standing on the Corner." Bob has a good line here: "Thirteen buttons on one pair of pants—no wonder they surprised us at Pearl Harbor." Playing his real-life role as a new producer for NBC ("To prop up Perry Como," snarls Bob), Ken Murray recommends that Bob hire more erudite writers, all played by juvenile actors. One tells Bob, "We just give you the chicken feed—you lay the eggs," which is the best line in the skit apart from ad-libs by Bob and Ken. And Pearl Bailey is more entertaining singing than enacting a skit wherein Bob cons her in Las Vegas to do his film, *That Certain Feeling*—yep, another unneeded plug.

Bob and Show: ***

### *The Sunday Spectacular Presents the Road to Hollywood*
June 17, 1956, Sunday 8-9:30 p.m.

Host: Steve Allen. Guests: Bob Hope, Betty Grable, George Sanders, Dorothy Lamour, Marilyn Maxwell, Jane Russell. Featured: Hy Averback, Joe Lilley, Peter Leeds, Jerry Mathers, Florenz Ames, John Bryant, Joseph Kearns, Charlotte Atkins. P: Jack Hope. D: Jack Shea. W: Lester White, John Rapp, Mort Lachman, Bill Larkin, Larry Marks. Choreographer: Jack Baker. Music: Les Brown.

A Bob Hope special in disguise, this shamelessly promotes *That Certain Feeling* with bloopers, a long clip, and much more. Even Bob interrupts Steve's opening monologue with "Either you plug my picture or I go home!" First Bob is in a story conference with the film's writers and Steve humorously translates what everyone really is saying. Next, Bob reprises the psychiatrist sketch from *The Bob Hope Show* on March 16, 1954 opposite George Sanders, his *That Certain Feeling* co-star. After the film's bloopers and a clip from *The Road to Bali* with Bing Crosby and Dorothy Lamour (who later has her own live production number), Bob has his best skit with Jerry Mathers as himself, deflating Hope's ego in the latter's dressing room (while mentioning working with him on *That Certain Feeling*), and Betty Grable as a starstruck fan who dances with six men in Bob Hope masks. Bob also has a cute bit with his four children, then plays the leading man to Dorothy, Betty, Marilyn

Maxwell, and Jane Russell in a series of skits that end with all exiting into a theater showing—what else?—*That Certain Feeling*. Finally, Bob promotes Steve's new show in this time slot next week, and Bob will guest there too!

Bob and Show: ***

**The Bob Hope Chevy Show**
Oct. 21, 1956, Sunday 8-9 p.m.

Desi Arnaz, Lucille Ball, James Cagney, Diana Dors, Don Larsen, William Frawley, Vivian Vance, The Hollywood Deb Stars. Choreographer: Bruce Baker.

After a standard monologue touching on the presidential election and more, Bob brings out curvaceous Diana Dors. "I'm not really what you Americans would call a square," she says. "No, we'd never say that!" Bob grins. Diana and Bob play a British couple, where there's a great bit involving her trying to take off his long-stretching socks, and a similar American one, where the automation extends to mass production of babies. This will be remade much less effectively on Bob's Feb. 15, 1967 special. Then Bob asks New York Yankee Don Larsen, the first man to pitch a no-hitter in the World Series, "Have you ever seen Little Leaguers in action?" "Why sure, Bob. We play Cleveland," he shoots back. Larsen delivers his lines naturally before he and Bob re-enact the last out. "That's a hitter?!" Don asks as he spots Bob quivering holding a bat. After the funny skit ends, Bob reveals *Sport* magazine has honored Don with a new car for his achievement, adding, "And while you're driving on a freeway, try for a no-hitter there!" Measuring six-foot-four, Don squeezes into the convertible just barely. James Cagney comes out to present the Hollywood Deb Stars and dances splendidly with Bob. The only weak part is Bob imagining himself in Desi Arnaz's role on *I Love Lucy* as Lucille Ball's husband and Desi playing Vivian Vance's husband in place of William Frawley. It's a poor takeoff spruced up only by Bob's quips. Still, the rest of this is top Bob in action.

Bob and Show: ****

***The Bob Hope Chevy Show***
Nov. 18, 1956, Sunday 9-10 p.m.

   Perry Como, Julie London, Joan Davis, John Cameron Swayze. Cameos: Milton Berle, Steve Allen. Featured: Stephen Chase, Fred Tozere, Ty Perry, The Ray Charles Singers.
   Live and lively from New York City, this is what a Bob Hope special should be. Bob scores with his recent guest shot on *The Perry Como Show* ("It's a live show, except for him") and *The Ten Commandments* ("It's a wonderful picture, and I recommend it very highly to anyone who has a free weekend" and "When I saw the picture, there was a short subject with it—*Gone With the Wind*"). Also sent up well is Elvis Presley and his hits. Of "Hound Dog," Bob says, "He sounds as if it just bit him!" Next is a wildly manic bit where a queen (Joan Davis) must wed a rich, narcissistic commoner (Bob) to save her kingdom, but he's unimpressed by her decaying castle. The great physical humor has Joan so desperate she sticks her head out of dresser drawers Bob examines to sway him. Also swell is the NBC-CBS programming "war" covered by John Cameron Swayze. Bob leads the fight for the former with Perry Como, Milton Berle arrives as a "battle casualty" ready to do a routine to Bob's chagrin, and Steve Allen accidentally drives a tank into the war room because CBS stole his glasses. Perry singing his latest record in a filmed bit and performing "Small Fry" as Bing Crosby and Bob as his son (a routine previously done on April 26, 1952) are nice too. Then Bob and Joan sing and dance about how they like working with each other in spite of their faults, a cute ending for a fantastic show.
   Bob and Show: *****


***The Bob Hope Chevy Show***
Dec. 28, 1956, Friday 9-10 p.m.

   Peggy King, Mickey Mantle, Hedda Hopper, Jerry Colonna, Miss Universe Carol Morris, The Del Rubio Triplets, The Purdue University Glee Club, Ginger Rogers, Peter Leeds, Milton Frome, Muriel Landers, Charles Cooley. Choreographer: Jack Baker.
   Touring Alaska, Bob jokes a lot about the territory and service life, such as "One nice thing about these men up here, they all volunteered. For Honolulu," and "I don't care what you've heard about the weather up here—it's true. Right now it's about 10 degrees below. I don't know what

it is outside." He calls Miss Universe Carol Morris the "57 model—sweet, smooth and sassy" and tells her to "Aim high," so she kisses his forehead during their fake interview. Hedda Hopper does well in her own comic interplay with Bob. "Don't open up your head just for me!" she responds when he proposes to show her his rock collection. The first skit remakes Bob's April 26, 1952 *All Star Revue* show, with a saloon dancer (Ginger Rogers) enlisting a bartender (Jerry Colonna) to draw a map on her back as part of her efforts to find a gold mine discovered by a prospector (Bob). It is pretty lively with good contemporary updates. After Hedda introduces the singing Del Rubio Sisters, "Master Sgt. T-Bone" Hope has Mickey Mantle as his new finicky inductee in an intermittently amusing bit. After music from the Purdue Glee Club ("White Christmas") and Peggy King ("I've Grown Accustomed to Your Face") and a song and dance by Bob and Ginger, Gen. Frank A. Armstrong of the Alaskan Command thanks Bob for his work. Bob makes a few plugs before the glee club hums "Thanks for the Memory" and his guests join him on stage to end a satisfactory USO Christmas show.

Bob: \*\*\*\*\* Show: \*\*\*


***The Bob Hope Chevy Show***
Jan. 25, 1957, Friday 9-10 p.m.

Eddie Fisher, Harry James, [Dan] Rowan and [Dick] Martin, Jack Kirkwood, Betty Grable. Featured: Peter Leeds, Johnny Peters, Charley Cooley, Bob Tafur, Sunny Boyne. Choreographer: Jack Baker.

The elements are here for a top show, but somewhat overlong sketches and Eddie's boring number hurt its overall impression. Bob's nice monologue covers President Eisenhower's inauguration and budget problems and promotes *The Iron Petticoat*: "It has youth, courage, daring, loveliness … Let's see, who else is in it besides me?" He gets applause for quipping, "I suppose you read where Elvis Presley passed his Army physical. I feel a lot safer now, don't you?" Laughter drowns out the punchline when Bob says, "They didn't bother giving him the regular thorough exam. They just waited a minute and decided anybody that could stand at attention and go on maneuvers at the same time …" The solid skits include two mild-mannered hillbillies (Bob and Eddie Fisher) who con a carnival barker and Dan Rowan and Dick Martin heckling Bob as he conducts a singer. Bob introduces the latter duo with "Two weeks ago in Las Vegas, I had the pleasure of seeing what promises to be the top comedy team of the year" (they weren't until

1968) and appears as himself being pandered by them amusingly backstage after their show. The best bit has an actor (Bob) sell his soul to the devil (Jack Kirkwood) to romance a rich starlet (Betty Grable). She in turn gets the devil to help when Bob double crosses her. Betty is excellent performing "Get Happy" with twelve dancers, as is her husband, Harry James, on the trumpet before Bob sings "Thanks for the Memory" at the end.

Bob: **** Show: ***


**The Bob Hope Chevy Show**
March 10, 1957, Sunday 9-10 p.m.

Rosemary Clooney, Wally Cox, Lana Turner (TV debut), Steve Allen (cameo). Featured: Hy Averback (also announcer), Jack Pepper, Charley Cooley, Sunny Boyne, Duke Johnson. Music: Gordon Jenkins. Choreographer: Jack Baker.

Bubbly guests and skits make this show, originally planned to air Jan. 10, 1957, a delight. Bob states that "The Academy Award nominations are out again. So am I." He concludes that Katharine Hepburn being nominated for *The Rainmaker* rather than her work with Bob on *The Iron Petticoat* means "They're trying to tell me something!" He received no Emmy nominations either, so he muses, "Of course, I did get an [honorary] Oscar back in Fifty-Three. If I ever get an Emmy, I'll breed 'em!" Also figuring in his monologue and first sketch is Elvis Presley. A shady talent agent (Bob) makes a singing telegram messenger (Wally Cox) a star when women go wild over Wally's wiggling Adam's apple. Wally yodels on *The Steve Allen Show* with his neck covered electronically by a censor while Bob steals from him. They fight until Bob drops Wally for another messenger whose ears wiggle to the delight of ladies. Also nice is "Breakfast for Three," Wally and Lana as newlyweds interrupted by Lana's missing amnesiac husband (Bob). Rosemary sings solo and works opposite Bob as good and bad twin cowboys in a fitfully funny filmed bit. Best of all is Lana's top singing, dancing and joking with Bob at the end. "How did you happen to pick my show for your first [TV] appearance?" he asks. "It was really very simple. I called up your last two guest stars, Ginger Rogers and Betty Grable, and I asked them about you." "And what did they say?" "What's the difference? I'm here anyway!"

Bob and Show: ****

### The Bob Hope Chevy Show
April 7, 1957, Sunday 9-10 p.m.

Janis Paige, Frank Sinatra, Natalie Wood. Featured: Jack Kirkwood, Peter Leeds, Eleanor Audley, Charley Cooley. Choreographer: Jack Baker.

The script fails Bob and the talent here to an extent. Saying the show needs to cut a commercial, Bob has the sponsor's logo shown on his forehead. His jokes mainly concern income tax and claims that for Elvis Presley, "They're letting him put down his sideburns as dependents." He did not get to see his tax expert because "It was after visiting hours" and adds, "Regardless of whether you're rich or poor, it gives you an equal chance at poverty." Then Bob and Frank Sinatra reprise their vain baseball players routine they did on May 28, 1950. Frank seems surprised at how well the jokes are received. After Janis Paige sings and dances with two men, Bob asks Natalie Wood if she'd work with a more "mature" leading man. She responds, "Tab Hunter is twenty-seven. How much more mature can you get?" He also quips, "What's with you and the Tennessee Twitcher?" in reference to Presley in a good bit of interplay here. Bob next appears as a very wealthy man trying to impress Janis ("Howard Hughes?" he sniffs. "We have him down for a CARE package."). In a corny denouement, they realize both are lower class and sing a song as they decide to stick together. Frank reminds Bob of his skinny jokes about the singer, like Frank had to swallow a walnut to keep his pants up, promotes his movie *The Joker is Wild*, and sings "The Lady is a Tramp." The latter is consistently excellent, something that is not true for everything on display here.

Bob: ***** Show: ***

### The Bob Hope Show
May 5, 1957, Sunday 9-10 p.m.

Cary Middlecoff, George Jessel, Sonny James, Shelley Winters. Featured: Hy Averback, Shirley Fells.

TV's tenth anniversary gives Bob a chance to mock its stars, from Hopalong Cassidy ("If you ever reached for the dial, he shot your arms off") to cleavage-bearing Faye Emerson ("For a while, the only thing on TV was the V"). He bemoans the release of more old movies to TV, noting that "I've been on so many channels at the same time you can flip the channels and see my hairline recede!" But, he added, "I saw something

I've never seen before—Gabby Hayes' chin!" The first two skits are spottily enjoyable—Bob has golf pro Cary Middlecoff (a good straight man) return to the latter's old job as a dentist to pull one of Bob's teeth, and he cajoles George Jessel to appear as himself in Bob's upcoming film *Beau James* (which Jessel really did). Things perk up when Sonny James does his current hit "Young Love," and a parody of the *Alfred Hitchcock Presents* TV series has Shelley and George generating laughs as they try to kill an unstoppable Bob, playing Shelley's husband. This is a remake from Bob's June 15, 1953 *Colgate Comedy Hour* installment. Shelley also gets a good line on Bob before he ends the show with "Thanks for the Memory" by quipping, "Have you ever done a straight, sad role? I mean intentionally."

Bob and Show: ***

**The Bob Hope Show**
Oct. 6, 1957, Sunday 9-10 p.m.

Eddie Fisher, Marie MacDonald, Ann Miller, Gary Crosby. Featured: Carol Brooks, Leroy Payant, Jess Hahn, Teddy Wimoness, Charles Cooley, Tony Hope. D: Mort Lachman. W: Gig Henry. Choreography: Hermes Pan.

From Casablanca, North Africa and French Morocco, Bob jokes about perspiring in the intense heat as he and his cast perform outdoors. "The whole country looks like they're in the shower and someone rang the doorbell!" He adds that in the desert, the grass serves as traps on golf games. His material isn't as hot until a skit where Bob quips after having to kiss Eddie Fisher's feet, "I hate to think what'll happen when I go on his show!" and "You know something? This is your best side!" More laughs come from his repartee with uniformed PFC Gary Crosby ("I never thought I'd see a Crosby who'd pass the physical"), who also gets "I remember you when you were knee high to Bing's wallet!" Gary sings as do the other guests, with none of it of note except for Bob claiming Eddie Fisher is "Here on a three-day pass from Debbie Reynolds" as the latter dutifully promotes Bob's latest film *Beau James*. A skit with Bob as a black market dealer who's so tough that he eats his own bullets is similarly disappointing. The soldiers who watch it all seem to lap it up nevertheless.

Bob and Show: ***

## The Bob Hope Show
Nov. 24, 1957, Sunday 7-8 p.m.

Sheree North, Rhonda Fleming, Francis X. Bushman, Danny Thomas, The Hollywood Deb Stars (Delores Hart, Diane Jergens, Ruta Lee, Peggy Conley, Erin O'Brien, Yvonne Craig, Gloria Winters, Jana Land, Joan Tabor). Featured: Peter Leeds, Alan Gifford, Billy Curtis, Rocky Carr, Billy Rhodes. Choreography: Bruce Baker. Sheree North's Choreography: Sonia Shaw.

Westerns and singers figure predominantly in the spoofing here, starting with Bob saying the two genres consume TV so much that "You've got your choice of being scalped or 'Tammy'-ed to death!" (The latter refers to Debbie Reynolds' hit record.) Joan Caulfield interrupts Bob's monologue to remind viewers that her sitcom *Sally* is usually in this slot Sundays. It doesn't help—*Sally* will end four months later. The spottily amusing first skit has three Martians shrink Bob down to their height to the shock of his wife (Rhonda Fleming). Sheree North's cha cha cha number is fine if a little coy. What really clicks is "Bad Day at NBC," where one TV sheriff (Danny Thomas) fights Wyatt Burp (Bob) for control of the airwaves. When Danny pokes Bob and the latter's holster falls to his knees, Bob ad libs, "Don't move, I got the drop on you! Wardrobe!" Danny retorts, "Don't blame wardrobe. You lost your hips in the market!" to general hysteria. The two have a showdown interrupted by the appearance of another cowpoke on TV, "Durango Durante" (a cameo by Jimmy Durante), prompting both men to shoot the set. Rhonda's song is overshadowed by Bob and Sheree's dance wherein viewers hear the "crew" make catty comments about them along with visual tricks. Danny returns to play Frank Sinatra to Bob's Perry Como in a segment with great parody lyrics to offset so-so impressions. Francis X. Bushman helps Bob introduce a talented crop of upcoming actresses before this satisfactory session ends.

Bob and Show: ***

## The Bob Hope Show
Jan. 17, 1958, Friday 8-9 p.m.

Jayne Mansfield, Hedda Hopper, Jerry Colonna, Erin O'Brien, Carol Jarvis, Arthur Duncan. Featured: Mike Connelly, Peter Leeds, Alan Gifford, Charles Cooley, Irving Kupcinet, Al Sharper, Terence O'Flaherty, Herb Krauch, Tony Hope, Les Brown Jr. D: Mort Lachman.

Touring the Pacific with a passel of newspaper columnists during the Yuletide season, Bob and his troupe visit soldiers first in Hawaii, where he cracks, "This looks like a live bait tank for Zsa Zsa Gabor!" He jokes about the islands, the Army-Navy game being played under recent budget cuts, and the plane the USO gave him ("Lindbergh's lunch was still in the seat"). Erin O'Brien's song after that pales in comparison, but Bob's bit with Jerry Colonna clicks. When Bob asks Jerry, "What were you in civilian life?" the mustachioed comedian shoots back, "Happy!" In Guam before 12,000 airmen, Hedda Hopper has a solid routine with Bob, claiming that she is with him because "I don't like to buy Christmas presents." But the real attraction is curvaceous Jayne Mansfield, who after many whistles from attendees tells Bob, "I think you were very nice to share your seatbelt with me." "General" Alan Gifford interrupts the talk to escort Jayne offstage, ostensibly to get to know her better. "I fill the tank and someone steals the car!" Bob grouses in response. Jerry shows up here too, as well as at Johnson Air Base in Tokyo, where Carol Jarvis sings and Bob plays a private on an eight-hour pass dating Jayne (Jayne: "I just threw this on"; Bob: "You about missed!"), and at the thirty-eighth parallel in Korea, where Arthur Duncan tap dances solo and with Bob. Though the music and some material are tired, Bob is always on top of presenting his parts, as is Jerry Colonna, making this acceptable overall.

Bob: \*\*\*\*\* Show: \*\*\*

**The Bob Hope Buick Show**
Feb. 6, 1958, Thursday 8:30-9:30 p.m.

Dorothy Malone, Wally Cox, Nick Todd. Featured: Doris Singleton.
"The Three Faces of Bob" spoofs *The Three Faces of Eve* by having Bob be the one with multiple personalities being treated by Dorothy Malone. He also promotes a song in his new film, *Paris Holiday*, while Nick Todd and even Wally Cox sing a few numbers.

**The Bob Hope Buick Show**
March 2, 1958, Sunday 9-10 p.m.

Anita Ekberg, Natalie Wood, Robert Wagner. D: Jim Jordan. Choreography: Jack Baker.

Partly because the guests deliver their lines strongly without cracking up at what Bob throws at them, this show rocks. Bob cracks that being sponsored by an outboard motor company here affected him so much "I dreamt that I have to pull my tie to get my head started." He remarks that "The Oscar nominations are out. So am I." Bob says he begged Paramount to call his last picture "Bridge Over Beau James" to qualify. His old foil is expecting a baby, so "Crosby's getting an award for the best supporting role in an independent production." Bob gets "Anita Ekberg—I thought she made quite a combination" past the censor before a very good sketch with Natalie Wood as a love-struck fan of Bob, a matinee idol popular throughout North America ("I'm very big around the border" he quips). She hides herself inside a TV and pretends to be a spokesman before Bob's butler (Robert Wagner) whisks her out. "That's the first time a television set left the room during a commercial!" Bob jests. When he opens a hidden cabinet to get his Oscar, he finds Bing Crosby cradling the statuette like a baby and saying, "I'm limbering up for next summer." Also great is Bob's repartee with his latest film's costar, telling Anita, "In *Paris Holiday*, you amazed me with your performance. You really proved you could act." "Oh Bob, next to you, anybody could look good," scoffs Ekberg. A great duet with Bob and Natalie doing "Two Sleepy People" from his film *The Big Broadcast of 1938* in various musical styles scores well, and to top it off at the end, Bing cracks up Bob by demanding an outboard motor and exclaiming, "I really think my appearance elevated the tone of this whole little shabby charade of yours!" Like most of this show, the bit is wonderful.

Bob and Show: \*\*\*\*

*The Bob Hope Show*
April 5, 1958, Saturday 8-9 p.m.

Popov the clown, David Raikin (comedian), Galena Ulanova (ballerina), David Oistrakh (violinist), The Ukraine State Dancers, Yuri Dorov's animals. D: Mort Lachman. W: Gig Henry. Background Music: Les Brown.

This classic Cold War relic has Bob visiting Russia ("The people just mobbed me" he sarcastically quips at the top) and acting like he's hosting a travelogue on *The Ed Sullivan Show* by showcasing top talent in Moscow for the first third. Then Bob does a wildly funny fourteen-minute set before the American, British and Canadian corps at the U.S. embassy. "With my kind of act, I need diplomatic immunity," he notes, adding that his passport photo looks like George Arliss. "You must be Democrats—why else would you be here?" Saying his flight arrived with a twenty-one-gun salute, he adds, "It would've been nicer if they waited until the plane landed." While claiming he was having no problem with the language ("Nobody speaks to me"), he did say that "I cleared my throat and my waitress slapped me." One more quotable quote was "I know it's spring—snow is turning green." He spends the last minutes ruminating on what he learned from five days and nights and what bonded the countries. "These days, when they're building a bomb for every letter in the alphabet, it's nice to know these are people still trying to develop friendship." He places his faith in hoping to reach the younger generation and adds, "I certainly don't envy Secretary (John Foster) Dulles with the job at hand, but it certainly could be nice to have a peaceful coexistence so that human beings like these don't become obsolete." NBC will rerun this acclaimed show within a year.

Bob: ***** Show: ****


*The Bob Hope Buick Show*: "Roberta"
Sept. 19, 1958, Friday 8-9:30 p.m.

Janis Paige, Anna Maria Alberghetti, Howard Keel. D: Dick McDonough. Music: Jerome Kern. Book and Lyrics: Otto Harbach, Dorothy Fields ("Lovely to Look At"). Adaptation: Bob's writers.

Bob stars in a color presentation of the musical that launched him into success on Broadway in 1935. He will remake the property once again eleven years later, and Janis Paige will rejoin him on it. For more details, see *Chrysler Presents the Bob Hope Special:* "Roberta" on Nov. 6, 1969 in the next chapter.


*The Bob Hope Buick Show*
Oct. 14, 1958, Tuesday 9-10 p.m.

Joan Crawford, Fernandel, Robert Strauss, The Bernard Brothers, Marian Ryan. Featured: Hillary Brooke, Betty Lou Gerson, Linda Sterling. D: Bill Ward, Jerry Hopper (Joan Crawford sketch).

Disjointedly edited and presented, this stinks apart from Bob's monologue. He jokes about his recent musical on NBC that "We used up so much color in *Roberta*, the peacock is pooped!" Regarding the space race against Russia, "I don't know why everyone is so anxious to get to the moon. There's nothing to do in the evenings." Of a gyrating music superstar, he says, "Did you hear about the Army shipping away Elvis to Germany? They just want to get him away from the old grind." Then the show bombs with Joan Crawford pretending her marriage with Bob is invalid and trying to spark his competitive ardor by romancing a confused TV repairman (Robert Strauss). Filmed without a studio audience but using canned laughter, this is like a stale sitcom. The rest apparently is filmed in Europe. Fernandel and Marion Ryan's boring singing appear before Bob is straight man to the Bernard Brothers in a pantomime which fails to play to his talents. It's fitfully amusing when Bob plays a tourist being conned by a French waiter (Fernandel) at the end, but not enough to compensate for overall disappointment.

Bob: *** Show: **


*The Bob Hope Show*
Nov. 21, 1958, Friday 8-9 p.m.

Gloria Swanson, Betty Grable, Wally Cox, Randy Sparks, The Hollywood Deb Stars. D: Bob Henry.

Besides the listed guests, this special also includes an appearance by Los Angeles Rams quarterback Jon Arnett. Gloria Swanson helps Bob in presenting the Hollywood Deb Stars, while Betty Grable and Wally Cox join Bob in the sketches.


*The Bob Hope Show*
Jan. 16, 1959, Friday 9-10 p.m.

Gina Lollobrigida, Molly Bee, Elaine Dunn, Hedda Hopper, Randy Sparks, Jerry Colonna. Featured: Peter Leeds, Ursula Halloran, Atra Baer, Eleanor Harris, Terry Fockler. D: Mort Lachman.

Bob is solid but unexceptional, and a D-list guest cast apart from Gina Lollobrigida drags down this Christmas tour of U.S. military bases of eight countries in Europe and Port Lyautey, Africa, over twelve days. In Berlin, Germany, there are jokes about Russian interference ("On our radar scope, we were getting *Amos and Andy*"), while Bob calls the USS

Forrestal carrier at Naples, Italy, "a floating crap game." He adds, "To give you an idea how long this is, one end is in Russia!" A sketch where Molly Bee recounts her love of Bob at a USO dance club in a role reversal is moderately amusing, but better laughs come with Bob's interplay with Gina in Spain. She says she's worried about singing to the soldiers and being compared to great American singers like "Peggy Como," to which Bob interjects, "Let's not forget Hilda Crosby!" He adds, "Why wouldn't they like your voice? Look where it's been!" When she does vocalize, Bob translates her words humorously into a western tale. Jerry Colonna also shines as a matador in the audience. The singing by Elaine Dunn and Randy Sparks are less impressive, and the last half of the show is pretty dull apart from Bob having a sharp joke about Elvis during a Q&A with the troops and Hedda Hopper: "When he started, he couldn't spell Tennessee. Now he owns it." Bob ends the show with a prayer for peace that of course did not last.

Bob and Show: ***


**The Bob Hope Show**
Feb. 10, 1959, Tuesday 9:30-10:30 p.m.

Maureen O'Hara, Danny Thomas, Carol Haney (also choreography). Featured: Hugh Lambert, Doris Singleton, Stephen Chase, Bob Jellison, Bill Arnold. Music: David Rose.

Great bits alternate with groaners here. The swell monologue ranges from Russia's defense problems ("They've been up in Siberia three weeks now trying to launch a hula hoop") to the proposed seventy-seven billion-dollar U.S. budget ("It may take both Desi and Lucy to pay for this," referencing Desi Arnaz and Lucille Ball's successful TV production empire). Of Danny Thomas being here after Bob appeared on *The Danny Thomas Show* (see Chapter 11), Bob claims, "He's on my show just for revenge." He adds, "We're happy to have David Rose and his 'Holiday for Les Brown' band." The geniality vanishes with a sexist skit of a congresswoman (Maureen O'Hara) who gives her aide her fur wrap and says "File this under natural resources" and complains to a military leader how the Army's tanks are "dank and dingy inside" while Bob is her henpecked husband. Carol Haney's dance number is an improvement, as is Bob and Danny as dueling cops. Danny cracks his knuckles rather than snapping his fingers to punctuate the theme of *77 Sunset Strip*, and more guffaws come as he and Bob fight over the rights to a dead body and plots before Nick Charles of *The Thin Man* (Peter Lawford in a surprise cameo) shoots them because his show is short of corpses. Also good is Maureen singing, but Bob and Carol as a beatnik couple and Danny and Bob's routine of how commercial jingles would sound if they used old pop hits are best forgotten. The final decision on this: a draw.

Bob and Show: ***

**The Bob Hope Show**
March 13, 1959, Friday 8-9 p.m.

Fess Parker, Chuck Connors, Julie London, Guy Mitchell, Gail Davis. Featured: Hy Averback, Walker Edmiston, Mike Ross, Joan Bradshaw, Bill Arnold, Peter Leeds.

Apart from a few bum music numbers, this is a joy. All the guests except Julie London appear on horseback in the opening, including Les Brown (!), and Bob has one of his best monologues ever. He went to New York to have his eyes examined because "you have to get out of Los Angeles to find out if your eyes are working." The facilities were so crowded that to be seen, "I'd either have to have a baby or wait for a room. (beat) It was a boy." Regarding the Oscar nominations, "Someone did throw a rock through David Niven's window last night. It's a shame too, because he's such a wonderful neighbor." Bob adds his eye problems are gone and he's fine. "So there's no need for you hanging around, sir," he tells Jack Paar, who walks away. Next is a rollicking skit where Bob, Julie, and Chuck Connors are the only people left on Earth. Bob loses Julie to Chuck naturally, then gets his hopes up by seeing another girl—but she's his sister. "Frontier Head-Shrinker" ("They hung his shingle and Tom Dooley at the same time") has Fess Parker as the title character trying to make peace between Annie Oakley (Gail Davis) and a Bat Masterson clone (Bob) in a wild and wooly western takeoff. The rest is mostly plugging for Bob's new film *Alias Jesse James*, including Guy Mitchell and Julie singing songs from the film and bantering between Bob and Fess and Chuck, all enjoyably presented.

Bob: ***** Show: ****

***The Bob Hope Buick Show***
April 15, 1959, Wednesday 9-10 p.m.

Jack Benny, Jerry Colonna, Ginger Rogers, Dodie Stevens, Milton Berle (cameo). Featured: Joseph Kearns, Joan Tabor, Janet Lord. Choreography: Dante DiPaolo.

Nearly everything clicks here as Bob brings up the recent Oscar ceremony ("Almost two hours of television without a horse or private eye") and congratulates host David Niven ("He was so refreshingly sincere, I almost forgot to hate him"). As for his lack of nominations, Bob grouses, "I've lost so often I feel like the district attorney on *Perry Mason*." He plugs his film *Alias Jesse James* a lot before discussing the space race and the upcoming baseball season ("The Dodgers won their opening game in Chicago. It was canceled."). From there comes a smart bit with Jack Benny surreptitiously filming Bob at his home to avoid paying Bob to be on his show. Their great reactions and wonderful lines make this hysterical, especially when Jack points a gun at Bob's crotch and threatens, "I'm going to blow your brains out!" Next, Ginger Rogers dances and duets with Bob on a record where the music was sped up intentionally, supposedly by Jerry Colonna, to their consternation. Bob and Ginger show up next as a beatnik couple expecting a child at the hospital assisted by Colonna. "Are you the baby doctor?" Hope asks. "No, I'm fully grown!" snaps Colonna. Jerry does his own funny number, then Jack is upset to learn he won't be getting more money for this appearance. He and Bob exchange jokes before a monkey that played the violin on Jack's last special comes out to take Jack offstage. Bob then promos Milton Berle's new novel *Earthquake* and Milton comes out to sign it to promote his show next week. Bob sings "Thanks for the Memory" and makes a pitch to fight cancer, ending a strong show.

Bob and Show: \*\*\*\*

***The Bob Hope Show***
May 15, 1959, Friday 8-9 p.m.

Rosemary Clooney, Joan Collins, Wendell Corey, Sam Snead. Featured: Jack Kirkwood, Peter Leeds, Joan Bradshaw, Tony Haig, Hank Brandt. Music: David Rose.

"Three weeks after my picture is released, I get an award for my contribution to television," wryly notes Bob in his opening monologue, referencing both *Alias Jesse James* (which will be promoted later in the show by Bob's co-star in the movie, Wendell Corey, introducing bloopers from filming) and the recent Emmy Awards. He does several jokes mixing TV with politics, such as saying of Desi Arnaz, "He does pretty good for a Cuban who shaves," referring to recent dictator Fidel Castro. This leads into two shaky sketches which nevertheless have their moments. A spoof of the TV series *All Star Golf* has Sam Snead face off against Hope, a golf pro at Knott's Berry Farm who sports a sexy girl caddy. Despite Bob having an oversized club, Sam wins the contest as Bob's ball is rejected by the eighteenth hole. Bob then appears with Joan Collins ("courtesy of the studio for *Say One for Me*," Bob says, referring to Bing Crosby's latest movie) in a so-so bit with them playing performers in a barn interrupted by a farmer milking a cow and other distractions. After such trivialities as Bob getting golf lessons from Sam Snead, the somewhat sloppily sung and present musical finale features Bob, Rosemary, Wendell and Joan. Bob plugs *Alias Jesse James* once more and notes he's on the cover of *TV Guide* before saying good night.

Bob: **** Show: ***

## *The Bob Hope Buick Show*
Oct. 8, 1959, Thursday 8-9 p.m.

Dean Martin, Natalie Wood, The Crosby Brothers (Gary, Dennis, Phillip and Lindsay). Featured: Peter Leeds, William Forrest, Dale Van Sickle. Music: David Rose. Choreographer: Nick Castle. Musical Arranger/Conductor for The Crosby Brothers: Dick Stabile.

Replacing *Bat Masterson* and *Staccato*, Bob mocks both by saying, "I can't shoot a gun, I can't ride a horse and I'm not a private eye ... Welcome to Frontier Coward." His strong monologue includes, "This has been some month, hasn't it? The Russians hit the moon, the Dodgers won the pennant, and Bing had a filly. And you know, it's hard to believe any of them!" Of Russian leader Nikita Khrushchev being denied a security clearance to a theme park in his visit to America, he says to applause, "I'd hate to go over war over Disneyland, wouldn't you?" After the Crosbys do "Mack the Knife," they play henchmen to Bob, who plans to take over NBC. The network's top cop star (Natalie Wood) must stop him from drowning Lawrence Welk in his own bubbles and starting game shows like "The Price Should Be Right." She seduces Bob in an enjoyably silly skit that touches most 1959 TV trends. Dean Martin is cute arguing with Bob over their competing restaurants before they sing. In a comedy fantasy, each of Bing's sons do a road picture with Bob every five years though 1980. Dean sings and then appears as a gondolier who shows Bob how to kiss Natalie. Bob takes his place steering and the boat splits, leaving Bob alone. Natalie does a great soft shoe to "Together" from *Gypsy* (ironically, she will be in that musical's 1962 movie adaptation in 1962) before Dean, Bob and the Crosbys join her to finish off the song. Bob's respectful patriotic pitch at the end closes a very nice show.

Bob and Show: \*\*\*\*

### The Bob Hope Show
Nov. 9, 1959, Monday 8:30-9:30 p.m.

Zsa Zsa Gabor, James Darren, Patti Page, May Britt, The Hollywood Deb Stars.

Patti Page and May Britt each appear in one skit with Bob on this show, while Zsa Zsa Gabor assists him in introducing the latest crop of Hollywood Deb Stars. James Darren participates in a spoof on rock and roll with Bob to round out this offering.

### The Bob Hope Show
Dec. 11, 1959, Friday 8:30-9:30 p.m.

Ernie Kovacs, Janis Paige, Rhonda Fleming, Rod Lauren. Featured: Peter Leeds, Jack Pepper, Audrey Saunders, Louise Vincent, Gary Menteer, Guy Chandler.

Were it not for the interesting and effective contrast between Ernie Kovacs' brand of humor with Bob's, this would be negligible. Bob gets in some good ones about the new movie *Scent of Mystery*, which pumps odors in theaters during showings ("What do you say to a girl now? 'Let's go down and sniff a double feature?!'") and payola ("Money can't buy a hit record. Nobody knows that better than I do."). However, his quip that "Dean [Martin] records on the Mafia label" gets shudders from the audience. Janis Paige's song and dance number in a cane and bowler with two men easily outshines vocal bits by Rod Lauren (doing his minor hit "If I Had a Girl") and Rhonda Fleming. A skit where a Beverly Hills cat burglar (Bob with a thin mustache) invades the home of a Hollywood star (Rhonda) and her press agent (Peter Leeds) wants to publicize the incident to his client's benefit waxes and wanes in effectiveness. Also mediocre plus dated is "The Beat Generation" with Bob and Janis as a beatnik couple. Ernie saves it all by playing a cliffside house dweller whose house is falling apart, but Bob buys it because it's over-insured, or so he thinks. The special effects showing the destruction and Bob and Ernie's takes are swell here. Ernie reappears as a lead investigator grilling a deejay (Bob) about pay-for-play record deals, which is richly funny too, but not enough to make this prime Bob watching.

Bob and Show: ***

Milton Berle (left) plays a nuclear chicken who meets a witch (Phyllis Diller, center) and a bat (Bob Hope), both from outer space, on Bob's Sept. 25, 1964 special. Phyllis and Milton appeared several times in occasionally stupid sketches like this that predominated on Bob's shows in the 1960s and relied more on star power and humorous costumes over witty lines and plots. Courtesy of Getty Images.

# 3   Specials – 1960s

"THIS IS MY FIFTEENTH YEAR in television. Imagine that—fifteen years of me. It's the longest stomach test in the history of show business. Of course, I started very young. You remember me. I was the first dropout on *Ding Dong School*."—Bob on his Sept. 25, 1964 special.

Credits for this decade are as follows (exceptions noted in shows when known): EP: Bob Hope. P: Jack Hope (1960-April 1962), George Hope (October 1962-April 1964), Mort Lachman (1964-1969; billed as associate producer until September 1968). D: Jack Shea (1960-1968), Dick McDonough (1968-1969). W: Norman Sullivan, Mort Lachman and Bill Larkin, Charles Lee and Gig Henry, Lester White and John Rapp (1960-1968), Larry Rhine (1968-1969), and Mel Tolkin (fall 1969), Gene Moss (fall 1969) and James Thurman (fall 1969). Music: Les Brown and His Band of Renown. Announcer: Frank Barton. Choreography: Jack Baker (1960-1961).

Bob started this decade with a notable honor, getting three stars on Feb. 8, 1960 on the Hollywood Walk of Fame marking his work in movies, radio and TV. He would also have another one for Live Performance/ Theater, but he never got one for the other category the Hollywood Walk of Fame honors, Recording, even though he did make *Billboard*'s singles chart in 1945 and 1950 and its album chart in 1976 with his Bicentennial comedy record *America is 200 Years Old … And There's Still Hope!*

On television, Bob kept chugging along on television strongly with the public too. He had three of the top six highest-rated specials of the 1960-1961 season. The next season, his January 1962 USO Christmas special got an impressive 35.2 rating (in contrast, the number one series on TV at the time, *Wagon Train*, averaged a 32.1).

Despite these accomplishments, Bob had sponsor troubles. Buick dropped him in the fall of 1961 for *Sing Along with Mitch*, a musical variety series hosted by conductor Mitch Miller. Bob's demand that Buick spend at least $50,000 in newspaper ads promoting each of his specials along with footing the specials' production expenses probably was the reason why. When the company made the move, Bob's jokes about it indicated some displeasure bubbling underneath a friendly veneer, as he could not find another sponsor for his show until 1961 almost was over.

"Welcome to the late late start," Bob cracks on the Dec. 13, 1961 show, his first that season. He says the delay was due to surgery he had in September: "I had a sponsor removed from my back." Pointedly, it had a skit about TV doctors where one bearded medic rhythmically moved needle and thread between his hands as the narrator calls his program "Stitch Along with Mitch."

The grumbling continued the rest of the season, as Bob quipped "Welcome to 'Swing Along with Mitchico!'" playing a Japanese house owner on his March 22, 1962 outing. He nicknamed his April 25, 1962 special "Chew Along with Bob" as a gum company sponsored him.

In the 1962-1963 season, Bob found trouble of a different sort when his appearances replacing *The Perry Como Show* struggled against the sitcom *The Beverly Hillbillies* on CBS, which went to number one shortly after its debut. For the first time ever, he lobbied NBC to move him to another time slot. He wasn't really joking when he quipped "It's a wonderful show. I just don't want to be against them anymore" when *The Beverly Hillbillies* won the Favorite New Series award on the *TV Guide* awards on his April 14, 1963 special.

**Bob Goes to a Series—Sort of**

Bob got that chance in the fall of 1963, when his specials began airing as part of a new anthology series known as *Bob Hope Presents The Chrysler Theatre*. More details on that can be found in Chapter Twelve, but it should be noted that the new sponsor bowed to the comedian's desire to make his annual USO Christmas tours run as a ninety-minute special each season rather sixty minutes to include more of the acts and highlights of the overseas trips.

In return, Bob helped the sponsor by ending most of his specials with a preview of next week's filmed drama. He also stopped thanking his guest stars for appearing on each show at the end, where he now often forced a smile and looking off stage to his right to see if the taping was over. It was not a graceful way to conclude his specials.

The dramatic presentations were filmed in color along with Bob's introductions to them while his specials continued to air in the cheaper black and white format. Though Bob joked on his 1965 season opener that the reason why was "It'd be silly for NBC to have two peacocks," it was no laughing matter for network executives. They had invested considerably in the technology, and by September 1965, the network was virtually all color all day. Bob's specials were about the only shows without the network's peacock spreading its feathers at the start to announce, "The following NBC program is brought to you in living color." NBC executives forced him to pay the extra cost and convert to using color cameras and videotape by the time of his December 1965 show and overseas specials. Bob would be in black and white no more on TV except reruns.

Two years later, *Bob Hope Presents The Chrysler Theatre* ended per the sponsor's wishes. However, Chrysler remained a regular sponsor on the series the rest of the decade, while Bob specials typically pre-empted *The Kraft Music Hall* on Wednesdays (the same slot *Bob Hope Presents The Chrysler Theatre* held from 1965-1967) or *NBC Monday Night at the Movies*.

**Minor Changeovers**

The key creative talent backstage on his shows stayed the same throughout all this except for producers. When Jack Hope died Aug. 6, 1962, another sibling of Bob's, George Hope, became his producer through the spring of 1964 before tiring of the responsibilities and assuming the less intensive role of Bob's production coordinator until his death on June 21, 1969. Bob's longtime writer Mort Lachman then became the producer, but he did not get the official title in the credits until the fall of 1968.

That same year, the writing lineup changed for the first time in a decade when Larry Rhine replaced John Rapp as Lester White's writing partner for a year, then Mel Tolkin assumed the role from Rhine a year later. The relatively stability may explain why Bob's comedy was becoming stale.

**Bob Becomes Square**

While Bob had mocked Elvis Presley and some other youth trends and fads into the early 1960s, there was a general display of gently needling these aspects of pop culture. That all changed when the Beatles making waves with a huge series of hits on the American music charts in 1964, and Bob reacted like a cranky, middle-aged fuddy-duddy to them over the next few years. In retrospect, it was the start of him losing the pulse of the younger generation as well as a sense of irreverence that had made him a top comic star over several decades.

One typical piece of sniping was his referring to the group and saying "What I fool I was, just trying to make it on talent" on his Sept. 23, 1964 special. Seven months later, discussing Beatles member Ringo Starr announcing his wife was pregnant, Bob cracked, "How do you think this baby is going to feel when they tell him his mother is the one with short hair?" He praises Frankie Avalon's style of singing later in the same show (Avalon had not been on the music charts for three years by this time) and tells him regarding the Rolling Stones, "They sound like a bad night at All Star Bowling!"

Even when they established themselves as the world's top musical act, Bob disdained John, Paul, George, and Ringo. "The Beatles have also been taking meditation lessons from this bearded yogi named Maharishi Mahesh, who sounds like he smokes his name," Bob said on his Oct. 16, 1967 special. "And according to Maharishi, yoga is a simple way of coming to that. I am that, you are that, this is that. You have to be a Beatle to understand it."

He was not finished with them there. Interviewing Sergio Mendes in 1969, he exclaimed, "You're selling more records than the Beatles!" The musician neutrally responded, "Why is that so phenomenal?" "Well, you did it with your clothes on!" says Bob.

Bob never booked the Beatles, nor any other English rock act. He would not have a British singer as a guest until Tom Jones on Oct. 13, 1969. Bob preferred to mock such musicians instead. For example, during his 1965 tour of Vietnam, he, Peter Leeds, and Jerry Colonna sported wigs to portray the rock trio the Rolling Rejects, a few seconds of which made Bob's 1966 TV special on the visit.

The development was embarrassing for a man claiming to bring the best entertainment to his audiences. In a decade rich with innovative memorable music in pop, rock, soul, jazz, and country, it is discouraging to note that the artist seen most often in Bob Hope specials was the blander than bland songstress Anita Bryant.

Bob's comedy was even more intransigent, turning reactionary and tone deaf toward Baby Boomers' opinions about what changes needed to occur in America. An early example was a skit on his Oct. 20, 1965 special where he and Carol Lawrence played college students carrying signs like "Draft Parents" and "Ban Outer Space" who complain they have run out of issues to protest.

For his 1967 season opener, Bob went in for the kill on long-haired protesters. "Los Angeles is becoming the hippie capital of the world, and I mean it. Even the smog has hair on it. Have you seen a hippie group? Looks like a rummage sale. With live rummage. What a sight, all those beards. One of them had a beard so long, you could barely see her mini-skirt. And the hippies are against all authority. They can smell a cop a mile away—and vice versa."

He kept getting worse. On Oct. 14, 1968, in a sketch mocking college students protesting the war, Bob introduces himself to one jailed man (John Davidson) and says, "I'm a professional picketer. Here's my card." He tries to convince John to continue demonstrating while polite guards offer them room service. When two sexy female guards release him, John disavows picketing while Bob blubbers, "I'm going to sit in the corner and pray for some police brutality!" Protesters jailed in the 1960s know that is a gross misrepresentation of what they encountered.

Topping that was a skit on March 19, 1969, where a new university president (Jimmy Durante, improbably wearing a beret) is greeted by a student (Bob in a long-haired wig), who unveils a sign that says "Keep the pot boiling." As Bob rides into Jimmy's office in a sidecar driven by a blonde, Jimmy thinks he's a girl as Bob gives a list of demands. These are horrible jokes, like when Bob wants both black and white studies, Jimmy responds, "All right, but most people are buying color sets!" Jimmy gets his revenge as he closes the school down and dances off with fawning female students while guards arrive to stop Hope. It's a middle-aged man's dream of what should have been occurring on campuses.

These attempts at humor happened concurrently with Bob's annual overseas tours to the military now being dominated by his appearances for troops at the Vietnam War. It was an increasingly unpopular conflict that brought him his first big wave of negative publicity, and Bob awkwardly tried to remedy the situation on his specials as activities escalated with no end in sight.

## Bob and Vietnam

Bob first visited in Vietnam for Christmas in 1964. He simply concluded the special with, "These are the kids we met face to face and had the privilege of entertaining. They sat in the rain, they sat in the heat, they sat in the snow. And they said thank you. I don't think any of us had a better Christmas present."

The conflict escalated sharply thereafter. In 1965, Bob and crew ran into another USO touring company with Martha Raye and Johnny Grant and got Eddie Fisher and John Bubbles to join in as guests on his shows at camps, while Gen. William Westmoreland acknowledged on the same special that troops in Vietnam had grown eightfold since Bob had been there a year earlier. Bob's 1966 special documenting that 1965 Christmas tour got a massive 35.5 rating, and he published a book, *Five Women I Love*, recounting his experiences there with Kaye Stevens, Carroll Baker, Joey Heatherton, Jill St. John and Janis Paige that he promoted on his specials too.

The next year, the special's rating was even higher at 38.0, but there were problems evident to any viewer. Jerry Colonna had suffered a stroke, and Bob included shots of him recuperating and grateful for gifts sent from the front in the special. More telling was Bob including some dark humor with a quiet air of disgust regarding the war. Regarding its coverage on American TV, he jested, "It's not bad, but it's not *Bonanza!*" He told said of peace negotiations that "I'm very happy about the truce. I only hope the snipers know about it." And Bob got applause when after musing about politicians in Washington, D.C., having problem budgeting the military conflict, he asked, "Wouldn't it be awful if they ran out of money and had to repossess the war?"

Even when Bob met with John Steinbeck in Vietnam during filming for the special, the reaction was not exactly what he anticipated. "I know you're a hawk," Bob told the novelist. "Well, no, but I'm not a pigeon either," Steinbeck said, sounding more tepid than pro-war. Yet Bob thought well enough of this statement to include it in the show.

In 1968, the show remained a top ratings attraction at 36.3. While proudly noting that many soldiers clamored to watch his shows in Vietnam, Bob did address the war's atmosphere in summarizing the trip. "The big topic of conversation here is 'How many days you got left?'" he noted. Visiting soldiers in hospitals, as he had always done previously, he noted that "A lot of their buddies didn't make it at all." Acknowledging the high number of casualties and agreeing that there was no easy resolution, Bob nonetheless gave much camera time to and placed faith in officers telling him that victory was on its way soon. The truth would prove to be quite different.

The 1969 show found Bob wistful. It ended poignantly as Bob emphasized the plight of Vietnamese youth as justification for the war while recognizing frustration over its progress. "I never dreamed back in 1964 that it would go on this long, take such a terrible toll," he said. He commended the dedicated efforts of young soldiers in battle and how resolute they remain before concluding, "We pray that this was the last of our trips to Vietnam." Sadly, it was not, and Vietnam would hang over him as much as the country in the early 1970s.

**Other Bob Business**

Apart from the controversies, Bob thrived in the 1960s, although his production company remained unable to sell any series beyond *Bob Hope Presents The Chrysler Theatre*. In 1962, Bob himself produced *Amy*, a sitcom starring Sharon Farrell as the title character, a 19-year-old who gets into misadventures in Boston. It failed to make the NBC schedule.

He fared better with the Emmys, winning a couple and having several other victories associated with himself. In 1961 *The Bob Hope Buick Show* was nominated for Outstanding Program Achievement in the Field of Humor, losing to *The Jack Benny Program*, while Jack Shea and Dick McDonough lost Outstanding Directorial Achievement in Comedy to Sheldon Leonard for *The Danny Thomas Show*. In 1965 he got an Emmy nomination for his comedy specials as well as producer of *Bob Hope Presents The Chrysler Theatre*. He won the Emmy for Outstanding Variety Special in 1965.

Also, several productions on *Bob Hope Presents The Chrysler Theatre* got wins, including acting for Shelley Winters (1964), Albert Paulsen (supporting role by an actor, 1964), Cliff Robertson (1966), and Simone Signoret (1966), Sidney Pollack for direction (1966) and Rod Serling for writing (1964). There were nominations as well for Rod Steiger as lead actor (1964), Shelley Winters as lead actress (1966), David Rayfiel (1964) and S. Lee Pogostin (1966) for writing, and Sydney Pollack for directing (1964).

Clearly, despite the war and his occasional stodginess, Bob remained a popular and respected figure on his specials throughout the 1960s. And while his creative spirit was not as strong as in the 1950s, he did produce several shows that are among his finest. Read on to find out which ones they were.

*The Bob Hope Buick Christmas Show*
Jan. 13, 1960, Wednesday 9-10 p.m.

Steve McQueen, Neile Adams, Jayne Mansfield, France Langford, Jerry Colonna, Tony Romano, Patty Thomas, Peter Leeds. Music: Skinnay Ennis.

Bob gets laughs from the U.S. military in Alaska by greeting them with "Thank you, tourists!" and tweaking the host state. "You hit a [golf] ball and before it stops rolling, it's an avalanche … The weather's been fine here. The other day, the temperature shot up to 30 below." He also hits on the aged aircraft he flew: "It was so old, all the 'No Smoking' signs were in Latin … It was the first time I saw a plane started by a whip." Bob then dances with a costumed bear (Patty Thomas), which surprisingly works well, and has delightful interplay with Frances Langford before she sings. A stumble occurs as Steve McQueen and Bob play Japanese soldiers stuck on an island fifteen years in a slow sketch whose big joke is that they see what their lives look like now and want to commit hari-kari. The show recovers as Jayne Mansfield assumes her dumb blonde routine with Bob before singing. Bob and Jerry Colonna kiss Tony Romano at the end of their song (!), then Jayne and Neile Adams (Steve's then-wife) whistle after sailors Bob and Steve in a funny role reversal of a skit from Bob's May 22, 1956 special. Jayne calls Bob "Snorkel Snoot" as she seduces him ("You're bending my tattoo!" he tells her), while two other women arrive and all fight for the men hilariously. Clips of other parts of the show, including Steve doing a swell Marlon Brando impersonation, round out a fine offering.

Bob: ***** Show: ****


**The Bob Hope Buick Show**
Feb. 22, 1960, Monday 8:30-9:30 p.m.

Ginger Rogers, Wally Cox, Jimmy Demaret. Featured: Peter Leeds, Danny DiPaolo, Betsy Duncan, Bob Harvey. Music: David Rose.

Lively guests and good material make this outing superior. Jack Paar exiting *The Tonight Show* temporarily over NBC censoring a joke prompts Bob to crack, "How about that Jack Paar walking out and leaving those commercials homeless?" He adds, "With all those western shows they've got, [NBC] still couldn't head him off at the pass!" Bob also ribs the struggling space program at Cape Canaveral. "One rocket's been in Florida so long it's got a tan." Bob also quips, "And of course, you've heard about the TV writers' striking. Heard about it?! You've been listening to it for ten minutes!" to applause. Ginger Rogers sleekly performs "I Got Rhythm" backed by a jazz trio, and Wally Cox shines as a meek bellhop recruited by a power broker (Bob) to run for president. Wally's deadpan interpretation of "Running Bear" backed by Bob and three other singers is even better. Ginger reappears as a senorita enticing dueling matadors (Bob and Wally) in energetic nonsense where Bob shoots too much shaving cream on Wally's face to everyone's delight. Also good is Jimmy Demaret as a golf pro whose rival (Bob) tries to seduce Jimmy's favorite student—Jimmy even sings decently! Next, Bob presents the thirty-ninth annual Photoplay Awards to Millie Perkins (outstanding new actress), Troy Donahue (outstanding new actor), producer Ross Hunter and director Michael Gordon for *Pillow Talk* (most popular picture), Gina Lollabrigida (outstanding foreign actress) and Tony Randall (special award). Bob and Ginger dance to "Ballin' the Jack" in tuxedo and gown for a classy end to a mostly stellar show.

Bob: ***** Show: ****


*The Bob Hope Buick Show*
April 20, 1960, Wednesday 9-10 p.m.

James Garner, Patti Page, Joan Caulfield. Featured: Stephen Chase, Peter Leeds, Sandra Gould, Joi Lansing, Lyle Moraine. Music: David Rose.

Fresh off receiving the Jean Hersholt Humanitarian Award at the Oscars, Bob says, "I won in a new category—miracles" and adds, "I honestly never expected to get an Oscar honestly." This leads a string of jokes ranging from his name being called ("They had to come get me out of the sulking room") to the win's confidence boost ("I hope they can get my whole head on the screen!"). He also muses about the space race, the candidacies of John F. Kennedy and Hubert Humphrey, and Prince Margaret's wedding ("It's the biggest celebration England's had since I left."). The rest of the show suffers in comparison, starting with a stupid skit with Dr. Sigmund Hope (Bob) treating James Garner for believing he's a horse. Jim maximizes what laughs there are, from calling Bob a Communist for not watching his series *Maverick* to saying that if Bob had raced him, "You'd have nosed me out!" His timing and singing excels too as an apprentice beatnik to Bob. Less impressive is "The Man with the Golden Tooth," where a comedian (Bob) must lose sixty pounds to placate his sponsor. He hides food from his wife (Joan Caulfield) amid lots of fat jokes. Bob also does a singing comedy duet with Patti Page interrupted when Jim romances her, sings a season-ending version of "Thanks for the Memory" and plugs *My Eyes are in My Heart*, sportscaster Ted Husing's new autobiography. It's an odd finish for a show full of quirks that don't quite pan out.

Bob: **** Show: ***

### The Bob Hope Buick Show
Oct. 3, 1960, Monday 8:30-9:30 p.m.

Joan Crawford, Bobby Darin, Patti Page, The Hollywood Deb Stars of 1960 (includes Paula Prentiss and Shelley Fabares). Music: David Rose. (Norman Sullivan not credited as a writer.)

This show gets sluggish as it progresses, as does Bob. He begins by saying, "Yes, I'm back, and don't look so surprised. Crime shows are big this year." Bob jokes a lot about the political conventions, quipping of the presidential candidates' youthfulness, "I've never voted for a candidate with hair." After the promising start is a so-so bit with Patti Page as a spaceship stewardess and Bob as a passenger who thought he was going to Glendale. His pilot is a monkey, his food is all contained in a pill, he and his cigar float in midair, and he learns Patti is a robot as he accidentally breaks her down. After Bobby Darin sings, he mocks Bob's record collection and splendidly imitates Bob closing out a show. Bob responds with a version of "Mack the Knife," leading to a duet on "Splish Splash" and "Sweet Alice Blue Gown," the latter with Bob interpolating "Itsy Bitsy Teenie Weenie Polka Dot Bikini" to great comic effect. Unfortunately, next is weak, overlong comedy in poor taste after Patti dresses as an Asian to sing "Two Different Worlds," as Bob sports a Fu Manchu moustache and has problems operating chopsticks. He attempts to woo Patti from Bobby, a painter outside Patti's Chinese restaurant, but fails as he accidentally poisons himself. Patti sings, then Joan Crawford describes the ten Hollywood Deb Stars as Bob does gags. Bob plugs the United Way, *Celebrity Golf* on NBC, his upcoming dates and his sponsor before ending this average outing.

Bob and Show: ***

### The Bob Hope Buick Show: "Potomac Madness"
Oct. 22, 1960, Saturday 8:30-9:30 p.m.

Ginger Rogers, Perry Como. Featured: Peter Leeds, Herb Vigran, Lisa Davis, J. Edward McKinley, Charlie Lung, Eddie Marr, Stephen Chase,

Lyle Moraine, Milton Frome, Frank Barton. Music: David Rose. Special Music and Lyrics: Sammy Cahn, James Van Heusen.

In this original musical, Ginger Money (Ginger), the most powerful woman in Washington, D.C., plans to date with Perry Crooner (Como) until she had to hold a party to introduce presidential candidate Gov. Gaylord Goober (Hope). The Southern politician, an obvious takeoff on Lyndon Johnson, nearly bombs when he tells the ritzy crowd he wants to tax the rich but recovers until pressed on his positions. The three sing "Playing Politics," then it's revealed that Ginger is using Goober in order to crush him. She has Perry dress up as a psychiatrist who tries to dig up dirt by asking Bob about his past, but he fails. Undaunted, Ginger has a woman at the convention pretend to be Goober's wife and claim to be mother of his child. Disgusted, delegates start casting votes for Perry instead, who picks Goober as his running mate, weds Ginger, and becomes president. Ginger books Perry solid for four years on performance dates, so Perry tells Goober to take his place in the White House. Instead, Ginger forces Goober out and does a musical number about her plans. Goober visits Perry in Vegas to complain, but Ginger tells Perry she hates her new power and wants him to be president instead. Bob rolls some dice and wins a budget before all three sing a number celebrating the USA. Nice sets, good use of stock footage, pretty catchy music, and a solid idea can't overcome an overall flat execution here, including some shaky camerawork and bad jokes involving a monkey.

Bob and Show: ***

*The Bob Hope Buick Show*
Nov. 16, 1960, Wednesday 9-10 p.m.

Steve McQueen, Neile Adams, Kay Starr, The Air Force Academy Band. Featured: Peter Leeds, Stephen Chase, Joan Tabor, John Gallaudet, Carrie Grace.

With a similar cast and setting to the January 13, 1960 show, this falls short in comparison, but everybody gives it their all. Visiting the Air Force Academy in Colorado Springs, Colorado, Bob remarks on its facilities ("They have 3,000 acres of windows over here! It's the first time I've ever seen a military greenhouse!") and location ("Last year four moose graduated"). Clips of the soldiers and activities at the base are interspersed during Bob's seven-minute monologue, followed by a redo of a skit from the Nov. 17, 1953 show with Steve McQueen trying to con his new roommate (Bob) into joining the Air Force football team. Steve is quite good "singing" and pretending to play the ukulele. Kay sings solo and with four men, then Bob is funny as a cowardly cadet in training tried by a court-martial for failure of duty for spending time with a stripper who consoled him in Las Vegas. Another song and dance, this time by Neile Adams, leads into Bob playing a cadet who finished 569$^{th}$ out of a class of 570. "So you see, there's a guy stupider than I," Bob quips and then salutes a soldier wearing an Alfred E. Neuman mask. The general's daughter (Kay) tries to seduce Bob but her father arrives home early, leading to some pretty humorous complications. The academy chorale joins Bob at the end for a special version of "Thanks for the Memory," and he thanks the academy for training men from across the globe.

Bob: **** Show: ***


**The Bob Hope Buick Show**
Dec. 12, 1960, Monday 9:30-10:30 p.m.

Jimmy Durante, Polly Bergen. Featured: Benny Rubin, Peter Leeds, Mike Ross. Music: David Rose.

The guests fight a losing battle against weak skits and bad musical numbers here. While Jimmy doing "September Song" is fine, Polly suffers in comparison to Judy Garland in doing "The Man That Got Away," and Bob, Jimmy and Polly doing "Triplets" cannot match how well Fred Astaire, Nanette Fabray and Jack Buchanan presented it in the movie *The Band Wagon*. This starts well, with Polly on *To Tell the Truth* introducing three contenders as Jimmy Durante—Bob Hope, David Rose, and Jimmy himself, who proclaims, "Two of us is liars!" Bob's monologue is nice too. Of votes in the presidential election, he quips, "This is the longest count since Jack Benny broke a hundred-dollar bill in the automat." The ultimate winner helps Bob promote his new movie, *The Facts of Life*: "It's for the whole family. And if you don't have a family, call the Kennedys!" It slumps from there. Bob is unbelievable and unfunny as a cerebral nuclear physicist facing a German agent posing as his wife (Polly) to steal atomic secrets. Jimmy and Bob get few laughs as overworked TV detectives trying to break out of a "jail" on a studio where they sleep at night. And "Lady Tolliwogger's Boo Boo," with Polly cheating on her husband (Bob) with the gardener (Jimmy) in the English countryside, not only has bad gags but also awkward

camerawork and several microphone shots. It looks like Bob and crew were trying to save money and time for the next special rather than on this miss.
Bob: *** Show: **


**The Bob Hope Christmas Show**
Jan. 11, 1961, Wednesday 9-10 p.m.

Janis Paige, Zsa Zsa Gabor, Anita Bryant, Jerry Colonna, Andy Williams. Featured: Peter Leeds, Delores Kaye (dancer), Butch [Stone] and Stumpy [Brown] (singers). (Delores, Butch and Stumpy appear only in film clips during the show.)

Bob first arrives in Panama, mocking water control efforts and the rainy season ("I'd hate to go out with a girl and have her rust on me"). Janis Paige tells Bob she's envious that he cheated on her with Lucille Ball on *The Facts of Life*. "Janis, there's nothing between us, at least on my side," Bob quips. They finish a show by flashlight in Antigua before going to Guantanamo Bay. Calling it "Cape Canaveral's ashtray," Bob quips, "It's very safe here. This is their (Cuba's) target area." He has a good exchange with Jerry Colonna dressed as Fidel Castro ("I ain't Gabby Hayes!"). In Puerto Rico, Bob references the weather ("Of course, if a hurricane's going in any direction, it's safer than any taxi!" to applause) before a pretty stagnant skit where Anita Bryant and Janis are WACs saying goodbye to their husbands (Bob and Andy). Returning to Gitmo, Bob duets with Andy on a number touching on Eddie Fisher's affair with Elizabeth Taylor and other topical issues. Zsa Zsa Gabor's low-cut gown bearing cleavage and accented delivery win over the crowd as well as her 38-22-36 measurements. "The girls I used to date were the same age all over!" Bob notes before joking about her wedding record. As everyone joins Anita singing "Silent Night" at the end, Bob narrates over them a lengthy tribute to "These boys at our tropical bases sweating out the Cold War" and others who contributed to the show.
Bob and Show: ***


**The Bob Hope Buick Sports Awards Show,** Feb. 15, 1961—See Chapter 9: Game Shows and Sports.

***The Bob Hope Buick Show***
April 12, 1961, Wednesday 9-10 p.m.

James Darren, Phil Harris, Patti Page. Featured: Julie Bennett, Beverly Gray, Mike Ross, Lyle Romaine, Billy Mumy.

Sloppy and intermittently enjoyable, one great sketch redeems this along with a typically solid monologue by Bob. Discussing the importance of the newly started Peace Corps, he notes, "Do you realize there are remote tribes in Africa that have never heard of Fabian?" He ruminates over baseball, President Kennedy's budget, taxes and of course the Oscars. "I didn't get a thing from the Academy. Not even a key to *The Apartment*," he says, referring to the 1960 Best Picture. The musical numbers are a bore—James Darren, who Bob calls "Jimmy," performs "Gidget Goes Hawaiian" and Patti Page does "Dondi," both mediocre title songs to their new pictures. However, Patti (who's on the show roughly seventy-five percent!) is wonderful as the mother of fifteen kids in a raucous bit on the population explosion, where so many children overrun a house that their dad (Bob, who has a great rapport with Patti and the youths) has to take a number to go to the bathroom. Less likable is "Patti Loves Philsy," a takeoff of the flop sitcom *Peter Loves Mary*, where Phil Harris is upset that Patti, his TV wife, has secretly married Bob in real life and disrupts their anniversary. Phil's delivery and a good ending barely salvage this sketch. Bob and Phil also have spotty success singing "Hey Look Me Over" as sailors on shore leave trying to attract girls. Bob ends this by doing "Thanks for the Memory" with lyrics to fight cancer.

Bob: \*\*\*\* Show: \*\*\*


***The Bob Hope Buick Show***
May 13, 1961, Saturday 8:30-9:30 p.m.

James Garner, Julie London, Juliet Prowse. Music: David Rose.

"I'll be back next season on a horse," vows Bob as this special replaces the westerns *The Tall Man* and *The Deputy*. "If you can't lick 'em, join 'em." His excellent monologue hits reruns on TV ("There was an awful mess on *Wagon Train*. They met themselves at the pass.") and Bob's latest honor ("After eleven years, I finally got an Emmy nomination. It's a new category—survival."). Bob also cleverly promotes his latest picture, *Bachelor in Paradise*, by claiming he sacrificed a fishing vacation in favor of making a film with Lana Turner. It's bumpy thereafter, starting with an odd skit where Bob and Juliet are a dance team bankrupted by the stock market who are stripped down to their skivvies while performing "Everything's Coming Up Roses" to confiscate their possessions. Juliet and Julie's boring production numbers are offset somewhat by a decent bit where a Los Angeles Dodgers scout (Bob) attempts to recruit a hillbilly (James, who has great comic delivery). Bob and James will remake this skit in a modified form on Oct. 20, 1965. Also enjoyable is Bob and Julie doing "Two Sleepy People" for two cocker spaniels who become attached to them to their amusement. The finale is best, as Bob appears as Alfred Hitchcock to introduce "Weird-O," a spoof of the movie *Psycho* where an axe-wielding hotel clerk (Bob) attempts to kill a woman (Julie) who encounters supernatural activity in her hotel room. Her boyfriend (James) comes to rescue her, but she decides to stick with Bob instead. The show could have used more of this wackiness.

Bob and Show: ***

### *The Bob Hope Show*
Dec. 13, 1961, Wednesday 9-10 p.m.

James Garner, Nancy Kwan, Danny Thomas, The 1961 Hollywood Deb Stars, The 1961 Look All-America Football Team. Featured: Peter Leeds, J. Edward McKinley. Music: David Rose. Choreography: Nick Castle.

The first face shown here is Barbara Britton, commercial spokesperson for sponsor Revlon. The latter apparently dictates that Bob only narrate introductions for the Hollywood Deb Stars, who include Cynthia Pepper, Noreen Corcoran, Cheryl Holdridge and Mary Jane Saunders. After this strange start, Bob strolls on stage to get in licks about Bing Crosby, his costar in the upcoming movie *The Road to Hong Kong*, becoming a father again. "While he was acting over there [in London], he was producing here," Bob quips. He adds that Bing wanted his regular makeup man from Madame Tussauds Wax Museum. After plugging his picture *Bachelor in Paradise* ("based on an idea by Frank Sinatra"), Bob cracks gags about the Twist dance craze, some good ("I don't know how to do it, but did you ever see a dog get out of water?"), some not ("The big hit was by Chubby Checker. Up until last week, I thought that was a fat taxicab.") Next comes Bob investigating the proliferation of doctor shows on TV with a star medic (Danny Thomas). It never quite catches fire, but the next skit does literally and figuratively, as a vain, glamorous Hollywood couple (Bob and Nancy Kwan) reject the help of a firefighter (James Garner) as their home is ablaze. Acceptable but not great is a parody of the movie *The Hustler* with Nancy, James and Bob (in Jackie Gleason's role). Bob introduces the team winners without jokes, then Barbara Britton comes out at the end to plug Revlon again, concluding an odd show to watch.

Bob and Show: ***


**The Bob Hope Christmas Show**
Jan. 24, 1962, Wednesday 9-10 p.m.

Dorothy Provine, Anita Bryant, Jerry Colonna, Miss World Rosemarie Frankland, Peter Leeds, Jayne Mansfield, Secretary of the Air Force Eugene Zuckert. Choreographer: Nick Castle.

For this USO tour, Bob and crew go to Harmon Air Force Base in Newfoundland first, where he quips that he previously appeared at Cuba and Berlin for Christmas and thinks what happened at those locations forced him to be shipped here. He encounters Jerry Colonna as a wisecracking pilot for a quick bit. At Goose Bay Labrador, Bob cracks about TV being so late here that "On *Gunsmoke*, Chester hadn't broken his leg yet." Dorothy Provine joins him dressed her period costume from *The Roaring Twenties* and wants Bob to do the Twist with her. "It's just like doing the Charleston only with a backfield in motion." He demurs, so she does the Charleston solo. He then pretends to play golf who is interrupted by a Mountie (Jerry), but that pales next to Jayne Mansfield. She is a delight as a sergeant appears next to her to enact Romeo and Juliet with Bob, who appears in drag as a nurse and snuggles up to Jayne's ample bosoms. At Soderstrum Air Base in Greenland, he jokes, "I was thrilled at the reception. I hear the caribou don't turn out for just anybody!" Frobisher Bay is even more remote, prompting Bob to say, "Which, if you remember your map, is a place that isn't on it!" Also visited is Naval Station Argentia Base in Newfoundland and Thule Air Base in Greenland. Bob is in great form, but apart from his monologues and the Jayne Mansfield bit, the other entertainment comes up short.

Bob: ***** Show: ***

## The Bob Hope Show
Feb. 27, 1962, Tuesday 9-10 p.m.

Steve Allen, Joan Collins, Joanie Sommers, Jack Paar, Bing Crosby. Featured: J. Edward McKinley, Joi Lansing, Mark Scofield, Dave Lund. Music: David Rose.

Watching the original host of *The Tonight Show* (Steve Allen) and his successor (Jack Paar) interact makes this fascinating albeit fitfully successful. Bob makes space jokes in honor of Col. John Glenn orbiting the Earth ("We've seen what happens when a capsule takes a man!") and rain in Los Angeles ("Maybe it's just fallout from Jayne Mansfield flopping in the ocean"). Of the First Lady's tour of the White House on TV, he notes, "Mrs. Kennedy said they were looking for paintings of authentic America history, like [Bing] Crosby with his first son." To promote *The Road to Hong Kong*, Bob introduces his costar, Joan Collins, who says, "I love to travel. It rounds you out." Bob responds, "I have a line here, but ..." That's better than when they play a lady customs inspector checking Bob's luggage for only spotty laughs. Longer and not any funnier is "Bicycle 54... Are You There?" with Steve and Bob as English bobbies investigating Joan as a suspect in her husband's death that ends with everybody dancing the Twist. Jack Paar is next, comparing New York City to Los Angeles before narrating an odd but amusing pantomimed taped piece of visiting Bob's house in Palm Springs where Steve walks by in flippers getting ready to spearfish in Bob's pool. Joanie Sommers sings "It's Love" before the last two skits with Jack and Steve—see more about them in the Talk Shows chapter introduction. The cast comes out to shake Bob's hands and bow at the end, giving this a warm feeling overall.

Bob and Show: \*\*\*\*

## The Bob Hope Show
March 22, 1962, Thursday 8:30-9:30 p.m.

Ethel Merman, Piper Laurie, Maximilian Schell, Fabian. Featured: Bob Harvey, Gino Condino. Music: David Rose.

Acknowledging the upcoming Oscars, Bob jests that "I'm coming to you in livid black and white." He calls himself "the Adlai Stevenson of the awards" and says of hosting the awards, "That's like being a driver on a busload of honeymooners. You're there, but something's missing." He also jibes the Chief Executive for planning to tour Palm Springs: "That's what I like about President Kennedy. He gives his personal attention to every disaster area." Bob even claims with some truth that teen idol Fabian is here "so we can get a rating." From there, he and Ethel Merman parody *A Majority of One*, with Ethel as a movie star who moves into a Japanese man's house (Bob) and becomes a geisha while he gets Americanized. Despite some politically incorrect humor, this gets some laughs. More guffaws come after Fabian sings "Kansas City" and Bob tells him he needs gimmicks to last. Bob's imitations of Frank Sinatra and Dean Martin are pretty good, as is his mockery of Fabian singing "Tiger" before both sing it. Ethel belts out a medley including "There's No Business Like Show Business" before a great send-up of Method acting with Maximilian as a teacher and Piper as a crazed Maggie from *Cat on a Hot Tin Roof*. Ethel cracks up everyone at the end by exclaiming to Piper, "I thought you were Peter Lorre!" She and Bob sparkle doing "It's De-lovely," then everyone has fun doing the Twist as the credits roll for this satisfying outing.

Bob and Show: \*\*\*\*

**The Bob Hope Show**
April 25, 1962, Wednesday 9-10 p.m.

Janis Paige, Dorothy Lamour, Frank Sinatra. Featured: Peter Leeds, Bill Arnold, Veronica Cartwright (as a Girl Scout). Music: David Rose. Choreographer: Tom Hansen.

Some old, some new, and some borrowed material will make one blue in parts here. Bob's strong monologue refers a lot to the Los Angeles Dodgers. "If you don't like the ball game, there's a little knob on your seat. You can switch the whole thing to *Wagon Train*." He complains about taxes and then the Academy Awards, where there was a gate crasher ("They said he was a nut. But so far, the only proof of that is that he gave me an Oscar"). Bob also mentions his new picture with Bing ("The *London Daily Mail* said 'funniest American comedy since *Judgment at Nuremberg*.'") and David Rose's hit new record "The Stripper." Numbers by Janis Paige (with four dancers) and Dorothy Lamour (a medley of tunes from her movies) pale next to Frank Sinatra's typically smooth job on "Goody Goody." Dorothy also jokes and does commentary with Bob for the trailer and some bloopers from their *The Road to Hong Kong* movie in an overlong sequence. Frank has hilarious byplay with Bob (including promoting the singer's cameo in *The Road to Hong Kong*) before the third time in ten years Bob does the "Small Fry" comic duet dressed as a Little Lord Fauntleroy costume with Frank. As for Janis, she plays Juliet opposite Bob's Romeo in a proposed new TV series, "And So They Were Married." This will be remade and updated for Bob's April 10, 1972 special. Like the rest of the show, it is spottily amusing at best.

Bob: **** Show: ***

*The Bob Hope Show*
Oct. 24, 1962, Wednesday 9-10 p.m.

Lucille Ball, Bing Crosby, Juliet Prowse. Featured: Milton Frome, Stephen Case, Bob Jellison, Eddie Marr, Phil Arnold.

"We're in black and white again—it's been that way ever since we tried to barbecue the [NBC] peacock," Bob remarks as he launches his thirteenth season on TV. He also skewers the new Telstar satellite that broadcast overseas ("Is the world ready for Soupy Sales?") in a good monologue that last only four and a half minutes. The acceptable skits start with a lady district attorney (Lucille Ball) and a mobster (Bob) bent on framing the other one. This is a repeat of a skit Bob did with Betty Hutton on his Nov. 15, 1955 special, but not quite as well executed. "Bananaz" follows Juliet's dance number and has her encountering Ben Cartwheel (Bing Crosby) and his sons Hoss, Adam and Little Joe (all played by Bob). "I'm almost too hammy for me," Bob admits in this spoof of *Bonanza*, which ends with Bing shooting his sons to get the hand of Juliet. Lucille rejoins Bob to set up bloopers from their film *Critic's Choice* and also cracks that "You've been on television since *The Flintstones* were on live!" Bob then introduces Bing by saying he discovered him singing at a car wash in Palm Springs where he was the head squeegee boy. "I've always had a soft spot in my head for you, Bob," ripostes Bing. They share more insults before promoting *The Road to Hong Kong* and singing "Put It There, Pal." The obvious use of post-production work dampens the sporadic fun on display here.

Bob: **** Show: ***

***The Bob Hope Show***
Nov. 29, 1962, Thursday 8:30-9:30 p.m.

Jack Benny, Bobby Darin, Ethel Merman. Featured: Peter Leeds, Milton Frome. Music: Skinnay Ennis.

In London filming *Call Me Bwana*, Bob appears with a monocle and cup of tea to talk about his third Command Performance before the queen at the Palladium and narrates film of her arrival before showing his monologue. Jokes tailored for the audience (e.g., how Americans aren't used to being commanded to do anything) have variable results. The best involve President John F. Kennedy: "He has a dry humor. Imagine—a dry Irishman … This is the first time in history we've had a president that's young enough to be drafted." Then it's back to America, first for the movie spoof "The Bird Brain of Alcatraz" with Jack Benny which gets lousy so quickly that when Jack remarks, "Well, somebody's laying eggs and it isn't me!" it comes across as a statement of fact. In contrast, Bobby Darin sparkles doing an "international hit parade" with Bob, each singing "Ahab the Arab," an Israel spoof of "They Call the Wind Maria," "Speedy Gonzalez," "The Monster Mash," "Papa Oo Mow Mow" and more. They enjoy the lively medley even with Bob laughing at the lyrics and straining to hit some notes. Also strong after Ethel Merman sings is Bobby playing Mack the Rat, a gambler on a riverboat with its owner, the Unsinkable Ethel. The two bamboozle Bob in a swell skit. At the end Jack banters with Bob in a bit as surprisingly sluggish as their earlier skit. Bob compliments all his guest stars in "Thanks for the Memory" quickly before leaving.

Bob and Show: ***


***The Bob Hope Christmas Show***
Jan. 16, 1963, Wednesday 9-10 p.m.

Anita Bryant, Jerry Colonna, Janis Paige, Lana Turner, Miss USA Amedee Chabot, Peter Leeds. Choreographer: Roland Dupree.

Showing highlights of fifteen shows done in ten days over 20,000 miles across Asia, this is the gold standard for Bob's overseas Christmas shows. He sparkles in ad libs ("Who's up in the balcony, the Republicans?" he cracks at his first stop in Korea) and his monologue ("It's been a slow year back home—only one Kennedy got elected"). Lana Turner gets a tremendous reception and is a good straight man. "I'm just an ordinary girl," she tells Bob. "Then I've been going out with sailors!" he responds. Les Brown gets in the act and breaks his baton to leave with Lana rather than conduct the orchestra. Bob's beatnik routine gets a good foil with Janis Paige as his long-haired wife dancing to his downbeat. Laughs continue in Japan with jokes like "I feel right at home. It's been bombed before," and Bob questioning Jerry Colonna disguised as a geisha girl at the Iwakuni Air Base. "What does the general say?" Bob says of Jerry's look. "Stay a little while, honey!" Jerry shoots back. The skit with Bob interrogating Lana as a spy crackles, as does the two of them dancing later on. Best of all is a hilarious bit with Bob and Miss USA enacting a scene with a wooden sailor aboard the Kitty Hawk aircraft carrier. After Anita sings "Silent Night" comes a scene of a Christmas tree being put up in a demilitarized zone and Bob concluding, "While it stands, there's hope for all." Fun, funny and patriotic, this is what Hope did best.

Bob and Show: *****

**The Bob Hope Show**
March 13, 1963, Wednesday 9-10 p.m.

Frank Sinatra, Robert Goulet, Brenda Lee, Edie Adams, The Hollywood Deb Stars (Susan Hart, Laurel Goodwin, Sheila James, Lana Wood, Lori Martin, Patty McCormack, Karyn Kupcinet, Sandra Descher, Sandra Gale Bettin, Roberta Shore, Mimsy Farmer, Joan Freeman).

This sprightly effort is hurt only by an overabundance of references that date it squarely to 1963. Bob hits President Kennedy's physical education campaign ("How did a guy in a rocking chair con everybody into walking?"), the Oscar nominations ("I've been left out more than the milk bottles at [Bing] Crosby's house"), and Elizabeth Taylor's love life ("I think *Lawrence of Arabia* was pretty good entertainment, but how about Richard [Burton] from Rome?"). Best of all, Bob sets up a joke by promoting his new movie, album, book (*I Owe Russia $1,200*) and sponsors and concludes, "Ask not what your comedian can do for you, but what you can do for your comedian." After Robert Goulet's number, "Teenage Tune Time" twinkles as hostess Brenda Lee interviews new singing star Bob, sporting a spit curl. His ad libs crack up Brenda often, and she fills in as a backup vocalist to do "Big Girls Don't Cry," with backup singers who add to the fun. Bob also has great interplay with Frank Sinatra ("He's been featured in quite a few short engagements"), who sings "Call Me Irresponsible" superbly. Next,

Bob fires an actor starring on a series (Robert) who then moans about the travails of TV. "What I need is steady employment," Robert grouses. "You should've been a flower girl for Liz Taylor!" Bob exclaims. A nice song by Brenda and a smooth presentation of the Hollywood Deb Stars by Edie Adams with Bob round out a fine show.

Bob and Show: ****


**The Bob Hope Show**
April 14, 1963, Sunday 9-10 p.m.

Dean Martin, Martha Raye. Featured: Cliff Norton, Peter Leeds, Bob Jellison. *TV Guide* Awards Presenters: James T. Quirk (publisher), Arthur A. Shulman (assistant to the publisher). D: Dick Schneider (New York awards segments). Music: David Rose.

A very TV-centric special starts with Bob hilariously riffing on the Oscars he did not host this year. "My annual humiliation is over ... I thought it was a wonderful five-hour show. That's how long it was for the losers. I watched it in color—green." Bob also references this show's *TV Guide* awards and asks, "If *The Defenders* lose, will they hire Perry Mason?" Then the chairman of a congressional subcommittee investigating TV ratings (Bob) discovers that the hearings are opposite TV's biggest show, "The Sicilian Hillbillies." That show's lead (Dean Martin in a beard and mountaineer clothes) appears on the stand, doing drunk jokes ("Do you know you're under oath?" "I might, if you hum a few bars!"). Bob switches outfits with him "To see what kind of rating I can get" to end a so-so skit. After Martha Raye sings, "Cedars of Paramount Studios" sends up TV medical shows. A nurse (Martha) and young Dr. Kilroy (Bob) fight for custody of a script with a new disease. Its writer falls down, and both demand to treat him even though he insists he's fine. Bob paints a line on the writer to indicate which side they get to operate before he and Martha fall in love. Martha and Bob's good interplay and delivery of lines make this a winner. Dean sings before Bob introduces James T. Quirk in Hollywood and Arthur Schulman in New York for the *TV Guide* Awards. One winner is *The Bob Hope Christmas Show* as best single dramatic, music or variety show. "No, no!" Bob exclaims as he gets whistles. "I hope this puts an end once and for all to the rumor that the people who watch my show can't read. And I'd like to be a gracious winner, but I haven't had the experience. This is actually my second year and I'm very grateful and, oh, how sneaky you are!" He thanks everyone connected to the show profusely, then after a few other awards congratulates everyone and says good night.

Bob and Show: ***

## *The Bob Hope Show*
May 15, 1963, Wednesday 9-10 p.m.

Fred MacMurray, Arnold Palmer, Patti Page. Featured: Peter Leeds, Quinn O'Hara, Eddie Marr. Music: David Rose.

"You all know me, the NBC hillbilly," cracks Bob, referencing his competition. His monologue ranges from his new book ("*Time* magazine said, 'Funnier than *The Robe!*'") to world leadership ("I see where Premier Khrushchev is turning in his shoe") to pregnancies among U.S. political dynasties ("It's spring in Washington. The cherry blossoms are in bloom, and so are the Kennedys."). He gets in good lines about his guests, Patti Page ("She's a singer-musician. That means she's a girl.") and golfer Arnold Palmer ("Let's see him get out of this trap!"). The strong start shines in comparison to the so-so, overlong skits that follow. Fred MacMurray is a Martian robot astronaut (you read right) looking for a female who Bob mistakes for a butler. The alleged comedy here includes Fred acting like a slot machine paying out money during the bit. Arnold Palmer has at least one good line about Bob's golf swing—"I've seen better on a condemned playground"—before showing supposed outtakes of Bob's efforts in *Call Me Bwana*, a new film that Arnold did with the comedian. And Patti Page is quite funny as the strict operator of a Soviet hotel where Bob feels uncomfortable as a patron. At the end, Bob muses about being a guest on Fred's series ("I'm not Fred Flintstone!" retorts Fred) and plugs his new article in *Readers Digest* and new book *I Owe Russia $1,200*. He just walks off the show before the credits roll, apparently glad to end a season running fruitlessly against *The Beverly Hillbillies*.

Bob: **** Show: ***

## *Chrysler Presents a Bob Hope Comedy Special*
Sept. 27, 1963, Friday 8:30-9:30 p.m.

Dean Martin, Barbra Streisand, Tuesday Weld, James Garner. Featured: Verna Felton, Peter Leeds, Jesse White, Butch Stone, Stumpy Brown, Bob Harvey.

The script lets down a wonderful cast to an extent, but this is not a total loss. In his monologue, to indicate how long he's been with NBC, Bob blows dust off the microphone. He also notes that "The Supreme Court ruled no more praying in school. From now on, the kids have to study to get good marks." A production number leads into Bob and Tuesday Weld play a married Hollywood couple with competing TV series who threaten to divorce until Bob's agent (Jesse White) tells him he need Tuesday to appears on his ratings-deprived series. It's a pretty raucous entry. Verna Felton plays their maid and gets applause plus delivers an in-joke by saying "I'm watching *The Flintstones!*" where she was the voice of Wilma's mother. Barbra Streisand introduces Dean Martin, then Tuesday says the Telstar satellite is beaming live from France a TV show starring James Garner as a psychiatrist and Bob as his patient. Spottily amusing, Barbra's rendition of "Any Place I Hang My Hat is Home" overshadows it and is one of the best vocal presentations ever on a Hope special. The good vibes continue with a spoof of *Hootenanny*, where James introduces Hog Chitlins and the Goat Grabbers Three. Barbra plays two washboards ("I'm in stereo") while Bob has a goatee as they sing a modified version of "Jimmy Crack Corn." The Surf Riders led by Dean join Bob to do takeoffs of other folk numbers too. The elements are here for a top show, but it never jells much beyond average.

Bob and Show: ***

**Chrysler Presents the Bob Hope Special**
Oct. 25, 1963, Friday 8:30-9:30 p.m.

Andy Griffith, Martha Raye, Jane Russell, Connie Haines, Meryl Davis, Los Angeles Dodgers Sandy Koufax, Don Drysdale, and Tommy Davis. Featured: Peter Leeds, Paula Lane, Charles Smith, Mike Ross.

Everything is disconnected as guests appear only in their own segments, making this a disjointed special to endure. It's dated too, starting with Bob's monologue on Joe Valachi's Mafia testimony, Nikita Khrushchev, Elizabeth Taylor's tour of London, and Christine Keeler and the Profumo affair. The jokes make little sense unless one has knowledge of the events. A spoof of *The Andy Griffith Show* follows as Bob plays a criminal on the lam who escapes to Mayberry. Andy Griffith is forced to play the broader version of himself from his series' early years in this semi-successful takeoff. Odder and longer (seven minutes) to endure is Jane Russell, Connie Haines, and Meryl Davis singing together. The juxtaposition of the trio decked out in gowns, furs and glitz while performing old time spirituals is hard to process. Worse is Martha Raye as Madame Foo, the dragon lady of Viet-Poo, who plans to kill her fiancé, Moo Goo Guy Foo (Bob) in an extended and only occasionally enjoyable outing, and Bob as a stereotyped Asian pretending to be guillotined is not funny. Still awkward but cuter and easier to watch are three L.A. Dodgers stars in top hats and canes reading scripted lines to Bob before singing a special version of "We're in the Money." It closes by promoting next week's drama on *Bob Hope Presents the Chrysler Theatre* with its star, Paul Lukas, forcing Bob to open a vault and see Peter Falk inside. One wonders who thought all this amounts to good entertainment.

Bob: *** Show: **


*Chrysler Presents the Bob Hope Special*
Dec. 13, 1963, Friday 8:30-9:30 p.m.

Jack Benny, Bing Crosby (guest hosts), Juliet Prowse.

Bob's eye treatment prevents him from hosting his Christmas show so Benny and Crosby fill in for him serviceably as host. "It was either this or send flowers," quips Benny, while Crosby presents the TV debut of his Christmas perennial anthem "Do You Hear What I Hear?" The show also repeats skits from previous Hope specials of Bob and Danny Thomas being competitive private eyes (Feb. 10, 1959) and Benny hiding cameras in his house to film an unaware Bob (April 15, 1959). Since there is no Bob here, there is no rating for this one.


*Chrysler Presents The Bob Hope Christmas Special*
Jan. 17, 1964, Friday 8:30-10 p.m.

Tuesday Weld, Anita Bryant, Jerry Colonna, Miss USA Michelle Metrinko, Philip Crosby, John Bubbles, The Earl Twins (Jane and Ruth Earl), Peter Leeds.

First on this USO tour is Wheelus Air Base in Tripoli, Libya, where Bob performs during a sandstorm. He references the rickety plane the troupe took before hilariously interviewing Jerry Colonna dressed as an Arab. Bob's repartee with Tuesday Weld has perfect timing by both. When she says, "You must know everything there is to know about handling women," Bob answers, "Richard Burton doesn't make a move without me!" From Incirlik Air Base and Ankara in Turkey, he jokes some before Anita Bryant sings "He's Got the Whole World in His Hands" slowly. At Iraklion Air Station in Crete, Bob quips, "I've never played an olive grove before" and introduces the dancing Earl Twins. In Athens, Greece, Bob notes its king and queen in the audience while riffing on its ancient history. He greets eight thousand at the NATO headquarters of the Mediterranean command in Naples, Italy, with "This is nice, we've been playing cow pastures!" Bob sings "You Make Me Feel So Young" to Miss USA Michelle Metrinko while delivering gags. "Funny, huh?" he says. "Everything about you is funny," she shoots back. Aboard the U.S.S. Shangri-La, Philip Crosby does "White Christmas" competently, but John Bubbles' song and tap dance solo and with Bob is superior. Bob as an airman meeting a dancing girl (Tuesday) who is a spy is an amusing update of his Nov. 26, 1950 skit with Marilyn Maxwell. Bits of other entertainment appear at the end along with Bob's traditional thanks to all involved and patriotic wrap-up. Apart for a few bum songs, this really clicks.

Bob and Show: \*\*\*\*


***Chrysler Presents a Bob Hope Comedy Special***
Feb. 14, 1964, Friday 8:30-9:30 p.m.

Anne Bancroft, Sergio Franchi, Janet Leigh, Julie London. Featured: Ray Kellogg, Peter Leeds, J. Edward McKinley, Stephen Chase, Lois Corbett.

Funny but flawed throughout, Bob nevertheless is in great spirits. He gets laughs but in retrospect comes off grumpy about a new musical group arriving from England. "The Beatles are kind of a barbershop quartet that couldn't get waited on ... They look like animated toadstools ... I can't believe their first record. It sounds like Yma Sumac and Jerry Colonna on a barbecue spit." He also jokes extensively about Elizabeth Taylor and Richard Burton doing Shakespeare in Canada and the Surgeon General's recent report linking smoking to cancer: "Overnight, America went from 'Ban the bomb' to 'Ban the butt.'" After his ten-minute set, Bob notes that as Sen. Margaret Chase Smith planned to run for president, "She couldn't decide what hat to throw in the ring." That sexist comment leads into a skit with Anne Bancroft as a chief executive who plans to paint the White House pink and worries about her fashion and looks. Her feminized husband (Bob) knits in protest before he says he's pregnant, prompting Anne to boast, "At last we beat the Russians at something!" Also intermittently amusing is Janet Leigh doing fine work as Bob's blonde wife and a brunette fooling him as his "mistress." For his musical guests, Julie London comes off better than Sergio Franchi. She and Bob have good jokes about her recent appearance in Vegas and her birth of twins ("She even has kids in stereo!"). The overall impression of this special is that it is disjointed from conception to execution.

Bob: ***** Show: ***


*Chrysler Presents a Bob Hope Comedy Special*
April 17, 1964, Friday 8:30-9:30 p.m.

Tony Randall, Martha Raye, Jack Jones. *TV Guide* Awards Presenters: James T. Quirk (publisher), Arthur A. Shulman (assistant to the publisher). D: Jack Schneider (New York awards segments).

"Good evening, Mr. and Mrs. America, and all our Oscars oversees," jests Bob about British wins four days earlier at the Academy Awards. He notes that "Seven guys split the award for art direction in *Cleopatra*, and a lot of sharing went on in that picture, I want to tell you that!" The audience howls in light of how Elizabeth Taylor and Richard Burton cheated on their spouses during filming. Bob scores with everything from "*Tom Jones* got ten nominations, each for a commandment they broke" to astronaut John Glenn's fall at home ("He stepped into a bathtub, said 'A-OK,' and that's what he landed on!"). The skits can't match this strong opening, but the *Tom Jones* spoof (with Martha as Tom's sister trying to hide her lovers from Bob as a squire) gets energy from Martha's mugging as she engages in nonsense like eating buttons noisily. Less effective are Tony and Bob's banter and Jack Jones' number. Better but racially insensitive is Bob and his guests playing the Japanese Beatles, with stereotypical makeup and jokes used before they sing "I Want to Hold Your Hand" and Japanese girls in the audience squeal with delight. It wraps up with the annual *TV Guide* awards, which includes a message from President Lyndon Johnson praising the networks' coverage of the John F. Kennedy assassination along with announcing the winners. The ceremony finishes early so Bob has to fill in with jokes, making a rather wobbly ending to a show that started strong.

Bob: ***** Show: ***

***Chrysler Presents a Bob Hope Comedy Special***
Sept. 25, 1964, Friday 8:30-9:30 p.m.

Dean Martin, Phyllis Diller, Milton Berle, Jack Benny.

Some great moments are undercut by a bad final skit. Bob's fine monologue focuses on the presidential campaign. "It looks like a big season on TV for comedy ... You've got your choice of 'I Love Barry' or 'Leave It to Lyndon.'" He references the "LBJ brand," and some start cracking up before the punchline due to President Lyndon B. Johnson's association with ranching, forcing Bob to say, "There's more! ... That's not easy when it's not on your arm." Jack Benny is in the audience and says Bob is the world's best comedian. Bob responds, "You're the funniest comedian in the world." Jack stands up and exclaims, "I stand corrected!" It is an amusing way for Bob to welcome Jack back to NBC. There is more rowdy fun with Phyllis Diller as a marriage counselor who claims her male clients fall in love with her to a doubting Bob. (Phyllis: "Kiss me." Bob: "You mean without an anesthetic?") When she learns Bob is rich, she tells him to divorce and manhandles him while Jack pops up playing the violin to serenade her efforts. Dean Martin sings "The Door is Still Open to My Heart" before Bob presents him with a gold record for "Everybody Loves Somebody," which he lip syncs. Then Phyllis plays a witch married to a large bat (Bob) when an oversized atomic chicken (Milton Berle) arrives to fight for her love. Everyone cracks up for no reason in this odd skit with a stupid ending using poor special effects. It seriously hampers an otherwise top show.

Bob and Show: ***


***Chrysler Presents a Bob Hope Comedy Special***
Nov. 20, 1964, Friday 8:30-9:30 p.m.

Richard Chamberlain, Annette Funicello, Trini Lopez, Donald O'Connor, Stella Stevens. Featured: Pat Priest, The Wellingtons. Choreography: Louis DaPron.

Bob really seems to love his guests here as tees off with a great opening set. He notes Lyndon Johnson's election as president ("Lady Bird, Lynda Bird and Lucy Bird are back in their nests") and roasts Barry Goldwater's huge loss ("Does Arizona qualify for foreign aid?"). Bobby Kennedy's win as senator from New York despite barely visiting the state prompts Bob to quip, "I know guys who've been stuck in the Holland Tunnel longer." For California's new senator, ex-actor George Murphy, Bob says, "What a great victory for the late late show!" The spotty and overlong skits have Stella as the in-flight entertainment on a plane arguing with an egotistical pilot (Bob), and Richard opposite Bob in "Bonzai Earp," a Japanese western take-off with awful stereotypes (Bob appears in Fu Manchu makeup and says lines like "Check, prease!"). Richard does have a great bit prior to the skit as Bob says, "People are always expecting me to be funny," and Richard responds, "That's what I mean—they expect the impossible!" Bob likes bantering as well with Trini (who does "Hello Dolly!" in Spanish) and Annette, who sings "Do the Clyde" with six guys in white tuxedos and has Bob duet with her by just crooning "Ooooo!" The most effective bit has Bob and Donald in a magic act where Donald is both a flamenco dancer and a knife thrower with Bob as his target. A clip of Jeffrey Hunter on next week's installment of *Bob Hope Presents The Chrysler Theatre* ends the show.

Bob: \*\*\*\*\* Show: \*\*\*


## *Chrysler Presents a Bob Hope Comedy Special*
Dec. 18, 1964, Friday 8:30-9:30 p.m.

Nancy Wilson, James Garner, Martha Raye, Kathryn Crosby, The Beach Boys. Featured: Jerome Cowan, Peter Leeds, Delores Faith, Eddie Marr.

The musical numbers and first and last skit give this one a passing grade. The obviously edited monologue scores with some swipes at Russia's recently deposed leader, Nikita Khrushchev. "They fired Khrushchev because his agricultural plan failed. None of the people he planted came up." Bob adds, "He is overexposed. It happens to all the big comedians." He then plays the King of Commercials whose wife (Kathryn Crosby) must break it to him that he is no longer in favor among advertisers. It's amusing with cleverly lines and good acting, whereas even the talented James Garner cannot help a bit where he plays Santa Claus being investigated as a spy captured flying over Moscow. It is a Cold War relic that creaks, especially with Bob's flailing attempt at a Russian accent. Bob does better as a teen on a skateboard in love with Martha Raye in "Pitiful Place," a spoof of *Peyton Place* as they throw their supposed baby back and forth. Then Bob appears as Martha's dad in a trick screenshot to grab the infant and marries them amid an unsuspecting younger Bob. Still, the lack of interaction between any of the guests beyond their spots makes this feel erratic, and it's not helped by Bob only announcing the performances of Nancy Wilson and the Beach Boys (performing "Dance Dance Dance"). Although only billed as featured, familiar character actor Jerome Cowan gets a nice round of applause as the doctor in "Pitiful Place."

Bob and Show: ***

## *Chrysler Presents the Bob Hope Christmas Special*
Jan. 15, 1965, Friday 8:30-10 p.m.

Janis Paige, Anna Maria Alberghetti, Anita Bryant, Jerry Colonna, John Bubbles, Miss World Ann Sydney, Peter Leeds, Tony Hope, Jill St. John.

Bob's first Vietnam War special, a 28,000-mile trek of the Far East, features five women who sing, act in skits and of course participate in suggestive banter with Bob on stage. For example, Jill St. John complains that while in Guam, "About four o'clock in the morning, a man knocked on my door and wouldn't stop! And he came back five times!" "Six," Bob immediately interjects. Apart from some dated stereotypes (Bob affects an Asian look in South Korea, Jerry Colonna plays half of a Siamese twin), this holds up well due both to its documentary feel of covering five shows in three days and its tight editing of lots of material. What is disquieting is amid Hope's relaxed demeanor on stage with a golf club and off stage meeting dignitaries such as Gen. William Westmoreland and the king and queen of Thailand, signs of guerrilla warfare appear near the troupe. For their Christmas Eve show in Vietnam, a bomb explodes near the hotel where they were staying, causing it to lose electricity and sustain glass damage. Bob then jovially tells the audience the next day that "We opened with a bang!" Some of the cast laughs nervously after a bad night of little sleep when Hope added with a sliver of truth, "Rough there, sleeping with a parachute on my back." Apart from this, soldiers clearly love the performances, taking pictures with their cameras and whistling at the women, and the cast is similarly committed to providing top entertainment. This got a huge 36.0 rating.

Bob: ***** Show: ****

## *Chrysler Presents a Bob Hope Comedy Special*
Feb. 12, 1965, Friday 8:30-9:30 p.m.

Johnny Carson, Louis Prima, Jack Jones, Gia Malone, Sam Butera and The Witnesses, Carroll Baker. Featured: Peter Leeds, Jane Dulo, Reta Shaw, Billy Curtis.

Except for one raucous spoof, this is a mediocrity from the music to a short (less than four minutes) monologue. There, Bob makes little impression with gags on Vietnam, Lyndon Baines Johnson's inauguration and the proposed $99 billion federal spending plan for 1965 ("Our budget may get to the moon before we do!"). "The Woman from A.U.N.T." mocks *The Man from U.N.C.L.E.* with Carroll Baker as the title spy taking on arch criminal Bob. It's moderately amusing but overlong at nearly fifteen minutes. Bob then shows his age by joking about teens and their wild crazes with Jack Jones, along with promoting Bob's latest movie *I'll Take Sweden*. Things finally perk up when Ed McMahon introduces "Bobby Carson" (Hope) in a delicious send-up of *The Tonight Show* that includes Les Brown with a fake goatee as bandleader "Snitch Henderson." "Bobby" brings out movie star Rock Carson (Johnny Carson in a dinner jacket), who kisses the camera and promotes his next TV appearance on *Rawhide* with the title emblazoned on his pants' buttocks. "Glad it wasn't *Naked City*!" cracks Bob. With commercial spoofs and great work by Jane Dulo (as a charwoman horny for "Rock") and Reta Shaw (as an audience member), this is wildly fun and funny. Too bad the show slumps thereafter with Louis Prima's forced number, Bob's fake banter with Carroll and promotion of her new movie, clips of the next *Bob Hope Presents The Chrysler Theatre* production and a plug for the Heart Fund by Bob before signing off.

Bob and Show: ***

## *Chrysler Presents a Bob Hope Comedy Special*
March 26, 1965, Friday 8:30-9:30 p.m.

Bill Mauldin.

Additional footage from the 1964 USO Christmas tour makes up the bulk of this show. Bob delivers a new monologue on current events plus shows famed editorial cartoonist Bill Mauldin films of his son overseas. Bob even releases a record album using material from this tour called *On the Road to Vietnam*.

## Chrysler Presents a Bob Hope Comedy Special
April 16, 1965, Friday 8:30-9:30 p.m.

Gina Lollobrigida, Nancy Wilson, Frankie Avalon, Pete Fountain. Featured: Pat Harrington Jr.

The jazz stylings of Nancy Wilson and Pete Fountain and great supporting work by Pat Harrington Jr. distinguish an otherwise average entry. At the top, Bob tackles taxes ("The government's being very cooperative this year. If you're late with your taxes, they'll give you more time. In fact, you can get up to ten years."), the Oscars ("Did you see Audrey Hepburn congratulating Julie Andrews? She won an Emmy right there!"), and Medicare. Nancy sings "The Grass is Greener" and "Who Can I Turn To," then Gina Lollobrigida sings Italian and Bob "translates" the lyrics into a stereotypical tale about a family that includes a "pizzaholic." After that groaner, Pete does a fine upbeat take on "Georgia on My Mind," followed by Bob and Frankie Avalon as bums basically as the pretext to do a duet on "King of the Road." Stock footage of Rome introduces an Italian film spoof with Bob as a vain movie star (no, not himself!) dealing with ramshackle conditions on the studio set with his director (Pat) and his co-star (Gina). The latter is a dowdy pickpocket Bob eventually transforms into a refined woman a la *My Fair Lady*, but she leaves with the director instead. It's sufficiently funny enough. Frankie presents the title song for *I'll Take Sweden*, his new movie with Bob, and the comedian quips about lots of footage (arguably too much) of Frankie and himself from the film afterward. Pete will work on another Bob Hope special in 1973, while Gina will have to wait until 1982.

Bob and Show: ***

## Chrysler Presents a Bob Hope Comedy Special
Sept. 29, 1965, Wednesday 9-10 p.m.

Douglas Fairbanks Jr., Beatrice Lillie, Dinah Shore, Andy Williams. Featured: Cliff Norton, Eddie Marr, J. Edward McKinley, Mike Ross, Bob Jellison, Phil Arnold.

Another season opener is another hot-and-cold session of entertainment. The monologue's highlights include shots at new TV series' titles like *My Mother the Car*, which Bob says CBS will copy as "My Father the Skateboard," and *Run for Your Life* ("It's about a Los Angeles pedestrian"). Less effective are ones on the Beatles. Bob claims no one knew the difference between them and the Mets playing at Shea Stadium and makes fun of Ringo Starr becoming a father ("The baby looks like Ringo, but they're keeping him anyway"). Bob's first skit has him and Douglas Fairbanks Jr. as bickering astronauts stuck in a capsule in space for three years. It has good special effects of Bob floating in space and pretty nice jokes overall. Dinah Shore shows up next as a spy for CBS in the offices of NBC who is being investigated by Bob in an acceptable bit with nothing really special happening. The same applies to Andy Williams singing "The Way You Look Tonight" solo before joshing Bob about his golf game and joining him to present "Heart" from the musical *Damn Yankees,* with Bob pretending to be Andy's son. Dinah's torchy take on "Any Place I Hang My Hat is Home" adds a skosh of excitement, but "Tiger Ballou," a spoof of *Cat Ballou,* fails even with Beatrice Lillie doing her best to squeeze out what good comic lines are there. Bob urges everyone to travel America before promoting next week's drama on *Bob Hope Presents The Chrysler Theatre.*

Bob and Show: ***


### *Chrysler Presents a Bob Hope Comedy Special*
Oct. 20, 1965, Wednesday 9-10 p.m.

James Garner, Carol Lawrence, Phyllis Diller, The We Five. Cameos: Johnny Carson, Robert Goulet. Choreography: Kevin Carlisle.

Most of this is good enough just to get by, including the monologue. Bob says Frank Sinatra had an accident with his young girlfriend, Mia Farrow, at the World Series: "He jumped up to cheer a play and speared himself on Mia's popsicle." He also notes that with the president's recent surgery, "His stitches now read, 'All the way with LBJ!'" Bob mocks Johnson's War on Poverty program as a senator approaching a hillbilly in a shack (James Garner). The set designers impressively put the scene on a large rotating turntable as Bob and James enter the house. For some reason, Johnny Carson appears shirtless in a moving bathtub during the rambling skit. Another jaw-dropping set has Carol Lawrence lowered on a lift to perform "Fascinating Rhythm" and "I Got Rhythm" with eight male dancers while musicians pretend to play on high risers. It's the show's best part. Bob as a peeping Tom who wants to possess Phyllis and then vice versa has its moments but no real ending. The We Five lip sync "You Were on My Mind" and "Small World" satisfactorily before Bob and Carol bore as college students in the 1920s compared to 1965. There is one good joke with Carol's husband, Robert Goulet, saying he's getting a book called *Try to Remember* by Francis Scott Key (Goulet had recently forgotten "The Star Spangled Banner" lyrics at an event). It ends with a monologue by Phyllis with lines like "I can make a TV dinner taste like radio." Like most of the show, it's adequate but not stellar.

Bob and Show: ***


## *Chrysler Presents a Bob Hope Comedy Special*
Dec. 15, 1965, Wednesday 9-10 p.m.

Jack Benny, Bing Crosby, Janet Leigh. Featured: Peter Leeds, Shirley Mitchell, J. Edward McKinley, Mike Ross.

"The jokes may not be funny, but they'll be pretty," quips Bob on his first starring special in color. He adds, "You can tell it's almost Christmas here in Los Angeles. The smog is turning green." Bob also touches on heavy rains in Los Angeles and the space race before appearing opposite Bing as the latter rents out his house to Bob. Prior to leaving, Bing learns a family plans to tour the facility even though Bob has signed a lease and wants to go to bed. When the family offers more money, Bing buys Bob out, but the clan was really just actors Bob hired to extort the money from Bing in this sporadically humorous segment. Jack Benny appears next as a convict who flies to the North Pole to rob Santa Claus (Bob). Turns out he had a traumatic experience and didn't get a stuffed bear. Santa gives him that gift, but seeing Santa has turned his reindeer into women, Jack takes them instead. Like the first skit, this leaves much to be desired. So does the next one, with Bob and Janet Leigh as married celebrities dueling for attention as they run for office until reconciling when Janet withdraws because she is pregnant. Thankfully, Bing's rendition of "Do You Hear What I Hear?" redeems the tedium, even with Bing lip syncing it. Unfortunately, Jack coming out to promote Bob's latest album before Bob promotes next week's drama brings things back down. That plus the underdone sketches make this one Christmas show to forget.

Bob: *** Show: **

***Chrysler Presents the Bob Hope Christmas Special***
Jan. 19, 1966, Wednesday 9-10:30 p.m.

Jack Jones, Joey Heatherton, Kaye Stevens, Anita Bryant, Jerry Colonna, The Nicholas Brothers, Miss USA Dianna Lynn Batts, Peter Leeds, Carroll Baker.

Some shaky camerawork and a recurring xenophobic streak mars an otherwise strong show from parts of Asia-Pacific. "The official meaning of the name Thailand is land of the free, but none of the native girls has discovered it yet," Bob says, referring to the country's prostitutes. He claims Bangkok's canals are known as sewers in America, and noting the defense of Guam, he cracks, "We wouldn't want the Communists to capture all this crabgrass, would we?" Otherwise, Bob has great interplay with his female guests, who mock his cheapness ("He promised me some genuine pearls. He gave me a dozen oysters and a hammer!" says Carroll Baker) and randy nature (Carroll: "Every glamour girl in Hollywood was begging to go on this trip with you." Bob: "Who told you that?" Carroll: "You did." Bob: "At least you heard it from a reliable source."). Some of Bob's best comic reactions ever occur as a hospital patient dealing with a crazy doctor (Jerry Colonna) and wartime bureaucracy. And of course, his monologues click. Of the trip's tight security, he quipped, "I've been frisked so many times, I'm beginning to like it!" However, the most memorable moment is Joey Heatherton dancing the Watusi with twelve Marines. One is black, making it one of TV's first times of interracial dancing. At the end, Bob claims that the soldiers "seem to be a lot more optimistic about this commitment than a lot of our citizens here at home" and says many would be willing to lay their lives to protect America. Sadly and unknowingly to him and millions more, many will do so over the next decade in Vietnam.

Bob: ***** Show: ****


***Chrysler Presents a Bob Hope Comedy Special***
Feb. 16, 1966, Wednesday 9-10 p.m.

Martha Raye, The Righteous Brothers, Jill St. John, Danny Thomas. Featured: Peter Leeds, Mike Ross, Bob Jellison, Phil Arnold, Kathryn Minner.

"It's nice to be back working for a civilian audience again," Bob says. "You don't laugh as easy, but you don't shoot as fast either." He scores with President Lyndon B. Johnson's $113 billion budget ("That's what happens when you give a Texan an expense account."), a golf game with Phyllis Diller as his caddy ("After I putted out in the greens, I kept sticking her back in the cup."), and rising skirt hemlines ("I like them. I'm for anything educational."). He warmly introduces Martha Raye, who says of her USO experience that "You'd be surprised how many GIs in Vietnam told me I was gorgeous." The audience applauds, then Bob quips, "Funny, the same thing happened to me!" She then plays Batgirl fighting the evil Lobsterman (Bob with a huge claw on his left hand and a pink outfit). A wonderful set, costumes, and props, including an oversized bat swatter, cannot overcome bad special effects and no real ending. The Righteous Brothers doing "You're My Soul and Inspiration" and "Turn On Your Lovelight" live is swell, but the show sags thereafter. A biker (Bob) with his new bride (Jill St. John) is sluggish and relies on lazy special effects designed to get laughs that do not emerge. Introducing Danny Thomas with "This is one of the few shows on TV you don't own," Bob is the stooge to a gambler (Danny) cheating in cards with the help of his girlfriend (Jill). It is overlong and under-funny like the other skits. Still, Bob has done worse shows.

Bob and Show: ***


**Chrysler Presents a Bob Hope Comedy Special**
April 13, 1966, Wednesday 9-10 p.m.

Phyllis Diller, Pete Fountain, Jonathan Winters, Lee Marvin. Featured: John Hoyt, Johnine Lee, Damian London.

Pre-empted four weeks earlier, this has a top monologue trying to compensate for the rest of the show. Citing a man rigging the Nielsen ratings, Bob says, "He now has a steady job. He's working for the Republicans." He riffs on the upcoming Oscars with "Only five more days, and we'll all know who to hate." About Richard Burton being a good lover, Bob responds, "You should catch me in my dressing room mirror. There's real passion!" He says taxes are so high that "Gomer Pyle is now Gomer Molehill." Hearing that some Mexican deejays are playing Frank Sinatra's records at the wrong speeds, Bob adds, "So he sounds exactly like [Bing] Crosby." Oscar nominee Lee Marvin tells Bob of his recent roles in *Ship of Fools* and *Cat Ballou* that "I was seasick for three months and hung over for four." In "The Rancid Six," Bob is somewhat offensive as a bandit with a stereotypical Spanish accent opposite Lee, a bounty hunter disguised as an effeminate traveler who gets fooled by Bob in the end. Lee's delivery is funny, but the skit drags. Better is an award nominee (Jonathan Winters) accused by a detective (Bob) of killing his competition. Jonathan's ad libbing and use of dialects to impersonate others helps. After Pete Fountain plays the clarinet nicely, "Pagoda Place" bombs as Japanese newlyweds (Bob and Phyllis Diller) argue about the arrival of Phyllis's other husband (Jonathan). It is messy and larded with dated, politically incorrect jokes. This show is not a total botch, but it sure ain't a triumph.

Bob and Show: ***

## *Chrysler Presents a Bob Hope Comedy Special*
Sept. 28, 1966, Wednesday 9-10 p.m.

Lucille Ball, Joan Caulfield, Joan Collins, Arlene Dahl, Phyllis Diller, Rhonda Fleming, Joan Fontaine, Signe Hasso, Hedy Lamarr, Dorothy Lamour, Marilyn Maxwell, Virginia Mayo, Dina Merrill, Vera Miles, Janis Paige, Jerry Colonna, Paul Lynde, Ken Murray. Featured: Peter Leeds, Mike Ross, Bob Jellison, Eddie Marr, Lilyan Chauvin, Phil Arnold, Ray Kellogg, Johnine Lee.

Noting he romances fifteen leading ladies from his movies, Bob quips, "The title of the show is 'Richard Burton, Eat Your Heart Out.'" His relatively short monologue includes new TV shows. "*Run Buddy Run* and the Fugitive had a head-on collision. And this season we have television in the round. Jackie Gleason is back." Then a network president (Ken Murray) tells Bob he needs a physical for insurance. A doctor (Paul Lynde) checks him out by hitting his own knee ("Mind your own business, I'm a masochist!"). Bob's obsession with his film costars leads to clips from his films and a depiction of his dream dancing with Marilyn Maxwell, Rhonda Fleming, and Arlene Dahl, who sing "I Believe in You" from *How to Succeed in Business Without Really Trying*. He runs into Virginia Mayo, who offers him a job, and Janis Paige and Joan Collins, who ignore his entreaties before doing "Big Spender." When word goes out that he plans to do a musical version of *Gone with the Wind*, the remaining women run to Bob's bedroom to make their pitches except for Lucille Ball, driven in on a bike by Jerry Colonna. She plays several moods to show Bob she should be his Scarlett O'Hara before all the ladies find out what each is doing. Bob ends up choosing Phyllis Diller, "Because if I picked a girl, they'd have killed me!" While Bob and Paul are great, the ladies' material is weak, though they each sing a line of a special version of "Thanks for the Memory" at the end.

Bob: **** Show: ***

***Chrysler Presents a Bob Hope Comedy Special*: "Murder at NBC"**
Oct. 19, 1966, Wednesday 9-10 p.m.

Don Adams, Milton Berle, Red Buttons, Johnny Carson, Jack Carter, Bill Cosby, Wally Cox, Bill Dana, Jimmy Durante, Don Rickles, Dan Rowan and Dick Martin, Soupy Sales, Dick Shawn, Jonathan Winters. Featured: Lee Giroux.

A mad scientist (Bob) kills an NBC reporter and plans to shrink everyone and … wait, let's mention the monologue first, which covers politics including President Lyndon B. Johnson and his daughters. "LBJ must be very happy. Luci's married, Linda's working. Now if he can only find something for [Vice President] Hubert [Humphrey] to do." After that, a brush salesman (Dick Shawn) and Charlie Chin (Jack Carter) discover what evil Bob is doing. Bob kills them, then his henchmen (Rowan and Martin) say that a special agent will be appearing on Johnny Carson's show tonight, along with a German professor (Jonathan Winters) whom Bob will replace to get on the program. The agent (Bill Cosby) finds out who Bob is, but Bob miniaturizes him and Johnny. Bob uses the shoe phone of secret agent Maxwell Smart (Don Adams), hijacks a plane with Don Rickles and Red Buttons as pilots, and goes to Tijuana. There, a waiter (Soupy Sales) contacts Mr. Big (Wally Cox), who passes the news to kill Bob. Bob confronts the bartender, Jose Jiminez (Bill Dana), for help on finding Mr. Big. Before Bob can kill Mr. Big, Rosita (Milton Berle) dances a number, and she attempts to kill him with a poisoned rose. She dies, as does the pianist (Jimmy Durante), but Wally Cox kills Bob in order to become host of *Bob Hope Presents The Chrysler Theatre*. Lots of dated stereotypes and few funny lines hurt this, but at least Bob does credibly appear insane and aggravated, for what that is worth.

Bob: *** Show: **

*Chrysler Presents a Bob Hope Special*
Nov. 16, 1966, Wednesday 9-10 p.m.

Bing Crosby, The New Faces of Hollywood (Donna Denton, Marilyn Devon, Marianne Gordon, Melodie Johnson, Chris Noel, Eileen O'Neill, Susan St. James, Benita Wolf), Miss Vietnam Bach Yen. Featured: Robert Foulk, Peter Leeds, Eleanor Audley, Sara Taft.

Bing is in most of this except for Bob's monologue, which has good jokes about Ronald Reagan's win as governor like "California's back to a two-party system—the Democrats and the Screen Actors Guild" and "You know, twenty governors got elected with no show business experience at all!" He also addresses shoppers complaining of air being injected into bread ("I believe it. This morning, my toast had a slow leak."). Bob promotes his new book, *Five Women I Love*, as "Based on a day in the life of Mickey Rooney." He introduces Bing straight but goes for a gag by looking at the singer and saying, "That Medicare really works!" Bing responds that their teaming always worked so well because Bob is everything Bing isn't. Their first skit, with Bing as a refined Englishman in a horse racing grandstand joined by a crude cowboy (Bob), is spotty. Better is "Journey through a Fantastic Stomach," a spoof of the movie *Fantastic Journey* where Bing and Bob are shrunk on a golf cart and injected into Jackie Gleason's gut. Broad asides in a wild set make this quite enjoyable. Bing nicely sings three Oscar-nominated songs he introduced before he escorts eight ingénues to talk with him and Bob. Bach Yen's bilingual song is anticlimactic, but Bing gets one final lick in by asking Bob for autographed copies of *Five Women I Love*. He deflates the comic by telling them they're all for his three children too young to read before Bob says good night.

Bob and Show: ***


*Chrysler Presents a Bob Hope Special*
Dec. 14, 1966, Wednesday 9-10 p.m.

Michael Caine, Cantinflas, Glenn Ford, Jayne Mansfield, Merle Oberon, Eva Renzi, Elke Sommer, Teddy Stauffer, Emily Kranz, Freddie Guzman, Ballet Folklorico de Acapulco.

There's no monologue at the start as Bob instead takes viewers on a tour of Acapulco with up-and-down entertainment offerings including obviously staged interviews with visiting American stars backed with canned laughter. All appear there apparently for a film festival, as is shown by footage of attendees John Gavin, Jeffrey Hunter, Louis Nizer, and Jack Valenti. The country seems filled with American influences, as Bob cracks that "I passed a shop that says, 'Spanish spoken here.'" He also notes its racy atmosphere: "Down here, *Playboy* is a comic book!" Mostly it's just people making promos, like Michael Caine for his movie *Alfie* and Elke Sommer to push her movie with Bob, *Boy, Have I Got a Wrong Number!* Weirdest of all, Bob does jokes for members of the Mexican Navy who don't understand him due to the language barrier, so he just interviews Emily Kranz, Eva Renzi, and Jayne Mansfield (in one of her last TV appearances) for similar lackluster results. Near the end, Bob observes, "You know, it's a rare privilege and real pleasure these days to visit a country and be greeted as a friend and feel that you are among friends." He says there are no demonstrations, embassies being stormed or "Yankee Go Home" signs. A promo for next week's presentation on *Bob Hope Presents The Chrysler Theatre* with George Maharis concludes this passable but unremarkable excursion, which at least has beautiful cinematography.

Bob and Show: ***

**Chrysler Presents the Bob Hope Christmas Special**
Jan. 18, 1967, Wednesday 9-10:30 p.m.

Vic Damone, Joey Heatherton, Anita Bryant, Miss World Reita Faria, The Korean Kittens, Diane Sheldon, Phyllis Diller. D: Mort Lachman. Choreography: Jack Baker, Bob Sidney (for Joey Heatherton only).

This inadvertently reflects America's growing weariness with the Vietnam War, mixing tired guests like Anita Bryant with obscurities like the Korean Kittens dancing female trio and fire baton twirler Diane Sheldon. Bob makes the best of it all with so-so results. Some top moments come from the soldiers, such as when a flying squadron plane greets Bob by loudspeaker. "Why don't you land and see the show, coward?" Bob quips back. Also enjoyable is Phyllis Diller. Bob describes her figure as "C rations" and compares her to the tour's other women: "Where they're curved, you're warped!" Phyllis gets off some good lines herself, like "I've been captured and released twice by both sides!" When Miss World Reita Faria of Bombay asks, "What do I do?" on stage, Bob scores with "You just stand here while the rest of us complete our world tour!" As always, Bob's monologues go well, like noting at an area affected by monsoons that "It really blows here!"

The rest of this feels like a retread, including crossing paths with Johnny Grant and Cardinal Spellman as in in earlier USO tours (the company also encounters Chris Noel, Diane McBain, Tippi Hedren, Chuck Yeager, and the Rev. Billy Graham). Bob ends by letting Marine Gen. Lew Walt explain that the war's goal is to make South Vietnam the cornerstone of freedom in southeast Asia. Then Bob notes a plane of dead soldiers followed the tour home. If he meant to reassure the American public about the war's progress and purpose, he miscalculates badly here.

Bob: ***** Show: ***

## *Chrysler Presents a Bob Hope Comedy Special*
Feb. 15, 1967, Wednesday 9-10 p.m.

Tony Bennett, Shirley Eaton, Jill St. John, Carol Lawrence. Featured: Peter Leeds. Choreographer: Tony Charmoli.

The music makes this show bearable. Bob promotes a little excessively here his book *Five Women I Love* plus his movie *Eight on the Lam* with Shirley Eaton and Jill St. John. Of the latter, he adds, "Wait until you see the love scenes with Phyllis Diller and Jonathan Winters … They make the orangutans [at the zoo] look like Liz and Richard." Shirley tells Bob, "I enjoy being here in the Colonies," before they contrast the ways British and America couples behave. Her jaunty delivery easily beats her flat dialogue. Carol Lawrence's lively "I'm a Brass Band" song and dance is a definite step up. Bob then enacts a supposed missing chapter from *Five Women I Love* where Bob learns his room in Vietnam is booby trapped. Jill St. John appears as the "chambermaid" who is a spy, and many other saboteurs hide in his room. He avoids her by planning to go to the PX where everything is half price, prompting all the spies to leave and check out the offering. This will be remade even more offensively on Bob's Nov. 7, 1971 special. Tony Bennett does two numbers superbly, then they talk about Bob having discovered Tony singing in Greenwich Village sixteen years earlier. Describing his success, Tony says, "People never get tired of hearing familiar things, things they've heard a thousand times. But I don't have to tell you that." He and Bob have an ease and natural humor that the skits needed more of here.

Bob and Show: ***

*Chrysler Presents the Bob Hope Show*: "Shades of Vaudeville"
Sept. 20, 1967, Wednesday 9-10 p.m.

Phyllis Diller, Dan Rowan and Dick Martin, Kaye Stevens, Jimmy Durante, Jack Jones, Rudy Vallee.

Bob's monologue is heavy mocking new TV series in this better-than-average outing. "*The Flying Nun* does impossible things including walking on water, and I hope DeGaulle doesn't sue. And there's a new show called *The Mothers-In-Law*. They needed something to replace *Combat*. And there's *He and She*, or as it's known in Greenwich Village, *The Odd Couple*." Of the finale of *The Fugitive*, Bob notes, "He was vindicated and canceled the same week. He was better off a murderer and working steady!" What follows is almost as good. Saying "I know something about vaudeville. I was one of its pallbearers," Bob reprises a routine he did on *The Ed Sullivan Show* in 1955. After Kaye Stevens sings "I Ain't Down Yet" from *The Unsinkable Molly Brown*, Bob conducts Rudy Vallee singing until Dan Rowan and Dick Martin heckle him from opera boxes. "I can't be listening to stuff like that," Bob tells them. "Why not? We've been listening to you!" Dan responds. Also nice is a comedy act with Bob and Kaye. "Are your intentions honorable or dishonorable?" she asks. "Do I have a choice?" he responds. Jimmy Durante doing "September Song," Phyllis Diller giving a monologue, and Jack Jones singing "The Days of Wine and Roses" are all swell. So is Dan Rowan playing charades with an overeager, dense Dick Martin and Jimmy, Jack and Bob singing together. Even Rock Hudson's promotion of his show next week on Hollywood musicals at the end is fun. As Rock leaves, Bob jests, "Poor kid. You know, without makeup, he looks just like Don Knotts!"

Bob: *** Show: ****


*Chrysler Presents the Bob Hope Show*: "Love In"
Oct. 16, 1967, Monday 9-10 p.m.

Steve Lawrence, Eydie Gorme, Debbie Reynolds. Featured: Milton Frome, Mike Ross, Eddie Marr, Lee Giroux, Harve Evans, Roy Fitzell. Debbie Reynolds' Choreographer: Bob Sidney.

After Bob jokes about NASA cutbacks ("The astronauts are really worried. Up until now, those space flights have been round trip."), the question of whether actors should be in politics ("They figure I can give an impartial answer, not being in either racket.") and the economy ("I think Charlton Heston could balance the budget. God knows it could take a miracle."), this show tanks. Eydie singing "When the World Was Young" is not a rousing start. Then a party boss (Bob) is upset that his competition, child actress Debbie Dimples (the first of several characters played by Debbie Reynolds), will be California's next congresswoman. He goes to recruit Debbie Gabor. "Were you ever married to me?" she asks Bob. No, he says, as he still has his house and bank account. He then tries Baby Doll Debbie, lying in bed with a Southern accent, and Debbie Diller, wearing a fright wig, before settling on the Flying Nun. Apart from Debbie's impersonations, this is long and choppy. Steve singing "I've Gotta Be Me" from his Broadway show *Golden Rainbow* gives one hope, but Bob and Eydie as an angry Hollywood couple who reconcile and find that her fiancé (Steve) is actually their child is a sputtering mess. After Debbie does a medley with two singer-dancers, Bob plays a hippie who gets a parking ticket for sleeping and plans to smoke a long banana. Steve and Eydie are high too, and they all have messy wigs and talk slow before singing "If They Could See Me Now." It is as bad as it sounds, but Bob will do worse in later specials.

Bob and Show: \*\*\*

***Chrysler Presents the Bob Hope Show*: "Shoot-In at NBC"**
Nov. 8, 1967, Wednesday 9-10 p.m.

Don Adams, Steve Allen, Raymond Burr, Rod Cameron, Philip Carey, Jack Carter, Perry Como, Wally Cox, Bill Dana, Richard Deacon, James Drury, Buddy Hackett, Jack Kelly, Paul Lynde, Doug McClure, Cameron Mitchell, Ken Murray, Jack Palance, Don Rickles, Dale Robertson, Dan Rowan and Dick Martin, Larry Storch, Danny Thomas, Forrest Tucker, Bobbie Gentry.

A meandering plot of westerns versus comedians and bad jokes sabotage this effort. The sufficient monologue scores best with one subject. "Hey, I have an announcement: The Zsa Zsa husband alumni association (laughter) will have their annual meeting and homecoming tomorrow at the coliseum," Bob says. "I see where Zsa Zsa is free again. I mean divorced. She's never been free. (applause) I just want one meaning to that joke!" Bob next consoles Steve Allen at a bar with Don Adams tended by Bill Dana (using his Jose Jiminez voice). Steve is down because a western pushed out his new show. Jack Kelly and Philip Carey arrive, brag about their show's success, and ask Bob, "Pardon me, ma'am, is this your purse?" They turn on the TV to see Bob Hope's show and Philip shoots the set. To summarize concisely and coherently the twists and turns afterward is tough. Don Rickles makes Bob disguise himself as a cowboy, attend a big western spectacular being filmed and find out their plans. Bob leads an attack of funny men against cowboys ("I'll schpritz those brutes to death!" Paul Lynde says, wielding a seltzer bottle in a rare truly funny moment here). Raymond Burr (as Ironside) shoots them all to get his own show. Amid in the inanity and insanity is a cutaway to Perry Como sleeping with a horse, Bobbie Gentry singing a special version of "Do Not Forsake Me" as a musical break from the standoff, and much more. What were the writers smoking when they came up with this?

Bob: *** Show: **


*Chrysler Presents the Bob Hope Show*
Nov. 29, 1967, Wednesday 9-10 p.m.

Jack Jones, David Janssen, Elke Sommer, The Kids Next Door, The Look All-American Football Team. Featured: Florence Lake. Choreography: Miriam Nelson.

Boring musical numbers combined with a sketch done previously on Nov. 17, 1953, and Nov. 16, 1960, make this a miss despite a good monologue and a pleasant change of venue in doing the show at UCLA. Introduced by the university's cheerleaders, Bob pithily assesses the current mood: "I think it's a wonderful world. It may destroy itself, but we'll be able to watch it on TV!" He calls Twiggy "the world's most successful X-ray" and notes racist Alabama Gov. George Wallace "made a tour around Watts—very around it." He gets away with saying "My great-grandfather was a lookout for Lady Chatterley" too. It goes downhill after that, with Jack Jones' decent set including his hit "The Impossible Dream" overshadowed by seven long minutes of Elke Sommer doing tunes from *Cabaret* with eight male dancers and Bob for the third time playing an unassuming quarterback being manipulated by his fellow athlete and roommate (David Janssen, who at least has fun pretending to play the ukulele and "sing" to Bob and Elke). The Kids Next Door (think Up with People) do a corny version of "Mame" in straw hats, and Bob's announcement of the top college football players (including O.J. Simpson) in a bit taped in New York City is tired too. Bob Thomas, chairman of the UCLA Alumni Association Committee, introduces Jill St. John to tell Bob he's become an honorary alumnus before everyone sings funny lyrics to "Thanks for the Memory," but it's too little too late.

Bob: *** Show: **


*Chrysler Presents the Bob Hope Show*
Dec. 14, 1967, Thursday 8:30-9:30 p.m.

Phil Silvers, Paul Lynde, Wally Cox, Jerry Colonna, The International Children's Choir, Ernest Borgnine, Don Adams. Featured: Phil Arnold, Joyce Jamison, Bob Jellison, Ray Kellogg, Florence Lake, Eddie Marr, Jack Pepper, Mike Ross, Billy Sands. D: Stan Harris.

One of Bob's best monologues ever on TV unfortunately is on a Christmas show that's more ho hum than ho ho ho. Discussing a family wedding, he quips, "My son Tony married a lovely girl he met at law school. And she's a lawyer too, so I'm not losing a son, I'm gaining another opinion." He also gets in good jabs about Lynda Bird Johnson's nuptials, General De Gaulle's inflated ego, Eugene McCarthy's presidential campaign, and even Martha Raye's tour of Vietnam. Then comes the slogging storyline with Santa Claus (Bob) causing a freeway traffic jam investigated by an irate patrolman (Phil Silvers). Everyone including others stuck in the mess sing "Silver Bells" before Santa is arrested for causing a public nuisance and goes to jail. There, two convicts (Ernest Borgnine and Wally Cox) plan to escape their cell along with their new inmate, but Santa gets stuck during the breakout. He visits the prison psychiatrist (Paul Lynde, who is especially prissy) and inspires the doctor to have more confidence via a duet. Santa then goes on trial in a court presided over by a crazy judge (Jerry Colonna) and a prosecuting attorney (Don Adams) who brings out a woman claiming to be Santa's wife. After Santa pleads with the court that someone must believe, out runs members of the International Children's Choir to sing "Santa Claus is Coming to Town," and he is freed. Despite a talented comic cast's best efforts, this drags, and Bob dressed as Santa throughout inhibits his comic delivery. Better luck next year.

Bob: *** Show: **

***Chrysler Presents the Bob Hope Christmas Special***
Jan. 18, 1968, Thursday 8:30-10 p.m.

Raquel Welch, Barbara McNair, Elaine Dunn, Miss World Madeline Hartog-Bel, Phil Crosby, Earl Wilson. D: Mort Lachman.

Raquel Welch's dynamic presence enlivens highlights of visits to twenty-two overseas bases. She dances with soldiers, gyrates and sings "You Make Me Feel So Young" with Bob (who takes comic offense when her rewritten lyrics mention Medicare), and plays Bob's straight woman. Reviewing her new movie role, Bob asks, "You're kidnapped by outlaws?! Who's the dum dum that says crime doesn't pay?!" He does well with Miss World too, responding when she gives her weight in stones that "What a wonderful way to get stoned!" However, Bob by himself really stands out. "I bring you great news from the land of liberty: it's still there," he says. "You may have to cross a picket line to see it, but it's there. But don't worry about those riots you hear about in the States. You'll be sent to survival school before they send you back there!" Many of his punch lines grimly wink at the war's reality. "Miniskirts are bigger than ever. Even some of the fellows are wearing them. Don't laugh. If you'd have thought of it, you wouldn't be here!" Regarding international relations, Bob noted, "Thailand is our strongest ally in Southeast Asia. It must be—our embassy here still has windows." He also shines with Bing's son Phil. "Dad's teaching you to act?" Bob asked. "That's like Twiggy coaching the Green Bay Packers!" When Phil notes his father has won an Oscar, Bob retorts, "He deserved it. *Birth of a Nation* was quite a movie," citing the 1915 silent film. Even so, author Erik Barnouw mocked Hope's gags such as "I hope your grandfather heard me at Appomattox. I was great," as examples of how out of touch the comedian had become to the younger generation in his 1970 book *The Image Empire*.

Bob: ***** Show: ****


***Chrysler Presents the Bob Hope Show***
Feb. 12, 1968, Monday 9-10 p.m.

Bing Crosby, Pearl Bailey, Barbara Eden, The West Point Glee Club, New York City Mayor John V. Lindsay, Rocky Marciano, Gene Tunney, Ed Sullivan, Jack Dempsey. Choreography: Miriam Nelson.

In a special taped at a newly refurbished Madison Square Garden, New York City Mayor John V. Lindsay provides the opening address.

"He's not only pretty, he's funny too!" quips Bob afterward, adding, "It's so refreshing to meet a Republican who's not running for president." He also needles the host city ("Never drive down Broadway in an open car during a garage strike."). The rest is solid if a little square musically—the West Point Glee Club singing "America the Beautiful" and "Anchors Aweigh," Pearl Bailey presenting "That's Life" along with comic patter, Barbara Eden doing a big production number. The superb comedy has Bing joining Bob in their first joint appearance in Manhattan since 1932 and handling their routines nimbly, like Bing telling Bob he should've stayed with singing and would've got more laughs that way. They are great singing "The Road to Morocco" and "Put It There," and Bob even offers his version of "White Christmas." Best of all, Bob is "Packy East" in oversized trunks opposite Rocky Marciano in a boxing match with Barbara ringside as Bob's nurse. The referee (Bing) assesses Bob before the fight and already calls Rocky the winner. It ends raucously with the men dancing joined by Ed Sullivan and other veteran fighters. Concluding the show, Gen. Emmett "Rosie" O'Donnell salutes Gen. Omar Bradley with a medal from the USO and says, "In these days of riots and marches and demonstrations, you can't do enough to encourage his kind of Americanism." Comedy plus patriotism remains Bob's strong suit.

Bob and Show: ****


**Chrysler Presents the Bob Hope Special**
March 20, 1968, Wednesday 9-10 p.m.

Anne Bancroft, Arnold Palmer, Lou Rawls, Paul Lynde, Jill St. John, [Dan] Rowan and [Dick] Martin, Jack Benny. Featured: Phil Arnold, Ray Kellogg, Johnine Lee, Eddie Marr. D: Stan Harris.

"I hear LBJ's trying to get rid of 150 pounds—Bobby Kennedy," cracks Hope at the top, starting off a barrage of jokes about the New Hampshire presidential primary results for a good monologue leading into another variable outing. He has a good new joke about the upcoming Oscars—"As it's known in our house, *Mission: Impossible*"—and mulls over some of the nominees before parodying one of them. "Bonnie and Clod" with Jill as Bonnie and Bob as Clod is a pretty good skit that has the *Laugh-In* pacing of cuts between bits and even a cameo by its stars when Bob cracks open a safe and gets Dick Martin telling Dan Rowan, "I told you he's been stealing for years!" Still, at twelve minutes, it should've been shortened. The same applies to the contrived banter Bob does separately with Arnold Palmer and Lou Rawls before it brightens at the end with a clever original skit. Paul Lynde is hysterical as Bob's doctor, notifying the latter that he is near death ("It's kaputzville, baby! Turn up your toes time!"). He suggests that Bob donate his heart to socialite Anne Bancroft and tells her, "I've found a ticky-boo for you!" Complications arise when Bob and Anne's respective dates (Jill and Jack Benny) see what's going on and plan to maximize the situation to their individual needs. It's funny enough to make this passable albeit unexceptional.

Bob and Show: ***


*Chrysler Presents a Bob Hope Special*: **"For Love or Money"**
April 11, 1968, Thursday 8:30-9:30 p.m.

Janet Leigh, Fernando Lamas, Eddie Mayehoff, Pat Harrington Jr., J. Carrol Naish. P/D: Jess Oppenheimer. W: Dean Hargrove.

In an hour-long book comedy from an outside writer, Bob plays an American caught up in a revolution in an unspecified foreign country. Since this was not viewed, there is no rating for it.


*Chrysler Presents the Bob Hope Special*
Sept. 25, 1968, Wednesday 9-10 p.m.

Carroll Baker, Vikki Carr, Cyd Charisse, Angie Dickinson, Jill St. John, Zsa Zsa Gabor. Cameos: Carol Burnett, Dean Martin. Featured: Jesse White, J. Edward McKinley, Edward Marr, Henry Corden, Ken Niles, Bob Jellison, Lee Giroux, Johnny Grant.

What appears to be a misfire barely becomes a winner in this outing with an extended storyline. First up is Bob's fine monologue on TV shows new ("*The Beautiful Phyllis Diller Show*, first known as *Mission: Impossible*" and "Doris Day is coming on to balance *Peyton Place*") and old ("*The Flying Nun* is back, although she had a very rough summer. Three times they tried to hijack her to Cuba."). As for politics, "I've been very busy this past month entertaining the troops at the Democratic convention." The campaign sets the scene as eligible bachelor presidential candidate Gaylord Goodfellow (Bob) becomes a ukulele-playing Tiny Tim wannabe, forcing his handlers to draft a lookalike cab driver in his place. The stand-in has women throwing themselves at him, including Vikki Carr, who sings her hit "It Must Be Him" to show her obsession. It's borderline boring until Angie Dickinson interviews Bob and tussles with a sharp-tongued Zsa Zsa Gabor. Bob tries to defuse the tension by telling Zsa Zsa, "Put the trash out," and she snaps back at Angie, "My dah-link, I'd love to, but she's your friend!" Bob tries to throw the election but gets the presidency and faces six potential brides clad in white as he takes the oath. Then Carol Burnett shows up as the cab driver's homely wife to remind him they're still married and have a baby, with a close-up of Dean Martin sucking a pacifier. It's a wild finish to a sometimes strained and flat show.

Bob and Show: ***

## *Chrysler Presents the Bob Hope Special*
Oct. 14, 1968, Monday 9-10 p.m.

Gwen Verdon, John Davidson, Jeannie C. Riley, Bob Fosse, World Series' pitchers Bob Gibson and Denny McLain. Cameo: Mitzi Gaynor. Featured: Lee Giroux, Bob Jellison, Mike Ross. Gwen Verdon's Choreography: Bob Fosse.

The guests are swell but the skits stink here. A generally good monologue covers the presidential election a lot. Speculating why Richard Nixon refuses to debate Hubert Humphrey, Bob says, "That's like asking why Rosemary won't have another baby." Some gags are dubious, like Bob saying of the Kenyan runners in the Olympics that "Their coach is a leopard." John Davidson is boring doing "Hey Jude," but Jeannie C. Riley is natural and funny talking about her sudden stardom with Bob. Noting her recent performance with Bing Crosby on *The Hollywood Palace*, Bob cracks, "The only original equipment he has left is his ears!" She lip syncs "Harper Valley P.T.A." later on the show. The show slumps again with a partial remake of Bob's June 1, 1954 spoof of *Queen for a Day*, this time mocking *The Dating Game* as dowdy Gwen wins a date with superstar Bob, who wants to avoid her. It's long and lumpy. Gwen redeems herself as she elegantly dances the flamenco to "Mexican Shuffle" with two men in sombreros under Bob Fosse's lead. The show hits rock bottom when a paid heckler (Bob) tries to convince a war protester in jail (John) to falsely claim cops beat him. More on this heinous bit can be found in this chapter's introduction. Better is Bob's banter with Bob Gibson and Denny McLain, followed by Mitzi Gaynor as a hick tourist on the NBC studio tour who thinks Bob is Dean Martin. Her special follows this, and it probably is an improvement too.

Bob and Show: ***

## *Chrysler Presents the Bob Hope Special*
Nov. 6, 1968, Wednesday 9-10 p.m.

Apollo Seven Astronauts Walt Cunningham, Donn F. Eisele and Walter Schirra, Barbara Eden, David Janssen.

From the NASA administrative headquarters in Houston, Texas, Bob's guests including the astronauts who orbited the Earth 163 times over eleven days. Besides the gags about them, Bob also touches on the marriage of Aristotle Onassis to Jacqueline Kennedy ("Whoever would think the Kennedys would be poor relations?"), and more. It includes an impressive live cut-in to Burbank so that Bob could quip on the close president election results the previous day where Richard Nixon won ("This may get him another guest shot on *Laugh-In*"). The first skit has the astronauts at the school for television, where they do nose jokes as Bob plays himself criticizing their TV appearance in space. "How do you think I've been a star for twenty-five years?" he tells them to emphasize his expertise. "Luck?" responds Walter Schirra. "Watch it, nobody likes a smart astronaut!" Bob responds, getting applause for playing off the "smart ass" pun. He laughs as Walt Cunningham awkwardly presents a comedy routine before the men put him in a spacesuit to fly on Apollo Eight. It is all fun and frisky. Barbara Eden performs "Don't Tell Mama" from *Cabaret*, then Bob introduces her to the astronauts in good, suggestive repartee ("I tell you, it was a thrill watching you up there," she tells Walter. "Thank you. It's not bad watching you down here!" he responds). Unfortunately, David Janssen and Bob as two astronauts suffering on an extended trip is long and spotty, rendering this mission as only a semi-success.

Bob: ***** Show: ***

## *Chrysler Presents the Bob Hope Special*
Nov. 27, 1968, Wednesday 9-10 p.m.

John Wayne, Eddie Fisher, Coach John McKay, James Garner, Juliet Prowse, Barbara McNair. Choreography: Larry Maldonado.

Amid shaky camerawork, University of Southern California cheerleaders escort Bob into the Los Angeles Sports Arena. "It's a pleasure to be here at OJU," he jokes regarding USC football star O.J. Simpson. Bob's monologue also praises USC for avoiding sit-ins and riots ("The parking is too rough for the outside agitators," he concludes), the recent election and Jacqueline Kennedy marrying Aristotle Onassis ("It's amazing what lengths a woman will go to get a boat for her son"). He notes Barbara McNair is a graduate of crosstown rival UCLA and a recent *Playboy* model before she sings. Bob then banters with USC Coach McKay and O.J., who is a little flat but gets laughs for saying that regarding his NFL prospects, "The money is unimportant." Momentum flags when Eddie Fisher sings "Rock-a-Bye Your Baby with a Dixie Melody" and Juliet dances but returns when James Garner plays coach of a dumb football team. His good delivery cracks up O.J. in the skit. The dean (a surprise cameo by Robert Stack) brings in new player P.J. Hope (Bob) from UCLA, and O.J. mocks Bob's age. Barbara and Juliet appear as cheerleaders, and another surprise cameo wraps up this raucous bit when USC alum Fess Parker hijacks Bob to Cuba. The fun dissipates when another USC alum, John Wayne, lectures students not to protest against the university ("This college is owned by the state of California!") and rails against affirmative action. It is a sour, preachy ending for an otherwise relatively enjoyable show.

Bob: **** Show: ***


*Chrysler Presents the Bob Hope Show*: "Mission: Ridiculous"
Dec. 19, 1968, Thursday 8:30-10 p.m.

Glen Campbell, Carol Lawrence, Nancy Ames, Wally Cox, Jerry Colonna, Janet Leigh, Robert Goulet (cameo). Featured: Henry Corden, Kathleen Freeman, Sid Haig, Luis Peralta, Jerry Maren, Billy Barty. Choreography: Kevin Carlisle.

Replete with ridiculous plotting and sexism, this does have a meaty monologue mainly on the new president. "You realize Dick Nixon once ran for governor here. Who realized the consolation prize would be the White House?" Then the stupidity begins as Bob learns that Santa Claus has been kidnapped by an organization called BROADS whose members include Janet Leigh and Carol Lawrence. At the North Pole, Mrs. Claus (Kathleen Freeman) reads to the elves (Jerry Maren, Billy Barty) when Janet holds them up at gunpoint. She impersonates Mrs. Claus to fool Bob before she gets away to Cuba. Bob hijacks his plane as a co-pilot (Robert Goulet) asks, "Coffee, tea or tequila?" In Havana, a judge (Jerry Colonna) throws Bob in jail with Glen Campbell, who says, "It's not the first time they've found Campbell in the can." ("Let's not get hostile out there, remember he's only a singer!" Bob tells the camera.) Glen sings before a blonde frees them. He says he will do *The Hollywood Palace* with Bing Crosby, and Bob responds, "Boy, what a horrible way to go!" In Hong Kong, Carol does a mod routine with dancers, and Bob disguises himself as a stereotyped Asian. He survives Carol's efforts to kill him but get shipped to BROADS headquarters. Janet tells him that "BROADS is a nonprofit organization whose sole purpose is to provide equal opportunity to women ... Why shouldn't Santa Claus be a woman?" Bob helps Santa (Wally Cox) escape to deliver presents, then stuffs all the BROADS into a trunk and locks himself up inside with them. Merry Christmas? Despite a stupid plot, this got a big 35.5 rating.

Bob: *** Show: **


*Chrysler Presents the Bob Hope Christmas Special*
Jan. 16, 1969, Thursday 8:30-10 p.m.

Ann-Margret, Rosey Grier, Linda Bennett, Miss World Penny Plummer, Dick Albers (a comic trampoline artist), The Golddiggers. D: Mort Lachman. W: Lee Hale, Trustin Howard, Ed Scharlach. Special Material: Jay Livingston, Ray Evans. Choreography: Jack Baker, Walter Painter (Ann-Margret only).

Strong jokes, enthusiastic performers and lively audiences make this the quintessential Bob Hope Christmas show. Bob cracks lively in Korea ("I don't know how close we are to Russia, but one of the medics is named Zhivago"), Vietnam ("I planned to spend Christmas in the States, but I can't stand violence"), and even a supply depot, where he lets loose with "They have more spare parts than [Bing] Crosby's doctor." His interplay with everyone is tops too. He enjoys bringing soldiers on stage to read letters from home as much as telling Miss World Penny Plummer that as a librarian, she's stacked in all the right places. For Ann-Margret, who whips one audience member in a frenzy with her frenetic version of "Dancing in the Streets," he recounts her similarly steamy number on the 1961 Oscars show. "It was the first time my cummerbund was welded to my navel!" For jokes at Bob's own expense, the best comes from football player Rosey Grier about the host's face: "You mean, those are Mother Nature's own cleat marks?" Other highlights include an impressive rendition of "Jingle Bells" in English done a capella by a Korean orphanage and Bob giving out the names of all the Golddiggers female dancers at the end in thanking in them for appearing. Thankfully, gags about the anti-war protesters are few and pretty tame (e.g., for students demanding to run college, Bob said, "That's like Gomer Pyle running the Pentagon."). All told, this is a triumph for all involved.

Bob and Show: *****

*Chrysler Presents the Bob Hope Special:* "Antics of 1931"
Feb. 17, 1969, Monday 9-10 p.m.

Bing Crosby, Martha Raye, George Burns, Diana Ross and the Supremes. Cameos: Dick Martin, Dan Rowan, Jo Anne Worley, Henry Gibson. Featured: Lisa Miller, Billy Curtis. Special Musical Material: Lee Hale.

The guest stars give it their all, while Bob is on only about a third of the show and suffers a little in comparison. His rather poor monologue covers everything from President Richard Nixon to heavy rains in Los Angeles ("Lawrence Welk was bubbling whether he wanted to or not."). To start the vaudeville revue, Dick Martin interrupts Bob selling food. When Bob learns Dick makes $200 a week, he switches places with him. The Supremes sing before Bob plays a magician with an assistant (Martha Raye) who unintentionally spoils his tricks. There are some stereotyped gags of them being Asian, but it is still pretty good if silly. After Bing Crosby croons "When the Red, Red Robin (Comes Bob, Bob, Bobbin' Along)," Martha complains to a theater manager (Dan Rowan) that the man next to her is fooling with her knee. "I'm the manager, and I'm not fooling!" he responds lecherously. Lisa Miller joins George Burns to fill in for his late wife and comic partner Gracie Allen. She is fine but is no Gracie. Martha sings "Mr. Paganini" comically, then a woman removes her hat and her wig along with it to show she is bald. Bing and Bob do gags about being old, corny puns, and a routine of different types of people meeting, plus a soft-shoe number. Diana sings solo along with Bob before Jo Anne Worley appears in the audience yelling for her baby. Henry Gibson throws one to her, but it's the wrong infant. It is a funny end to an enjoyable program—even when Bob shows up.

Bob: *** Show: ****

***Chrysler Presents The Bob Hope Show***
March 19, 1969, Wednesday 9-10 p.m.

Cyd Charisse, Ray Charles, Jimmy Durante, Nancy Sinatra. Featured: Milton Frome, Bob Jellison, Eddie Marr, Lee Giroux, Mike Ross, Louise Lawson, Damian London, Don Crichton (uncredited). Cyd Charisse's Choreography: Eugene Loring.

Great music and so-so comedy make up this outing. Bob's better lines in his monologues involve Jeanne Dixon predicting California will fall into the ocean ("Now we know what Howard Hughes is doing. He wants a seaport."), President Richard Nixon visiting France's leader ("DeGaulle told Nixon what a great man DeGaulle was."), and Vice President Spiro Agnew being hurt because "He slipped at the airport on some ice the Democrats left behind." After Nancy Sinatra sings, Bob and Jimmy Durante do a horrible sendup on campus unrest. At least both men seem to like the nose jokes they make about each other. Cyd Charisse has a nice dance number with Don Crichton, then Bob plays a cowboy who sees a frontier psychiatrist (Nancy) pulling her own couch. They duet on "Headshrinker," a decent comical country-pop music number. Saying one of his favorite albums is *The Genius of Ray Charles*, Bob adds, "Ray Charles is just that. He writes, he arranges, he plays and he sings, and he does them all superbly." Ray also jokes well with Bob while showing he clearly merits all the praise with a rollicking, swinging version of "Bright Lights and You Girl." It ends with a clunker as Bob and Cyd are members of Waist Watchers who find romance in their group but are both too stout to kiss each other. On their honeymoon, Bob is so hungry trying to lose weight that he steals a turkey, only to see the Flying Nun hijack it. That summary shows just how comedy deprived this program is.

Bob and Show: ***

***Chrysler Presents the Bob Hope Special***
April 17, 1969, Thursday 8:30-9:30 p.m.

Patti Page, Jack Nicklaus, Louis Nye, Tina Louise, Maureen Arthur, Jane Wyman, Sergio Mendes and Brasil 66. Featured: Reta Shaw, Henry Corden, Victoria Carroll, Ray Kellogg, Eddie Marr, Roy Mitchell, Jack Pepper, Mike Wagner.

Specials – 1960s • 139

This is a really up-and-down special, uneven throughout including Bob's monologue. He jokes variably about the weather, summer vacation and hippies. Describing paying taxes, he claims, "I felt like I visited the blood bank and forgot to say when." He gets applause by saying of the surprise cancellation of *The Smothers Brothers Comedy Hour* that "This is the biggest TV scandal since they discovered Ed Sullivan's knuckles were cracking dirty jokes in Morse code." Next, he and Patti Page are a Southern California suburban couple preparing to survive natural disasters. Many board their manmade raft, including a blonde who Bob insists on keeping. Making this somewhat tolerable is veteran character actress Reta Shaw providing strong delivery for her weak jokes. After Bob and Sergio Mendes perform "Pretty World," a lame bit follows where Jack Nicklaus meets Bob on a golf course and they compare honors. When Bob tries to teach a redhead how to golf instead of Jack, Jack challenges Bob on his abilities, and Bob slices one to the highway and causes a crash. Then, an extended promo for Bob's new movie has a film editor (Louis Nye) showing clips of *How to Commit Marriage* while telling Bob the film is two minutes overlong. Bob says in turn take out his costars Jane Wyman, Maureen Arthur, and Tina Louise, each of whom objects, as does a chimp in the picture at the end. Patti sings and Bob pays tribute to Dwight Eisenhower, who died on March 28, before this erratic show ends.
Bob and Show: \*\*\*


*Chrysler Presents The Bob Hope Special*
Sept. 22, 1969, Monday 9-10 p.m.

Marty Allen, Steve Allen, Shelley Berman, Red Buttons, Sid Caesar, Johnny Carson, Jack Carter, Jerry Colonna, Wally Cox, Bill Dana, Richard Deacon, George Gobel, Shecky Greene, Buddy Hackett, Jack E. Leonard, Pat Paulsen, Nipsey Russell, Soupy Sales, Phil Silvers, Danny Thomas, Flip Wilson. Unbilled Cameos: David Brinkley, Chet Huntley, Tom and Dick Smothers, Dan Rowan and Dick Martin. Featured: Julie Bennett, Henry Corden, Billy Curtis, Bob Jellison, Ray Kellogg, Jack Pepper, Billy Sands.

The fast pacing of *Rowan and Martin's Laugh-In*, which this follows, occurs here after Bob's ten-minute monologue. He discusses the new TV series ("There's *The Jim Nabors Hour*, or Gomer makes a pile… *Love American Style*, about a man and his car… *The Survivors*, about two guys who try to take a pizza away from Jackie Gleason."), the cost and results of astronauts landing on the moon ("Twenty-four billion, and we got back eight pounds of rocks."), and more. As Chet Huntley and David Brinkley report about free speech on TV, an NBC executive (Richard Deacon) cuts Bob's script. Bob plans to say "Bottoms up," but Richard interjects, "No more bottoms!" Then come a series of blackouts depicting other censorship, including Jack E. Leonard appearing in drag opposite Sid Caesar in a *Peyton Place* spoof; Tarzan (Wally Cox) rescuing Steve Allen and Nipsey Russell tied together on a stake above a flaming pit (Steve tells Wally, "You look more like Jane."); Red Buttons accused of sucking jam out of donuts in a nonviolent western with Shelley Berman; and Phil Silvers pleading for Flip Wilson to stop running with a football. Disgusted, Bob leaves NBC, and Johnny Carson must book has-been guests on *The Tonight Show*. More blackouts occur, culminating with Bob, Jack Carter, Shecky Greene, Marty Allen, and Jimmy Durante forcing Richard to rehire them at NBC. Dan Rowan and Dick Martin then appear as janitors because as, Dick says of NBC, "They finally found out what a bippy meant!" and punished them. As the description implies, this is all spottily enjoyable.

Bob and Show: ***


**Chrysler Presents the Bob Hope Special**
Oct. 13, 1969, Monday 9-10 p.m.

Jimmy Durante, Barbara McNair, Donald O'Connor, Tom Jones, Mitzi Gaynor. Featured: Louise Lawson. Choreography: Louis DaPron.

Bob talks about appearing in Texas, seeing the "miracle Mets" winning the World Series and playing golf with Vice President Spiro Agnew. He has a good line about Jacqueline Onassis giving a judo chop to a member of the paparazzi: "He was lucky. She could've hit him with one of her rings." He concludes his set with riffs about Jackie Gleason losing sixty pounds ("CBS insisted he do something. He was being seen on all three networks.") and that if Don Knotts did the same, he'd need to gain five back to stay alive. Following this promising start comes two tired remakes—Jimmy Durante trying to hide a seal from the *I Love Lucy* spoof from Oct. 21, 1956, and Donald O'Connor reprising his comic magic act he did with Bob originally on the Nov. 20, 1964 special. O'Connor does better when he dances with his uncooperative shadow.

The only highlight is Bob and Tom Jones as a vaudeville song-and-dance duo. They sing, alternate in doing punchlines, trade suggestive lines with two ladies and have a dance-off. It's pretty enjoyable, as is Tom singing "Fly Me to the Moon" in his own hip style. Barbara McNair sings too, but it's unmemorable. Mitzi Gaynor appears at the end to promote her *Mitzi's 2nd Special* following this show, and Bob makes a pitch to support the American Cancer Fund before signing off.

Bob and Show: ***

*Chrysler Presents the Bob Hope Special*: "Roberta"
Nov. 6, 1969, Thursday 8:30-10 p.m.

Janis Paige, John Davidson, Michele Lee. Featured: Laura Miller, Irene Hervey, Eve McVeagh, Ann Shoemaker, Chris Carter, Hugh Dempster, Wayne Dugger, John McLaren, Jack Pepper, Bob Street, Clifford David. Music: Jerome Kern. Book and Lyrics: Otto Harbach, Dorothy Fields ("Lovely to Look At"). Adaptation: Bob's writers plus Gene Moss and James Thurman. Choreography: Bob Sidney.

Taped before a live audience at Southern Methodist University's Bob Hope Theatre, this odd juxtaposition of material from the Broadway musical that starred Bob in 1933 combined with topical gags is unsatisfying and not helped by muddy audio, static staging, and awkward lighting. Bob is too old to be playing John Davidson's college pal, though he's energetic as ever, and his incongruous contemporary quips amid the old fashioned setting are forced. For example, after John has an argument with his girlfriend, Bob chimes in, "Welcome to the Paris peace talks." To supplement the musical, John sings "Lovely to Look at," a Best Song Oscar nominee from the 1935 movie version of *Roberta*, and Janis Paige performs "I Won't Dance," also taken from the film. Michele Lee, who pines for John, gets to do the show's hit, "Smoke Gets in Your Eyes." Bob does shine some in doing a monologue as host of a fashion show, and he clearly appears to be happy doing this. However, the musical's book really creaks with tedious exposition and dialogue, and the show sags whenever Bob isn't on stage. At the curtain call, Bob thanks the university and its drama program for their support in making this production a reality.

Bob: *** Show: **

***Chrysler Presents the Bob Hope Special***
Nov. 24, 1969, Sunday 9-10 p.m.

Danny Thomas, Steve Lawrence, Eydie Gorme, Virna Lisi. Featured: The Clingers, Henry Corden, Chanin Hale, Bob Jellison, Eddie Marr, John McLaren.

With a huge 32.0 rating, one wonders how many viewers wound up disappointed by the limp sketches and music offered here. The monologue is fine, as Bob jabs the vice president's fight against the news media ("Did you hear [Spiro] Agnew's going to have a new show, 'Beat the Press?'") to a *Time* magazine story on California's sex scene ("My neighborhood is so dull, my Avon lady is a man."). "And California's running out of everything too," he adds. "It's getting to be you have to go to Phoenix to breathe, Tahoe if you want a drink, and Tijuana if you have nothing else in mind." Also amusing is Virna Lisi talking to Bob about American men. "They are wonderful. Big, strong, and good looking too. And very intelligent." "True, true," says Bob. "What country are you from?" responds Virna. Things sag with "The Secret of Santa Pasta," a so-so spoof of Virna's current film *The Secret of Santa Vittoria* with an Italian village hiding its pizza from a Nazi colonel (Bob). Eydie and Steve's solo numbers are unmemorable, as are skits following them. Danny Thomas as an Alaskan native is slow to endure until Bob shows up as his freewheeling son leading four girls in a rock group, which results in them singing corny songs. Arguably worse is the closer with a bartender at last call (Bob) dealing with an arguing couple (Steve and Eydie), an attempted robbery, and inept firefighters. This sputters along, as does the show in general.

Bob: *** Show: **


***Chrysler Presents the Bob Hope Special***
Dec. 18, 1969, Thursday 8:30-9:30 p.m.

Andy Williams, Elke Sommer, Anthony Newley. Cameos: Bing Crosby, Dean Martin.

Saying there are nineteen series booking some 6,000 guests a year, Bob introduces a skit saying everyone is trying to get Elke to do their shows. Andy Williams presents flowers to her, but she first thinks he's Tiny Tim. She tells him she's already agreed to do Bob's show and he tells her to beware. He sees it's a bad check and promises to help her get out of the spot. He disguises himself as Dr. Sigmund Fruit and lets Bob in. Andy tells Bob Elke has gone crazy, and she pretends Bob is part of her family. She talks into a statue like it's a phone and talks to an imaginary person who she pretends to kill. Elke then talks to Bob about her elaborate plans which scare Bob off. Andy runs away too when she learns Elke claims to really want do those things. She then summons Dean Martin, who says, "I think we can work something out" as he kisses her. This is funny in a silly way, thanks to Andy committing himself to the idiocy. Additionally, Anthony Newley sings "There's No Such Thing as Love." Because not all of the episode is available for review, there are no ratings for this.

Jackie Gleason looks unimpressed as Bob Hope checks out his outfit as the comedians play two police officers going undercover as women to capture muggers in Central Park in Bob's 1974 season opener taped on location. Courtesy of Getty Images.

# 4 Specials – 1970s

"**IN TWENTY-FIVE YEARS,** I've never missed a show because to illness. No matter how sick NBC gets of me, I show up."—Bob on *Highlights of a Quarter Century of Bob Hope on Television*, Oct. 24, 1975.

Credits for this decade are as follows (exceptions noted in shows when known): EP: Bob Hope. P: Mort Lachman (1970-1975), Linda Hope (1979). D: Dick McDonough (1970-1978). W: Gig Henry, Charlie Lee (1970-1978), Norman Sullivan, Mort Lachman (1970-1975), Mel Tolkin (1970-1975), Lester White (1970-1975), Bill Larkin (1970-1971), Ray Parker (1970-1972), Raymond Siller (1972-1974), Steve White (1973-1975), Jeffrey Barron (1975-1977), Leona Toppel (1975-1976), Katherine Green (1976-1977), Robert L. Mills (1977-1979), Fred S. Fox (1978-1979), Seaman Jacobs (1978-1979). Conductor: Les Brown, Bob Alberti (1974-1979). Announcer: Frank Barton (1970-1974), John Harlan (1973-1979).

Bob came roaring into 1970 amassing some of his hugest ratings ever— 46.6 on Jan. 15, 35.7 on Feb. 16, and 33.4 on his last special of the season on April 13. He would come close to equaling those mind-bending figures through 1972. However, while his numbers were stratospheric, his comedy often was diametrically opposed, sinking to its lowest quality on TV ever.

Particularly in the fall of 1970, Bob faltered horribly with two specials that had comedy so reactionary that one can understand how politically correct speech came into vogue years later. His season opener was an hour-long mockery of the Women's Liberation movement that assumes total role reversals by the genders if those rights are achieved in show business. Bob wears an apron cleaning dishes and accidentally burns a chicken when talk show host Virginia Graham visits his kitchen and wonders what's going on. He recounts the supposedly hilarious indignities of the changing times, such as Minnie Huntley (Minnie Pearl) and Granny Brinkley (Irene Ryan) now delivering the news.

When Bob says to Zsa Zsa Gabor at one point, "Don't you think a woman's place is in the kitchen?" and addresses Nanette Fabray, the new head of NBC West Coast programming, with "A woman in charge?! Women make a mess of everything!" he says both matter-of-factly, as if they are statements of truth. He and the rest of the creative staff failed to realize what was going on in the culture at the time—this was the same month *The Mary Tyler Moore Show* debuted—and the result was one of Bob's worst specials.

Just as painful—if not more so—is Bob's monologue two months later, where he spends an excruciating ninety seconds of homophobic jokes. "Now gay liberation is demanding the rights of whatever they are. Now we've got something else to worry about—sissy power. Their leaders are really tough. They wear leather pantyhose." Bob continues by noting how some gay men attempted to take over Alpine County in California by describing their sheriff thusly: "He had boots, chaps, buckskin jackets. and pearls." The comedian exaggerates the last word with a sibilant "s," an old stereotype even by 1970.

What makes both efforts so disheartening is that Bob had worked with successful independent actresses and gay men and women previously, so he and his crew should have known better than to do this. There is a big irony to all this: On the 1970 season opener, Bob quips how he thinks there's nothing wrong with being a woman, "I just wouldn't want my daughter to marry one!" As it later turned out, his daughter Linda Hope did in fact become romantically entwined with a woman, actress turned producer/director Nancy Malone, and the two would produce Bob's last specials. Sometimes real life gets the last laugh.

Bob continued an antifeminist approach on his Nov. 7, 1971 special, saying if a woman ever did make the U.S. Supreme Court, he'd prefer Raquel Welch over Margaret Mitchell. Bob even half-joked about the notion of women being "Supreme Court justices wearing pants" on his 1973 season opener and how only women should be flight attendants because he couldn't imagine hearing, "I'm Irving—come fly me." This is after Billie Jean King beat Bobby Riggs in tennis.

By the time of that joke, many in the United States were preoccupied as to whether their president, Richard Nixon, was guilty of illegal activity as part of the Watergate hearings. Everybody but Bob, it seemed, since he remained a steadfast supporter of the president, even at the expense of his comic chops.

**Bob Ignores Watergate**

Bob dropped a lot of the impartiality he maintained for the occupant of the Oval Office when Richard Nixon took office in 1969, and his actions grew more favorable to him in the 1970s. At the end of his 1971-1972 season opener, Bob took a minute from his comedy to praise President Nixon's executive order to impose 90-day wage and price controls in order to stall inflation.

During that season, the person who bore the brunt of his jokes Nixon administration was not the president but Attorney General John Mitchell's loose-lipped wife Martha, whose propensity to phone the media about her suspicions of wrongdoing in the government made her the bane of the chief executive's office. On his Sept. 13, 1971 show, Bob says he saw Martha Mitchell in Washington, D.C., but "I didn't recognize her without her dial tone." A nastier comment came six months later, when he mentioned the Chinese practice of binding women's feet: "John Mitchell just tried it on Martha's mouth."

After Nixon's re-election in November 1972, Bob wholeheartedly endorsed the president and became virtually the only comedian on television who didn't do jokes about the Watergate scandal that emerged in 1973. He would make some defense for the president or mock the Senate committee members investigating the cover-up, if he mentioned it at all. As a result, his monologues until Nixon resigned in August 1974 were some of his weakest and worst ever.

For example, Bob implicitly endorsed book burning with his limp crack on how Richard Nixon was handling the energy crisis during his Nov. 13, 1973 special: "The president is worried about freezing. He says he can always throw an extra *Time* magazine at the fireplace." Even worse, Bob actually had Shirley Jones enact that joke on his next special less than a month later, playing Pat Nixon at the start of a skit on the First Family coping with the energy crisis. It was just as tepidly received—and deservedly so—the second time around.

Then there was his jibe at the looks of the lead senator of the hearings on the April 19, 1974 show. "Personally, I'm against rerunning last summer's big hit, Sam Ervin presents the Watergate singers. I mean, when you've seen one eyebrow twitch, you've seen them all."

He was just as toothless when it came to Vice President Spiro Agnew. Bob remarked wise about Agnew's bad golfing game but remained quiet when the executive was investigated and resigned over bribery charges on Oct. 10, 1973.

Fortunately for Bob, Nixon's resignation occurred before his 1974 season opener and thus did not force him to joke about it. He had bigger things to concern himself with at that time, in fact.

**The Big Deal**

In the fall of 1974, Texaco came to Bob and offered to sponsor him exclusively starting in September 1975 for seven hours of programming (meaning roughly five comedy specials annually, allowing for some ninety-minute and two-hour specials) over three years at $3.15 million a year, plus $250,000 more for him to film commercials for the oil company. Bob jumped for the opportunity, even though there were some strings attached, for a few reasons.

By the 1971-1972 season, Chrysler ended being a regular sponsor of Bob's specials. Several other companies took their place in serving as the sole advertiser on individual specials, but Bob missed the appeal of being identified exclusively with one product, like he had been going all the way back to his radio days promoting Pepsodent. Given that, Texaco's offer appealed to him that way.

Around the same time, in early 1975, he renegotiated with NBC to end its longstanding co-ownership of Hope Enterprises, then got a new contract of $18 million for the next three years with the network. However, both NBC and Texaco wanted a new look for his shows. It was a valid criticism with his monologue at least, as Bob came out and stood in front of the same curtain in Burbank, and the studio shows were starting to be as generic as their shared title—*The Bob Hope Special*. Texaco even insisted he fire his old writing team as part of the revamp.

Bob conceded to the parties, but the news leaked out before Bob was able to tell it personally to Mort Lachman and Lester White, each released after more than a quarter century with Bob, along with Mel Tolkin, who had joined Bob in the 1960s. Three other veterans—Gig Henry, Charlie Lee, and Norman Sullivan—learned their layoffs were only temporary due to problems transitioning new writers to handle Bob's style, and they were rehired.

The news shocked some in the industry, but several factors played into why Bob decided to work with Texaco and NBC this way. He had to consider the following:

Variety series were looking bad in the fall of 1974—only *The Carol Burnett Show* and *The Sonny Comedy Revue* were on the networks, and the latter was bombing. If variety series were on the wane, variety specials were next on the chopping block.

Bob saw his contemporaries either scrounging for guest work, like Jerry Lewis and Danny Thomas on *The Tony Orlando and Dawn Rainbow Hour;* retired like Red Skelton (who mounted a middling comeback effort that included working with Bob in 1978); stuck doing gunk like the increasingly tiresome comedy roasts Dean Martin endured; or had recently died, like Ed Sullivan and Jack Benny did in 1974.

Bob was not getting much love from the Academy of Television Arts and Sciences. The last Emmy nomination connected to him was for Outstanding Achievement in Film Editing for Entertainment Programming for *Chrysler Presents the Bob Hope Christmas Special* in 1970.

Yet all the supposed changes Bob was doing to "modernize" his programs in 1975 were mostly superficial. After a two-hour retrospective of his TV work kicked off the season in September (*Highlights of a Quarter Century of Bob Hope on Television*, which nabbed an Emmy nomination for Outstanding Film Editing for a Limited Series or Special), the main alterations viewers noticed were that the backdrops behind him during the monologue were decorated to whatever season or theme the show was emphasizing, the monologues no longer opened every special, and the shows themselves were becoming longer. Now it was more common for Bob to appear ninety minutes or two hours when he did show up on the schedule.

While not forcing Bob's writers to do its commercials, Texaco did insist on using a variety of producers for his specials, apparently in an effort to keep him on his toes. The process generated more inconsistency than spontaneity, and Bob finally put his foot down and had his daughter, Linda Hope, come aboard as his regular producer before the end of the decade. In the interim from 1975-1979, Bob went through several producers who worked only a few shows for him for various reasons, which often meant more writers working for Bob as well.

**In and Out with the Writers**

One of the first writers to last only a season in this period (1975-1976) was Leona Toppel, who says one of her professional contacts informed Bob what a good comedy writer she was, and his office asked her to submit some sample lines for his monologue. "I wrote a bit for him recalling his days in school as a kid," Toppel says. "It was very well acted." However, she discovered she could not meet his needs for a full-time writer because "I could not go to California because I had a family with children." Toppel stayed in the Midwest as a freelancer after just a couple of shows with Bob.

An even shorter stint occurred for veteran comedy writer/actor Bo Kaprall, who did only Bob's 1975 Christmas show. Enlisted to write for the special by former *Rowan and Martin's Laugh-In* writer turned producer Chris Bearde ("He was a crazy man," notes Kaprall), he was shocked by Bob's reaction to the way an elephant in a scene with Redd Foxx kept sticking its trunk into Bob's crotch. While everybody looking on laughed, by the third time it happened, Bob was irritated. He privately summoned his writers including Kaprall, cursed about the situation and demanded "Write him out of the script!"

As Bearde only produced that one show for Bob, Kaprall was not retained for future shows, and he did not care to write for Bob anymore anyhow seeing that outburst. He did work some on developing potential sitcoms for NBC with Bob's daughter, Linda Hope, who he liked a lot, but he was unimpressed by her father after seeing him act up close. "It's just reading cue cards," says Kaprall of Bob's work on his specials. "Well, who can't do that?"

A writer more admiring of Bob was Howard Albrecht, who says, "When I was a kid, Bob Hope was my idol on the radio." Albrecht began his professional comedy writing career teaming with Sol Weinstein in New York City, where they began working for Milton Berle. Describing how he and Weinstein collaborated, Albrecht says, "I used to sit around the typewriter, and he would roam around the room or sit on the couch, and we'd come up with jokes."

After nearly twenty years in the Big Apple, their friend, producer Sheldon Keller, convinced them to come work for him in Hollywood in 1968 on *The Jonathan Winters Show*. They did, only to find out that Keller was fired after the first season, leaving them without a job. Still, they persevered, and Keller retained them when he was hired to produce several Bob Hope specials from 1976-1978. (They had tried to work for Bob when Mort Lachman was his producer, but he declined adding the duo.)

"Bob was really a pleasure to work for, because he adapted to what the producer wanted him to do," says Albrecht. He also like the writing situation. "Each team would write their stuff, and we'd all pitch in on it, and if somebody wrote a better joke for it, that got in. It was a happy time."

There was one drawback Albrecht felt Bob displayed. "He was a slave to the cue cards. We used to do a joke that Bob had cue cards on his honeymoon, and he said, 'I have a headache.' And Dolores said, 'Bob, you're reading my line!'"

Albrecht says his tenure with Bob was relatively short because he and Weinstein became attached to being part of Sheldon Keller being producer. "Sheldon went on to other things, another producer came in, and you just go on," he says. Ironically, his son, Richard Albrecht, teamed with Sheldon's son, Casey Keller, to write some specials for Bob in the mid-1980s!

**The Writers Who Lasted**

A lawyer turned comedy writer (it happens!), Robert L. "Bob" Mills had been collaborating with the more experienced Gene Perret when producer Carolyn Raskin called Perret in 1975 and asked him to craft a monologue for Dinah Shore's stage show. Perret was too busy working on *The Carol Burnett Show* then, so he recommended Mills for the job instead. From there, Mills got a regular job on Shore's daytime talk show *Dinah!*, followed by work on Dean Martin's roast specials that led him to be hired by Bob.

Mills joined veteran Hope scripters Gig Henry and Charles Lee on the payroll on August 1977, along with Norman Sullivan, who as in years past only did jokes for Bob's monologue. He worked forty weeks a year exclusively for Bob, and he made it a point to let Bob know he went to bed at 10 p.m. and not to call him past that time (Bob obeyed this all but once in their fifteen-year working relationship).

Crafting the material for Bob followed a set pattern, according to Mills. "We submitted a list of topics we thought were good for the monologue. He pick those he liked and a new master list was typed up and sent to the writers … Sketch ideas were submitted the same way. He picked the ideas he liked and the chosen ones we began working on. Of course, there were sketches somebody else had submitted and that you didn't care for."

Mills adds that "Once in a while, Hope would think of a title himself and have us come up with an idea that fit it. Like for a show in Paris [in 1989], he thought of 'The Hunchback of Maître D'.' So we set the sketch in a restaurant with Quasimodo ordering. Conversely, you could sell Hope on a sketch idea with just the title. For a special in the Bahamas [also in 1989], I once suggested 'Nassaublanca' as a title, he picked it and we had to force a sketch around it. It didn't work very well, and I regretted suggesting it."

There was one joke Mills crafted in his first year with Bob—on 1978's *Bob Hope's All-Star Comedy Salute to the 75<sup>th</sup> Anniversary of the World Series*—that he said prompted so much laughter that they had to stop tape for the audience to settle down. It went, "With the series in L.A., there has never been so many celebrities in the stands. I sat in the shade. I had a box seat right in front of Dolly Parton's." According to Mills, this got a big laugh, but that's just the setup. The payoff was: "In the third inning, Dolly caught a pop foul, and Steve Yeager is still looking for it."

When Charles Lee retired in 1978, Gig Henry stayed on, and Bob replaced them by hiring Seaman Jacobs and Fred S. Fox, who had written for sitcoms like *Bachelor Father*, *The Andy Griffith Show* and *Here's Lucy* as well as variety shows like *The Red Skelton Hour* and specials like *The George Burns One-Man Show*, which earned them their only Emmy nomination. Jacobs stayed on with Mills to work for Bob through 1992, while Fox ended his tenure a little earlier in 1990. Bob would add a few more writers in the 1980s, but these gentlemen served as his nucleus into that decade.

**Changing Directions**

Also altering frequently in the 1970s was the director's chair. Dick McDonough had served as assistant director to Sid Smith before becoming Bob's primary director in 1968. When McDonough could not make some shows in the early 1970s, Mort Lachman would summon Smith to replace him. "But it was always two days before a show, and I did not like to do that kind of a thing ... So, I refused him several times, like four or five times, then finally he said, 'You must come, I got nobody than I can get that can do it, so you've got to do me a favor,'" Smith told the Archive of American Television.

Reluctantly, Smith agreed to direct in 1974, and "That's when I discovered, hey, that's the way that show always is. If you had been there a week it doesn't matter, because the show is going to change the day before you do it! New sketches, new lines, new script. So I learned to go with the flow of comedy." He would serve as the main director of Bob's Christmas show into the 1990s, long after McDonough had left, while the series would use other directors in the 1980s.

Smith also tried to change the location of where Barney McNulty held Bob's cue cards to make it appear more like Bob was looking into the camera, but Bob refused. Bob's contemporary, Steve Allen, hated the setup too, noting in his book *More Funny People* that "Hope and his guest literally seem to look in two separate directions. It is almost as if Hope is standing on home plate, the person he's speaking to is on the pitcher's mound, and the man with Bob's cue cards is standing on first base."

Allen also despised the heavy and obvious use of a laugh track, which Barney McNulty recognized too. "The laughs in the sketches were mostly added later during audio sweetening, using canned laughter from industrial-size cans," McNulty told veteran network announcer Randy West. "Hope's canned laughter was spread so liberally, it might have been shipped in fifty-five-gallon drums."

Slathering on such a loud laugh track while guests obviously read cue cards, Bob's shows in the 1970s became artificial and aggravating to watch. As Bob was executive producer signing off on it all, it was what he wanted to present, even if it was not the optimal way to watch him.

**Changing Content**

Bob did have to reorient his comedy somewhat in the 1970s due to outside factors. One was his dying motion picture career. The disastrous filming of and reception for his 1972 film *Cancel My Reservation* led him to not have any of its cast on his specials and barely mentioning it as well, plus it curtailed Bob's movie work to a handful of cameos thereafter.

Another was not having Bing Crosby as a frequent source for punch lines when the crooner died in 1977. His passing resulted in one of Bob's best shows, *Texaco Presents Bob Hope in a Very Special Special: On the Road with Bing*, where Bob brilliantly eulogized his frequent partner at the end. "Who would've thought that a flop-eared kid from Tacoma with a name out of a comic strip would end up making the words 'show business' synonymous with love? With the mischievous twinkle in his eyes and a jaunty whistle on his lips, Ol' Dad was everybody's favorite Irish uncle." He offered much more effusive praise before concluding, "As long as the blue of the night meets the gold of the day, Bing will live forever." The superb tribute earned an Emmy nomination for Outstanding Film Editing for a Limited Series or Special.

Bob also switched out targets if someone else became prominent in the same way he joked about a person. For example, by 1977, Orson Welles had replaced Jackie Gleason for fat jokes from Bob and would continue to do so occasionally through his 1984 Christmas special (Welles would die ten months later). Other targets he just adjusted based on their activities, like favoring plastic surgery jokes about Phyllis Diller rather than ones calling her ugly, although he used though as needed.

New guests were mainly ones with recent success in entertainment or sports. Olympic winner Mark Spitz fit the bill for the latter and made a highly seen and ultimately disastrous acting debut on Bob's

1972 season opener. He stepped on one line, used a slow delivery, and obviously relied on the cue cards almost as much as Bob. The Olympic swimmer couldn't even mime drying off properly. His skit is not as bad as its reputation suggests, but it was notorious enough among casting directors and producers to prevent Spitz from being the next Johnny Weissmuller.

As for music, Bob looked to be moving in a more adventurous direction in the 1974-1975 season, using current hit makers Chaka Khan and Rufus, America, and Aretha Franklin as guests. Alas, it was a temporary aberration, as he would go back to favoring Las Vegas-style numbers thereafter, with viewers more likely to see Charo than Chaka.

The most ambitious show Bob did after dropping his old crew in terms of star power was 1976's *Joys!* The title was a spoof on the movie *Jaws*, not that many recognized it, since the antagonist here was not a shark but a killer targeting more than thirty comedians playing themselves. Bob tantalizingly promoted it the night before it aired on *The Tonight Show Starring Johnny Carson*, showing a blooper with Don Knotts and Angie Dickinson that was the last part they had to tape in the wee hours of the morning, and it had the last TV acting appearances of Desi Arnaz and a barely-with-it Groucho Marx. The storyline had a solid payoff, but it was uneven getting there.

Bob's specials were not getting better with pressure from Texaco and NBC, they were just differing more in what worked and what did not. It soon clicked that his birthday shows were a big draw following his seventy-fifth one in 1978, and doing it from a military setting like was done in 1979 was even better, so that became a new annual tradition during the 1980s.

**Bob Beyond the Specials**

Hope Enterprises, Bob's production company, stayed busy on a few projects outside his specials, but mostly like previous decades, hardly anything clicked. Bob himself appeared in *The Bluffers*, which aired as a special on NBC in 1974, but it failed to sell. See Chapter Eleven for more information on it.

Two years later, his production company offered *Shaughnessy*, a sitcom pilot that sounds remarkably similar in basics to *Taxi* two years later, although the lead title character, played by Pat McCormick, was a cab company dispatcher in Chicago. NBC aired the failed series effort on Sept. 6, 1976.

A sale finally occurred on a sitcom called *Joe and Valerie*, but it ran for only two abbreviated seasons on NBC in 1979-1980. Hope Enterprises would not be able to sell another series after this, but not for lack of trying.

**Bob's Big Bash**

Any disappointments regarding Hope Enterprises simmered in 1978, when Bob agreed to do his seventy-fifth birthday celebration as a fundraiser for the USO in Washington, D.C. Gerald Rafshoon, serving as the White House Communications Director for President Jimmy Carter, says the event grew out of his first production for that administration.

"When Carter ran for president and he got elected, we had an inaugural gala Jan. 19 [1977] in the Kennedy Center, and it was the first time it had been televised," he says. "He wanted everything to be subsidized." Rafshoon managed to sell the idea of airing the gala to CBS, and the network picked up the tab for that privilege.

"That was successful, and a few months later, I got a call from a woman in Chicago who was a supporter of Carter," Rafshoon continues. "The USO was her organization, and it was its anniversary, and she wanted to raise money. Bob Hope had been attached to the USO for many years, since World War II, and his seventy-fifth birthday was coming up, so I was commissioned to do that event." He made James Lipton his co-executive producer because the latter had helped produce the inaugural for CBS.

Rafshoon and Lipton learned that President Carter had to attend a sudden engagement the day of the taping, so a reception honoring Bob at the White House occurred the day before with the president thanking Bob on behalf of the nation. The next day, First Lady Rosalyn Carter attended the festivities with former President Gerald Ford and his wife Betty alongside Bob in a viewing box at what officially was termed the Opera House at John F. Kennedy Center.

One person hired by Lipton was veteran orchestra leader Donn Trenner, who had to scramble to nail down all the music he had to conduct for the elaborate production. "Some wasn't available until the last minute, which is typical in our business," he notes. "A lot of writing had to be done during the two weeks before the show."

Trenner particularly remembers how nervous the opener for the show was. "I had to soothe Pearl Bailey, she was so kind to me, and she was grateful," he says. By airtime with Trenner's assurances, she delivered a rousing start singing "Hello, Dolly" with military bands, with lyrics adapted to salute Bob. Rafshoon says it was his idea to have her do what became known as "Hello, Bobby" based on her starring in the musical in the 1960s.

Bob looked ecstatic at Bailey and the other talent that paid tribute to him throughout the show. Inserts for the show came from Las Vegas, Nevada, where Donny and Marie Osmond recorded a brief routine that included singing Bob's hits, and on the West Coast, where Sammy Davis Jr. did two songs, George Burns did a music and comic patter routine, and via satellite from Newport Beach, Calif., John Wayne talked about the USO and showed clips of Bob in action in World War II followed by clips through the Vietnam War. More than twenty stars appeared in person at the Kennedy Center.

"It cost two million dollars," Rafshoon said of the production. It could have been more had the talent not waived their usual fees except for expenses related to their appearances. Elizabeth Taylor was easy to obtain because she was married to U.S. Senator John Warner at the time.

Celebrating Bob would become the theme of a lot of his specials in the 1980s. Like a lot of his work in the 1970s, it kept him popular but came across often as wasted opportunities for what a top comic could and should do on TV, though a few shows were nice exceptions to that belief.

***Chrysler Presents the Bob Hope Christmas Special*: "Around the World with the USO"**
Jan. 15, 1970, Thursday 8:30-10 p.m.

Neil Armstrong, Teresa Graves, The Piero Brothers, Romy Schneider, Miss World Eva Rueber-Staier, Connie Stevens. D: Mort Lachman. W: Gene Moss, James Thurman.

Details on this special can be found in the Preface.
Bob: **** Show: ***

***Chrysler Presents the Bob Hope Special*: "Five Stars for a Five Star Man"**
Feb. 16, 1970, Monday 9-10 p.m.

Ray Bolger, Johnny Carson, Johnny Cash, Bing Crosby, Raquel Welch. Featured: The West Point Glee Club, Oleg Cassini. W: Gene Moss, James Thurman.

A $1,000-a-plate gala benefit for the Eisenhower Medical Center in Palm Springs, this somewhat stuffy affair is taped January 27, 1970 at the Grand Ballroom of the Waldorf-Astoria in New York City. New York Gov. Nelson Rockefeller welcomes the assembled guests before introducing Bob, who gets a standing ovation. "I feel as though I'm really ready for New York," Bob tells the crowd. "I just spent two weeks in Vietnam." He mentions the president's state of the union speech stopping pollution and other topical concerns before saluting David Eisenhower and Julie Nixon and guest of honor Mamie Eisenhower. Thereafter, Bob name drops attendees before and after Bing Crosby sings and Bob suggestively jokes with Raquel Welch before they do a special version of "My Kind of Town." Ray Bolger's hoofing is great but long (over four minutes), and Oleg Cassini's fashion presentation is tedious even with Bob injecting his comments. Johnny Cash singing a medley of hits is much better, as is Johnny Carson deflating some of the pomposity with gags before introducing Bob and Bing in a solid set of comedy. President Richard Nixon (an honorary chairman of the event along with former Presidents Lyndon Johnson and Harry Truman) appears on film to praise Bob before Bob, Bing, Raquel, Ray and the West Point Glee Club sing a tribute to Mamie. The West Pointers also sing "America the Beautiful" behind Bob as the latter praises the late President Dwight Eisenhower at the end.

Bob and Show: ***


*Chrysler Presents the Bob Hope Special*
March 18, 1970, Wednesday 9-10 p.m.

Billy Casper, Tony Curtis, Perry Como, Barbara Eden, Jo Anne Worley. Featured: Henry Corden, Walker Edmiston, Lee Giroux, Ray Kellogg, Eddie Marr, John McLaren, Nancie Phillips, Sandy Roberts, Mike Ross, Benny Rubin, Herb Vigran. Choreographer: Roland Dupree. W: Gene Moss, James Thurman.

Everybody's going through the motions here, with flaccid concepts enacted messily in overextended skits and blah musical numbers like Barbara's bland "Spinning Wheel." Bob's monologue is similarly no classic, with so-so gags about recent TV cancellations including *The Jackie Gleason Show* ("Jackie said, 'Away we go,' and he went!") and others, such as "Whoever thought they'd shoot down the Flying Nun?" He did get laughs with a joke about Tiny Tim's wife: "Miss Vicki is expecting.

Of course, we still don't know what!" After that, Bob stumbles as a man who tries to avoid having sex with Barbara to avoid overpopulation and somehow winds up married to Jo Anne Worley, as a luckless astronaut along with Perry Como trying to leave Saturn, and as a guy quitting smoking who's hampered by an assistant (Tony Curtis) who unwittingly undermines his efforts. For example, Tony tries to take Bob's mind off cigarettes by reading the TV listings, but *Gunsmoke* and *Tobacco Road* remind Bob of his craving. Hoo boy. At least Bob is sincere at the end thanking the public for their support of funding the Eisenhower Medical Center in Palm Springs in honor of the late president.

Bob: *** Show: **

## *Chrysler Presents the Bob Hope Special*
April 13, 1970, Monday 9-10 p.m.

Phyllis Diller, Buddy Greco, Ann-Margret, The Spurrlows, Jerry Colonna. Cameo: Wally Cox.

Bob's opening jokes about how celebrities are handling their taxes, the Oscars, and fashions are all no more than moderately amusing. Ann-Margret does a sultry take on "It All Depends on You" with six male dancers in several different settings and outfits in a five-minute production number. Then Bob learns his co-pilot is Phyllis Diller, who proclaims her demand for equal rights. Phyllis helps Bob fly, but they are interrupted by a hijacker (Wally Cox) who jumps to his death rather than get kissed by Phyllis. The trivial sketch ends stupidly with Bob promising to date Phyllis until they learn they don't have to do an emergency landing. Buddy Greco's horrible medley of contemporary hits like "Aquarius" and "Spinning Wheel" precedes "Odd Squad," a long, sputtering spoof of *The Mod Squad* with Bob and Ann-Margret going undercover at a biker bar to find a missing chopper. Bob's repartee with Jerry Colonna and overall delivery fall short of the usual caliber, and it has another weak ending, this time with all of the "bikers" revealing themselves to be undercover cops. Buddy returns, and after Bob rubs his shirt and says "You were a flower girl at Tiny Tim's wedding," they do comic country western numbers solo and together, such as "Tennessee Bird Walk." They're having a good time even if the songs aren't much. The upbeat youthful gospel group the Spurrlows perform at the end, capping off a competent but unexciting show.

Bob and Show: ***

## Chrysler Presents the Bob Hope Special
Oct. 5, 1970, Monday 9-10 p.m.

Edie Adams, Kaye Ballard, Ruth Buzzi, Imogene Coca, Phyllis Diller, Nanette Fabray, Totie Fields, Zsa Zsa Gabor, Virginia Graham, Teresa Graves, Sheila MacRae, Minnie Pearl, Martha Raye, Irene Ryan, Connie Stevens, Nancy Walker, Jo Anne Worley. Cameo: Don Knotts. Featured: Mary Ann Beck, Henry Corden, Bob Jellison, Eddie Marr, Toni DuPre. W: Lloyd Turner, Gordon Mitchell.

An antifeminist relic, this special is amusing only from the monologue and the hardworking comic actresses who deserve better treatment than this material. Bob does his opening jokes in New York and muses about returning TV stars like Doris Day ("They rearranged her freckles"), new security measures in airports, and Nixon's peace talks in Paris. Referring to Vice President Spiro Agnew's sophisticated vocabulary, he says, "It takes two days to know if you've been insulted." Insulting describes the rest of the show, as Bob frets to Virginia Graham about women being in power as taxi drivers (Totie Fields) and cops (Nancy Walker) and learns from his agent (Ruth Buzzi) that he's been replaced by Phyllis Diller as females take over TV. This is shown by a distaff version of *Bonanza* with Jo Anne Worley as Hoss, Imogene Coca as Little Josie and Kaye Ballard as Ma, with the first two hitting each other with purses. Desperate for work, Bob dresses up as a Playboy bunny and gets sexually harassed by Sheila MacRae, Connie Stevens, and Edie Adams at a club. Bob and his writers unwittingly reveal here the real discrimination women face from men, but like the rest of the show, it's not very hilarious. As Bob ends telling his story to Virginia, he commiserates with fellow "housewife" Don Knotts, who comes into his kitchen knitting. This is the type of show that makes some use "a Bob Hope special" as a pejorative term.

Bob: *** Show: **

## Chrysler Presents the Bob Hope Special
Nov. 16, 1970, Monday 9-10 p.m.

Lucille Ball, George Burns, Tom Jones, Danny Thomas, Lisa Miller. Featured: Elvia Allman, Linda Avery, Timothy Blake, Roberta Collins, Jackie Giroux, Florence Halop, Brad Logan, Eddie Marr, Mike Ross. W: Lloyd Turner, Gordon Mitchell.

If one ignores the hateful gay "jokes" in the monologue (see the chapter introduction for more information) and a bad one at hippies not voting due to the booths since "It reminds them too much of a shower curtain," this is a tolerable vaudeville installment. Bob's set does have a few good jibes like how early election results make you feel like you've bought a wedding gift for Elizabeth Taylor and Eddie Fisher and how for nude show raids in California, "The cops came from as far away as Minnesota." Bob then clearly enjoys joking with his cast and giving them a chance to shine individually, like Tom Jones singing and George Burns using Lisa Miller as his new Gracie (she's fine, but the original is still the greatest). The material is so-so, however. While Danny Thomas scores as a candy vendor heckling Bob on stage, Lucille Ball and Bob struggle to generate their usual magic as an unwilling frump (Lucy) working with a hypnotist (Bob). It is padded too—the bit with Danny, Lucy and Bob as competitive child actors at a competition is a redo from Bob's Feb. 27, 1962 special.

Bob: \*\*\*\* Show: \*\*\*

**Chrysler Presents the Bob Hope Special**
Dec. 7, 1970, Monday 9-10 p.m.

Jack Benny, Dorothy Lamour, Elke Sommer, Engelbert Humperdinck, The Look All-America Football Team. Featured: Maurice Dallimore, J. Edward McKinley, Mike Ross, Christianne Schmidtmer.

The first third of this show looks like a winner, but sexism, a remake, and general boredom defeat it. Bob's sprightly monologue hits Christmas in Hollywood, Nikita Khrushchev's memoirs and the shortage of acting jobs ("That's why there's so many nude movies today. That's all the wardrobe budget will allow"). On co-ed dorms, he notes, "Psychologists say the kids are much happier this way," then chuckles, "I could've guessed that way!" Bob then gets ready to go overseas when Jack Benny returns a lawnmower and accidentally cuts Bob's rug. Jack plans to have a party at Bob's house during the latter's absence and even asks Bob for a kidney in an amusing play on Jack's cheap reputation. Then things sag. Engelbert Humperdinck's song bores. The presentation of the football players ends limply with them running scared off the stage due to women's libbers supposedly coming their way. Bob, Jack and Elke Sommer wanly redo "Breakfast for Three" from Bob's Jan. 10, 1957 special. "Humpy the

Terrible" has Engelbert fretting he has to let go of Bob, his butler, and his other servant, a sexy maid, from attending him in his decrepit castle. After singing a comic version of "Those Were the Days" with Engelbert, Bob says has been able to buy the castle because "I'm also the bail bondsman for the Rolling Stones." Ho hum. Finally, Mrs. Claus (Dorothy Lamour) demands equal rights from her chauvinistic husband (Bob) before they duet on "Santa Claus is Coming to Town," ending a rather tired Yuletide special.

Bob: *** Show: **

***The Bob Hope Christmas Special*: "Around the Globe with the USO"**
Jan. 14, 1971, Thursday 8:30-10 p.m.

Ursula Andress, Johnny Bench, Lola Falana, The Golddiggers, Gloria Loring, Bobbi Martin, The Ding-a-Lings, Miss World Jennifer Hosten, Miss United Kingdom Yvonne Ormes. D: Mort Lachman. W: Stan Dreben, Jim Carlson, Lee Hale (special material). Choreography: Jack Baker, Jonathan Lucas.

Bob's got a paunch as his troupe leaves Los Angeles greeted by Mayor Sam Yorty and Jack Benny as Santa. He wows cadets at West Point with lines like "I haven't seen so much gray since I passed out at the Letter Carriers Convention!" Next are England and Germany, where at the latter Ursula Andress gets a rapturous reception while saying, "I can't sing and I can't dance!" "Just stand there. They'll do the singing and dancing," Bob retorts. At the John F. Kennedy carrier near Crete, Bob says, "I've played golf courses smaller than this!" and in Thailand, he solidly banters with baseball MVP Johnny Bench. Bob scores in Vietnam mocking the war's length ("It was nice of you guys to stick around with me"), dancing with Lola Falana and joshing with Gloria Loring, who gets a soldier tongue-tied talking to her. His women's lib jokes with Miss World flop, however. After everyone sings "Silent Night" on stage in Alaska, Bob emphasizes peace and support for soldiers and Vietnamese children. "We can't run out ... With God's help, this war will end in the next year," he says (it doesn't). Sloppy editing with awkward cutaways hurt this otherwise okay show, which scored a huge 45.0 rating.

Bob: **** Show: ***

*Chrysler Presents the Bob Hope Special*
Feb. 15, 1971, Monday 9-10 p.m.

Bing Crosby, Teresa Graves, Petula Clark, Jo Anne Worley. Featured: Reta Shaw, Henry Corden, Morgan Farley, Sandra Gould, Ray Kellogg, Mike Ross, Jerry Colonna.

Given a longer than usual monologue (nine minutes), Bob gets in some good jibes here. Of hot pants, he says, "I remember when you got your face slapped just for saying it ... They make the miniskirt look like a muumuu! ... On larger types, it's like trying to cover Mount Rainier with a doily!" Assessing Nixon running a budget deficit, he cracks, "Do you think he's trying to be a Democratic president too?" And a recent earthquake in California prompts him to say, "My zip code changed three times, and I was still in bed!" Almost as enjoyable is the first skit with Bing. "I'll do anything to bolster your ratings," the crooner quips. "Then you're not going to sing?" Bob zings back. The momentum falters thereafter with songs by Petula and Bing bookending a long, so-so routine with Bob as a house burglar stopped in his tracks by a loud baby (Jo Anne Worley, sounding a lot like her fellow *Laugh-In* star Lily Tomlin as Edith Anne). A remake from April 13, 1954 with Petula assuming Rosemary Clooney's role in conning Bob into marrying her doesn't help matters either, but Bob's bubbly banter with an animated, fun Teresa Graves before she dances bring it back into being satisfactory overall.

Bob: **** Show: ***


*Chrysler Presents the Bob Hope Special*
April 5, 1971, Monday 9-10 p.m.

Lee Marvin, Shirley Jones, Wally Cox, Sammy Davis Jr., Joe Frazier. Featured: Don Davis, Stephanie Evans, Sid Haig, Ray Kellogg, Michael Link, Eddie Marr, Fayard Nicholas, Billy Sands.

The guest stars' solo turns are livelier than a sluggish Bob, who is seen getting a drink from a stagehand as part of just a five-minute monologue. A few lines do score, like Bob saying why he won't retire from show business like Frank Sinatra just did: "It'd be too much to lose two sex symbols in one year." On being denied an Oscar nomination again, he says, "I made an obscene phone call to Dial a Prayer." He also reviews some of the series canceled, including "Old Stone Face" Ed Sullivan ("He just applied for

Mount Rushmore") and *Green Acres* ("Arnold the Pig was having a real good time, and then they put an apple in his mouth"). Following this is "Flossie," a tired spoof of *Lassie* where Shirley Jones and Wally Cox play the on-screen parents of Bob and try to get the latter fired as the "juvenile actor" has outgrown his part. Much better is Sammy Davis Jr. singing, dancing and doing impersonations, and even Shirley doing her version of "Where Do I Begin? (Theme from *Love Story*)." Lee Marvin shines too in a pretty good skit of pilots in a plane with live entertainment. Most impressively, Joe Frazier gets a huge reception after having won the "Fight of the Century" a few weeks earlier against Muhammad Ali, and he even does a decent job singing "My Way" too. Bob plugs his summer dates before signing off, and presumably he was more engaged on those appearances than he was here.

Bob: ** Show: ***

**The Bob Hope Show**
Sept. 13, 1971, Monday 9-10 p.m.

Edie Adams, Dr. Joyce Brothers, Imogene Coca, Linda Cristal, Angie Dickinson, Phyllis Diller, Nanette Fabray, Zsa Zsa Gabor, Sue Lyon, Rose Marie, Barbara McNair, Phyllis Newman, Martha Raye, Jill St. John, Sally Struthers, Jacqueline Susann, Edy Williams, Jo Anne Worley. Featured: Ray Kellogg, Les Morrell, Janos Prohaska, Bill Zuckert.

This *Planet of the Apes* spoof is less offensive than the previous season opener but is still somewhat sexist. It comes after a weak, prudish monologue that includes jokes about Cass Elliot's weight and Martha Mitchell's mouth, plus Bob boasting that he's making another picture without profanity, nudity or pornography. From there, Bob somehow lassoed NBC newsmen Frank McGee and Sander Vanocur to play themselves announcing how Bob is lost in space. He lands on Venus interrogated by Sally Struthers, Edy Williams, Rose Marie and Phyllis Newman when during his interrogation a man wearing an Alfred E. Neuman mask shows up ("How'd Crosby get here?" cracks Bob). After further interrogation by Edie Adams and Dr. Joyce Brothers, Bob is put in a zoo cage by Phyllis Diller, and he calls her a hyena. Bob tries to plead his case in court, but in another dated gag, Barbara McNair, Jacqueline Susann, and Nanette Fabray are more interested in what Jill St. John carries in her purse. Eventually Imogene Coca drags Bob back to her mistress, Zsa Zsa Gabor, who makes him her maid and says she doesn't know about men, love and marriage (gales of laughter follow that). He faces the queen (Angie Dickinson) and prime minister (Martha Raye) before being saved by Linda Cristal, but another astronaut arrives and takes all the women except one, leaving Bob on Venus with his sister. The script is nowhere near as good as the actresses who give their best despite what's written here.

Bob and Show: ***


### *The Bob Hope Special*
Nov. 7, 1971, Sunday 9-10 p.m.

Jack Benny, John Wayne, Debbie Reynolds, The Osmonds. Featured: Allison McKay, Joanna Cameron, Jerry Colonna. W: Ray Parker. Choreographer: Jaime Rogers.

"I'd rather be a tardy pumpkin than an early turkey," Bob quips in this post-Halloween, pre-Thanksgiving special. His nine-minute monologue is so crammed that Bob doesn't bow at the end. Some of it is sexist, like "Adding a woman on the [Supreme] Court is a great idea, but I pity those eight old men all wanting to get into the bathroom." Going lower, Bob says President Nixon considered Cass Elliot, "But he doesn't want to pack the court." He also disappoints with "Spiro Agnew was surprised by his welcome in Athens. He thought the Greek soldiers were pickets from women's lib." Bob is better riffing on an American pastime: "I watched so much football last weekend, I almost wore out my end zone." Nothing really shines thereafter except "All in the West," a rowdy *All in the Family* spoof with John Wayne as a bigoted father who hates his peace-loving son (Bob) until he learns the family of Bob's Indian fiancée owns oil wells and John eagerly sends out smoke signals to announce the wedding. Less impressive is "Carnal College," a 15-minute *Carnal Knowledge* parody set in the 1920s with Bob, Jack Benny and Debbie Reynolds; a presidential advisor (Bob) being spied on in China (with Debbie in offensive multiple Asian roles); and songs by Debbie and the Osmonds. The latter do "Down by the Lazy River" and duet with Bob Hope on "I Want a Girl (Just Like The Girl That Married Dear Old Dad)." This got a huge 31.8 rating.

Bob and Show: ***

*The Bob Hope Special*
Dec. 9, 1971, Tuesday 9-10 p.m.

Lee Marvin, Robert Goulet, Barbara Eden, Smokey Robinson & The Miracles, The AP All-America Football Team. Featured: Julie Bennett, Timothy Blake, Henry Corden, Bob Jellison, Ray Kellogg, Eddie Marr, Paul Sorenson.

Lee Marvin, the Miracles, and the team winners are great, and the rest are just sufficient in another ratings hit (33.7). Bob promotes his upcoming USO jaunt with "We're entering every war zone except New Hampshire [home of the first presidential primary] … Jim Nabors is going with us, or Gomer shifts his pile." Other targets are presidential candidates like Hubert Humphrey (Bob calls the talkative politician "Minnesota Chats"), Timothy Leary, and President Nixon's talks with Russia and China. This leads into Robert Goulet singing and then Lee Marvin playing a doctor who treats oil millionaire J. Paul Rich (Bob). Lee's comic chops are tops here, but this is overshadowed by Bob's exchanges with the honored football players like future *Hill Street Blues* star Ed Marinaro ("Ed's had longer runs than *Fiddler on the Roof* and is tougher to get down"). Bob also has a surprisingly strong rapport with Smokey Robinson, who jokes that he thought of Bob while writing "Tears of a Clown." The Miracles do a splendid job of singing that hit live. The show sags as Bob and Robert Goulet play two Red China delegates in Central Park in a messy bit, but it rebounds with the musical spoof "Yes Yes Nanette" featuring Lee Marvin as the hilariously grimacing criminal Mad Dog, whose hijinks including an elaborate death scene crack up Bob often. Bob thanks Earl Wilson for the latter's nice words about the comedian in his new book before saying good night.

Bob and Show: ***


*The Bob Hope Christmas Special*: "Around the Globe with the USO"
Jan. 17, 1972, Monday 9:30-11 p.m.

Jim Nabors, Jill St. John, Charley Pride, The Hollywood Deb Stars, Vida Blue, Jan Daley, Sunday's Child, Suzanne Charny, Miss World USA Karen Brucene Smith, Carmen Sevilla, The Blue Streaks (Bob Bell and Louise Edwards), Rear Adm. Alan Shepard. D: Mort Lachman. W: Ed Weinberger. Choreographer: Jack Baker.

Gen. William Westmoreland and Glen Campbell as Santa say goodbye as this group leaves for Waikiki, Hawaii, where Bob wears a loud outfit he calls "Liberace's pajamas." Next is the Far East, where all that scores is a pot joke ("I'm not too thrilled with an audience higher than I am!") and a crack at Miss World that "If you're just another girl, the Astrodome is a pup tent!" When he follows the soul teenage trio Sunday's Child dancing with soldiers on stage with "We had more stomping than a Gay Lib convention!" one wonders if Bob has lost his touch. Once he leaves Asia (and shows Martha Raye and Johnny Grant on tour), he sparkles in Europe joshing with Vida Blue and Jill St. John. Noting the show's lineup, Jill remarks, "I feel like excess baggage." Bob responds, "How about that? Do I know how to pack!?" For the last show in Guantanamo Bay, the crowd is enthusiastic for him and former astronaut Rear Adm. Alan Shepard. Bob follows Jan Daley singing "Silent Night" by thanking members of the military and the USO effusively and claiming "We're all anti-war." Noting the empty seats and happier soldiers as signs of progress, he tells Americans to remain committed to those still in Vietnam. "They're laying it all on the line for us. God bless them."

Bob and Show: ***

## *The Bob Hope Special*
Feb. 27, 1972, Sunday 9-10 p.m.

Milton Berle, Petula Clark, Sammy Davis Jr., Juliet Prowse. Featured: Eddie Marr. W: Ed. Weinberger.

Airing just two weeks before another Hope special, this vaudeville-style revue looks and feels like a rush job, and dated jokes and music (almost all the songs were at least five years old) do not help. Neither does Bob starting his monologue with a Chinese impersonation saying he's coming from the People's Republic of Burbank, a cheesy nod to the president's recent diplomatic excursion. His set is obviously edited and misses considerably, save for some gags about Phyllis Diller's recent plastic surgery: "Her skin is so tight now that every time she sits down, her mouth slams shut!" Nothing special happens afterward. Bob and Petula play bums who bond and sing "King of the Road" in what could be a leftover Freddie the Freeloader bit from Red Skelton. Sammy Davis Jr. does an embarrassing "hep cat" version of the Ides of March rock hit "Vehicle." Milton Berle heckles Bob on stage as has been done on previous specials back to the 1950s. Petula sings three Beatles tunes unremarkably. Bob and Sammy exchange tiresome lines (Bob—"Lots of children are left for adoption." Sammy—"At a dog pound?"). Juliet Prowse dances a tribute to Irving Berlin with video effects vainly trying to spice it up. It ends with Petula playing the teacher enduring the rest of the cast as rowdy, wisecracking pupils amid awkward editing and camerawork. Bob seems to know this one is a dog, as he doesn't even sing "Thanks for the Memory" at the end.

Bob: *** Show: **

*Chrysler Presents the Bob Hope Special*
March 13, 1972, Monday 9-10 p.m.

Dyan Cannon, Eva Gabor, Elke Sommer, Connie Stevens, Danny Thomas (cameo). Featured: Henry Corden, Bob Jellison, Peter Leeds, Eddie Marr, George Wintour. W: Ed. Weinberger.

Bob does some of his best acting ever for a special here, but once again the script doesn't quite measure up to what he's doing. It's an assortment of parodies of Oscar-nominated films, and that subject appears in Bob's monologue too. Of this year's contenders, Bob says, "The only two who were missing were me and Willard the rat." Surveying what did qualify, he vows that "Next year, I'm going to play a ninety-one-year-old homosexual cop with three Jewish daughters, and I'm going to refuse to accept the Oscar. What do you think of that?" The first takeoff, "Summer of 52," with Bob as a teenager seduced by an older woman (Dyan Cannon), is tedious except for Dyan's joke about available men to date: "This is the last summer I'm ever going to spend on Fire Island." Elke Sommer singing doesn't help matters, but "The Polish Connection" is a surprisingly jovial effort with Bob as a tough but dumb cop who harasses his wife (Connie Stevens), the mailman, the grocery man, and even his son. Also enjoyable is "Krutch," with Bob as a senior citizen who weds a pregnant woman (Elke) as she goes into labor. Connie sings before Bob and Eva Gabor star as husband and wife in "Nicky and Alex or They Loved Me in St. Petersburg," where they are upstaged by some truly impressive set design, costumes and makeup—and Danny Thomas as Rasputin. Dyan sings and banters with Bob before this installment ends.

Bob: **** Show: ***

***The Bob Hope Special***
April 10, 1972, Monday 9-10 p.m.

Ingrid Bergman ("in a rare television appearance," the announcer notes), Barbara McNair, Ray Milland, Shirley Jones. Featured: Bryan Clark, Eddie Marr. W: Ed. Weinberger.

Ingrid Bergman and a great monologue compensate for the deficits here. Airing before the Oscars in the East and Midwest, Bob looks at himself and sighs, "My favorite actor didn't win." He also ribs commercials, inflation ("Restaurant are substituting cheaper cuts of meat. The other night I ordered a steak and I got the part of the bull the matador never sees."), and Burt Reynolds' magazine layout ("One newsstand on Hollywood Boulevard sold out in fifteen minutes. And women liked it too!") Bob visits Washington, D.C., where a chic Ingrid is appearing on stage, and she handles jokes well. "This is the top comedy show on television, isn't it?" she asks. "Well, we like to think so," Bob responds. "Well, when do I get to meet Flip Wilson?" Ingrid answers. Of working with Bing Crosby in *The Bells of St. Mary's*, she says, "Oh, he gave such a great performance." Bob cracks back, "He sure did. How a man with all those kids could play a priest, I'll never know." However, Bob and Shirley Jones as a married "Romeo and Juliet," a redo from Bob's April 25, 1962 special, is middling, as is *The Lost Weekend* spoof with Ray Milland being addicted to women instead of booze. It recovers as Ingrid and Bob play a smug Hollywood couple. "Peers? Darling, we don't have any," says Ingrid. When she wins an Academy Award, they argue about their acting talent until he gets George C. Scott's Oscar and all is well with them. It's a funny end to a nice installment.

Bob and Show: \*\*\*\*

***The Bob Hope Special***
April 27, 1972, Thursday 9-10 p.m.

Carol Lawrence, Dorothy Lamour, Vic Damone, Glen Campbell, Sugar Ray Robinson. Featured: Bob Jellison, Ray Kellogg, Eddie Marr, Belle Mitchell, Jack Pepper, Benny Rubin, Dan Seymour. W: Ed. Weinberger.

A wan season ender starts promisingly by Bob noting "We're filling in tonight for *Ironside*, who's out having his tires rotated," before doing so-so gags on the Democratic presidential candidates, the Apollo flight, and *The Godfather*. He sends up that movie playing the title character in a tolerable Marlon Brando Italian dialect opposite Vic Damone as his longhaired son. It's only sporadically funny. Vic has his own singing spot as do Carol Lawrence and Glen Campbell (doing Nilsson's hit "Without You"), but none dazzle. Carol and Glen are in the first skit with Bob, where Bob and Glen play vain, stupid policemen in Beverly Hills. For example, when Glen responds to calls in their patrol car with "Roger," Bob says, "Tell them to call Roger!" They arrest Carol for killing her husband in a tedious effort that at least has a clever ending: When Glen sings with the voice of Robert Goulet (Carol's then-husband in real life), she begs Bob to take her to jail. Bob's bit with Dorothy Lamour as his new neighbor complaining of his hitting golf balls and encouraging fans to visit is as stale and rife with dated references as the rest of the show, including plugging his new picture *Cancel My Reservation*. The only one who comes off well is former boxer Sugar Ray Robinson, talking with Bob about their recent charity match. "They used to call me the Cleveland Bomber," Bob says. "They still do," says Sugar Ray. He's right in using that to describe this show.

Bob: \*\*\* Show: \*\*


**The Bob Hope Special**
Oct. 5, 1972, Thursday 9-10 p.m.

The Carpenters, David Cassidy, Bobby Fischer, Alexis Smith, Mark Spitz. Featured: Julie Bennett, Henry Corden, Peter Leeds, Eddie Marr. W: Buddy Arnold.

A stellar guest lineup contributes to this having a deservedly huge 32.3 rating, as Bob seems energized by the new talent. His monologue runs from plugging his new picture *Cancel My Reservation* to noting Johnny Carson's new marriage ("I guess after ten years, he wanted a different kind of late show"). Bob's running joke of a Russian waiting to play chess opposite champ Bobby Fischer is broken up by nice bits, the first being a comic sing-off with David Cassidy (Bob does "Tennessee Bird Walk" to David's Partridge Family hit "I Think I Love You"). Next, Bob is a superstar whose wife is running for governor in a lively skit thanks in part to Alexis Smith's comic chops. The Carpenters similarly shine performing "Top of the World" and "A Song for You" while joking about Bob's singing and "hip talk." Mark Spitz gets a standing ovation as Bob says, "You look good with your clothes on too!" Spitz says he's making his show business debut here because "My agent said the way to the top is to start at the bottom." The good repartee is overshadowed by a poorly written skit with Spitz as a dentist, who acts badly. That weak spot is forgotten as Bobby Fischer arrives and jokes, "That's why I like it here. The audience is so quiet." He's good with the banter, like saying of his date last night, "I beat her in four moves." Fischer and Spitz take bows at the end, and wisely the cameras stay on them as the credits roll for a mostly smooth hour.

Bob and Show: ****

**The Bob Hope Special**
Dec. 10, 1972, Sunday 9-10 p.m.

Redd Foxx, Phyllis Diller, Elke Sommer, Gloria Loring, The AP All America Football Team. Featured: Milton Frome, Eddie Marr, Karen Anders.

"I want to thank Bing for doing my warmup tonight," Bob quips at the top, citing Bing Crosby and his family preceding this show. "You all saw his special, the musical version of *The Brady Bunch*?" Bob jokes more about Bing before delving into Christmas shopping, resignations in Nixon's administration, peace talks, Apollo 17 and the Rose Bowl, all of which are mild. The rest is much better, starting with the first skit that has Bob at home alone on Christmas Eve when a curious Santa (Redd Foxx) arrives and strips Bob down to his undergarments to get presents for others. Redd's snappy delivery of lines make this a keeper. Gloria does swinging renditions of "Song Sung Blue" and "As Time Goes By" that actually work, then Phyllis Diller comes out in a Santa outfit to joke with Bob. She muses about her recent plastic surgery ("Don't touch my dimple! I don't want to tell you what that used to be!") and delivers a monologue on Christmas that's enjoyable. The AP All America Football Team includes Randy Gradishar, who will later appear on Bob's 1983 Super Bowl special, and Bob clearly enjoys clowning with the men. Bob and Gloria do "Silver Bells" delightfully, and he and Elke are charming as a tacky entertainment act on a plane with turbulence. This beaming outing got a big 38.1 rating thanks in part to Redd Foxx's popularity on *Sanford and Son* on the time, and he will appear on Bob's next show.

Bob and Show: ****

## *The Bob Hope Christmas Special*
Jan. 17, 1973, Wednesday 8:30-10 p.m.

Redd Foxx, Lola Falana, Roman Gabriel, Fran Jeffries, Rudy Cardenas, Miss World Belinda Green. D: Mort Lachman. Choreographer: Jack Baker.

Jim Nabors and Merlin Olsen send off seventy-eight people bound for a location in Japan Bob calls "the only place in the world where you can get a Purple Heart for breathing." Next are Korea and Thailand, where astronaut Don Isley and Bob's wife Delores appear and Bob gets a cane adorned in the shape of a snake. "Reminds me, I've got to get a Christmas card for Don Rickles!" he says. In Vietnam, he notes it's his ninth and last visit there and says "Try not to cry!" Bob is especially festive here and across Asia, with a great skit with Redd Foxx as two privates swabbing some barracks and wonderful interplay with the twelve bathing beauties (including twin future actresses Cyb and Trish Barnstable), Miss World, Roman Gabriel and Lola Falana, hoofing it up well with the latter. At the last show in Guam, Fran Jeffries sings "Silent Night" while Bob recalls serving war audiences during Christmas going back to 1941. "We'll never forget them," he says, as clips of the last previous eight Christmas specials appear as he thanks those and others connected to them. It's a stirring finale to a series of specials that for better and worse established Hope's legacy as Vietnam's top comedian.

Bob: ***** Show: ****


## *The Bob Hope Special*
Feb. 8, 1973, Thursday 9-10 p.m.

Marty Allen, Steve Allen, Jack Benny, Red Buttons, Jack Carter, Jerry Colonna, Howard Cosell, Bill Dana, Joe Flynn, George Foreman, Shecky Greene, Merv Griffin, Arte Johnson, Corbett Monica, Jan Murray, Ken Murray, Louis Nye, Tony Randall, Don Rickles, Nipsey Russell, Danny Thomas, Jo Anne Worley. Featured: Pamela Collins, John Harlan (also announcer).

This energy crunch takeoff needs a few comedic jolts. After Bob's mild monologue, Arte Johnson, Jo Anne Worley, and Merv Griffin report on the crisis (Arte: "Petroleum is so scarce in Russia, they're running their tractors with borscht!") before Dr. Paranoid (Bob) unveils his energy grabber device. Jan Murray is his monster assistant, while Louis Nye is a flaming fashion reporter who squeals, "Ooo, your laboratory is darling!" When Dr. Paranoid zaps the Super Bowl, Howard Cosell has to call plays by candlelight as do Red Buttons, Marty Allen and Shecky Greene in a huddle, with few laughs. Upset with the outage, the president (Danny Thomas) calls in "three of the greatest handicapped detectives on television," but Dr. Paranoid infiltrates the White House to take out the power of body fat in Cannon (Arte Johnson), the accent of Charlie Chan (Jack Carter), and the electricity in the chair of Ironbottom (Ken Murray). Things get even dumber as Joe Flynn (in drag as a manicurist) tries to use a killer anchovy to eat the doctor's fingers in a *Mission: Impossible* spoof with Tony Randall and Nipsey Russell; Jose Jiminez (Bill Dana) pitches George Foreman as Dr. Paranoid's potential bodyguard; and the doctor tricks Detective Poopeye (Don Rickles) to eat uranium. Game show host Monty Benny (Jack Benny) gets the doctor arrested, followed by Bob and eight other comedians singing "Thanks for the Memory" with lyrics about their work on the show. George Foreman's amiable banter with Bob at the end is a relief from an often clunky show.

Bob and Show: ***


*The Bob Hope Special*
March 7, 1973, Wednesday 8:30-9:30 p.m.

Phil Harris, Al Hirt, Pete Fountain.
This shows highlights of Bob's activities as the King of Bacchus at New Orleans Mardi Gras held a few days prior to airing. Jazz artists Al Hirt and Pete Fountain contribute music to this hard-to-find special, which was unavailable for viewing.


*Bob Hope Presents the Cavalcade of Champions,* March 27, 1973—See Chapter 9: Game Shows and Sports.


*The Bob Hope Special*
April 19, 1973, Thursday 9-10 p.m.

Milton Berle, Glen Campbell, Joey Heatherton, The Supremes. Featured: Karen Anders, Norman Andrews, Bob Jellison, Dan Seymour, Doodles Weaver, Clifford Allen, Bob Romaniak.

This somewhat lackluster vaudeville show starts with a promising monologue about tax season, Howard Cosell ("a tongue sandwich"), the meat shortage ("My goldfish was beginning to cringe every time I looked in his bowl") and recent TV cancellations. For *Rowan and Martin's Laugh-In*, Bob says, there was "No notice, they just enlarged the trap door." He mentions overhearing an explicit radio show discussing sex and adds, "It's embarrassing, especially when you hear your wife's voice!" The energy ebbs with Joey Heatherton's strained singing and dancing to "Sunny" and Bob being heckled by Milton Berle before Glen Campbell comes to Bob's defense. More singing and bantering with Joey and Glen occurs before the Supremes thankfully jolt the atmosphere to life doing "Bad Weather" and having a great time singing along with Bob, who at one point even breaks into doing a bit of "I Feel Pretty." Then it's off to an extended but generally winning skit with elaborate plotting involving Milton pretending to be a mannequin as he has an affair with Joey that's interrupted by her husband (Bob) coming home early. Bob is a scientist who transfers patients' ailments onto the dummy, so that means Milton contracts a cold, itching, and effeminate behavior and does a great job mugging for each condition. The ending is strong too—turns out Joey has been cheating on Bob with other men too. Bob ends the show warmly by sincerely thanking his crew and sponsors for a great season.

Bob and Show: ***


**The Bob Hope Show**
Sept. 26, 1973, Wednesday 8:30-9:30 p.m.

Ann-Margret, John Denver, Bobby Riggs, The Jackson Five.

This soars and sinks artistically and aesthetically, even within the monologue. Great lines (of the new TV schedule having twenty-five crime dramas, Bob exclaims, "Last night I had to change channels and almost got caught in the crossfire!") alternate with clinkers (on oil drilling in Israel: "So far they've only struck chicken soup") with obviously heavy editing. He does get a huge laugh referring to the recent writers' strike and adding, "Fortunately I have never had to depend on writers." The skits look cheap—the backdrops are painted flat—and everyone's reading cue cards with stilted deliveries. The one with Bob playing Bobby Riggs to Ann-Margret's Billie Jean King is stupidly sexist, with Ann-Margret strenuously losing her set to a bored Bob but winning by stripping down to a bikini. Her slow medley of "You Are the Sunshine of My Life," "Killing Me Softly" and "I Won't Last a Day Without You" doesn't help matters. Riggs plays himself in a somewhat better sketch with Bob as an airport security guard interrogating the tennis player about his loss. The best moments are Bob dressing like John Denver and having a good interplay with him in and out of song, and the Jackson Five smoothly presenting "Get It Together" and "Dancing Machine." Between the numbers, Michael Jackson tells Bob, "You're lucky that you're a comedian, Mr. Hope. People seem to laugh at the same things for years." It sure seems that way here more than it should for a season opener.

Bob and Show: ***

**The Bob Hope Show**
Nov. 13, 1973, Wednesday 9-10 p.m.

The Carpenters, Mike Connors, Joey Heatherton, Don Rickles. Featured: Donna Douglas, John Roberts.

"I may be the only turkey you can afford," proclaims Bob at the outset of a show that comes close to being a turkey itself. Pluses are the Carpenters doing "We've Only Just Begun" and "Top of the World" and bantering well with Bob, and a decent monologue focused on a recent TV technicians strike ("Marcus Welby performed brain surgery with an ice cream scoop") and the energy crisis. Minuses are just about everything else, from Joey Heatherton's blasé singing to Mannix (Mike Connors) facing off against a fat cop (Bob) for thirteen long minutes. It even reuses the "Assault with a dead weapon" joke from Bob's 1971 season opener. Another ho hum skit has Joey as an alien, and just as dull is Don Rickles wasted as a football coach looking to find his top draft pick, O.J. Hope (Bob), in the Ozarks. Donna Douglas appears as a mountain girl not too far removed from her Elly May character on *The Beverly Hillbillies*. Nobody seems to be caring much for what's going on here, and that includes the technical crew, as a boom mike clearly can be seen in one shot. What a mess this is.

Bob: *** Show: **

### *The Bob Hope Special*
Dec. 9, 1973, Sunday 9-10 p.m.

Lucille Ball, Shirley Jones, Marie Osmond, The AP All America Football Team. Featured: Gary Morton, Doris Singleton, Millie Slavin.

Bob takes advantage of this airing after *Bing Crosby's Sun Valley Christmas Show* and references its star at the top with "It's nice to see that the old rule 'Age before beauty' still applies." Other lines don't fare as well, like Bob's comment on Japan's efforts to combat the energy crisis: "Did you ever try to dig an oil well with chopsticks?" About as dated is when discussing not driving Sundays to save gas, he says, "How are all the Saturday night drunks going to get home?" The skits aren't much either. Bob hides a bracelet he buys at Lucille Ball's home, but Lucy opens it and thinks it's Bob's way of saying he loves her before Bob straightens things out. Apart from Lucy doing her patented cry and acting opposite her frequent costar Doris Singleton, this is a slog. Scant laughs occur too as Bob and Shirley Jones play President and Mrs. Nixon struggling to keep the White House warm (for example, Shirley makes Bob grimace when she asks if he wants to hear "something on tape" to relax). Saving this are good musical moments with Shirley and Marie Osmond, the latter performing her hit "Paper Roses" and singing "Silver Bells" with Bob after saying he booked her instead of her brothers because "I don't have to split the money five ways." The AP team has a few familiar names like Lynn Swann and Tony Dungy, and it's okay. This relative disappointment nonetheless had a huge 34.7 rating.

Bob and Show: ***

### *The Bob Hope Special*
Jan. 24, 1974, Thursday 9-10 p.m.

Dyan Cannon, Dionne Warwicke, Burt Reynolds. Featured: Peter Leeds, Eddie Marr, Mike Ross.

One of Bob's worst monologues makes his guests look better than him in this otherwise quite entertaining show. His set ranges far and wide and scores very little, like the spotty gags about the horror movie *The Exorcist*: "The child grows up to be Don Rickles … Even the Godfather walked out on it … The guy sitting next to me kept getting his tail into my popcorn." Luckily his guests give better than this, including Burt Reynolds, a nice substitute for Peter Sellers, who Bob claimed at the end of his last show would be his guest here. He's a winning stooge opposite con artists Bob and Dyan Cannon in a very funny parody of *Paper Moon*. Bob lets him steal the scenes in another effective movie sendup, this time of *Papillon*, as Burt ends up tunneling back to their jail cell every time he tries to escape. The music is contemporary and top notch—Dionne Warwicke sparkles doing "Promises Promises," "My Love" (the Paul McCartney hit) and even a comic version of "Those Were the Days" with Bob, while Dyan's take on "I Won't Last a Day Without You" is similarly easy on the ears. At the end, Bob smartly gives out flowers to the trio for their excellent work here, and they all do "Elegance" from *Hello, Dolly!* to top it off. If Bob had been as sharp at the start as they were, this easily would have been a five-star special.

Bob: *** Show: ****


**The Bob Hope Special**
March 1, 1974, Friday 8:30-9:30 p.m.

Debbie Reynolds, Charley Pride, Juliet Prowse, Ara Parseghian, Robert Goulet. Juliet Prowse's Choreographer: Ron Field.

"Nice to be back here at Vatican West," Bob quips at the start of this special taped at Notre Dame's Athletic and Convocation Center in South Bend, Indiana. It's part of his college visit, but there's little here designed to appeal to youth with the middle-aged guest lineup. There are many Catholic jokes, references to Bing Crosby and streaking gags, none special, before Robert Goulet sings "Melinda" and banters with Bob. "We've had you three times," Bob says. "And you phrased it perfectly," Robert retorts. They sing special lyrics to "Applause" from the Broadway show of the same name that are funnier than most of their earlier banter. Juliet Prowse sings "Let Yourself Go" with two men in gymnast outfits in some interesting choreography that includes them on parallel bars, but its length (six minutes) and Vegas-style orchestrations work against its effectiveness. Things improve somewhat with Notre Dame football coach Ara Parseghian playing himself meeting a hillbilly prospect (Bob) and his mother (Debbie Reynolds). It's got humorous moments by all concerned, but it runs too long and is tiresome by the end. After Charley Pride sings, Bob and Juliet appear as a priest and nun waiting in lines to see Bob perform at Notre Dame in line before doing a song and dance routine at the end. Like the

rest of the show, the self-referential bit is not as good as one hopes. Debbie's singing closing out is nice but cannot save this disappointment.
Bob: *** Show: **


**Bob Hope Presents the Cavalcade of Champions,** April 2, 1974—See Chapter 9: Game Shows and Sports.


***The Bob Hope Special***
April 19, 1974, Friday 8:30-9:30 p.m.

Ann-Margret, George Foreman, Bob Newhart, Charlie Rich. Featured: Mel Blanc (voice of parrot), Johnny Grant (voice of Wolfman Jack). Choreographer: Louis DaPron.

The guests seem more invested in this special than the star, especially Bob Newhart's surprisingly committed acting. Describing himself as "either the first sparrow of summer or the last egg of Easter," Bob is both with his monologue. He scores on the Oscars ("I loaned my tux to Tatum O'Neal") and Henry Aaron's home run streak ("Records were made to be broken. If you don't believe me, ask Crosby's neighbors"). However, he bombs with his anachronistic mention of "long-haired hippies" and mean jokes about overweight flight attendants ("I sympathize with the chubbies"). In "Burbank Graffiti," a spoof of *American Graffiti*, he is a pompadoured biker who competes with Bob Newhart for Ann-Margret at a drive-in. Newhart tells her he wants to be a big successful psychiatrist. "Who wouldn't, following Mary Tyler Moore?" she cracks about the real-life scheduling of Bob's CBS sitcom. He gets the upper hand by leaving and giving his car to Bob in exchange for the latter not to date Ann-Margret. After this sparkling bit are duds with a promoter (Bob) fleecing George Foreman after a boxing match and Ann-Margret doing a boring ballad. Better is Newhart as a pet shop owner who sells a vaudevillian (Bob) a wisecracking parrot and Charlie Rich performing his hit "Behind Closed Doors" smashingly with a band onstage. Bob finally comes to full life singing and hoofing excellently on "The Two of Us" with Ann-Margret (who relies too much on cue cards throughout the show), but the special ends shortly thereafter.
Bob and Show: ***

***The Bob Hope Special***
Sept. 25, 1974, Wednesday 9-10 p.m.

    Glen Campbell, Carol Channing, Jackie Gleason, Chaka Khan and Rufus, Miss America Shirley Cothran. Featured: Patrick Hines. D: Sid Smith.
    A change of scenery by taping in Central Park in New York City does Bob and his format a world of good, as almost everything is fresh, fast and funny. His short but sweet monologue gets a good reception from the crowd, with the biggest laugh being "It's the first time that I've played to an audience on grass—that I know about." Jackie Gleason comes out to rapturous applause and Bob interjects, "It's a long time since they've seen so much meat!" The repartee and duet about New York by the two sparkle. After Glen Campbell plays the theme from *Bonanza*, Jackie plays a Wall Street broker ready to jump from a ledge ("How sour it is!" he proclaims) when a priest (Bob) offers comfort in an amusing bit. Other skits have Bob as a guy trying to fleece Glen at Grant's Tomb who has the tables turned on him and as a hammy actor exchanging words with his costar (Carol) backstage after both acted in Shakespeare in the Park. All flow well, and a performance taped separately of Chaka Khan and Rufus doing their funky hit "Tell Me Something Good" enhances the mood. A chat with the new Miss America goes much better than usual, and best of all, Bob and Jackie are hysterical as cops dressed in drags to stop criminals in Central Park. Bob thanks the New York park department and cops and brings out Jackie for a final bow to conclude this great affair.
    Bob: \*\*\*\* Show: \*\*\*\*\*

***The 1974 Las Vegas Entertainment Awards,*** Nov. 20, 1974—See Chapter 7: Awards and Telethon Shows.

***The Bob Hope Special***
Dec. 15, 1974, Sunday 9-10 p.m.

    Dyan Cannon, Dean Martin, Olivia Newton-John, The Singing Angels youth choir, The AP All America Football Team. Featured: Joanne Corcoran, Eddie Marr, Tracy Newman, Bill Zuckert.
    This good but not great Christmas special by Bob garners a huge 34.9 rating. He is back into doing more political jokes, quipping that Japan and

Russia were the only places to vote for Republicans following the party's many losses in November, and has a good one on inflation: "Prices are so high this year, some folks are doing comparison shoplifting." Bob plugs his new book about his Vietnam tours, *The Last Christmas Show*, with "Jack Benny really liked my book. I know because he called me up from the library." (Benny will die two weeks after this telecast.) The music by the guests is fine, particularly Olivia Newton-John with her hit "I Honestly Love You" and in a duet with Bob as two hobos singing "Silver Bells." The skits are okay too. Bob plays a swinging singles apartment resident with permed blond hair who eventually admits to his neighbor (Dyan Cannon) that he's her former fat husband (Bob's picture as a fat cop from the Nov. 13, 1973 special is reused here to show what he used to resemble). He and Dean co-pilot a flight sending up disaster movies where they hit a bus at high altitude, deal with a singing nun in the cockpit and finally end up landing on top of the Towering Inferno. The AP Team has a humorous unison singing of "Deck the Tube with Football Bowl Games" as well. It ends with the Singing Angels performing Christmas carols at the credits roll, all nice but not spectacular.

Bob and Show: \*\*\*


***Bob Hope Presents the Cavalcade of Champions,*** April 8, 1975—see Chapter 9: Game Shows and Sports.


***Bob Hope on Campus***
April 17, 1975, Thursday 8-9 p.m.

John Wayne, Aretha Franklin, America, Flip Wilson. Featured: Florence Lake. Choreographer: Jack Baker.

The main show at UCLA is interspersed with filmed inserts of Bob's conversations at other institutes of higher learning to show he's still relevant to the younger generation. He is bubbly and engaged throughout, starting with a monologue in an auditorium ("No matter where I turn, there's an audience behind me!") on concerns like co-ed dorms. In Bob's day, he says, "We weren't even allowed to share the biology rooms." When he gets boos mentioning the recent Oscars, he asks, "You didn't win either?" Playing retiring UCLA basketball coach John Wooden, John Wayne sees Bob is his successor and quips, "It's like replacing Air Force One with a skateboard!" John also plugs his new movie, *Brannigan*, before UCLA players cart Bob off. Better is Aretha Franklin singing solo and along with Bob wonderfully on hit songs associated with him including of course "Thanks for the Memory." An extended skit with Bob as a neat UCLA student thrown off by a hip roommate (Flip Wilson) is only fair, but it is cute at the end to see John Wayne bump hips with Flip. America performs "Sister Golden Hair" and joins everyone at the end to tell students how they personally overcame challenges in their lives and sing in unison "It's Not Where You Start, It's Where You Finish." Between all this, students Bob interviews at Vassar, Howard Page and more offer hopeful opinions about the future that Bob seems to appreciate (e.g., "'America—love it or change it' is what it should be").

Bob: \*\*\*\* Show: \*\*\*


## *Highlights of a Quarter Century of Bob Hope on Television*
Oct. 24, 1975, Friday 8-10 p.m.

Bing Crosby, Frank Sinatra, John Wayne. P/W: Paul W. Keyes.

Bob gets a standing ovation and cracks "Some fine acting!" He jokes about the networks cancelling new TV series and New York being bankrupt before previewing this program. "And there's a lot of history in this show. You'll see what Phyllis Diller looked like before she got younger." He shows the first special with his monologue and Dinah Shore from 1950, Lee Marvin in 1971, Perry Como in 1970, his 1951 "bon voyage" show, Flip Wilson in 1975, John Denver in 1973, and John Wayne in 1971. Wayne shows up to reminisce with Bob trivially, then comes Shirley MacLaine in 1955, the *I Love Lucy* skit in 1956, Jackie Gleason in 1974, Redd Foxx in 1972, Robert Goulet in 1971, and the 1968 presidential marriage bit. Bing Crosby shows up and bobbles saying "Hollywood Scares" instead of *Hollywood Squares* before taunting Bob with "I was a star when you were sewing up torn chicken livers in your brother's butcher shop in Cleveland!" A segment of jokes about the presidents appear before Gwen Verdon's dance number in 1968, Rosemary Clooney in 1954, Shirley Jones and Mike Connors in 1973, Mayor John Lindsay in 1968, the Carpenters in 1973, Jack Benny in 1964, Ann-Margret and Bob Newhart in 1974, Steve McQueen in 1960, Janis Paige and David Niven in 1954, Milton Berle and Petula Clark in 1972, Danny Thomas in 1959, Ingrid Bergman in 1972, Wally Cox and Phyllis Diller in 1970, Jonathan Winters in 1966,

Dan Rowan and Dick Martin in 1957, and Jimmy Durante in 1967. Frank Sinatra complains he is upset with Bob showing him when he was skinny and attacks his lines vigorously, which is pretty funny. Bob does show Frank from 1957, then Ginger Rogers from 1956, Sammy Davis Jr. from 1971, Nelson Rockefeller and Raquel Welch from 1970, Debbie Reynolds from 1974, Andy Williams from 1965, Natalie Wood in 1958, and Johnny Carson and Bing Crosby in 1970. Then U.S. Senators Edward Brooke and Stuart Symington reveal a unanimous Senate proclamation honoring Bob. Bob lets all of his writers' names crawl on the left side of the screen to thank for the jokes before this ends.

Bob and Show: ***

## *Bob Hope's NBC Christmas Party*
Dec. 14, 1975, Sunday 8-9 p.m.

Angie Dickinson, Redd Foxx, Donny and Marie Osmond, Sandy Duncan, Dorothy Lamour, Paul Lynde, Dean Martin, Danny Thomas, Jimmie Walker, The Rose Queen and Court, The AP All America Football Team. Featured: Fred Pinkard, Nichelle Nichols. P: Chris Bearde. W: Pat Proft, Bo Kaprall, Ira Nickerson, Mark Klingman, Buzzy Linhart.

The guests listed after Donny and Marie Osmond are just here for a quick cameo to plug their upcoming TV shows or make a mediocre joke at Bob's holiday celebration. The exception is Paul Lynde, who draws cackles for saying in his distinctive voice, "I wanted your party to be a big success, so I came!" The show opens with Bob and Redd Foxx grumbling about being Santa's reindeer. Bob's monologue follows with some good jibes about rain in California and reduced speed limits ("The houses can only slide down the mountains at fifty-five miles per hour") and Christmas itself ("It's the only time of the year Americans give things to Americans"). Bob then tries to get Redd Foxx to come to his party while Foxx is more interested in his lady (Nichelle Nichols). Redd cracks up Bob with his delivery of "When you started, the only repairman was Marconi!" Back at the party, Donny and Marie sing "Deep Purple" and banter with Bob before he does "Silver Bells" with Marie. Then he visits Angie Dickinson's set for *Police Woman*, where she wants him to play a different kind of villain—a junk food junkie. Next, Bob introduces the All America team, with lots of applause for two-time Heisman Trophy winner Archie Griffin, of whom Bob quips, "He's got more moves than [stripper] Fanne Foxe at a Shriner's convention!" Bob returns to the party to sing "Friends" (the Bette Midler song) with Redd, Angie and Donny and Marie. As typical for a Bob Hope Christmas show, this earned a big 33.1 rating.

Bob and Show: \*\*\*


**Joys!**
March 5, 1976, Friday 8:30-10 p.m.

Don Adams, Jack Albertson, Marty Allen, Steve Allen, Desi Arnaz, Rona Barrett, Billy Barty, Milton Berle, Foster Brooks, George Burns, Red Buttons, Pat Buttram, John Byner, Sammy Cahn, Glen Campbell, Jack Carter, Charo, Jerry Colonna, Mike Connors, Scatman Crothers, Bill Dana, Angie Dickinson, Phyllis Diller, Jamie Farr, George Gobel, Jim Hutton, David Janssen, Arte Johnson, Alan King, George Kirby, Don Knotts, Fred MacMurray, Dean Martin, Groucho Marx, Jan Murray, Wayne Newton, Vincent Price, Freddie Prinze, Don Rickles, Harry Ritz, Telly Savalas, Phil Silvers, Larry Storch, Abe Vigoda, Jimmie Walker, Flip Wilson. Cameo: Johnny Carson. Featured: Chanin Hale, Milton Frome, Andy Albin. P/W: Hal Kanter. W: Ben Starr, Paul Pumpian, Harvey Weitzman, Ruth Batchelor. Concept: Ben Starr.

Vincent Price sets the scene of this murder mystery, where Phil Silvers bullies his way into being the first guest to Bob's party. Bob delivers his monologue at NBC with mostly dated jokes, then Jack Albertson tells Bob backstage he cannot make his celebration. Bob claims he has no party planned, then learns that Jerry Colonna was invited too, so a concerned Bob heads home with a drunk Foster Brooks. At the house, Milton Berle, Jack Carter, and Alan King argue over why they have all been invited before Milton makes a move on a woman (Milton in drag!), and George Burns learns a frail Groucho Marx uses Billy Barty to play himself as a young boy. Bob arrives and sees Don Rickles is his butler and Don Knotts is carrying cue cards. Don prompts Dean Martin what to say, while Phyllis Diller tells Bob Jerry Colonna vanished. David Janssen checks things over before he is taken too. After Rona Barrett reports on the murders, Telly Savalas sends over Abe Vigoda to investigate. Bob suspects Glen Campbell, Fred MacMurray, and Flip Wilson, because they were upset that he cheated in their golf game. As Abe investigates, there is casual chit chat between comedians, and Milton and Jamie Farr learn they are wearing the same dress. Abe labels George Kirby as a person of interest before they both disappear. A German professor (Arte Johnson) helps Bob while Harry Ritz leads Jan, Jack, and Marty Allen in doing shtick while Sammy Cahn plays piano before all are killed. More deaths occur, and TV detectives Don Adams, Mike Connors, Angie Dickinson and Jim Hutton are as useless as the professor in discovering whodunit. Everyone dies before Bob's house is blown up. In heaven, Bob as an angel learns the killer is Johnny Carson, who wanted to kill off the rest from guest hosting *The Tonight Show*. Overlong, choppy, and chock full of inserts due to guests appearing at different times, nonetheless the concept is different, there is a lot going on to keep one interested, and some of it is pretty funny, including the denouement.

Bob and Show: ***

*The Bob Hope Olympic Benefit Special*
April 21, 1976, Wednesday 8-9:30 p.m.

Shirley Jones, Jesse Owens, Freddie Prinze, Bing Crosby, Lynn Anderson. P/D: Bob Wynn. W: Sheldon Keller. Choreographer: Jack Baker.

Appearing at the Montreal Forum, Bob arrives swinging a hockey stick and speaking badly accented French before pointing to his head and saying, "That's using the old derriere!" He mocks the summer Olympics host country's chilly spring weather, such as "That's when you get your thermal underwear open with an ice pick" and "Everybody's out in their gardens, spreading the same stuff as the presidential candidates." The very good set leads into a show stretched so thin it reprises "Small Fry" from the Nov. 18, 1956, special, with Freddie Prinze playing Bob's father (!). Freddie's bit trying to get Bob to be bilingual and Shirley Jones' solo and duet with Bob are just adequate. Country artist Lynn Anderson's takes on the pop hits "Never Can Say Goodbye" and "Feelings" fail to impress, as does Canadian juvenile singer René Simard's half-English, half-French version of "I Write the Songs." Better is Bob's interactions with Olympians to pledge for donations to the U.S. and Canadian teams. For example, when he tells eighteen-year-old Canadian slalom champ Kathy Kreiner, "I'm forty," she shoots back with "And I'm Tatum O'Neal!" Bob shines saying, "How do you introduce Bing Crosby, a man I've admired since I was a boy?" "I knew that your words would eventually hit the fan," Bing retorts happily as he sings solo and with Bob. They work well together as two Canadian Mounties on the prowl for Shirley and Lynn against a fur trapper (Freddie) and redeem an otherwise shaky show.

Bob and Show: \*\*\*


## Bob Hope's Bicentennial Star-Spangled Spectacular
July 4, 1976, Sunday 8:30-10 p.m.

Sammy Davis Jr., The Captain and Tennille, Debbie Reynolds, Donny and Marie Osmond, Steve Allen, Angie Dickinson, Phyllis Diller, Ron Howard, Don Knotts, Ed McMahon, [Dan] Rowan and [Dick] Martin, Doc Severinsen, Jimmie Walker, Henny Youngman. P/W: Paul W. Keyes. W: Terry Hart, Bob Keane, Paul Pumpian, Harvey Weitzman. Special Lyrics: Sammy Cahn.

Bob gets a prime spot on NBC's lineup saluting the country's 200th anniversary and gives America a fine show in return. His monologue is strongest if a little sexist addressing President Jimmy Carter's effort to address recent sex scandals involving congressmen's secretaries: "He's having their wives pick their secretaries, which may be a big break for Phyllis Diller and Ruth Buzzi … They can't type, they can't answer the phone, can't keep a secret. I hardly had a chance to see *All the President's Men* because I was hearing about the Congress's women! One thing's for sure—we can't call this a do-nothing Congress!" The sketches start with Bob and Sammy Davis Jr. as anchors for the evening news of July 4, 1776, interrupted by cameos like Dick Martin as Paul Revere suggestively announcing "I aroused a few villagers myself!" Sammy's delivery is so sharp that Bob ad libs, "You worked that up to a nice guest shot!" Pretty enjoyable numbers by the Captain and Tennille ("Shop Around") and Donny and Marie Osmond break up the other skits. Debbie Reynolds has a dead-on Louise Lasser impersonation in a Revolutionary War-style spoof of *Mary Hartman, Mary Hartman*, and Bob's *Tonight Show* set in the same era uses its announcer (Ed McMahon) and bandleader (Doc Severinsen) as it sends up all of its conventions. After Sammy and Debbie do their individual song and dance numbers, Bob wraps it up summarizing accomplishments by famous and not-so-famous Americans. However, Sammy has the best line in the special about America's future potential: "For as long as we can laugh at our problems and smile at each other, you know something? We're home free, baby."

Bob and Show: \*\*\*\*

## Bob Hope's World of Comedy
Oct. 29, 1976, Friday 8-10 p.m.

Lucille Ball, Norman Lear, Don Rickles, Neil Simon, Big Bird. P/D/W: Jack Haley Jr.

"With Barbara Walters gone, I'm the only sex symbol NBC has left," jokes Bob at the top of this mostly retrospective special. He also touches on the upcoming election, Halloween, and Zsa Zsa Gabor's latest marriage ("She's the only one I know who keeps the justice of peace on permanent retainer"). Big Bird amuses Bob with great delivery and physical humor as they lead into eight clips with actors with animals on Bob's specials, including a chimp playing golf with Jackie Gleason in the 1969 film *How to Commit Marriage*, followed by another eight clips focused on international guest stars. Lucille Ball zings Bob when he asks, "If you couldn't do comedy, what would you do?" with "Probably what you do." Bob plays back their 1962 skit, and they actually seem to have a real conversation afterward. Three clips of slapstick comedy bits follow. Neil Simon says he does not think one can learn how to write comedy and provides more insights before Bob cuts the discussion short to show four vaudeville-style sketches. Don Rickles bobbles his prepared lines to the audience's amusement before devoting more of his time to promoting his new series *CPO Sharkey*. Bob shows approximately fifteen guests insulting him before bringing out Norman Lear, who is surprisingly relaxed and informative in talking with the host. Bob even says to Lear, "You are a great product of America, and America is proud of you for your accomplishments." This leads to four more parodies and four dance numbers before Bob pays homage to dozens of comic actors and actresses who have passed away to conclude the program. Bob has some of his best interactions with guests here that it's a shame so much of the show consisted of repeated materials—or in some cases, re-repeated materials.

Bob and Show: ***

## Bob Hope's Comedy Christmas Special
Dec. 13, 1976, Monday 8:30-10 p.m.

Dyan Cannon, Neil Sedaka, Lola Falana, John Wayne, Kate Jackson, The AP All America Team, The Rose Queen, Miss Teenage America Rebecca Ann Reid, Miss America Dorothy Kathleen Benham. P: Sheldon Keller. W: Howard Albrecht, Sol Weinstein.

A surprisingly enjoyable if overstuffed show, this opens with Santa (Bob) leading his sleigh with ladies as his reindeer, only to see Mrs. Claus (Dyan) force him to pull everyone else instead. It's a good twist on the sexist skits of the past. Bob's monologue after this in front of a colorful, seasonal curtain excels, first by mocking new President Jimmy Carter from Georgia. "The national anthem will start, 'Oh say, can y'all see?'" Remarking on Carter talking to former Secretary of State Henry Kissinger, Bob quips, "They had a wonderful meeting, the two of them and their interpreters." The president's brother, Billy Carter, also gets ribbed with "He bought new overalls for the inauguration." Also not spared is Elizabeth Taylor and her seventh marriage ("Liz just yells, 'One more time!'") and a prediction of an earthquake for California ("I won't go to a restroom without air bags"). It's mostly music and banter after that, but almost all of it clicks, from Neil Sedaka doing his slow version of "Breaking Up is Hard to Do" and a "Calendar Girl" duet with Bob to Lola Falana's collection of Christmas carols. The only skits are a cute bit with Bob and Kate Jackson playing Ken and Barbie dolls and a decent one with John Wayne as a psychiatrist helping Ebenezer Scrooge (Bob) cope with his dislike of Christmas. Bob seems to be having fun here due to good new guests, strong returning ones, and nice new material to boot.

Bob and Show: \*\*\*\*

**Bob Hope's All Star Comedy Spectacular**
Jan. 21, 1977, Friday 8:30-10 p.m.

Ann-Margret, Charo, Mac Davis, Sammy Davis Jr., Dean Martin, Super Bowl quarterbacks Ken Stabler and Fran Tarkenton. Cameos: Muhammad Ali, Red Buttons, Howard Cosell. Featured: Eddie Marr. P/W: Sheldon Keller. W: Howard Albrecht, Sol Weinstein.

Bob kicks off this special first dressed as an Indian as "Son of Cochise" in the forests of Lake Tahoe, then "Robin Hood of Tahoe Forest" opposite Ann-Margret, Clark Gable in "Gone with the Tahoe" opposite Charo, a golfer in "The Arnold Tahoe Story" and the start of "The Last Tango in Tahoe" with Ann-Margret. Anyone thinks the titles are funny will think the skits are too. Calling the area "Las Vegas with thermal underwear," he riffs on it before talking about rising coffee prices and President Jimmy Carter's inauguration, all pretty mild (sample: "It's the first time I've ever heard 'Hail to the Chief' played on the jug and wash bucket"). Sammy Davis Jr. does "Kiss Today Goodbye" fine if rather upbeat before Bob and Ann-Margret do "A Star is Torn," a parody of the Barbra Streisand film that moves well even if it is very broad. The Mac Davis number with Strut is visually engaging, and Dean doing "I've Grown Accustomed to Her Face" is good too, especially with it revealed that he's singing to himself. The banter Bob has with Fran Tarkenton and Kenny Stabler is forced though they deliver the lines well. Ann-Margret does "All By Myself" rather melodramatically, but she and Bob singing "One" is great. Bob appears in "Son of Rocky" with Howard Cosell announcing his fight against Sammy Davis Jr. and Ann-Margret acting hilariously as Rocky's homely girlfriend. It's raucous, and Muhammad Ali coming out to stop them to save his industry—acting—is a great ending. Charo does "Fernando," then Bob talks to her ("You make Tom Jones look like Perry Como"), and she's excited to be here with him. Bob banters with Mac Davis before he sings an okay song, then Bob and Sammy play correspondents for the inauguration, and it's fairly amusing. Even more enjoyable is Bob and Dean as Lewis and Clark pelted with fake snow and spotting Charo in a sarong. Sammy and Bob do a great soft shoe number, then "The Bob Hope Roast" has as its honored guest King Kong, which also scores with Red Buttons doing his "never got a dinner" routine before Dean. Bob gives a nice tribute to the transfer of power at the end for a better-than-usual special.

Bob and Show: \*\*\*\*

### Bob Hope's All Star Comedy Tribute to Vaudeville
March 25, 1977, Friday 8:30-10 p.m.

Jack Albertson, Lucille Ball, The Captain and Tennille, Bernadette Peters, Vivian Reed. Cameo: Jimmie Walker. Featured: Vanda Barra, Jeffrey Barron, Chaz Chase, Sid Gould, Isobel McCloskey. P/W: Sheldon Keller. W: Howard Albrecht, Sol Weinstein. Choreographer: Jack Baker.

With five consecutive musical numbers, plus two others in the show, this special makes one question its title. True, there is humor in Bob's monologue, with several jabs at President Jimmy Carter's Southern heritage ("Mr. Carter is the first president we've had who considers a three-piece suit a sweater and two elbow patches"), along with quips about the California drought and the Oscars, all of which gets good response. Bernadette Peters plays a neglected wife in the first skit who literally rips the shirt off the back of the ice delivery man (Bob) to get her husband's attention. It's pretty funny. The Captain and Tennille do their new hit, "Can't Stop Dancing," then Jack Albertson does an original song and dance with Bob as well as reprise the routines of vaudeville stars. Jack doing Eddie Cantor performing "If You Knew Susie" and Bob doing Al Jolson presenting "Toot Toot Tootsie" is either cute or eye-rolling, depending on one's tolerance for so-so imitations. Lucille Ball and Bob play housecleaners who attack each other at work for some good slapstick and some bad lines that ends stupidly with a Jimmy Carter impersonator. Vivian Reed from *Bubbling Brown Sugar* on Broadway does a number with four male dancers, then comes a torch song from Bernadette, a forgotten tune from the Captain and Tennille and a Sophie Tucker impersonation from Lucy before returning to Vivian to do "God Bless the Child" from her Broadway show. Next, Bob and Bernadette do "We're Couple of Swells," which is fine but can't match the original done by Fred Astaire and Judy Garland in *Easter Parade*. "The Hospital" has Bernadette as a nurse, Lucy as a crazed physician and Bob as a wisecracking patient. It's pretty good, with Jimmie Walker in a funny cameo and an incredible bit by vaudeville veteran Chaz Chase eating everything in sight. However, Bob's blah song finale on an empty stage leaves a barren taste at the end of this.

Bob and Show: ***

***Texaco Presents Bob Hope in a Very Special Special: On the Road with Bing***
Oct. 28, 1977, Friday 8-10 p.m.

Bing Crosby. P/D: Howard W. Koch.

This tribute to Bob's recently deceased longtime professional partner begins with their number "Teamwork" from 1962's *The Road to Hong Kong* before Bob comes out and eschews his monologue for some heartfelt words. "Bing always topped me, you know. Here I'm working, and he's up there swinging on a star. You know, when someone of Bing's stature leaves us, we say we've lost a good man. Not this time. With all of his glorious records, great films, we haven't lost Bing at all. He's still with us. From hence on, he's our show." Clips come from the Road movies plus Bing and Bob's joint appearances on the 1955 Oscars and Bob's March 2, 1958, March 22, 1962, Oct. 24, 1962, Dec. 15, 1965, and Feb. 16, 1970 specials. Apart from those specials, there is no laughter heard, even though Bob speaks before a live studio audience. That includes his two-minute benediction after Bing sings "Do You Hear What I Hear?" from the Dec. 13, 1963 special. Discussing this special, Bob says, "In some ways, it was the most difficult one, but in other ways the most joyful. For we all had some time to spend with a friend whose philosophy of life was 'Let's get on with it, but let's have some fun along the way.'" The show could have used some editing (particularly the tepid 1962 *Bonanza* parody), but mostly it shows Bing at peak form with Bob, who honors his fellow comrade well with his remembrance.

Bob: ***** Show: ****


### *Texaco Presents the Bob Hope All Star Christmas Comedy Special*
Dec. 19, 1977, Monday 8-9 p.m.

Perry Como, Mark Hamill, Olivia Newton-John, The AP All America Football Team, The Muppets (Frank Oz, Jerry Nelson, Richard Hunt, Dave Goelz, Jim Henson). P/W: Sheldon Keller. W: Howard Albrecht, Sol Weinstein.

The bonhomie permeating throughout this special by the guests make this a delightful seasonal installment. For his monologue, Bob mentions Christmas at the White House (everything has peanuts for President Jimmy Carter), Anita Bryant's campaign against gay rights ("They're going to name a street after Anita in Miami. Of course, it'll only go one way"), and more. It is par for the course, but the Muppets overshadow it. Miss Piggy throws herself at Bob to leave the gang and nearly does until she learns she has to be his personal servant, so she karate chops Bob. He apologizes, says he wants everyone to stay together, and sings "Have Yourself a Merry Little Christmas" with the Muppets to end a superb segment. The strong AP All America Football Team has Ozzie Newsome, Earl Campbell, Doug Williams, and Jerry Robinson with Bob's usual quips. Mark Hamill talks with Bob before they play two kids locked overnight in a toy store, wear hats to play the likes of Sherlock Holmes and Dr. Watson, and even do a soft-shoe routine. Next, "Scar Wars" has a princess (Olivia Newton-John) and Luke Sleepwalker (Perry Como) trying to help Santa Claus hijacked by Barth Vader (Bob). Bob's ad libs crack up Olivia and Perry frequently, and Mark does show up as Luke Skywalker to arrest Bob for making fun of his movie in a satisfying wrap-up. Olivia gets to sing "Silver Bells" with Bob too. Apparently this is what the public wanted, as it earns a huge 34.0 rating.

Bob: *** Show: ****

**Texaco Presents the Bob Hope Show All Star Comedy Tribute to the Palace Theatre**
Jan. 8, 1978, Sunday 8-9:30 p.m.

George Burns, Sammy Davis Jr., Carol Lawrence, Steve Lawrence, Donny and Marie Osmond. Cameos: Johnny Carson, Jimmie Walker, Milton Berle, Phyllis Diller. Featured: Sid Gould, Bobby Ramsen. P/W: Sheldon Keller. Writers: Howard Albrecht, Sol Weinstein. Choreographer for Carol Lawrence: Louis DaPron.

This barely gets by mainly on the strength of George Burns and Sammy Davis Jr., whom Bob obviously adores, and surprise guest shots. Bob starts with a solid monologue covering topics from the end of college football ("Nobody knows who's number one. It's a lot like Cher's love life.") to Johnny Carson's beneficial terms from his new NBC contract ("This afternoon, my parking spot had a meter on it."). His song and dance turn with Burns is warm and funny, but the musical numbers after it flounder. Donny and Marie's take on "You're My Soul and Inspiration" pales next to the Righteous Brothers' original, while Carol Lawrence is no Barbra Streisand playing Fanny Brice opposite Bob's Flo Ziegfeld and doing "I'm the Greatest Star" and "My Man." Steve and Eydie's so-so solos are overshadowed by their skit with Queen Guinevere (Eydie) ignoring Lancelot (Steve) and King Arthur (Bob) for Sir Carsolot (Johnny Carson), who quips, "There goes one of my (k)nights off!" Sammy and Bob have fun reprising comic duos, like Bob as Dean Martin in a curly wig opposite Sammy's manic Jerry Lewis. The finale, with Carol as a jungle goddess attempting to capture an English hunter (Bob), is stupid until Jimmie Walker amuses Bob as king of the jungle, as does Milton Berle in drag as a sacrificial maiden and Phyllis Diller as a new goddess. Bob sings a tribute in honor of the recently deceased Charlie Chaplin at the end, which smooths out a sometimes rough special.

Bob: **** Show: ***

## *The Bob Hope Classic Comedy Special from Palm Springs*
Feb. 13, 1978, Monday 8-9 p.m.

Roy Clark, Phyllis Diller, Telly Savalas, Raquel Welch, Andy Williams, Flip Wilson. Special Musical Material: Ray Charles.

A rather staid entry, this comes off like a pale imitation of *The Ed Sullivan Show*, with Bob introducing mostly middle-aged talent doing their usual routines to a mostly middle-aged audience that includes former President Gerald Ford, Johnny Bench and Fred MacMurray. Bob's monologue notes how rich the crowd is that's watching him at the Pelican Hotel at the Desert Classic Ball in Palm Springs ("They send food stamps to Texas") and covers several current topics including the King Tut exhibit ("Dead for 5,000 years and still on tour. That's what I call having a good agent."). Afterward he mostly introduces acts that are largely going through the motions. Andy Williams, Raquel Welch, and Telly Savalas lend their vocals to unexciting presentations and Roy Clark presents a "Jambalaya (on the Bayou)" with little spice to it, while Flip Wilson and Phyllis Diller do slightly better with their monologues. Flip needles the mostly white crowd's perspective, saying that "I went to the men's room and I made twelve dollars" because they that he was an attendant. Phyllis cracks that "Raquel Welch is afraid to be in the same room with me. She thinks what I have is catching!" The only spark of excitement comes near the end when Bob sports a dark toupee, dresses like John Travolta in *Saturday Night Fever* and bumps hips with Raquel as they do a funny, energetic take on "Staying Alive." Alas, it just proves how dead the rest of the show is in comparison.

Bob: *** Show: **


## *The Bob Hope All Star Comedy Special from Australia*
April 15, 1978, Saturday 8-9:30 p.m.

Charo, Barbara Eden, Florence Henderson, Kamahl, The Four Kinsmen, Mary Anne Davidson, Miss Australia Gloria Krope. P: Chris Bearde. W: David Letterman.

Bob goes Down Under—as well as to New Zealand—in this outing, with a featured skit being Charo grilling him as a customs officer. He and the cast also interact with kangaroos and koala bears in several sketches and song. As this was not viewed, there is no rating for this entry.

## Happy Birthday Bob
May 29, 1978, Monday 8-11 p.m.

George C. Scott, Pearl Bailey with The U.S. Army Band and Chorus, The U.S. Marine Band, The U.S. Marine Drum and Bugle Corps, The U.S. Navy Band and Sea Chanters, The U.S. Air Force and the Singing Sergeants, The U.S. Coast Guard Band, Jim Henson's Muppets with Frank Oz, Mac Davis, Redd Foxx, KC and the Sunshine Band, Elliott Gould, Donny and Marie Osmond, Charles Nelson Reilly and Fred Travalena, Sammy Davis Jr., Lucille Ball, Fred MacMurray, Bert Convy, Carol Lawrence, Telly Savalas, Danny Thomas, Lynn Anderson, Shields and Yarnell, Dorothy Lamour, George Burns, David Soul, Alan King, Charo, Kathryn Crosby, Elizabeth Taylor, Peter Jay, Tony Orlando, John Wayne. Announcer: Norman Rose. EP: James Lipton, Gerald Rafshoon. P/D: Bob Wynn. Co-P: John Hamlin. W: Bob Arnott, James Lipton. Music: Les Brown, Donn Trenner. Choreographer: Carl Jablonski.

"How do you take the measure of a man?" George C. Scott intones at this mega-production's outset. "It's a nationwide, worldwide birthday party for Bob Hope. And he's agreed to mark the seventy-fifth anniversary of his birth by giving it to us, to America and to the institution with which his name and his heart have been linked for half of his lifetime, thirty-seven years—the USO." Pearl Bailey's special "Hello, Dolly" delivers a rousing start, as does a funny routine as Miss Piggy forces Kermit the Frog to pretend to be Bob introducing her song. She does "Secret Love," then karate chops and stomps on Kermit before blowing kisses to Bob. Other songs at the opera house come from Mac Davis, Bert Convy, Carol Lawrence, KC and the Sunshine Band, Lynn Anderson, David Soul, Charo, and Tony Orlando. Comic bits include Redd Foxx presenting a pretty good monologue about military life as the Chairman of the Joint Chiefs of Staff; Charles Nelson Reilly interviewing President Carter (Fred Travalena), claiming that he was Bob's caddy who is cloned, in a sporadically amusing bit; and Danny Thomas recounting Bob's jokes at his expense and claiming falsely he and Bob do not cheat on their wives. The best is Alan King, who says Bob was born in 1897 and "The first troops he entertained were the Hessians." Recounting Bob's marriage to Delores, he asks, "Why the hell anyone would want to get married in Erie, Pennsylvania?! The people in Erie, Pennsylvania, don't get married in Erie, Pennsylvania!" and jokes some more before adding, "I'd like to make you an honorary Jew." Also good is Shields and Yarnell's funny pantomime of a female dummy who menaces her ventriloquist. Reminiscing warmly about old times with Bob are Lucille Ball, Fred MacMurray, Dorothy Lamour, and Kathryn Crosby. So does Delores Hope, who joins Kathryn, gets a standing ovation, and recalls how she met Bing in 1932 before singing Bob's favorite song "On a Clear Day You Can See Forever" beautifully. Elizabeth Taylor notes Bob had been honored by every president since Franklin Delano Roosevelt and introduces Peter Jay, the ambassador of Great Britain, who relays a note from Queen Elizabeth congratulating Hope on his birthday saying, "We thank you for your invaluable contribution to our vitality and our freedom." USO President Gen. Michael Davison then reveals the organization's new building will be called the Bob Hope USO Center.

After all this, Bob comes down to the stage, warmly thanks everyone, and naturally launches into a routine. Of the White House, he says, "Whoever thought that government housing could be that elegant?" Bob claims Roosevelt once told him, "Son, the only thing we have to fear is your act." On his own golf game, he quips, "I beat [Dwight] Eisenhower once. Mamie had an off day." Regarding his age, Bob notes, "Being seventy-five is watching *Charlie's Angels* and following the plot." He pretends to forget the names of his four children, then has Sen. Stuart Symington take a bow in the audience for starting the USO tours for Bob. ("He saved me a fortune in Christmas presents," he claims.) Bob adds some serious words about the purposed USO during peacetime ("I assure you that the USO is still with us and is just as ready to help whenever and wherever it is needed.") before concluding with, "Speaking for myself, Les Brown and his wonderful band that traveled with us all those years, and all the wonderful artists who've traveled with me over the years, I just want to say it's been an honor and a great privilege to have been a part of this great organization. And needless to say, this has been an event I will always remember and one that has touched me deeply." He then does "Thanks for the Memory" before shaking the hands of all who appeared. Like most big birthday parties, this lasts a little too long but still is a fun experience overall.

Bob: ***** Show: ****

*Bob Hope's All-Star Comedy Salute to the 75th Anniversary of the World Series*
Oct. 15, 1978, Sunday 8-10 p.m.

Danny Kaye, Glen Campbell, Charo, Howard Cosell, Billy Martin, Steve Martin, The Muppets (Frank Oz and Jim Henson), Cheryl Tiegs. P: Don Ohlmeyer. D: Sid Smith. W: Marty Farrell. Howard's "Dead Sea Scrolls" Material: Monty Hall. Choreographer: Jack Baker. EP of Baseball Clips provided by MLB Productions: Larry Parker.

Bob's show is as is fitfully funny as his monologue. He addresses Los Angeles being so hot that "Paul Williams bought an ice cream cone and climbed in" (a joke he will reuse in 1988, replacing Paul with Emmanuel Lewis) and more, and he gets the most laughs about pretending to be sixty ("I've lied to so many girls"). His guests appear between montages of major league baseball errors. First, Danny Kaye jokes with Bob about women reporters in locker rooms before they depict conversations between pitchers and managers in Great Britain (funny), Japanese (dated), and Germany (midway between both). Glen Campbell does "Southern Nights" live, then Bob talks to Kermit the Frog about becoming a player for the Cleveland Indians with Miss Piggy acting as Kermit's agent. Both are solid. After a 1963 flashback for Bob, Billy Martin is funny mocking his managing woes with the Yankees with Bob. Glen as a hick prospect sought by a baseball agent (Bob) has its moments (even though it is just an updated remake of what Bob last did with James Garner in 1965), but Steve Martin as a vendor competing with Bob with crazy items for sale is better. After a trivial interview, Cheryl Tiegs "acts" as a psychiatrist to a distraught umpire (Bob), which echoes a funnier bit Bob did on his June 15, 1952 show. Charo's disco bullfight number with five male dancers surprisingly works well, and Danny's variation on "Trouble" from *The Music Man* combined with "Take Me Out to the Ballgame" is cute. Less enjoyable is Charo pleading to be put on Bob's team, but Howard Cosell's sharply comic and pretentious "sermon" on baseball's history followed with banter with Bob makes up for it. Danny and Bob do a nice "Thanks for the Memory" referencing highlights of the sports and honor its stars with vintage footage, leaving this special with a nice glow despite its faults.

Bob and Show: ***

## *Bob Hope Salutes the Ohio Jubilee*
Dec. 3, 1978, Sunday 8-9 p.m.

Lucille Ball, Vic Damone, Donny and Marie Osmond, Ginger Rogers. Larry Merritt, President Gerald Ford. Cameo: Danny Thomas. D: Bill Hobin.

In a show originally planned for March 3, 1978 but delayed by organizers, Bob celebrates fifty years of the Ohio Theatre in Columbus with a vaudeville show mostly old in content and style. At least the middling monologue is contemporary. Bob mentions attendee Sen. John Glenn along with other native Ohioans Danny Thomas and Dean Martin ("He could stagger before he could walk"), plus Betty and Gerald Ford. Bob then sports a huge beer belly as a football-watching TV addict whose wife (Lucille Ball) cannot get his attention even parading around in a negligee. Lucy seduces a plumber (Danny Thomas) until the latter joins Bob to watch the game. She hoses both men down in response, and Bob and Danny's reaction to the squirting water is the funniest part of a bit that never really jells. Donny and Marie do their last top forty hit, the disco-flavored "On the Shelf," then Ginger Rogers does a fine dance routine. Vic Damone and Bob come out as the Happiness Boys to sing and tell unexceptional jokes. Bob talks to Ginger in the usual forced scripting and cutesy musical number. A skit with pet shop operators Bob and Donny trying to sell Marie a dancing bear is stupid and not up to a similar one Bob did on April 19, 1974. Lucy's talk with Bob about beauty secrets, her husband, and Nashville is dull too. Thankfully, President Gerald Ford is amusing in thanking Bob for appearing at the theater, and Bob's parting words are nice as well. Still, this show is forgettable.

Bob: *** Show: **


## *The Bob Hope All Star Christmas Special*
Dec. 22, 1978, Friday 8-9 p.m.

Andy Gibb, Delores Hope, Red Skelton, Dionne Warwick, The AP All America Football Team, The Rose Queen and Her Court. Featured: J. Edward McKinley. P/D: Bill Hobin. W: Red Skelton.

A Yuletide special with occasional cheer, this begins with Bob jesting about Christmas in Beverly Hills ("It's pitiful, watching children try to make a snowman out of smog"), the high prices of gifts, the popularity of albums (including a bad gay joke of "I bought an album by Queen and beat it to death with my purse"), and the *Superman* movie before unveiling the AP All America Football Team, which includes Heisman Trophy winner Billy Sims. Dionne Warwick sings "What the World Needs Now," then Andy Gibb talks with Bob with several cracks involving Bob's age. Andy then lip syncs to "Shadow Dancing" on a set strewn with oversized snowflakes. The only skit has Freddie the Freeloader (Red Skelton) getting a visit in his shack from his fellow hobo Robert (Bob). Bob accidentally calls him "Red," cracking up the latter, before Santa Claus visits them as they plan to eat a measly bird. "We have to have a funny Santa Claus?!" Bob ad libs, amusing Red again, until finally they learn their bird has been transformed to a meaty one by Santa. Dionne joins Bob to talk some before they do a disco version of "Jingle Bells" with new lyrics. However, it is Delores Hope who does "Silver Bells" with Bob. The Rose Queen and six girls of her court have to endure the dumbest lines in the script talking to Bob before he brings Red out for a special bow and wishes everyone a merry Christmas. It's all watchable but feels slightly stale nonetheless.

Bob and Show: ***


## *The Bob Hope Cavalcade of Comedy*
Jan. 28, 1979, Sunday 10-11 p.m.

Debby Boone, Pat Boone, Sammy Davis Jr., Debbie Reynolds. Cameo: Kathryn Crosby. P/W: Buz Kohan. D: Walter C. Miller. W: Bob Arnott. Special Musical Material: Ray Charles. Choreographer: Louis DaPron.

Two Debbies plus two Boones equals too bland here, even with Sammy Davis Jr. The guests sing lines to spell out Bob's surname before he comes onstage in Pasadena, California, for the Bing Crosby Youth Fund. "The money here is so old, they tip in gold nuggets," quips Bob as he muses on the Super Bowl ("The worst injury was on a thrown-out hip, and that was one of the cheerleaders"), Chinese Vice Premier Deng Xiaoping and his entourage's visit to Washington, D.C., (with a questionable quip of "One guy looked at the Washington Monument and said, 'Ooo, biggest chopstick I ever saw!'") and more. Then Bob, Sammy and Debbie Reynolds play actors who put on lampshades on their heads and get gonged on stage after singing the first line of "You Light Up My Life." This should've been gonged itself. Debby Boone sings (no, not "You Light Up My Life") before Bob and Sammy do a peppy song and dance to "Me and My Shadow." Debbie's medley of standards is okay, but she can't salvage a long, deadly skit as Lois Inane investigating a mad doctor (Pat Boone) and his assistant (Debby) until she's saved by Superior Man (Bob) and his clone (Sammy). Sammy goes all out performing "Birth of the Blues," but it follows Pat and Debby's flat medley of rock tunes. The finale with everyone singing and clowning and Bing's widow Kathryn Crosby graciously accepting the funds raised, is better, but by then the show is a lost cause.

Bob: *** Show: **

*Bob Hope American Youth Awards,* March 2, 1979—See Chapter 9: Game Shows and Sports.

*Bob Hope An Evening at the Palladium, A Lifetime of Laughter*
May 14, 1979, Monday 8-9 p.m.

Richard Burton, Raquel Welch, Susan George, Leslie Uggams, Leif Garrett.

Bob returns to his native country with a half-American, half-English guest star lineup. Among the skits, "Backstairs at the Palace" has Bob as a butler married to a maid (Susan George) while another maid (Leslie Uggams) brings in Princess Anne's baby. Richard Burton arrives as himself and kisses Susan and Leslie before the four all sing a song to end the so-so sketch. (Originally Richard was to kiss Raquel Welch, but his new wife opposed him doing so, forcing Bob's people to draft Susan George as an acceptable emergency replacement.) Better is Bob's byplay with Richard, with both singing "How to Handle a Woman" and joking well. Richard sports a dry, witty delivery, such as when Bob asks, "This is your first appearance on a comedy show, isn't it?" and he murmurs, "Well, that reminds to be proven." As only part of this special was available for review, no ratings are given for it.

## *All Star Birthday Party for Bob Hope*
May 30, 1979, Wednesday 8-9:30 p.m.

Diahann Carroll, Charo, the cast of Broadway's *Dancin'*, Dr. Henry Kissinger, Don Knotts, Sarah Jessica Parker, The U.S. Marine Drum and Bugle Corps, The Village People. EP: Linda Hope. P/D: Bob Wynn. W: James Lipton.

The guests bring their A games and force Bob to give more than usual, making this seventy-sixth birthday party quite enjoyable. Aboard the USS Iwo Jima, the U.S. Marine Drum and Bugle Corps play "New York, New York" to herald Bob's arrival and emphasize where the aircraft carrier is docked. "All of you are here because they cancelled shore leave, right?" Bob jests as he zings Billy Carter's drinking and preparation for his trip to China. There's plenty of Navy jokes too, including a few dated ones about females joining the service ("They have enough accidents with one hammock!"). Bob enjoys hamming it with the Village People, as lead singer Victor Willis "recruits" Bob while the group performs "In the Navy," and he is swell as a straight man interviewing Don Knotts as a cowardly helicopter pilot. Doing duets, he's relaxed with Diahann Carroll on "How About You" and Sarah Jessica Parker on "I Don't Need Anything but You" from *Annie*, where she is starring on Broadway (she also sings that show's hit "Tomorrow" solo). The numbers bookend Charo having fun inviting servicemen to dance with her onstage. Bob then is a lieutenant marooned on an island with another castaway (Don, with impeccable timing and delivery) so weary that he thinks his servant (Charo) is a man. Bob has a nice time chatting with the Village People before they do "Go West," then introduces what he calls the brilliant cast of *Dancin'* from Broadway doing a number. Former Secretary of State Henry Kissinger stolidly praising Bob at the end decreases the fun, but otherwise it's a solid party.

Bob and Show: \*\*\*\*

## *Bob Hope on the Road to China*
Sept. 16, 1979, Sunday 8-11 p.m.

Mikhail Baryshnikov, Crystal Gayle, Shields and Yarnell, Big Bird, Peaches & Herb, Delores Hope, The Philadelphia Boys Choir and Men's Chorale, artists of the Peking Opera, students of the Peking Opera

School. EP: James Lipton, Linda Hope. P/D: Bob Wynn. W: James Lipton. Choreographer: Carl Jablonski.

Swinging a golf club while singing on the Great Wall of China, Bob launches an audacious mix of diplomacy and entertainment that mostly succeeds, even if it's tiring to absorb it all in three hours. Bob stands at Tiananmen Square and says the show's mission is to get to know the country's customs and people. Since he doesn't speak the native tongue, Bob relies on a translator while doing his monologue, and the delays are distracting in this portion and when he uses the translator again for a Q&A after a screening of his old film *Monsieur Beaucaire*, as he has to explain some references to the natives. He fares better cracking children up as he loses to them playing ping pong and gamely trying tai chi in the morning. For his supporting cast, mimes Shields and Yarnell act as animated mannequins to confused and bemused shoppers, Mikhail Baryshnikov tutors a female dancer, and Big Bird interacts comically with a 7-foot-5 basketball player. Even without doing their hits, Crystal Gayle and Peaches & Herb provide enjoyable musical interludes too. Bob donning a Fu Manchu mustache to do a comic number with six Peking male dancers is dicey, but it's thankfully overshadowed by Bob doing comic business with three male Chinese comics and Delores Hope singing "Do Re Mi" with children. It ends very movingly with the Philadelphia Boys Choir and Men's Chorale doing patriotic tunes and Bob thanking the cast and crew on stage for touring with him for three weeks.

Bob: ***** Show: ****


*Bob Hope on Campus*
Nov. 19, 1979, Monday 9-11 p.m.

Bear Bryant, Erik Estrada, France Joli, Melissa Manchester, Joe Namath, Tony Randall, Tanya Tucker, The Village People, Dionne Warwick. P: Linda Hope. Co-P: Frank Badami II. D: Bill Hobin. W: Casey Keller, Richard Albrecht, Stephen Perani, Pacy Markman.

Cheerleaders at USC give Bob a lively welcome in a special apparently designed to show Bob still has appeal with the collegiate set. He seems invigorated by his appearances that go over well with material specially tailored for each locale—the weather at USC ("You can tell Thanksgiving is here. The frost is on the smog."), the culture at Harvard

("Seven people from Harvard wrote the Declaration of Independence. Three are still here."), the party atmosphere at Florida's Gator Growl ("Where else is going to class an extracurricular activity?"), the industrial pollution near Indiana State University ("It must be tough on you students, going four years without inhaling."), the reverence for Coach Bear Bryant at Alabama ("Before I speak to him, I have to kneel and kiss his ring. I wish it wasn't in his back pocket.") and the quietness of Hamilton near Colgate ("The meter maid doubles as a SWAT team."). The other comedy is tops too, whether Bob is bantering at USC with *CHiPs* star Erik Estrada's recovery after a recent accident (Erik: "Somebody up there likes me." Bob: "Yeah, [NBC President] Fred Silverman!") or acting opposite Tony Randall as statues commenting on current events at Harvard. The musical acts, all in peak form, appear at USC except for Tanya Tucker (Indiana), Frances Joli (Colgate) and the Village People (NBC's Burbank studios). Some overused references to *Animal House* and Paul Williams being short are the only big drawbacks to an otherwise top special.

Bob: ***** Show: ****


**Bob Hope's Merry All Star Christmas Special**
Dec. 13, 1979, Thursday 9-10 p.m.

The 1979 AP All America Football Team, Kathryn Crosby, Angie Dickinson, Bonnie Franklin, Adam Rich, The Rose Queen and Her Court. P: Linda Hope. D: Sid Smith. W: Casey Keller, Richard Albrecht, Stephen Perani, Pacy Markman.

Bob's guests try hard but get a lump of coal with the writing for this Yuletide outing. His decent but short opening monologue (less than five minutes) covers rumored presidential candidates and new Christmas toys: "Ever since those [electronic] games have come out, staying at home is more fun. You and your date can sit in front of the set and push each other's buttons." Then Santa Claus (Bob) is arrested by a police officer (Angie Dickinson) who interrogates him for being an imposter. She ends up wanting him badly, but he has to campaign to be both the Democratic and Republican candidate for president. In terms of humor, this is more cheesy than cheery. The football team is big on talent (Heisman Trophy winners Billy Sims and Charles White) but short on laughs. Bonnie Franklin does the best with her scripted jokes about acting in the theater before she and Bob appear as juveniles, with Bob in a Little Lord Fauntleroy outfit. She one ups Bob until they learn through all their parents' marriages that they are actually brother and sister in a time-killing segment. Then a hobo (Bob) convinces a runaway (Nicholas Rich) to return home, and the runaway has him join him in a slushy bit. Kathryn Crosby endures corny lines before doing "Silver Bells" with Bob. Bonnie singing "My Ship" and the Rose Queen and Her Court introducing themselves do not bring any excitement either. It adds up to a weak wave goodbye to the Seventies.

Bob: *** Show: **

Gina Lollobrigida, right, gets the attention of Bob Hope and Marie Osmond while Delores Hope (far left) and Lucille Ball prepare for a group shot promoting their special *Bob Hope's Women I Love Beautiful But Funny*, which aired Feb. 28, 1982. Bob's specials in the 1980s tended to be focused on gorgeous costars bantering with the host and clips of his old work, and this one plenty had both. Courtesy of Getty Images.

# 5  Specials – 1980s

"**For thirty-five years,** I've been doing these specials on NBC. Who says crime doesn't pay?"—Bob on his Sept. 24, 1984 special.

Credits for this decade are as follows (exceptions noted in shows when known): EP: Bob Hope. P: Linda Hope (1980-1981), Elliott Kozak (co-producer 1984-1986, producer 1986-1989). D: Tim Kiley (1981-1989). W: Robert L. Mills, Fred S. Fox, Seaman Jacobs, Gig Henry (1980-1983), Gene Perret (1981-1989), Martha Bolton (1986-1989), Jeffrey Barron (1988-1989).

Bob kicked off the 1980s with an unbelievable achievement: He got six hours of time on NBC basically devoted to a clip show. *Bob Hope's Overseas Christmas Tours Parts One and Two*: "Around the World with the Troops" took over two Sunday nights on the network's schedule in February 1980 during a time when NBC needed the ratings boosts.

"It was something that was very important to Bob," recalls the mega-production's producer, writer and director Andrew Solt. "Bob for years had mentioned this show, but NBC wanted three hours, and he said, 'No, no, this is too big. I want six to do it.' He was denied it for years until [then NBC Entertainment president] Fred Silverman said yes in the summer of 1979."

Bob's producer at the time, his daughter Linda Hope, knew that it was an intensive show to handle, so she sought the help of Solt and his partner, Malcolm Leo, who had produced the acclaimed 1977 documentary "Life Goes to War" for *The Big Event* on NBC. "Linda spoke to our agent at William Morris," Solt says. "We had twelve weeks to do it." They worked seven days a week and had to cut physically on three-quarter-inch cassettes to make innumerable edits.

Dealing with approximately 100 hours of footage, Solt and Leo did have an advantage in using their previous work along with what Bob had compiled. "There was material in there that Malcolm knew from researching 'Life Goes to War,'" says Solt. "It was basically a history of the troops being entertained during the wars. It didn't always depend on Bob being there."

Bob did participate considerably in the development of the special, according to Solt. Usually twice a week, he and Leo met him in the morning at his home in Toluca Lake to go over what film to use. "It was fun to see his reactions looking at materials and telling stories about them," notes Solt.

Solt also received the privilege of supervising Bob's monologues at NBC Studios at Burbank to install at the start of both parts of the special. "He was always prepared, always funny, the consummate entertainer," Solt says. "It was a real honor to direct him in the monologues."

The impressive special earned an Emmy nomination for Outstanding Achievement in Special Events for its editing. It also set a tradition or an irritation, depending on one's perspective, of using old footage on many of Bob's specials this decade. Often this gave viewers the impression that Bob was coasting on his reputation and was lax if not indifferent to the idea of performing any new comedy, much less anything regarded as cutting edge. Indeed, Bob's shows that had all new comedy ranged everywhere from enjoyable from intolerable.

**Other Top Specials**

During the 1980s, visits to locales away from Burbank became the norm, particularly for Bob's birthday shows. That was true for his extravagant eightieth birthday gala, which like Bob's first big celebration five years earlier took place at the Kennedy Center in Washington, D.C., with James Lipton again serving as executive producer.

Joining Lipton as producer and director was Don Mischer, whom Lipton recruited after Mischer had already won two Emmys and six other nominations for his work in those roles. "Jim was instrumental in trying to get on board," says Mischer. "I don't know if Bob was really aware of anything I'd done."

Excited by the offer ("Working with Bob Hope was a real honor. I grew up listening to him"), Mischer says he and Lipton were in tune about getting an emotional response for the event. "Jim had specific ideas about who he wanted to book, and we would exchange ideas. It was a good creative relationship."

The preproduction for the gala was as elaborate as the program itself. "It's a couple of months that you work on this, and Jim booked the venue, but together we had to come up with a crew with the right video trucks, a music director, production truck, writers," notes Mischer. "The first step is putting together a creative team to execute this. Then there's booking. And there was no one who would say no to perform for Bob." However, he added, some individuals asked to perform did have prior commitments that they could not cancel and thus missed the special.

Mischer spent three weeks doing the staging as well as at least a week going over technical concerns. "That's when the director kind of takes over the running of the show," he notes. There was also an unusual choice he and Lipton employed during the taping.

"We made a decision to do it like a live show. And when we get to where there are commercial breaks, we're going to keep going. It generates an electricity you don't get with stop-and-start television style," he says. It went off without a hitch until Lucille Ball bobbled her presentation. "Lucy came out said, 'I have to stop and start over again' after thirty seconds, and I worried the spontaneity would be lost, but it wasn't. Other than that, I just remember it was fun."

Mischer was especially happy given the reaction of his two biggest critics, one being Bob himself. "We were editing this pretty quickly, working through the night, and Bob came to the editing room, probably two o'clock in the morning, and he told me, 'They told me you were really expensive, but you were worth the money.'" The other one was a family member who had never been impressed with Mischer being a TV producer and director. He noted that after watching that special, "My dad said, 'Well, I think you finally made it.'"

While that celebration was a ratings bonanza, one might argue that the best show where Bob sat back to watch performers entertain him before he did a concluding monologue in the 1980s was *America's Tribute to Bob Hope* in 1988, a cultural appreciation of his activities. "That was a good show," says Buz Kohan, who wrote special lyrics to "Thanks for the Memory" for celebrities to sing (for lack of a better term) in appreciation of Bob. "Nancy Reagan was there, and I have a picture of me and Nancy Reagan shaking hands in the hall, and looking ten feet away with a look of jealousy was Van Cliburn."

Bob also had a huge triumph in Christmas of 1983, risking his safety by taking a troupe to entertain men stationed in Beirut who had just faced a horrific terrorist attack that killed hundreds of men. Recalling that time as a participant, Cathy Lee Crosby says, "It was an amazing experience, to say the least. From all of the cast and crew leaving Los Angeles on a huge camouflaged jet accompanied by two military fighter jets, this was definitely not business as usual. I only began to get scared when they wouldn't let anyone on the plane who hadn't made out a will, which had obviously never entered my mind. There I was, talking through my tears on video, saying goodbye to my family and friends, telling them who gets what of my earthly possessions and telling them how I wanted to be buried. Yikes! But, with my will in order, off to the Mediterranean Sea we were.

"Then there was the in-flight, plane-to-plane transfer of fuel. Fascinating but scary, with a plane flying directly over you at the exact same speed, at what seemed like mere feet above us, filling our empty tank with gas! Another scary moment was being forced down on a landing field in Turkey—or Syria, I've forgotten—and held hostage until the U.S. government or someone in power could get us clearance to leave and continue on our way. It was tense there for a few anxious hours. Then there was an 'all hands on deck' emergency siren alert on board the ship we were living on for the three-week tour. On our hands and knees, we all followed the red lights along the floor—up six flights of stairs in our pajamas underneath our floatable flak vests and helmets, by the way—till we arrived on the top deck and directed to hunch down on the floor. There we were, like sitting ducks really, watching the bombs and flashes of light go back and forth on the shore in front of us.

"It's funny, but I wouldn't have traded any of the experience for the world, because in spite of the danger and cramped quarters, etc., being with and interacting with the servicemen and women on all the ships we visited made up for everything that was uncomfortable in spades. They were the real people risking their lives, not us!"

*Bob Hope's USO Christmas in Beirut* went off despite such hitches, proving Bob could still handle war-torn areas even at age eighty-one (and landing an Emmy nomination for Outstanding Technical Direction, Camerawork or Video Control For A Miniseries, Movie Or A Special). He performed it with the help of two new important contributors.

**The New Scripters**

As a contributing writer to Phyllis Diller, Gene Perret impressed the comedienne, so she recommended him to Bob, who asked him to submit some jokes for Bob to use at the Oscars in 1969. Hope said ten of them on the telecast and requested more material, but Perret had other regular comedy writing commitments preventing him from joining Hope full time. Instead, according to Perret, "I worked for Hope part time during those years because I was usually working on other shows." Those included *Rowan and Martin's Laugh-In* from 1971-1973 and *The Carol Burnett Show* from 1973-1978. Ironically, his time devoted to the latter allowed his protégé, Bob Mills, to join Hope in 1977.

In the fall of 1978, says Perret, "I began producing *Welcome Back, Kotter*, and retired from working for Hope for a brief period, because I wanted to devote all of my efforts to producing. However, a few topics came up that I couldn't resist, so I began sending material to Hope again. After *Kotter* [in 1979], I produced *Three's Company*, and then began working on Tim Conway's variety show. One of Hope's writers dropped out (I forget why), and I went full time with Hope." The writer was Bob's longtime contributor to his monologue, Norman Sullivan.

Perret says working for Bob was an enjoyable regular assignment with a possible exception. "If I had to decide on one challenge, it would probably be that often it was hard to understand exactly what Bob Hope wanted. Often he would have an idea in his head, but wouldn't be able to verbalize it to the writers. In those cases, we'd try to deliver what we thought he was expected, but sometimes didn't. That meant we'd have to run it through the typewriter again. Eventually, we would hit on the exact idea that he had in mind, but it was largely through trial and error. It seemed like a lot of wasted effort."

Perret says that the changeover in producers during the 1980s through 1990s did not affect him. "For me, and for most writers, the producers weren't that much of a factor. Not that they didn't work hard and work effectively, but Hope was the real producer. We generally worked for him."

As for Perret producing the show himself, like he did with *Welcome Back, Kotter*, he says, "I'm not sure Bob Hope would have wanted me to produce his shows. I may have been a little bit too laid back to produce his specials. He hinted at it a few times with me, but never made a formal offer. I especially enjoyed working with and writing for Bob Hope, so I was content to stay active on his show rather than try to find work producing."

Perret did assume one title by the end of the 1980s, however. As he explains, "Hope never really had a functioning head writer. So, no one coordinated the rewrites and the consolidation of the different pieces being written except Bob Hope. Normally, he did an excellent job, because he really cared about the quality of the writing on his shows. Sometimes, though, he would get overwhelmed with work and get careless. I think that's when I got the assignment of being the acting head writer (although the WGA insisted that I have a different title, as the term 'head writer' had become obsolete according to them). Hope would often have me coordinate some of the writing, both on the monologues and on the sketches."

Also joining Bob as a writer was Doug Gamble, who started contributing to his monologues in 1983, though he would not get credit on screen until the end of his tenure in 1992, when the main writing team brought Gamble in to do sketch writing as well. "I was among his last gang of writers," Gamble notes. "How many people start a job when their boss is eighty?"

Gamble had been writing for other comedians such as Phyllis Diller and Joan Rivers when word of his work came to Gene Perret, who was looking for new writers for Bob. His work first appeared in Bob's Sept. 19, 1983 show, when the comedian used four of his gags. The special included what Gamble says was his favorite joke to write for Bob, which involved preparations for the summer Olympics in Los Angeles: "A lot of people are worried about what might happen if terrorists come to L.A. My attitude is, if they get mugged, they get mugged!"

He learned a few basic rules from the veteran writers, like Bob did not like to talk much about himself in the monologue and how to adapt to Bob's rhythm and speech pattern in delivering jokes. "There was very little collaboration," Gamble adds. "Everybody worked out of their houses independently. He thought he could get the best out of the writers this way."

He also learned to expect being given a list of topics for a monologue at 1 p.m. and be expected to deliver his set of jokes to Bob by 5 p.m. (in the pre-fax and internet days, Gamble was grateful that he lived in Studio City at the time, taking him only ten minutes to get to Bob's home in Toluca Lake). Gene Perret concurs about the rather tight timeline: "Most of the writing we got was expected to get done as soon as possible. Bob lost all concept of how much time it took quickly."

Like the other writers, Gamble went to the tapings for Bob's specials at NBC, and the incident he remembers most vividly is when Lucille Ball taped a new number with eight dancers for Bob's eightieth birthday in 1988. "They kept having technical troubles. They had to stop and start three or four times. I was really concerned for Lucy." She was worn out from the lengthy delays at the end, but despite what some reports say, Gamble says she did not collapse, leave the show, and suffer a mild stroke thereafter.

Besides Perret and Gamble, no other longtime writers joined Bob's crew in the 1980s until Jeffrey Barron, a former writer with the *Second City TV* series who worked for Bob previously in the mid-1970s, and Martha Bolton, Bob's sole female writer, who had contributed captions to cartoons as well as created inspirational Christian books. Perret showed Bolton's work to Bob, who was impressed enough to hire her full time. "She was hired to add a softer touch to the material," says longtime Hope writer Bob Mills. "Hope was eighty-six and slowing down."

Meanwhile, on a sadder note, most of the old guard who had been with Hope virtually since he started TV in 1950 passed away. Norman Sullivan was the first to depart, in 1984. Charles Lee predeceased his former longtime writer Gig Henry by a year, dying in 1988 followed by Henry in 1989. Only Mort Lachman survived and thrived, serving as executive producer to the hit sitcoms *Gimme a Break!* and *Kate & Allie* before retiring in the early 1990s. He would die in 2009.

**Burbank Blahs**

Despite the influx of newer writers, Bob's shows taped at Burbank during the 1980s were often partial successes at best, even by relying on one theme attached to the sketches throughout. Sometimes the theming itself was limp. For example, after the mediocre *Bob Hope Lampoons Television 1985* special aired, Bob and crew revisited similar subject matter two months later with *Bob Hope's Comedy Salute to the Soaps*, and the results were just as unimpressive.

For a true change of pace, Bob allowed his writers to pursue a few mini-musicals with books, like a condensed Broadway production with a storyline. The results varied widely from arguably Bob's worst special (*Bob Hope in the Starmakers* in 1980) to one of his best (*NBC Investigates Bob Hope* in 1987). The latter has an interesting story from one of its writers.

"I resisted that idea from the beginning," says Gene Perret about doing a full-length parody of the Iran-Contra hearings. "In fact, I tried to talk Hope out of it, but there was no way. It was too current for him to abandon it."

Perret's objection was that the show's premise was unclear to him whether it was prosecuting or defending the behavior of Bob, playing a substitute for Col. Oliver North. "As I argued with Hope about it, he said, 'Well, fix it.' So I wrote a song called 'A Man is Innocent Until He's Proven Guilty.'" Fellow Hope writer Martha Bolton contributed to it, while Bob Alberti did an arrangement where the entire jury and courtroom became the backup singers. It earned all three Emmy nominations for Outstanding Original Music and Lyrics, the first time a Bob Hope special had appeared in the creative side of the Emmys since 1968. (Besides one technical nomination each for *Bob Hope's Overseas Christmas Tours Parts One and Two* in 1980 and *Bob Hope's USO Christmas in Beirut* in 1984, the other Emmy nomination this decade came for *Bob Hope's USO Christmas Show from the Persian Gulf* for Outstanding Sound Mixing For A Variety Series Or Special in 1988.)

Unfortunately, most of the writing was not as consistently pleasurable. Some of that had to do with restrictions Bob placed on content for his specials. His Christmas shows deepened a rut that had developed in 1975, with Bob insisting they always carry his duet with a female guest on "Silver Bells," the presentation of the AP All America Football Team, and worst of all Bob interviewing the Rose Queen, hardly a source for hilarity. Longtime Hope writer Bob Mills loathed handling the latter two assignments, which he said his boss would not change because the ratings for the Christmas shows were always strong.

"Hope interviewed the Queen, a seventeen- to eighteen-year-old rich kid from Pasadena or La Canada Flintridge, bastions of WASPism. It was murder coming up with that routine every year," he says. "The other one was the AP All America Football Team. Same format every year. Each player trotted out when his name was called, and Hope made a clever and hilarious remark. How many football jokes are there?"

Some of the inconsistency in scripting can be blamed in the first part of the decade to the producers Bob employed. He fired his daughter Linda Hope as producer, feeling she was not watching the budget as carefully as he wanted, and used a few freelance producers until relying mainly on Elliott Kozak. Those producers varied widely into how successful they worked with Hope, and the results of their relationship with Bob (or lack of one) often appeared on screen.

Bob also can be blamed for sometimes being a poor judge of what was funny to include on his specials. He allowed sexism to continue to creep in and demean his sets, as when Bob discussed an amendment to draft women in the Army on his Feb. 3, 1980 show ("Women soldiers can be very useful. They can stand behind a driver in a tank and tell him he's going the wrong way."). Also, an AIDS joke he told during a Liberty Weekend gala in New York City in 1986 was not televised, but many attendees were so offended and complained loudly enough that he had to apologize and do benefits raising funds for the cause.

In addition, Bob now cared very little about getting Emmy nominations for his work. He just gauged the quality of what he did on the number of viewers who turned out to see him. "Yes, he watched the ratings carefully," says Mills. "If a show failed, he'd always blame himself for not promoting it enough. Never blamed us."

Judging from the kind of ratings Bob got in the 1980s, he must have been doing a lot of blaming on himself.

**Bob's Numbers Become Iffy**

When the decade dawned, NBC, third among the three networks and desperate for a hit, had Bob make seven to eight specials each season in the early 1980s—amounts not seen since his early 1970s heyday—and make roughly half them ninety minutes or longer. Viewers were not only seeing more of Bob, they also were seeing more of him when they saw him. The overexposure made his ratings shaky, and soon Bob's specials were no longer a sure thing for the network.

The first big shock came on Nov. 21, 1982, when for the first time a Bob Hope special finished third in its time slot, running against *Gloria* on CBS and *Matt Houston* and the movie *Escape from Alcatraz* on ABC. However, at the end of the season, Bob rebounded, with his eightieth birthday special in May 1983 finishing number three for the week.

The up-and-down pattern continued over the next few seasons. His 1983 season opener fell in second place to a rerun of the season finale of *M*A*S*H*. *Bob Hope Goes to College* finished behind its ABC competition *The Fall Guy* two months later, while *Bob Hope's USO Christmas in Beirut* on Jan. 15, 1984 came in second to *The Jeffersons* and *Trapper John, M.D.*, opposite it on CBS. While Bob's 1984 birthday special finished fourteenth for the week, *The Concorde—Airport '79* debut on ABC beat it to finish third overall. At the start of the next season (1984-1985), *Bob Hope's Hilarious Unrehearsed Antics of the Stars* scored lower numbers than its competition on ABC, *Benson* and *Webster*, but his 1984 Christmas special three months later ranked third for the week.

Indeed, the Yuletide and birthday installments were the only real draws for big audiences to watch Bob by the mid-1980s. "The Christmas and birthday were probably more special because the occasion was more special," opines longtime Hope writer Gene Perret. "You had unique premises for the monologues, and you had plenty of idea for the sketches, too. You're right, these did often result in more attractive guests."

In the 1984-1985 season, NBC cut Bob back to just five specials a year—usually a season opener along with two specials between the Christmas and birthday shows—at the same time it zoomed up to number one in the network ratings race with hits like *The Cosby Show*, *Cheers*, *The A-Team*, *Highway to Heaven*, and more. NBC's decline in Bob's appearances soon coincided with less desire for viewers to watch him thereafter.

As confirmation of this development, a Nielsen rating survey for the 1986-1987 season found that while two of Bob's shows were among the top ten specials of the period, they were behind such offerings as the animated Garfield Christmas show and David Letterman's sixth anniversary celebration. Stuck in time slots considered conducive for success like on Thursdays following the runaway hit *The Cosby Show* or Saturdays after *The Golden Girls*, Bob's specials would finish in the top ten or twenty. Such was the case for his eighty-fifth birthday show in May 1988, when he replaced the hit *ALF* and more on Monday night and got a sixth-place finish as a result. (On the eve of that special, Bob admitted to a reporter that ABC had wooed him to join the network a few years earlier. "I thought I was going to go," he said without divulging why he stayed with NBC.)

However, when pre-empting a series not as strong, as Bob did in January and March 1989 with the struggling sitcom *227*, his ratings would slump to number twenty-eight and thirty-six, respectively. Bob's annual birthday celebration on NBC's weak Wednesday in May 1989 was similarly disappointing, finishing thirty-fifth for the week and coming in third in its time slot.

Texaco apparently was fine with the yo-yo ratings, as it remained a sponsor throughout the decade and continued using Bob as its commercial spokesman, making the company Bob's longest advertiser ever. Network executives did not share the same enthusiasm, however.

Taking stock of Bob's results, and keen on promoting an up-and-coming comedian NBC had signed, programming head Warren Littlefield decided during the 1989-1990 season that Bob would have two hours less airtime in order for the network to afford producing four half-hour trial episodes of a new series. The project was *Seinfeld*, named in honor of its star, Jerry Seinfeld.

Inadvertently, Bob had given NBC its biggest hit comedy of the 1990s. That same decade would prove to be more problematic for him. Even given that, Bob entered it from the end of the 1980s as a comedy giant, though not necessarily an idol that many other comedians wanted to emulate, due to the tired sketches and forced humor increasingly on display in his specials that weighed them down. Luckily, that was not the case for everything, including his first one of the decade.

## *The Bob Hope Special*: "Hope, Women and Song"
Jan. 21, 1980, Monday 9-10 p.m.

Beatrice Arthur, Debby Boone, Diahann Carroll, Shirley Jones. Cameo: Kathryn Crosby.

A vaudeville-style Bob Hope special taped in Pasadena, California, for the Bing Crosby Youth Fund, this is quite enjoyable given that Bob and the ladies are bringing their talents full throttle to the event. Bob presents a monologue that includes references to Pat Boone (Debby's father) before he sports a top hat and cane to do an opening song and dance number with his guest stars. Then Bob dons a straw hat to do some old routines with them interrupting him as well, such as Beatrice Arthur slowly walking across the stage with a glass of water and stopping to stare at Bob repeatedly. During her fourth pass by him, Bob asks what's she is doing, and she tells him she is putting out a fire in her room. It's the same joke Sid Gould did during the hospital sketch on Bob's March 25, 1977 special, but Bea's delivery makes it fresh and enjoyable. Numbers by Diahann Carroll, Shirley Jones, Bea and Debby follow, with Bob joining Shirley and Debby for duets, and all look and sound glamorous and vivacious. Bob then recreates doing his old radio show with the cast, and they score even with reading the scripts into a mike like old times sake. There is mostly more singing after that by all involved, which usually can be wearying on a Hope special, but the camaraderie and chemistry on display overcome such complaints. Kathryn Crosby thanking Bob for the money he has helped raise is a delight as well.

Bob and Show: \*\*\*\*

## *Bob Hope's Overseas Christmas Tours Parts One and Two*: "Around the World with the Troops"
Feb. 3 and 10, 1980, Sunday 8-11 p.m.

P/D: Andrew Solt, Malcolm Leo. W: Andrew Solt (additional material). Background Music: Bob Alberti.

A warmly nostalgic if slightly overextended series of filmed highlights focusing on Bob's USO work going back to the 1940s (including years when America was not at war), these two weeks of specials have new monologues recorded at the start of each before showing a barrage of clips. For the first, Bob says, "I just want to also warn you that this is the start of a three-hour show, and next Sunday, we do three hours more. Imagine six hours of me?" He takes stock of Paul McCartney's drug bust in Japan, the presidential election campaign, and the Olympics in a mild set. At the outset of the second show, Bob wryly notes, "Just to stay in the mood, I've been sleeping in a foxhole." He also has a string of odd jokes about stamps before mentioning a new one has been issued commemorating W.C. Fields, with whom Bob co-starred in *The Big Broadcast of 1938*. "It's not true that he hated children. He liked me!" Bob adds. The rest is expertly edited pieces of shows over forty years with some theming given, such as a salute to Jerry Colonna, along with new narration by Bob.

Bob: *** Show: ****

**Bob Hope in the Starmakers**
March 17, 1980, Monday 9-10 p.m.

Cast: Bob Hope (Miles Badeuk), Bernadette Peters (Sally the secretary), Robert Urich (Ace Robbins), Linda Gray (Wendy Truesdale), Robert Guillaume (actor), Gallagher (himself), Elaine Joyce (actress), Conrad Janis (Roman Lear). EP: Linda Hope. P/W: Sheldon Keller. D: Sid Smith. W: Bryan Blackburn. Choreography: Carl Jablonski.

Any special that includes among its guests the ape from *B.J. and the Bear* and dubs in applause for the creature's appearance is asking for trouble. One of Bob's worst ever outings, its storyline is trite and stretched thin, and its nonstop parade of "jokes" thud when delivered. Bob plays talent agent Miles, whose company is in a slump until actor Ace Robbins offers him $5,000 to become his partner in the venture. Sally, Miles' secretary, fantasizes about being with Ace, but the actor only has eyes for Wendy Truesdale, a star on "Levitz's Lovelies" who left Miles when she became a success but now offers him a shot at the big time by casting a replacement on her series. This involves interviewing a lot of ladies in bathing suits including Elaine Joyce, but none work out. It takes producer Roman Lear to inform everyone that Sally can and should do the role, leading to the unsurprising finish of Ace falling in love with Sally and Miles reconciling with Wendy. Between everything, Robert Guillaume sings and comedian Gallagher does his shtick to an unimpressed Miles. This is an awful videotaped mess, cheaply and quickly shot on mostly two sets, and Bob's supposedly dramatic moments with Linda Gray lack credibility. Plus, with innumerable bad one liners like Miles telling Ace, "You're the only Texan I've met who's got a ten-gallon tongue," the entire enterprise is unworthy of both Bob and the audience's time.

Bob: ** Show: *

*Bob Hope's All Star Comedy Birthday Party*: "A USO Salute"
May 28, 1980, Wednesday 9:30-11 p.m.

Loni Anderson, Andy Gibb, Randy Gardner and Tai Babilonia, Andy Gibb, Delores Hope, Barbara Mandrell, Diana Ross, Admiral Alan Shepard, Kenneth Mars, The Air Force Academy Choir. EP/W: James Lipton (special material). P: Linda Hope. D: Kip Walton.

At the U.S. Air Force Academy in Colorado Springs, Colorado, Bob appears to parachute from the sky before starting his monologue, a trick that will be reprised in his 1982 birthday special. He jokes about the altitude ("I'm sharing an oxygen tent with Loni Anderson"), weather ("They have four seasons up here: June, winter, winter and winter"), and more before hitting on the presidential election. It is all strong. Diana Ross sings "Ain't No Mountain High Enough" magnificently before she and Bob do a rousing medley of "flying" songs. Next, the commandant (Kenneth Mars) meets a new colonel (Loni Anderson) to investigate the academy's oldest cadet (Bob). She tries to seduce him, then plays a word association game where his wacky answers make her conclude, "You are definitely officer material!" Andy Gibb sings "Desire," and Randy Gardner and Tai Babilonia perform a fine ice skating pairs routine. Loni has suggestive dialogue with Bob and even gives him a kiss because it's his birthday. "Maybe it was a little underhanded, but it was the result that counts!" he tells the audience. "The fantastic Barbara Mandrell" sings her country hit "Crackers" before Bob plays a hillbilly singer recruited by a talent scout (Andy) to the pleasure of Bob's mom (Loni) and Bob's girlfriend (Barbara). This bit creaks along. After Diana gets audience members to sing "Reach Out and Touch Somebody's Hand" and the Air Force Academy Choir presents patriotic tunes, Admiral Alan Shepard introduces Delores Hope to sing "The Best is Yet to Come," and she sings "Happy Birthday To You" to her husband after his traditional special lyrics for "Thanks for the Memory" close a fairly breezy ninety minutes.

Bob and Show: ****

## *Bob Hope's All Star Look at TV's Prime Time Wars*
Sept. 6, 1980, Saturday 9-10 p.m.

Willie Aames, Claude Akins, Loni Anderson, Cathy Lee Crosby, Howard Duff, Barbara Eden, Erik Estrada, Gil Gerard, Charlotte Rae, Brooke Shields, Stella Stevens, Danny Thomas, Larry Wilcox.

Bob calls the actors strike "Stars Wars" and says all are picketing from their good side. He says Shelley Winters will not take the situation lying down, referencing the many sexual escapades in her new memoirs. Also mentioned are summer movies, the presidential election, and drugs among professional basketball players in a very good set. For skits, first up is "Amarillo," a spoof of *Dallas* with Charlotte Rae as the mom, Danny Thomas as the dad, Loni Anderson as "Dew Melon," and Bob as the evil B.H., who was a flasher when he was six years old. His daughter is Brooke Shields, and her boyfriend is Erik Estrada. All are suspects in shooting B.H., but they determine the audience is doing it instead. It is rollicking good fun, but the rest isn't. "That's Impossible" has Cathy Lee Crosby parodying her show *That's Incredible* with things like Claude Akins trying to open a childproof bottle, and Bob interviews conjoined twins Danny and Howard Duff, who constantly bicker. Imagining a newscast as a variety show already was done better on *Rowan and Martin's Laugh-In*, and adding the dog from *Here's Boomer* does not help, no matter how much the laugh track squeals. Barbara Eden's take on "Come in from the Rain" is better than the off-and-on *Charlie's Angels* spoof with Bob, Danny and Larry Wilcox as the ladies. If everything had been on the level of the monologue and the first skit, this would have been possibly five stars instead of three.

Bob and Show: ***


## *Hope for President*
Nov. 1, 1980, Saturday 8-10 p.m.

Tracey Austin, Mr. Bill, Johnny Carson, Sammy Davis Jr., Angie Dickinson, Lou Ferrigno, President Gerald Ford, Senator Henry Jackson, Barbara Jordan, Jayne Kennedy, Harvey Korman, Louis Nye, Gary Owens, Miss America Susan Powell, Stefanie Powers, Tony Randall, Vidal Sassoon, Brooke Shields, Toni Tennille, The UCLA Fife and Drums Corps, Jonathan Winters. EP: Linda Hope. P/Special Musical Material: Ken

Welch, Mitzie Welch. D: Kip Walton. W: Stan Hart, Chris Hart, Mitzie Welch, Stephen Perani, Pacy Markman. Choreographer: Don Crichton.

Too many flaccid bits over two hours makes this a bomb. After classic clips with Bob's quips about previous presidents, the host takes shots at Halloween, the new TV season, and of course the presidential election ("The debate was held in Cleveland. That's the greatest thing to happen there since I left."). Then planted actors in the audience yell out for Bob to run for president, and the studio seating transforms into a convention with the UCLA Fife and Drums Corps leading a big production number. From there, Tony Randall wears down Bob to be his campaign manager in a deadly dull bit. It perks up with Johnny Carson putting Bob's name into nomination and humorously giving Bob's biography in the process, and the clay figure Mr. Bill getting electrocuted by Mr. Hand for voting for Bob. The show stumbles thereafter. Toni Tennille interviews people on the street for support of Bob. Sammy Davis Jr. does a long song and dance routine in concert with Bob as the latter unsuccessfully woos him to be his vice presidential pick. Gary Owens, a cohost of "Showdown 80" with Jayne Kennedy, interviews Jonathan Winters as several characters about Hope, while Bob cannot get a disgusted Gerald Ford nor Senator Henry Jackson nor Barbara Jordan to run with him. Tony directs Bob in a campaign commercial, but Bob is so dependent on cue cards that he confuses a black man (an unbilled Meshach Taylor) with a Jewish supporter, then gets sick from of all the ethnic foods he eats. Celebrities do cameos to endorse Bob, while Angie Dickinson and Stefanie Powers have problems marketing Bob to women's groups until Miss America Susan Powell accepts being his running mate. Large crowds support Bob at places he visits across America, and he demurs from using the tedious dirty tricks Louis Nye offers him to assure a win. But a boy notes that since Bob was born in England, he cannot be president. A contrite Bob then urges Americans to get out and vote. This is almost as enervating to watch as a real presidential campaign.

Bob: *** Show: **


***Bob Hope's All Star Comedy Christmas Special***
Dec. 16, 1980, Tuesday 8-9 p.m.

Loni Anderson, Larry Gatlin and the Gatlin Brothers Band, Loretta Swit, The AP All America Football Team, The Rose Queen and Her Court. P: Linda Hope. D: Sid Smith. W: Gail Lawrence, Pete T. Rich.

After a good monologue, the rest is too mild to make much of an impression. Bob manages to combine Ronald Reagan beating Jimmy Carter for president with the highly-watched "Who Shot J.R.?" episode of *Dallas* with "Did you know that more people watch Kristin shoot J.R. than voted for president?! I guess it was sort of the same thing though. Two Southerners were put out of work." Then, to celebrate the hundredth anniversary of the Salvation Army, Loni Anderson plays a bell ringer opposite Bob as a rundown gambling addict who impersonates Fu Manchu and even Santa Claus to get $200 from Loni's organization. It never sparks. Many of the AP All America Football Team members, which include Herschel Walker and Lawrence Taylor, deservedly give Bob a double take for his exaggerated comments about how strong and tough they are. The most hilarious part is them singing new lyrics to "Deck the Halls" in honor of bowl games. After the Rose Queen and Her Court appear, Loretta Swit chats amiably with Bob about her experience playing a nurse on *M\*A\*S\*H* and her work for animal rights. Larry Gatlin and the Gatlin Brothers Band sing their country hit "Take Me to Your Lovin' Place" before Larry jokes with Bob, and Loni's recent TV-movie role as Jayne Mansfield gets Bob to reminisce fondly about working with her. Bob and Loretta play mannequins who come to life after a store closes before both sing "Silver Bells," and that's about it. And that ain't much.

Bob: \*\*\* Show: \*\*

## *Bob Hope's 30th Anniversary Television Special*
Jan. 18, 1981, Sunday 9-11 p.m.

Ann-Margret, Lucille Ball, Milton Berle, George Burns, Glen Campbell, Sammy Davis Jr., Douglas Fairbanks Jr., Eydie Gorme, Steve Lawrence, Marie Osmond, Brooke Shields, Fred Silverman, Danny Thomas, Tanya Tucker, Robert Urich. P: Linda Hope. D: Kip Walton.

This is another clip show broken up by brief new bits by mostly returning guests plus Fred Silverman, then the president of NBC at the time (he would lose the job later this year due to NBC being in third place among the networks). Since it was not viewed, it is not rated.

*Bob Hope's Funny Valentine*
Feb. 11, 1981, Wednesday 9-10 p.m.

Dr. Joyce Brothers, Cathy Lee Crosby, Phyllis Diller, Barbara Mandrell, Charlene Tilton. W: Bob Keane. Choreography: Don Crichton.

The video equivalent of a stale box of chocolates, this show uses the pretext of Bob writing a romance newspaper column called "Dear Bob, Advice to the Lovelorn." Stumped on how to answer a letter, Dr. Joyce Brothers appears and gives Bob lines to set up jokes. Impressed, Bob even makes a pass at her which she quickly rebuffs. Getting back to his correspondence, Bob imagines he is dating Cathy Lee Crosby as Donald Drab. This is fairly funny, but his next vision of being a vain quarterback disdaining an admirer (Charlene Tilton) is deadly, as is Bob's fake banter and duet with Barbara Mandrell. Better is Phyllis Diller as a princess who kisses a frog (Bob) that still acts like one while being a man. He tells her he likes her because she draws flies. It ends with them kissing again and Phyllis becoming a frog. Phyllis also gets to play the piano and do an amusing monologue. Unfortunately, negating much of this is an irritating bit where Bob asks innumerable questions of Cathy Lee Crosby to make her say the name of her series, *That's Incredible*, along with a lousy skit of Bob, Charlene, and Cathy at a florist shop where they all sing "My Funny Valentine" weakly. Bob's monologue has largely mediocre jokes too about the Reagans, the Oscars, and female mud wrestling ("You don't know what you've got till you hose her down."). If this show were a Valentine's Day gift card, most would return it or crumple it up.

Bob: *** Show: **


*Bob Hope's Spring Fling*
April 13, 1981, Monday 9-10 p.m.

Loni Anderson, Brooke Shields, Jill St. John, Melissa Manchester, Teri Copley, Donna Dixon. D: Norman Abbott. W: Bob Keane. Bob Hope credited as producer, no EP listed.

Spring flop is more like it. After a short six-minute monologue, Bob talks with Brooke Shields before they enact "Lady Di, or Not So Ordinary People," with Brooke as Princess Diana encountering an elderly fox hunter (Bob). Brooke is still learning her comedic chops, and the sketch is static in its staging for what is supposed to be a race. Melissa

Manchester appears next in a tuxedo under a soft-focus lens performing "As Time Goes By" in a setting designed to approximate *Casablanca*—if *Casablanca* had been shot in color. Then it is the standard byplay between Bob and Loni Anderson, followed by "8:30 to 5:30, or Beauty & the Beast, Part II," a takeoff on the movie *9 to 5* with Bob as a lecherous boss in lustful pursuit of his secretary (Loni). He even uses a rope to trip her so that she lands in his arms. However, Loni gets revenge by gluing Bob to a chair, spraying him with water. spreading food on his face, and fooling him to kiss an inflatable woman. This childish slapstick feels longer than the full-length feature it spoofs. Morgan Fairchild, Donna Dixon and Teri Copley appear during individual "photo shoots" to stop and talk with Bob. All are weak in generating laughs. Melissa reappears to sing solo and with Bob, then it's Jill St. John's turn to work with Bob in "Bunnies or You Light Up My Hutch," where the duo play rabbits making their rounds for Easter. That kind of humor makes this fling deserve to be flung away.

Bob: \*\*\* Show: \*\*


***Bob Hope's All-Star Comedy Birthday Party at West Point*: "A USO Salute"**
May 25, 1981, Monday 8-10 p.m.

Glen Campbell, Delores Hope, Sugar Ray Leonard, Mary Martin, Marie Osmond, Mickey Rooney, George C. Scott, Brooke Shields, Robert Urich, the cast of *42$^{nd}$ Street*. EP/W: James Lipton. P: Mike Gargiulo. W: Charles Isaacs. Choreographer: Carl Jablonski.

"All of you are here because you couldn't get three-day passes, right?" Bob asks the cadets. His jokes about their outfits and life in general all score well. After that, Marie Osmond does "Mr. Sandman" and "Celebration" joined by nearly forty midshipmen on stage dancing in formation with her. George C. Scott gets a standing ovation, then barks at Bob, "You're slouching!" in the manner of his famous role in *Patton*. His interplay with Bob is golden, including their discussion about George's refusal to accept the Oscar for Best Actor for the movie and Bob saying he would take the statuette under any circumstances. A similar talk with Glen Campbell has the latter bemoaning his touring schedule before doing "Rhinestone Cowboy." Bob plays the new roommate for Marie and Brooke Shields, until Glen busts him. It's sporadically funny, as is Bob's dialogue with Sugar Ray Leonard and

Mary Martin. The latter's song is upstaged by the Broadway cast of *42nd Street* superbly performing a big production number of "We're in the Money" from the musical. Bob, Glen and Robert Urich play hapless cadets in West Point's first class of 1802 under the leadership of Mickey Rooney until an Indian (George) and his daughter (Brooke) want to take back their land and plan condos. It's very good thanks to George and Mickey's acting. Mickey is also sprightly talking to Bob, Robert and Brooke are less so. Delores Hope sings "Young at Heart" before Lt. Gen. Andrew J. Goodpaster, superintendent of West Point, introduces Vice President George H.W. Bush, who pays tribute to Bob. Everyone gets a piece of cake as this variably enjoyable affair ends.

Bob: **** Show: ***


***Bob Hope's All-Star Comedy Look at the New Season*: "It's Still Free and Well Worth It!"**
Sept. 27, 1981, Sunday 8-9 p.m.

Loni Anderson. Cathy Lee Crosby, Barbara Eden, Linda Evans, Bruce Jenner, Merlin Olsen, Cheryl Tiegs. Featured: Kelly Lange. D: Kip Walton. W: Jeffrey Barron. No producer listed.

Apart from seeing Bruce Jenner in drag prior to transitioning to Caitlyn Jenner (as one of the "Mandrake Sisters" along with Bob and Merlin Olsen doing "Take This Job and Shove It" to send up *Barbara Mandrell and The Mandrell Sisters*), this is trivial. Bob's solid monologue hits award shows ("I love spectator sports"), *Superman II* (where he reuses his Dec. 22, 1978 special joke on the first *Superman* movie: "Why pay to see a guy in tight leotards when you can cruise Hollywood Boulevard for nothing?") and politics ("In Washington, Nancy Reagan has come up with a new china policy"). He scores highly with, "My wife Delores went on the grapefruit diet. That was murder. Every time I hugged her, she squirted in my eye." Then newscaster Kelly Lange interviews Barbara Eden, Linda Evans, Cathy Lee Crosby, and Loni Anderson on strike over women being exploited on TV. They call for gender reversals that are enacted, like "Ms.M*A*S*H" with the ladies as doctors and Bob as "Hot Hips"; "Bonnie Miller" with Barbara in the title role; and "The Duchesses of Hazzard" with Linda and Loni as the Duchess sisters and Barbara as Boss Hogg. All are bad, as is "Six Minutes" (Merlin talking to Bob, an unimpressed coot) and "Son of Shogun" (Bob avoid Merlin's efforts to kill him and marries three women). Bob makes a strong pitch for the "Get High on Yourself" campaign with Cathy Lee and Cheryl Tiegs at the end. Committed to his characters in every skit, he is great, but the show grates.

Bob: **** Show: **

*A Bob Hope Celebration*
Oct. 22, 1981, Thursday 8-10 p.m.

Pearl Bailey, Debby Boone, Foster Brooks, Glen Campbell, Sammy Davis Jr., Betty Ford (unbilled), Gordon MacRae, Tony Orlando, Mark Russell, Danny Thomas, The U.S. Air Force Presidential Drill Team, The U.S. Army Chorus, The University of Michigan Marching Band. P: William O. Harbach. D: Tony Charmoli. Special Musical Material: Ray Charles.

Promoting the dedication of the Gerald R. Ford Museum in Grand Rapids, Michigan, the ex-president tours the facility with Bob between entertainment meant to please an upscale middle-aged and older audience. President Ronald Reagan, First Lady Nancy Reagan, Vice President George W. Bush, Lady Bird Johnson and more stand for the national anthem before the high-stepping University of Michigan Marching Band plays its fight song and exits around Bob when he enters. His monologue about the honoree's career and bad golf game as well as the current president are pretty funny, but at twelve minutes, it nearly overstays its welcome. Sammy Davis Jr., Glen Campbell, and Danny Thomas join Bob to talk and sing about golf tournaments they each host. After Pearl Bailey presents "One Day at a Time" in her own inimitable style, Foster Brooks gives a wonderful drunk routine. Tony Orlando and Debby Boone do "Tie a Yellow Ribbon Round the Ole Oak Tree" and "Home" from *The Wiz* respectively before Mark Russell gently needles the politicos. In a charming moment, Bob does "Once in Love with Amy" with lyrics retitled for him to dance with Betty Ford. The U.S. Air Force Presidential Drill Team precedes Glen doing "All the Way" and Gordon MacRae offering "New York New York" (two Sinatra tunes without Frank—hmm…). Danny's somewhat sanctimonious routine about his life is a weak point, as his talk with Bob afterward. Sammy getting everyone to clap with him on "The Birth of the Blues" is the closest thing to a showstopper here, but his routine with Bob joking about furniture stops the show in a different way. The U.S. Army Chorus perform "The Battle

Hymn of the Republic" and Bob does "Thanks for the Memory" with new lyrics to end a long, choppy, occasionally enjoyable show.

Bob and Show: ***

**Bob Hope's Stand up and Cheer National Football League's 60*th* Year**
Nov. 22, 1981, Sunday 8-10 p.m.

Elizabeth Taylor, O.J. Simpson, Olivia Newton-John, Barbara Mandrell, Howard Cosell, Michael Conrad, Susan Anton, Joe Namath, Don Knotts, George Gobel, Betty White, Roger Staubach, Rosey Grier, George Allen, George Blanda, Dick Butkus, Weeb Ewbank, Bob Lilly, Hank Stram, Garo Yepremian. Featured: Fritzi Burr, Terry Burns, John Harlan. P: Jane Upton Bell. D: Dick Harwood. W: Harvey Berger, Ivan Ladizinsky. Special Musical Material: Ray Charles. Olivia Newton-John's Choreography: Kenny Ortega.

Classic NFL clips and a lively score help this long and lumpy show. Bob jokes about Thanksgiving, football, and Princess Diana's first child, then tells Olivia Newton-John he will star in a sequel to her movie *Grease* called "Lard." She does "Physical" with Dick Butkus, Rosey Grier and Bob Lilly working out in a stylized gym along with four male dancers in skimpy football outfits. Next, the Shady Glen Rest Home for Coaches has George Allen, Weeb Ewbank, Hank Stram, and Bob faking being crazy to Betty White to get more time to play poker. It's modestly funny. After he narrates old NFL clips and photos with O.J. Simpson, Bob enacts a sloppy skit as a quarterback with a girlfriend (Barbara Mandrell) and tough coach (Michael Conrad). Howard Cosell has good chitchat with Bob before playing himself at home with his wife (Betty), who talks over Howard using his usual flowery language for mild results. Better is Don Knotts as a beleaguered referee, who's so good Bob has him bow at the end. After a two-minute montage of O.J.'s highlights and more film clips, George Gobel serves as an interpreter for a Polish placekicker (Garo Yepremian). It's amusing, as is Garo singing with Bob and George. Then the NFL's first female commissioner (Elizabeth Taylor) hears complaints about a team owner (Bob) from O.J., George Blanda and Joe Namath in a silly skit where she ends up mesmerized by the men. Elizabeth's banter with Bob afterward is better. A Barbara Mandrell song, more clips, and Bob doing "Button Up Your Overcoat" with Susan Anton are acceptable, but Dick, Rosey, and Bob Lilly "singing" a spoof of "Nine to Five" to lineman who block and tackle is an assault on the ears that should have been penalized fifteen yards. Roger Staubach bantering with Bob is surprisingly funny ("You ever play football, Bob?" "Yeah, when I was a kid." "No, I mean since they made the ball pointy."). Bob's talk with George Allen, Weeb and Hank is better in the unscripted parts, but his new lyrics to "Thanks for the Memory" and warm words to the NFL at the end give this a nice glow at the end.

Bob and Show: ***


***Bob Hope's Christmas Special*: "A Time of Cheer, A Time for Hope"**
Dec. 20, 1981, Sunday 8-9 p.m.

Loni Anderson, The AP All America Football Team, Brooke Shields, The Rose Queen and Her Court, Andy Williams. Featured: Joan Crosby, Eddie Marr, Danny Rodgers. D: Kip Walton. W: Charles Lee. Bob Hope credited as both P and EP.

Apart from the team players, this show coasts on the seasonal goodwill for its meager appeal. His monologue about Washington, D.C. ("It's nice for a change, they have nature provide the snow job."), football ("There's a Fruit Bowl too. There's no running, everybody skips.") and fog in Los Angeles go over better then than now. Bob and Loni Anderson then play astronauts on the space shuttle, and Bob gets away with saying his favorite radio station is "WKRP in Uranus." He paws her constantly, but she is more upset he made their re-entry mechanism into a Christmas tree, preventing them from getting back to Earth. Between lines like Loni saying "Santa is based solely on conjecture" and Bob responding, "Really? I thought he was based on the North Pole," and short aliens arriving to wish them peace and sing "Jingle Bells," this stinks. The AP All America Football Team, including Jim McMahon, Herschel Walker, and Marcus Allen, has more chuckles than usual, and the audience loves it too. Andy Williams sings a new Christmas song and plugs his upcoming golf tournament with Bob with trivial dialogue before they do "Small Fry," the fourth time Bob has done this routine in as many decades. Bob does a nice soft-shoe routine with the Rose Queen, but otherwise the segment is negligible entertainment. So is Bob as a shabby tenant with a genie (Brooke Shields) who helps him deal with his crabby landlord. Loni joins Bob to do "Silver Bells" before this Yuletide yawner ends.

Bob: *** Show: **

## Bob Hope's Women I Love Beautiful But Funny
Feb. 28, 1982, Sunday 8-10 p.m.

Lucille Ball, Milton Berle, Delores Hope, Gina Lollobrigida, Marie Osmond. P: Robert D. Hussey. D: Kip Walton.

With references to miniskirts, the movie *Tora! Tora! Tora!* (which Bob says with one "Tora!" omitted), and Bob saying his swing is like Shirley Jones's, some comedy here seems stuck in 1970 rather than 1982. It definitely is sexist, as a show saluting the fairer sex has as one guest Milton Berle in drag ("They did name a pansy after me," he coos, showing the gay humor is circa 1970 too). The plusses are a beautiful set without the usual curtain behind Bob, a few good lines by the host ("Goose bumps on Dolly Parton—that'd be like a snowflake on the Matterhorn") and great jobs with fake banter by Lucille Ball and Milton. Bob talks with them between mostly good clips of more than seventy female guests since 1951 including Lassie, and Delores does fine singing "Just the Way You Are." It's nice but not essential Bob Hope. Still, Marie Osmond says of all the Bob Hope specials she did, "That was the best. Lucille Ball was one of my favorites of all time. She was absolutely intelligent, she knew what she was doing, and she was so smart in her comedy. And I loved Gina Lollobrigida, because she was very nice."

Bob and Show: ***

## Bob Hope Laughs with the Movie Awards
March 28, 1982, Sunday 8-9 p.m.

Pat Boone, George Burns, Ann Jillian, Lee Marvin. Featured: Joe Donte, Lance Gordon. D: Sid Smith. No producer listed.

George Burns and Lee Marvin are the only reasons that prevent this collection of mundane movie sendups from getting one star. Bob first disdains the Oscars with quips like "Just getting a bunch of votes doesn't prove you're an actor. Look at Ronald Reagan." He follows it with jabs at taxes ("This is when our government of the people, by the people and for the people does it to the people"), heavy rain in California ("My star in Hollywood is now in Tijuana"), diets and more. It's a funny set that flows well, neither of which applies to a spoof of *Reds* called "Pinks" with Pat Boone, Ann Jillian and Bob as a Russian, nor of "Frantic City," a takeoff of *Atlantic City* with Bob and Ann. George's amusing talk with Bob about his recent visit to England is a definite improvement (Bob: "Did you curtsy when you met [Princess Diana]?" George: "No, if I got down, I'd still be there, trying to get up."). However, Ann singing "I'm Coming Home Again" offers little excitement, while a twelve-minute parody of *Wings* (the first Academy Award winner for Best Picture) gets its only spark by Lee as a cranky leader and makes one yearn for how *The Carol Burnett Show* did this better. "Chariots of Ire" with Bob, Pat and Lee have them playing prissy English athletes to dismal results too. Ann comes out as Mae West to promote her upcoming TV-movie on the actress near the end, but even her swagger cannot save this sluggish show.

Bob: *** Show: **

*Bob Hope Stars Over Texas*
May 3, 1982, Monday 9-10 p.m.

Jack Lemmon, Morgan Fairchild, Larry Gatlin and the Gatlin Brothers, Dottie West, Miss Texas Lu Ann Caughey.

Bob hosts a show at the University of Texas in Austin with a slant toward country music in this installment. It honors the Senior Tour players in the Legends of Golf tournament, which explains the inclusion of amateur duffer Jack Lemmon.

*All Hands on Deck for Bob Hope's All Star Birthday Party at Annapolis*
May 25, 1982, Tuesday 8-10 p.m.

Christie Brinkley, James Coburn, Secretary of State Alexander Haig, Charlton Heston, Delores Hope, Leslie Nielsen, Bernadette Peters, Brooke Shields, Roger Staubach, Hinton Battle, Gregg Burge, Phyllis Hyman, Gerry Cooney, Larry Holmes, Sammy Davis Jr., Robert Goulet, Don King. Featured: Eddie Marr. EP/W: James Lipton. Music: Bob Alberti. Choreography: Carl Jablonski.

Bob's monologue and performances by Hinton Battle, Gregg Burge, and Phyllis Hyman from Broadway's *Sophisticated Ladies* are about all to enjoy for this tired and tiring entry. The host wins over everyone at the start with "Annapolis—that's an old Indian word meaning, 'Warden, get me out of here!'" He says honoring the Navy for his party was strategic: "We wanted to do my birthday show near water in case they light all the candles in the cake." He cedes the stage for Bernadette Peters to do a good routine to "We're in the Money" with six midshipmen. Then come stale skits. Brooke Shields and Christie Brinkley are the first female plebes under a senior officer (Bob), who is warned by James Coburn about the arrival of a new female commander (Bernadette), who's really an actress who fools Bob out of leadership. Bob banters with Brooke and then Roger Staubach, who badly plays a recruit tempted to play football for Navy by Bob and Bernadette and for Notre Dame by James and Christie. Another bit of interplay with Bob and a guest is forced (James Coburn on *The Magnificent Seven*: "The only bright spot in our cast was Yul Brynner's head!"). Much worse is Bob playing Washington crossing the Delaware and, in segments taped in Palm Springs and Las Vegas, a boxer opposite Larry Holmes and Gerry Cooney, with Leslie Nielsen and Charlton Heston as his trainers and Robert Goulet, Sammy Davis Jr. and Don King as themselves in cameos. Secretary of State Alexander Haig trying to be funny adds to the pain until the cast finally cuts a giant cake to celebrate the occasion and end the show.

Bob: **** Show: **

### *Bob Hope's Star-Studded Spoof of the New TV Season*: "G Rated—with Glamour, Glitter and Gags"
Oct. 3, 1982, Sunday 8-9 p.m.

Elizabeth Taylor, Richard Burton, Tom Selleck, Linda Evans, Brooke Shields, Ricky Schroder, Milton Berle, Glenn Ford, Tony Geary, Gavin MacLeod, Billy Barty. Featured: Doris Roberts.

In this special's featured sketch, a spoof on *General Hospital*, Bob plays an incompetent surgeon assisted by two nurses, Doris Roberts and Elizabeth Taylor. Elizabeth throws herself at Glenn Ford and then Tony Geary, both hidden, and promises to go to Acapulco with each one separately once the operation is over. Bob is oblivious to what is happening, believing Elizabeth really loves him. He finishes the surgery and gets Richard Burton up off his feet, who takes Elizabeth in his hands and plans to go to Puerto Vallarta with her. Bob will manage to get Taylor to do his show one more time, for his 1986 birthday special.

## Bob Hope's Pink Panther Thanksgiving Gala
Nov. 21, 1982, Sunday 8-10 p.m.

Julie Andrews, Dean Martin, Dudley Moore, Willie Nelson, Bernadette Peters, Robert Preston, Robert Wagner. Featured: Richard Adams, Tom Grantham, Tim Stone. P: William O. Harbach. Co-P: Rita Scott. D: Tony Charmoli. Special Musical Material: Jay Livingston.

The animated cartoon version of the Panther appears in the titles in this odd promotion for *Trail of the Pink Panther*, an attempted continuation of the series following Peter Sellers' death. Bob muses about President Ronald Reagan ("I think he'll run again. Actors love reruns."), Thanksgiving ("You know what a turkey is? That's an eagle designed by Congress"), and other topics. Bernadette Peters does Cole Porter's "Let's Misbehave" with two male dancers before Bob introduces the first of several clips from the Panther pictures interspersed here. Bob, Dean Martin, Robert Preston and Robert Wagner play pro football players singing about their strike. They are upstaged by Willie Nelson performing his hit "Always on My Mind." Following another clip, Julie Andrews sings a "citified" country tune, but surprisingly her banter with Bob is more fun. A skit with President Reagan (Bob in a black toupee), Nancy Reagan (Bernadette), Vice President George H.W. Bush (Dean), David Stockman (Robert Wagner) and Senator Ed O'Neill (Robert Preston) flounders badly. Dudley Moore plays the theme from the movie *10* before he unveils his dry wit opposite Bob. Dean sings "Bumming Around" and jokes with Bob. Julie and Robert Preston do "You and Me" from *Victor/Victoria*, then Robert talks with Bob for some laughs, as does Robert Wagner. Willie Nelson sings again, then a clip from the new film plays, concluding a choppy preview combined with a typical Hope special and Bob stumbling a lot through his introductions. For better and more consistent laughs, watch any Pink Panther movie with Peter Sellers instead of this.

Bob and Show: **

## The Merriest of the Merry: Bob Hope's Christmas Show: "A Bagful of Comedy"
Dec. 20, 1982, Monday 8-9 p.m.

Mac Davis, Loni Anderson, The AP All America Football Team, Phyllis Diller, The Rose Queen and Her Court, Olivia Newton-John. D: Sid Smith. No producer credited.

Another year, another disappointing Hope Yuletide special. Bob talks about Christmas, taxes on gasoline ("And you know, there's a lot of Sunday drivers around nowadays? That's because it takes six days to save up enough to go for a ride."), new books and airline price wars. Then a new talking robot (Loni Anderson) meets a battling couple (Bob and Phyllis Diller) at Santa's workshop. Phyllis responds to Loni's taunts by leaving with a polar bear. It's that kind of a skit. Bob asks Herschel Walker, part of the AP All America Football Team, "How do you feel about winning the Heisman [Award]?" Herschel responds, "The same way you do when you when an Oscar." Also seen are Eric Dickerson, John Elway, and Wilber Marshall. The Rose Queen bit is a bore, as is Mac Davis singing his minor country song "Lying Here Lying." A monologue by Phyllis gives the show its only spark, as she jokes about her husband ("Once he took the kids and me out for donuts and coffee. The kids loved it because they had never given blood before.") and her looks ("Last time I had a physical exam, I had to coax the doctor off the ledge."). Olivia Newton-John sings "Silver Bells" with Bob before Loni tells Bob she is just good friends with future husband Burt Reynolds in an otherwise dull segment. Mac's "Christmas is for Kids" is forgettable, and the show is so desperate to fill time that it repeats a bit from 1978 with John Wayne. Bagful of comedy? Ho ho no!

Bob: \*\*\* Show: \*\*

## Bob Hope's All-Star Super Bowl Party
Jan. 29, 1983, Saturday 8-9 p.m.

Lola Falana, Ann Jillian, Audrey Landers, Merlin Olsen, Don Rickles, Miss America Debra Sue Moffett. Football Players: Dwight Clark, Randy Gradishar, Dan Hampton, Ted Hendricks, John Jefferson, Steve Largent, Anthony Munoz, Ozzie Newsome, Lawrence Taylor, Doug Wilkerson. D: Tony Charmoli. No producer credited.

This is one Bob Hope special that classifies as gay camp. Bob and Don Rickles appear in drag ("I look like ET's sister!" quips Don) to join an all-women's football team in "Footsie," a spoof of *Tootsie*, which ends with Don revealing Bob is a man but insisting on dating Merlin Olsen. Ann Jillian sings "Why Do Fools Fall in Love?" with Dwight Clark, John Jefferson, Steve Largent, and Ozzie Newsome wearing outfits that display their chests like Chippendale's strippers. To top it off, Randy Gradishar, Dan Hampton, Ted Hendricks, Anthony Munoz, Lawrence

Taylor, and Doug Wilkerson don wigs and dress like Shirley Temple to sing "Animal Crackers in My Soup" and "On the Good Ship Lollipop," plus do a kick line! It's wild but it all works somehow thanks to everyone having a playful spirit including Bob, who clearly is enjoying the comedy including his in the monologue before an audience in Pasadena, California. Football jokes predominates, including the playoffs' rough play: "There were more people on their backs than in *Dynasty*!" He also mentions budget cutbacks at the White House ("For the next state dinner, Nancy [Reagan] is using Caviar Helper") and George Burns ("He's the only one around who still calls me kid"). Also included is Lola Falana, Audrey Landers, and Miss America Debra Sue Moffett singing, Don hilariously defending his losing record as a coach to Merlin, and Bob warmly giving a paean to the Super Bowl before bringing out the cast for a deserved final bow.

Bob: ***** Show: ****


**Bob Hope's Road to Hollywood**
March 2, 1983, Wednesday 9-11 p.m.

Lucille Ball, George Burns, Rosemary Clooney, Rhonda Fleming, Martha Hyer, Dorothy Lamour, Virginia Mayo, Dina Merrill, Janis Paige, Martha Raye, Jane Russell, Jill St. John. P: Carolyn Raskin. D: Kip Walton.

A rather unimaginative compilation, this special ain't much apart from the film clips of Bob and his leading ladies. That includes Bob's monologue, where he discusses Oscar prospects including *Tootsie* ("Dustin [Hoffman] did a lot of research for the part. One night he cruised Hollywood Boulevard, picked up a guy and took him to his hotel room. Then he took off his wig and yelled, 'Surprise!' I almost fainted."), California's financial difficulties, and more. Bob shows his short movies *Going Spanish* (1934) and *Old Grey Mayor* (1935) before Martha Raye comes out to talk prior to clips from *The Big Broadcast of 1938* and *Never Say Die*. She has a strained, artificial dialogue with Bob that plagues all the other presenters. They and the films they are introduce are Jane Russell for *The Paleface*; George Burns for his late wife Gracie opposite Bob in *College Swing*; Rhonda Fleming for *Alias Jesse James*; Rosemary Clooney for *Here Come the Girls*; Dina Merrill for Bob's dancing in *The Seven Little Foys* and *Beau James* (apparently he did not want to show their collaboration on *I'll Take Sweden*); Lucille Ball for *Fancy Pants* and *The Facts of Life*; Jill St. John for *Eight on the Lam*; Virginia Mayo for *The Princess and the Pirate*; Dorothy Lamour for the Road pictures (naturally); Martha Hyer for *Paris Holiday*; and Janis Paige for *Bachelor in Paradise*. Interestingly, Bob shows his much-derided *The Iron Petticoat* and thanks Katharine Hepburn for her work there. Other films also appear, but this is mostly a mediocre overview of Bob's movie output.

Bob: *** Show: **

*Texaco Star Theatre*: "Bob Hope in 'Who Makes the World Laugh… At Itself'"
April 20, 1983, Wednesday 8-9 p.m.

Jonathan Winters, Erma Bombeck, Art Buchwald, Skip Stephenson. P/W: Marshall Flaum. D: Sid Smith.

Saluting American comedy in clips from Mark Twain (in an astounding rare piece of film captured by Thomas Edison) to Robert Klein, Richard Pryor, George Carlin and Eddie Murphy—all of whom never did a Bob Hope special—this is an enjoyable stroll down memory lane. Bob kicks it off in excellent fashion with a monologue centered on the Oscars. He calls Best Picture winner *Gandhi* a movie with "a sheet with only one person under it" and says that he was worried about giving the special Academy Award to Mickey Rooney: "It was taller than him!" Bob gets a big round of applause and smiles apparently in satisfaction when he takes aim at Gary Crosby's new tell-all book *Going My Own Way*, which charged his late father Bing Crosby with child abuse, and quips, "Bing used to sing to me too, but I don't think it was necessary to write a book!" The clips are all enjoyable as are most of the guests. Erma Bombeck garners plenty of chuckles talking about coping with adult children living in her house, and Jonathan Winters is wildly inventive portraying obscure people running for president. The only weak parts are Art Buchwald, whose segment via satellite is less effective because of his garbled pronunciation of words, and Skip Stephenson, who Bob mentions how he liked working with him at a recent telethon, yet Stephenson comes off as less funny than the others seen here. A sequel to this will air April 4, 1984.

Bob and Show: ****

***Happy Birthday Bob***
May 23, 1983, Monday 8-11 p.m.

Lucille Ball, Christie Brinkley, George Burns, Lynda Carter, Howard Cosell, Kathryn Crosby, Phyllis Diller, Roberto Duran, Sheena Easton, Marvelous Marvin Hagler, Delores Hope, Julio Iglesias, Ann Jillian, Jim Henson (as Kermit the Frog), Loretta Lynn, Barbara Mandrell, Dudley Moore, Nancy Reagan, Ronald Reagan, George C. Scott, Tom Selleck, Brooke Shields, Cheryl Tiegs, Tommy Tune, Twiggy, The U.S. Army, Navy, Air Force and Marines Bands, Flip Wilson. EP/W: James Lipton. P/D: Don Mischer. Choreographer: Charles Jablonski. Announcer: Bob Fitzsimmons.

Bob and Ronald Reagan reminisce in the Lincoln Bedroom prior to appearing at the Kennedy Center, where Lynda Carter and four military bands present "Hey Big Spender" with special lyrics to start Bob's birthday celebration. Tom Selleck summarizes Bob's life before Flip Wilson has a great set as Geraldine and Sheena Easton performs "When He Shines." Howard Cosell announces a match between Roberto Duran and Marvelous Marvin Hagler surrounded by dancers making moves during the "warmup," which comes across as *Flashdance* meets *Rocky*. Geraldine intervenes when Hagler and Duran fight, and Cosell announces that Bob is the winner. At least Bob laughs at that. What follows are good songs by Loretta Lynn, Julio Iglesias (in Spanish), Lucille Ball (with special lyrics to "Hey Look Me Over"), Ann Jillian (leading a USO production routine), Barbara Mandrell (two production numbers including a gospel rave), and Tommy Tune and Twiggy from the Broadway hit *My One and Only*. Also fine are comic bits by George Burns, Phyllis Diller, and Dudley Moore. The only awkward missteps are Kermit the Frog romancing Sheena before she kisses him to see if he will become a prince (he does not), and Christie Brinkley, Brooke Shields, and Cheryl Tiegs as 1933 models all in love with Bob who sing "You Made Me Love You" as clumsily as they act. Words of thanks come from Kathryn Crosby (recounting how Bob met Delores before the latter sings "What Are You Doing the Rest of Your Life?"), George C. Scott (bringing greetings from world leaders including the Pope, plus a birthday card signed by the governor of Ohio, the Cleveland Indians baseball team, and more than fifty thousand others) and President Reagan. At the end, Bob cracks, "I hope you enjoyed our miniseries tonight" and adds, "I'm glad Tom Selleck participated tonight. I needed another sex symbol here to take the pressure off me." Bob also jokes about what being eighty means ("Did you ever try blowing into someone's hearing aid?"), and staying in the White House before "Thanks for the Memory" with new lyrics and cake cutting end a mostly enjoyable celebration.

Bob and Show: ****

*Bob Hope Salutes NASA:* "25 Years of Reaching for the Stars"
Sept. 19, 1983, Monday 8-9:30 p.m.

John Denver, Marie Osmond, astronauts Neil Armstrong, Guion Bluford, Robert Crippen, Alan Shepard. Co-P: Elliott Kozak. Film Sequences P: Phil Savenick. D: Stan Harris. Special Musical Material: Ray Charles.

Astounding space footage plus decent interviews with astronauts equals a passing grade for this. Bob has a strong monologue encompassing his years with NBC to the Statue of Liberty before he narrates a history of flight and NASA and brings out one of the latter's biggest boosters, John Denver, who talks about his ambitions to go to the moon in a decent bit of repartee. He presents a song based on a poem from a pilot who died in a plane crash (sadly, the same will happen to Denver in 1997). Clips from Bob's Nov. 6, 1968 special where he interacted with Apollo Astronauts Walt Cunningham, Donn F. Eisele and Walter Schirra and his Sept. 29, 1965 space sketch with Douglas Fairbanks Jr. bookend classic film of astronauts in action. Marie Osmond talks about her new marriage and baby before she and Bob do a cute medley of songs with "Moon" in their titles. Stirring archival recordings of the Apollo Eleven follow along with an interview with its lead astronaut, Neil Armstrong, who's great in delivering canned dialogue (Bob: "You're not afraid to face danger, are you?" Neil: "Well, I'm here …"). So are Guion Bluford and Robert Crippen (together) and Alan Shepard after Bob narrates a review of women in the NASA program. Armstrong and Shepard also appear in clips from Bob's Vietnam specials. There also a repeat of Bob's Dec. 19, 1977 *Star Wars* parody, which illustrates this show's main flaw of too much old Hope to fill out ninety minutes.

Bob and Show: ***

### Bob Hope Goes to College
Nov. 23, 1983, Wednesday 8-10 p.m.

Kareem Abdul-Jabbar, Irene Cara, Morgan Fairchild, Joe Montana, Eddie Rabbitt, [Bill] Skiles and [Pete] Henderson, Taco, Bonnie Tyler, Dionne Warwick, Miss America Vanessa Williams. Co-P: Elliott Kozak.

Mediocre comedy burdens this jaunt to eight institutes of higher learning. Bob starts with a good monologue at SMU in Texas and clever dialogue with SMU grad Morgan Fairchild and Bonnie Tyler (Bonnie to Bob: "I know all your hits. I'm a great trivia buff."). The latter sings "Total Eclipse of the Heart" before an erratic skit where a police chief (Bob) deals with a new addition, "Parking Tag Tessie" (Morgan), who leaves with SMU football star Craig James. At Clemson, Bob disses the bad food on campus before doing a cute duet with Eddie Rabbitt on the latter's hit "I Love a Rainy Night." Bob's clever byplay with Joe Montana after Dionne Warwick sings at Notre Dame devolves into silliness as Bob and Joe play athletes dealing with a coach (Dionne) and team members who are female. For UCLA, Bob talks with Kareem Abdul-Jabbar before Taco does "Puttin' on the Ritz." At Syracuse, Miss America Vanessa Williams sings "Happy Days Are Here Again" before joining Bob in a swell comic duet. Irene Cara's presentation of "Flashdance" is the highlight of the University of Florida in Gainesville, while Bob has a great line at Utah State: "Among Mormons, 'Not tonight, I have a headache' is blasphemy." It culminates in Vail, Colorado, where Bob presents what he says is one of his favorite acts, Skiles and Henderson, but the duo is more forced than funny. If the comedy were as strong as most of the music here, this would have merited another star.

Bob: **** Show: ***

### Bob Hope's Merry Christmas Show
Dec. 19, 1983, Monday 8-9 p.m.

Catherine Bach, John Forsythe, Brooke Shields, The Rose Queen and Her Court, The AP All America Team. D: Sid Smith.

In this Yuletide special's centerpiece skit, Catherine Bach and Brooke Shields play life-sized talking dolls who became enamored with Bob and John Forsythe, two hoods who discover them when casing a joint. The two successfully plead for the two men to adopt them. Catherine also joins Bob in doing the traditional duet of "Silver Bells."

## Bob Hope's USO Christmas in Beirut
Jan. 15, 1984, Sunday 9-11 p.m.

Cathy Lee Crosby, Vic Damone, Miss USA Julie Hayek, Ann Jillian, George Kirby, Brooke Shields, The 6th Fleet Show Band. Co-P: Elliott Kozak. D: Sid Smith.

Entertaining troops at the USS Guam and other warships off the coast of Lebanon in the wake of a horrific terrorist attack on U.S. Marines in October 1982 (the mainland was considered too unsafe to do shows), Bob offers a change of pace this time with George Kirby showing up to impersonate everyone from Walter Brennan to Pearl Bailey. Ann Jillian gets to sing "Silent Night" at the end of this trek. Cathy Lee Crosby recalls of this visit that "the guys in the audience went crazy and would yell out some pretty outrageous things like 'I want Cathy Lee for Christmas!' Bob wouldn't hesitate to grab the opportunity to go off script, and his replies would be hilarious! I don't remember anything being actually cut from a broadcast, because Bob was never verbally crude. That was not his style. I think what happened on set was just so priceless that producers took a chance that everything would pass the censors."

## Bob Hope's Wicky-Wacky Special in Waikiki
Feb. 27, 1984, Monday 9-10 p.m.

Loni Anderson, Tom Selleck, Mr. T, Miss Venus USA Bonnie DeFinizio. P: Carolyn Raskin, Elliott Kozak.

Beautiful cinematography of Hawaii to celebrate its quarter century of being the fiftieth state in the union cannot compensate for a lot of flat entertainment. Holding his monologue outdoors, Bob wows the crowd with lines like "I tried talking to a tourist the other day, but his shirt was so loud, he couldn't hear me." Some parts don't date well, like his off-color take on the melding of cultures on the islands to produce things like a pineapple burrito: "You still get the trots, but you do the hula to the bathroom." He does mock the former star of *Hawaii Five-O*, who is in the audience. "The other day, the winds got so bad, Jack Lord's hair almost moved!" The first skit strains with Bob as a vacationer who meets a goddess of volcanoes (Loni Anderson in a sarong). Bad lines abound, like Bob saying, "I wasn't born yesterday, you know." "Oh?" asks Loni. "No, my birthday's May 30th," replies Bob. Bob's banter with Mr. T is slightly better thanks to the guest's deadpan angry attitude, and Loni and Bob have fun singing together and joking about their setting ("These people here are so laidback, they make Dean Martin look like Richard Simmons," quips Bob). Then Bob's interview with Tom Selleck on the set of *Magnum P.I.* is tedious, as is his banter with Miss Venus USA. Mr. T does elicit smiles showing Bob how to dance the hula, but it can't stop viewers from wanting to say "Aloha" to this as soon as possible.

Bob: *** Show: **

## Bob Hope's Who Makes the World Laugh? Volume Two
April 4, 1984, Wednesday 9-10 p.m.

Lucille Ball, George Burns, Paul Rodriguez, Mickey Rooney. P/W: Marshall Flaum. Announcer: Donald Rickles (not the comedian).

While everyone is nice and happy here, the bulk of the show is really a compilation of comic filmed and taped bits narrated by Bob between presentations, making it look like he and the cast are phoning this in. When Bob's on screen, however, he does glow, starting with his monologue on the Oscars (denied a nod again, he calls it "The Big Chill" in honor of one of the nominees), the Democratic presidential candidates, quarterback Steve Young's payout, Michael Jackson's concert tour, and Easter and taxes being due the same time this year ("You roll the eggs, the government rolls you."). He adds, "I don't mind sending money to Washington. It's where I get most of my jokes." From there, it's vintage pieces of humor broken up by visits with the guests. George Burns gets Bob to wear a fur piece to play dumb like his later partner and wife, Gracie Allen, and the routine holds up well before they dance to "Tea for Two." Lucille Ball has great rapport with Bob and delivers her scripted lines well while cackling about her love scenes with him and other jokes at his expense. She mentions being proud that she never used a stuntwoman in all her years in Hollywood. Mickey Rooney goes off script with Bob as they recount their misadventures in vaudeville, and Bob accurately predicts Paul Rodriguez will be a big hit in the future before the latter comedian performs a set. In all, this is funny but only occasionally fun.

Bob: **** Show: ***

*Super Birthday: A World's Fair Salute to Bob Hope*
May 28, 1984, Monday 9-11 p.m.

The World's Fair Aquacade, Red Buttons, June Carter, Johnny Cash, Dick Cavett, Placido Domingo, Marvelous Marvin Hagler, Delores Hope, Sugar Ray Leonard, David Letterman, John Ritter, Brooke Shields, Mr. T, Twiggy. EP/W: James Lipton. P: Elliott Kozak. D: Sid Smith. Aquacade Choreography: Ron Field. Announcer: Donald Rickles (not the comedian).

The World's Fair is at New Orleans, so Bob jokes about its rowdy reputation ("The crowds on the street are incredible. I tried to put my hand in my pocket and had to wait my turn."), among other topics. Bob and Mr. T do a few semi-successful jokes before and after the World's Fair Aquacade members perform synchronized swimming and diving. David Letterman does his best to make his lines sound like natural conversation before conducting hilarious interviews with people at the fair interspersed through the show. Twiggy sings a number from Broadway's *My One and Only*, then talks to Bob before they sing moon-themed songs next to the space shuttle. Brooke Shields discusses her first year in college, which leads into "The Road to New Orleans," with Bob, Brooke, and Placido Domingo as crooked riverboat gamblers, Red Buttons as the ship captain, Twiggy as first mate, and John Ritter as a patsy. Shot on location, it's fourteen minutes long on music and short on comedy. Bob's conversation with John prefaces Bob as Tom Sawyer to John's Huck Finn, Brooke's Becky and Mr. T's Jim. It is a time waster, as is Bob's banter with Placido at an Italian villa until Placido's fine singing takes over. Also an improvement is Johnny Cash singing an amusing variation on his hit "A Boy Named Sue" and Red Buttons cleverly talking about how some of the biggest people in the world never had a birthday party like this. Dick Cavett pops up as a reporter covering a big fight with John as the referee, Bob as a promoter, Brooke as his bimbo girlfriend, and Marvin Hagler and Sugar Ray Leonard snarling at each other. Red interrupts the frenzied atmosphere to offer a million dollars to the winner of the match, provided he can come out without bruises. The two fighters become friends even with John trying to incite aggression between them. Both Marvin and Sugar Ray talk to Bob about the latter's boxing career in an amusing fashion, and Johnny and June Carter Cash's version of "Jackson" is an audience pleaser. Delores does her standard ballad before Bob wraps it up with new verses to "Thanks for the Memory" and cuts pieces of the cake for everyone in the cast while fireworks go off. It's a warm ending to a somewhat clunky show.

Bob and Show: ***

## Bob Hope Presents the Hilarious Unrehearsed Antics of the Stars
Sept. 28, 1984, Friday 8-9 p.m.

Lucille Ball, Milton Berle, Angie Dickinson, Lee Marvin. D: Sid Smith. Announcer: Donald Rickles.

As blooper TV series are the current rage, Bob does one as well in this relatively painless but pointless outing. In his monologue, he talks about the summer Olympics producing a $150 million surplus for Los Angeles, Prince Charles and Diana's new baby, celebrity workout tapes ("I figure if God meant for us to touch our toes, he would've put them further up on our body"), the planned presidential debate, and more. Between clips of mistakes on Bob's specials mostly from the last twenty years, plus Bob's surprise appearance on *The Tonight Show* in 1975 with Don Rickles as host, Angie Dickinson talks about bloopers that happened on her series *Police Woman*, Lee Marvin discusses how he got into acting and his Oscar win for *Cat Ballou*, Lucille Ball recounts her audition as Scarlett O'Hara for *Gone with the Wind*, and Milton Berle recalls a live sketch with Jack Benny when a phone rang that should not have done so. It is all modestly amusing like most of the clips themselves, but it is a lazy way to serve as a season opener as well, and some of these clips are on their third run or more on Bob's shows.

Bob and Show: ***


## It's Ho-Ho Hope's Jolly Christmas Hour
Dec. 16, 1984, Sunday 9:30-10:30 p.m.

Brooke Shields, Mary Lou Retton, Shirley Jones, The AP All America Football Team, Joey Lawrence, The International Children's Choir of America, The Rose Queen and Her Court. Featured: Peter Leeds. D: Sid Smith. Announcer: Don Stanley.

A by-the-book Yuletide special, this stresses cuteness to the detriment of its effectiveness. Bob jokes about Christmas presents ("Trivial Pursuit— that's a guy chasing Phyllis Diller"), the White House dog, George Burns' new movie, and President Reagan's second term inauguration. He interviews an adorable Mary Lou Retton on her Olympics gold medal win in gymnastics. It leads into Bob playing a toy department clerk who must sell a life-sized doll doing tumbling moves (Mary Lou) before midnight when a snooty customer (Shirley Jones) arrives. Inexplicably, Bob rekindles an old romance with Shirley and they plan to adopt Mary Lou in an overdone, contrived finale. Shirley then sings "Let There Be Peace on Earth" with the International Children's Choir of America, which is a direct steal from Bob's appearance on *Here's Edie* in 1963. Brooke joins Bob to set up a clumsy, largely unfunny sketch where Ebenezer Scrooge (Bob) visits a psychiatrist. At least the AP team has Bruce Smith, Heisman Trophy winner Doug Flutie, and other players who mostly deservedly give Bob looks back for his often corny comments. Shirley gets to join Bob to do "Silver Bells" in a fake snow scene before Joey Lawrence hams it up singing and dancing "Give My Regards to Broadway." Bob joins him to tap dance to "Tea for Two" as well. A blasé bit with the Rose Queen and Her Court and tired new verses to "Thanks for the Memory" wrap up a special that reeks of being regifted from previous Bob Hope shows.

Bob: *** Show: **

*Bob Hope Lampoons Television 1985*
Feb. 24, 1985, Sunday 8-9 p.m.

Elvira, Morgan Fairchild, Hal Linden, Donna Mills. Cameos: George Burns, Mr. T. Featured: Peter Leeds, Michael Morrison, Gary Owens, Fredd Wayne.

These spoofs range from brilliant to brittle. Perhaps sensing the problem, Bob's monologue runs longer than usual at ten minutes, but it's good. Musing on recent cold weather, he quips, "In Nebraska, I saw a mink wearing a fat lady." He says the Oscars are known as "The Killing Fields" in his house, mentioning one Best Picture nominee, and he scoffs at comparisons that Paul Newman is sexier than he is. This leads into the show's best parody, "Freeway to Heaven," with Bob sporting a wig resembling the locks of Michael Landon as he ineptly tries to help a couple (Donna Mills and Peter Leeds) keep their farm solvent. "I'm not the man I was when I was a man," he says when Donna calls him useless, but Bob is able to summon God (George Burns), who tells Bob to stop beeping him for help. Hal Linden and Morgan Fairchild then join Bob and Donna to sing a specialty number setting up several send-ups of commercials with mixed results. Gary Owens introduces the cast doing *Cheers* set in colonial times, but even Elvira as a customer can't make this exciting. *The A-Team* with Hal as the group leader and Bob as Mr. T grappling with the series' cancellation amuses only when the real Mr. T shows up and bellows at Bob, "Mom wants you home for dinner now!" The rest is a wash, with more lame commercial blackouts and a stupid mockery of *Dynasty* with Bob, Donna, and Morgan.

Bob and Show: ***


**Bob Hope's Comedy Salute to the Soaps**
April 15, 1985, Monday 8-9 p.m.

Morgan Brittany, Diahann Carroll, Deidre Hall, Peter Reckell, Joan Van Ark, Jack Wagner. Featured: Joan Crosby, Ronald Anderson, Walter Harrah, Rob Tro. P: K.D. Peel. Co-P: Elliott Kozak.

Any goodwill one has for Bob and an attractive cast is sorely tested here, with all barely getting a thumbs up in the end. Bob's monologue is generally fine, with good licks on the miniseries *A.D.* ("They hired George Burns as technical advisor"), MX missiles Russia has designed to harm America ("They have them aimed at Japan"), and the big charity record to benefit African famine victims, "We Are the World." So many celebrities sing on the latter that it "scared the hell out of the Mormon Tabernacle Choir," quips Bob, adding that artists who didn't appear on it are recording a new album titled "We Are the Rest." Then Bob, Morgan Brittany, Diahann Carroll, Peter Reckell and Joan Van Ark sing about how they cannot watch their soap operas while on the job in an extended tiresome number. Similarly long and only intermittently funny is Peter and Jack Wagner as soap writers quizzing an actor (Bob) on ways to stage an accidental death before he realizes that they're trying to write him out. The show bounces back with clever byplay between Bob and Joan (learning that Bob came over from England at age four, she exclaims, "I didn't know they deported minors!") and a hilarious bit with Bob, Peter and Morgan doing a soap opera as if singing a real opera. However, Bob overhearing Joan and Deidre Hall discuss how they'd murder someone and thinking they plan to kill him bombs, as does his individual bantering with Morgan and Deidre. As a genre tribute, this needs more work.

Bob and Show: ***

*The Royal London Gala for Bob Hope's Happy Birthday Homecoming*
May 28, 1985, Tuesday 9-11 p.m.

Michael Caine, Chevy Chase, Phyllis Diller, Duran Duran, Crystal Gayle, Marvelous Marvin Hagler, Charlton Heston, Delores Hope, Julio Iglesias, Kermit the Frog (Jim Henson), Ben Kingsley, Miss Piggy (Frank Oz), Bernadette Peters, Debbie Reynolds, Brooke Shields, Ray Alan, Rowan Atkinson, Spike Milligan, Mike Yarwood. EP/W: James Lipton. D: Dwight Hemion. Music: Allyn Ferguson. Choreographer: Brian Rogers. Announcer: Patrick Allen.

Bob appears in a box seat with Prince Philip as Ben Kingsley bows to them to start the show. Sitting underneath the prince, Miss Piggy thinks the honor was for her, to the embarrassment of Kermit the Frog. Chevy Chase is interrupted by an alien (Rowan Atkinson) whose English translation box keeps misfiring. Bernadette Peters sings and dances to Noel Coward's "Mad Dog and Englishmen," "Nina," and "Mad About the Boy" to Bob's delight. Michael Caine recalls how Bob's donation to his boys' club saved it and thanked him again for that as he did as a child. Unfortunately, after Mike Yarwood does a solid Bob Hope impersonation, the show moves at a crawl. Charlton Heston and Marvelous Marvin Hagler talk too long about the boxer's recent win and pay tribute to Bob's skits with fighters over the years. Kermit driving Brooke Shields along with an envious Miss Piggy is unfunny, Debbie Reynolds' medley of love songs and Crystal Gayle's ballad are both pallid, and Ray Alan and his drunk dummy Lord Charles are tiresome. Phyllis Diller shakes away the growing torpor by saying, "Think of me as the sex symbol for men who just don't give a damn!" in an okay set, and Duran Duran adds some excitement doing "A View to a Kill" (in its worldwide TV debut!), only to have Ben Kingsley's windy note of appreciation to Bob slow things down again. Bob improves things somewhat at the end (one joke is "I visit my birthplace once in a while to see if the manger is still intact."). Still, it isn't one of his best monologues, and it confirms this as a disappointing birthday special.

Bob: *** Show: **

## Bob Hope Buys NBC?
Sept. 17, 1985, Tuesday 9-10 p.m.

Lucille Ball, Milton Berle, George Burns, Johnny Carson, Lynda Carter, Dick Cavett, Phyllis Diller, Phil Donahue, Elvira, President Gerald Ford, Michael J. Fox, Delores Hope, Lee Iacocca, Michael Landon, Dean Martin, Ed McMahon, Mr. T, Ricky Schroder, Tom Selleck, Brandon Tartikoff, Danny Thomas, Ted Turner. D: Walter C. Miller. Special Musical Material: Jay Livingston, Ray Evans.

Spoofing a wave of recent corporate takeovers, Bob employs a storyline of rumors he will run the network to allow for a lot of comic cameos including network honchos like NBC Entertainment president Brandon Tartikoff. It also makes time for its featured talent to shine as well, such as letting Lynda Carter do two songs and discuss what she likes about living in Washington, D.C., before she sings "You Make Me Feel So Young" with Bob.

## The Bob Hope Christmas Show
Dec. 15, 1985, Sunday 9-10 p.m.

The AP All America Football Team, Barbara Eden, Emmanuel Lewis, William "Refrigerator" Perry, The Rose Queen and Her Court, Brooke Shields.

Lots of good spirits by all participants make this a delight. Bob discusses everything from how Christmas is different in Beverly Hills ("It's the only city in the world where bag ladies wear minks") to the soap opera *Dynasty* in an assured, very 1980s monologue. In "Miami Nice, he and Emmanuel Lewis must interrogate Brooke Shields without using violence to squeeze out a confession. With smart lines and acting, this moves well. Emmanuel then jokes, sings and dances to "Me and My Shadow" with Bob, and he is charming and talented throughout. (When Emmanuel says, "I'm almost over the hill," Bob cracks back, "If you're over the hill, then I'm over the creek!"). The AP All America Football Team includes Tim Green, Brian Bosworth, and Heisman Trophy winner Bo Jackson, and the lines are better than usual. Bob even cracks up Baylor free safety Thomas Everett with "Tom hits a runner, he leaves a black and blue mark so big, it has to be continued on a friend!" Brooke's repartee with Bob is sharp too, and they both have a hard time keeping composed amid their dialogue. The same applies to his banter with Barbara Eden, who sings "Silver Bells" with Bob, William "the Refrigerator" Perry and even the Rose Queen, all loose and lively. The sole drawback is Bob, Emmanuel, and Brooke as the last dolls stuck at a toy store who sing "Side by Side" at the end. It is silly and tiresome. Still, this generally is what a great Bob Hope Christmas special should be.

Bob: \*\*\*\*\* Show: \*\*\*\*

*Bob Hope's All Star Super Bowl Party*
Jan. 25, 1986, Saturday 8-9 p.m.

Diahann Carroll, Donna Mills, Don Rickles, Miss America Susan Akin, Russ Bollinger, Russ Francis, Mike Haynes, Howie Long, Tony Eason, Jim McMahon.

Six NFL players join Bob to salute the big game in a special last seen three years earlier when NBC was airing it (and yes, the next edition will not be until 1989). And as in 1983, Bob appears in drag to be part of Diahann Carroll and Donna Mills' all-female football team. Bob likes another person appearing in this sketch, Miss America Susan Akin, enough to invite her back next year for his special *From Tahiti, Bob Hope's Tropical Comedy Special*.

*Bob Hope's Royal Command Performance from Sweden*
March 19, 1986, Wednesday 8-9 p.m.

Liv Ullman, Omar Sharif, Shirley Jones, Glen Campbell, Emmanuel Lewis, Dolph Lundgren, Boy George and Culture Club, Scott Grimes, Miss Universe 1984 Yvonne Riding. P: Elliott Kozak, Dick Arlett. D: Sid Smith.

From the Oscars Theater in Stockholm, Bob dances with Emmanuel Lewis and does comic conversation with Liv Ullman and Omar Sharif while letting the other guests strut their talents in this command performance before King Carl Gustav and Queen Sylvia. This taping was a disaster because before Bob's cast and crew left for Europe, word came that a murderer assassinated Olaf Palme, the prime minister of Sweden. The king and queen insisted that the show must go on, but few were laughing at the jokes, and worse yet, Bob and the writers failed to realize the name of his character in one of the skits was Olaf, forcing Bob to apologize for the gaffe during a break. Summarizing the situation in his book *The Laugh Makers*, Bob Mills astutely noted, "It was like watching the lounge act on the Hindenburg. It was a wake with entertainment."

### Bob Hope's High-Flying Birthday Extravaganza
May 26, 1986, Monday 8-10 p.m.

Elizabeth Taylor, Sammy Davis Jr., Jonathan Winters, Don Johnson, Phylicia Rashad, Brooke Shields, Barbara Mandrell, Mac Davis, Patti Andrews, Delores Hope, The Pensacola Naval Aviation Station Training Command Choir. EP: James Lipton.

Taped aboard the USS Lexington, this celebration of Bob turning eighty-three includes a spoof of *An Officer and a Gentlemen* with Hope joined by Sammy Davis Jr., Mac Davis and Jonathan Winters; songs by Sammy, Mac, Barbara Mandrell, Brooke Shields, and Delores Hope; and Elizabeth Taylor, well, just being Elizabeth Taylor.

### Bob Hope Lampoons the New TV Scene
Sept. 15, 1986, Monday 8-9 p.m.

George Burns, Ann Jillian, Tony Randall, Danny Thomas. Cameos: John Davidson, Estelle Getty. D: Kip Walton.

Bob, George Burns, and Danny Thomas play the male equivalent of *The Golden Girls*, spoofing a series produced by Danny's son Tony that is Bob's favorite TV show. Estelle Getty shows up at the end of "The Golden Boys" sketch to accost Bob. Also sent up are *Moonlighting*, *Night Court*, and *Dallas*.

### Bob Hope's Bagful of Christmas Cheer
Dec. 21, 1986, Sunday 9-10 p.m.

The AP All-America Football Team, Crystal Gayle, Donna Mills, The Osmond Boys Second Generation, The 1987 Tournament of Roses Queen and Her Court, Brooke Shields. Featured: Fredd Wayne, Stephen Henry. D: Sid Smith.

There's little cheer here, despite what the title says. Bob's monologue targets Christmas shopping, football bowls, Joan Collins divorcing her younger husband ("She got tired of him cutting his teeth on her jewelry") and Johnny Carson taking his fourth wife ("The first three took him") in a passing set. Donna Mills does "Silver Bells" with Bob and then introduces a Beverly Hills couple (Bob and Brooke Shields) so rich that they take pity on Santa Claus and give him money. This is ho ho hum. The Osmond Boys (all Alan Osmond's sons) are a barbershop quintet long on cuteness and short on talent. The Associated Press All-America Football Team includes Brian Bosworth, Cris Carter, and Vinnie Testaverde and is the funniest part of the show—the audience cheers a lot and even the players are laughing at some of the lines. Following it is deadly banter with Brooke, then Bob reprises singing "I Want a Girl (Just Like the Girl That Married Dear Old Dad)" with the Osmond Boys like he did with the Osmonds on his Nov. 7, 1971 show. A *Crocodile Dundee* spoof with Bob and Donna bombs too. Crystal Gayle talks with Bob fine before she does "Have Yourself a Merry Little Christmas" well enough. Near the end, the Tournament of Roses Queen asks Bob, "You've never skied before?" and he responds, "Honey, in show business, downhill is one direction you never want to go." Unfortunately, that's exactly where most of this not-so-special ends up heading.

Bob: *** Show: **

*From Tahiti, Bob Hope's Tropical Comedy Special*
Feb. 23, 1987, Monday 8-9 p.m.

John Denver, Morgan Brittany, Howard Keel, Jonathan Winters, Miss Tahiti Bohi Luana, Miss America Susan Akin. P: Elliott Kozak, Dick Arlett. D: Walter C. Miller.

This special got a lot of critical derision from *Variety* for its lackadaisical presentation, and some of Bob's assistants responded by making up an ad with fake raves for it in the same publication. For his part, writer Bob Mills says the monologue went disastrously, with Bob making sex jokes on a cruise shop where most guests were senior citizens who did not laugh at the material, and the bad weather and poor accommodations made shooting on the island something less than a tropical paradise. Nearly everyone breaks into song at some point (even actress Morgan Brittany sings "Everything Old is New Again" to a group of native children), Jonathan Winters plays two sketches without being allowed to improvise, and a spoof of *Mutiny on the Bounty* with Winters as a tribal chief and Bob as Captain Bligh lamely ends with Howard Keel pairing up with Miss America Susan Akin, John Denver doing the same with Miss Tahiti Bohi Luana, and Bob having to settle for a missionary (Morgan).

### *Bob Hope with His Easter Bunnies and Other Friends*
April 19, 1987, Sunday 9-10 p.m.

Lynda Carter, Stepfanie Kramer, Gloria Loring, Vanna White. Cameos: Jack Carter, Scott Grimes.

The main sketch of this seasonal special has Lynda Carter playing a psychiatrist treating the Easter Bunny (Bob), who feels fatigued and ignored. At the end, she sympathizes with him because she has a tail too. Lynda also sings "Great Balls of Fire" and "I'm All Right" from *Caddyshack*, while Gloria Loring does "Change of Heart" and Stepfanie Kramer joins Bob to perform "If I Could Be With You (One Hour Tonight)." At the end, Bob does "Easter Parade" and other seasonal songs with Lynda, Stepfanie, Gloria, and Vanna White, who shows she lacks the vocal chops of Bob's other female guests.

### *Bob Hope's High-Flying Birthday Extravaganza*
May 25, 1987, Monday 8-10 p.m.

Alabama, Lucille Ball, Kirk Cameron, Glen Campbell, Phyllis Diller, Delores Hope, Don Johnson, Emmanuel Lewis, Barbara Mandrell, Phylicia Rashad, President Ronald Reagan, Brooke Shields. EP/W: James Lipton.

Celebrating the fortieth anniversary of the U.S. Air Force along with Bob's birthday, this enthusiastic offering is at Pope Air Force Base in Fayetteville, North Carolina, and has a lot of laughs at the expense of Jim and Tammy Faye Bakker, plus other topics like short skirts, in a strong set. He has a warm rapport with Barbara Mandrell, who sings and dances with a military man from the audience. Then Bob plays Orville Wright planning to fly at Kitty Hawk with his brother Wilbur (Glen Campbell), who wants a nervous Orville to fly their plane. Barbara and Brooke Shields play two women who convince him to do otherwise, and it is funny. Lucy and Bob's banter sparkles recounting their work together in the movies before doing special lyrics with "I Remember It Well." Don Johnson gets a rousing reception for his chitchat with Bob. Phyllis, Phylicia, Barbara, and Brooke do a funny number about searching for a man in uniform, and Bob joins them to extol the virtues of Air Force men. Phyllis then talks about doing strip poker with the guys who forced her to wear eighteen blouses and aluminum siding in a good set. Bob plays a paratrooper who drops into a hillbilly family of Brooke, Barbara and Phyllis and their mom, Lucy, who forces Bob to marry Phyllis with Emmanuel Lewis as the preacher. Alabama sings "Happy Birthday" to Bob and does a number, then Emmanuel talks with Bob, and they do a great song and dance to "Carolina in the Morning." Then Bob banters with Phylicia and Glen before they do songs, and he has a similar routine with Brooke and Kirk Cameron. Delores Hope sings before President Reagan jokes with the honoree and even leads everyone singing "Happy Birthday" to Bob as a big cake comes out and the cast serves it to the audience. It's a corny but cute ending to a nice outing.

Bob: \*\*\*\*\* Show: \*\*\*\*

### NBC Investigates Bob Hope
Sept. 17, 1987, Thursday 8:30-9:30 p.m.

Milton Berle, Jack Carter, Peter Leeds, Louis Nye, Tony Randall, Danny Thomas. Cameos: Army Archerd, George Burns, Phil Donahue, Gerald Ford, Fred Hunter, Stepfanie Kramer, Michael Landon, Gary Owens, Tom Selleck, Todd Susman, Brandon Tartikoff. Featured: Fred Soloff, Fredd Wayne, The Gene Merlino Choir. D: Bob Henry. W: Jeffrey Barron.

An unexpected laugh riot based on the Iran-Contra hearings, this is on point in every aspect. After Bob's monologue sends up the new TV season ("Dolly Parton's going to have her own variety show this year. They should be a hit"), the Pope's visit to America ("He's going to meet with 40,000 Japanese tourists. He's going to Disneyland."), and California's recent heat wave ("God waits till it's closer to Christmas to bake his fruitcakes"), NBC head of programming Brandon Tartikoff wonderfully plays himself and says that Bob has been accused of diverting jokes from the network to the enemy—cable TV. In NBC's basement, Bob and his new sexy blonde secretary sell gags to a cleaning lady (Louis Nye in drag) until they're discovered. Gary Owens introduces the hearing where Bob and his lawyer (Tony Randall) face a committee led by Peter Leeds whose other members (Milton Berle, Jack Carter, and Danny Thomas) bear the surnames of Bob's writers as an in-joke. Bob addresses the committee with "To the best of my recollection, I can't recall remembering" while its members snipe at each other as well as Bob. After seven celebrities defend Bob humorously in cameos, Army Archerd reports "Hopemania" has taken over America to support Bob. The jury sings "The Battle Hymn of the Republic" behind Bob as he proclaims the jokes he was sold were idle and needed to be shared to bring laughter and peace on Earth, which wins over the committee. This is one of Bob's best ever.

Bob and Show: *****


*The Bob Hope Christmas Show*: "A Snow Job in Florida"
Dec. 19, 1987, Saturday 8-9 p.m.

Morgan Fairchild, Reba McEntire, Brooke Shields, Tony Randall, The Rose Queen and The Orange Queen, The AP All America Football Team.

Another year, another Yuletide special with the usual elements this time has a twist because it is recorded in Fort Lauderdale during its Winterfest event. That means with the Orange Bowl coming up, it is only fair to have the Orange Queen appear along with the Rose Queen. Bob also plays Santa Claus running for president assisted by a consultant (Tony Randall), campaign manager (Morgan Fairchild), and speechwriter (Brooke Shields). By the time this airs, Bob is already overseas again to do his next special.


*Bob Hope's USO Christmas Show from the Persian Gulf*: "Around the World in Eight Days"
Jan. 9, 1988, Saturday 9:30-11 p.m.

Barbara Eden, Lee Greenwood, Connie Stevens and her daughters Joely Fisher and Tricia Leigh Fisher, Miss USA Michelle Royer, The Super Bowl Dancers.

With Bob narrating and Johnny Grant and Phyllis Diller wishing Bob and the group safe travels as they go first to Honolulu, plus the appearances of Barbara Eden and Connie Stevens, this feels like one of Bob's Vietnam specials from the 1960s, which is a mixed blessing. Bob as always is in his element, with lots of jokes that land well and good comebacks when the troops ask him questions, and his interplay with Miss USA is amusing in its suggestive dialogue. However, the numbers by Barbara and Connie Stevens and her daughters are nothing exceptional, nor is the hoofing by the Super Bowl Dancers, although they look smashing even when not in motion. Even so, Barbara does impress with her version of "One" from *A Chorus Line* in a duet with Bob, and Connie singing "Silent Night" at the end remains as moving as when she did it nearly two decades earlier. Stops include the USS Midway in the Philippines, the USS Okinawa and Bahrain.

Bob: ***** Show: ***


*America's Tribute to Bob Hope*
March 5, 1988, Saturday 10-11 p.m.

The Alvin Ailey American Dance Theater, Lucille Ball, Steve Barton, Sarah Brightman, Diahann Carroll, Van Cliburn, Vic Damone, John Forsythe, Leila Josefowicz, Andrew Lloyd Webber. Special Appearances: Ann-Margret, George Burns, Johnny Carson, Phyllis Diller, Delores Hope, Alan King, Barbara Mandrell, Donald O'Connor, President Ronald Reagan and Nancy Reagan, Dinah Shore, O.J. Simpson, Danny Thomas. EP: Gregory J. Willenborg. P: Gary Smith. P/D: Dwight Hemion. W/ Special Lyrics: Buz Kohan. Music: Ian Fraser. Special Musical Material: Larry Grossman.

An atypically classy if a little stuffy lineup of artists doing their best at opening night for the new Bob Hope Cultural Center in Palm Springs, California, is a welcome break from the usual Hope special. Lucille Ball calls Bob America's most-loved comedian before welcoming the Alvin Ailey American Dance Theater's stupendous footwork. Classical pianist Van Cliburn makes his first network TV performance since the 1960s playing Robert Schumann's composition "Dedication." John Forsythe, who alternates hosting with Lucille, introduces Diahann Carroll and Vic Damone singing Broadway hits, and the President and the First Lady are seen holding hands at one point. Next up is 10-year-old violinist Leila Josefowicz, whose spellbinding precise playing earns a standing ovation. Andrew Lloyd Webber comes out after a film clip of "Music of the Night" from the musical *The Phantom of the Opera*, performed by Michael Crawford and directed by Ken Russell. He sets the scene for his wife, Sarah Brightman, and Steve Barton to sing more from that show. Capping it off are in order George Burns, Ann-Margret, Phyllis Diller, the U.S. military band, Johnny Carson, Barbara Mandrell, Dinah Shore, Delta crew members, O.J. Simpson, Alan King, Donald O'Connor, Danny Thomas, and as a surprise to Bob, Delores Hope live next to him singing new lyrics to "Thanks for the Memory." President Ronald Reagan presents the inaugural Bob Hope Humanitarian Award to Bob (later known as America's Hope Award), who responds, "I appreciate the nice things he's said about me, even if I'm not Russian" and makes other jokes before accepting it and ending a swell show.

Bob: *** Show: ****

*Happy Birthday Bob*: "50 Stars Salute Your 50 Years With NBC"
May 16, 1988, Monday 8-11 p.m.

ALF, Steve Allen, Lucille Ball, Milton Berle, George Burns, Kirk Cameron, Diahann Carroll, Bert Convy, Sammy Davis Jr., Angie Dickinson, Phyllis Diller, John Forsythe, Delores Hope, Ann Jillian, Jack Jones, Stepfanie Kramer, Dorothy Lamour, Michael Landon, Jay Leno, Shelley Long, Reba McEntire, Donald O'Connor, Marie Osmond, Tony Randall, Nancy Reagan, President Ronald Reagan, Don Rickles, Brooke Shields, Dinah Shore, James Stewart, Brandon Tartikoff, Danny Thomas, Leslie Uggams, Betty White, Jonathan Winters. EP: James Lipton. Music and Lyrics: James Lipton, Cy Coleman. Choreographer: Walter Painter.

ALF discusses Bob's party with Kirk Cameron before the long cast list appears and Sammy Davis Jr. leads a song and dance number introducing Stepfanie Kramer, Leslie Uggams, and finally Bob himself to the party, which includes several celebrities in the audience including Glenn Ford, Foster Brooks, Stella Stevens, Pat Sajak, Don Adams, Jamie Farr, Red Button, Hal Linden, Loretta Swit and more. Cut to a montage of more than six minutes of old monologues, followed by a cute poem by Jimmy Stewart. A duet by Marie Osmond and Kirk Cameron with a new song leads to old clips of performers. After Lucille Ball and Reba McIntire, Jay Leno has a great monologue blistering the modern day movie theater experience, and Sammy Davis Jr. is electrifying tap dancing to "Yankee Doodle Dandy." Much less fascinating is Brooke Shields and Michael Landon with their duet. Luckily, Jonathan Winters' hilarious routine enacting several baseball players make one forget that experience quickly. As she did on Bob's party in 1983, Ann Jillian leads a salute to the USO, and some clips of overseas tours follow. Milton Berle is amusing in his monologue and song, but Stepfanie Kramer's non-hit is embarrassing. Better is Jack Jones as a reporter interviewing Oscar nominees Betty White, Bert Convy, Marie, Brooke, Phyllis Diller and Angie Dickinson in a song with clever lyrics, with of course clips from Bob at the Academy Awards. George Burns is adorable as always joking and singing, and Steve Allen does a smart salute to Bob too. Diahann Carroll sings strongly, then Betty joins Donald O'Connor and Tony Randall to a tribute to vaudeville. Don Rickles tells Bob, "It's all over ... You have nothing!" and Dinah Shore sings well before singers with Bob appear. Shelley Long does limericks (?), then Dorothy Lamour introduces the Road pictures. Delores does "It Had to Be You." NBC President Brandon Tartikoff is funny and announces Burbank is renaming one street Bob Hope Drive. John Forsythe reads messages from England, China, and ex-presidents Nixon, Carter and Ford. President Ronald Reagan appears on tape, and his wife stuns everyone by showing up in person to sing "Thanks for the Memory." Bob gets the Bob Hope Comedy Fund in his honor at Yale and gently needles everyone fo a nice ending.

Bob: *** Show: ****


*Stand By for the HNN ... The Hope News Network*
Sept. 8, 1988, Thursday 8:30-9:30 p.m.

Phyllis Diller, Morgan Fairchild, Tony Randall, Brooke Shields, Yakov Smirnoff. Cameo: Ted Turner. Featured: Fritz Coleman, Michael Chan, Glenn Chin. D: Walter C. Miller. Special Musical Material: Jay Livingston, Ray Evans.

Bob and his crew take a swing at TV reporting and pretty much whiff it here with horrible jokes and a vaguely xenophobic edge to boot. He does kill in his monologue on the Republican candidate for vice president ("I wouldn't mind sending a [Dan] Quayle to Washington. We've already sent enough turkeys") and America's economy ("The most prosperous beggars are being bought out by other beggars"), among others. Then Ted Turner blandly says from his CNN headquarters that

Bob has set up his own headline network, leading into Bob, Phyllis Diller, Morgan Fairchild, Tony Randall, and Brooke Shields doing a long, wan musical introduction on a set with a long desk. They introduce bad bits from correspondents in Japan, where the reporter says the country's tallest person is five foot six, and the People's Republic of China, where an actor has to say, "Though we are Chinese, we have very little news to go." Yakov Smirnoff's coverage from Russia is better, with a few good jokes at Mikhail Gorbachev, and there's intermittent pleasure with Phyllis as a 131-year-old woman who keeps nodding off when interviewed by Bob, plus Tony, Bob, Morgan, and Brooke as political consultants trying to one up their candidates over the competition. Unfortunately, loser bits like Bob promoting the Iran Express card as the Ayatollah Khomeini and Brooke saying it was so hot that Emmanuel Lewis bought ice cream and moved into the cone appear too much, making this media mockery a muddled mess.

Bob: *** Show: **

### *Bob Hope's Jolly Christmas Show with the All America Champs*
Dec. 17, 1988, Monday 8-9 p.m.

Dolly Parton, Don Johnson, Florence Griffith-Joyner., Orel Hershiser, The AP All America Football Team, The Rose Queen. D: Sid Smith.

A tedious talk with Don Johnson and Dolly joining Bob to do "Silver Bells" are about the sole distinguishing features of this otherwise forgotten Yuletide installment.

### *Bob Hope Super Bowl Party*
Jan. 29, 1989, Saturday 8-9 p.m.

George Burns, Sammy Davis Jr., Shelley Long, Tiffany, Joe Montana, Boomer Esiason.

This tribute in advance of the "big game" included skits with George Burns as one of the surviving first football players and Shelley Long as a mentally deranged woman whose comments distract Bob and Sammy Davis Jr. as they watch the game.

## *Bob Hope's Easter Vacation in the Bahamas*
March 25, 1989, Saturday 8-9 p.m.

La Toya Jackson, Barbara Mandrell, Andy Williams, Tony Randall. La Toya's Dancers: Melvin Lewis, Timothy Richard.

Nassau's Crystal Palace Resort hosts this alternately interesting and innocuous installment. Noting the locale has casinos, Bob jests, "I went into one for a free beer and spent $2,700." He quips of the skimpy bikinis, "They're not big enough to hold a label," while back in the United States, "It was so cold the Golden Girls had to be jump started." The monologue's clever lines disappear when Bob banters with Barbara Mandrell so she can promote her new album, but they return when Bob interviews pretentious Gov. Gen. Sir Reginald Thisdale (Tony Randall), sporting a trimmed beard and monocle. "You needn't curtsy," he tells Bob as he refers to America as "the Colonies" and claims the Revolutionary War got an assist because Paul Revere's horse was on steroids. Andy Williams lip syncing his old hit "Theme from Love Story" brings down the excitement, but things rebound with a funny bit as the Easter bunny (Bob) encounters difficulties going through customs with an official (Tony). Then La Toya Jackson converses with Bob, who references her recent *Playboy* nude pictorial spread. "You sure topped your brother Michael," he says. "How so?" she asks. "He only took off one glove!" Bob answers. The whole cast appears in "Nassaublanca," a funny if silly spoof of *Casablanca* with Bob as the café owner. The rest of the show, with Bob joking about golf with Andy, Tony playing a scuba diver talking to a local fisherman (Tony), and La Toya performing at the Straw Market, is okay but unremarkable.

Bob and Show: ***

## *Bob Hope's Birthday Spectacular in Paris*
May 24, 1989, Wednesday 8-10 p.m.

Bea Arthur, Sid Caesar, Linda Evans, John Forsythe, The Gipsy Kings, Dolores Hope, Ann Jillian, Louis Jordan, Melissa Manchester, Brooke Shields, Randy Travis. EP/W: James Lipton. D: Dwight Hemion.

The stars sing a line of "I Love Paris" in the introduction before the show officially begins at the Champs Elysées Theatre to celebrate France's bicentennial. Bob discusses the country's history, relationship with America ("I saw a sign this morning that said, 'Yankee go home.

But not until you finish your shopping.'"), driving ("People who think Chuck Yeager was the first man to break the sound barrier have never had a ride in a Paris taxi."), and more in an impressive set. Louis Jordan appears in several blackouts as a gendarme dealing with Bob as the target for a firing squad. Bob and Bea Arthur banter and sing outdoors before he presents the Gipsy Kings in a lively performance. The Hunchback of Notre Dame (Sid Caesar) serves Bob and Bea in a long, lumbering sketch. Better is Melissa Manchester, who after singing a song straight hilariously creates a dialogue alternating famous lyrics with Bob as he attempts to impress her. Linda Evans and John Forsythe talk trivially with Bob, then things improve as Ann Jillian sings "Autumn Leaves" and Sid does a swell double talk routine in many languages. However, whoever came up with the tedious skit with Marie Antoinette (Ann), Louis XVI (Bob), Louis's lover (Brooke Shields), Louis's confidante (Louis), Louis's captain (Sid) and a peasant (Bea) should have been overthrown themselves. An eight-minute fashion show narrated by Brooke and Bob does not help, although it marks one of the last public appearances by designer Patrick Kelly before his death. Bob and Louis sing "Thank Heaven for Little Girls" from Louis's movie *Gigi*, and Randy Travis superbly presents "It's Just a Matter of Time" before Brooke tries to teach Bob French in another overextended routine. Ann's song and dance number with Bob on "It's De-Lovely" perks up things, and Delores Hope's rendition of "Our Love is Here to Stay" is fine too. At the end, Bob gets an endowment fund in his name to foster artistic exchange between France and the United States, and he sings a touching bilingual version of "Thanks for the Memory." Even with all that, this is another two-hour show that feels like it would have been much better at ninety minutes—or sixty. Bob also is beginning to show his age, as he slurs a little during his introductions and is obviously dubbed some.

Bob: *** Show: **

## *Bob Hope's Love Affair with Lucy*
Sept. 23, 1989, Saturday 9:30-11 p.m.

George Burns, Kirk Cameron, Danny Thomas, Betty White. D: Ellen Brown.

After a montage of entrances by Lucy on Bob's previous specials backed by the *I Love Lucy* theme, Bob comes out to say he is not doing a monologue in order to honor Lucy. He notes that "Lucy handled the medium of television like she handled everything else—with grace and style. And a richness of color that didn't need any help from the peacock." Clips are from Dec. 9, 1973, Oct. 24, 1962, Oct. 21, 1956, May 16, 1988, March 25, 1977, May 25, 1987, and Bob and Lucy's movies *The Facts of Life*, *Fancy Pants* and *Sorrowful Jones*, plus the 1989 Academy Awards. Danny Thomas talks about doing his series on Desilu Studios, calls Lucy a great clown while recounting working with her and adds, "I owed her a lot, especially a lasting friendship." Kirk Cameron shares his memories from their times doing Bob Hope's May 25, 1987 and May 16, 1988 shows, while George Burns talks movingly of working with her. Betty White is best, discussing her first meeting Lucy when Betty was filming her sitcom *A Date with the Angels* and the importance of *I Love Lucy* in establishing the multiple-camera format for doing television. Bob reappears at the end and warmly rhapsodizes, "Whoever thought that this little girl from Celeron, New York would grow into a talent that would dazzle the world?... Thanks, Lucille, for making life a ball." It's all nice, but Lucy will be remembered better for her work away from Bob.

Bob and Show: ***

## *Bob Hope's Christmas Show from Waikoloa, Hawaii*
Dec. 16, 1989, Saturday 10-11 p.m.

Ashley and Wynonna Judd, Barbara Eden, The AP All America Team, The Rose Queen. D: Sid Smith.

Barbara gets to sing "Silver Bells" with Bob in this tropical outing, which includes him appearing in drag with her and the Judds in a parody of *Steel Magnolias*. A clip of John Wayne from 1978 is included too, just as it was in the Christmas show of 1982.

Bob is beginning to show his age even in publicity photos, seen here with Loni Anderson during a break for taping *Bob Hope's Bag Full of Christmas Memories*, which aired on Dec. 15, 1993 to Bob's last highest ratings. Courtesy of Getty Images

# 6  Specials – 1990s

"I REMEMBER SEEING a couple of those Bob Hope specials and saying, 'Gee, I wish he would quit.'"—Bob's former writer Howard Albrecht on watching the comedian in the 1990s.

Credits for this decade are as follows (exceptions noted in shows when known): EP: Bob Hope. P: Elliott Kozak (1990), Linda Hope (1990-1996). D: Tim Kiley (1990-1992). W: Gene Perret, Martha Bolton, Robert L. Mills (1990-1992), Seaman Jacobs (1990-1992), Jeffrey Barron (1990-1992), Fred Fox (1990), Doug Gamble (1992). Announcer: John Harlan. Music: Les Brown, Bob Alberti (1990-1992), Nick Perito (1993-1995).

Discussing growing older with Dick Hobson in *Los Angeles* magazine in April 1979, Johnny Carson said, "Jeez, Bob Hope was on the show last week, and he's like a kid running around. He's 76 going on 77, but I don't anybody considers Bob Hope an elderly man. In the entertainment business, nobody comes in and tells you that it's time to get your gold watch."

Oh, what a difference a decade made.

By 1990 it was obvious to anyone seeing his specials that Bob was not the robust man he had been for decades, as he was losing his hearing and vision and slowing his delivery. Those witnessing that included Carson, who saw how Hope had declined and considered that as a factor when he decided to retire from hosting *The Tonight Show* in 1992, when he was 67.

NBC did its part to ease its workload on Bob, cutting him from five to four specials each season starting in 1990-1991, but that reduction could not hide how Bob was deteriorating even by taking a casual look at his shows. By 1991, he was balding, slurring, sounding more nasal, and looking disoriented frequently.

Hope's team recognized this too and tried to adjust to help him where possible, but it added to their problem in doing the specials. "Part of the problem was his very poor eyesight," says writer Doug Gamble, looking back at Bob's difficulties at the time. "The printing on the cue cards became enormous, and it slowed production down."

"Mostly, the adjustments were realizing that we were working with an elderly star," says Gene Perret. "There were certain physical gags that we just couldn't put into the script." They also changed the concepts to make the shows easier for Hope, like letting other comedians do their routines and bringing in guests to help Bob introduce the talent.

While these additions and compensations helped somewhat, a few other things hampered Bob as well. One was that his material unfortunately could be just as sexist as decades earlier. For example, on his Feb. 17, 1990 special, he cracked of female soldiers, "I hate to pick on women, but how can we have an invasion where our troops storm ashore and then change their minds? I mean, putting women in combat could change the whole look of warfare. You know, curtains in the foxholes, taffeta flak jackets, open-toe combat boots. But anybody who thinks women can't fight hasn't been to a January white sale! ... I knew there were women in combat in Panama when I saw a tank make a left turn without signaling." To anyone familiar with how women had fought to get the right to serve with men, these retrograde gags were staggeringly unfunny.

His guest list was getting pretty stale too. On his May 19, 1990 special, Brooke Shields noted that this was her twenty-fourth special with Bob. Holdovers like Ann Jillian and Phyllis Diller stayed on despite having low-key professional careers at the time simply because Bob liked and trusted them. Some big newbies did show up, like Macaulay Culkin, but one was more apt to encounter Milton Berle than these types on Bob's 1990s shows.

With all these factors in play, ratings unsurprisingly continued to be a hit-or-miss affair—sometimes with big misses. Things looked dire when Bob's April 9, 1990 special scored a new low of forty-fifth place, placing third in its time slot behind *MacGyver* on ABC and *Major Dad* on CBS. However, his first two specials the next season bounced back into the top twenty-five, and Bob even soared to number nine on a wave of patriotism with his special entertaining troops in the Persian Gulf War in January 1991. To many, it reminded them of what Bob did best.

## Going Back to War

Participating in *Bob Hope's Christmas Cheer in Saudi Arabia* was Marie Osmond. Bob had asked her to go overseas with him for his USO trek in December 1987, but she was pregnant and had to decline. Now she could join him, but the country's strict standards of clothing prompted Bob to have a good laugh at Marie's expense.

"We were told we had to wear dresses up to our necks and long sleeves and no shorts at one base where they were taping," she recalls. "I came out of my dressing room, and he took one look at my red dresses and just busted out and said, 'That's my girl!' It definitely was long."

Bob was more serious in informing Marie prior to the trip, "You'll know why I'm going over. I love these men and women." He told her to explore the camp to get a better sense of what was happening in the lead-up to the war that would be known as Operation Desert Storm.

"I remember I walked into a huge tent, and it was all connected. There weren't that many people. It was a hospital. I said, 'What are all those boxes?' And he said, 'It's for blood plasma. We're preparing for the war,'" says Marie. The official's statement brought home to her Bob's knowledge about what the military was facing in its fighting. "It was one of those things that I don't think I would've had an experience if he didn't have me wander."

Marie also took home video footage of her experience, which proved to be invaluable for the special when Bob's daughter producer, Linda Hope, said they had lost some footage shot in Saudi Arabia and wanted to use some of what she had for the special. "You'll see certain pieces with time codes on it, and that's mine!" she says. She adds that she later learned that "The first guns fired in the war were right there where I was standing on the USS Wisconsin."

Alas, a special celebrating the end of that war just three months later sunk to thirtieth place, even with a goodly amount of big-name celebrities. Bob also was starting to show his age there too, relying on his guest stars to do most of the work. It was a sign of things to come.

## Bringing on the Youngsters

Bob rebounded somewhat in the 1991-1992 season. There was good news in that his Christmas show made the top twenty and that a new style of special, *Bob Hope and Other Young Comedians*: "The World Laughs, Young and Old," won its time slot on March 14, 1992. As its name implied, the special featured up-and-coming talent including comedic juggler Mark Nizer.

"He was a huge inspiration to me," Nizer says, adding that he met Bob first at the American Collegiate Talent Showcase program for aspiring performers, where he got to talk with Bob's manager, advertisers, musicians and others as well as Bob to discuss plans for their careers. "I remember having a private session with Bob Hope. We would get to sit down and ask questions of people in the program. He said that show business is two words—show and business. And as a juggler/comedian, I had only thought about show… He taught me that you've have the two pieces of the puzzle, or you'll be in your garage."

Booked on Bob's special, Mark had a great time. "He was very kind, very funny," he says "I got my first job because I got a video of Bob putting his arm around me praising me. He really gave me the jump that start me going." In fact, he became Bob's opening act on tour until the comedian could no longer remember his jokes and punch lines, and Nizer believes he did the last live performance Bob gave.

Also appearing some with Bob in this period was Carol Siskind, who appeared in an all-female edition following this special on Nov. 28, 1992, *Bob Hope Presents Ladies of Laughter*, which had a surprisingly strong showing of number eighteen in the ratings. She got word from her management that "Bob watched your tapes and wants to works with you," and soon she appeared with him in Washington, D.C. and a benefit at Branson, Missouri.

"He was winding down, but I feel very fortunate to have spent time with him," she says. "It was like traveling with the Pope. You never saw anything like it… Anywhere we would go with him, he got a standing ovation going into the room."

While acknowledging Bob's timing was not as sharp as in the past, Siskind claims he still had his wit ready to go. She recalls one funny spontaneous moment at a press conference held at his house in Toluca Lake for their special. "I turned to him and said, 'Is this a good time to ask you for some cash?' And he said, 'Oh, this would be the time!'"

Wendy Liebman was part of *Bob Hope Presents Ladies of Laughter* too, and the appearance gave her burgeoning career a big boost. "I had just moved out to L.A. after doing a spot on *The Tonight Show Starring Johnny Carson*," she recalls. "My agent was Rick Greenstein at William Morris, and I believe he gave me the offer."

Liebman learned she needed to do a six-minute set of her material. "I think the producers watched my set and approved the jokes—all from my regular routine," she says. She used her standard opening joke of "Some guy thought I was Ruth Buzzi, is she pretty?" eagerly at the start of her set, and from there, the laughs just kept flowing easily during her segment.

Introducing Liebman on the special was Phyllis Diller, who impressed her. "When I was eleven, I saw Phyllis being interviewed, and she said something like, 'You have to make the audience laugh, and just when they think they're done laughing, you have to hit 'em again.' And I thought to myself, 'I know what you mean, Phyllis!' She was speaking my language! So, meeting her was an absolute thrill! I just loved Phyllis Diller. Her humor, her art, her music."

She has fond memories of the show's host too. "I was fortunate enough to open for Bob Hope in Indianapolis in an outdoor tent for 5,000 people after doing his special. It was the biggest audience I had ever performed for. Both Mr. and Mrs. Hope were so sweet to me. And I got to watch him perform a whole set live, which was surreal having seen him on TV and in movies. Phyllis Diller and Bob Hope both had perfect timing. And when I think about them, I can hear their voices and their laughs, and I picture their eyes and their smiles, smiles of great comedians who just told the funniest jokes."

Liebman adds that her appearance on this special reaped big dividends for her career. "Being on the show gave me a huge credit I could use to get gigs! And just knowing I was a part of a Bob Hope special made me feel special."

Yet as successful as these young comedians specials were, Bob still had general ratings problems. His 1991 fall opening show finished second in its time slot against *Knots Landing* on CBS, and his birthday show in 1992 collapsed to fiftieth place. By the time of that special, titled *Bob Hope's America*: "Red, White and Beautiful—The Swimsuit Edition," Bob could barely get through the taping of the segments, and it appalled his writer of fifteen years, Bob Mills.

"I just couldn't bear to see him deteriorate like that," Mills said. "I didn't push to renew my contract for the 1992-1993 season. [Jeffrey] Barron couldn't take it anymore, either [sadly, Barron would die of a heart attack three years later]. [Martha] Bolton and [Gene] Perret stayed on for a couple of more seasons too many."

Bob's overall performance also unnerved NBC executives in preparation for the 1992-1993 season, so they took considerable action to remedy the flagging numbers. One was when the network's New York City flagship station announced it would carry the New York Knicks-Boston Celtics basketball game on Dec. 18, 1992, NBC leaders decided to move the Bob Hope Christmas special scheduled for that day to Dec. 19 to get a better shot at a decent national rating, which it did receive.

Another was that for his ninetieth birthday in 1993, they insisted Bob honor the occasion with an all-star party extravaganza rather than his suggestion of doing a planned travelogue recapping his overseas tours called "Around the World with Bob Hope." The efforts paid off for both, and the three-hour celebration *Bob Hope: The First 90 Years* finished at seventeenth place.

**Bob Turns the Big Ninety**

Don Mischer produced and directed the mammoth production as he had done for Bob's eightieth birthday, which many consider to be Bob's last big hurrah. "Linda Hope asked me if I would produce that show with her," he recalls. "And I remember it being a lot of fun and I remember a lot of people wanting to take a part of it and to cover so many ways Bob influenced this country."

This celebration required him to work more with Bob than the earlier one did, and its importance arguably was even bigger because for many in the entertainment industry, they realized this probably would be their last chance to thank Bob in public. Regarding his approach to it in pre-production, Mischer says, "You never consciously shut your family out or anybody else out, but what happens in these situations, you get so preoccupied with things and you have a list of things you have to do, and you work for two to three weeks, and you never take a moment to say, 'God, I'm working with a guy I listened to when I was eight or nine years old!'"

Meeting often with Linda and Bob at the latter's Toluca Lake estate, Mischer helped determine the guest lists of who to perform and what to cover, and one was a huge "get" for them. "I remember many times I tried to book Johnny Carson for other stuff. He didn't like the other stuff and usually bowed out," notes Mischer. "In this instance, he didn't!" In fact, Johnny's monologue at the start of the special was the only time he performed on TV after retiring from *The Tonight Show* in 1992.

Mischer adds that doing the special, "I remember being concerned about Bob's hearing. I knew that if he couldn't hear, we wouldn't get the same kind of reactions. First, I went to Bob's house, and we talked about the hearing issue. I said 'Bob, have you thought about wearing a hearing aid?' He looked at me and said, 'I'm saving that for a special occasion!'"

It took some effort to conquer that obstacle in rehearsals. "I had speakers down on him that were massive, like two-and-a-half-feet high, very heavy. We tried and tried, but Bob really had a hard time hearing," Mischer says. They ultimately used on Bob an in-ear earpiece with very high frequency. "In the control room, Linda could talk to Bob directly, if she felt like he wasn't understanding something. From the expressions we got on his face, I got the impression he understood what was going on and appreciated it."

Buz Kohan, who came in two weeks before the show and wrote with bandleader Ray Charles (not the blind one) the Emmy-nominated opening production number, "Where There's Life, There's Hope," has a different recollection of Bob's demeanor during the taping. "Linda Hope was in the director's room, and she was on a microphone and she was telling him what to do," Kohan says. "He was like literally an automaton, doing whatever she said from the control room."

Shooting the program at NBC's Burbank studios, Linda Hope and Mischer planned to conclude the opening ceremonies held on the outside lot and hosted by Jay Leno with a special tribute to Bob. "Before we went into the studio to do the show, we had a military salute for him, and we wanted to get the Blue Angels to fly into the entrance into Studio One at NBC," Mischer says. "We had spotters on the roof to try to direct this. Jay did the lead-up and said, 'Here they are!' but they did not fly over NBC, they went the wrong direction. We redid it, and Jay started to make sure that those guys weren't lost. Jay did the same introduction, and once again, they were on the other side of Burbank!" The planes eventually were inserted into the show in post-production, making it look like Bob was seeing them overhead for the first time even thought that was not the case.

Mischer spent the taping cutting often to Bob for reactions and for planned quips in response to what had been presented. To supervise a large-scale production that took three hours and hundreds of guests to appear on stage would stagger many producers and directors, but Mischer said he thrives on it.

"I like bringing on choirs and teens carrying flags, giving it some scale and importance, and all aspects of Bob's life lent him to do it … What really pays off is when you can trigger some kind of an emotion that touches you and makes you think a little different about the person up there," he says.

The hard work paid off by winning an Emmy for Outstanding Musical or Comedy Special, the first win for a Hope special since 1966. The special also garnered Emmy nominations for Outstanding Choreography (Don Crichton), Music and Lyrics (Ray Charles and Buz Kohan), and Multi Camera Picture Editing For A Special Miniseries Or A Movie.

## Going Forward Unsteadily

Most familiar with Bob's work agree that *Bob Hope: The First 90 Years* should have been his last special, as it was respectful to him despite the fact that Bob's increasing infirmities were apparent. However, he was determined to keep doing TV, and with no one at NBC willing to say no to him—even though that same network had announced a year earlier of counting only viewers in the eighteen- to forty-nine-year-old age bracket to measure its rating success, a group where Bob was in serious trouble of attracting—he was able to eke out a few more shows, to the chagrin of many.

His writers, which now were down to just Gene Perret and Martha Bolton, tried to accommodate Bob as best as possible. At least one of them defends Bob continuing to do specials in his nineties.

"I don't feel that any of us have the right to tell a performer like Bob Hope when is the time to quit performing," says Perret. "He enjoyed it so much that I wouldn't want to deny him that pleasure. Yes, he did slow down and had some problems reading the cue cards or remembering lines, but audiences still loved seeing him. If I had the power, I doubt if I would have forced him to do anything differently."

The first reaction by the public of Bob's circumstances on his specials was quite different. The overpromoted, underproduced *Bob Hope's Bag Full of Christmas Memories* aired on Dec. 15, 1993 to excellent ratings of number eleven for the week and horrible notices about how out of it Bob looked during the show. Viewers were shocked of what little of Bob they saw, having difficulty making conversation with guests and reacting slowly to the world around him, and nobody seem to like it much (well, maybe Warden Neil, who somehow got an Emmy nomination for Outstanding Costumes For A Miniseries Movie Or A Special from doing it). Ratings for Bob's next specials cratered over the next two years in the wake of this show.

First up was *Bob Hope's Birthday Memories* in May 1994, which came in third in its slot with a rating of 8.5 and prompted *Daily Variety* to add, "It was also Hope's lowest-rated first-run special in at least twelve years and possible ever." The news got worse in succeeding installments. Bob's August 1994 outing scored a measly 6.9 rating even though it aired against repeats. His 1994 Christmas show had twenty-five percent fewer viewers than Bob's previous Yuletide entry. The March 1995 special emerged a horrible eighty-first place out of ninety-one network shows ranked the week it aired, and the next show five months later scored even lower ratings than its predecessor.

With this track record, some wondered whether it was Bob or NBC calling the shots when it was announced he would not host a Christmas special for the first time since he started TV in 1950. Matters were not helped in 1996 when tabloids characterized Bob virtually at death's door. Writing for *TV Guide* in August 1996 for a now-rare interview with the star, Mary Murphy scoffed at those reports, but she acknowledged he was far from 100 percent: "Sometimes Hope remembers events clearly, sometimes he needs to be gently reminded. At other moments, his apparent lack of focus is due to his refusal to wear a hearing aid."

In the summer of 1996, Bob finished taping his part for a new special. It occurred at the White House with Tony Danza assisting Bob. Gloria Loring recalls that when she went to a show in Pensacola, Florida, celebrating the Bob Hope Village and Delores Hope All Faiths Chapel at the Air Force Enlisted Village, Delores told her a story that showed Bob still had some wit during that taping. "Delores mentioned Bob being at the White House for all his service and taking pictures, and on the way out of the office, Bob said, 'Who was that?' And Delores said, 'Bob, that was the president.' He said, 'Oh, maybe I should make another entrance!'"

An October news release announced that this would be Bob's last special for NBC (even though he was under contract through 1997) and would air in November. It brought attention to *Bob Hope ... Laughing with the Presidents*, which would prove to be Bob's last starring finale, but it was not a rousing windup with the critics or general public. While Bob's rating of 9.1 was the highest he had in at least three years, it still was less than the 9.4 *Dr. Quinn Medicine Woman* got in the same time slot against him on CBS. For a man who dominated TV for decades, it seemed a sad finish.

**TV After the Specials**

The only TV job Bob had thereafter was a commercial he filmed for Kmart in 1997, not surprisingly saying and doing very little (according to Loring, Bob was somewhat deaf and nearly blind by this time). His next TV appearance was in the news, as someone at the Associated Press accidentally announced incorrectly that Bob was dead on June 4, 1998 and the family had to clarify that was wrong.

Three months later, at the fiftieth annual Emmy Awards held Sept. 13, 1998, Bob sat in a director's chair and waved on stage along with Milton Berle and Sid Caesar as a tribute to the founding comedy talent on TV during the 1950s. They did not speak, but they did get a healthy round of applause from a standing ovation lasting more than a minute. That was Bob's last appearance on an entertainment show.

In June 2000, he went to Washington to the unveiling of the Bob Hope

Gallery of American Entertainment, which was his last public appearance. Bob already had shown up at a few other events during the second term of President Bill Clinton's administration with drooping eyes that looked like he was ready to fall asleep at any second. One such moment of being named an honorary veteran in 1997 was caught on camera and rebroadcast as the "moment of Zen" on Comedy Central's *The Daily Show*—a cruel use of footage against Bob.

Bob got a respectful remembrance from his former costars and admirers a few years later when Linda Hope served as co-executive producer with Gary Smith of a birthday special called *100 Years of Hope and Humor*, where nearly forty celebrities recalled their memories and encounters with Bob. Given Bob's frail condition, there was no new footage of him included. It aired on NBC on April 20, 2003 and got an Emmy nomination incongruously in the category of Outstanding Reality/Competition Program.

Three months later, on July 27, 2003, Bob passed away peacefully at home with his family. News about it came out the following morning. To its everlasting shame, NBC only showed a brief few seconds in tribute to him on TV that night, preferring to keep its regularly scheduled program of a repeat of the tacky reality show *Fear Factor*. Thankfully, CBS installed a special edition of its newsmagazine *48 Hours* to honor Bob, and that show beat all its competitors—including *Fear Factor*.

If one looks at it this way, Bob went out on TV a winner. It's probably best to do so, given what passes for entertainment on most of his 1990s specials. For anyone who knows Bob and his legacy, they are tough to withstand watching, and for those who do not know him, they are a poor representation of what a truly talented comedian, singer, and dancer he was.

### *Bob Hope Lampoons Show Business*
Feb. 17, 1990, Saturday 10-11 p.m.

Michael Crawford, Norm Crosby, Morgan Fairchild, John Forsythe. Featured: Peter Leeds, Dale Kristien.

Everyone is energetic and half the skits work, so this gets mild approval. Bob's monologue covers Mike Tyson's surprising loss in boxing ("Tyson knew he was in trouble when he looked over and saw [ex-wife] Robin Givens in Buster Douglas's corner"), the Oscars ("As they're known in my house, *Field of Dreams*"), Roseanne Barr's marriage to Tom Arnold ("Tom is still laid up with the five hernias he got from carrying Roseanne over the threshold") and more. Except for mocking women in combat, this is one of Bob's best ever. John Forsythe, Morgan Fairchild, Michael Crawford, and Bob sing a forgettable opening tune before Bob and Morgan play a tacky couple who earned fifty million dollars from John's sweepstakes contest. It is pretty funny, as is Norm Crosby as a shady real estate promoter. Next, Bob and John are the Constitution's signers reviewing TV ratings reports to determine what language to use in the document in an uninteresting sketch. Michael does a number from his hit musical *The Phantom of the Opera* with costar Dale Kristien before joining Bob to deliver "Rap News," which is more odd than funny. A spoof of *Love Connection* with Morgan and Bob telling John about their lousy date flails, as does John pitching cemetery plots, Mikhail Gorbachev (Bob) promoting his "greatest hits" album, and Batman (Michael) and the Joker (Bob) interrupting a dinner between Lois Lane (Morgan) and Superman (John). However, John, Morgan, and Michael's funny lyrics along with Bob on "Thanks for the Memory" makes this end on a high note.

Bob: **** Show: ***

*Bob Hope's Spring Fling of Comedy and Music from Acapulco*
April 9, 1990, Monday 8-9 p.m.

Clint Black, Kirk Cameron, Phyllis Diller, Ann Jillian, The Hollywood Swimsuit Models. D: Greg V. Fera. "Hot Tamale" Music and Lyrics: William Dunham, Marilyn Hooven.

Since Bob is not seen walking out for his entrance and the monologue is taped at two different locations—with several cutaways to the audience—one fears that he will be in poor shape here, but thankfully that's not the case. The weak monologue has odd targets like the increase in stamp costs ("And you still have to provide your own spit!"), but Bob is fine as the Hollywood Swimsuit Models go so crazy over Kirk Cameron that Bob quips, "Am I in this scene?!" Phyllis Diller joins Kirk in interviewing matador Don Manuel Labor (Bob) about what is the most dangerous part of his job. "Getting into these pants," he responds. Phyllis has an amusing routine targeting everyone from her imaginary husband ("Fang is so dumb, he thinks Joan of Arc is Noah's wife") to ex-President Ronald Reagan ("He's so old, he can remember when two white guys fight!"). Kirk and Bob putting on sombreros and singing "Hot Tamales" would not pass muster today and lacks laughs too, and Bob's banter with Clint Black before the latter sings is not much better. Just as the show looks ready to sink, Bob excellently mocks future President Donald Trump as Donald Frump, who keeps making passes at women while his wife (Ann Jillian) is nearby. Ann is great here, and she gets revenge by handing Bob over to Phyllis. Bob also has time to do a routine on the nearby USS Belleau Wood before bidding adios here.

Bob and Show: ***


***Bob Hope's USO Road to the Berlin Wall and Moscow***
May 19, 1990, Saturday 9-11 p.m.

Rosemary Clooney, Yakov Smirnoff, Delores Hope, La Toya Jackson, Brooks Shields, Miss Universe Mona Grudt.

This trek to entertain U.S. military troops begins at Milton Hall Royal Air Base in England, where Bob references his birthplace. "I love to come back and try to find the doctor that delivered me by the nose," he says. Rosemary Clooney joins him to muse about her family and their former co-star. "Bing [Crosby] had a way of making anyone he worked with look like a bigger star than they really were. But you know that," she jabs at Bob. They do a medley with special lyrics. With La Toya Jackson, Bob makes innuendos out of what she says about her love of planes before letting her perform. In West Berlin, Bob cracks them up with "I knew I was in Germany when I turned on my shower and beer came out," and Rosemary sings "The Way We Were." Yakov Smirnoff's so-so monologue is long and reuses a joke he told on Bob's Sept. 8, 1988 special. Bob makes a detour to greet two men on the other side of the Berlin Wall helping to take it down. He returns to Moscow for the first time since his 1958 special and lets Brooke Shields sing "Reach Out and Touch (Somebody's Hand)" to the natives in an odd number. Brooke also promotes her new movie, *Backstreet Dreams*, with Bob at Rhein-Main Air Force Base in Frankfurt, Germany, then Delores Hope sings "Just the Way You Are" and Miss Universe Mona Grudt does the usual chitchat with Bob before this decent but long entry ends.

Bob: **** Show: ***


***Bob Hope: Don't Shoot, It's Only Me***
Sept. 15, 1990, Saturday 10-11 p.m.

Milton Berle, George Burns, Dr. Henry Kissinger, Frances Langford, Gloria Loring, Connie Stevens, Danny Thomas. Featured: Elvia Allman. D: Ellen Brown. W: Melville Shavelson (special material).

With three comedians with an average age of eighty-five and three singers with the youngest being in her mid-forties, this infomercial for Bob's latest book has little youth appeal. A little old lady (Elvia Allman) wants an autograph from Bob for her mother (oh boy), then Henry Kissinger shows up in the queue and is actually funny delivering his lines. Delores is waiting too ("I heard you were in town"). Bob mocks upcoming awards ("The Emmys—to me, that's a spectator sport."), President Bush, Iraq, oil prices, Saddam Hussein, and more. The special pretends to be like the book and covers chapters in Bob's life starting with vaudeville, with a clip from the Jan. 8, 1978 special with George Burns shown before George joins Bob in a routine where Bob plays Gracie's role, not as well as Gracie did unfortunately. Nonetheless, they get claps for their patter and song and dance. Next is radio, with plenty of film clips of Bob's USO shows and even speeches by President Franklin D. Roosevelt. Frances Langford obviously reads her "memories" of their wartime activities but delivers them well. For TV, Bob shows clips of Danny Thomas from Nov. 24, 1957 and Milton Berle from Oct. 19, 1966 before they come out to mock argue over about their legacies. Inexplicably, Bob calls them part of the "Mount Rushmore of comedy." Next are the Christmas shows, where Gloria Loring speaks movingly of their work in Vietnam, and finally the Middle East, with Connie Stevens being bubbly. Bob defends his efforts for the military before thanking everyone.

Bob and Show: ***


***Bob Hope's Christmas Show from Bermuda***
Dec. 15, 1990, Saturday 10-11 p.m.

Loni Anderson, Dixie Carter, Joan Van Ark, The AP All America Football Team, The Rose Queen. D: Sid Smith.

Being escorted to stage, Bob does a little shuffle while sporting white shorts to show he is ready to work. He jokes about the island's mopeds ("bicycles on steroids"), President George Bush visiting the troops in the Middle East, and a musical duo lying about singing on their records ("Any two grown men who call themselves Milli Vanilli should have been investigated long ago!") in two different locations. He talks and sings with Loni Anderson in front of an audience, which is better than his boring interplay with Joan Van Ark of both wearing hats to play characters like a sheriff and a bandit. Dixie Carter is delightful bantering with Bob (Bob: "It's hard for me to believe that you've two daughters old enough to be in college." Dixie: "Oh yeah. Mating season in the South comes early and often!") as well as singing "I'll

Be Home for Christmas." The Rose Queen segment is funnier than usual, and the All Americans, including Heisman Trophy winner Ty Detmer, clearly love joking with Bob too. After Dixie does "Silver Bells" with Bob, a dumb skit recreates English colonists discovering Bermuda in a shipwreck in 1609, with Bob as the captain and Joan and Loni as passengers fighting over him. A repeat of Bing Crosby singing "White Christmas" from 1965 leads to a tribute by Bob that feels somewhat like filler. Still, this special has more good than bad moments overall, and its lush scenery is a nice change of pace for the Yuletide season.

Bob and Show: ***

## Bob Hope's Christmas Cheer in Saudi Arabia
Jan. 12, 1991, Saturday 9:30-11 p.m.

Johnny Bench, Khrystyne Haje, Delores Hope, Ann Jillian, Marie Osmond, The Pointer Sisters, Aaron Tippin.

The minister of information of Bahrain and honorary mayor of Hollywood Johnny Grant introduce Bob, who mocks Saddam Hussein by saying he'd like to see him interviewed by Geraldo Rivera and hit with a chair. Mentioning how Steve Martin was turned down to do a show overseas, he says, "They said they didn't want entertainment, but they still wanted me." The set is good, and the Pointer Sisters get the energy flowing by presenting "I'm So Excited," prompting Bob to say, "What a kick to have these girls here. I can't thank you enough." He cracks about going to the desert before introducing Johnny Bench, who jokes about being conned by Bob into joining him there. They present soldiers with gifts from back home. Due to local customs restricting their ability to perform, the women entertained on the ships only, with Ann Jillian substituting for Bob there as emcee. She joins Bob for a comic exchange that's better than usual due to Ann's comic timing before they do "The Two of Us." Gen. Norman Schwarzkopf introduces Bob at another location, who in turn introduces Marie Osmond for some fun. Bob eats at "Tent City" before doing a night show with Johnny and scores with jokes about the men being sex starved and racing camels in the desert before Johnny does his jesting (Bob: "You ever thought about becoming an actor like me?" Johnny: "You're an actor?"). The fun continues with Bob bantering with Khrystyne Haje as if she was Brooke Shields and Marie Osmond singing "Crazy" with a soldier for a moment that's alternating comic, romantic and touching. After Ann sings "Silent Night," Bob recounts the trip and thanks all involved. It's a solid show, and Bob gives his best too, but he is showing his age with his delivery throughout.

Bob: *** Show: ****

## Bob Hope's Yellow Ribbon Celebration
April 6, 1991, Saturday 9:30-11 p.m.

Clint Black, Delta Burke, Betty Ford, President Gerald Ford, Clint Holmes, Dolores Hope, Ann Jillian, Patti LaBelle, Ed McMahon, Gerald McRaney, Marie Osmond, Brooke Shields, James Stewart.

Bob hosts the troops at Palm Springs in this patriotic, flag-waving celebration of the end of Operation Desert Storm. Apart from his jokes, it is heavy on music from everyone from Patti LaBelle to Bob's wife Delores, plus James Stewart does his slow talking routine as he compares Saddam Hussein to Hitler and Mussolini. Also seen on tape thanking the military men and women are President George W. Bush and Gens. Colin Powell and Norman Schwarzkopf.

## Bob Hope & Friends... Making New Memories
Sept. 12, 1991, Thursday 10-11 p.m.

Roseanne and Tom Arnold, Garth Brooks, Angela Lansbury, Burt Reynolds, Dorothy Lamour, Jane Russell, Debbie Reynolds, The Hollywood Deb Stars (Martha Byrne, Sondra Sprigg, Karenjo Goodwin, Jennie Garth, Monika Schnarre, Cheryl Richardson, Laura Piper, Raquel Gardner, Alex Dotrice). Featured: Peter Leeds, Jane Dulo, Ed Evanko, Jean Sincere. D: John Bowab.

Bob moves and talks slower than ever at times and looks a little frail. Perhaps knowing this, his guest stars are quite lively to compensate and make this tolerable. Bob's monologue does him no favors. Hearing Bob jest about Pee Wee Herman's arrest in an X-rated theater ("At least now we know how he got his nickname!") is jarring, like listening to someone's grandfather tell a dirty joke. Several old clips pad out the time between new segments, the first with Dorothy Lamour, Jane Russell, and Debbie Reynolds listlessly spouting their memories of Bob contacting them only when he needed a favor and being so cheap that he charges for parking at his house. Bob is absent here, but he's engaged with Angela Lansbury, the first time they have worked together professionally. She's very animated too, and their song and dance to "Well,

Did You Evah?" has a sparkle the show needs, even if Bob is a little stiff. Bob has a tougher time as he and Burt Reynolds play waiters trying to impress a studio head (Peter Leeds), bobbling a line badly. It stays in the show rather than do a retake, as would have been done in the past. Garth Brooks croons fine, and Bob is okay introducing the Hollywood Deb Stars and playing the Sheriff of Nottingham opposite Robin Hood (Tom Arnold) and Maid Marion (Roseanne, who keeps giggling). Still, Bob sounds tired as he thanks everyone for forty-two great years on TV at the end.

Bob: ** Show: ***


## Bob Hope's Cross-Country Christmas Special
Dec. 18, 1991, Wednesday 9-10 p.m.

Macaulay Culkin, Reba McEntire, Delores Hope, Miss America Suzanne Sapp, The Rose Queen, The AP All America Football Team. D: Sid Smith.

Shot at Opryland in Nashville, Tennessee, and the U.S. Air Force Academy in Colorado, this Yuletide special is enjoyable if one makes allowances for it and its host. Bob's delivery is slow and slurred noticeably throughout, and his monologue runs under three minutes, yet nonetheless he gets a standing ovation. He does have one good line here about the recent Persian Gulf War and a short-live musical duo: "Saddam Hussein disappeared faster than Milli Vanilli." Bob talks to Reba McEntire barely beyond a minute before she sings her latest Christmas song, then speaks more and has fun in a cute routine of showing dance moves to Macaulay Culkin. In a swell spoof of *A Christmas Carol*, Tiny Tim (Macaulay) defends Scrooge (Bob) to Sally Cratchitt (Reba) before they all sing new lyrics to "Joy to the World." The appearance of cheerleaders on a football field to greet members of the AP All America Football Team perks up Bob as well as he introduces Marshall Faulk, Ty Detmer, and others. The excitement levels off thereafter. Bob and Delores Hope perform "Silver Bells" rather sedately on a horse-driven sleigh in Colorado. He does a monologue designed for Air Force cadets, then plays a hotel doorman who meets Miss America Suzanne Sapp and sings "Button Up Your Overcoat" with her. After bantering with the Rose Queen, Bob plays a clip of Redd Foxx as Santa from his Dec. 10, 1972 special to honor the recently deceased star and end a decent but unspectacular show.

Bob and Show: ***

***Bob Hope and Other Young Comedians:*** **"The World Laughs, Young and Old"**
March 14, 1992, Saturday 10-11 p.m.

Co-Hosts: Milton Berle, Phyllis Diller, Betty White. Comedians: Max Alexander, Jeff Cesario, Jeff Dunham, Jeff Foxworthy, John Henton, Carol Leifer, Mark Nizer, Pam Stone.

To help out Bob here, the co-hosts and comedians do most of the work, and the lessened workload frees him greatly. It opens with ventriloquist Jeff Dunham's curmudgeon dummy Walter seeing Betty White and saying since Bob is next to her, she must be Brooke Shields. For his monologue, though Bob enters a little slowly, his sting is still there despite a few stumbles. "Delores has started spring cleaning," he notes. "This morning she did my wallet." He gets applause for saying of the presidential campaign, "No one party can fool all of the people all of the time." He is a little winded introducing Jeff Cesario, who scores with a bit on how to make classic books appeal to more people by making them sound like tabloid headlines. Betty White joins Bob ("I kept telling them, 'Get *Vanna* White!'" he mock protests), and she is wonderful in coaxing Bob to speak unscripted about his memories of doing standup and *Roberta* on stage. She introduces Max Alexander (doing diet jokes) and Jeff Dunham before Milton Berle takes her place and reminisces about old times with Bob. He introduces John Henton and Carol Leifer, both hilarious, then Phyllis takes over with Bob and cracks up over Jeff Foxworthy ("You're funny!" she exclaims after his "You might be a redneck ..." routine), Pam Stone (introduced by Bob alone) and prop comic Mark Nizer. "Keep laughing, will you? It'll keep me working," Bob quips at the end before getting a deserved standing ovation for this.

Bob and Show: \*\*\*\*


***Bob Hope's America:*** **"Red, White and Beautiful—The Swimsuit Edition"**
May 16, 1992, Saturday 9:30-11 p.m.

Boyz II Men, Barbara Bush, Michael Feinstein, Delores Hope, Elle MacPherson, Dolly Parton, Rita Rudner, Loretta Swit.

Taped in Columbus, Ohio, Bob does only one sketch, as a person phoning a doctor (Dolly Parton) with multiple concerns about his health. Otherwise, he does a monologue ("Johnny Carson goes off the air next week—another flash in the pan"), talks with Barbara Bush (who had to read Bob his lines because he could not see the cue cards) and sings with Delores while mostly letting the other guests participate in their own numbers. Despite what the title suggests, it is not a parade of pulchritude, as Loretta Swit introduces women who are doing their part in the military, and Rita Rudner provides females can be as funny as Bob too.

### *Bob Hope Presents Ladies of Laughter*
Nov. 28, 1992, Saturday 10-11 p.m.

Co-Hosts: Crystal Bernard, Phyllis Diller, Rue McClanahan. Comediennes: Margaret Cho, Wendy Liebman, Carol Siskind, Anita Wise.

A redo of Bob's March 14, 1992 special, this time with just the distaff side performing, this cannot hide Bob's increasing problems as he grows older. He is slow in walking out and delivering some lines, even halting and stumbling at points that apparently could not be edited out. Still, when he is able to comment on the battle of the sexes with "If there is, I want to be a prisoner of war," it does remind one of the Bob Hope of days past. He's also pretty comfortable reminiscing off the cuff with his co-hosts, starting with telling Phyllis Diller of a time when he bombed on stage in 1928. After recounting her jokes on cooking, Phyllis introduces Carol Siskind, who does a decent set comparing how women do tasks versus men. Phyllis also introduces Margaret Cho and then Wendy Liebman, who goes over best of all because her quick-fire approach with strong one-liners resembles that of Bob and Phyllis. After seeming to strain to read her introduction, Bob recalls his first jokes while on stage to Crystal Bernard, who appeared with Bob at the show's opening asking for his autograph and saying "My grandmother's going to love this!" She introduces Kathleen Madigan, then passes the baton to Rue McClanahan, who prods Bob's memories about working with Fanny Brice and Beatrice Lillie before bringing out Anita Wise. All the comediennes have solid sets and Bob's memories are sweet, making this a breezy hour in general despite his missteps.

Bob: *** Show: ****

## Bob Hope's Four-Star Christmas Fiesta from San Antonio
Dec. 19, 1992, Saturday 8-9 p.m.

Rita Rudner, Clint Black, Phylicia Rashad, Dolores Hope, The Rose Queen, The AP All America Football Team, Gen. William Westmoreland, U.S. Navy Admiral Wallace B. Short, Gen. Louis H. Wilson, U.S. Air Force Chief of Staff Merrill A. McPeak, U.S. Secretary of Defense Dick Cheney. D: Sid Smith.

Held at Kelly Field in San Antonio, Texas, Bob is saluted by military leaders plus Secretary of Defense Dick Cheney, who dubs Bob "America's Four-Star Hero" with a presentation. Bob gives a minute-long monologue thanking the service members, his guests, and Texas before this ends.

## Bob Hope: The First 90 Years
May 14, 1993, Friday 8-11 p.m.

Guests: Paula Abdul, Lucie Arnaz, Roseanne and Tom Arnold, Milton Berle, Les Brown, George Burns, Kirk Cameron, Johnny Carson, Chevy Chase, Walter Cronkite, Whoopi Goldberg, Phil Hartman, Florence Henderson, Dorothy Lamour, Angela Lansbury, Jay Leno, Paul Reiser, Michael Richards, Tom Selleck, Brooke Shields, Dave Thomas, Raquel Welch, Betty White. On Film and Tape: Candice Bergen, Martha Bolton, Garth Brooks, George H.W. Bush, Jimmy Carter, Bill Clinton, Gerald Ford, Mort Lachman, Richard Nixon, Gene Perret, Ronald Reagan, Sherwood Schwartz, Mel Shavelson. P/D: Don Mischer (segments). D: Allan Kartun, Nancy Malone (segments). W: Linda Perret, Buz Kohan. Music: Nick Perito. Choreographer: Don Crichton. Special Musical Material: Ray Charles.

At NBC Burbank Studios, Jay Leno addresses a crowd outside and notes, "You realize Bob Hope is still singing 'Thanks for the Memory' at an age when most guys don't even have a memory!" Inside, Johnny Carson surprises everyone and says, "Well, now that my vacation is over, I can't wait to get back to *The Tonight Show* Monday. Just kidding, Jay, just kidding!" He introduces the first appearance of Bob on KTLA in 1947 and more early clips. Bob says some words of thanks to Johnny on air after that. Angela Lansbury recounts Bob's early years, then Paula Abdul talks about Bob's dance moves, Whoopi Goldberg does a routine, and Betty White recounts Bob's radio days with comments from Bob and Candice Bergen. John Denver introduces Bob's friendship with George Burns and brings the ninety-seven-year-old down to sit with Bob. "I came here to help you blow out the candles. I understand your blower is gone," George quips. Tom Selleck brings out Dorothy Lamour, who tells Bob "Let me get my joke in" as he attempts to comment about their relationship in a fun reunion. Chevy Chase introduces clips of Bob on the Oscars, then Paul Reiser does the same for Bob's monologues. Mel Shavelson recounts how Bob used to test his material with fellow writers Martha Bolton, Mort Lachman, Gene Perret, and Sherwood Schwartz. "I owe everything I have to my writers, and I can't tell you how hard they tried to get it," Bob quips afterward. All surviving presidents record thanks for him next. Phil Hartman and Michael Richards play two veterans of the Civil War who thank Bob comically before Raquel Welch recounts his work for the USO and introduces Florence Henderson, Kirk Cameron, and Les Brown. Roseanne and Tom Arnold introduce Bob's sketches. Walter Cronkite shows Bob's tours of World War II and Vietnam and introduces the color guards of the U.S. armed forces plus bands from them as well, and veterans from World War II, Korea, Vietnam, and Operation Desert Storm. One man saw Bob in Vietnam and said his father saw Bob in World War II and his son the same in Operation Desert Storm. Milton Berle pays his respects ("Bob has said some of the funniest jokes I've used"), and Lucie Arnaz introduces funny moments with her mother, Lucille Ball, and Bob. Dave Thomas plays Chester Hope, Bob's nephew, in a perfect sendup of his monologues. Brooke Shields pays tribute to Bob's wife Delores. Walter Cronkite brings on people who worked with Bob, which is the warmest and best. "What a party, huh?" Bob remarks. He slurs a little and says, "I've got everybody here I love" in a short statement at the end.

Bob and Show: ****


## Bob Hope's Bag Full of Christmas Memories
Dec. 15, 1993, Monday 8-10 p.m.

Loni Anderson, Delores Hope, Barbara Eden, Naomi and Wynonna Judd, Joey Lawrence, Ed Marinaro, Lynn Swann, The AP All America Team. D: Sid Smith. Choreographer: Susan Donovan.

Bob tries to lip sync a new song as Loni Anderson brings her family as the first guests at Bob's home (actually a stage set). The other guests except the AP All America Team appear in order of the cast list, plus some of Bob's grandchildren. The show alternates between clips like Barbara Eden's 1988 USO tour appearance with Bob and present-day activity like the Judds recalling their 1989 parody of *Steel Magnolias* with Bob in drag. Interspersed between it all are Bob's monologues on Christmas over the years. Some clips are longer than others, like almost the full skits of Bob with Red Skelton in 1978 and with Jack Benny in 1965, while in the present, members of Bob's family deliver lines weakly. Bob does come to life briefly at his party as he recounts a Christmas story from the war to James Bacon and other members of the press. Also wonderful is the Judds singing "Beautiful Star of Bethlehem," but that's about it for highlights. After a montage of Bob's USO Christmas tours, Bob and Delores lip sync at the house party to "Silver Bells" before it quickly fades to him doing it with other women back to Gale Storm in 1953. Next up are Lucille Ball in 1973, Lee Marvin in 1971, and John Wayne in 1976 before Bob lip syncs to "I Wish It Could Be Christmas Forever" with still shots of family and friends shown as the show closes. The total screen time of Bob and his guests is less than twenty-five percent of this show, and Bob has reached the point where he cannot introduce each member of the AP All America Team—they do it themselves instead. One can see why audiences began avoiding Hope's specials thereafter with the awkward, forced atmosphere of gaiety on display here, led by a host who looks to be struggling the fleeting moments when he is seen.

Bob: * Show: **

## *Bob Hope's Birthday Memories*
May 11, 1994, Saturday 8-10 p.m.

Bea Arthur, Angie Dickinson, Phyllis Diller, Delores Hope, John Forsythe, Sugar Ray Leonard, Leslie Nielsen, John Ritter, Betty White, Jonathan Winters.

Bob celebrates turning ninety-one by reminiscing about his life and career with guests visiting him. Most of the material is recycled footage from previous specials.

## *Bob Hope's Young Comedians Making America Laugh*
Aug. 27, 1994, Saturday 10-11 p.m.

Cohosts: Dave Thomas, Crystal Bernard. Comedians: Henry Cho, Dana Gould, Anthony Griffith, Susie Loucks, Susan Norfleet, Gregg Rodell.

This third go-round of comedians reportedly had Bob get into a spat with his daughter Linda about how to end the show. She wanted a simple goodbye, he insisted on more and at least got it taped (not seeing the final version, it is hard to determine who won out when it aired).

**Bob Hope's Christmas Show: "Hopes For The Holidays"**
Dec. 14, 1994, Wednesday 9-10 p.m.

Tony Bennett, Kaitlin Cullum, Mark Curry, Delores Hope, Lindsay Wagner, The Rose Queen, The AP All America Football Team. D: Nancy Malone.

This lifeless clip-heavy special zooms in from an aerial view of Bob's estate on a mountain in Palm Springs to show him and Delores trimming the tree. He unsteadily sets up clips as "Christmas memories." They include him as Santa Claus opposite Paul Lynde (1967), Dorothy Lamour (1970), Angie Dickinson (1979), and Dyan Cannon (1976). When Mark Curry visits, Bob recounts being lifted by Joan Rhodes lifting him in 1955 and the clip follows, along with Loni Anderson (1982), Miss Piggy (1977), Brooke Shields (1987), Dionne Warwick (1978), Barbara Eden (1985), and Dixie Carter (1990). Delores talks some, then more "memories" appear from ten of Bob's Christmas shows from 1953-1985. Kaitlin Cullum plays "Jingle Bells" on a toy piano as she, Delores and Bob sing it together. Next are other child stars appearing with Bob over the years—Sarah Jessica Parker (1979), Emmanuel Lewis (1985), the Osmond Boys (1986), Marie Osmond (1973), Frank "Sugar Chile" Robinson (1953), Ricky Schroder (1982), Macaulay Culkin (1991), and Adam Rich (1979). The Rose Queen shows Bob the AP All America Team introduced by John Harlan and including Warren Sapp and Kerry Collins. Bob briefly becomes animated recalling his first time seeing Tony Bennett perform, followed by a flashback to Tony's appearance on Bob's 1967 Christmas show before Tony sings a song. Lindsay Wagner speaks pretentiously about the real meaning of Christmas before more clips appear. At the end, Kaitlin sets up a nativity scene with Delores as they sing "Do You See What I See?" Bob joins in only at the last line, then waves merry Christmas afterward. If this description needs any more added about how bad it is, consider that Bob sings "Silver Bells" to his dogs as they howl along with him as well. It's rather depressing, even without a laugh track.

Bob: ** Show: *

Specials – 1990s • 279

*Bob Hope's Young Comedians:* "A New Generation of Laughs"
March 25, 1995, Saturday 10-11 p.m.

Phyllis Diller, Alan Thicke. Comedians: Wayne Cotter, Karen Kilgariff, Sue Kolinsky, Kevin Meany, Mark Pitta, Margaret Smith. D: Patricia Eyerman.

Appearing before a live audience for the last time on one of his specials, Bob tells everyone they're going to see a lot of great talent without delivering a monologue. In a roundtable discussion about comedy with the cast in a rehearsal hall, he jokes about Shakespeare being his writer but mostly rambles as others interject in bits interspersed throughout the show. On stage, Kevin Meany and Sue Kolinsky are up first and are mild and erratic. Much better are Margaret Smith, who complains about her visiting parents, underwear inspectors, bodybuilders at the gym ("If your neck is as wide as your head, take a day off!") and mammograms, and Mark Pitta, who discusses recording over rented VHS sex tapes with *The Wizard of Oz* to confuse people and giving bad answers with the names of people you know as you are losing *Jeopardy!* Karen Kilgariff is fine enough, but Wayne Cotter outshines her with a tight set about physical checkups and more. Bob has some fleeting moments of fun at the roundtable, like mentioning how an older brother dismissed his career until he earned his first big paycheck and playing golf with Jack Benny and Danny Kaye with all three cursing how bad their shots were until people recognized them and they had to curb their words, but otherwise Phyllis Diller and Alan Thicke carry the conversation. At the end, Bob offers appreciation to everyone without doing "Thanks for the Memory" and says that they will do another special like this. But they do not. Seeing what little Bob does here, one understands why.

Bob: * Show: **

*Bob Hope: Memories of World War II*
Aug. 5, 1995, Saturday 10-11 p.m.

Delores Hope, Frances Langford, Patty Thomas.

Narration of soldiers' letters occurs over still pictures and films of Bob on tour in the 1940s to start this program. He briefly talks about how treasures those letters before telling how the war affected him first in 1939, when he took the Queen Mary from England as Germany began attacking the country. Everyone worried that the Nazis would bomb the vessel, so Bob did a performance and wrote a special version of "Thanks for the Memory" to calm their nerves. He mostly narrates this with clips of his radio show touring camp shows. Frances Langford recounts her memories too. Delores shares an album of photos from the victory caravan with Bob. She looks like she is prodding him for memories. He talks about appearing in Royal Albert Hall and then North Africa and meeting Gen. Dwight Eisenhower. A replay of his show on June 6, 1944, recounting what had happened hours earlier at D-Day is very moving. Patty Thomas speaks about touring the Pacific theater, where Bob got jungle rot. He recalls how as a young lieutenant, President John F. Kennedy attended one of Bob's show. There's more film through the war's conclusion, then more letters of thanks are narrated. Historians of Bob, the war, and classic radio will find much of this fascinating, but for most it will feel like a flaccid documentary. And Bob barely appears on camera after the first twenty minutes, making one wonder where he is and how he is doing. One is left impressed by all of what Bob and his entourage did fifty years earlier and how he is struggling to get by in the present.

Bob and Show: **

**Bob Hope... Laughing with the Presidents**
Nov. 23, 1996, Saturday 8-9 p.m.

Tony Danza, President Bill Clinton, First Lady Hilary Rodham Clinton, President George Bush, Barbara Bush, President Gerald Ford, Betty Ford, David Eisenhower, Julie Nixon Eisenhower, Ann-Margret, Don Johnson, Naomi Judd, Tom Selleck. P: George Paige. D/W: Daniel Helfgott. Music: Steven Orich.

After some new shots of the White House and old clips of Bob, the chair behind the desk at the Oval Office turns, and it's Bob sitting in it in different views in a series of quick cuts. Tony Danza walks in and says, "Okay, so it's not the president. But this man probably has as much right to sit behind that desk as anyone." Bob twiddles with a golf club and loudly tells Tony he did a show with George Washington at Valley Forge, then adds he has been visiting the presidents since 1941 before letting Tony do the talking. What follows is commentary by Tony linking the footage of Bob talking with and about former chief executives going back to Franklin Delano Roosevelt. While it is fascinating to hear Bob tell the jokes about him and his successor, Harry Truman, the remaining clips from Dwight D. Eisenhower onward are familiar ones to longtime viewers, and the commentary by all guests including the ex-presidents are rather innocuous. Bob's own statements on each president is brief, and he is seen on camera talking less than a minute total in favor of voiceovers. The need to fill time is so desperate here that the special even shows a minute of bloopers of Barbara Bush telling a story. Combine that with enduring cheesy, irritating background music (alas, no Les Brown here) and watching a hunched-over Bob clutching onto Tony as they head out of the Oval Office, and the result is one sad fadeout for Hope specials.

Bob: * Show: **

Nobody donned more tuxedos to host more awards on TV than Bob. Here he comically tries to grab the one honor he wanted the most but never got from Best Actor Oscar winner Rod Steiger, being hugged at the waist by actress Claire Bloom, his then-wife, backstage at the 1968 Academy Awards ceremony. Courtesy of Getty Images.

# 7
# Awards and Telethon Shows

**ASKED BY A REPORTER** if there was anything he wanted to do, Bob said seriously, "I'd like to win an Oscar."

This was in 1993, when Bob was ninety.

Yes, though he often joked about it, Bob's desire for an Academy Award was real. It was the only major entertainment honor that he never received (he was not going to do Broadway again, so the Tony was of no concern for him, and even he realized his recorded output had little likelihood of meriting a Grammy). He had to settle instead for being the ceremony's most frequently used host—six times on radio and fourteen on TV.

Bob was the first emcee of the Oscars on TV in 1953 (actually co-host, as Conrad Nagel assisted him) and received raves plus high ratings for his work. He looked like a lock for the job, but conflicts between the sponsors of his specials and the Academy Awards prevented him from doing the show in 1954, 1956, and 1957. And when he did host the show in the 1950s, he had to split duties with others.

Finally, starting in 1960, Bob was the sole host of the Oscars, and he held the position until the Academy tried Frank Sinatra in 1963 and Jack Lemmon in 1964. Bob returned as host the next four years until a majority of the organization's leaders decided a change of pace was in order, possibly due to negative reviews about Bob's performance in 1968. He came back as a co-host in 1971 and 1975 and as a solo host in 1978, and he showed up as a presenter in 1969, 1984, 1986, 1989, and 1991.

Because of the high number of people involved in presenting and receiving Oscars—not to mention what feels like an eternity getting through each ceremony—this section will limit itself to Bob's performances on them only for the sake of brevity. Keep in mind that the times listed are for the East Coast, so because the ceremonies typically took place live from Los Angeles, the "real" start and end times are three hours earlier for the West Coast.

Bob participated in a few other awards shows over the years, mainly as an honoree. A selection of those appear in this section as well. The exceptions are the five sports awards shows he produced and hosted from 1961-1979. They appear in Chapter 9: Game Shows and Sports.

Also included in this chapter is another all-star affair over which Bob presided, the telethon. Only a few national ones are listed here, but Bob's work in this area for local and regional TV is extensive. For example, Bob hosted telethons to raise money for cerebral palsy in Los Angeles in 1952 and 1954, for arthritis on WAVE Louisville, Kentucky on April 30, 1954 and for relief of victims of two different hurricanes, one a six-station hookup based in WHTN Meridian, Mississippi, on Aug. 23, 1969 and the other seen in 20 cities along the East Coast based in WBAL Baltimore, Maryland, on July 21, 1972. He truly gave back his time and talent when possible to help others.

Incidentally, despite doing twenty-five movies when he hosted the show off and on TV from 1953-1978, Bob's only films to get nominations by the Academy Awards in this period were *The Seven Little Foys* in 1955 (Story and Screenplay), *The Facts of Life* in 1960 (win for Black and White Costume Design, and nominations for Story and Screenplay Written Directly for the Screen, Black and White Cinematography, Black and White Art Direction-Set Direction and Song), and *Bachelor in Paradise* in 1961 (Song). If one counts cameos with Bob, add *The Five Pennies* in 1959 (Color Cinematography, Song, Scoring of a Musical Picture and Color Costume Design), and *The Oscar* in 1966 (Color Art Direction-Set Direction and Color Costume Design). The latter had Bob play himself as emcee of a fictional Academy Awards presentation.

Additionally, Bob can claim that he earned five honorary Oscars, including two given to him by surprise on TV—the Jean Hersholt Humanitarian Award in 1959 for his charitable efforts and a gold medal in 1966 "for unique and distinguished service to our industry and the Academy." Not too bad for someone who did not win a "real" Oscar in competition.

## U.S. Olympic Team Telethon
June 21-22, 1952, NBC and CBS, 14 ½ hours

Hosts: Bob Hope, Bing Crosby. Guests Included: Frank Sinatra, George Burns and Gracie Allen, Milton Berle, Peggy Lee, Frankie Laine, Donald O'Connor, Eddie Cantor, George Jessel, The Ritz Brothers, Abbott and Costello, many more.

This special marks the national TV debuts of Bing Crosby, singer Phil Harris, gossip columnist Louella Parsons, and actor Walter Pidgeon, among dozens of other entertainment acts and figures who contribute their time to raise funds for American athletes to go to the summer Olympics. A highlight is when Dean Martin and Jerry Lewis join the hosts for the festivities. Jerry hugs his entire body around Hope and kisses him while Dean shakes Crosby's hand. "It's time for the old timers to sit down!" pronounces Jerry as he asked for a little wake-up music as he and Dean danced. Bob returns as Jerry and Dean yell for Bing to come back too. He does not, so Jerry overtakes the camera as Dean sings "When You're Smiling." The show is in shambles for another ten minutes or so as he and Dean do a medley of commercial jingles. Bing might have rethought about making his debut this way.

Bob: ***** Show: ****


## The 25th Annual Academy Awards
March 19, 1953, Thursday 10:30 p.m.-Midnight (approximately)

Hosts: Bob Hope, Conrad Nagel.

"Good evening, ladies and gentlemen. Welcome to *Suspense*," quips Bob, referring to a dramatic radio/TV program to laughter at this ceremony's outset. He also gets laughs for saying "I want to thank all the wrestlers for relinquishing their time so we could give these awards. Just shows you that there's nothing one group of actors won't do for another." After acknowledging humorously how the marriage with TV is paying for the ceremony, Bob tells viewers you'll see "New faces like Mary Pickford, Janet Gaynor, Ronald Colman and Jean Hersholt" in relation to previous winners showing up as presenters tonight. He cracks about how TV have made stars out of Hopalong Cassidy and the Bowery Boys. "The whole thing's like a big maternity ward. Everybody's expecting." He adds, "I like to be here just in case ..." and looks over at the Oscars on display. Bob has a pretty good start with a little shakiness. He also could take satisfaction in knowing that appeared in a cameo in this year's Best Picture winner, *The Greatest Show on Earth*.

Bob: \*\*\*\*


## The 27th Annual Academy Awards
March 30, 1955, Wednesday 10:30 p.m.-12:20 a.m. (approximately)

Hosts: Bob Hope, Thelma Ritter.

"I was a little worried last year when the Oscars came through in a kneeling position," Bob jokes about competition from TV at the start. There is lots of applause for his monologue, and he has great rapport with presenters like Humphrey Bogart. His chemistry with Crosby is fluid amid the scripted lines too. Referencing Bing's Oscar-nominated role in *The Country Girl*, Bob talks about his dramatic work on *The Seven Little Foys* and says, "I do it without a drink." "You know, that might be your problem," Bing zings him back and leaves by flipping his tails on his tux. But Bob as co-emcee gets to have the last words. He says Bing called him needing help—"He didn't know whether the tails went inside or outside"—and adds, "He was born on the stage, you know. I think it went from Tulsa to Dodge City." It's a wonderful outing for him.

Bob: \*\*\*\*\*


## The 30th Annual Academy Awards
March 26, 1958, Wednesday 10:30 p.m.-1:10 a.m. (approximately)

"This is the nicest group of filthy capitalists I've ever seen," says Bob as he mentions his recent trip to Moscow in depth. "They have a TV in every room, only it watches you." He remains disappointed by his chances of getting an Oscar, noting that "If someone should suddenly explode a bomb and blow up every big star in this theatre, I still wouldn't get an award ... I haven't won an award in fifteen years, and I've been trying very hard. And I just want to say to my producers, directors, and cameramen that I could never have done it alone. You all helped!" As just one of five emcees this year—and the last one on the show—his monologue is shorter than usual but not significantly better than usual either.

Bob: \*\*\*

## *The 31ˢᵗ Annual Academy Awards*
April 6, 1959, Monday 10:30 p.m.-12:25 a.m. (approximately)

"I'm here tonight against my doctor's orders. He wanted my tickets," notes Bob. He sets the mood—"You can feel the tension in the air. This makes Cape Canaveral look like a rest home."—and comments on the other hosts of the show as well as the British stars backstage. Bob reviews the Best Actress nominees' roles as hookers, addicts, and troubled souls and quips "Put them all together, they spell mother." He also jests about the frequency and bad editing of old movies on TV ("I saw an old Road picture last night and Bing and I aren't even in it"). This is pretty lumpy but gets by in the end.
Bob: ***


## *The 11ᵗʰ Annual Emmy Awards*
May 6, 1959, Wednesday 10-11:30 p.m.

Jack Benny presents the Trustees Award to Bob, who strolls down the aisle and grabs the statuette from Jack before the latter insists on reading the citation aloud. Bob mockingly tells Jack to read the honor slower. "I guess this is one that *Gigi* in New York didn't want," Bob cracks. "Believe me, I should be speechless, but I'm not. I've had an acceptance speech written for nine years." He says Jack also gave an award to Marconi for starting broadcasting before adding, "I've always wanted one of these things to go with my honorary Oscar. You get so lopsided wearing one earring." Bob receives his award near the end, right before Fred Astaire completed winning lots of statuettes for his special *An Evening with Fred Astaire* and getting lots of applause for it.
Bob: ****


## *The 32ⁿᵈ Annual Academy Awards*
April 4, 1960, Monday 10:30 p.m.-12:10 a.m. (approximately)

Bob references the actors strike ("Who else would give up working for Lent?") before getting into tonight's contest. "For many, there'll be heartbreak and tears, for others, fame and fortune. I can go any way." He mentions several actors up for Oscars ("Jack Lemmon was nominated for impersonating a girl. I remember when you used to get arrested for that"), as well as failed trends like Smellovision ("Pictures that smell—isn't that wonderful? I remember when you had to wait for the reviews!"). Regarding the awards overseers, Price Waterhouse, Bob says, "I can vouch for their honesty. Believe me, if they'd ever take a bribe, I'd be the first to know." Bob scores very well, even if there are a few bombs where he has to use savers, and his acceptance of the Jean Hersholt Humanitarian Award later in the show, which he had no idea about getting ("I'll get you for this!... I don't know what to say. I don't have writers for this type of work!") is short and sweet too, making this a treat.

Bob: *****

## *The 33rd Annual Academy Awards*
April 17, 1961, ABC Monday 10:30 p.m.-12:35 a.m. (approximately)

Assessing the atmosphere of the awards, Bob says, "I wouldn't say feeling has been running high, but if *The Alamo* doesn't win, they may do it over again live right here." He notes the awards are now from Santa Monica and jokes about it being near the ocean, as well as even the Russians being the first in space ("It just proves one thing: Their German scientists are better than our German scientists"). Bob then launches into reviewing the year's pictures and nominees ("We all know how Jack Lemmon got in there, lending his apartment to members of the Academy"). This is one monologue where most of his jokes either land strongly or crater upon arrival, and luckily for him, the former somewhat predominates.

Bob: ***

## *The 13th Annual Emmy Awards*
May 16, 1961, Thursday 10-11:30 p.m.

Bob appears in the audience as a nominee for Outstanding Program Achievement in the Field of Humor for *The Bob Hope Buick Show*. Alas, he does not win.

## *The 34th Annual Academy Awards*
April 9, 1962, ABC Monday 10:30 p.m.-12:40 a.m. (approximately)

"This is an exciting night, the moment we've been all waiting for. In just a few hours, the Dodgers' new ballpark will be open," quips Bob. He says this year he is a two-time loser, for he's not only not nominated but also a manhole cover has been placed over his star on Hollywood Boulevard. Bob muses about George C. Scott saying he would decline receiving a statuette if he wins ("If enough people refuse an Oscar, maybe I'll get one"), Princess Grace of Monaco coming to Hollywood, and the other actor and picture nominees ("Sophia Loren was nominated for *Two Women*, and I certainly think she is"), plus several about the cost and extramarital romance of Elizabeth Taylor and Richard Burton occurring in next year's Best Picture nominee, *Cleopatra* ("I don't know how the picture is, but I'd like to make a deal for the outtakes"). It's hit or miss overall, but more hits than misses.
Bob: ***

## *The 37th Annual Academy Awards*
April 5, 1965, ABC Monday 10 p.m.-12:50 a.m. (approximately)

"It's envy time and I'm your host, the jolly green emcee," Bob tells those assembled at Santa Monica Civic Auditorium. He later adds, "This is the night war and politics are forgotten, and we find out who we truly hate." Bob describes the prayers of nominees as "Thousands of voices saying silently, 'Let it be me. But if it can't be me, not him!'" He even makes a clever joke about Bing Crosby before going into the British onslaught. "Twelve of the twenty acting nominations went to foreigners, but we're not worried. We still lead the world in the production of popcorn! ... There'll always been an England, even if it's in Hollywood." Bob has sharp lines and even sharper delivery for most of this program, making it one of his top outings.
Bob: ****

## *The 38th Annual Academy Awards*
April 18, 1966, ABC Monday 10 p.m.-12:55 a.m. (approximately)

Calling the gathering a chance to create new feuds, Bob says, "I'm delighted to be back here for my twelfth year of penance." He notes that while viewers await the winners, psychiatrists in Beverly Hills anticipate the losers. Later, Academy President Arthur Freed catches Bob off guard before the presentation of Best Picture with the board of governors presenting him with the organization's first gold medal. "That's a beautiful thing, and it's got a little Oscar. How much do you think to pump that up?" he asks presenter Jack Lemmon before offering sincere thanks for the honor.

Bob: ***

**The Best on Record**
May 16, 1966, Monday 9-10 p.m.

Presenters: Bob Hope, Bill Dana, Dan Rowan and Dick Martin, Steve Allen, Henry Mancini, Bobby Darin, Don Adams, Godfrey Cambridge, Perry Como, Diahann Carroll, Dinah Shore. Performers: Herb Alpert and the Tijuana Brass, Tony Bennett, Petula Clark, Bill Cosby, Duke Ellington and His Orchestra, Robert Goulet, The Anita Kerr Singers, Jody Miller, Roger Miller. EP: Ted Bergmann. P: George Schlatter. D: Bill Hobin, John Dorsey. Music: Les Brown.

In his book *Broken Record*, author Henry Schipper incorrectly assumes that when Bob says here "Welcome to the award show that dares to be similar," the comedian means the bland honorees that the Grammys often recognized. He actually is citing his inability to win an Oscar, as he adds, "I didn't win anything here either ... I know I'm already going home alone." This taped respective honoring winners of Grammys announced two months earlier (the ceremony did not go live on TV until 1971) uses many stars like Hope with little relation to the recording industry to introduce performers. His monologue reflects that ignorance, as he says this has "just about every great artist in the musical world with the exception of Sonny and Cher. We hoped to have them, but Sonny didn't have a tuxedo, and Cher wouldn't lend him hers." Between that and a line about Bing Crosby winning for best performance by a 60-year-old newlywed, this is best forgotten.

Bob: **

## The 39th Annual Academy Awards
April 10, 1967, ABC Monday 10 p.m.-12:30 a.m. (approximately)

A technicians strike nearly prevented this show from airing, so Bob makes comments about that situation before getting back to the usual industry jokes. "So once again, the fantastic facilities of television and the great artistry of the motion picture industry are blended so you in your home can cut to your neighbor and say, 'They cut *Rat Patrol* for this?!'" He mentions politics mingling with the awards, the British influence on filmmaking, and specific picture like *Alfie* ("I thought Michael Caine was wonderful as me") and *Who's Afraid of Virginia Woolf* ("that wonderful sequel to *Bambi*"). The monologue is good overall but has a few rough patches.

Bob: ***

## The 40th Annual Academy Awards
April 10, 1968, ABC Wednesday 10-11:50 p.m. (approximately)

Bob's opening joke paraphrases one he first said on his April 14, 1963 special regarding the Academy Awards—"It was Passover for me too." It gets applause, but his next line about the nominees seems insensitive in light of the show being delayed two days due to the assassination of Martin Luther King Jr.: "How would you like to spend two days in a crouch?" So did saying that ABC executives planned "mass hara-kiri" in response to lost revenue from the switch. He recovers somewhat after that including a Bing Crosby gag (he was there to greet Adolph Zukor when the latter arrived in Hollywood in 1928), but still some do not land well, like ones involving transcendental meditation and the trends for adult pictures. Then there was this one for an actress playing the blind heroine in *Wait Until Dark*: "Audrey Hepburn knocks off a nomination with her eyes shut" (Audrey forces a smile in the audience, but no one laughs). He does have a good line summarizing what his new role will be next year based on this year's nominees, but it is too little too late to save his bad start.

Bob: **

## The 20th Annual Emmy Awards
May 19, 1968, Sunday 9-11 p.m.

Bob is a presenter at this event.

## The 41st Annual Academy Awards
April 14, 1969, ABC Monday 10 p.m.-12:35 a.m. (approximately)

"I finally made it. I've been waiting at the Santa Monica Auditorium!" Bob says at the start of his presentation of the Jean Hersholt Humanitarian Award to his old pal Martha Raye (the Oscars moved to the Dorothy Chandler Pavilion this year). Of not hosting this year, he says, "I feel like the third Smothers Brother. I've been on this late in this show. Are we still on in prime time?" He does a great monologue touching on current concerns, his perpetual Oscar envy, this year's contenders ("I can't believe them nominating *Romeo and Juliet* as Best Picture. It's such an obvious steal from *West Side Story*!"). He said he was not going to be on the show until the producers told him they were honoring Martha Raye, and he praises her to the hilt. This is one of Bob's best Oscar appearances ever.
Bob: *****

## The 42nd Annual Academy Awards
April 7, 1970, ABC Tuesday 10 p.m.-12:25 a.m. (approximately)

Calling Bob "America's ambassador of laughter," John Wayne introduces Bob Hope, who sports an eyepatch the way Wayne did in *True Grit*. "I didn't think you'd show," he cracks as Wayne laughs and leaves. Bob cleverly references the top films of the year in his monologue ("It's so crowded, Bob and Carol and Ted and Alice had to sit in the same seat") as well as the occasion's pretensions ("This is a beautifully gowned, elegantly coiffured gathering dedicated to the proposition that jealousy and envy shall not perish from the earth"). He also brings up his Oscar hopes with "I hope your favorite wins tonight, although I know mine won't." Also figuring into it is runaway productions and movie nudity and adult trends, where he bears a moralistic bent that hurts the jokes' effectiveness somewhat. Still, more works than fails overall in this effort.
Bob: ***

## *The 43rd Annual Academy Awards*
April 15, 1971, Tuesday 10 p.m.-1 a.m. (approximately)

Bob bombs pretty badly here, coming across as smug, self-obsessed about his previous lack of recognition and really out of touch, with audience members greeting him with much forced laughs and stony silence during his eight-minute monologue. In reference to the slew of hosts on hand, he quips, "I'm your next friend of the Oscar … And after what he's done for me the last thirty years, you might say we're enemies." He refers to the awards as "the final stop for midget talents to have their egos inflated," which goes over poorly, and flops with a *Love Story* joke ("Imagine having the courage, the audacity and the daring in today's market to make a picture about a boy falling in love with a girl"). And then there are lines like these: "With the kind of pictures they're making these days, you can win an Oscar without getting out of bed." "I know this is the year of kinky sex, but *The Owl and the Pussycat*? And how about *Cold Turkey*—did you think you could make a picture out of a frigid bird?" "For the first time, the Academy has come up for something for the losers—a free scholarship to a skydiving school." "I met a panhandler the other day and I said, 'Why don't you get yourself a job?' And he said, 'What, and give up show business?!'" Regarding Hollywood insiders meeting with the President for a tax break, he notes, "We sent all of the heads of the studios to plead poverty. Mr. Nixon looked out the window at their cars, and they were bigger than Air Force One." There is no reaction to this at all. Seeing this set, it's understandable how the show would not invite Bob back until 1975.

Bob: \*\*

## *Zenith Presents a Salute to Television's 25th Anniversary*
Sept. 10, 1972, ABC Sunday 8:30-10 p.m.

Host: Robert Young. Guests: Dame Judith Anderson, James Arness, Lucille Ball, Milton Berle, Sid Caesar, Jimmy Durante, Lorne Greene, Florence Henderson, Bob Hope, Harry Reasoner, Rod Serling, Dinah Shore, Ed Sullivan. EP: Bob Finkel. P/D: Marty Pasetta. Choreographer: Jaime Rogers. Music Arranger/Conductors: Jack Elliott, Allyn Ferguson. Choral Director: Alan Copeland.

This disjointed special uncomfortably mixes long production numbers (including Florence Henderson's flashy opening routine, George Chakiris dancing as the lead in various scenarios like westerns and mysteries, and a reunion of the *Your Hit Parade* cast singing the top tunes of the 1950s) with grainy, aged film clips of classic TV series and canned acceptance speeches by honorees, all with dubbed applause and laughter. Robert Young informs viewers that the Academy of Television Arts and Sciences is honoring a quarter century of commercial television with the presentation of silver medallions to select honorees among 101 series and individuals honored for the impact, popularity, longevity, innovation and substance they have provided the medium. For example, James Arness accepts an award for *Gunsmoke*, and Lorne Greene does the same for *Bonanza*. Rod Serling hands out the medallions for the last three honorees, Ed Sullivan, Lucille Ball and Bob Hope, and it's obvious that all except Lucy and Bob (who enter together) were taped at separate times. Getting his honor from Rod after old footage from his specials airs, Bob asks, "Where does it say 'Spooky writer tells jokes?'" and pretends to snipe with Lucy before saying goodbye with "Thanks for the memory." For an observance of TV history, this is a pretty messy affair to endure, so it's hard to blame Bob for not mustering any clever things to say on it besides what he does contribute.

Bob: **


## The 1974 Las Vegas Entertainment Awards
Nov. 20, 1974, Wednesday 10-11 p.m.

Host: Bob Hope. Presenters/Winners: Marty Allen, Paul Anka, Ann-Margret, Carol Channing, Charo, Roy Clark, Sammy Davis Jr., Zsa Zsa Gabor, Mitzi Gaynor, Bobbie Gentry, Robert Goulet, Shecky Greene, Alan King, Rich Little, Liza Minnelli, Wayne Newton, Juliet Prowse. Music: Les Brown and His Band of Renown. EP: Bob Hope. P: Mort Lachman, Norman Sedawic. D: Dick McDonough. W: Lester White, Mel Tolkin, Charles Lee, Gig Henry, Mort Lachman, Steve White, Norman Sullivan.

The formation of the Academy of Variety and Cabaret Artists created this event, which basically resembles a Bob Hope special with awards. His set is one of his best ever in his lifetime (see the introduction for examples), and his familiarity with the presenters gives him wonderful opportunities to banter with them. With Bob's long monologue and numbers by Bobbie Gentry, Sammy Davis Jr., Juliet Prowse, and Roy Clark and Robert Goulet (together), the awards themselves get short shrift, with several winners standing in the audience at the end to acknowledge their wins as the credits roll. That could be why this did not become a recurring awards show on network TV.

Bob: *****


## The People's Choice Awards
March 3, 1975, CBS Tuesday 9-11 p.m.

Faye Dunaway announces Bob has been voted Favorite All Around Male Entertainer, and he accepts with "This proves Abraham Lincoln is wrong—you can fool them all of the time. And I would like to thank a lot of people who made this possible, but I can't think of them. I did it all myself! And how can we get Jimmie Walker out of this business?!" He adds, "I'm not going to hide this kid, because it's really a goodie. I think I may have this duplicated and have my ears pierced." There is lots of laughter throughout, including his incredulous look when motioned to stretch his speech a little. He concludes by thanking the voters and quipping, "You've showed that you're real connoisseurs of fine entertainment."

Bob: *****


## The 47th Annual Academy Awards
April 8, 1975, Tuesday 9:30 p.m.-12:50 p.m. (approximately)

"I'm here again for my annual exercise in masochism," Bob greets the audience. He later adds, "But don't get me wrong. There's not a jealous bone in my body. But some of my flab is furious." Commenting on the nominees, Bob notes, "*The Towering Inferno* was a most unusual disaster film. Imagine all those people being saved without Charlton Heston." Fred Astaire has a best supporting actor nod for that movie, prompting Bob to say, "You know, it's easy to dance good when the floor below you is on fire." The adult themes continue to vex him half seriously: "Movies have become so permissive these days things I used to be too young to see, I'm too old to do." Bob seems uneasy at a few points here, and later in the show, he got into a controversy demanding co-host Frank Sinatra read a disclaimer about Best Documentary winner Bert Schneider's statements on Vietnam (which Frank did to cheers and boos), making this a mixed success at best.

Bob: ***

## The 2nd People's Choice Awards
Feb. 19, 1976, CBS Thursday 9-11 p.m.

Presenter Rod Steiger announces Bob's tie with Tony Orlando for Favorite All Around Male Entertainer with this statement: "The first winner is a gentleman who has given us pleasure for many, many years, and I hope he continues to do so, Mr. Bob Hope." "This is a tie?" he asks Steiger in mock surprise. "I wouldn't have come! … I won this last year alone! Now I know how Ford feels about Reagan." He adds, "I'm just so thrilled to be able to get up those steps … I hope the Oscar people are watching this." The other winner, Tony Orlando, then comes on stage, greets Bob and praises him by saying, "You do and always will stand alone."
Bob: *****

## The 3rd People's Choice Award
March 5, 1977, CBS Thursday 9-11 p.m.

Former President Gerald Ford gets a half-minute standing ovation before he tells the audience, "The first time I saw tonight's winner was in New Haven, Connecticut, back in the 1930s. I was struggling through Yale Law School, and he was struggling through a production called *Red Hot and Blue*. He became number one in the entertainment world and still is." Ford commends Bob's work during wartime ("When home was so far away, there was this man, making life more bearable.") and his charitable acts, and he calls him a true friend. Bob cracks up Ford by saying "Yesterday you wouldn't give me a two-foot putt!" He says he appreciates the award because "It's not from a little group of arrogant, pretentious, supercilious snobs (laughter) who have turned their awards into a ridiculous farce. And I want to thank George C. Scott for lending me his speech." Also, "How about John Denver and me being in the same category? That's like Farrah Fawcett and Phyllis Diller fighting over the same T-shirt at Frederick's of Hollywood." Before he leaves, he tells Ford, "We're all grateful for your wonderful record of public service. I mean that."
Bob: ****

## *The 50th Annual Academy Awards*
April 3, 1978, ABC Monday 10 p.m.-1:30 a.m. (approximately)

After a long twelve-minute opening, Bob finally emerges to say, "You're too kind. Well, maybe not too kind, but you're wonderful." He comes on stage following a presentation of former honorees, leading him to note, "Some of these people have won two and three Oscars each. Their names have been taken, and there'll be getting their obscene phone calls in due time." Bob sets the scene inside and outside the venue too. "The first time when I arrived here tonight, my car was surrounded by packs of screaming women, clawing to get at me. If you don't believe me, just ask my driver, John Travolta." Of the nominated movies, he says, "*Julia*, I love. I like a good cry. But that's pretty obvious. Why else would I be here?" His monologue is spotty, and there appears to be a generation gap as much of the younger audience members barely smile much less laugh at his cracks. Still, he has sentimental appeal and keeps the show moving despite its slow start.

Bob: ***

## *Footlights! (The 32nd Annual Tony Awards)*
June 4, 1978, CBS Sunday 9:30-11 p.m.

Bob comes out thirty-four minutes into the show amid sustained applause, then says, "I suppose you all are wondering what I'm doing here tonight on this show that celebrates theatre. How soon they forget (laughter). You know, in 1927 I did a show called *Sidewalks of New York* at the Knickerbocker Theater ... My goodness, what a thrill it was to see my name up in candles." He warmly recounts his other appearances in the 1930s and gets applause for saying "This is where I belong, back on Broadway." Bob follows it with much smiling and praise for Irving Berlin before giving him the Laurence Langner Memorial Award for distinguished lifetime achievement (Berlin was not there to accept it). At the end, Bob joins the other presenters to sing "There's No Business Like Show Business."

Bob: ****

## The Grammy Hall of Fame
May 18, 1981, CBS Monday 10-11 p.m.

Host: Andy Williams. Guests: Peter Allen, Count Basie, Natalie Cole, Mary Crosby, Ella Fitzgerald, Andy Gibb, Bob Hope, Celeste Holm, John Raitt, Joe Williams. EP: Pierre Cossette. D: Walter C. Miller. W: Marty Farrell.

More of a tribute show than an awards presentation, this features Bob and Mary Crosby doing a salute to Bing Crosby during the inductions for recordings and artists selected to be honored.

## The 55th Annual Academy Awards
April 11, 1983, ABC Monday 9 p.m.-12:15 a.m. (approximately)

"This is a unique role for me, giving instead of accepting," jokes Bob after getting a standing ovation. He later continues, "When a man gets to my age—which I intend to do shortly—he realizes there's more to life than awards. There's the esteem of your fellow man, the respect of your colleagues, the admiration of your peers, none of which I have. But this was my most successful year at the movie box office. They lowered the price for senior citizens." Shortly thereafter, he presents a fine introduction to Mickey Rooney, the winner of the Jean Hersholt Humanitarian Award. Short and sweet, Bob sparkles here.

Bob: ****

## The 11th People's Choice Awards
March 14, 1985, CBS Thursday 9-11 p.m.

Fred MacMurray comes out of retirement to introduce Bob as the winner of the new All-Time Favorite Entertainer award, with clips of Bob's previous acceptance speeches from the event. "I've been suffering from laryngitis the last ten days. It's nothing serious. It just happens every time the writers go out on strike," Bob says. He adds, "I'd like to be humble about it, but they asked me to be myself." Bob warmly recalls fifty years ago how he and Fred did *Roberta* on Broadway, thanks everyone and kisses them in a short (less than two minutes) speech.

Bob: ****

## The 8th Annual Kennedy Center Honors
Dec. 27, 1985, CBS Friday 9-11 p.m.

Host: Walter Cronkite. Honorees: Merce Cunningham, Irene Dunne, Bob Hope, Alan Jay Lerner, Frederick Loewe, Beverly Sills. Presenters for Bob's Segment: Kirk Douglas, Chevy Chase.

"It's quite possible that no one in history has gotten more laughs than Bob Hope," Kirk Douglas tells a star-studded audience. "Why, even his pauses are funnier than most people's punchlines." Bob appreciates Kirk's sentiments before a five-minute compilation of his movies and life story appear. The audience gives him a standing ovation, then Chevy Chase does pratfalls and says "Very sorry, wrong president," to Bob's amusement. He does a hilarious monologue often promoting himself and adds, "I've stolen much of his stuff, and I think he knows it by now." All branches of the military then sing a salute, followed by eight former service members who recalled their memories of him performing during their wartime service, causing Bob to tear up. The military choruses end by singing a special version of "Thanks for the Memory" that clearly moves him as part of a classy tribute show.

Bob: *****

## The 58th Annual Academy Awards
March 24, 1986, ABC Monday 9 p.m.-12:05 a.m. (approximately)

On his record-breaking twenty-fifth appearance on the Oscars, Bob brings out the Passover joke again and congratulates Don Ameche on his win before reading words of praise to Charles "Buddy" Rogers as he presents him with the Jean Hersholt Humanitarian Award. It is nothing special, but it is a fine presentation by Bob nonetheless.

Bob: ***

## The 4th Annual Television Academy Hall of Fame
Nov. 30, 1987, Fox Monday 8-10 p.m.

Bob is one of the five inductees for this presentation from the Academy of Television Arts and Sciences.

### The 5th Annual Television Academy Hall of Fame
Jan. 23, 1989, Fox Monday 8-10 p.m.

>Presenters Include: Bob Hope.
>Bob introduces Red Skelton as an inductee.

### The 61st Annual Academy Awards
March 29, 1989, ABC 9 p.m.-12:20 a.m. (approximately)

"Tonight, it is my privilege to introduce two people who not only personify comedy greatness, who not only are beloved by millions of people in virtually every corner of the globe, who not only have been delighting audiences for half of this century, but who are among the only people I can think of who could get me to come here from Pacoima to make this introduction," Walter Matthau says. Bob and Lucille Ball walk out and appreciate the large applause and standing ovation. Lucy is amused by Bob's cracks, then interjects after he notes that "Lucy and I made four pictures together" with "Yeah, talk about *Dangerous Liaisons!*" (the latter was one of the Best Picture nominees). They're relaxed and happy and show off their talents naturally, unlike the nineteen young actors they introduce as the "stars of tomorrow" (most of them were not). Lucy dies a few weeks after this appearance.
Bob: ***

### The 41st Primetime Emmy Awards
Sept. 17, 1989, Fox Sunday 8-11 p.m.

Bob pays tribute to Lucille Ball as he introduces a montage of her TV work and presents the award to her widower, Gary Morton. He is sincere, low-key, and excellent in his delivery here.
Bob: ****

### The 63rd Annual Academy Awards
March 25, 1991, ABC 9 p.m.-12:35 a.m. (approximately)

Bob gets lots of applause but no standing ovation before he begins his set. "Remember me, the Macaulay Culkin of 1927? I was home alone too," he says unsteadily. He gets more claps for saying, "I couldn't be here in spirit, so I'm in person." He welcomes back soldiers from Saudi Arabia ("I think it was a tough fight, but CNN won.") before introducing a montage of celebrities remembering the first movies they saw. Bob's delivery is slow, but his material generally is good.

Bob: ***

### *The 65th Annual Academy Awards*
March 29, 1993, ABC 9 p.m.-12:35 a.m. (approximately)

Host Billy Crystal points out Bob in the audience, and Bob stands up and waves, prompting a standing ovation. Given Bob's deteriorating condition at this point, having him just do that was probably a wise move. Buz Kohan, a writer for this show, says he told Billy to acknowledge Bob during the show to get the audience on his side and keep a lengthy show lively. He adds that Bob saw him at the end of the telecast backstage and the comedian joked, "Are you staying for the second half?"

Bob: ***

### *The 50th Annual Emmy Awards*
Sept. 13, 1998, Sunday 7-11 p.m.

Introduced as TV legends by Jay Leno, Bob sits in a chair between Milton Berle and Sid Caesar, and all wave to the audience without speaking. They get lots of applause, and it is a nice tribute to three men who meant so much to the medium, especially NBC, which is hosting this show. Some might have been saddened by Bob's physical condition, but he actually was looking a little better than he did in his last specials.

Bob: ***

Talk show hosts Jack Paar (left) and Steve Allen (right) flank Bob Hope and Bing Crosby as they perform a comic kick line during the taping of Bob's Feb. 27, 1962 special. Paar hated doing this sketch so much that he banned Hope from his talk show, even though it only ran until 1965, while Allen had no such problem and continued working professionally with Bob as a guest on his talk shows and on Bob's specials into the 1980s. Courtesy of Getty Images.

# 8 Talk Shows

BOB ALREADY KNEW the promotional power of radio when he came to television. The rise of the talk show format in the 1950s was a perfect vehicle for him to do a few jokes written by his writers before plugging his latest book, album, movie, TV show, personal appearance or anything else. He realized this quickly and leveraged virtually every opportunity to show up any talk show that would have him. All of them wanted him, of course.

How busy was he? A survey in *The Book of Lists #2* of most appearances by performers on major TV talk shows between the start of 1976 and July 31, 1979 found Bob tied in seventh place, with fifty-four guest shots—thirteen on *Dinah!*, twelve on *The Mike Douglas Show*, nine on *The Merv Griffin Show*, and twenty on *The Tonight Show Starring Johnny Carson*—in just that three-and-a-half-year period alone.

On these guest shots, Bob had a general pattern of staying throughout the show if it was centered on him or had other guests he loved or wanted to meet, like a two-year-old golf prodigy named Tiger Woods on *The Mike Douglas Show* in 1978. For *The Tonight Show Starring Johnny Carson*, however, Bob usually was the first guest to arrive and leave from 1972 onward, even though he lived just a ten-minute drive from the Burbank studios where the show was taped.

While producers and hosts were happy to have such a recognized and loved guest, Bob was no sure thing to make a talk show work. For example, while he did appear on the pilot to launch the short-lived *The Toni Tennille Show* in 1980, his guest shot in 1971 on *Phyllis Diller Kitchen Kween*, a pilot for a syndicated daytime talk show starring the title comedienne, was not enough to sell it as a series, and this appearance by Bob never made it to air.

There was at least one talk show host not enamored with Hope. Jack Paar told Robert Metz in the latter's book on *The Tonight Show* in 1980 that Bob had him come out to Hollywood in a deal where he had to rehearse for a week without being paid Bob's normal rate of $10,000 for a guest spot in exchange for Bob appearing on his show without cost, which was only $320 for *The Tonight Show* at the time. Adding to Paar's discomfort was the fact that Bob booked his predecessor, Steve Allen, as a guest too and wanted Paar to come out in a Little Lord Fauntleroy outfit, which he hated. He added that that appearance started the show and it bombed.

The truth is quite different from what Paar recollected. First, the sketch came at the end of the special, not the start; second, it got lots of laughs; and three, not only Jack but also Bob, Steve and surprise guest Bing Crosby donned the foppish look, all playing child actors auditioning for a vaudeville routine (Crosby gets the biggest laughs when he enters after being named the final choice and says, "My name is Harry Lillis Crosby. I sing, dance and babysit!").

Jack also has a cordial rapport on the show during other skits with the men, including one precluding the child actors audition where Steve and Bob pine to replace Jack on *The Tonight Show*, although some of their lines may have made him wince. For example, Bob gets applause for "Are you really quitting, Jack, or are you going to replay the tape of your last walkout?" while Steve hits the number of commercials Paar does on *The Tonight Show* with "After all, Jack, what would happen to the country if you stop selling deodorant?"

Nonetheless, for the other side of the deal, Paar said, "We wanted Hope, but he said he wouldn't come until he did a picture [he could plug] and then he said, 'I won't follow Paar with a monologue.' He wanted to sit and talk for a $320 show." Paar responded by calling Bob's office and saying, "You tell Bob Hope to send me $10,000. I don't want him on my show." It did not matter, though—Paar appeared on Hope's special on Feb. 27, 1962, and left hosting *The Tonight Show* a month later on March 30. Also, Bob was one of several celebrities on tape bidding Paar farewell to boot. Paar did do a weekly talk show on NBC from 1962-1965 and an occasional one on ABC from 1973-1974, but he was true to his word about not having Bob as a guest on them.

As for the other guest on the special, Steve Allen interviewed and worked with Bob on his syndicated talk shows for decades, yet Allen admitted he had a hard time understanding "the real Bob Hope," so to speak. While the comedian always came across friendly and amiable when they met, he did so usually with an ulterior motive of promoting some project, with the feeling "that one has the sense of conversing with a sort of affable charm-machine rather than just one of the guys," noted Allen in his book *More Funny People*. Allen concluded that "the world is rarely permitted to see the self of the man. All one gets is that good-looking, glib, likable front."

Indeed, watching Bob on a talk show critically can reveal that he would do anything to deflect the conversation from being of a personal nature. He would praise guests on his specials with colloquial phrases like "Idn't that something?" (not "isn't," but always the idiomatic "idn't"), throw gag lines in response to serious questions, and rehash old stories about his life and career. Sometimes he would register an opinion on current events, but he often found those did not get the universal praise and acceptance he came to expect, so his responses would be measured at best. The general impression left was that Bob was no more and no less than a happy comedian who loved his work, his family, and his country, and he was fine preserving that image.

Having said that, Bob was seemingly ubiquitous in this genre, making an estimated 140 appearances on *The Tonight Show* alone, where Paar's replacement, Johnny Carson, had a grin-and-bear-it attitude sometimes to Bob's incessant guest shots. As NBC's number one prime time star, Bob could and did request to show up whenever he wanted to promote a project, and that often meant Carson had to bump another guest or change the show's lineup at the last minute. Bob easily appeared much more on other daytime and nighttime national talk shows (and if one added local and regional talk shows like Ruth Lyons and Paul Dixon in Ohio, that figure probably would be in the thousands).

To save space, this section will concentrate mostly on confirmed dates for major occasions where Bob showed up, as well as a healthy sampling of Bob on *The Tonight Show*. Only shows that have been viewed are rated, and they are just by Bob's appearance in this section.

Besides those talk shows previously mentioned and to be discussed more in depth shortly, other notable appearances by Bob on national talk shows include *The Steve Allen Show* several times starting in 1963, *Kup's Show* (Irv Kupcinet) in the 1960s and 1970s, *The Phil Donahue Show* (later just *Donahue*) from the 1960s through 1980s, *The Pat Boone Show* in 1966 and 1967 (and its syndicated follow-up, *Pat Boone in Hollywood*, in 1969), *The Rosey Grier Show* in 1969, *Dinah's Place* (the forerunner to *Dinah!*, which ran from 1974-1980) in 1971, *The John Davidson Show* in 1981 and

1982, *Larry King Live* in 1985, and *The Tonight Show With Jay Leno, Live with Regis and Kathie Lee*, and *Vicki!* (with Vicki Lawrence as host) in the 1990s.

By the time of some of the latter appearances, Bob was so feeble that his wife Delores joined him as his escort and helper. Watching him try to answer and looking out of it all was painful for viewers to withstand, so this section ends with Bob's last set of solo appearances in the 1990s.

### *Meet The Veep*
March 8, 1953, Sunday 5:30-5:45 p.m.

> Host: Earl Godwin. Interviewer: Alben W. Barkley. Guest: Bob Hope.

Alben W. Barkley, the vice president under Harry S. Truman, talks with Bob mostly for laughs in this early interview show.

### *Home*
Aug. 9, 1957, Friday 10-11 a.m.

> Hostess: Arlene Francis.

Bob showed up several times during the daytime series' three-year run, and a clip of one of those occasions appears in this finale.

### *The Tonight Show Starring Jack Paar*
March 29, 1962, Thursday 11:15 p.m.-1 a.m.

Bob appears in a recorded bit to bid Jack Paar farewell from late night TV on NBC.

### *The Tonight Show Starring Johnny Carson*
May 2, 1963, Thursday 11:15 p.m.-1 a.m.

After waiting to come out after opera singer Patrice Munsel and writer William Saroyan, Bob talks with Johnny Carson for the first time on this series. He recalls his sponsors over the years on radio with good humor, noting that most of them were associated with being in the bathroom.

"I'm back with Pepsodent this year, in case you're wondering where the yellow went," he quips. Bob mentions about how Phil Silvers topped him in the ratings in 1956, then after noting he has been with NBC since 1938, a woman applauds, and Bob says, "Thank you, mother." He reviews all the perks he's gotten from the relationship before adding, "And all because I saw [NBC president] Bob Sarnoff coming out of that hotel," which knocks out the audience and Johnny. It is a great debut for Bob with Johnny.

Bob: \*\*\*\*

## *Today*
Nov. 29, 1967, Wednesday 7-9 a.m.

The series devotes its entire show in advance of Bob's latest special airing that evening, supposedly to honor his thirtieth anniversary of working with NBC, even though that mark does not really occur until the fall of 1968. The presentation includes recorded interviews with Bob and Bing Crosby as well as a talk with Bob.

## *Here's Dick Cavett*
June 14, 1968, ABC Friday 7:30-8 p.m.

Clips showing highlights of Cavett's short-lived ABC daytime show include an appearance by Bob, where he quipped of his boxing career, "I was the only fighter in Cleveland history who fought with a rearview mirror."

## *The Tonight Show Starring Johnny Carson*
March 6, 1969, Thursday 11:30 p.m.-1 a.m.

A relaxed Bob with a golf club in hand comes on after Louis Dawson and Buddy Rich play drums and Judy Carne talks about *Laugh-In* to make a joke about short-lived *Turn On* is. "It's the only show that got canceled during a commercial!" Johnny adds. He says Jack Benny has the pretty legs in Sun City. "He's one of my favorites among the older fellas." Johnny then introduces George Gobel when to everyone's surprise Dean Martin joins them to shoot the breeze and they all have great comic interplay.

Bob cracks up seeing Dean flick his ashes into George's beer cup, while George causes hysterical laughter when he surveys the A list guest couch and says, "Did you ever get the feeling that the world was a tuxedo and you were a pair of brown shoes?" This is one of the most frequently repeated guest shots ever on *The Tonight Show Starring Johnny Carson*.

Bob: \*\*\*\*

### *The Tonight Show Starring Johnny Carson*
June 30, 1970, Tuesday 11:30 p.m.-1 a.m.

Guest host Jerry Lewis, smoking up a storm, occasionally calls Bob "Robert" as the latter starts by making these jokes about the Italian-American Civil Rights Parade to the host's amusement: "I thought it was an annual outing of the George Raft Fan Club ... They were lassoing people with spaghetti. And they all stopped at Doubleday and autographed copies of *The Godfather*." He says he waved to Jerry's ex-partner Dean Martin in the parade and Dean weaved back, which cracks up Jerry a little. After the discussion ambles, a person at one point applauds Jerry, prompting Bob to say, "You've got a hell of a fan out there." Bob clearly dislikes the gender-bending movies *Myra Breckenridge* and *The Christine Jorgensen Story* being made at Paramount as he and Jerry reminisce about their days there. "I can't accept some of these parts because I'm not going to strip for any kind of money. I just will not," Bob says of current films. "And I'd hate to see Crosby go nude." He says the nudity trend will continue onto television where "I can see Ed Sullivan coming out and saying, 'There's a big one tonight, folks!'" which shocks and amuses the studio audience. Praising the youth of America, Bob ends by mentioning the stars coming to the July 4 patriotic event he is hosting in Washington, D.C., which he boasts will give a lift to the country before leaving.

Bob: \*\*\*

### *The Tonight Show Starring Johnny Carson*
May 6, 1971, Thursday 11:30 p.m.-1 a.m.

Woody Allen, serving as guest host, says, "This next gentleman is certainly one of my great idols. I mean, I spent my whole childhood seeing his move over and over again. And you'll notice if you watch *Bananas* how much I've secretly copied and been influenced by him." Bob comes out in a tux as Woody tells him how he'd pretend to be Bob when dating girls. "Don't tell me you scored better than I did!" Bob responds. It is a mutual admiration society, as Bob mentions how Woody submitted a script to his radio show with another guy. "I love this guy. This is one of the finest young talents on our show. You're a great delight," Bob says. He quips of New York City, "These glass buildings intrigue. I'm afraid to go to the men's room." After talking about how he works with his writers, Bob mentions playing golf with Billy Graham: "He's a little bit of a showoff, walking across water hazards ... And he hits that ball pretty good from a fellow playing from a kneeling position." As to whether the reverend cursed on the course, Bob says, "Not openly. But his lips move." He adds that of his pictures, *The Paleface*, *The Seven Little Foys*, *The Facts of Life* and the Road pictures are his favorites. Bob even stays on for the next guest and compliments James Coco's work on *Last of the Red Hot Lovers*, who he saw the previous week ("You were so great, Jim").

Bob: \*\*\*\*


## *Today*
Oct. 11, 1971, Monday 7-9 a.m.

Bob appears on tape to bid farewell to Hugh Downs' last day as host.


## *The David Frost Show*: "600th Broadcast"
Nov. 1, 1971, Syndicated 90 minutes

A clip of Bob from an earlier show appears as part of this retrospective.


## *The Dick Cavett Show*
Oct. 4, 1972, ABC Wednesday 11:30 p.m.-1 a.m.

Dick devotes his entire show to talking to Bob. The latter says he loves his peripatetic work schedule ("I get a lot of therapy from getting around.") and misses working on the New York stage. "I would really—I'm serious about this—in the next year, I'd like to come back and do a show on Broadway." (He never does.) Bob recalls protecting his dog when he was a child and being injured other times as a child, even showing Dick scars on his face from the experiences. Career-wise, he discusses the time when an NBC censor forbid him to say on radio, "We want to help Kate Smith get her moon over the mountain." Dick prods Bob to bring up the latter's days teaching dancing, prompting Bob to say, "Geez, you've got a nasty memory!" Bob has a fantastic rapport with Dick (when he drops the latter's notes, he apologizes wittily with "I didn't mean to move your career!"), and he loves hearing the band play music from his musical *Roberta*. Even Bob admits he really enjoyed the experience.

Bob: *****


*The Tonight Show Starring Johnny Carson*
Dec. 7, 1972, Thursday 11:30 a.m.-1 p.m.

Bob's taping his Christmas special across the hall from this show, and Bob mock complains about having to make room for Carson ("I've got to work in some toilet"). He says it's an excellent studio "no matter how your monologue plays." Bob dominates the conversation and asks announcer Ed McMahon about his nightclub act and does in-jokes until Johnny shows a painting from a museum in Florence with a person looking remarkably like Bob. That gets some favorable response from Bob, but he deflects Johnny's question about researching his family history. Bob does better joking about the recent election, saying that George McGovern was so out of money at the end of his presidential bid that he mugged an Avon lady, before plugging his Vietnam tour too.

Bob: ***


*The Merv Griffin Show*
Oct. 12, 1973, Syndicated 90 minutes

In a tribute to Lucille Ball that has most of her immediate family plus longtime co-star Gale Gordon, Bob fondly remembers working together with Lucy on three out of four pictures. Regarding the one that bombed, he says, "*Critic's Choice*, oh my God, after the thing, the manager of the theater came up, pressed something into my hand. It was a .38 [special]!" He calls Lucy a delight and a perfectionist and seems happy to be talking about her.

Bob: ****

*The Tonight Show Starring Johnny Carson*
May 21, 1974, Tuesday 11:30 p.m.-1 a.m.

Coping with a musicians strike in its third week along with an audience composed largely of executives from NBC affiliates seems to frazzle Johnny Carson introducing Bob, who calls him his next guest when Ed McMahon corrects him that Bob will be his first one. Ed is a little cranky, as after Johnny says Bob needs no introduction, he interjects, "Just bring him out here if needs no introduction!" On stage, Bob and Johnny exchange pleasantries about NBC executive David Tebet and Secretary of State Henry Kissinger's travels before Bob plugs his new special *The Bluffers* so intently that he reads the guest list aloud before playing nearly five minutes from the show. After that ends and Bob asks Johnny, "I read that whole cast to you, didn't I?" he adds that he forgot to mention David Niven as host and thanks the affiliate representatives before leaving. His segment is funny, but most of the enjoyment comes from other people and not Hope here.
Bob: ***

*The Tonight Show Starring Johnny Carson 12th Anniversary Special*
Oct. 1, 1974, Tuesday 11:30 p.m.-1 a.m.

This includes a clip from Bob's appearance on the March 3, 1969 show.

*The Tonight Show Starring Johnny Carson*
Dec. 12, 1974, Thursday 11:30 p.m.-1 a.m.

"This Christmas, Bob is going to be entertaining our fighting men and women at the supermarket checkout line," Johnny Carson says in introducing the comedian for an unusually rowdy and delightful visit. Bob gets so much applause that he offers to throw out money to the audience, then jests some with Richard Harris (Johnny's first guest) as he recalls saying "Son of a bitch!" when being harassed by Laurence Olivier before the two met the king and queen of England in 1947 (Bob's phrased got bleeped on the air, of course). To top that, Bob tells of meeting a restaurateur in the Midwest who told him, "When you get back to Johnny

Carson's show, you tell him it's so windy here in Hays, Kansas, that we have white caps in the toilet!" As Bob is promoting his book *The Last Christmas Show* along with his upcoming special, Johnny offers to read jokes from Bob's first TV Yuletide program in 1950, but Bob jabs him by suggesting Ed should read them instead since Johnny's monologue bombed. The bloopers from his upcoming show are funny this go-round too, with Bob quipping in one scene in a curly wig opposite Dyan Cannon that "I look like Helen Reddy."

Bob: \*\*\*\*

### *The Tonight Show Starring Johnny Carson*
Oct. 15, 1975, Wednesday 11:30 p.m.-1 a.m.

While taping Bob's first show of the season next door, Bob, Bing Crosby, and John Wayne make a surprise visit on guest host Don Rickles. John is scared to get into a battle of insults with Don, but not Bob, who says "By the way, your wife just called. Your crocodile got loose again." However, Bing gets the most applause when plugging his new project with "I thought Mr. Carson would be here, but I'll take what I got."

Bob: \*\*\*\*

### *The Tonight Show Starring Johnny Carson*
March 4, 1976, Thursday 11:30 p.m.-1 a.m.

"Why do you give me this spot? I mean, after the hatchet?" Bob asks Johnny as he follows Don Rickles. Commenting on Johnny singing "Rhinestone Cowboy," Bob says he has a Midwest voice: "I didn't know Nebraska was so flat!" Bob promotes his special on the next night, *Joys!*, and Johnny shows outtakes after Bob mock complains that Johnny didn't do his show. After that, he tells Johnny, "I'm like you, I just do one show a month" to audience laughter. Don laughs hysterically at Bob's cracks. When Desi Arnaz follows, Bob is amusing interjecting his days of having Desi as his bandleader on the radio too. This is a hit-or-miss appearance.

Bob: \*\*\*

*The Tonight Show Starring Johnny Carson*
Oct. 28, 1976, Thursday 11:30 p.m.-1 a.m.

Bob follows Jim Fowler exhibiting animals as Johnny's first guest and quips, "You have to be careful where you step back there!" Johnny and Bob shoot the breeze about their hair color before Bob promotes his special airing the next night, *Bob Hope's World of Comedy*, and how tough it was to edit down to eighty-five comedians appearing on it from his previous specials: "We chopped out twenty-nine minutes last night." He adds, "Looking through that stuff is like Zsa Zsa [Gabor] going through her old wedding albums." Bob relays how movie producer Harry Saltzman tried to get the Pope lined up for one of Bob's specials unsuccessfully, and he and Johnny both agree that they have tried and failed to get Cary Grant too. It gets dull then until Johnny convinces a reluctant Bob to do a soft shoe routine to "Tea for Two." "I'll be in an iron lung later," Bob says afterward, but Johnny gets the last laugh as Bob exits and says, "I know you'll be on *Sermonette* later!"
Bob: ***

*The Tonight Show Starring Johnny Carson*
Jan. 14, 1977, Friday 11:30 p.m.-1 a.m.

Bob follows Angie Dickinson, who he warmly hugs, before he laughs as Johnny presents him with a man-sized pencil prop to tap like Bob does all the time on the show. He is here to promote his special airing in a week, *Bob Hope's All Star Comedy Spectacular* from Lake Tahoe, but he does get in a bleeped gay joke as Johnny cracks, "Every comedian has a little hint of mint." He talks about his golf handicap and some childhood memories while showing clips in a visit that's easy to take but has no real substance to it.
Bob: ***

*The Barbara Walters Special*
May 31, 1977, Tuesday ABC 10-11 p.m.

Host: Barbara Walters. Interviewees: Bob Hope, Bing Crosby, Redd Foxx. P: Daniel Wilson. D: Don Mischer.

Barbara's third of her long-running series of specials (they continued for nearly forty years) has Bob and Bing Crosby interviewed separately. Bing's comments regarding drugs and sex here raised several eyebrows among viewers shocked by his answers.

### Dinah!
July 5, 1977, Syndicated 90 minutes

Hostess: Dinah Shore. Guests: Bob Hope, Lucille Ball, Rosemary Clooney, Jane Russell, Rhonda Fleming.
"He was much older, and I thought it was his last chance," Bob says on why Bing Crosby always wound up with the girls in their movies in this meeting with his former leading ladies on screen. Lucille Ball amusingly feigns being ticked off when Rhonda Fleming notes how many times Bob wanted to rehearse her love scenes with him. "Far into the night!" Bob adds. He speaks of overdoing their lip movements when lip syncing due to their love scenes. Dinah quips, "Try to remember" when asking about Bob's sex appeal, prompting him to stand up and say, "I'd like my money, I want to get the hell out of here!" to much laughter and applause. Rhonda asks, "How did you get the name 'Rapid Robert?'" to hysteria, and Bob responds, "Keep this up, Anita Bryant will be my enemy!"
Bob: *****

### The Tonight Show Starring Johnny Carson
Oct. 13, 1978, Friday 11:30 a.m.-1 p.m.

Promoting his upcoming World Series special, Bob is pretty loose but seems appalled by the concept of male strippers. This interview was repeated on *Carson on TCM* on March 11, 2014.
Bob: ***

### The Tonight Show 17th Anniversary Special
Oct. 1, 1979, Monday 9-11 p.m.

The clip from the March 3, 1969 show reappears in this celebration, as it did five years earlier on the 12th anniversary special.

*The Tonight Show Starring Johnny Carson*
Feb. 1, 1980, Friday 11:30 p.m.-1 a.m.

"I am a great admirer of Bob Hope," Johnny prefaces in his introduction that earns Bob a huge round of applause even by his standards. "Do me a favor, when you're dying out there, don't mention my name?" Bob tells Johnny in reference to his so-so monologue. He confides that he did 109 jokes for the taping of his upcoming two-part special and acknowledges, "I've used this audience a lot of times. After you've mangled them for about three hours, then I get them. They're in great shape! We have to wire the seats to get them to sit up!" Bob says his biggest bomb in America was in Lafayette Park in Buffalo in 1945, when he appeared before 175,000 people and the microphone died. "I haven't been back to Buffalo since," he added. He recalls his entertaining before military troops including a close call on a visit to Alaska. After a commercial break, he continues reminiscing and looks deadpan into the camera to say, "I had eighteen gorgeous gals in the last five trips, and I'd do it again for my country." A three-minute clip of the special plays and then Bob talks about how great the audiences were. He concludes with funny memories he shared of the recently deceased Jimmy Durante before leaving.

Bob: ****

*The Tonight Show Starring Johnny Carson*
Sept. 5, 1980, Friday 11:30 p.m.-1 a.m.

Bob is in concert in Los Angeles for the first time in forty years. He and Johnny discuss why some British comics don't do as well as American comics do in England and mentions his experience in China: "Nine hundred million people who didn't know me and didn't give a damn." Bob mentions about planning the seating of this studio and how his new special came about when talking to the writers and one mentioned, "Who shot B.H.?" as a parody of "Who Shot J.R.?" on *Dallas*. After showing bloopers from his upcoming special, he quips that "Danny Thomas, he slowed us up. Blessed the camera before every take." He also talks about upcoming trips to Russia and England before leaving, though he does tell Johnny to give his best to the next guest, Richard Pryor. This is one of Johnny's last shows to run ninety minutes.

Bob: ***

*The Tonight Show Starring Johnny Carson*
Oct. 31, 1980, Friday 11:30 p.m.-12:30 a.m.

Bob's special tomorrow night (*Hope for President*) was originally set to air four days earlier but was pushed back due to the presidential debates, prompting some jokes between him and Johnny Carson about the situation. When Johnny asks Bob if he'd run for president, the latter demurs with "The money's not right." Apart from a questionable crack about his appearance in one war zone ("It had a big effect on me. The first time I stayed there, I woke up in the morning and went to the telephone and freed my writers"), there's nothing much of interest here beyond a standard visit by Bob.
Bob: ***


*The Tonight Show Starring Johnny Carson*
Jan. 16, 1981, Friday 11:30 p.m.-12:30 a.m.

Bob promotes his special two days from now and recalls his early days on TV followed by comments on his golf game and his upcoming inaugural appearance, as well as his experiences with previous presidents. He's very loose and funny here, even when Johnny shows pictures of Bob at seven and seventeen, and ends strong with a joke about Jack Nicklaus telling him to try marijuana to boost his game on the links.
Bob: *****


*Tomorrow Coast to Coast*
Feb. 2, 1981, Monday 12:30-2 a.m.

Emerging to a standing ovation, Bob tells host Tom Snyder and his audience in New York City how he did his radio show in the same studio in the 1930s before sharing a secret about his recent thirtieth anniversary special. "There's a couple of years where they burned up some old kinescopes… two or three years," he said. While denying he lets his celebrity go to his head, he noted how some people react to him when a cabbie saw him and asked, "Are you alive?!" Regarding his specials, he says, "Every show is a challenge, and you've got to try and do it better." Bob adds he wasn't bothered by a recent negative article on him in *Rolling Stone* and does not think about death unless it happens to family and friends.

Bob: ****


*The Tonight Show Starring Johnny Carson*
Nov. 20, 1981, Friday 11:30 p.m.-12:30 a.m.

Plugging his NFL sixtieth anniversary special on two nights later, Bob tells Johnny how the Los Angeles Rams pro team was one of his better tax deductions from 1948-1962. He also played football in high school: "I was very limber. I could go around my own end." Bob tells a joke about President Ford playing golf that makes everyone crack up on the straight line. A clip is shown, Bob promotes a personal visit to Villanova, and that's that. All this goes down easily.

Bob: ****


*Late Night with David Letterman*
Nov. 29, 1984, Thursday 12:30-1:30 a.m.

Bob, a surprise guest, comes through the exit doors and after a standing ovation chats six minutes. With his hairline receding, he mentions his first show in 1934, then discusses a recent appearance at Carnegie Hall. Dave prods him about Christmas and hanging out with regular folks. He says what he gets for Christmas is "money and stuff" and admits he drives his kids crazy when shopping for him. Bob is happy that's he's off the Forbes richest list after it revised its original estimate of his worth ("200 million?! I don't even play basketball!") and jokes about investing in Joan Crawford day care centers, which gets some audience reaction, as well as Gerald Ford's golf game. David is perplexed by Bob going to the Army-Navy game with Dick Cavett, but Bob tells him it is for an article (Cavett later claims he had no idea he was doing that until Bob said so on the show). Bob exclaims, "You have a hell of a holiday, David!" before leaving.

Bob: ***

*The Tonight Show Starring Johnny Carson*
April 17, 1987, Friday 11:30 p.m.-12:30 a.m.

After mentioning Bob's first TV appearance on KTLA in 1947, Johnny asks him, "What keeps you going?" and Bob responds by asking him the same question. "Alimony," zings back Johnny. However, Bob tops him with "How do you like him building me up for the straight line?" He muses of his beautiful co-stars, "I put on more makeup than they did," and of his days as an amateur boxer, "I found out you weren't allowed to hit below the belt, so I wore my trunks as a hat." Johnny shows some old pictures of Bob in wild outfits, and Bob makes clever comments because he cannot remember most of them. A two-minute clip of his next special runs before Bob runs off.
Bob: \*\*\*\*

*The Tonight Show Starring Johnny Carson 25th Anniversary*
Oct. 1, 1987, Thursday 9:30-11 p.m.

"Do you realize I've said to Bob Hope 3,000 times, 'Well, I know you gotta run, Bob!'" jokes Johnny in the opening monologue to this extended special of highlights on his show. Bob in fact appears early on in a clip from 1982 singing all of "Thanks for the Memory," which Johnny adds here was a spontaneous event.
Bob: \*\*\*

*The Tonight Show Starring Johnny Carson*
Dec. 18, 1987, Friday 11:30 p.m.-12:30 a.m.

Following the manic moves of Robin Williams promoting his new movie *Good Morning Vietnam*, Bob cracks, "Thank you, John, and I want to thank you for this spot. That's the damndest warm-up I've ever had!" He talks about his Persian Gulf tour starting soon with some interjections by Robin, who Bob admits he'd love to have on one of his tours. About running for office, he says the money isn't right and "Delores wouldn't want to move to a smaller house." The inevitable Christmas show clip follows with some jokes at Johnny's expense ("You know, Rich Little does you more than you do you!"), and Bob sticks around to hear Tony Bennett sing "White Christmas." Tony recounts how Bob gave him his professional name and helped boost his stock. Even there, Robin slips in a few jokes.

Bob: ***


## *Late Night with David Letterman*
June 16, 1989, Monday 12:30-1:30 a.m.

Fresh from his eighty-sixth birthday celebration, Bob is a little shaky but becomes chipper enough to slap Dave's desk for emphasis in their conversation. Dave has a mission with Bob: to crash the taping of *Live at 5*, the news show at NBC's New York City affiliate that tapes across the hall from his show. They used to let Dave do so freely, but then they banned him. As Dave tries to find a back door to enter, Bob quips, "I love this!" and when they can't access the studio, he adds "I've never been locked out!" Dave grouses that "Those people are wimpy!" as they return to the desk, where Bob recalls doing his radio show in the 1930s from the studio, playing golf in Paris and a new course in Japan, and doing a speech for his granddaughter for an easy session of discussion and some laughs.

Bob: ****


## *The Tonight Show Starring Johnny Carson*
Feb. 16, 1990, Friday 11:30 p.m.-12:30 a.m.

Bob gets so much applause that he stands up after sitting down to acknowledge it. His special airing tomorrow night is the first one he was able to do at NBC's Burbank studio in several years, and his answers to Johnny's questions are terse. However, he comes alive talking about how Donald Trump's wife wants seven hundred million dollars for alimony and his boxing career before a rather long clip of his special plays and then Bob exits.

Bob: ***

***The Tonight Show Starring Johnny Carson***
Sept. 14, 1990, Friday 11:30 p.m.-12:30 a.m.

"I've never seen you wear sneakers!" Johnny Carson proclaims as Bob enters to promote his new special *Bob Hope: Don't Shoot, It's Only Me*. Bob insists he has, then rambles on about his days in vaudeville and other guest shots. He gets in a good one noting Carson's younger days as an amateur magician and contrasting it with the host's marital record: "You used to saw a woman in half, and now their lawyers are doing that to you!" He also scores on explaining why he doesn't plan to tour Saudi Arabia with "I don't go to that much sand without a caddy."
Bob: ***


***The Tonight Show Starring Johnny Carson***
Jan. 11, 1991, Friday 11:30 p.m.-12:30 a.m.

Back from the Persian Gulf a week earlier—a twenty-hour time difference, notes Johnny Carson—Bob looks none the worse from the wear of it all to promote his special on it tomorrow night. "I'm still tired, but it's a gorgeous thing to see those guys." He calls Saddam Hussein "Madass," claiming it's just the leader's name backwards, and he jokes that the men fighting overseas are so longing for female companionship that "They save the buns from their hamburgers and hang them up in their lockers." Bob also mentions talking to the president when he got back to America in an otherwise standard guest spot.
Bob: ***


***The Tonight Show Starring Johnny Carson***
May 15, 1992, Friday 11:35 p.m.-12:35 a.m.

Following Clint Eastwood and David Letterman, Bob comes on last and talks about a fifty-fourth honorary degree from a college he's getting. "Yep. What are you going to do?" he tells Johnny. He does not have much to say to the graduating class in 1992, as he rambles some and stumbles a little about how good he was in school. Discussing today's politicians, he thinks Ross Perot should run with Johnny and buy the White House. Bob is more animated talking about his upcoming special, which runs ninety seconds and includes his joke about Johnny being old enough now that he can't do anything three times a week. Overall though, it is Bob who is hard of hearing and sluggish here. It is his final appearance with Johnny on this series.

Bob: **

Bob has to hit a shot out of the bunker on a course while playing golf in 1961. Courtesy of Getty Imagers.

# Game Shows and Sports

**A GAME AND SPORTS ENTHUSIAST,** Bob not only was an amateur boxer, he also was a part owner of the Cleveland Indians baseball team from 1946 onward. He was particularly identified with golf too, seen constantly in participating in celebrity and pro-am events on TV from the 1950s through the 1990s. He became so identified with his participation in the Palm Springs Classic, which started in 1960, that in 1964, officials renamed the golf tournament the Bob Hope Desert Classic in his honor. To list all of his golf tournament appearances there and elsewhere would be redundant and overwhelm this book, so only a few highlights here will suffice, along with a sampling of occasions when Bob was interviewed as a guest at the World Series and the Super Bowl.

For game shows, Bob mainly served as a guest attraction, and almost always he appeared when he had a movie or other project to promote. Besides the game shows listed in this chapter, Bob is said to have appeared as a guest on *I've Got a Secret* in 1957, *Take Two* in 1963, *Snap Judgment* and *Art Linkletter's House Party* in 1967, *The Hollywood Squares* three times from 1967-1969 (as a celebrity contestant, not as a "square"), *The Movie Game* in 1970, and *This is Your Life* tributes to General Omar Bradley (1971) and Ethel Merman (1972).

Bob also hosted awards shows dedicated to honor sports in 1961, 1973-1975, and 1979. Those are included here as well.

## Kay Kyser's Kollege of Musical Knowledge
Nov. 23, 1950, Thursday 9-10 p.m.

Host: Kay Kyser. Guest: Bob Hope.
Bob appears on this mixture of comedy, variety and game show to promote his upcoming appearance on *The Colgate Comedy Hour*.


## The Jimmy Demaret Show
June 1954, Syndicated 15 minutes

Host: Jimmy Demaret. Guest: Bob Hope. P: J. Milton Salzburg. D: Marvin Rothenberg. W: Bob Brumley.
A series filmed in color (rare for TV at the time), this features professional duffer Jimmy Demaret, who just appeared on *I Love Lucy* as himself a month before this first went into circulation. Jimmy instructs one male celebrity per episode such as Bob on how to improve his swing in addition to chatting casually for each of the series' thirteen installments.


## What's My Line?
Dec. 12, 1954, CBS Sunday 10:30-11 p.m.

Host: John Charles Daly. Regular Panelists: Fred Allen, Bennett Cerf, Arlene Francis, Dorothy Kilgallen. Mystery Guest: Bob Hope. EP: Gil Fates. D: Franklin Heller.
This classic episode of four celebrities guessing a person's profession (or identity, in the case of Bob) starts with Clarence Nash, voice of Donald Duck. It's a humorous interrogation thanks to Bennett Cerf inadvertently throwing the panel off. "It's made in California?" Arlene Francis says of Nash's "product," then memorably quips, "So many people are." John Charles Daly ends the game after five minutes as all were off the track, and Nash does the Donald voice saying what a pleasure it was to be here. Next, a handsome, muscular man who is a sewer cleaner from Akron, Ohio, generates much humor, along with John's conferences and clarifications. Fred Allen even offers to pay sixty dollars instead of making the panel guess amid great interplay. Then Bob signs in as Bing Crosby and affects a low drawl. Arlene identifies him as a comic and asks, "Is your hair thinning a little?" Bob smiles and adjusts his hairline before saying yes. "I'll take a

wild guess. Are you Bing Crosby?" Bob and Daly die laughing along with the audience. Bennett nails him after that. Bob reveals that he did the Bing Crosby signing on the version of *What's My Line?* in England too, while John mentions Bob doing *Producers' Showcase*: "Dateline," which will air on NBC the next night, and promotes Bob's book *Have Tux, Will Travel* too. Before leaving, Bob adds, "I can't tell you how happy I am to finally appear on this show. I watch it all the time."

Bob: \*\*\*\* Show: \*\*\*\*\*


**It Could Be You**
June 4, 1956, Monday 12:30-1 p.m.

Host: Bill Leyden. Announcer/Assistant: Wendell Niles. P: Ralph Edwards.

Bob makes a guest walk-on on the debut of this daytime wish fulfillment series, which ran until Dec. 29, 1961, for a woman who wanted to meet a celebrity. It also lets him promote his new movie, *That Certain Feeling*.


**What's My Line?**
June 24, 1956, CBS Sunday 10:30-11 p.m.

Host: John Charles Daly. Panelists: Bennett Cerf, Arlene Francis, Dorothy Kilgallen, Paul Winchell. Mystery Guests: The Cincinnati Reds, Bob and Linda Hope. EP: Gil Fates. D: Franklin Heller.

Wonder what Bob thought about being on the same show as the eleven members of the Cincinnati Reds baseball team, in-state rivals of his beloved Cleveland Indians? They kick off this program. Paul Winchell has an amusing bit throwing his voice during questioning, wherein John gives the panel a big hint that the mystery guest is more than one person. Following that is a photographer who took Bennett's passport picture in Oxford, Ohio. The panel fails to identify him. Next is Bob and his daughter. Bob amusingly tried to make his voice sound high, but Arlene recognizes there are two of them. "They sound to me like two ladies," says Dorothy to general laughter. They determine it involves promoting a movie, and Arlene says, "I have a certain feeling I know who this is," in reference to Bob's new film *That Certain Feeling*. The whole panel guesses wrong intentionally to let Bob win, and Arlene tells John afterward, "He needs the money, that's why wouldn't guess him!" Nonetheless, Bob does have plenty of time to promote his picture plus explain how he got a sunburn and the fun time he had earlier with Steve Allen. He is a good sport here.

Bob and Show: \*\*\*\*


***Bing Crosby and His Friends***
Jan. 12, 1958, CBS Sunday 5:30-7 p.m.

Host: Bing Crosby. Commentators: Tom Harmon, Roy Storey. Guests: Bob Hope, Red Skelton, Kathryn Grant (Mrs. Bing Crosby), Fred MacMurray. P: Cecil Barker. D: Seymour Berns, Bob Quinlan. W: Jack Quinlan. Music: Buddy Cole.

Bing attempts to spruce up coverage of the Bing Crosby National Pro-Am Golf Championship with this odd mixture of recorded bits and live coverage. After action amid such players as Guy Madison, John Charles Daly is in the clubhouse to introduce a filmed clip of Bing with Bob on the links. Bob promotes his new film, *Paris Holiday*, by saying it was nice working with a talented partner for once. He surveys Crosby's outfit and quips, "Hey, is that a Liberace reject?" At one point, Bob seems to forget what he needs to say and comically snarls back to Bing, "Don't cue me!" He jokes about Bing's riches and claims big-breasted stars like Jayne Mansfield held up his progress on the court, all of which amuses Bing.

Bob: \*\*\*\* Show: \*\*\*


***What's My Line?***
April 13, 1958, CBS Sunday 10:30-11 p.m.

Guest Host: Clifton Fadiman. Panelists: Bennett Cerf, Arlene Francis, Dorothy Kilgallen, Cesar Romero. Mystery Guest: Bob Hope. EP: Gil Fates. D: Franklin Heller.

As John Charles Daly is flying to Europe, Clifton is his substitute—a little shaky but serviceable. First up is a female human cannonball. Bennett asks if she's connected to any kind of transportation, generating laughs, as well as Clifton doing his John Daly best of interpretation. Incredibly, Arlene nails it after Bennett finally gets a no, in part because the circus is in New York and it inspired her. Next is a woman who makes glamorous collars for poodles. Cesar does a good job narrowing it down to a canine after the other panelists do their part, and Bennett nails it soon thereafter. The audience applauds when Dorothy thinks Bob's reception could indicate he could run for president. When Cesar asks, "Do I know you personally?" Dorothy quips, "That's going to be a great help to us, Cesar!" Bob answers "Oui" and "Non" so Bennett asks, "Are you not French?" A few questions later, Arlene exclaims, "I'm not so sure it's a man!" She misses, so Clifton turns the cards. Bob is astonished they missed him. Bob cracks everyone up by saying, "I came in last night and I was on *The Perry Como Show* last night and had a nice rest." Clifton has to prod him to tell the name of his new picture, *Paris Holiday*, before Bob leaves happily.

Bob and Show: \*\*\*\*

## *Celebrity Golf*
Sept. 25, 1960, Sunday 5-5:30 p.m.

Regulars: Sam Snead, Harry Von Zell. Guest: Bob Hope. P: Norman Blackburn, Jack Hope. D: Norman McLeod. W: Victor McLeod.

Bob faces off against Sam Snead on the links for nine holes while Harry Von Zell covers the action in the opener of this filmed sports series that ran for eight months. Bob's brother serves as co-producer here, so that may have played a part on getting him to guest on this.

## *This is Your Life*: "Johnny Grant" and "Jayne Mansfield"
Dec. 11 and 18, 1960, Sunday 10:30-11 p.m.

Host: Ralph Edwards. Announcer/Assistant: Bob Warren. P: Axel Gruenberg. D: Richard Gottlieb.

While Bob appears as a surprise guest for Johnny Grant on the first episode, Ralph throws another twist by telling fellow guest Jayne Mansfield that she is to be profiled as well. "Bob, did you think it might be you?" Edwards asks. "Oh no, not at all!" Bob says with a mock mortified look on his face. His work adds to the humor of a pretty good installment, and it is repeated on the next week's show at the start of profiling Jayne.

Bob: \*\*\*\* Show: \*\*\*

### The Bob Hope Buick Sports Awards Show
Feb. 15, 1961, Wednesday 9-10 p.m.

Host: Bob Hope. Honorees: Joe Bellino, Norman Van Brocklin, Wilt Chamberlain, Pancho Gonzalez, Dick Groat, Rafer Johnson, Jerry Lucas, Barry Mackay, Roger Maris, Arnold Palmer, Floyd Patterson. Presenters: Dana Andrews, Lucille Ball, Julie London, Jayne Mansfield, Dean Martin, Ronald Reagan, Ginger Rogers, Jane Russell, Tuesday Weld, Esther Williams, Jane Wyman. P: Jack Hope. D: Jack Shea. W: Mort Lachman, Bill Larkin, Charles Lee, Lester White, John Rapp, Norman Sullivan, Gig Henry. Music: David Rose.

Bob's monologue lays into Jackie Gleason's recent show *You're in the Picture*, which ended after one show. "Gleason laid such a large bomb on his new show, he's been living for three weeks on the fallout. He dropped the show, but the apologies were picked up for thirty-nine weeks. It was one of the shortest runs on television. By the time Jackie said, 'And away we go,' the show was gone." He also jokes about Jackie's weight, the space race, and ex-President Dwight Eisenhower. Bob reads a telegram from President John F. Kennedy lauding him for focusing on athletic accomplishments, then chides the chief executive for doing so much in office the first month with "I wonder whose job he's after?" The first presentation to tall basketball player Wilt Chamberlain ("Now I know how Mickey Rooney feels," quips Bob) by Jayne Mansfield, another physically impressive specimen, is the show's longest and funniest segment, thanks to all involved. Other winners and their categories and presenters are Pancho Gonzalez, tennis, Julie London; Joe Bellino, football, Tuesday Weld; Pittsburgh Pirates captain Dick Groat, World Series, Dana Andrews; Roger Maris, baseball, Jane Wyman; Jerry Lucas, college basketball, Esther Williams; Floyd Patterson, boxing, Lucille Ball; Barry Mackay, amateur tennis, Ginger Rogers; Rafer Johnson, track and field, Ronald Reagan; Norman Van Brocklin, pro football, Jane Russell; and Arnold Palmer, golfing, Dean Martin. Bob narrates clips of each athlete in action as well. While everyone reads cue cards, the jokes are pretty good (for example, Rafer telling Ronald Reagan he hopes to be as good an actor as him, causing Bob to get some laughs), so this is easy to take.

Bob: **** Show: ***

*What's My Line?*
Nov. 19, 1961, CBS Sunday 10:30-11 p.m.

Host: John Daly. Panelists: Dorothy Kilgallen, Martin Gabel, Arlene Francis, Bennett Cerf. EP: Gil Fates. D: Franklin Heller.

The first contestant is the Duke of Bedford, who runs his ancestral estate as a tourist attraction. The panel is blindfolded just to make sure they don't recognize him. It takes some time, given his American dialect, but Dorothy nails him before the tenth "No" answer. A woman who owns and operates a cranberry bog is found out pretty quickly when Arlene gets her to acknowledge her product is used for Thanksgiving. There is some good interplay when Bennett makes a pun after the segment. Then Bob uses a German dialect to everyone's delight, and questions like Dorothy's "Did your address book ever fall out of a helicopter while you were over Greece?" add to the fun (she was thinking of Anthony Perkins). They get him after only two "No" answers. John praises Bob's latest movie, *Bachelor in Paradise*, and Bob brings out money to pay him off comically. The panel is close to identifying a subway policewoman with the New York Transit Authority before the fun show runs out of time.

Bob and Show: \*\*\*\*


*The Bing Crosby Celebrity Golf Tournament*
Jan. 19 and 20, 1963, Syndicated Saturday 3:30-4:30 p.m. and Sunday 5-6:30 p.m.

Host: Bing Crosby. Commentator: Jimmy Demaret. Participants included Bob Hope. P: John Vrba, Walter Gould.

One of the first syndicated events to be shown live to the top 100 markets in the United States, this followed the first year of the networks inexplicably declining to carry the popular event since the 1950s. It will return to the networks for coverage in succeeding decades.


*What's My Line?*
May 5, 1963, CBS Sunday 10:30-11 p.m.

Host: John Daly. Panelists: Arlene Francis, Bennett Cerf, Dorothy Kilgallen, Buddy Hackett. EP: Gil Fates. D: Franklin Heller.

After Arlene introduces Buddy Hackett, a befuddled Joey Bishop comes out with Buddy following him and yelling, "You're on next week!" There's a bad Bennett Cerf pun too before John Daly has some amusing dialogue with Buddy. First up is a female dog catcher. Bennett nails her after two rounds. Next is a woman who makes diet bread, and Arlene gets her after two rounds. They identify Bob and Lucy (who sign in as "Bob Ball" and "Lucy Hope") immediately because the duo had been going around promoting *Critic's Choice*, their new film. After one go-round, Dorothy gets them with, "Are one of you redhead and the other a ski nose?" Bob promotes his book *I Owe Russia $1,200*, and there is lots of good interplay, with John complimenting Bob on getting a gold medal from the USO from a ceremony John hosted. The audience gives them a long round of applause as they leave, and Bob is very friendly toward Buddy and Arlene especially. There is time for one more game after Bob and Lucy leave.

Bob and Show: *****


## *Super Bowl I*
Jan. 15, 1967, Sunday 4-7 p.m. (approximately)

Curt Gowdy (play-by-play), Paul Christman (analyst), Jim Simpson (sideline reporter).

Bob is interviewed during the proceedings of the inaugural sporting event on the NBC telecast (CBS also shows the program with its own hosts as part of the deal for covering the contest).


## *Super Bowl III*
Jan. 12, 1969, Sunday 3-6 p.m. (approximately)

Curt Gowdy (play-by-play), Kyle Rote, Al DeRogatis (analysts), Jim Simpson (sideline reporter).

Shortly after the halftime ends, Jim Simpson tells the home audience that "Our special guest is the nation's number one comedian and turning out, Bob Hope, to be the number one sports fan. We see you at the World Series and now the Super Bowl." Bob shows he's been keeping track of the action by saying, "I'm really shocked by this game today. These Jets are really something today, aren't they? ... I think the Jets forgot to read the papers." After suggesting that he bet on the Baltimore Colts to win over the New York Jets, he adds, "This is a thrilling game, Jim, I'll tell you that" before promoting his next special on NBC. (The Jets do win in a surprise victory.)

*Bob Hope Presents the Cavalcade of Champions*
March 27, 1973, Tuesday 9-10 p.m.

Host: Bob Hope: Presenters: Barbara Eden, Mitzi Gaynor, Fred MacMurray, Darren McGavin, Dinah Shore, Danny Thomas, John Wayne. P: Mort Lachman. D: Dick McDonough. W: Charles Lee, Gig Henry, Mort Lachman, Lester White, Mel Tolkin, Raymond Siller, Norman Sullivan. Music: Les Brown.

Preceding the Oscars in the East and Central time zones (as it will in 1974 and 1975), this awards show starts with a good Hope monologue about the time of year ("Remember when a sure sign of spring was the first robin? Now it's the first rerun."), the TV writers strike and how protesters are trying to sabotage series ("Ironside took tap dancing"), high food prices, slow mail service ("This morning I just got an invitation to Zsa Zsa's first marriage"), and movies (he says of *Deep Throat*, "I thought it was giraffes!"). More than 800 voters participated in selecting the honorees—for more on the process, see the next entry. Winners and their categories and presenters are Steve Carlton, Pro Baseball Player, Danny Thomas; Jerry West, Pro Basketball Player, Mitzi Gaynor; Jack Nicklaus, Pro Golfer, Barbara Eden (presented while he is on tour in Palm Beach, Florida); Larry Brown, Pro Football Player, Dinah Shore; Mark Spitz, Amateur Athlete, John Wayne (who gets the longest round of applause); Bobby Orr, Pro Boxing, Tennis and Hockey, Darren McGavin (Bobby appears on satellite on a rink while Darren is in the studio with Bob); and Billie Jean King, Woman Athlete, Fred MacMurray. Gillette president Bill Salatich presents the Athlete of the Year honor (as he will in 1974 and 1975) to Mark Spitz. There's passable scripted lines between Bob and the honorees first and then the presenters with Bob and the winners, making this a nice way to pass an hour.

Bob and Show: ***

## Bob Hope Presents the Cavalcade of Champions
April 2, 1974, Tuesday 9-10 p.m.

Host: Bob Hope. Presenters: Carol Channing, Tony Curtis, William Holden, Dorothy Lamour, Karl Malden, Tony Randall, Alexis Smith. D: Dick McDonough. W: Mel Tolkin, Lester White, Mort Lachman, Gig Henry, Charles Lee, Raymond Siller, Norman Sullivan. Music: Bob Alberti.

This opens with Bob's jests about Easter and income taxes ("while you roll Easter eggs, the government rolls you!"), his sponsor (Gillette) and the gas shortage ("This morning I jogged ten miles. I was siphoning and got my lip caught in the gas tank." and "People are leaving their cars home and streak to work. Traffic that used to be bumper to bumper is now cheek to cheek!"). He then explains that more than 1,000 sports experts ranging from sports columnists to Hall of Famers nominated athletes and sports fans voted their favorites, with each winner receiving a $5,000 check to donate to a favorite youth organization. Bob narrates films of each category's top three nominees in action and lists their accomplishments before introducing each winner and presenter. Winners and their categories and presenters are Reggie Jackson, Baseball Player, Karl Malden; Basketball Player, Walt Frazier, Carol Channing; O.J. Simpson, Football Player, William Holden (who will costar with Simpson in the film *The Towering Inferno* later in 1974); Billie Jean King, Female Athlete, Tony Randall; Jack Nicklaus, Golfer, Dorothy Lamour (in a remote from New Orleans); Bill Walton, Male Amateur Athlete, Tony Curtis (accepted by Walton's coach, John Wooden of UCLA); and Phil Esposito, Pro in Hockey, Tennis and Horse Racing, Alexis Smith. Simpson also wins Athlete of the Year. It's passable but unmemorable entertainment. Bob accidentally calls Bob Alberti "Les" for his final music cue—it's obviously going to take some doing to forget his longtime conductor.

Bob and Show: ***

## Bob Hope Presents the Cavalcade of Champions
April 8, 1975, Tuesday 8-9:30 p.m.

Hosts: Bob Hope, Barbara Walters. Presenters: Steve Allen, Dyan Cannon, Eva Gabor, Zsa Zsa Gabor, David Janssen, Alan King, Dean Martin, Jennifer O'Neill, Tony Randall. EP: Bob Hope. P: Mort Lachman.

D: Dick McDonough. W: Mel Tolkin, Lester White, Mort Lachman, Gig Henry, Charles Lee, Steve White, Norman Sullivan. Music: Les Brown.

This prerecorded special is enjoyable despite some latent sexism (Barbara Walters handles honors only in the women sports categories). Bob's solid monologue hits spring weather ("So the younger generation will understand, Mother Nature's on an upper"), taxes ("This is the time of year when you put your hand in your pocket and there's another hand"), and his sponsor, Gillette ("Do you realize how much it takes for me to be this close to a razor on Academy Awards night?!"). The criteria and process for choosing honorees are the same as in 1974. Winners and their categories and presenters are Ken Stabler, Football Player, Jennifer O'Neill; John Havlicek, Basketball Player, Dyan Cannon; Male Golfer, Johnny Miller, Dean Martin; Female Golfer, Sandra Haynie, Tony Randall; Baseball Player, Lou Brock, David Janssen; Hockey Player, Bobby Orr, Eva Gabor; Female Tennis Player, Chris Evert, Alan King; Male Tennis Player, Jimmy Connors, Chris Evert (she and Connors were dating at the time); Male Amateur Athlete, Archie Griffin, Steve Allen; and Boxer, Muhammad Ali, Zsa Zsa Gabor. Barbara and Bob jointly present the Female Swimming, Tennis, Field and Gym award to gymnast Olga Korbut, who accepts via satellite to her native Russia with help from an interpreter. Johnny Miller also wins the Champion of Champions award presented at the end of this relatively breezy awards show, where everybody gets a few laughs, even Barbara Walters (when Bob asks her how she manages her busy schedule, she deadpans, "I do my own hair").

Bob and Show: \*\*\*\*


**Bob Hope American Youth Awards**
March 2, 1979, Friday 8:30-9:30 p.m.

Host: Bob Hope. Presenters Include: George Burns, Chris Evert, Ron Howard, Dinah Shore.

These awards include honoring students who excel in academic and artistic accomplishments along with athletic achievements.

Bob adjusts the napkin around the neck of his old comic sparring partner Bing Crosby in a surprise cameo on *The Carol Burnett Show* on Nov. 10, 1969. Carol (on right, playing a waitress who bothers Crosby for requests) invited Hope to show up at the end of the sketch without Crosby's knowledge, and Bob eagerly agreed. Courtesy of Getty Images.

# 10 Guest Shots – Variety Series and Specials

**BESIDES HIS OWN SPECIALS,** Bob made nearly two hundred guest shots on variety shows and specials from 1948-1995. For the sake of brevity, only the ones that could be viewed are listed in detail in this chapter. Besides those, Bob also appeared on the following series:

*The Toast of the Town*, Sept. 27, 1948, CBS Sunday 9-10 p.m., Host: Ed Sullivan. Bob does an unscheduled walk-on without makeup and jokes with Jerry Colonna before leaving in this early installment of what will become better known as *The Ed Sullivan Show*. The other, low-wattage acts include comic Al Bernie, Brazilian vocal quintet Los Angels du Inferno, and dancers.

*The Red Skelton Show*, Nov. 25, 1951, Sunday 10-10:30 p.m., Host: Red Skelton.

*The Buick-Berle Show*, June 8, 1954, Tuesday 8-9 p.m., Host: Milton Berle.

*The Jimmy Durante Show*, Feb. 26, 1955, Saturday 9:30-10 p.m., Regulars: Jimmy Durante, Eddie Jackson.

*The Chevy Show*, Oct. 25, 1955, Tuesday 8-9 p.m., Hostess: Betty Hutton. Bob does a monologue at the top of the show and then reappears at the end clowning with Betty Hutton and her other guest, Jimmy Durante. Betty will return the favor and show up as a guest when Bob hosts *The Chevy Show* three weeks later.

*The Amazing Dunninger*, June 27, 1956, ABC Wednesday 8:30-9 p.m., Host: "The Amazing" Joseph Dunninger. Apparently eager to promote his film *That Certain Feeling* anywhere, Bob joins pretentious telepathic Joseph Dunninger for a session of attempted mind reading in exchange for plugging his picture.

*The Steve Allen Show*, June 30, 1957, Sunday 8-9 p.m.

*Club Oasis*, Oct. 26, 1957, Saturday 9-9:30 p.m., Guests: Jimmy Durante, Vivian Blaine, Hy Gardner. This biweekly musical variety series employs different hosts (here it is Jimmy Durante). Bob and Danny Thomas make surprise cameos.

*The Eddie Fisher Show*, Dec. 10, 1957, Tuesday 8-9 p.m., Regulars: Eddie Fisher, George Gobel.

*The Polly Bergen Show*, April 19, 1958, Saturday 9-9:30 p.m. Hostess: Polly Bergen.

*The Eddie Fisher Show*, April 29, 1958, Tuesday 8-9 p.m., Regulars: Eddie Fisher, George Gobel.

*The Big Record*, May 7, 1958, CBS Wednesday 8:30-9 p.m., Hostess: Patti Page.

*The Dick Clark Show*, May 10, 1958, ABC Saturday 7:30-8 p.m., Host: Dick Clark.

*Perry Como's Kraft Music Hall*, Nov. 30, 1960, Wednesday 9-10 p.m., Host: Perry Como.

*The Kraft Music Hall*, Oct. 25, 1967, Wednesday 9-10 p.m. With Mike Douglas, Hugh Masekela, and Sonny and Cher.

*Rowan and Martin's Laugh-In*, Sept. 30, 1968, Monday 8-9 p.m., Hosts: Dan Rowan, Dick Martin.

*The Andy Williams Show*, Nov. 29, 1969, Saturday 7:30-8:30 p.m., Host: Andy Williams.

*This is Tom Jones*, March 5, 1970, ABC Thursday 9-10 p.m., Host: Tom Jones.

*The Ed Sullivan Show*: "The Georgies," Sept. 20, 1970, CBS Sunday 8-9 p.m., Host: Ed Sullivan.

*Rowan and Martin's Laugh-In*, Sept. 13, 1971, Monday 8-9 p.m., Hosts: Dan Rowan, Dick Martin.

*The ABC Comedy Hour*: "Something Funny Happened on the Way to the Special," March 15, 1972, ABC Wednesday 8:30-9:30 p.m., Host: Danny Thomas.

*Saturday Night Live with Howard Cosell*, Nov. 29, 1975, ABC Saturday 8-9 p.m., Host: Howard Cosell.

*The Rich Little Show*, March 22, 1976, Monday 8-9 p.m., Host: Rich Little.

*The Mac Davis Show*, March 25, 1976, Thursday 8-9 p.m. Host: Mac Davis.

*Star Search*, Jan. 13, 1985, Syndicated One hour, Host: Ed McMahon.

Additionally, Bob guest starred on the following variety specials unable to be viewed:

*GM Motorama*, Jan. 19, 1955, Wednesday 10-11 p.m., Bob Hope, Harlow Curtice. Music: Victor Young. Bob hosts this infomercial for new vehicles from his sponsor, General Motors, with comments from company president Harlow Curtice. A *Daily Variety* reviewer roasted this but loved Bob's quips, particularly one about a car with a TV set in the back: "Now you can be arrested for speeding and watch your case on *Dragnet!*"

*Frances Langford Presents*, March 15, 1959, Sunday 10-11 p.m., Hostess: Frances Langford.

*The Dean Martin Show*, May 3, 1959, Sunday 8-9 p.m., Host: Dean Martin.

*Eleanor Roosevelt's Diamond Jubilee Plus One,* Oct. 7, 1960, Friday 9-10 p.m., Host: Bob Hope.

*The Bing Crosby Show,* Dec. 11, 1961, ABC Monday 9-10 p.m., Host: Bing Crosby.

*The Jo Stafford Show,* Aug. 18, 1963, CBS Sunday 9-10 p.m., Hostess: Jo Stafford.

*The Danny Thomas Show,* April 23, 1965, Friday 8:30-9:30 p.m., Host: Danny Thomas.

*Up With People,* Aug. 23, 1968, Friday 10-11 p.m., Host: Bob Hope (he introduces the title group).

*Tournament of Roses Parade,* Jan. 1, 1969, CBS and NBC, Wednesday 10 a.m.-Noon. As grand marshals of the parade, Bob and Delores Hope are interviewed during their procession by the networks covering it live at their own reviewing stands.

*Danny Thomas Looks at Yesterday, Today and Tomorrow,* Jan. 28, 1970, CBS Wednesday 9-10 p.m., Host: Danny Thomas.

*Raquel,* April 26, 1970, CBS Sunday 9-10 p.m., Hostess: Raquel Welch.

*Honor America Day,* July 4, 1970, NBC and CBS Saturday morning/afternoon

*A Royal Gala,* April 7, 1971, Wednesday 9:25-10:25 p.m., Host: Rex Harrison. Queen Elizabeth is among the guests in this special, which shows highlights of transatlantic stars in performance at a World Wildlife Fund charity event held five months earlier. This starts at the odd time due to a pre-emption by President Richard Nixon addressing troop withdrawals in Vietnam.

*Festival at Ford's,* Nov. 15, 1971, Monday 10-11 p.m., Hosts/Narrators: Bob Hope, Raymond Burr.

*The Dinah Shore Special:* "How to Handle a Woman," Oct. 20, 1972, Friday 9-10 p.m., Hostess: Dinah Shore.

*Ken Berry's Wow:* "A Wacky Look at Yesterday," March 21, 1972, Tuesday 8:30-9:30 p.m., Host: Ken Berry. A special for NBC with several celebrity cameos including Bob and written by the team behind *The Sonny and Cher Comedy Hour* on CBS, this somehow led to a summer series on ABC four months later called *The Ken Berry Wow Show*. Got all that?

*The American Film Institute Presents a Salute to John Ford*, April 2, 1973, CBS Monday 9:30-11 p.m., Host: Danny Kaye.

*A Show Business Salute to Milton Berle*, Nov. 27, 1973, ABC Tuesday 9-10 p.m., Host: Sammy Davis Jr.

*Bing Crosby and His Friends*, Oct. 9, 1974, CBS Wednesday 9-10 p.m., Host: Bing Crosby. Because this has the same cast except for Sandy Duncan in place of Carol Burnett, some confuse this with Bing's 1972 special of the same name, but they are different. See the 1972 special's entry in this chapter for more information.

*The Flip Wilson Comedy Special*, Nov. 11, 1975, CBS Tuesday 9-10 p.m., Host: Flip Wilson.

*The 16th Annual Miss Teenage America Pageant*, Nov. 27, 1976, Saturday 10-11 p.m., Host: Bob Hope. The winner, Rebecca Ann Reid, appears opposite Bob on his Christmas special two weeks later.

*Paul Anka: Music My Way*, April 25, 1977, ABC Monday 10-11 p.m., Host: Paul Anka.

*America Salutes the Queen*, Nov. 29, 1977, Tuesday 8-11 p.m.

*Pat Boone and Family Thanksgiving Special*, Nov. 12, 1978, ABC Sunday 7-8 p.m.

*Danny Thomas: Young and Foolish*, Dec. 8, 1978, CBS Friday 9-10 p.m., Host: Danny Thomas.

*Lucy Moves to NBC*, Feb. 8, 1980, Friday 8:30-10 p.m.

*The Anita Bryant Spectacular*, March 1980, Syndicated Two hours, Hostess: Anita Bryant.

*Debby Boone: The Same Brand Old New Me*, June 23, 1980, Monday 9-10 p.m., Hostess: Debby Boone.

*NBC Star Salute to 1981*, Jan. 1, 1981, Thursday 10-11:30 a.m.

*All-Star Salute to Mother's Day*, May 10, 1981, Sunday 9-11 p.m., Hosts: Ed McMahon, Jayne Kennedy.

*An NBC Family Christmas*, Dec. 18, 1981, Friday 10-11 p.m.

*Salute!:* "Gladys Knight and the Pips," November 1983, Syndicated 60 minutes, Host: Dick Clark.

*America's All-Star Tribute to Elizabeth Taylor*, March 9, 1989, ABC Thursday 9-10 p.m., Host: Charles Bronson.

This compilation also does not include appearances that could not be confirmed by more than one recognized source at this writing, such as on *Dick Clark's Live Wednesday* in the fall of 1978 and *NBC Star Salute to 1980* on the morning of New Year's Day. Still, there is plenty to review in this section.

 As to why Bob did so many of these, most of the time, he wanted to promote an upcoming project, or NBC wanted him to promote a show, or he owed a favor to the talent involved, or he just thought it might be fun, like surprising Bing Crosby on *The Hollywood Palace* and *The Carol Burnett Show*. He usually only had to do a quick monologue and/or song with the host or hostess to do that. Coming from vaudeville, he enjoyed the format immensely too.

 Consider Bob's four appearances on *Donny & Marie* including its pilot or test show. According to costar Marie Osmond, Bob came aboard simply by her request. "I asked him to the *Donny & Marie* pilot because we were friends, and he liked me," she says, adding with a smile that Bob always asked to work with her and not her brother, Donny Osmond.

She knew about his propensity to ad lib (he showed advanced scripts of shows where he was a guest to his writers to come up with several clever alternate lines he could insert), but that fact never bothered her or Donny. "Bob was so brilliant. He would make us laugh and get off script, and Bob always knew how to get off it, but always get back on it, unlike Milton Berle," she says.

Marie acknowledges that while ad-libbing generally was discouraged for the series' guests, she and the rest of the cast and crew came to expect and enjoy his contributions. "The producers were sometimes like, 'Uh, this will be an editing nightmare,' but not with Bob. The directors and everybody would be like, 'Oh, we're having fun.'"

Bob did have a lot of fun for a long time on TV variety series and specials. He guest starred on virtually all the major variety series on NBC (with the notable exceptions of *The Dinah Shore Chevy Show*, *The Flip Wilson Show*, and *Saturday Night Live*) and many more shows and specials on all the networks. Take a deep breath before reading this section, as it is the longest one in the book, but these entries show in some ways the depth and breadth of Bob's talent better even than his own specials did at the same time.

*Texaco Star Theatre*
Dec. 19, 1950, Tuesday 8-9 p.m.

Host: Milton Berle. Guests: Toni Harper, Sam Levene, Mary Hatcher, Bob Hope, The Dunhills, Robert Merrill, J. Fred Coots, Verna Raymond. Cameo: Frank Gallop. Music: Alan Schwartz.

Coming out as a mermaid, Milton Berle does a monologue on Christmas shopping with a near-equal combination of good and bad puns before introducing eleven-year-old singer Toni Harper and appearing as a five-time murderer pretending to be his victims to the inspector (Sam Levene) in a long (ten minutes) spoof of the creepy anthology series *Lights Out* that includes an introduction by that show's host, Frank Gallop. After Mary Hatcher sings, she appears with Milton as his newlywed bride in a hotel room that includes Bob Hope's joke files that Milton owns. Uncle Miltie opens the cabinet and Bob is seen typing. He comes out and sings to Milton he's going to steal the latter's wife for all the gags the comedian has purloined from him. When it ends, Milton has Bob take a bow and plug his new special along with his sponsors before praising Milton for how hard the latter worked in rehearsal. After Bob leaves, Milton quips, "He's a comer" to much laughter. The Dunhills, a three-man team, dance, then Robert Merrill croons operatically before Milton joins him with J. Fred Coots, the songwriter behind "Santa Claus is Coming to Town." All three sing "The First Noel" before Milton appears as Santa before a young girl. The sentimental ending, coupled with Bob's sharp delivery in his appearance, redeem what is otherwise a rocky show to watch.

Bob and Show: ***

*All Star Revue*: "The Ed Wynn Show"
Nov. 10, 1951, Saturday 8-9 p.m.

Host: Ed Wynn. Guests: Dorothy Lamour (TV debut), Buster Keaton, The Nicholas Brothers, The De Mattiattzes, Chick Chandler. Cameo: Bob Hope. D/W: Leo Solomon. Production Supervisor: Pet Barnum. W: Hal Goodman, Bob Fisher. Music: Lou Bring. Choreographer: Dick Barstow.

In his short time here, Bob is much better than most of the material on display, which peaks and dips irregularly throughout. First, Ed Wynn explains how to create a TV show in a lengthy setup showing the individuals involved before scoring with a convoluted Rube Goldberg-type display of how they all work together. The Nicholas Brothers stun with their acrobatically amazing dance routine, and it's always a pleasure to see Buster Keaton in a pantomime as well, even if his role as an inept baker's helper who ends up accidentally shoving himself into an oven when baking a pizza isn't on par with what he did in movies in the 1920s. Tedium predominates the next fifteen minutes, even with Dorothy Lamour singing and dancing, until Ed and Dorothy star as Samson and Delilah in a silent movie rendition where the players flash signs to express their thoughts. It's fun, and midway through, Bob shows up to tap Dorothy on her shoulder and kiss her. Interrupted from doing this, Bob holds up a sign telling Ed, "Pardon me ... I thought this was *The Road to Morocco*" and leaves. It's a great cameo that for once doesn't involve Bob plugging anything.

Bob and Show: ***

## The Kate Smith Evening Hour
Jan. 9, 1952, Wednesday 8-9 p.m.

Kate Smith, Ted Collins. Guests: The Hamilton Trio, Bob Hope, The Billy Williams Quartet.

Hosting the *Look* Second Annual Television Awards, Ted Collins introduces star Kate Smith singing "There's No Business Like Show Business" before giving honors to Alex Segal for Best Director and Max Liebman for Best Producer and Best Variety Show (*Your Show of Shows*). The latter's stars, Sid Caesar and Imogene Coca, perform a funny pantomime of two lonely people at a diner before Kate awards them with Best Comedy Team. After the Hamilton Trio's jazz dance, Kate introduces Kukla, Fran and Ollie doing "Cherchez La Femme" before Burr Tillstrom accepts the Best Children's Show statuette. Kate sings and then announces Best Dramatic Program is *Studio One*, which its producer, Worthington Minor, accepts. Ted presents awards to sportscasters Jack Brickhouse, Jimmy Powers, and Jimmy Britt for *Cavalcade of Sports*, Marlin Perkins for Best Educational Program (*Zoo Parade*) and John Cameron Swayze for Best News Program (*Camel News Caravan*). The Billy Williams Quartet performs between the sports and educational awards. Bob finally appears live from California and says he was tricked: "I find out I'm giving [awards] again … I'm used to giving to this man anyway." That comment brings laughter from his studio audience. Bob praises Milton Berle but adds, "I watch you every Tuesday night. I love to sit here and see how my jokes are doing." Milton calls Bob both Bing [Crosby] and Jerry [Lewis] before sincerely thanking *Look* and Kate for the award. Kate gets the award for Best New Nighttime Show from *Look* Editor Gardner Cowles too, but it can't save the show from cancellation in June 1952.

Bob and Show: ***

## The All Star Revue
Jan. 26, 1952, Saturday 8-9 p.m.

Jimmy Durante, Eddie Jackson, Jules Buffano, Jack Roth. Guests: Bob Hope, Mickey Rooney, Doris Singleton, Butch Austin, Candy Candido, Rafael Mendez, Jimmy Rae. P/D: Joseph Santley. D: Sid Smith. W: Charlie Isaacs, Jack Elinson, Norman Paul (additional dialogue). Music: Roy Bargy. Choreographer: Aida Broadbent.

Mickey Rooney's TV debut and Bob's cameo are the only distinguishing features of a wan offering despite Jimmy Durante's best efforts. It starts well, with Jimmy spoofing *The Continental* by pretending to be a suave lover saying good night to his imaginary date before he sings and jokes in the audience. An indignant NBC executive (played by an unidentified actor) stops the proceedings to summon Jimmy's replacement, Bob, who gets a huge reception as he stares at the audience. He then kisses Jimmy before the latter pushes him off stage. Though brief, Bob's moment is charming, unlike the rest of the show, a belabored skit where Jimmy visits Palm Springs and Mickey rooms with him in his hotel to keep the comedian from carousing. Mickey and Jimmy try valiantly, but they only get scattered laughs, mostly from ad-libbing following prop failures.

Bob: *** Show: **


***The All Star Revue***
Feb. 28, 1953, Saturday 8-9 p.m.

George Jessel. Guests: Bob Hope, Fred Allen, Sue Allen, Hilde Gueden, Diane Sinclair, Ken Spaulding, Sara Berner, Sam Carlton, Toots Shor. EP: Sam Fuller. P/D: Joseph Santley. D: Grey Lockwood. W: George Jessel, Mannie Manheim, Sam Carlton. Music: Al Goodman.

"A dinner without Jessel nearby is like a wedding without Tommy Manville," cracks Bob at the top of the host, adding "Nowadays, when he takes a girl out, he brings a menu!" He also claims that the "Toastmaster General" is so old, he was in New York City when it was called New Amsterdam. Jessel, who will guest on Bob's *Colgate Comedy Hour* tomorrow night, takes the jabs well even when he sings a special version of "Thanks for the Memory" to Bob and the latter interjects, "He's on key tonight!" As Bob leaves, George quips, "He'll be back, we have prunes!" What follows is anticlimactic singing and comedy except for a good monologue by Fred Allen about his hometown. In a thirteen-minute skit near the end, Bob plays the president briefly opposite Fred. George concludes with more singing and speechifying that weigh down the show overall.

Bob: *** Show: **

*Producers' Showcase*: "Dateline"
Dec. 13, 1954, Monday 8:30-10 p.m.

Host: John Daly. Cast: Marian Anderson, Hal Boyle, Sid Caesar, Milton Caniff, Perry Como, Bob Considine, Fleur Cowles, Eddie Fisher, Ben Grauer, Bob Hope, H.V. Kaltenborn, Elsa Maxwell, Martha Raye, Carl Reiner, Richard Rodgers, Carl Sandburg, Lawrence Spivak, Robert Sherwood, Ray Walston (as Ernie Pyle), David White (unbilled). P: Fred Coe. D: Alan Handley. W: Mel Tolkin, Robert Sherwood. Music: Harry Sosnik, Mitchell Ayres, Axel Stordahl.

This live "spectacular" unevenly mixes drama with comedy to honor fallen members of the Overseas Press Club, which produces this show, and let Carl Sandburg dedicate the club's new memorial building. Bob's monologue comes early and sparkles starting with "Remember, this is a charity affair, so your applause and laughter will be deductible." Noting it's his color television debut, he says, "This isn't an announcement, this is a warning." Of comedians on TV this season, "The new ones are so young, the makeup men don't know which end to put on the powder." He commends club members by saying if it weren't for them, how would Americans know how amorous Errol Flynn and Marlon Brando had been doing overseas? Bob's delivery and material is crisp and fresh. Too bad much of the rest of the show isn't the same.

Bob: ***** Show: ***


*Entertainment 1955*
March 27, 1955, Sunday 7:30-9 p.m.

Hosts: Fred Allen, Ralph Edwards, Helen Hayes. Cast: Earl Barton, Malcolm Broderick, Pat Carroll, Nancy Coleman, John Derek, The Double Daters, B.A. Graham, George Grizzard, Buddy Hackett, Joseph Hayes, Judy Holliday, Tom Holmes, Bob Hope, Karl Malden, George Mathews, Elizabeth Montgomery, Paul Newman, Patricia Peardon, Leontyne Price, Cesar Romero, NBC Executive Vice President Robert Sarnoff, Dinah Shore, The Skylarks, NBC President Pat Weaver, Josh Wheeler, Adolph Zukor. P/D: Bob Banner. *Tosca* P: Samuel Chotzinoff. New York D: Norman Felton. *Tosca* D: Kirk Browning. M: Henri René. Choreographer: Nick Castle.

A live, all-star extravaganza spotlighting the opening of a new color TV studio in Hollywood for NBC, this is predictably uneven as it ranges from the cultural (Leontyne Price and Josh Wheeler singing arias from the opera *Tosca*; Nancy Coleman, Karl Malden and Paul Newman acting in an excerpt from the Broadway drama *The Desperate Hours*) to the ponderous (NBC executives Pat Weaver and Robert Sarnoff joining B.A. Graham, president of Sunbeam, in awkwardly christening the opening). Bob's appearance is somewhere in the middle both in appeal and order of appearance. Ralph Edwards introduces Paramount Pictures Chairman Adolph Zukor, who praises Bob as an actor who can make people laugh and cry. "And that's why he's so wonderful as Eddie Foy in this new picture he's just completed," Zukor says, cuing Bob to enter and promote *The Seven Little Foys* along with a hit-or-miss monologue. His most audacious joke is mentioning Eddie Foy's primary field of entertainment and quipping, "Vaudeville—that's like *The Toast of the Town* without Ed Sullivan." (The latter series runs opposite this special on the Eastern and Central time zones, and Bob will appear on it three months later.) A bit of the picture is shown, supposedly being the first film clip ever shown on color on television, then Bob talks a little more with Ralph and Adolph before leaving and letting the men talk to Paramount's new star hire, John Derek. There's more after that, but nothing particularly of note.

Bob and Show: ★★★

## *The Toast of the Town*
June 26, 1955, CBS Sunday 8-9 p.m.

Ed Sullivan, The June Taylor Dancers. Guests: Bob Hope, Will Jordan, Smith and Dale, Pearl Bailey, Tony Bennett, Polly Bergen, Victor Borge, Charles Coburn, Eddie Fisher, Burl Ives, Eartha Kitt, Julius LaRosa, Johnny Ray, Phil Silvers. Music: Ray Bloch.

Celebrating its seventh anniversary (and readying to change its name to *The Ed Sullivan Show* in the fall), this program secures an ex-competitor of *The Colgate Comedy Hour* by letting Bob plug his new film, *The Seven Little Foys*. He also does an amusing part of his old vaudeville routine with conductor Ray Bloch. The rest of the program includes comic bits by Will Jordan (the foremost impersonator of Sullivan) and the vaudeville team of Smith and Dale. Pearl Bailey also sings some and joins celebrities following her in the listing who pay tribute to Sullivan at the top of the show.

Bob and Show: ★★★

## *The Perry Como Show*
March 17, 1956, Saturday 8-9 p.m.

Perry Como, The Ray Charles Singers, The Louis DaPron Dancers. Guests: Bob Hope. Announcer: Frank Gallop.

Bob joins Perry to quip about Elvis Presley being a wild singer ("Sort of a hillbilly with hydromatics" and "Presley has more hair on his sideburns than Crosby has on his head"). There are more cracks about Bing Crosby before Bob introduces Perry doing "True Love." The clip with Bob's appearance is the only one in circulation, hence no rating here for the show.

Bob: \*\*\*

## *The Patti Page Show*
June 23, 1956, Saturday 8-9 p.m.

Patti Page, The Spellbinders (a three-man, two-woman singing group). Guests: The Christianis, Walter Dare Wahl and Emmet Oldfield, Joe Maize and His Chordsmen, Guy Mitchell, Bob Hope. Announcer: Don Pardo. P: Norman Frank. D: Grey Lockwood. W: Bob Corcoran, James Shelton. Music: Carl Hoff. Choreographer: Frank Lewis.

For five minutes Patti sings before the Christianis (three men and two women) do acrobatic tricks, Walter Dare Wahl and Emmet Oldfield clown around comically, and both Joe Maize and His Chordsmen, a four-piece instrumental group including an accordionist, and Guy Mitchell offer some music. Patti singing "The Wayward Wind" between the first two guest spots is the best thing amid these contrived efforts. Bob finally joins Patti two-thirds into the show, cleverly drops the name of his film *That Certain Feeling*, and shows a clip from it before Patti lets him do a monologue. He talks of his flight to New York and his interaction with the stewardess. "She didn't like the way I fastened my safety belt. She wanted to move around." He jokes about talent that appeared at the Paramount Theater in New York previously ("Remember when Artie Shaw played there and all the girls wanted to marry him—and did?") as well as Elvis Presley. Bob repeats his "Sort of a hillbilly with hydromatics" line he did in March on *The Perry Como Show* (for which this series is a summer replacement) and adds, "A few month ago, he couldn't spell Kentucky. Now he owns it!" He also hits on New York traffic and of course Mr. Crosby ("Bing got his start here. Of course, it was called New Amsterdam then."). It's a tight set, and Bob clearly loves Patti as well. If only the rest of the show was up to his level.

Bob: **** Show: **


## The Steve Allen Show
June 24, 1956, Sunday 8-9 p.m.

Host: Steve Allen. Regulars: Louis Nye, Don Knotts, Tom Poston, Dayton Allen. Guests: The Will Mastin Trio Starring Sammy Davis Jr., Kim Novak, Vincent Price, Wally Cox, Dane Clark, Bambi Lynn and Rod Alexander, Roy Eldridge, Coleman Hawkins. Cameos: Jerry Lewis, Bob Hope. Announcer: Gene Rayburn. P: Nick Vanoff. D: Dwight Hemion. W: Steve Allen, Stan Burns, Mike Marmer, Herbert Sargent, Don Hinkley.

On the title comedian's new series debut, the first image is Jerry Lewis pretending to be Steve to many laughs. Steve shows up next to do his impersonation of Bob Hope, whereupon the shot cuts to another camera of Bob turning around and joining Steve. "I'm here with thousands of your friends because this is your big night," Bob says. "And I know you're starting your series here on *The Colgate Comedy* [*Hour*], I mean, uh, the thing ..." There's much laughter, as the latter held the same time slot until cancelled six months earlier. Bob then gives Steve an award by the producers of Bob's new picture, *That Certain Feeling*, lists the film's credits and ends with saying the host gets the award "Because Steve Allen is the TV star who gives most people that certain feeling." The clever, funny plug sets the tone for a solid hour of comedy and music.

Bob and Show: ****


## The Perry Como Show
Nov. 10, 1956, Saturday 8-9 p.m.

Perry Como, The Ray Charles Singers, The Louis DaPron Dancers. Guests: Bob Hope, Yvonne De Carlo, Glenn Derringer, Robert Lamouret. Announcer: Frank Gallop.

"Bob, do you mind if I take my show back?" Perry quips good naturedly following one of many interjections made by the bubbly comedian here. After a rousing introductory production number of "Another Op'nin', Another Show" from *Kiss Me Kate*, Perry elaborately introduces his other guests, prompting Bob to ask, "What's he got out there? A long-playing cue card?" Bob comes out after eleven-year-old organist Glenn Derringer wows the crowd. "Bob Hope! Are you the star of that new MGM picture *The Iron Petticoat*?!" Derringer exclaims as he keeps plugging, leading Bob to add, "This kid is getting taller with every line!" Bob is loose as Glenn blows a few lines ("Speak, Derringer, speak!") and then leaves after Bob pays him while Bob asks, "He's not coming on any more, is he?" He joins Perry and Yvonne in a funny road picture tribute that's well sung and danced by all (Bob alone dances a salsa, flirts with Yvonne, pretends to swat flies, and tries to step on Perry's feet). Also amusing is Bob lustfully describing Yvonne while Perry thinks he's getting golf tips instead. Bob's final bit has him emerge from his dressing room with the star on his door falling off to say "Subway Entrance" earlier than planned, amusing him and Perry and Bob. Showing Perry his new golf swing, Bob supposedly busts a camera lens, prompting Perry to remove his check before Bob exits. Bob is in top form here, and the show comes close to matching him.

Bob: ***** Show: ****


**The Steve Allen Show**
Nov. 18, 1956, Sunday 8-9 p.m.

Host: Steve Allen. Regulars: Louis Nye, Don Knotts, Tom Poston, Dayton Allen. Guests: The Duke Ellington Orchestra, [Ole] Olsen and [Chic] Johnson, Gene Nelson, Betty Walker, Erin O'Brien, Bob Hope, George Hamilton IV. Announcer: Gene Rayburn. P: Nick Vanoff. D: Dwight Hemion. W: Steve Allen, Stan Burns, Mike Marmer, Herbert Sargent, Don Hinkley.

A quarter hour into a good but not great mix of songs and humor, Bob pops up as a surprise guest to promote his live special following this show tonight (each show is based in New York City this time). Of his upcoming guest, Perry Como, Bob quips, "Right before rehearsal, he fell awake," then launches into some jokes he said he could not fit into his upcoming presentation. The first two bomb, so he throws them away, but he scores after mentioning Elvis Presley has become a millionaire: "Just shows you what clean living can do." Most of his other efforts are forgettable, and when Steve rejoins him for a final, also variable bit where Bob translates what movie ad lines really mean, Bob greets him with "You saved me!" The talents of and rapport between Steve and Bob salvage some humor here despite the missteps.

Bob and Show: ***

## The Edsel Show
Oct. 13, 1957, CBS Sunday 8-9 p.m.

Bing Crosby, Frank Sinatra, Rosemary Clooney, Louis Armstrong, Lindsay Crosby, The Four Preps, Mr. Conn and Mr. Mann. Cameo: Bob Hope. P/W: Bill Morrow. D: Seymour Berns. Music: Camarata, Buddy Cole, The Norman Luboff Choir. Choreography: Eugene Loring.

Frank is told to take Bob's part in "The Road to Morocco" duet with Bing, but Bob interrupts them by whistling and grabs both men. "You're singing our song to him!" he tells Bing. "After all, Dean wouldn't do this to Jerry!" He grabs leis they are wearing and says, "You look like two flower girls left over from Marlon's wedding!" cracking them up. "This will get them out on the highways!" After several crackups by all, the trio finish the song. It is a fun part of a lively special that is nominated for an Emmy. Too bad the title vehicle it introduces is one of the automotive industry's biggest bombs ever.

Bob and Show: ****

## The Frank Sinatra Show
Oct. 18, 1957, ABC Friday 9-9:30 p.m.

Frank Sinatra. Guests: Bob Hope, Kim Novak, Peggy Lee. P: William Self. D: Kirk Browning. W: Hal Goodman, Larry Klein. Music: Nelson Riddle.

This disappointing opener for Sinatra's one-season series has Frank singing "I Get a Kick Out of You" before Bob emerges from behind a blowup of his new LP *Bob Hope Sings the Best of Radio*. He says to Frank, "I know what a thrill it is for you to step out here on the stage in front of millions of people and know that deep down in your heart, you're insecure." After Bob adds, "I can't wait to see you die in living color," he and Frank proceed to do just that, as their interplay gets little reaction before Peggy Lee sings and then banters awkwardly with Frank, who speaks low using cue cards. Kim Novak kisses Frank and looks at him longingly while he sings in an effective bit before Frank and Bob emerge in tuxes and tails. Bob asks for a key to open the keyboard after mock cracking his knuckles, then Frank sings "Autumn Leaves" while leaves falls on him and Bob, which is pretty funny. After Frank sings "All the Way," he lassos Bob, who jokes about Frank's cowboy movie *Johnny Concho*, Frank's travels, other movies Frank's done and Bob's new movie in a deadly exchange. The duo then enacts "The Pride and the Passport," with Kim being wooed by both Frank and Bob. Bob's wisecracks, sharp delivery and ad libs can't save a sluggish sketch. Kim chooses Jeff Chandler (in a cameo), leaving Bob and Frank to say lamely, "That's all, folks!" At the end, Bob asks for money, grabs the singer's arms and says, "Good night, Bones." It's funny, but not enough to save the show.

Bob: **** Show: ***


***The Perry Como Show***
April 12, 1958, Saturday 8-9 p.m.

Perry Como. Guests: Bob Hope, Carol Channing, Johnny Puleo. Announcer: Frank Gallop. P: Bob Finkel. D: Grey Lockwood. W: Goodman Ace, Jay Burton, Mort Green, George Foster. Music: Mitchell Ayres.

Bob is surprisingly weak here, promoting his recent efforts with little verve amid great work by everyone else. After the opening number, Perry introduces Bob, who mentions his recent special on his trip to Russia, where that country's supposed top ten list mocks Perry's hits, like "Catch a Falling Czar." After the others perform, Bob provides more puny rejoinders with Perry except for some good cracks at Bing Crosby. He and Perry duet on "Nothing in Common" from Bob's film *Paris Holiday*, and apart from saying "Stop shaking the cards, will you?" to a card holder, there's little joy from this. Bob also does a stilted routine with Frank Gallop interjecting a promotion for *Paris Holiday* before the comedian says goodbye at the end with one more plug for the movie. His going through the motions routine drags down an otherwise solid hour of comedy and music.

Bob: ** Show: ***

*The Steve Allen Show*
April 20, 1958, Sunday 8-9 p.m.

Steve Allen, Louis Nye, Tom Poston, Don Knotts, Gene Rayburn. Guests: Bob Hope, Ray Anthony, Patrice Munsel, Johnny Haymer, David Allen. Filmed Guests: Willie Mays, Duke Snider, Lou Burdette, Fred Haney. P: William O. Harbach. D: Dwight Hemion. W: Leonard Stern, Stan Burns, Herbert Sargent, Bill Dana, Don Hinkley, Hal Goodman, Larry Klein. Music: Skitch Henderson.

Bob appears a lot in this overstuffed show. At the start, he, Ray Anthony and Patrice Munsel suggest answers for a Mad Libs story involving them and builds on the laughs created by the juxtapositions with his own quips. Later, he talks to Steve about his recent trip to Russia. "Don't you ever get any rest?" Steve asks. "Oh yes, last week I was on the Como show," Bob responds. His targets include Bing Crosby's recent wedding ("It was a very intimate affair. Only the immediate money was present") and, to plug his new film, *Paris Holiday*, Europe ("It's a great place, Paris. If you're not with a girl, they'll arrest you."). Next is a funny filmed comic bit with four baseball stars cut out of his recent special. He even does a live watch commercial! Too bad the rest of the show isn't quite as spry as he is.

Bob: \*\*\*\*\* Show: \*\*\*


*The Steve Allen Show*
Sept. 21, 1958, Sunday 8-9 p.m.

Steve Allen, Louis Nye. Guests: Ronnie Burns, Bob Cummings, Ralph Edwards, George Gobel, Bob Hope, Peter Lawford, Lee Marvin, George Nader. Announcer: Gene Rayburn. P: Nick Vanoff. D: Dwight Hemion. W: Steve Allen, Stan Burns, Mike Marmer, Herbert Sargent, Don Hinkley, Bill Dana.

Steve and company get spotty laughs in skits promoting NBC's new fall season, with the best being Louis Nye as an effeminate TV western fan. Bob arrives forty-five minutes in to tear up the joint with an extended monologue. He pretends to complain about his late appearance ("This is like getting the punch bowl after Dean Martin") and has risqué lines about a new NBC western, "The Gay Caballero." "Other cowboys wear high heeled boots. This one carries a purse," he snarks, adding, "The series is also in color. It's in surprise pink." He also unnerves the censor by asking how come Tonto in *The Lone Ranger* was "bar mitzvahed." One more TV cowboy reference has truth behind it: "They keep shooting Indians, but all they're burying is comedians." Bob gets in a gag about Bing Crosby becoming a new father ("Our scientists are studying that now") before ending this strong set.

Bob: **** Show: ***


*Milton Berle Starring in the Kraft Music Hall*
Oct. 8, 1958, Wednesday 9-9:30 p.m.

Host: Milton Berle. Guests: Gene Barry, The Dunhills, Bob Hope, Sam Levene, Tony Roberts. Announcer: Ken Carpenter. P/D/W: Hal Kanter. D: Selwyn Touber. W: Hal Goodman, Larry Klein, Milt Josefsberg. M: Billy May.

Two years after ending his TV series, Milton Berle returns to the medium in a show whose roots go back to radio. In fact, this premiere references that fact by having a Bing Crosby impersonator "sing" into a microphone in the shadows as Ken Carpenter narrates how the series ended on radio in 1946 with Crosby but Milton will now preside over its return. Milton waits outside a door where Bob enters and says, "Bing asked me to give you the keys to the hall." He sincerely wishes Milton a lot of luck on his new show, which Milton appreciates until Bob walks off and the host cracks that Secretary of State John Foster Dulles always says "You're on the plane again?!" when he sees Bob on tour overseas with him. The rest of the show has occasional moments of fun like this, such as Gene Barry popping up as his Bat Masterson character to remind viewers that show follows this one, but it's not a stunning opener, and the series will survive only one year before Milton and Kraft part ways.

Bob and Show: ***


*Some of Manie's Friends*
March 3, 1959, Tuesday 7:30-9 p.m.

Host: Perry Como. Guests: Sid Caesar, Rosemary Clooney, Nat King Cole, Eddie Fisher, Bob Hope, Harry James, Tony Martin, Dinah Shore, Frank Sinatra, Kay Starr, Danny Thomas, Jack Webb, Jane Wyman. P/D: Bob Finkel, Grey Lockwood, Bob Henry. W: Herbert Baker. Music: Axel Stordahl.

Manie Sacks was an NBC and RCA vice president who died in 1958. This live color tribute with filmed inserts raises more than $200,000 for his medical research foundation thanks to contributions from talent who knew and loved him for helping their show business careers, including Bob. Dinah Shore thanks him for encouraging her to record "Buttons and Bows" and performs it, as do Eddie Fisher for "Wish You Were Here" and Kay Starr for "Rock 'n' Roll Waltz." The latter joins Jane Wyman to do a good rendition of "Side by Side." Sid Caesar offers a funny pantomime of a pianist's first concert. Bob arrives nearly two-thirds of the way through to say there's so much talent backstage that Ed Sullivan has a net to try to trap them. He gets laughs about a cut in the transatlantic cable and how Manie "guided Sinatra through thin and thin." Bob adds, "I'd hate to think where I'd be if he hadn't shown up with the bail money." He even jokes about how Alvin and the Chipmunks could be investigated for payola in a solid set delivered well. After this, Frank Sinatra speaks glowingly of what Manie did for him before he and Dinah do a medley from Dinah's first hour show. Danny Thomas wraps this up by telling about the foundation's work. It's a nice tribute unfortunately hampered by awkward cuts between live and filmed segments.

Bob: **** Show: ***


**The Jack Benny Hour**
March 18, 1959, CBS Wednesday 10-11 p.m.

Host: Jack Benny. Guests: Bob Hope, Mitzi Gaynor, Senor Wences, The Marquis Family, The Youth Band Council of Southern California. P/D: Bud Yorkin. W: George Balzer, Sam Perrin, Al Gordon, Hal Goldman. M: David Rose. Choreographer: George Sidney.

A big dance number with a marching band that goes down the aisles overwhelms Jack at the start, along with other attractions coming on. It's pretty funny given Jack's bemused reaction. After Mitzi Gaynor makes her live TV debut singing "I'm in Love with a Wonderful Guy" from her movie *South Pacific*, Jack recounts visiting Bob Hope's house. Bob jokes about TV westerns and encourages a wrong caller to go see *Alias Jesse James*, his latest movie. When Jack starts humming, Bob ad libs, "Don't sing, I haven't been well." Jack is shocked to find a live girl model on top of Bob's calendar and loses his composure again as Bob ad libs his explanation that "Dad told me to make every day count!" For Senor Wences' bit, Jack appears as the head in the box and aggravates the ventriloquist enough that Wences nails the box shut. Even better is the Marquis Family, three chimps who mock Jack's movements for lots of comic mayhem. Bob emerges after that and quips, "I want to thank the producers for this spot. Imagine following four monkeys?" His solid monologue about the upcoming Oscars is interrupted by Jack pretending to be Jerry Colonna. Jack says he is following Bob's advice to insert himself more in his show. "I haven't been that wrong since I went on that blind date in Denmark," retorts Bob, alluding to the country doing sex change operations. If only the rest of the special were as strong as Jack and Bob are here.

Bob: **** Show: ***


*Hedda Hopper's Hollywood*
Jan. 10, 1960, Sunday 8-9 p.m.

Hostess: Hedda Hopper. Guests: Lucille Ball, Anne Bauchens, Stephen Boyd, Francis X. Bushman, John Cassavettes, Gary Cooper, Ricardo Cortez, Bob Cummings, William Daniels, Marion Davies, Walt Disney, Janet Gaynor, Bob Hope, Hope Lange, Harold Lloyd, Jody McCrea, Liza Minnelli, Don Murray, Ramon Navarro, Anthony Perkins, Debbie Reynolds, Teddy Rooney, Venetia Stevenson, James Stewart, Gloria Swanson, King Vidor, The Westmore Brothers. P: Michael Abbott. D: William Corrigan. W: Sumner Locke Elliott. Composer-Conductor: Axel Stordahl.

An ominous fanfare of horns and strings backs the opening and sets the artificial tone of this special as Hedda in her characteristic large hat and fur wrap sits near a mountain cliff with Hollywood behind her and proclaims, "This is my town." The staged interviews have many guests addressing the camera directly with stilted comments and delivery and Hedda nowhere to be found. Bob doesn't show up until the end but gets five minutes and redeems it somewhat. "Many ugly lies are created about Hollywood, which later turn out to be true," he quips amid a set filled with suitcases behind him. He claims the columnists say the gossip right to your face rather than behind your back and praises the makeup men for putting sequins in Doris Day's freckles. "Some stars have to depend on looks to get parts—poor slobs," he adds in a theme of mock humility as he promotes his upcoming special. He gets in some good licks on payola as well before praising Hedda and enlivening a mostly dull show.

Bob: **** Show: ***

## The Arthur Murray Party
March 15 and 22, 1960, Tuesday 9:30-10 p.m.

Kathryn Murray, Arthur Murray. Guests: Bob Hope, Cliff Arquette (as Charley Weaver), Jon Arnett, Tony Bennett, Johnny Carson, Dorothy Collins, Gloria DeHaven, Jimmy Demaret, Rocky Graziano, Alan King, Dorothy Lamour, Jayne Mansfield, Mickey Mantle, Ethel Merman, Jane Russell, Earl Wilson.

This filmed "roast" of Hope pre-empts this series' regular musical variety format for two weeks to raise $100,000 for Fight for Sight, a blindness prevention charity. "I'm about as nervous as a mink being led to Zsa Zsa Gabor," Bob cracks at the outset. The best presentations are Johnny Carson's monologue sending up Bob's wartime service and Dorothy Lamour and Jayne Mansfield's sprightly duet singing new lyrics to songs from Bob's movies and showing off their ample physiques in the process. Bob hilariously mocks staid Arthur Murray and sums it all up with a great quip: "In conclusion, I want to say that I thoroughly enjoyed this pile of filth for my wake." It has its moments, but this is so scripted (by Bob's writers) and overdone with audience responses that the enthusiasm generated for it and Bob is muted.

Bob and Show: ***

## Bobby Darin and Friends
Jan. 31, 1961, Tuesday 9-10 p.m.

Bobby Darin, Joanie Sommers, The Jud Conlon Singers, Bob Hope. P/D: Bud Yorkin. P/W: Norman Lear. Music: Billy May.

Bobby interminably sings, dances and acts in a slight sketch with Joanie Sommers as high school lovers before Ol' Ski Nose appears. He is busy with nailing benefit dates and pretending to do a monologue for the Boy Scouts over the phone ("I wanted to be a Girl Scout, but I couldn't pass the physical.") Bobby asks him to go on stage, and Bob launches into an assured five-minute monologue with inauguration jokes which generate many belly laughs. Then it's back to wan production numbers before Bob and Bobby do comic routines by wearing different hats. A sample: Bobby asks, "What would a cannibal be if he ate his mother-in-law?" "Gladiator," Bob answers. Bob cracks up several times before he and Bobby duet on "Down by the Old Mill Stream" and dance with Joanie. If only they and the rest of the show were as excellent as Bob is here.

Bob: ***** Show: **


***The Jimmy Durante Show***
Aug. 9, 1961, Wednesday 10-11 p.m.

Jimmy Durante, Garry Moore, Janice Rule, Bob Hope, Grady Sutton (as the hotel clerk). EP: Bob Braun. P/D: Norman Jewison. W: Goodman Ace, Selma Diamond, Jay Burton, Frank Peppiatt, John Aylesworth. Music: Roy Bargy. Choreographers: Marc Breaux, Dee Dee Wood.

Jimmy jokes that this special will cover the American husband's evolution and improve TV's quality. Sure, Jimmy. He, Bob and Garry have spotty success as they tell their wives, all played variably by Janice Rule, that they are going away for the weekend. The men enjoy dancing, singing and joking together, although their performances tend to be sloppy. When they arrive at a hotel, Bob launches into a monologue where one line dies ("I'll wait" he says to the audience, prompting some sympathetic guffaws) and another gets mangled as he calls Bat Masterson Bass Matterson. That becomes a running gag and is better than much of the other material here. Indeed, Bob ad libs often, breaking up Jimmy when he asks, "Is that your nose or one of the Guns of Navarone?" Bob sings new tailored lyrics to "Thanks for the Memory" before saying goodbye on this spotty special.

Bob and Show: ***


***The Ed Sullivan Show***
Oct. 1, 1961, CBS Sunday 8-9 p.m.

Ed Sullivan, Julia Meade, The June Taylor Dancers. Guests: Nancy Dussault, The McGuire Sisters, Peter Nero, John Reardon, Phil Silvers, Louis Armstrong, Brigitte Bardot, Bing Crosby, Jackie Gleason, Bob Hope, Gene Kelly, Paul Newman, Sidney Poitier. P: Bob Precht. D: Tim Kiley. Music: Ray Bloch.

For what's billed as his fourteenth anniversary show, Ed shows film clips of his tour of Hong Kong, Berlin, Paris (where he interviewed Jackie Gleason and Brigitte Bardot and showed Gene Kelly directing, along with Louis Armstrong, Paul Newman and Sidney Poitier in their new movie) and London. At the latter, he visits Bob on the set of *The Road to Hong Kong*. Bob cracks wise with Ed and his co-star, Bing Crosby, at an outside table. Screenwriters Norman Panama and Melvin Frank say they need to cut 30 minutes out of the script, so Ed removes parts to go that "upset" Bob and Bing, and they leave in mock protest. Regarding this intermittently humorous bit, Ed insists that "The amazing thing about this sequence, it was completely ad lib." Besides Ed, the only performers seen live are the first five guests (with Phil Silvers especially funny, promoting his musical *Do Re Mi* along with his costars Nancy Dussault and John Reardon) and commercial spokesperson Julia Meade.

Bob and Show: ***

**At This Very Moment!**
April 1, 1962, ABC Sunday 9-10 p.m.

Host: Burt Lancaster. Guests: Harry Belafonte, Bobby Darin, Jimmy Durante, Connie Francis, Greer Garson, Charlton Heston, Bob Hope, Lena Horne, Rock Hudson, The Kingston Trio, Paul Newman, Jack Paar, Edward G. Robinson, Dinah Shore, Danny Thomas, Joanne Woodward. Also Appearing: President John F. Kennedy, Vice President Lyndon B. Johnson, Eleanor Roosevelt. P: Michael Abbott. D: Dick Schneider. W: Arnold Peyser, Lois Peyser.

"At this very moment, this first Sunday in April, we are going to try to save your life," intones Burt Lancaster at the start of this well-meaning but stilted presentation of gains made in fighting cancer since 1947. Produced on behalf of the American Cancer Society and the Eleanor Roosevelt Cancer Foundation, it's mostly stars making shallow observations and introducing each other in bits filmed at different times. Fighting the ennui early on, Bob tells how he became involved here ("They were so persistent. They answered my calls") and grandly sends up the pretentiousness. "I'd like to thank Frank Sinatra for allowing his president to appear here tonight" goes one observation. He feels as out of place as "Truman Capote at Vic Tanny's [gym] and Carl Sandburg at the Peppermint Lounge." Other good lines are "Khrushchev might be a smash on American TV. Fred Flintstone made it," and in reference of a tidal wave in Miami, "I thought Jayne Mansfield fell in again." Then it's back to mostly boredom, unfortunately.

Bob: **** Show: **

## *The Bing Crosby Show*
May 14, 1962, ABC Monday 10-11 p.m.

Host: Bing Crosby. Guests: Bob Hope, Edie Adams, Gary Crosby, Pete Fountain, The Smothers Brothers. Music: David Rose.

This special focused on leisure pursuits opens with Bob putting on makeup and saying, "Mirror mirror on the wall, who's the fairest?" A quick fade out and in has Bing showing up saying "Oh man, you got a lot of nerve" before returning to Bob, who shrugs and leaves. Bing then shows some items and mentions "America's favorite outdoor sport" as Bob pops up to kiss Edie behind a haystack. Bing ad libs, "If you find a needle in there, take a tuck in your lips." "I got a writer under here, and I'll be right back!" Bob chimes in. Dancers do a production number while Bing, Edie and Gary sing new vacation-themed lyrics to "America" from *West Side Story*, joined by Bob in the finale, who playfully lays his legs on top of Gary at the end. After a long, overdone number with Edie, Bob and Bing sing "Teamwork" from *The Road to Hong Kong*, and Bing sings "Let's Not Be Sensible" from the same movie. Bob then is ignored for mostly songs and dances with Pete Fountain (who plays "I Got Rhythm" in a fine upbeat manner with a combo), Gary and Bing (who duet on "Play a Simple Melody" with Pete and the orchestra them) and the Smothers Brothers (who provide an okay campsite song). When Bing does "Zing a Little Zong" with the dancers, Edie and finally Bob join them to sing along. Bob does fine, but this show wastes his talent (and time) as a comedian.

Bob: *** Show: **


## *The Andy Williams Show*
Jan. 31, 1963, Thursday 10-11 p.m.

Andy Williams, Marian Mercer, R.G. Brown. Guests: Bob Hope, Dan Blocker, Lorne Green, Ann Sothern, The New Christy Minstrels, The Osmond Brothers. EP: Bud Yorkin, Norman Lear. P: Bob Finkel. D: Robert Scheerer. W: Mort Green, Bill Persky, Sam Denoff, James Murray, Harry Crane. Musical Director: Colin Romoff. Chorale Director and Additional Vocal Material: George Wyle.

After some music and bad skits with Andy talking to Marian Mercer and R.G. Brown as stereotyped Indians and Lorne Greene and

Dan Blocker as Andy's writers trying to come up with skits for the stars of *Bonanza* (a self-referential mess), Bob demolishes the tedium twenty-four minutes into the show. He tells Andy he's doing a special with Robert Goulet ("I hate him too," he quips to the host) and says Bing Crosby is down in Palm Springs, "working on his tax deductions," in reference to the latter's new children. Andy scores with some jokes too, so Bob mock threatens, "Keep it up, and I may learn to hate you too!" Bob disappears, but the mood still sparkles as five-year-old Donny Osmond makes his TV debut joining his brothers to sing with Andy. Too bad blah singing and comedy with Ann Sothern follow, making this a flat program overall.

Bob: *** Show: **


**Here's Edie**
June 18, 1963, ABC Tuesday 10:30-11 p.m.

Hostess: Edie Adams. Guests: Bob Hope, Lionel Hampton, The United Nations Children's Choir. D: Steve Binder. Special Material: Mort Lachman. Music: Jerry Fielding. Choreographer: Earl Burton.

After two solos and two instrumentals with Lionel Hampton on the xylophone and drums, Bob finally emerges midway through the show after a brief tease at the top to promote his new book, *I Owe Russia $1,200*, and movie, *Call Me Bwana*, where Edie is his costar. "What a plot—Edie Adams and Anita Ekberg fighting for my love!" he says of the film. "It's a comedy," adds Edie. Bob jokes about President Kennedy and the First Family too, noting that "They certainly take wonderful care of the [White] House, considering they're only renters," and that he's like the Chief Executive in one way: "We both have all our brothers on the payroll." He then duets with Edie on "(Let's Turn the Record to the) Flip Side," which is mildly entertaining like the rest of his appearance. However, the show's best moment is the end with Edie singing "Let There Be Peace on Earth" with the United Nations Children's Choir dressed in their native clothes, which is a moving plea for unity.

Bob and Show: ***

## *The Bing Crosby Show*
Feb. 15, 1964, CBS Saturday 8:30-9:30 p.m.

Host: Bing Crosby. Guests: Kathryn Crosby, Rosemary Clooney, Bob Hope, Dean Martin, Frank Sinatra, The Earl Brown Singers. P/D: Nick Vanoff. P: William O. Harbach, Bing Crosby. W: Howard Leeds, Sid Dorfman, Bob Rodgers, Bill Morrow, Mort Lachman, Bill Larkin. Special Material: Earl Brown, Billy Barnes. Music: John Scott Trotter. Choreographers: Marc Breaux, Dee Dee Wood.

Designed to promote Bing's new movie *Robin and the Seven Hoods* with costars Dean Martin and Frank Sinatra, this special is an easygoing trifle where Bob appears after Bing's opening song. Calling Bing "Tijuana's answer to Medicare" and ad-libbing, Bob promotes his TV series and exchanges pleasantries before he and Bing duet on "I Believe in You" from *How to Succeed Business Without Really Trying*, with Bob squeaking in things like "I'm auditioning for the Beatles." After lots of dancing and singing (including Bing with his wife, Kathryn), Bob plays Bing's new caddy in a "flashback" of how they met. Bob fawns over Bing when learning who he is, and they crack up during their interplay. Bob then claims he met Bing at Paramount when the latter shined his shoes. Bob's ad-libs enliven the proceedings, and even Bing slyly promotes Bob's new movie, *A Global Affair*. Unfortunately, then it's back to mostly boring musical productions.

Bob and Show: ***

## *The Andy Williams Show*
Oct. 11, 1965, Monday 9-10 p.m.

Andy Williams, The Goodtime Singers. Guests: Bob Hope, Mary Tyler Moore, Roger Miller. P: Bob Finkel. D: Bob Henry. W: Harry Crane, Don Hinkley. Musical Arranger and Conductor: Jack Elliott. Chorale Director and Additional Vocal Material: George Wyle. Additional Musical Arrangers: Dave Grusin, Allyn Ferguson, Bob Florence, Billy May. Choreographer: Nick Castle.

Everyone's at near peak form here having fun singing, dancing and joking throughout, and that includes Bob, a last-minute replacement for Joey Bishop, who hurt his back. "It's great to be here on the Osmond Brothers show," he cracks regarding Andy's frequent guests. He also jests about the show's runway entrance as being more appropriate for strippers and Bing Crosby's fecundity ("Last time I saw him was about three kids ago"). Andy laughs so hard that he falls off his stool at one point, plus delivers some comebacks so well that Bob says he'll put moths in the host's sweater drawer and adds, "How'd you get that line?!" They "call" Joey Bishop at home, who remarks that he saw one of Bob's pictures with silent movie star Mary Pickford before Joey vows to do the show soon, then Bob and Andy do a great duet to end their segment.

Bob and Show: ****


**The Jack Benny Hour**
Nov. 3, 1965, Wednesday 9-10 p.m.

Host: Jack Benny. Guests: Bob Hope, The Beach Boys, Elke Sommer, Walt Disney. Featured: Naomi Stevens, Lee Patterson, Bill Baldwin, Bob Garrett. EP: Irving Fein. P/D: Ralph Levy. W: George Balzer, Sam Perrin, Al Gordon, Hal Goldman. M: Dave Grusin. Choreographer: Paul Godkin.

At the top, Jack saunters so long to the stage that Bob appears on stage left before the curtain to complain about it. He's so bored that he brings out Elke himself to tell her she's made such an impression in American that there's already a TV series about her—*The Long Hot Summer*. Jack finally arrives and does a routine and a sendup of the plots of current TV series, both so-so. Next, the Beach Boys play "California Girls," and at the end, Jack and Bob show up in a hot rod as surfers in long wigs. They talk to the Beach Boys about where to do the best surfing before leaving in an okay bit. Jack then banters with Elke before she does a long production number. He has another monologue followed by the Beach Boys singing "Barbara Ann" and a filmed bit where Jack visits Walt Disney for a sluggish effort to get group discount tickets to Disneyland to treat everyone after his latest special. Bob finally reappears for an Italian movie spoof where he plays a chauffeur being hit on by an amorous wife. He and Jack have lousy accents, especially compared to fluent Elke, whose governess character has a sexy outfit that she uses to seduce both Jack and Bob. This choppy *Mary Poppins* takeoff has just enough laughs in it and by Bob to give three stars to each—but just barely.

Bob and Show: ***

## The Hollywood Palace
Nov. 20, 1965, ABC Saturday 9:30-10:30 p.m.

Host: Bing Crosby. Guests: The Black Theater of Prague, Diahann Carroll, Desmond and Marks, Hendra and Ullett, The Kessler Twins, Charlie Manna. Cameos: Bob Hope, Willie Mays. P: Nick Vanoff. D: Grey Lockwood. W: Joe Bigelow, Jay Burton. Music: Mitchell Ayres.

Bob comes out when Bing makes reference to Thanksgiving and the turkey. He calls the set "Jerry Lewis's old garage" (it was home to the disastrous *Jerry Lewis Show* in 1963 before this series launched in 1964) and gets Bing to promote Bob's new album of Vietnam tour highlights. Bob brings out Willie Mays to congratulate him on being named baseball's Most Valuable Player, and the latter does well joking with both men. Bob's able to get a bar mitzvah gag into the mix. Bob shows up toward the end, still in fine form with great lines for both. "You've got the nose for drilling," Bing says in reference to Bob's success in investing in oil. Bob shoots back, "You get pretty funky around White Christmas time!"

Bob: \*\*\*\* Show: \*\*\*


## The Dean Martin Show
Feb. 3, 1966, Thursday 10-11 p.m.

Dean Martin. Guests: Bob Hope, Juliet Prowse, Joel Grey, Pete Fountain, The Lively Set. P/D: Greg Garrison. W: Harry Crane.

"Here's the world's best friend," Dino says as he introduces Bob, who quips of the host, "He's got so much hair, it almost looks real, doesn't it?" He describes Dean as so relaxed, "He makes Perry Como look like he's doing the Frug." Bob claims to be avoiding doing booze jokes at Dean's request but alludes to the topic, then midway through switches to gags about golf and spy movies and TV shows, all pretty mediocre. Later and better, Bob joins Dean and Juliet Prowse in a loose conversation (Bob: "I haven't been this happy since I sat on a Bing Crosby record!") before the trio dances and sings a delightful medley of "The French Lesson/Brush Up Your Shakespeare." With her own separate dance medley with Dean on the show, Juliet comes off better than Bob here.

Bob and Show: \*\*\*

***The Danny Thomas Show*: "The Road to Lebanon"**
April 20, 1966, Wednesday 10-11 p.m.

Danny Thomas. Guests: Claudine Auger, Bing Crosby, Hugh Downs. Host/Narrator: Sheldon Leonard (as Hamid the storyteller). EP: Danny Thomas. Music: Harper Mackay.

Bob's presence temporarily enlivens this tiresome collection of excessive production numbers and flat comedy. It starts with Bing waking up a tired Hugh Downs hosting *Today* by singing his new song, "The Road to Lebanon," which he plans for a new road picture with Bob. Bing then informs Hugh that Bob is overworked and may not be able to do it, even though Bing keeps forgetting the words to "White Christmas" (a running gag that never goes anywhere here). Meanwhile in Lebanon, a sheik (Danny Thomas) orders his "son" (Claudine Auger) to kill his visiting relative, Danny Thomas, because the latter's great-great-grandfather got a nose job when the latter went to America. When Bing encounters Danny, they get abducted by Claudine and make weak jokes referencing previous road pictures while trying to survive. Three-quarters into the show, the men are buried to their necks in sand when Bob pulls up in a golf cart and quips, "Boy, I'll never be able to get out of this sand trap!" Calling Bing "Benedict Arnold," he nevertheless saves both men and somehow whips out a picture of Danny's great-great-grandfather that showed the ancestor actually made his nose larger. Bob leaves with four dancing girls to let the men fend for themselves in the inevitable happy ending and comes off looking better than most who are involved in this sorry excuse for entertainment.

Bob: *** Show: **


**The Milton Berle Show**
Sept. 30, 1966, ABC Friday 9-10 p.m.

Milton Berle. Guests: Bob Hope, Larry Storch, Forrest Tucker. P: Bill Dana, William O. Harbach, Nick Vanoff.

Bob comes out when Milton's name is called at the start of the show and mocks his bow, performing style, the way he holds his cigar, even his duck walk. He kills it imitating Berle, who similarly sends up Hope. Bob says he's here because "President Johnson asked me to play only the most dangerous areas." After a few more laughs, they sing "Bosom Buddies" from *Mame* (including the "somewhere between forty and death" line). It is a pretty funny and loose show overall.

Bob: **** Show: ***


***The Hollywood Palace*: "Happy Birthday"**
Jan. 14, 1967, ABC Saturday 9:30-10:30 p.m.

Host: Bing Crosby. Guests: Edie Adams, Tim Conway, Sen. Everett Dirksen, Jimmy Durante, Swordsmen of the Lido, Bob Hope, The James Joyce Singers. EP: Nicholas Vanoff. P: William O. Harbach. D: Grey Lockwood. W: Joe Bigelow, Bernie Orenstein, Jay Burton. Music: Mitchell Ayres. Choreographer: Rod Alexander.

The series celebrates its fourth anniversary starting with a long filmed introduction of Bing leading a parade of stars to the studio and then singing special words to "Put on a Happy Face" (the program's theme). As Bing does a monologue, Bob interrupts him wearing a tux and quips, "Hurry, I've got to get back into the window." He says he was on Hollywood Boulevard, "dusting his star," and wanted to see where they were taking Bing. They talk about who they favor for the Super Bowl, then Bob brings out Kansas City Chiefs Coach Hank Stram and Mike Garrett, a running on the team, for some alternately funny and awkward banter. It's variable entertainment after that, with Tim Conway and Jimmy Durante coming off best. Bob joins Bing and Jimmy to bring out the anniversary cake he claims has Mickey Rooney inside and amuses everyone with more ad libs before they sing "Inka Dinka Doo" and Bob bear hugs Jimmy.

Bob and Show: ***


***The Dean Martin Show***
Nov. 30, 1967, Thursday 10-11 p.m.

Dean Martin, Ken Lane. Guests: Lena Horne, The Andrews Sisters, Don Rickles, Bob Hope, Don Adams, Polly Bergen, Pat Boone, Barbara Eden, Joey Heatherton, Rose Marie, Ross Martin, Ricardo Montalban, Danny Thomas, Bob Newhart, MacDonald Carey, Dom DeLuise, Ernest Borgnine, Guy Marks, Caterina Valente.

Dean offers Don Rickles great early TV exposure to do his insult routine in an audience packed with celebrities (all the ones following him in the guest list). He sends them up for twelve minutes before Bob arrives late in the pack and starts cracking up while lighting a cigarette. "All right, what are you, seals?" Don says to Bob's strong round of applause. "You think somebody came in—why is he here? Is the war over?" Bob loses it along with everyone else. He adds how Bob can't do anything without cue cards and how he'll be at the old actor's home saying "There goes George Burns!" Bob enjoyed this roasting so much, he recounted the experience in his interview with *Playboy* in 1973.

Bob and Show: \*\*\*\*


## *The Danny Thomas Hour*: "The Royal Follies of 1933"
Dec. 11, 1967, Monday 9-10 p.m.

Host/Narrator: Johnny Carson. Cast: Danny Thomas (Prince Wolfgang), Hans Conreid (Von Pickle), Kurt Kasznar (Hansie), Shirley Jones (Peggy), Gale Gordon (Mr. Baxter), Ken Berry (Skip), Jackie Joseph (Suzie). Cameos: Eve Arden (Thelda), Bob Hope (makeup man). P/D: Alan Handley. W: Sheldon Keller.

Calling himself a model for thermal underwear, Johnny Carson oversees this underwhelming musical comedy wherein a prince of a bankrupt kingdom refuses to meet Thelda, a meat heiress who wants to wed him only for his title. He watches a Broadway show featuring Peggy, Skip and Suzie, and its producer, Mr. Baxter, mistakenly assumes he is an actor playing a prince and adds him to the cast. The prince falls in love with Peggy, but the antics of Thelda and her stooges plus some gangsters threaten their happiness. Bob shows up near the end as the prince's makeup man to shoot a few lines about making Danny's prominent nose even bigger to play Cyrano de Bergerac ("If I put on any more, you'll need a caddy!") before disappearing. This flat parody is tough to endure despite abundant talent.

Bob and Show: \*\*


## *Jack Benny's Carnival Nights*
March 20, 1968, Wednesday 10-11 p.m.

Jack Benny. Guests: Lucille Ball, Johnny Carson, Paul Revere and the Raiders, Ben Blue, The Earl Brown Singers. Cameos: Bob Hope, Danny Thomas, The Smothers Brothers, Dean Martin, Don Drysdale, George

Burns. Featured: Sid Fields, Herb Vigran, Larry Blake, Benny Rubin, Almira Sessions. EP: Irving Fein. P/D: Fred De Cordova. W: Hal Goldman, Al Gordon, Hilliard Marks, Milt Josefsberg (script consultant). Conductors/Arrangers: Jack Elliott, Allyn Ferguson. Choreographer: Jack Regas.

Bob and Danny play billboard hangers dressed in work clothes at the show's start. Bob says he's doing it because Jack threatened to foreclose on his house, while Danny says Jack threatened to foreclose on NBC. Bob admires the guest lineup and Danny says that Jack was determined to have a great show by hook or by crook. The audience is already laughing before Bob cracks, "Let's keep our noses out of this, huh?" When Bob learns he and Danny don't have time to do a monologue, they paint over the faces of Jack, Lucy and Johnny on the billboard. Jack jokes in his monologue that by having Bob and Danny, "That bit alone cost me $170." Some guests have a few good moments, including Tom and Dick Smothers as a two-headed man, where Tom insists Mom liked his brother's head best; the Raiders, who do "Too Much Talk" and "Him or Me" as con man Jack pretends to be a group member; and George Burns as a cigar-smoking bearded lady. However, they're interrupted and weighed down by tedious production numbers and two long, unfunny bits with Ben Blue. With the talent involved, this should have been better.

Bob: *** Show: **


*... And Debbie Makes Six*
ABC, March 7, 1968, Thursday 8-9 p.m.

Hostess: Debbie Reynolds. Guests: Bob Hope, Jim Nabors. P/D: Joe Layton. D: Walter C. Miller. W: Milt Rosen, Billy Barnes, Bob Rodgers, Gerald Gardner, Dee Caruso. Music: Jerry Fielding, Ralph Carmichael (arrangements).

Debbie Reynolds impersonates Barbra Streisand, Pearl Bailey (!) and Julie Andrews before she plays herself singing on an empty stage to dubbed applause. She has variably enjoyable skits with her five male guests. The first, Milt Rosen's "Fort Mudlark," has Debbie leading "Tia Juana and Her Hot Tomatoes," an all-woman musical group entertaining bored servicemen. A captain (Jim Nabors) sings "Mame" with Debbie before Bob arrives as Private Hope in a fur coat. "What were you in civilian life?" Debbie asks Bob. "Unemployed. But happy," he answers. He said he was drafted because "LBJ caught me wearing a [George] Romney button." Debbie thinks he's sexy, but he already has a girlfriend—a seal, who hilariously refuses to stay on stage for Bob's lines. "Which of you is Les Brown?" Bob ad libs to laughter from the crew before leaving. Like the rest of the show, this is a hit-and-miss affair.

Bob and Show: ***

***The Ed Sullivan Show***: **"The Tribute to Irving Berlin on His 80th Birthday"**
May 5, 1968, CBS Sunday 8-9:30 p.m.

Host: Ed Sullivan. Guests: Bob Hope, Robert Goulet, Harry James, Bing Crosby, Fred Waring, Irving Berlin, Lyndon B. Johnson, Ethel Merman, The Supremes. P: Bob Precht. D: John Moffitt.

Ed breaks out his tuxedo and adds an extra half hour to his usual show to salute one of the greatest songwriters of all time. Among the added attractions besides comments of appreciation from President Johnson is a six-minute monologue by Bob. He touches on the host ("The Ed Sullivan Theatre. I always figured that would be a wax museum!" and "You know the first time I was on television, it was for Ed. It's true. And for the same money"), heart transplants ("I always knew medical science could perform miracles. Did you see [Bing] Crosby?"), *Time* magazine ("They said I had five hundred million dollars. I wish my writers were that funny!"), Charles DeGaulle, and the troubles in New York City ("I was here a few weeks ago and I'll never forget it. I got towed away and wasn't even in a car!"). He then praises the honoree comically ("He's to music what Bing is to children. But enough about the miracle worker …") and seriously ("Irving Berlin did more for the American flag than Betsy Ross, and he gave us 'God Bless America.' And I say, 'God bless America for giving us Irving Berlin.'"). Bob adds to the classiness of this patriotic celebration, one of Ed's best.

Bob and Show: ****


***Rowan and Martin's Laugh-In***
Sept. 16, 1968, Monday 8-9 p.m.

Dan Rowan, Dick Martin, Judy Carne, Arte Johnson, Ruth Buzzi, Henry Gibson, Goldie Hawn, Dave Madden, Pigmeat Markham, Alan Sues, "Sweet Brother" Dick Whittington, Jo Anne Worley, Gary Owens, Chelsea Brown, Byron Gilliam. Guest: Barbara Feldon. Cameos: Bob

Hope, Zsa Zsa Gabor, Hugh Hefner, Jack Lemmon, Sonny Tufts, John Wayne. EP: George Schlatter. P/W: Paul W. Keyes. Co-P: Carolyn Raskin. D: Gordon Wiles. W: Hugh Wedlock Jr., Allan Manings, Chris Bearde, David Panich, Coslough Johnson, Marc London, Dave Cox, Jim Carlson, Jack Mendelsohn, Jim Mulligan, Phil Hahn, Jack Hanrahan.

This is the quintessence of the rapid-fire comedy series in content (Richard Nixon says, "Sock it to me?" which many believe helped him win the 1968 presidential election) and coverage (*Time* magazine quoted it extensively for a cover story). It introduces the Fickle Finger of Fate dubious achievement award, dresses up the females as Tiny Tim to introduce the news sketch, has quick bits flash on screen ("George Wallace, your sheets are ready") and even mocks its competition (Jack Lemmon: "You mean I could be at home watching *Gunsmoke* right now?"). Bob's part is tiny but effective in joking about his USO work: At the show's start, Arte Johnson's German soldier character Wolfgang greets him with "Every Christmas I waited for you." Chelsea Brown and Byron Gilliam are not credited in the opening titles while Charlie Brill and Mitzi McCall are, even though the latter do not appear.

Bob: \*\*\* Show: \*\*\*\*\*

*The Bing Crosby Show*
Oct. 23, 1968, ABC Wednesday 10-11 p.m.

Host: Bing Crosby. Guests: Bob Hope, Jose Feliciano, The Supremes, Stella Stevens, Dorothy Lamour.

Bing and Bob seek producer Marshall (McLean Stevenson) on a studio lot to pitch a new Road picture in this artificial comedy filmed without an audience. They crack age jokes (Bob calls Bing "the Tiny Tim of his day") and run into musical guest stars who unfortunately are singing other people's hits with and without Bing. Stella Stevens must choose which of the two men old enough to be her grandfather is the better kisser ("You must've forgotten your prune juice," Bob snipes when Bing loses), then participates in their "nonviolent western" complete with gay stereotypes. "I just may whip you with my pussy willow!" hisses Bob. Bing lisps back with "Well, I'll slam you with my purse!" Dorothy Lamour also shows up as a belly dancer before viewers agree with the producer at the end that any Road picture reunion like this mess would be a bad idea.

Bob: \*\*\* Show: \*\*

## The Ann-Margret Show
Dec. 1, 1968, CBS Sunday 9-10 p.m.

Hostess: Ann-Margret. Guests: Jack Benny, Carol Burnett, Bob Hope, Danny Thomas. EP: Burt Rosen. P/D: David Winters. W: Robert Wells, Larry Alexander, Marc B. Ray. Arranger/Conductor: Billy Goldenberg. Choral Director: Earl Brown. Special Musical Arrangements: David Grusin, Jack Elliot, Bob Florence.

Ann-Margret does a fair amount of comedy between some vibrant singing and dancing numbers with elaborate costume, lighting and set changes. Introducing Bob as "Mr. Cary Grant," he comes back crowing about his virility by saying "Once a week I Indian wrestle with Margaret Rutherford" and "You're looking at the Tiny Tim of Senior City!" They do a corny but effective soft shoe singalong to "With a Little Help from My Friends" before she does other numbers and banter with Danny Thomas, who she introduces as Cary Grant as well. Bob reappears as himself in a skit about a 1930s vaudeville show, where Jack Benny is host and Carol Burnett appears as Ann-Margret's dresser. He invokes some jokes set at the time ("I've been drinking so much bathtub gin, my glass has a ring around it") in a pretty good monologue that enhances a sometimes too flashy, "Vegas-y" production.

Bob: **** Show: ***

## The Carol Burnett Show
Dec. 16, 1968, CBS Monday 10-11 p.m.

Regulars: Carol Burnett, Harvey Korman, Vicki Lawrence, Lyle Waggoner. Guests: Marilyn Horne, Eileen Farrell, Bob Hope (cameo). EP: Joe Hamilton. D: Dave Powers. W: Arnie Rosen, Stan Burns, Mike Marmer, Don Hinkley, Kenny Solms, Gail Parent, Buz Kohan, Bill Angelos, Artie Malvin, Hal Goodman, Al Gordon. Music: Harry Zimmerman. Choreographer: Ernie Flatt.

To pay Carol back for her cameo on his first special of the 1968-1969 season, Bob pretends to be what a handsome movie star (Lyle Waggoner) looks like after he supposedly removes various accoutrements behind a curtain. Besides promoting his upcoming special, Bob puts the audience in hysterics by repeating a line Carol inexplicably told them during her question-and-answer session at the start of the show—"Uncross your

legs!" The rest of the show has similar bonhomie throughout.
Bob and Show: ****


## *The Don Rickles Show*
Jan. 17, 1969, ABC Friday 9-9:30 p.m.

Don Rickles, Pat McCormick. Guests: Bob Hope, Jim Nabors, Frank Sutton. EP: Joseph Scandore, Harris Katleman. P: Frank Wayne. D: Dick Carson.

This series' sixteenth and penultimate episode occurs as everyone knows it's canceled, so there's a wonderfully lackadaisical spirit by the star that leaves everyone laughing hysterically at Don's antics. He mocks apparently real Marines as a drill instructor and has problems with his props. Then Pat McCormick, his sidekick, pleads for Don to let him introduce a young comedian, "Leslie Townes" (Bob's real name). A jovial Bob savoring the setup comes out and says, "I couldn't miss this. I saw the Marines and I came right down." He tells Don, "I just found out you were on television" and dispenses other good insults delivered sweetly, like "I'm sorry I couldn't get down here to save you." He does praise Don warmly before leaving as a class act, but the show continues to be a laugh riot even with his absence.

Bob: ***** Show: ****


## *Here Come The Stars*
March 9, 1969, Syndicated 60 minutes

Host: George Jessel. Honoree: Bob Hope. Guests: Shani Wallis, Bob Crane, Phyllis Diller, Gene Baylos, Morey Amsterdam, Dick Patterson, Gary Crosby, Mickey Rooney, Jan Daley. P: Ernest D. Glucksman. D: Dick Ross.

Everyone's dressed up for what Jessel hyperbolically calls "this most stellar cast of some of the greatest artists that have ever appeared before anyone and also the most beloved buffoon actor/comedian of our time." From there, it is a pretty good roast. For example, Bob Crane says he feels like Elizabeth Taylor's next husband following the other comics: "I know what I'm supposed to do, but how do I make it interesting?" He also mocks Bob's NBC bio to Bob's amusement. "He'll someday be the first comedian on the moon even if they don't have a war going on up there." Bob seems to be having a good time throughout the show.

Bob: **** Show: ***


## *Rowan and Martin's Laugh-In*
Sept. 22, 1969, Monday 8-9 p.m.

Dan Rowan, Dick Martin, Judy Carne, Arte Johnson, Ruth Buzzi, Henry Gibson, Goldie Hawn, Alan Sues, Jo Anne Worley, Teresa Graves, Pamela Rodgers, Jeremy Lloyd, Byron Gilliam, Gary Owens. Guests: Diana Ross, Michael Caine. Cameo: Bob Hope. EP: George Schlatter. P/W: Paul W. Keyes. Co-P: Carolyn Raskin. D: Mark Warren. W: Paul W. Keyes, David Panich, Coslough Johnson, Marc London, Jim Carlson, Jim Mulligan, John Carsey, Gene Farmer, Jeremy Lloyd, John Rappaport, Stephen Spears, Jack Douglas, Allan Manings.

Loaded with jokes that alternately make one smile or wonder why they are supposed to be funny, this show does give Diana Ross a serviceable platform to show she can sing, dance and joke just fine without the Supremes, the group she is leaving for a solo career in 1970. Bob once again is with Arte Johnson's Wolfgang German soldier, and their exchange is enjoyably silly as it sets up Bob's special following this show. Wolfgang: "Good night to you too, Lucy and Gary [referring to Lucille Ball on *Here's Lucy* opposite this show, which is produced by her husband, Gary Morton]." Bob with a vaguely Teutonic accent and green combat outfit: "Oh Lucy, let Gary see my show. Have him stay up there, would you please?" "Your show?! When is it at?!" "Well, I'm next on NBC." "Oh no, Bob Hope is next on NBC!" "Well, I'm Bob Hope!" "No, you're not! Bob Hope is up there!" Wolfgang points to the sky, and Bob looks up and asks, "Where?" as Wolfgang hits him with a hammer on his helmet and exclaims "Gotcha!" Bob then breaks up before the show signs off.

Bob and Show: ***


## *Jimmy Durante Presents the Lennon Sisters Hour*
Oct. 24, 1969, ABC Friday 10-11 p.m.

Jimmy Durante, The Lennon Sisters (Dianne, Peggy, Kathy, and Janet). Guests: Bob Hope, Andy Williams, The Osmond Brothers. EP:

Harold D. Cohen. P/W: Bernie Kukoff, Jeff Harris. W: Hugh Wedlock, Jr., Bill Box, Don Reo. Music: George Wyle, Jack Regas.

After twenty minutes of the regulars and the Osmonds singing and doing lame comic bits, the Lennon Sisters introduce Bob, who muses of them that "They make Mary Poppins look like Myra Breckinridge ... I hope I'm not keeping you girls up. It's an hour past *Captain Kangaroo*." He's stunned by applause after commending them for presenting entertainment for the whole family. Next, he and Jimmy do proboscis jokes ("I love yours, James, every square foot of it") and sing "Be Nice to Your Noses" after they rub theirs together. Following more square singing, Bob is a jungle explorer tied to a stake in "The Road to Pago Pago," with one of the Lennons as a native woman who wants to marry him. Dorothy Lamour pops up to surprise Bob at the sketch's end, but there's little serendipity otherwise in watching this forced, antiseptic, unfunny one-season flop.

Bob: **** Show: **


*The Carol Burnett Show*
Nov. 10, 1969, CBS Monday 10-11 p.m.

Regulars: Carol Burnett, Harvey Korman, Vicki Lawrence, Lyle Waggoner. Guests: Bing Crosby, Ella Fitzgerald, Dan Rowan, Dick Martin, Bob Hope (cameo). EP: Joe Hamilton. D: Dave Powers. W: Arnie Rosen, Stan Burns, Mike Marmer, Don Hinkley, Buz Kohan, Bill Angelos, Artie Malvin, Hal Goodman, Al Gordon. Music: Harry Zimmerman. Choreographer: Ernie Flatt.

An incredible guest lineup combines with superb writing to make this a classic episode for this series. As a favor to Carol, Bob does his part by surprising Bing at the end of a restaurant sketch where Carol plays a pushy waitress bothering him while he eats. Bob enters beaming, but it is Bing who ad libs the best line against Bob. Too bad Bob does not have more to do to join in the fun here, particularly since the show includes a tribute to his longtime movie studio Paramount.

Bob: *** Show: *****

## The Barbara McNair Show
Nov. 16, 1969, Syndicated 60 minutes

Hostess: Barbara McNair. Guests: Bob Hope, Jeannine Burnier, Joanie Sommers, The Watts 103rd Street Rhythm Band. EP: Burt Rosen, David Winters. P/D: Jorn Winther. W: Alex Barris. Music: Donn Trenner. Choreographer: Joseph Cassini.

The unique set design (a large stage towering over an audience sitting around tables like a Las Vegas presentation) and Bob's appearance are about all to make an impact in this early episode of the two-season (1969-1971) series, unless one is a fan of the other music acts or Barbara, none of whom sing their hits. Comedienne Jeannine Burnier has an intermittently funny monologue, but Bob overshadows it with some witty rejoinders as Barbara interviews him midway through the show. Reminiscing about his childhood, he quips, "I left England early because I knew there was little chance of me becoming king." His thoughts on miniskirts: "I kind of like them, and all I want to say is I don't know what the fellas are looking for these days, but if they don't see what they're looking for, they're in trouble!" He acknowledges his heavy work schedule by noting today prior to this taping he had done three luncheons and a guest spot on *Rowan and Martin's Laugh-In* and will appearing at the Hollywood Bowl in the evening. As to why he's there, Bob says he saw Barbara appear at the College Town nightclub in Chicago and she asked him backstage to do this show and he agreed. It was that simple.

Bob: *** Show: **


## The Many Moods of Perry Como
Feb. 22, 1970, Sunday 10-11 p.m.

Perry Como. Guests: Bob Hope, Nancy Sinatra, Bobby Sherman, Flip Wilson. Music: Nick Perito. P/D: Bob Henry. W: Herbert Baker, Treva Silverman. Special Musical Material: Ray Charles. Choreographer: Jack Regas.

Surveying his special's title, Perry Como cracks, "You have to admit, that's pretty funny right there. I mean, you know me, one mood," and he pretends to sleep. Bob comes on stage to wake him up but Perry protests, "I'm right in the middle of my opening number!" He does a song where some lyrics are enacted in quick comic bits like on *Rowan and Martin's Laugh-In*. It's cute, but it tries too hard to be "mod," as does most of this program, where only half the elements click. Bob is among the former, where he starts by telling the audience to hold its applause: "Let's not wake the star." He adds, "This is the first time I've done a walk-on to a sleep-in" and notes the inappropriate title of the show with "That's like hiring William F. Buckley for *Gomer Pyle*!" His discussion of sex in films is funny but prudish, touching on Raquel Welch playing a man in *Myra Breckenridge* ("I love science fiction") and saying "There's so much nudity in movies lately that people in drive-in theaters are watching the movies!" Following his excellent set is everything from a hilarious skit with Perry earning ire from his secretary Geraldine (Flip Wilson) by making her stay late to work to a boring duet by Perry and Nancy Sinatra. Bob rejoins Perry near the end to discuss old family pictures shown on the air and his memories of vaudeville. Like the rest of the show, their discussion is only intermittently enjoyable and often rambles.

Bob and Show: ***

**The Johnny Cash Show**
Feb. 25, 1970, ABC Wednesday 9-10 p.m.

Host: Johnny Cash. Guests: Bob Hope, Cass Elliot, Kenny Rogers and The First Edition, The Statler Brothers, June Carter Cash, Carl Perkins, The Carter Family, The Tennessee Three.

Visiting Johnny Cash at the latter's TV studio in Nashville, Bob gets a tepid reception with the audience in a monologue focusing on the city's country-western scene with some weak jokes likes "Kids learn to twang before they talk." He refers to guitars as "GEE-tars" (with a hard "G") irritatingly several times, making it sound condescending, and has a gag about *Hee Haw*—"I think we need something to balance William F. Buckley"—that draws crickets. Cracks about Johnny Cash's riches, looks ("He's sort of a Rod McKuen with muscles") and appearances at prisons draw similar mild reactions. He redeems things somewhat by making jokes about himself between Johnny singing "A Boy Named Sue." Bob's appearance is also obviously cut and sweetened with laughs and applause at points. His bit is the weakest part of an otherwise fine installment of Cash's musical variety that ran from 1969-1971, including Kenny Rogers and the First Edition doing their hit "Something's Burning" here.

Bob: *** Show: ****

**The Bob Goulet Show**
April 7, 1970, ABC Tuesday 9-10 p.m.

Robert Goulet, Bob Denver, Jo Anne Worley, The Clara Ward Singers, Diahann Carroll, Bob Hope, Kyra Carleton. Cameos: Joey Bishop, Godfrey Cambridge, Jimmy Durante, Carol Lawrence. EP: Norman Rosemont. P/W: Sam Bobrick, Ron Clark. D/W: Marty Pasetta. Music: Joe Guercio, Bill Reddle. Choreographer: Claude Thompson.

This musical comedy special begins with the expected scripted banter and songs with guests, including ones Bob Goulet popularized in the Broadway musical *Camelot* like "If Ever I Would Leave You." Then, in an unusually insulting repartee with the host more akin to Don Rickles, Hope zings the other Bob with lines like "You've got to stop having your head spray waxed at the car wash" and "You can always go back to being a gigolo at Sun City!" He also calls Goulet a "plastic covered wallet photo" and "Wrong Note" before singing his own version of "How to Handle a Woman" with a pretty woman appearing. At the end, Jimmy Durante arrives to claim the female away from Bob. It's all fairly funny albeit unexpected but a little off here, as is most of the special's other comedy. Bob also does a meaningless cameo as a paratrooper.

Bob and Show: ***


**This is Tom Jones**
Oct. 9, 1970, ABC Friday 10-11 p.m.

Host: Tom Jones. Guests: Bob Hope, Aretha Franklin, The Ace Trucking Company (Patti Deutsch, Michael Mislove, Bill Saluga, George Terry, Fred Willard). P/D: Jon Scoffield. W: Tom Waldman, Frank Waldman, Ronnie Cass, Donald Ross. Music: Johnnie Spence. Choreographer: Norman Maen.

Aretha Franklin outshines Bob here—in fact, she outshines everything on this show. She sings "I Say a Little Prayer" live electrifyingly and gets a rave-up going when she and Tom duet on "It's Not Unusual" and "See Saw," plus does "Spirit in the Dark" as a spiritual. As for Bob, he provides lots of tittering but few real solid laughs. After calling the series "ABC's answer to women's liberation," he has some clinkers like "I'm British too, you know. In fact, that's what started World War II—Hitler leaked it to the press." Bob does earn applause after quipping about Tom's recent hospital stay that "They had to operate to get his pants on." Of the new TV series this fall, he says, "There's a lot of new faces, most of them on the same old bodies." His best bits here involve *Gunsmoke* ("Doc finally prescribed the pill to Kitty."), *Hee Haw* planning to do jokes again viewers missed the first time, "And of course Danny Thomas is back, living humble." However, an uncharacteristically long, involved joke about Andy Griffith fares poorly, and Bob knows it ("That's a nice book," he says afterward), and one doubts that he could get away today by saying that black is so in that Slappy White is thinking about changing his name to Slappy Brown.

Bob and Show: \*\*\*

*The Dean Martin Show*
Nov. 5, 1970, Thursday 10-11 p.m.

Dean Martin, The Golddiggers, Ken Lane, Jackie Vernon. Guests: Ernest Borgnine, Alan Sues, The Everly Brothers, Sugar Ray Robinson. Featured: Billy Baxter, Bob Hope, Wilfred Hyde-White. Music: Les Brown. P/D: Greg Garrison. W: Harry Crane, Stan Daniels, Tom Tenowich, Norm Liebmann, Rod Porter, George Bloom, Ed Schurlach, Jay Burton, Bernie Rothman, Jack Wohl. Choral Director for The Golddiggers: Jack Halloran. Musical Arrangements: Van Alexander. Special Musical Material: Lee Hale. Choreographer: Jonathan Lucas. Assistant Choreographer: Tommy Tune.

Bob drops in as a surprise guest behind the closet on Dean's living room set. After the applause subsides, Bob quips, "I was taking a shortcut to the men's room, Dean, but I will tell you something. I go around and visit a lot of colleges and see a lot of young people. And they want me to ask you if you would lead their sexual revolution." "I guess so," replies Dean. "Good, here's your uniform," says Bob as he gives Dean a hanger and leaves, followed by Dean promoting Bob's next special. That's it for Hope on this rather overloaded show brimming with silly skits ending in freeze frame, some successful, some not. There's Dean confusing the Everly Brothers with the Smothers Brothers before all sing "Bye Bye Love"; Billy Baxter delivering a good but long monologue on the differences between his native England and the United States; Wilfred Hyde-White playing a befuddled Interpol inspector who calls Dean his wife; and Sugar Ray Robinson unexpectedly dancing and singing well with Dean and the Golddiggers. Also, the writers seem to be telling viewers that Alan Sues is gay by having him play an effeminate Julius Caesar in one sketch ("Boy, have I had a day!" he proclaims as he enters) and act like he is being seduced when Ernest Borgnine mugs him.

Bob and Show: ***


## The Jack Benny 20th Anniversary TV Special
Nov. 16, 1970, Monday 10-11 p.m.

Host: Jack Benny. Guests: Eddie "Rochester" Anderson, Dennis Day, Bob Hope, Dinah Shore, Don Wilson. Cameos: Dean Martin, Red Skelton.

Jack reunites with old cast members and A-list guests add spice in this lively outing. Bob arrives midway through and announces, "It was either this or send a present. Jack went into TV just about the time Dr. Kildare delivered Marcus Welby ... People keep saying, 'For a man his age, he looks remarkable.' Anything his age looks remarkable! We have redwood trees in California that are not that old. Or that wrinkled." He spouts out more at the host's expense, including "He ought to team up with Perry Como and make still pictures," before "surprising" Jack with a plaque and singing "Thanks for the Memory" with him. His live 1954 appearance on Jack's sitcom appears in a retrospective of clips too. Finally, Bob is in a skit where Jack imagines what his crew will be like twenty years from now (he will be the only one in the sketch to actually live that long). He memorably quips, "This is Bob 'Road to Medicare' Hope. A funny thing happened to me on my way over here—I made it."

Bob: ***** Show: ****


## Swing Out Sweet Land
Nov. 29, 1970, Sunday 8:30-10 p.m.

Host: John Wayne. Guests: Ann-Margret, Lucille Ball, Jack Benny, Dan Blocker, Roscoe Lee Browne, George Burns, Glen Campbell, Johnny Cash, Roy Clark, Bing Crosby, Phyllis Diller, The Doodletown Pipers, Lorne Greene, Celeste Holm, Bob Hope, Michael Landon, Dean Martin, Dick Martin, Ross Martin, Ed McMahon, Greg Morris, David Nelson, Rick Nelson, Hugh O'Brian, Dan Rowan, William Shatner, Red Skelton, Tom Smothers, Leslie Uggams, Dennis Weaver. EP: Nick Vanoff, William O. Harbach. P/W: Paul Keyes. D: Stan Harris.

Cross a weak episode of *Rowan and Martin's Laugh-In* with an extended American history lesson, and the result is this celebrity-laden hodgepodge that varies so erratically in tone and content that is difficult to accept it either as entertainment or education. Bob is one of its precious few highlights. He has a funny monologue near the start playing himself entertaining the Revolutionary War troops at Valley Forge with contemporary references including a Bing Crosby joke. Bob also introduces Ann-Margret as a dancer entertaining the men with "She's a real patriot. I ought to know. At three o'clock this morning in my room, she declared her independence!" It's fun, but combine it with a depiction of the Civil War showing Rick and David Nelson fighting opposite sides, hokey musical interludes by the Doodletown Pipers and others, pretentious lines spouted by John Wayne and much more, and the result is patriotic claptrap.

Bob: **** Show: **

***The Red Skelton Show***
Dec. 28, 1970, Monday 7:30-8 p.m.

Red Skelton: Guests: Walter Brennan, Bob Hope (cameo). Featured: Chanin Hale, Jan Arvan, Brad Logan, Bern Hoffman, Pat Campbell, The Burgundy Street Singers. EP: Guy Della Cioppa. P: Perry Cross. D: Terry Kyne. Co-P/Script Supervisors: Gerald Gardner, Dee Caruso. W: Mort Green, Pat McCormick, Jeffery Barron, Lionel Bart, Red Skelton.

"Ladies and gentlemen, here's one of America's favorite clowns, certainly one of mine, Red Skelton!" intones Bob from a bit taped at one of his specials to introduce this tired edition of a series in its twentieth and final season. Red is past his prime, doing bits he could have done better ten years earlier. He starts with a long, sappy meditation on being a grandfather, then plays Sheriff Deadeye who, with his partner, Doc (Walter Brennan), attempts to evade outlaws in a western bar by dressing in drag. The weary festivities conclude with "The Silent Spot" featuring Red as a man retaliating against a fellow noisy camper in the woods in pantomime. It stinks too, making this a worn-out disappointment.

Bob: *** Show: **

## Everything You Always Wanted to Know About Jack Benny But Were Afraid to Ask
March 10, 1971, Wednesday 9-10 p.m.

Host: Jack Benny. Guests: Lucille Ball, George Burns, Phil Harris, Bob Hope, Dr. David Reuben, Dionne Warwick, John Wayne. EP: Irving Fein. P/D: Norman Abbott. W: Al Gordon, Hal Goldman, Hilliard Marks, Hugh Wedlock Jr., Bucky Searles.

Jack Benny has sporadic success with this special that paraphrases the title of a current best seller by Dr. David Reuben. He nervously giggles as he spells out "S-E-X," the word used in the original title in place of his name, as he talks to Reuben as his first guest. They are interrupted by Phil Harris for a long routine, followed by Jack and George Burns exchanging jokes and George taking planted questions from the audience about Jack. George mentions how he first met Jack and recalls that "There was a juggling act that was the worst." The next shot is of Bob bobbling balls backstage before he disappears. That's all he does, with no dialogue, and though he does get laughs, there's not much to it beyond that. The same can be said mostly about the rest of this show.

Bob: ** Show: ***

## Plimpton: Did You Hear the One About?
April 2, 1971, ABC Friday 9-10 p.m.

George Plimpton, Steve Allen, Woody Allen, Milton Berle, Jack Carter, Dick Cavett, Phyllis Diller, David Frye, Buddy Hackett, Bob Hope, Phil Silvers, Jonathan Winters. P/D/W: William Kronick. W: George Plimpton, Marc London, David Panich.

As part of his effort to have a successful standup comedy act like Woody Allen and David Frye (both of whom are seen in action), George Plimpton enlists the help of Steve Allen and humor writers Marc London and David Panich to develop his routine in this fascinating special. George also consults with Phyllis Diller, Phil Silvers, and Buddy Hackett before talking with Bob about how to prepare. "I think experience and more exposure to audiences help you," he advises after they finish a round of golf. Regarding timing, he says "It's a gift," and he notes how he appreciates the work of Jack Benny and Milton Berle equally, even though they have vastly different comic styles. It's insightful commentary that George incorporates as he pursues his challenging goal of being funny on stage by himself.

Bob and Show: ****


***The Stars and Stripes Show***
July 4, 1971, Syndicated, 90 minutes

Bob Hope, Dale Robertson, Kay Starr, Les Brown and His Band of Renown, The New Christy Minstrels, Chill Wills, Capt. Eugene Cernan U.S.N., The Cookie Bear, Johnny Unitas, Don Klosterman, Phyllis George, Steve Owens, Mickey Mantle, The U.S. Army Band, The U.S. Army Chorus. EP: Lee Allan Smith. P: Dick Schneider. D: Bill Thrash. W: Dennis Marks.

Dale leads everyone in the Pledge of Allegiance as host of what he acknowledges is a patriotic festival. This special, taped in Oklahoma and seen on other stations a few weeks later, has a distinct "America—love it or leave it" tone. For example, Chill Wills does a melodramatic monologue about being a soldier on D-Day, while astronaut Capt. Cernan reminds viewers of men who gave their lives for the country. Bob doesn't come on until a third of the way through. He's lively, but his material drags like the rest of the show. Of astronauts, he says, "They make Superman look like Truman Capote." His jokes include some local flavor plus ones of Jack Benny being cheap and Bing Crosby being old, and lots of flag waving, not much of it successful. He gets crickets when he quips, "Our Declaration of Independence states that all men are created equal. Of course, that was long before women's liberation. Not to mention Tom Jones." Bob adds that everything he says tonight is top secret. "I say that because I want all the newspapers to print it." He calls sex education "Ridiculous. It's embarrassing when a five-year-old kid knows more than you do," and claims Ralph Nader recalled Tricia Nixon's wedding cake. It's pretty painful, especially as Bob pontificates at the end about what being an American is before "The Battle Hymn of the Republic" follows him to conclude a thick layer of jingoism.

Bob and Show: **

## *Make Your Own Kind of Music*
July 20, 1971, Tuesday 8-9 p.m.

The Carpenters, Mark Lindsay, Al Hirt. Guests Include: Bob Hope. P: Ernest Chambers.

A surprisingly enjoyable summertime series, this debut installment features the Carpenters, Mark Lindsay and Al Hirt in peak form performing their recent hits, broken up by amusing comic pieces featuring (Jay) Tarses and (Tom) Patchett, who would go on to become leading comedy writers and producers for other TV series. Helping to keep the show on pace is having every letter of the alphabet serve as an introduction to a song, blackout or skit, with several celebrities commenting on them. One of them of course is Bob, who in a bit taped at one of his specials mockingly complains, "You dragged me to Burbank to say 'O'?! Must have a sexier letter!"

Bob and Show: \*\*\*\*

## *The Glen Campbell Goodtime Hour*
Sept. 21, 1971, CBS Tuesday 7:30-8:30 p.m.

Glen Campbell. Guests: Bob Hope, Dionne Warwick, Eddie Mayehoff, The Smothers Brothers, R.G. Brown.

Bob and Glen are on a golf hole and Bob cracks, "I went to see that movie *Shaft* because I thought it was the Sam Snead story." They talk about bad golfers like Spiro Agnew and Jack Benny ("He's so cheap, every time he tees off, he yells, 'Three!'") and Bob's favorite foursome ("Ann-Margret and Raquel Welch… and their agents."). The two then sing a takeoff of "Sixteen Tons" called "Eighteen Holes," which is okay enough. Also, the Smothers Brothers perform and Tommy thinks other men are their brothers including Bob Hope, who joins him on the cello to do "Matilda." He tries to prove it to Dick but he fails, as does the routine overall. Both Bob and the show are up and down throughout. Interestingly, though he did this show only one time, longtime Hope writer Bob Mills insists that Bob told him this was one of his favorite guest spots.

Bob and Show: \*\*\*

## *The Wonderful World of Disney*: "The Grand Opening of Walt Disney World"
Oct. 29, 1971, Sunday 7-8:30 p.m.

Julie Andrews, Glen Campbell, Buddy Hackett, Jonathan Winters, Bob Hope. EP/W: Bill Walsh. EP: Ron Miller. P/D: Robert Scheerer. Music: Arthur Fiedler.

To celebrate the opening of what became the United States' most heavily attended tourist attraction, this sometimes strange but fascinating show includes lots of singing and commentary by Julie and Glen, good but not great comedy bits by Buddy and Jonathan, and a monologue by Bob Hope "in special tribute to Walt Disney," as the credits read. He rides in on a monorail to the Contemporary Hotel and jokes about how big it is ("Here, Billy Graham comes up and reads [the Bible] to you") as well as mentions some Disney characters and Vice President Spiro Agnew. Some click, others are clinkers. Bob returns near the end to promote the park with a heartfelt spiel, saying "This is where the fun is. This is the place to relive your youth." This program is worth a look to see a lot of attractions that have changed or no longer exist at the park.

Bob: *** Show: ****


## *Bing Crosby and His Friends*
Feb. 27, 1972, Sunday 10-11 p.m.

Host: Bing Crosby: Guests: Pearl Bailey, Carol Burnett, Bob Hope. Music: Nick Perito. P: Bob Finkel. D: Marty Pasetta. W: Harry Crane, Marty Farrell, Norman Barasch, Carroll Moore, Bob Ellison. Special Musical Material: Ray Charles. Choreographer: Robert Sidney.

Given the level of talent involved, this is a relative disappointment, with contrived sketches involving the star quartet, unmemorable songs from its star and an obtrusive laugh track in place of a studio audience. The writers apparently did not get a note about the program's title, as Bing Crosby says "You've Got Good Friends" while backstage Bob and Pearl Bailey vow never to work with him again at the start of the show. That leads into the foursome supposedly getting stuck in an elevator after rehearsal, making Carol Burnett hysterical. "We're going to die!" she screams. "I know how she feels, we're the same age," pipes in Bob. It's pretty funny despite the fake circumstances, but Bing doing the deadly speech "Desiderata" afterward negates its impact. Carol and Pearl do a nice rendition of "The Little Things You Do Together" from the musical *Company* before the two and Bob learn that all three must share the same dressing room for the show. Bob's best bit here has him aggravate Carol by suggesting Lucille Ball replace her on the show. This is another moderately amusing yet too self-referential bit that ends with a reprise of "You've Got Good Friends." Thereafter it's mostly musical numbers with the stars broken up by some dialogue, such as Bing singing "Apalachicola, Florida" with Bob and telling the latter, "The first troops you entertained surrendered to Genghis Khan!" Bob is only as good as his material here, which is occasionally enjoyable, but one expects more from all this.

Bob and Show: ***

### *The Stars and Stripes Show*
July 4, 1972, Tuesday 9:30-10:30 p.m.

Host: Ed McMahon. Guests: Bob Hope, Chill Wills, Anita Bryant, Nancy Wilson, Kenny Rogers and The First Edition, Mickey Newbury, Miss World USA Karen Brucene Smith, The Johnny Mann Singers, Mickey Mantle, Johnny Unitas, Bobby Anderson, Paul "Bear" Bryant, Anne Henning, Steve Owens, Greg Landry, Allie Reynolds, Happy Hairston, Roger Staubach. EP: Lee Allan Smith. P: Dick Schneider. D: Bill Thrash. W: Dennis Marks.

NBC decides to carry this show's edition this year rather than have their star performer appear on it in syndication again. Still taped in Oklahoma, this has iffy production values while retaining the previous installment's off-putting hyper-patriotic tone. Ed McMahon isn't funny, the music is perfunctory, Chill Wills' melodramatic monologue is mushy, and the voiceovers done by athletes (the cast members listed after the Johnny Mann Singers) over video of their faces are stilted. Bob seems more partisan than usual, cracking about Oklahoma Gov. David Hall that "It's nice to see a Democrat who's working" and that this show emphasizes music because "They figure you'd get enough comedy next week from Miami" (referring to the 1972 Democratic national convention). Gags about hijacking and Nixon's visit to China bomb, which don't help. Bob concludes the show with a few digs at Democrats and rhapsodizes about soldiers in Vietnam at the end for a long, preachy, and tedious conclusion.

Bob and Show: **

## Jack Benny's First Farewell Special
Jan. 18, 1973, Thursday 9-10 p.m.

Host: Jack Benny. Guests: Johnny Carson, Isaac Hayes, Joey Heatherton, Dean Martin, Lee Trevino, Flip Wilson, George Burns (unbilled), Gov. Ronald Reagan (unbilled). EP: Irving Fein. P/D: Norman Abbott. W: Al Gordon, Hal Goldman, Hilliard Marks, Hugh Wedlock Jr., Stan Daniels, Tom Tenowich. Music Arrangers/Conductors: Jack Elliot, Allyn Ferguson.

This high-rated special's recurring joke is how guests including Bob assume Jack is retiring from show business. This setup has variable results in humor, as do the musical numbers (Isaac Hayes coolly performing "Shaft" and "The Look of Love" puts Joey Heatherton to shame). Bob largely succeeds, noting that "I do Jack's show once a year, usually around Lent. That's when I give up money." He carps that Jack gives him gifts like pens to dip into inkwells, adding "This year, I understand I'm getting the ink." He credits Jack's longevity to transplants: "One year he sold a kidney." When Jack joins him and Bob laughs after cracking that Jack can't tint his jokes like his hair, Jack ad-libs, "You like that joke?" After Bob exits, Jack gets the last laugh with "Wait till he needs a liver!" Their rapport highlights this so-so special pre-empting *Ironside*, which Jack parodies with Flip before the show ends.

Bob: \*\*\*\* Show: \*\*\*

## Ann-Margret—When You're Smiling
April 4, 1973, Wednesday 10-11 p.m.

Hostess: Ann-Margret. Guests: George Burns, Bob Hope. EP: Joseph Cates, Allan Carr. P/W: Roger Smith. D: Art Fisher. W: Allan Carr, Fred Ebb, Marvin Hamlisch, Hilliard Marks. Music: Lenny Stack.

About a third of the way through this taped concert of the title star's Las Vegas show, Bob and George Burns appear in a booth marveling at the performance. "Isn't Ann-Margret great? … Let's hope the government never devalues that!" cracks Bob. Soon he and George argue over who really made her popular in the 1960s. "She was one of my many discoveries, like Bing Crosby and Dorothy Lamour!" exclaims Bob before conceding to George that he discovered her—and as such, George should pay their tab. The duo appears near the end riding in on motorcycles and mod outfits to exchange pleasantries with Ann-Margret before she goes offstage for a final costume change, and they sing about how they taught her everything she knows. It's cute but doesn't make much of an impression, which unfortunately applies to much of this show, as the material and its presentation often comes short in matching the star's dynamic personality.

Bob and Show: ***

**The Stars & Stripes Show**
July 3, 1973, Tuesday 10-11 p.m.

Host: Tennessee Ernie Ford. Cast: Bob Hope. Anita Bryant, Lou Rawls, Les Brown, Today's Children, Doc Severinsen and His Now Generation Brass, The Strategic Air Command Band conducted by Lt. Col. Jim Owen, The U.S. Army Chorus, The Dancing Westchester Wranglerettes. EP: Lee Allan Smith. P: Dick Schneider. D: Bill Thrash. W: Barry Downes.

Col. Robinson Reisner, a POW from Vietnam, opens the show, which still has traces of previous editions' relentless "America first" approach, and Mickey Mantle, Greg Landry and others in the audience are seen with hokey voiceovers explaining their love for the country. The music remains square despite more contemporary tunes used, with the exception of an impassioned Lou Rawls, and choppy editing destroys the impact of Col. Reisner telling his story. Bob comes on earlier this time than in 1972 (less than a third into it rather than halfway), and his cracks about Martha Mitchell's mouth and Oklahoma do pretty well. Lots of jokes about meat prices, football, and planes vary greatly in quality, however. The sloppy editing and ultrapatriotic overkill atmosphere detract from the presentation greatly, but Bob does better here because he sticks more towards the principles of America's founding rather than assessing current problems.

Bob: *** Show: **

**American Film Institute Salutes James Cagney**
March 18, 1974, CBS Monday 9:30-11 p.m.

Host: Frank Sinatra. Honoree: James Cagney. Guests: Bob Hope, Charlton Heston, John Wayne, Gov. Ronald Reagan, Doris Day, Shirley

MacLaine, Jack Lemmon, Kirk Douglas, Frank Gorshin, George Segal.

Appearing after a clip from *The Seven Little Foys*, Bob jokes that he came to this great screen actor's tribute rather than go streaking at UCLA. He says he has always admired Cagney "for his wonderful impression of Frank Gorshin." His grade A-plus material, including "For Cagney, a love scene was when he let the other guy live," makes Paul Newman, Danny Kaye and more guffaw. Once he finishes with "I was going to conclude my remarks by saying that everything I know about dancing and acting, I learned from Jimmy Cagney, but AFI said 'Look, it's his night, why depress him?'" Bob has generated more laughs than the nearly ten minutes he did on the 1971 Oscars. This wonderfully warm, classy show has lots of fond memories by all plus a very gracious recipient.

Bob and Show: *****


*The Bluffers*
May 28, 1974, Tuesday 8-9 p.m.

Host: David Niven. Guests: Bob Hope, Ed Asner, Jack Benny, Michael Bentine, Ernest Borgnine, Johnny Carson, Angie Dickinson, Sandy Duncan, Glenn Ford, Zsa Zsa Gabor, Merv Griffin, Pat Harrington Jr., Ed McMahon, Carl Reiner, Bobby Riggs, Karen Valentine. The Bluffers Repertory Company: Jennifer Darling, Arlene Golonka, Ronny Graham, Chuck McCann, Barbara Rhoades, Bob Ridgely.

"How refreshing to hear that familiar music and not have him show up," David Niven quips in this special's intro as he comes out to "Thanks for the Memory." Bob shows up on tape to respond, "He once bluffed Hollywood into voting him an Oscar." They explain that the sketches will show how everyone gets around tricky situations by appearing confident despite the challenges they face. The variable amusing setups include a priest (Chuck McCann) losing his composure as he presides over the wedding of a bride he once dated and a TV commentator (Michael Bentine) getting no one to open the door of a London museum he is covering, so he breaks in and accidentally sets it on fire. This semi-successful pilot made a pitch for viewers to let NBC know what they thought of it at the end to see more episodes, and *Variety* reported the results were discouraging, hence no sale.

Bob and Show: ***

***The Stars & Stripes Show***
July 4, 1974, Thursday 10-11 p.m.

    Host: Tennessee Ernie Ford. Cast: Bob Hope, Dionne Warwick, Ricky Segall, Telly Savalas, Bob Feller, Mickey Mantle, The Singing Super Sportsmen, 1974 Miss America Becky King, The Texas Boys Choir, The Strategic Air Command Band conducted by Lt. Col. Jim Owen, The Mike Curb Congregation, The Dancing Westchester Wranglerettes. Announcer: Johnny Olsen. EP: Lee Allan Smith. P: Dick Schneider. D: Bill Thrash. W: Barry Downes. Music: Les Brown.
    Tennessee Ernie Ford introduces the Mike Curb Congregation doing a cheesy song and dance routine to kick off this annual clumsily edited, grade D Independence Day special. Dionne Warwick injects some liveliness with a medley of her Burt Bacharach and Hal David hits, but Ford, child star Ricky Segall, and the Dancing Westchester Wranglerettes performing "Yankee Doodle Dandy" puts this back in cornball country. Bob comes out with a cold to banter with 1974 Miss America Becky King ("I wish the country was in that shape") and joke hit and miss about the Elizabeth Taylor-Richard Burton breakup, President Nixon's overseas trips, the gas crisis, and small cars. Bob probably regrets saying "Mama Cass [Elliot] got into a Honda. It took her three days to get out," as the singer dies less than four weeks later. Things get really tiresome as Miss America tells Ricky Segall the story of America and the cast sings parts of it, followed by more artificial songs by the Mike Curb Congregation and even worse singing by Ricky, the Singing Super Sportsmen (which includes football star Mean Joe Greene), and Telly Savalas. Bob returns for a sticky five-minute spot about what makes America great before Dionne Warwick sings "The Battle Hymn of the Republic." This is the last edition of this special to run on NBC, but Bob will appear on it in 1975 when it is shown in Oklahoma only.
    Bob and Show: **


***Dean Martin's Celebrity Roast of Bob Hope***
Oct. 31, 1974, Thursday 10-11 p.m.

    Host: Dean Martin. Honoree: Bob Hope. Guests: Neil Armstrong, Johnny Bench, Jack Benny, Milton Berle, Gen. Omar Bradley, Foster Brooks, Howard Cosell, Phyllis Diller, Zsa Zsa Gabor, Rev. Billy Graham,

Delores Hope, Rich Little, Gov. Ronald Reagan, Don Rickles, Sugar Ray Robinson, Ginger Rogers, Nipsey Russell, Mark Spitz, James Stewart, Flip Wilson. On Film: Secretary of State Henry Kissinger, John Wayne. P/D: Greg Garrison. W: Harry Crane, George Bloom, Tom Tenowich, Milt Rosen, Don Hinkley, Peter Gallay, Stan Burns, Mike Marmer.

Formerly a segment on the last season of *The Dean Martin Show* (1965-1974), this series of specials has the host preside over guests delivering zingers to and about the guest of honor, in this case Bob. The funniest roasters here are Ronald Reagan ("He's entertained six presidents. He's performed for twelve."), Foster Brooks, Rich Little (impersonating most of the dais), Howard Cosell, Jack Benny ("He even used cue cards on his wedding night"), Nipsey Russell, Phyllis Diller, Don Rickles, and surprisingly James Stewart, Gen. Omar Bradley and the Rev. Billy Graham, mocking Bob's golf game. At the end, Bob hits back comically at all who roasted him ("Jimmy had me over the house last week, and what a thrilling evening. He showed slides of his last trip to Fresno"). Bob will reappear as a guest on three more of these specials through 1984.

Bob and Show: \*\*\*\*

### *Dean Martin's Celebrity Roast of Lucille Ball*
Feb. 7, 1975, Friday 10-11 p.m.

Host: Dean Martin. Honoree: Lucille Ball. Guests: Jack Benny, Foster Brooks, Ruth Buzzi (as Gladys Ormphby), Phyllis Diller, Totie Fields, Henry Fonda, Gale Gordon, Bob Hope, Rich Little, Gary Morton, Don Rickles, Ginger Rogers, [Dan] Rowan and [Dick] Martin, Nipsey Russell, Vivian Vance. P/D: Greg Garrison. W: Harry Crane, George Bloom, Tom Tenowich, Milt Rosen, Don Hinkley, Peter Gallay, Stan Burns, Mike Marmer.

Bob appears rather early on this program and hits Dean Martin with several drunk jokes before aiming at Lucille Ball. He says her series were able to easily beat such competition as "Charo Sings Cole Porter" and remarks of her ex-husband Desi Arnaz, "She got him a job as dialogue coach on *Chico and the Man*. And she still keeps up the payments on his bongos." It's pretty good, but most of the other participants including Dean are even better and frequently hysterical, including Don Rickles, who ribs Bob too. Throughout it all, Lucy is a delight.

Bob: \*\*\* Show: \*\*\*\*

***Mitzi... and 100 Guys***
March 24, 1975, CBS Monday 9-10 p.m.

Hostess: Mitzi Gaynor. Guests: Jack Albertson, Michael Landon. Appearing: Marty Allen, Steve Allen, Tige Andrews, Ed Asner, Ken Berry, Carl Betz, Bill Bixby, Tom Bosley, Mike Connors, Bob Crane, Bill Dana, Clifton Davis, James Farentino, Christopher George, Andy Griffith, Monty Hall, Bob Hope, Ross Hunter, Dean Jones, Tom Kennedy, Ted Knight, Rich Little, Allen Ludden, Gavin MacLeod, Monte Markham, Peter Marshall, Ross Martin, Strother Martin, Jim McKrell, Greg Morris, Jim Nabors, Leonard Nimoy, Louis Nye, William Shatner, Lyle Waggoner. EP: Jack Bean. P: Mort Green. D: Tony Charmoli. W: Jerry Mayer. Music: Bill Byers, J. Hill.

Thanks to its star, who knows how to sing and dance wonderfully and has a great sense of humor, this sparkling special is contemporary and captivating rather than condescending or corny. Mitzi really gets into the spirit of every number, starting with the "I Got the Music in Me" opener, where she dances with most of her male guests, all tuxedoed and looking ecstatic to be with her. In a bit obviously taped separately from her other guests, Bob arrives midway through the show for a quick soft shoe that lasts only thirty seconds, but he does get to be the last one at the end to kiss her goodbye. Even without doing a routine, Bob comes off well here.

Bob: **** Show: *****


***Perry Como's Lake Tahoe Holiday***
Oct. 28, 1975, CBS Tuesday 9-10 p.m.

Perry Como. Guests: Bob Hope, Anne Murray, Billie Jean King, Sandra Palmer, Suzy Chaffee, hang gliding champion Tina Trefethen, skateboard champs Robin Alaway and Desiree Von Essen.

Both Perry and Bob have performed better than in this spotty outing, wherein Perry sings bland tunes and visits female athletes in their venues outside in the California mountain area. This includes Anne Murray, who is seen on stage performing "Danny's Song" and offstage fishing with Perry for some reason and singing with him on "Catch a Falling Star." Bob appears in the middle of this quixotic muddle to do his routine, kicking off by saying he wins so many rounds of golf defeating Perry that he gets into a higher tax bracket from the earnings. His set references Tahoe's smog-free atmosphere ("I don't trust air I can't feel. No one for Los Angeles is allowed to exhale") and how to deal with sharks in light of the recent scary movie *Jaws* ("Bathe with someone who tastes better than you"). Otherwise, this appearance and special are best forgotten.

Bob and Show: ***

***Donny & Marie***
Nov. 16, 1975, ABC Sunday 7-8 p.m.

Hosts: Donny Osmond, Marie Osmond. Guests: Bob Hope, Paul Lynde, Lee Majors, The Osmond Brothers, Kate Smith, Chuck Norris, The Ice Follies.

This pilot is just as irritatingly cutesy and artificial as the 1975-1979 series of the same name it launched. After an insipid rendition of "It Takes Two" and blah comic dialogue, the brother and sister join Bob dressed in Elton John's Captain Fantastic outfit. "I'm either Elton John or a nightlight for Liberace," he quips, adding, "If my pants catch on fire, no one will ever notice!" Donny and Marie crack up at his ad libs (when a ball from his hat hits Donny's face, he says, "I feel like a walking pawnshop!") before Bob sings "Play a Simple Melody" with them. Bob has fun in spite of his material, as does Paul Lynde as a snarky gorilla hunter. Otherwise, it's bad comic bits and often dubious musical moments like Kate Smith doing "Crocodile Rock." Bob hightails it before the patriotic medley finale of "Stars and Stripes Forever" and "God Bless America" is performed by the rest of the cast except Lee Majors and Chuck Norris, who do cameos.

Bob: **** Show: **

***Merry Christmas, Fred, from the Crosbys***
Dec. 3, 1975, CBS Wednesday 9-10 p.m.

Bing Crosby, Kathryn Crosby, Harry Crosby, Mary Frances Crosby, Nathaniel Crosby, Fred Astaire, The Young Americans, Joe Bushkin. Cameo: Bob Hope. EP: Gary Smith. EP/D: Dwight Hemion. W: Buz Kohan. Music: Ian Fraser. Special Musical Material: Larry Grossman.

Choreographer: Peter Gennaro.

Bing phones Fred Astaire to cut an album with him, during which they sing each other's praises. The other Crosbys sing a tune interpolated with Bing's "We Need a Little Christmas" before Fred and Bing review what to record with pianist Joe Bushkin. They decide on "Sing" (the Carpenters' hit), but progress stops when the Young Americans visit the Crosbys to sing and dance a medley that includes "Love Will Keep Us Together." Back with Bing and Fred, the latter encourages Bing and Kathryn to re-enact being Bing, Bob Hope, and Dorothy Lamour singing tunes from the Road pictures. When they finish, Bob appears in top hat, tails, and cane and says, "Pardon me, but I'm looking for Ginger Rogers." "Well, what a present surprise," says Bing. "Yeah, that's what Custer said at Little Big Horn," snaps Bob. "You talk about surprises! The minute my back is turned, you go looking for my replacement! Don't you have any sense of loyalty?" "I would never presume to replace you," interjects Fred. "Why, you're an American institution!" "Yeah, so is Sing Sing!" Bob shoots back. Fred then claims he should be replacing Bing instead of Fred, and he and Kathryn dance off with Bob. It is contrived but easy to take, as is most of this special, with Bing and Fred reprising songs from their films *Blue Skies* and *White Christmas*, including the latter's title tune of course.

Bob and Show: ***


## *Donny & Marie*
Jan. 30, 1976, ABC Friday 8-9 p.m.

Hosts: Donny Osmond, Marie Osmond. Guests: Bob Hope, The Harlem Globetrotters, Ted Knight. Also Appearing: Jim Connell, Judy and Vicki Denton, Hank Garcia, The Estancia Marching High School Band. EP: Raymond Katz. P: Sid and Marty Krofft. D: Art Fisher. W: Sandy Krinski, Chet Dowling, Bill Larkin, Audrey Tadman, Garry Ferrier, Wally Dalton, Shelly Zellman.

How do the Harlem Globetrotters rate as special guests and Ted Knight as "very special guest" on a show with Bob Hope? That's one of this show's many mysteries, including why Bob appears as an obese Carmen Miranda in the first skit. He goes off joking on Danny Thomas's nose and Bing Crosby's age before singing off inconsequentially. Bob reappears later and does a solid set pretending to entertain some troops in a tropical island setting ("It's the only spot in the world where you have to save up a month to spit.") before joining everyone in a patriotic finale. The rest is mostly mediocre music and unfunny bits, from watching the Harlem Globetrotters try to deliver dialogue convincingly to Ted Knight being a barber attempting to style a werewolf's hair.

Bob: *** Show: **

## *The Dean Martin Celebrity Roast of Dean Martin*
Feb. 27, 1976, Friday 9-11 p.m.

Host: Don Rickles. Honoree: Dean Martin. Guests: Bob Hope, Orson Welles, James Stewart, Gene Kelly, John Wayne, Muhammad Ali, Gabe Kaplan, Tony Orlando, Howard Cosell, Dan Rowan and Dick Martin, Sen. Barry Goldwater, Joe Namath, Rich Little, Angie Dickinson, Joey Bishop, Sen. Hubert Humphrey, Foster Brooks, Paul Lynde, Georgia Engel, Nipsey Russell. Cameos: Charlie Callas (as Dean's producer), Ruth Buzzi (as Gladys Ormphby). P/D: Greg Garrison. W: Harry Crane, Bill Daley, Howard Albrecht, Sol Weinstein, Milt Rosen, Larry Markes, Terry Hart, Jeffrey Barron, Stan Burns, Mike Marmer.

The zenith of 1970s politically incorrect humor on TV, this special is quite delightful if one accepts it on those terms. Don Rickles is at his hysterically rude best ("Ladies and gentlemen, we make fun of Howard Cosell, and why not? Look at him!") and introduces particularly hilarious remarks by Orson Welles (mocking "That's Amore"), Paul Lynde, Rich Little, Ruth Buzzi (hitting everyone with her purse), Foster Brooks (as a drunk Scoutmaster), and of course Bob, who gets the last spot. He mocks the occasion ("This night is about as exciting watching the Walton family paper train their pet rock") as well as the honoree ("He's sort of a marinated Burt Reynolds"). Even such non-comedians as Sen. Barry Goldwater, Muhammad Ali, and Angie Dickinson are amusing with their strong scripted material here.

Bob: **** Show: *****

## *Captain & Tennille*
Sept. 27, 1976, ABC Monday 8-9 p.m.

The Captain (Daryl Dragon), Toni Tennille. Guests: Redd Foxx, Bob Hope, John Travolta. Featured: Joel Lawrence. EP: Alan Bernard. P: Bob

Henry. D: Tony Charmoli. W: John Boni, Norman Stiles, Stephen Spears, Thad Mumford, Tom Dunsmuir, Ed Hider, Ruth Merithew. Music: Lenny Stack. Choreographer: Bob Thompson.

This slice of pure Seventies cheese has an ever-smiling hostess awkwardly belting out "Honky Cat," "You Don't Mess Around with Jim," "Boogie Fever," and "Don't Go Breakin' My Heart" (with John Travolta), while her husband and cohost is ill at ease saying lines and trying to do comedy. Bob appears on this one-season series' second show and, apparently having judged this as a lost cause, delivers his repartee with the least amount of effort needed. To be fair, given clunkers like saying of fellow guest Redd Foxx that "He makes more money than Jimmy Carter's dentist" and having to hit yourself with a pie at the end of hosting "Masterjoke Theatre," that may be a wise choice. Still, his lack of chemistry bantering and acting with the duo within a skit as a nervous diamond cutter allows Redd to do a better job of getting what scant laughs there are here.

Bob and Show: **


## *The Sonny and Cher Show*
Oct. 10, 1976, CBS Sunday 8-9 p.m.

Sonny Bono, Cher, Ted Ziegler. Guests: Bob Hope, The Jacksons. EP: Nick Vanoff. P/W: Phil Hahn, Frank Peppiatt. D: Tim Kiley. W: Barry Adelman, Bob Arnott, John Aylesworth, Jeannine Burnier, Stuart Gillard, Coslough Johnson, Barry Silver, Iris Rainer.

Sonny talks about how he supports Gerald Ford for president and Cher supports Jimmy Carter and CBS being upset with the political humor. "Hey, if they don't like it, why don't they get Bob Hope?" Cher quips. Instantly Bob appears to much applause. "And Kissinger thinks he pops up in strange places!" Bob reacts. He calls Sonny "Tony" (as in Tony Orlando), jokes how Sonny's mustache is older than Donny and Marie and asks, "Hey, I stopped buying the *National Enquirer*. Are you two still married?" Cher laughs while semi-grimacing. On learning Cher's new baby was named Elijah Blue, a stunned Bob quips, "And I thought Bing was a silly name!" Following this feisty opening where Bob has a good time, he appears in a sketch with Sonny as King Arthur, Cher as Guinevere and Bob as Sir Lancelot. Dolled up in a suit of armor with pink shirt and pants underneath, Bob launches into a typical monologue he would be doing in medieval times. Cher kisses Bob so much that steam emerges from his outfit. With the Jacksons appearing too, this is a surprisingly lively and fun installment of the series as it nears its end.

Bob: ***** Show: ****


*All-Star Tribute to John Wayne*
Nov. 26, 1976, ABC Friday 8-9 p.m.

Host: Frank Sinatra. Honoree: John Wayne. Guests: Charles Bronson, John Byner, Glen Campbell, Sammy Davis Jr., Angie Dickinson, Monty Hall, Bob Hope, Ron Howard, Lee Marvin, Maureen O'Hara, Dan Rowan and Dick Martin, James Stewart, Claire Trevor, Henry Winkler. P/W: Paul Keyes. Co-P/W: Marc London. D: Dick McDonough. Music: Nelson Riddle.

This early installment of Variety Clubs International paying honor to a superstar allows pretaped bits by Bob along with John Byner, Sammy Davis Jr., Lee Marvin, and James Stewart, something that will be avoided for only in-person salutes thereafter. Bob is in fine form, saying that the Duke says so young in part because he uses only older horses. Of Wayne's films, Bob quips, "My favorite is *Road to Morocco*." How does Wayne relax? "He goes to South Dakota and punches Mount Rushmore in the noses." As for his children, "He has seven of them, one for each day of the week. Man, that must've been some week, Duke!" The short and sweet set ends with Bob doing a special version of "Thanks for the Memory" for the honoree.

Bob: **** Show: ***


*CBS Salutes Lucy: The First 25 Years*
Nov. 28, 1976, CBS Sunday 8-10 p.m.

Desi Arnaz, Lucille Ball, Carol Burnett, Richard Burton, Johnny Carson, Sammy Davis Jr., Gale Gordon, Bob Hope, Danny Kaye, Dean Martin, James Stewart, Danny Thomas, Vivian Vance, Dick Van Dyke, John Wayne. EP: Gary Morton. P/W: Sheldon Keller.

This celebration of Lucille Ball's work is richly enjoyable in capturing virtually all the memorably funny and occasionally touching bits of her acting across two and a half decades, with participants including a rare on-camera appearance by CBS President Bill Paley extending his thanks to TV's favorite redhead as well. Taped on the set of one of his specials, Bob introduces a segment showing an extended clip of his appearance on *I Love Lucy*. He's fine if not effectively insightful in his comments.

Bob: *** Show: *****

***Steve Lawrence and Eydie Gorme: From This Moment On... Cole Porter***
March 10, 1977, Thursday 10-11 p.m.

Hosts: Steve Lawrence, Eydie Gorme. Guests: Ethel Merman, Swingle Singers II, Natalie Marakova, The Cambridge University Glee Club, Bob Hope. P/D: Dwight Hemion. Co-P: Gary Smith. W: Harry Crane, Buz Kohan. Special Musical Material: Larry Grossman. Musical Director: Allyn Ferguson. Conductor: Jack Parnell. Concert Arrangement: Don Costa. Concert Vocal Arrangement: Artie Malvin. Choreographer: Norman Maen.

Steve and Eydie and other sing ad nauseam what sounds like the title songwriter's entire catalog in a tribute that falls way short of what the lead duo did better as guests on *The Carol Burnett Show* (Buz Kohan and Artie Malvin worked on the latter, incidentally). The taped British production uses extensive changes in costumes, settings, and lighting, but all that truly sparkles involves Bob (billed as special guest star) in a "flashback" rehearsing Porter's musical *Red, Hot and Blue* in the 1930s with a pianist (Steve). "It's the last time people have ever walked out on me during rehearsals," frets Bob as he struggles to shine in his role. With Steve's encouragement, he belts out "It's D'Lovely," and it is, as Bob does a swell soft-shoe routine with Steve and then duets on it with Ethel Merman as she joins him in the theater. As for the rest of the show, it's pretty much d'lousy.

Bob: **** Show: **

***Shirley MacLaine: Where Do We Go From Here?***
March 12, 1977, CBS Saturday 10-11 p.m.

Shirley MacLaine, Les Ballet Trockadero de Monte Carlo. Cameos: Bob Hope, Don Rickles, James Stewart, Jimmie Walker, Orson Welles. P/W: George Schlatter. D: Tony Charmoli. W: Digby Wolfe. Music: Donn

Trenner. Choreographer: Alan Johnson.

Shirley's special is a product of its time, with sometimes gaudy visuals and variably enjoyable segments. The latter applies to Bob's jokes, which like with the other cameos is taped elsewhere and edited quickly to resemble producer George Schlatter's *Laugh-In* series. Bob misses with dated gags on gays ("With the dismal condition of the British economy, they can't afford to support two queens") and women ("With more and more women entering the priesthood, they've changed the whole idea of confession. You go in feeling good and come out feeling guilty."), but scores with "Just this week, the Boy Scouts offered to make Raquel Welch an official honorary Boy Scout. Unfortunately, Raquel refused to go along with their good deed for the day." Shirley's dancing with four men and two women plus the all-male Les Ballet Trockadero outshine everything else. She will redo a weird routine where she makes a salad while dancing to "The Stripper" and wearing an old lady outfit on Schlatter's *The First Annual American Comedy Awards* on May 19, 1987.

Bob and Show: ***

*Bing! A 50<sup>th</sup> Anniversary Special*
March 20, 1977, CBS Sunday 9-10:30 p.m.

Host: Bing Crosby. Guests: Paul Anka, Pearl Bailey, Rosemary Clooney, Kathryn Crosby, Harry Crosby, Mary Frances Crosby, Nathaniel Crosby, Sandy Duncan, Bob Hope, Bette Midler, The Mills Brothers, Donald O'Connor, Martha Raye, Debbie Reynolds, Anson Williams, The Joe Bushkin Trio. EP: Frank Konigsberg. P/D: Marty Pasetta. W: Buz Kohan.

Bing is in great voice and Bob is in great form in this affectionate tribute to Crosby. Bob steals the show with a monologue that includes him presenting a special award to Bing, "the Crummy." He amuses himself with lines like, "For those of you who are unfamiliar with Mr. Crosby's career—and there must be millions of you—let me say that no one has ever done so much with so little for so long for so much." Bob gets applause for this as does Bing when he joins them, leading Bob to say, "Americans really root for the underdog." "I guess they asked the previous year's winner to present it," Bing says in response to Bob giving him the Crummy. Bob then narrates Bing's life story over old pictures and films, with jokes interjected by Bing along with Bob. It is a delight.

Bob and Show: *****

***3 Girls 3***
March 30, 1977, Wednesday 9-10 p.m.

Debbie Allen, Ellen Foley, Mimi Kennedy. Guests: Carol Burnett, Zsa Zsa Gabor, Florence Henderson, Bob Hope, Larry Kert. EP: Gary Smith, Dwight Hemion. P: Kenny Solms, Gail Parent. D: Tony Mordente.

The opening show of a series featuring three promising newcomers alternately clicks and croaks in its presentation, and unfortunately Bob's spot is one of the latter. A quarter of the way into the action, the trio pass by Bob, supposedly in an NBC hallway talking on the phone. "Norm, I'm doing Carson tonight. I need jokes," he says. Mimi Kennedy interrupts him to say that she, Debbie Allen and Ellen Foley are doing a new program for the network and would love for him to take part. He reviews the script, tears it up, and announces, "I wish I could, but I have a big part on *Zoo Parade II*." *Zoo Parade* had been off the air for 20 years, so the joke was dated as well as tired. One can sympathize with Bob perfunctorily making his appearance here given material like this. In its defense, the show does have some fun moments, like when the leading ladies learn at the start they are auditioning for their roles opposite Carol Burnett, Zsa Zsa Gabor, and Florence Henderson, and when Larry Kert gets fed up with the ladies trying to hog the spotlight as they join him to perform two numbers from *A Chorus Line*. However, dead bits like Bob's pop up enough that one can understand why this lasted only four episodes despite all the talent involved.

Bob: ** Show: ***

***Ann-Margret: Rhinestone Cowgirl***
April 26, 1977, Tuesday 9-10 p.m.

Ann-Margret. Guests: Chet Akins, Perry Como, Bob Hope, Minnie Pearl. Music: Bill Walker. P: Gary Smith, Dwight Hemion. D: Dwight Hemion. W: Buz Kohan. Special Musical Material: Larry Grossman. Choreographer: Rob Iscove.

This "countrypolitan" special is beautifully written, directed and edited in presenting glitz with downhome entertainment. Ann-Margret performs "Thank God I'm a Country Girl" with ten dancers, then lovingly reviews the history of the Grand Ole Opry, where this is taped, before being joined by Minnie Pearl. "I know this is an important show, so I raised the price tag on my hat," she jokes as they do a comic duet before Bob arrives. Sporting a Nudie suit bedazzled with chuck wagon emblems, Bob cracks, "I just got finished with the plow and didn't have time to change" and "I look like Elton John's nightlight." He says he has loved country music since Dolly Parton was wearing a training bra, prompting audience hysteria, and warns that "This outfit goes back to Liberace, and he hates fingerprints in his rhinestones." Ann-Margret mentions *The Paleface* and asks, "Do you remember the big duet in that movie?" "I already told you, Jane Russell!" Bob shoots back. He superbly does "Buttons and Bows" with Ann-Margret as a round and dances part of it as well. Bob is just as energetic later when he and Perry Como appear in bib overalls to join Minnie and Ann-Margret to do a number, and he jokes that he made Donna Fargo the happiest girl in the whole USA, paraphrasing that singer's hit. Add to that Perry and Chet Atkins doing "And I Love Her So" and more great dancing and singing, and the result is a splendid special.

Bob: ***** Show: ****


*Donny & Marie*
Nov. 11, 1977, ABC Friday 8-9 p.m.

Donny Osmond, Marie Osmond, The Ice Capades. Guests: Ruth Buzzi, Bob Hope, Cheryl Ladd. Also Appearing: The Beattys, Johnny Dark, Denny Evans, Rod Gist. EP: Raymond Katz, The Osmond Brothers. P/D: Art Fisher. P/W: Arnie Kogen. W: Rod Warren, Mort Scharfman, Bill Dana, Paul Pumpian, Harvey Weitzman, Bruce Vilanch, Ed Hider.

Tedious dialogue and songs abound until Bob and Ruth Buzzi show up ten minutes into this episode as bikers in black leather. They sing "Bad Bad Leroy Brown" and do the Twist with the rest of the cast while spouting lame lines in a weak beach movie spoof. He then appears in a tux with a golf club to joke about President Jimmy Carter, challenges Donny in a swinging match ("You know you'd get better distance if you'd use a ball?" he ad-libs) and even mocks NBC's struggling ratings. Bob reappears in the final skit as Sherlock Holmes in a musical comedy English murder mystery. Like most of the rest of the show, it's just overdone, soulless music and stupidity and mugging masking as humor, with few funny lines for Bob.

Bob: *** Show: **

### The George Burns One-Man Show
Nov. 23, 1977, CBS Wednesday 10-11 p.m.

George Burns, Bob Hope, The Captain and Tennille, Gladys Knight and the Pips, Ann-Margret, John Denver (cameo). EP: Irving Fein. P/D: Stan Harris. W: Elon Packard, Fred S. Fox, Seaman Jacobs. Music: Jack Elliott, Allyn Ferguson.

George says he faked a cough to con Bob into appearing on this supposed one-man show as a backup. Hope allegedly contacted the other talent to show up to help if needed. This contrivance nevertheless works well, with George sharply delivering some fairly risqué jokes amid good banter with his guests, all who score in their bits and performances save for the Captain and Tennille's forgettable number. Bob strolls onto the stage midway with an unnamed actress playing George's nurse, and as the host leaves with her, Bob quips, "The last nurse who found his pulse was Florence Nightingale." His decent monologue pales to what George offers but has two great lines: "(George) once told Noah he doesn't play cruises" and "You know, when one reaches a certain age, sex and violence become the same thing."

Bob: *** Show: ****


### All-Star Tribute to Elizabeth Taylor
Dec. 1, 1977, CBS Thursday 9-10 p.m.

Host: John Wayne. Guests: Elizabeth Taylor, June Allyson, Robert Blake, Debby Boone, Tom Drake, Henry Fonda, Frank Gorshin, Monty Hall, Bob Hope, Rock Hudson, Janet Leigh, Jimmy Lydon, Roddy McDowall, Paul Newman, Margaret O'Brien, Carroll O'Connor, Dan Rowan and Dick Martin. P/W: Paul W. Keyes. Co-P/W: Marc London, Bob Howard. D: Dick McDonough. Music: Nelson Riddle.

Bob helps the great film star in and out of her chair several times besides performing a smooth set here. "Thank you very much for that applause... It's much more than I deserve and considerably less than I expected," he says to the star-studded audience's amusement. "You have no idea what a thrill it is to stand here and see Elizabeth Taylor just to the left of John Wayne (last year's honoree). But then, who isn't?" he jokes of Wayne's right-wing politics. He said he left England like Taylor because

"I found out I couldn't be queen. Of course, the way things are changing in the world today..." He brings out Billy Carter, the brother of President Jimmy Carter and a surprisingly adept comic foil ("I always wanted to meet John Warner!" he says of Taylor's current husband). Others try as hard as Bob to be entertaining and most succeed, making this a winning effort overall.

Bob: ***** Show: ****


*The Kraft 75th Anniversary Show*
Jan. 24, 1978, CBS Tuesday 9:30-11 p.m.

Host: Bob Hope. Guests: Edgar Bergen, Milton Berle, Roy Clark, Bob Crosby, Alan King, Donna McKechnie, Hal Peary, Leslie Uggams. Music: Ian Fraser. P/D: Dwight Hemion. P: Gary Smith. W: Buz Kohan, Jerry Perzigian, Don Seigel, Marty Farrell. Special Musical Material: Earl Brown. Choreographer: Ron Field.

"It was an honor and a privilege to fill in for Bing this evening," Bob concludes at the end of this special that he knew should have been hosted by Bing Crosby, given the late performer's success on radio hosting *The Kraft Music Hall* from 1936-1946. He does a masterful, classy job as host, singing a new song about the history of Kraft and *The Kraft Music Hall*, and he is animated recalling highlights of the show and its performances, as well as introducing clips from *Kraft Television Theatre* (1947-1958). Bob has a wonderful time reminiscing with classic radio stars Edgar Bergen, Hal Peary, and Bob Crosby, joking with the latter that he didn't know the bandleader was Bing's son (Bob is actually Bing's brother). This is also the special where he and Milton Berle dressed in drag as two ladies in the supermarket, which gets a lot of repeat showing on Bob's specials and elsewhere in the 1980s and 1990s. It is a breezy hour and a half of memories and fun, and Bob enjoys recounting the old and presenting new songs and comedy from Roy Clark, Leslie Uggams, and Alan King so much that it even hard to tell at points if he's really relying on cue cards like he normally does. Buz Kohan adds that for this special, "I had written something for Bob saying that never a day goes by without him thinking about Bing, but he told me, 'You know, some days go by that I don't think of Bing.' So we changed it."

Bob: ***** Show: ****

### The Muppet Show
Feb. 11, 1978, Syndicated 30 minutes

Muppeteers: Frank Oz, Jerry Nelson, Richard Hunt, Dave Goelz, Jim Henson. Guest Star: Bob Hope. P: Jim Henson. D: Peter Harris. W: Jerry Juhl, Joseph A. Bailey, Jim Henson, Don Hinkley.

This marvelous piece of silliness and slight insanity includes a Bob Hope nose joke at the start, Animal going crazy about Bob being on the show, Miss Piggy doing a calypso number, and Bob having to leave to do different benefits for groups who come to see him on the show. Included among the latter is the Flying Zucchini Brothers human cannonball act, which attacks and launches Bob out. The suitably goofball plot also mixes bits like field rodents singing "For What It's Worth" while trying to hide from hunters and lots of blackouts. Bob does relatively little on the show apart from a few bits and a version of "Don't Fence Me In" riding a dumb talking horse, but it's all solid, and he reacts perfectly to all the wacky occurrences. "This isn't happening, this is just a hangover," Bob quips about the wildness amid him at the closing.

Bob: **** Show: *****

### The Osmond Brothers Special
May 26, 1978, ABC Friday 8-9 p.m.

The Osmond Brothers (Alan, Wayne, Merrill, Jay). Guests: Crystal Gayle, Andy Gibb, Bob Hope, The Knudsen Brothers, Jimmie Walker, The Dallas Cowboy Cheerleaders, Donny Osmond, Marie Osmond. P: The Osmond Brothers, Art Fisher. D: Art Fisher. W: James Parker, Michael Kagan.

Apart from Bob's on-point monologue, most of this show is so antiseptic that it makes *Mary Poppins* look like a war film. Bob follows an excruciating extended opening number involving limp scripted lines among Donny's four older brothers. He jokes about the family's size and teeth, President Jimmy Carter's problems, the TV schedule, and the slowness of Provo, Utah, where this special is taped ("*The Tonight Show* comes on at noon… This is the only town in the country where the Salvation Army has a jug band.") Bob then humorously interacts with the brothers and joins them in performing "I Want a Girl (Just Like the Girl

That Married Dear Old Dad)." Andy Gibb and Crystal Gayle's numbers are fine, but otherwise, eh. Donny and Marie appear in a segment taped in Hawaii, wisely avoiding most of this mess their brothers made on screen.

Bob: **** Show: **


*NBC Salutes the 25th Anniversary of the Wonderful World of Disney*
Sept. 13, 1978, Wednesday 8-10 p.m. and Sept. 17, 1978, Sunday 7-9 p.m.

Hosts: Ron Howard, Suzanne Somers. Guests: Edward Asner, Valerie Bertinelli, Big Bird, Bill Bixby, Ray Charles, Scatman Crothers, Buddy Ebsen, Crystal Gayle, Melissa Gilbert, Dan Haggerty, Phil Harris, Bob Hope, Bruce Jenner, Gavin MacLeod, Fred MacMurray, Ricardo Montalban, Fess Parker. EP/W: Ernest Chambers. P/W: Rocco Urbisci. D: Art Fisher. W: Hal Kanter, Rick Kellard, Bob Comfort, Dennis Landa, Tom Adair. Music: Jack Elliott, Allyn Ferguson.

An unwieldy four-hour salute to the first quarter century of the family anthology series, this has plenty of lame new comedy that weigh down some nice, appealing vintage footage of the series. Besides singing some new lyrics to "Heigh-Ho," Bob provides a fond introduction to the show's last host and namesake, Walt Disney.

Bob: **** Show: ***


*Donny & Marie*
Sept. 22, 1978, ABC Friday 8-9 p.m.

Donny Osmond, Marie Osmond. Guests: Bob Hope, KC and the Sunshine Band, Olivia Newton-John. Cameos: Robert Conrad, Betty White, Dick Van Patten, Lassie, John Wayne. EP: The Osmond Brothers, Raymond Katz. P/D: Art Fisher. W: Phil Hahn, Paul Pumpian, Ed Hider, Franelle Silver, Steven Adams, Bruce Kirschbaum, Scott McGibbon, Earl Brown.

The opener of this series' fourth and last season has Olivia, KC and Bob cutting a ribbon announcing the new show, only to have a quake hit and Bob left to fend for himself as the stage splits in two. After that feeble kickoff, the hosts do an embarrassing version of "Disco Inferno," banter lamely and bomb in a *60 Minutes* spoof with Johnny Dark enlivened only by slightly amusing guest cameos. Bob is part of that as a wisecracking surgeon who at least delivers his silly lines well. The show does get energized as KC and the Sunshine Band and Olivia lively perform their hits and more solo and with the hosts. Unfortunately, lousy skits including Bob at a roller skating party at the White House (with President and Mrs. Carter impersonators) predominate. Everyone participates in the "Pharaoh Follies" musical finale, where Bob plays King Tut and sings a refashioned rendition of "Diamonds are a Girl's Best Friend" to emphasize his gold holdings and does some more shtick. Bob looks like he's having fun despite the often stupid material and canned laughter around him.

Bob: **** Show: ***


### *General Electric's All-Star Anniversary*
Sept. 29, 1978, ABC Friday 9-11 p.m.

Host: John Wayne. Guests: Lucille Ball, Albert Brooks, Henry Fonda, Alex Haley, Pat Hingle, Bob Hope, Cheryl Ladd, Michael Landon, Penny Marshall, Donny Osmond, Marie Osmond, Charley Pride, John Ritter, Sha Na Na, Red Skelton, Suzanne Somers, James Stewart, Elizabeth Taylor, James Whitmore, Cindy Williams, Henry Winkler. P: Paul W. Keyes, Bob Howard. D: Dick McDonough. W: Jeffrey Barron, Monty Aidem.

Another celebrity-packed festival whose whole is less successful than the sum of its parts, this hauls out everything from impersonations (Pat Hingle as Thomas Edison, James Stewart as Mark Twain, James Whitmore as Will Rogers) to songs by Donny and Marie Osmond, all to celebrate 100 years of "progress for people," the slogan for General Electric (that company actually was eighty-four years old when this first aired). It also features comedy segments, and Bob's is the best. He jests about President Jimmy Carter's problems with his beer-drinking brother and says the Chief Executive tells his staff that "If Billy calls, I'm out!" Bob claims he's spent many hours worried that he can't become president because of his being born in England but Alice Cooper can. Noting the municipality's recent financial troubles, he quips, "Who would've thought that when we bought New York City that we'd need the twenty-four dollars back?" He puts the kidding aside at the end with "I'd rather have a bad year in America than a good year anywhere else." Host John Wayne joins him for some scripted lines afterward and gets in a good one about Bob's idea that they do a film together: "I guess I could handle the comedy right if you could handle the straight stuff." Wayne later thanks Bob for his work on the USO tours on the special as well.

Bob: \*\*\*\* Show: \*\*\*

## *The Wonderful World of Disney*: "Mickey's 50"
Nov. 19, 1978, Sunday 7-9 p.m.

Jack Albertson, Ed Asner, Anne Bancroft, Edgar Bergen, Ken Berry, Jacqueline Bisset, Mel Brooks, Carol Burnett, LeVar Burton, Red Buttons, Ruth Buzzi, Dyan Cannon, Cantinflas, The Carpenters, Johnny Carson, Charo, Dick Clark, Susan Clark, Hans Conried, Phyllis Diller, Dale Evans, Sally Field, President Gerald Ford, Jodie Foster, Annette Funicello, Eva Gabor, Steve Garvey, Elliott Gould, The Rev. Billy Graham, Goldie Hawn, Helen Hayes, Jim Henson, Sterling Holloway, Bob Hope, Bruce Jenner, Elton John, Dean Jones, Shirley Jones, Alex Karras, Gene Kelly, Cheryl Ladd, Christopher Lee, Rich Little, Roger Miller, Anne Murray, Joe Namath, Willie Nelson, Gary Owens, Gregory Peck, Helen Reddy, Burt Reynolds, Adam Rich, Kenny Rogers, Roy Rogers, Mickey Rooney, Ronnie Schell, Peter Sellers, Doc Severinsen, Shields and Yarnell, O.J. Simpson, James Stewart, Peter Strauss, Dick Van Patten, Jan-Michael Vincent, Barbara Walters, Raquel Welch, Lawrence Welk, Henry Winkler, Jonathan Winters, Jo Anne Worley. EP: Ron Miller. P/W/D: Phil May. W: Nicholas Harvey Bennion.

What appears to be half of Hollywood (including Chewbecca and R2D2 from *Star Wars*) turns out mostly to make cameos congratulating Mickey Mouse on reaching the half-century mark in this sometimes clever, sometimes clunky celebration. Bob shows up roughly midway through to say "Happy birthday, Mickey, though I must say it's disturbing that here you are, fifty years old, and your hairline has not receded one bit. How do you do that? Many happy returns, you little rascal!"

Bob and Show: \*\*\*

## *Steve Martin: A Wild and Crazy Guy*
Nov. 22, 1978, Wednesday 10-11 p.m.

Host: Steve Martin. Guests: Milton Berle, George Burns, Johnny Cash, Bob Hope, Strother Martin, Henry Winkler. Featured: Maryedith

Burrell, David Dozer, Joy Garrett, Jay Gerber, Philip Baker Hall, Zale Kessler, Tom Lillard, Michael McManus, Anna Rodzianko. Music: John McEuen. EP: Steve Martin, Marty Klein. P: Joe Cates. D: Gary Weis. W: Michael Elias, Alan Metter, Jack Handey. Choreographer: Scott Salmon.

An up-and-down special featuring the hottest comic of the time starts with Steve supposedly a nervous wreck prior to going out on stage. Milton Berle and Bob Hope try to coax Steve out of the latter's dressing room, and when Milton leaves, Bob has a breakthrough of sorts with Steve—literally, as the worried comedian busts his hand through the door to thank Bob for talking him out of his fears. Bob reminds Steve that all the comedians attending the show tonight are right behind him but adds, "And next time, we'd like seats in front!" Like the rest of the show, Bob's bit has its moments but could and should have been better.

Bob and Show: \*\*\*

*George Burns' 100th Birthday Party*
Jan. 22, 1979, CBS Monday 8-9 p.m.

George Burns. Guests: Milton Berle, Debby Boone, Pat Boone, Johnny Carson, Andy Gibb, Goldie Hawn, Bob Hope, George Jessel, Dean Martin, Steve Martin, Gregory Peck, Helen Reddy, Don Rickles, James Stewart, Gloria Stewart, Henny Youngman. EP: Irving Fein. P/D: Stan Harris. W: Fred S. Fox, Hal Goldman, Seaman Jacobs.

Bob Hope and Johnny Carson open this special with a bit taped during a recent appearance by Bob on *The Tonight Show* couch. "Bob, how about that George Burns, celebrating his 100th birthday?" "Yeah, they talk about the second half, this guy's on his third half!" "Yeah, it just shows you straight men live longer." "You ought to know." Johnny hits back with implying he's younger than Bob, who responds, "You know, you could be replaced. And you usually are." It's good interplay between the two here and sets up a show where George (actually eighty-three) is more endearing than the scripted lines he and many of his guests dispense.

Bob: \*\*\*\* Show: \*\*\*

## The Leif Garrett Special
May 18, 1979, CBS Friday 8-9 p.m.

Host: Leif Garrett. Guests: Bob Hope, Marie Osmond, Brooke Shields, Pink Lady, Flip Wilson. EP: Syd Vinnedge, Tony Scotti. P/D: Bob Henry. W: Rod Warren, Stephen Spears. Music: Michael Lloyd. Choreographer: Scott Salmon.

Amid many dim moments here—a messy U.S. debut of Pink Lady, a Japanese singing duo who a year later starred in *Pink Lady and Jeff*, one of the worst TV shows ever; Flip Wilson in drag as Geraldine, dancing with 17-year-old Leif as the latter lip syncs to "Runaround Sue"; Leif singing a ballad of undying love to both Brooke Shields and Marie Osmond simultaneously—Bob is incandescent. He opens the special with "I've never been on a show hosted by someone so young. I didn't know whether to applaud or burp him!" Bob reappears after Leif performs "I Was Made for Dancing" and shows clips from his show business career, including his audition as Lucille Ball's son in the movie *Mame* (!). As legendary bluesman Howling Wolf Hope ("My real name's Priscilla"), Bob cracks up Leif describing his tough neighborhood ("Anybody with teeth was a coward!"). He worked in a joint so cheap the stripper and his bass player had to use the same G string, and his steadiest job was flower girl for Mickey Rooney's wedding reception. Bob commits to this character well, helped by sporting dark glasses that cover his eyes looking at cue cards. Later he does a monologue and quips, "We teenage idols have to stick together" but mocks Leif's long blond locks with "He has a family of four living in his hair," along with dance crazes, recent films and more. Bob's set is fantastic—and much better than this froth deserves.

Bob: ***** Show: **

## Barbara Mandrell & the Mandrell Sisters
Jan. 3, 1981, Saturday 8-9 p.m.

Barbara Mandrell, Irlene Mandrell, Louise Mandrell. Guests: Bob Hope, Marty Robbins. P: Sid & Marty Krofft.

Barbara calls Bob "a big city boy" as he comes out in an orange cowboy hat and beige leisure suit. He tells her he could've been J.R.

Ewing on *Dallas* before she mockingly complains about the outfit she had to wear on his special in 1980 made her look like a boy ("Twelve-year-old boy?! Fourteen, maybe!" he says to her hysteria). He clearly loves talking to her and hugging her and singing "Buttons and Bows" with her. Bob is even more enchanting later when her two sisters join them ("A smorgasbord!") and they all joke as they fawn over him. Too bad the skits involving Irlene (playing dumb) are loud and unfunny. The musical numbers by Robbins and "Truck Shackley and the Texas Critters" (a five-piece country band composed of puppets) are a mixed bag too, as is this show.

Bob: ***** Show: ***

*All-Star Inaugural Gala*
Jan. 19, 1981, ABC Monday 10-11 p.m.

Host: Johnny Carson. Performers: Debby Boone, Grace Bumbry, Charlton Heston, Bob Hope, Rich Little, Dean Martin, Ethel Merman, Donny and Marie Osmond, Charley Pride, James Stewart, Mel Tillis, Ben Vereen. Special Guest: Gen. Omar Bradley. EP/D: Marty Pasetta. P: Michael Seligman.

Fine work by Bob, Johnny Carson, Ethel Merman and Frank Sinatra (the show's "producer/director and director of entertainment") cannot compensate for the other acts' overlong, bland sets in this salute to incoming President Ronald Reagan. It's particularly bad seeing Ben Vereen dressed in blackface as vaudeville minstrel comic Bert Williams. That aside, Bob fares well in a condensed set with jabs at Carson ("He seldom appears on a network he doesn't own.") and the actor turned incoming chief executive ("It's the greatest victory for Hollywood since George Burns became God."). His best if somewhat partisan laughs are at Washington, D.C. "Where else would a welfare office have valet parking?" he asks, adding that former Democratic presidential candidate George McGovern was his usher. Bob's real drawback is relying heavily on cue cards, though thankfully less so when he gives a warm introduction to James Stewart and a wheelchair-bound Gen. Omar Bradley.

Bob: **** Show: **

### *A Love Letter to Jack Benny*
Feb. 5, 1981, Thursday 9-11 p.m.

Hosts: George Burns, Johnny Carson, Bob Hope. P: Frederick de Cordova, Irving Fein. D: Norman Abbott. W: Hal Goldman, Hugh Wedlock Jr.

The three hosts read scripted lines to a laugh track in introducing skits from the 1960s and 1970s color specials of Jack Benny. Bob fumbles one line early and Johnny mocks it, prompting Bob to mock protest, "You don't like my timing?" Otherwise, the hosts muster as much enthusiasm as they can between bits sitting in chairs. This is occasionally funny, but it could have been much better if they showed Benny's best work from his 1950-1965 regular TV series.

Bob and Show: ***

### *Marie*
Sept. 12, 1981, Saturday 9-10 p.m.

Hostess: Marie Osmond. Guests: Nell [Ruth] Carter, Bob Hope, Jimmy Osmond.

After performing "Celebration," Marie Osmond prepares to introduce her show when a tuxedoed Bob yells out "Fore!" and carries a golf club with him on stage. She does a nose joke about him and he responds, "A nasty Osmond!" He calls *The Shining* a movie made about Marie's teeth, while she says *The Big Red One* was inspired by his proboscis. "That's two!" Bob responds. Later, Bob meets Marie during an airport sketch as themselves and they sing and dance to "On the Road Again" and "Gotta Travel On." As with her previous series *Donny & Marie*, the overall emphasis is on cuteness that overwhelms its effectiveness, and this series will end its abbreviated second season just two weeks after this show, but Bob's contribution is fine, and his adoration for Marie is obvious throughout.

Bob: *** Show: **

### *Get High on Yourself*
Sept. 20, 1981, Sunday 8-9 p.m.

Participants: Cathy Lee Crosby, Muhammad Ali, Carol Burnett,

Andrae Crouch, John Davidson, Julius Erving, Andy Gibb, Linda Gray, Rosey Grier, Dorothy Hamill, Bob Hope, Al Jarreau, Earvin "Magic" Johnson, Paul Newman, Ted Nugent, Peaches and Herb, Victoria Principal, Henry Winkler. EP: Cathy Lee Crosby, David Tate. P: Robert Evans, Tony Lombardo.

Larry Wilcox, star of *CHiPs* (whose show is pre-empted by this special), tells viewers at the outset that this program kicks off "Get High on Yourself" week on NBC. Henry Winkler explains its purpose more explicitly: to get Americans to care more about their children to reject drugs. Movie executive Robert Evans produces this special to fulfill his own substance abuse issues, and it is sincere if somewhat forced in having everything from Burt Reynolds talking to teens about their challenges to an all-star cast recording the campaign's theme song. Bob gets applause when he arrives at the taping and sings with Muhammad Ali, garnering laughs when he says Ali has "the Rudy Vallee key" in the number. He also dances with Cheryl Tiegs and some children and has a jubilant time recording with everyone in the studio for the chorus. This is fairly entertaining for an explicitly anti-drug public service show.

Bob and Show: ***


*George Burns' Early, Early, Early Christmas Special*
Nov. 16, 1981, CBS Monday 9-10 p.m.

George Burns. Guests: Bob Hope, The Playboy Playmates, Hans Conried, The Hawkins Family, Ann-Margret. EP: Irving Fein. P/D: Walter C. Miller. W: Fred S. Fox, Hal Goldman, Seaman Jacobs. Music: Jack Elliott.

This special is so convoluted that it incongruously pairs the spiritual Hawkins Family with five buxom and talent challenged Playboy Playmates to sing "Jingle Bells" at the end. In fact, the Playmates open the show pulling George in a sleigh and even sing and do a soft shoe routine with George with sand on the stage! Between them and Ann-Margret doing banter with George and a number with singers, Bob's role here is small. Calling the host "the Peter Pan of the prune juice set," his monologue ranges from solid ("This year I'm staying in California to entertain a complete group of strangers—my family") to shaky (a tired Phyllis Diller reference that even he apologizes for doing afterward). He and George do a tiresome bit where George implies he's entertained troops all the way back to the Revolutionary War and has Bob leave by supposedly playing a fife as part of a three-man band. His appearance as Santa near the end is similarly inconsequential. George is fine as always, including interacting with Scrooge (Hans Conried in one of the latter's last TV appearances before his death on Jan. 5, 1982).

Bob and Show: ***

## *American Film Institute Salutes Frank Capra*
April 4, 1982, CBS Sunday 9:30-11 p.m.

Host: James Stewart. Guests: Frank Capra, Claudette Colbert, Bette Davis, Peter Falk, Bob Hope, Jack Lemmon, Steve Martin, Donna Reed, Telly Savalas.

Hope is sitting at the honoree's table and drops the humor in favor of heartfelt comments about how he loves the legendary director and reads a telegram from President Ronald Reagan. This is a nice moment, and the other reminisces are even better.

Bob: *** Show: ****

## *NBC All Star Hour*
Sept. 12, 1983, Monday 8-9 p.m.

Cast: Ted Danson (Sam Malone), Shelley Long (Diane Chambers), Rhea Perlman (Carla Tortelli), Nicholas Colasanto ("Coach" Ernie Pantusso), John Ratzenberger (Cliff Clavin), George Wendt (Norm Peterson). Presenters: Byron Allen, Conrad Bain, Ed Begley Jr., Pierce Brosnan, Nell Carter, Gary Coleman, Erin Gray, David Hasselhoff, Joel Higgins, Ann Jillian, Vicki Lawrence, Sarah Purcell, Skip Stephenson, Dolph Sweet, Michael Warren, Betty White, Stephanie Zimbalist. Featured: Army Archerd, Tom Byrd, Johnny Carson, Bob Hope, David Letterman. EP: Peter Calabrese, Don Mischer (also D). W: Bob Sand, Tom Leopold, Dennis Rinsler, Marc Warren, Arlene Sand, Richard Steel.

*Mr. Smith, Jennifer Slept Here, We Got It Made, Manimal, Boone, The Rousters, For Love and Honor, The Yellow Rose*, and *Bay City Blues* comprised one of the worst new slates of fall TV programs ever. Johnny Carson (who appears briefly here as Carnac) astutely noted after they flopped that "NBC stands for Nine Bombs Cancelled." That's more entertaining than most of this preview special. The flimsy setup has the gang from the sitcom *Cheers* watching this show from their bar as Diane the waitress dreams that she is in it to pitch her series idea. The film portion goes to a bright videotape as current NBC series stars introduce clips and cast members from the new shows while the *Cheers* crew play themselves at the party. As part of the forced frivolity, Bob encounters the latter to exchange mostly lame gags. "I haven't had this much fun since I short sheeted Dorothy Lamour's sarong," he tells Norm, who offers to become Bob's new accountant. "I don't think I'll be interested, but maybe Carson needs somebody," Bob weakly responds. After being befuddled by Coach, Bob quips, "There are place in that guy's brain where no man should go." Carla's encounter lets Bob promote his special that will be in this slot next week. Clad in a tuxedo, Bob delivers all his lines with a minimum of effort. Given the overall cheesy quality of the comedy, singing and dancing here, it's hard to blame him for doing so.

Bob and Show: **

## *George Burns Celebrates 80 Years in Show Business*
Sept. 19, 1983, Monday 9:30-11 p.m.

Host: John Forsythe. Honoree: George Burns. Guests: Ann-Margret, Milton Berle, Red Buttons, Johnny Carson, Jack Carter, Carol Channing, Phyllis Diller, Larry Gatlin and the Gatlin Brothers, The Rev. Billy Graham, Shecky Greene, Buddy Hackett, Bob Hope, Bernadette Peters, Don Rickles, Kenny Rogers, Danny Thomas, Fred Travalena, Dionne Warwick. P: Irving Fein, Walter C. Miller. D: Walter C. Miller. W: Hal Goldman, Fred S. Fox, Seaman Jacobs. Music: Peter Matz.

This feels like an All-Star Tribute show, as celebrity guests stand up at tables facing the stage to do variable bits for the title honoree, with John Forsythe saddled with corny commentary. After Buddy Hackett, Danny Thomas, and Milton Berle do unlikely sex jokes, and Kenny Rogers and Bernadette Peters sing five songs, Bob provides a needed jolt with a superb set. Noting that in attendance is "Rev. Graham, St. Thomas [a reference to Danny's Catholicism] and God [George's movie role]," Bob riffs sweetly on George's age. "George is funny, but he'd rather be a sex symbol. A few of us have the good fortune to be both." Bob then smiles nervously, getting more laughs. He adds, "George has written a book offering sex advice. Along from his other talents, he has a great memory." He ends with a special version of "Thanks for the Memory" with warm lyrics that he sings very well. Only Red Buttons and Shecky Greene match him here for laughs. The segments with Johnny Carson, Carol Channing and Don Rickles are obviously taped separately, adding to this special's disjointed nature. The oddest moment has to be seeing soul superstar Marvin Gaye sitting in the audience just months before his untimely death. Why he was there and what he thought about the show is anyone's guess.

Bob: **** Show: ***

*Here's Television Entertainment*
Dec. 4, 1983, Sunday 9-11 p.m.

Steve Allen, Burt Bacharach, Carol Burnett, Dick Clark, Bob Hope, Michael Landon, Marie Osmond, Patti Page, Carol Bayer Sager, Dinah Shore, Ben Vereen, Dionne Warwick. P/D: Dwight Hemion. P: Gary Smith. W: Larry Grossman, Buz Kohan.

A tribute to the musical variety genre, this is loaded with classic clips between the guests. They are in order Dinah Shore singing about the difficulty of doing musical numbers live; Patti Page introducing vocalists' early TV appearances; Steve Allen doing the same for musicians; Carol Burnett surveying Emmy-winning variety series and specials; Dick Clark narrating rock and roll appearances; Michael Landon showing examples of actors who tried to croon; Marie Osmond singing as well as showing family musical acts; Ben Vereen tripping the light fantastic amid recordings of older production numbers; Burt Bacharach and Carol Bayer Sager spotlighting composers and lyricists whose work appeared on the medium along with singer/songwriters; Dionne Warwick remembering those who were lost; and Bob warmly wrapping it all up. Some of the commentary and presentations are too precious, but the rare clips are expertly presented, and Dionne's song "Gone Too Soon" will later become a familiar ballad when Michael Jackson sings it on his 1993 album *Dangerous* (and ironically, Usher will sing it at Jackson's funeral in 2009).

Bob: *** Show: ****

***The Dean Martin Celebrity Roast of Mr. T***
March 14, 1984, Wednesday 8-9 p.m.

Host: Dean Martin. Honoree. Mr. T. Guests: Bob Hope, George Peppard, Don Rickles, Gary Coleman, Nell Carter, Ann Jillian, Gavin MacLeod, Ricky Schroder, Howard Cosell, Rich Little, Maureen Murphy, Red Buttons, Dick Shawn, Slappy White. EP/D: Greg Garrison. P: Lee Hale. W: Harry Crane, Tom Finnigan, Howard Albrecht, Sol Weinstein, Bill Box, Jay Burton, David Axlerod, Stan Burns.

This is near the end of the line for these kind of roasts, and it shows. Dean Martin barely feigns interest in delivering his lines, and the guests who are not comedians are nearly intolerable to watch (for example, Gary Coleman wears gold chains around his neck to pretend he is the guest of honor, and Ricky Schroder could not get away today with his politically incorrect version of "Little Red Riding Hood"). Nearly halfway through, Bob delivers a mild monologue that nevertheless is better than the show overall, with lines like "He's an intimidating young man. When we were in Hawaii, I took him to a luau, and when we sat down, the pig choked on the apple" and "He's got muscles in places where I don't have places." At least Mr. T laughs at the jokes thrown at him more realistically than most of the other attendees.

Bob: *** Show: **

***George Burns How to Live to Be 100***
Sept. 17, 1984, CBS Monday 10-11 p.m.

Host: George Burns. Guests: Catharine Bach, Diahann Carroll, Bob Hope, Arte Johnson, The Los Angeles Rams Cheerleaders. Sketch Performers: Lou Felder, Jerome Guardino, Janet Hillis, Cynthia Songe, Todd Susman, Wayne Ward, Lucy Webb. P: Irving Fein, Walter C. Miller. D: Walter C. Miller. W: Hal Goldman, Fred S. Fox, Seaman Jacobs, Harvey Berger. Music: Peter Matz.

George introduces deadly dull and dumb skits that weigh down this special (e.g., Arte Johnson plays his old man character Tyrone from *Laugh-In* sexually harassing Dr. Joyce Brothers in a cameo appearance). Disrupting the torpor at the twenty-four-minute mark is Bob, who gets a standing ovation and is ready to roll about the host with great lines. "Last week George tried to get into the Beverly Hills Senior Citizens Club, but they wouldn't take him because he passed the physical ... He was one of the original Minute Men. Now he's down to five seconds." Bob says George once worked with a woman named Margarita and "You couldn't kiss her unless she had salt on her lips." He adds, "He tried to get a transplant, but he has body parts they don't make any more." The men sing together and hug afterward. Bob reappears to deliver the capper for an awful sketch to humorously plug his upcoming bloopers special. He's much better than the alleged comedy shown here, apart from George's typically solid work.

Bob: **** Show: **

### *The Third Annual NBC All Star Hour*
Sept. 16, 1985, Monday 8-9 p.m.

Guests Include: Nell Carter, Don Johnson, Philip Michael Thomas, Saundra Santiago, Olivia Brown, Beatrice Arthur, Betty White, Rue McClanahan, Estelle Getty, Lisa Bonet, Kim Fields, Charlotte Rae, Perry King, Don Penny, Thom Bray, Bob Hope, Stepfanie Kramer, George Peppard, Keshia Knight Pulliam. P: Peter Calabrese. D: Don Mischer. W: Doug Steckler, Mitzie Welch, Ken Welch, Mason Williams. Music: Bob Rozario. Choreographer: Walter Painter.

The last installment of the network's annual variety special/fall preview is cheesy kitsch from watching Nell Carter trying to emulate Patti LaBelle doing "New Attitude" at the start to all of the black tie audience getting on stage to "sing" and clap that year's theme song, "Let's All Be There." Bob shows up in good spirits to tell the regulars on *Riptide* (Perry King, Don Penny, and Thom Bray) he plans to take over the network and will reveal more on his special airing on NBC tomorrow night before introducing Stepfanie Kramer, Saundra Santiago, and Olivia Brown performing Glenn Frey's hit "The Heat is On" with male dancers dressed like cops. It's that kind of a show.

Bob and Show: ***

### *George Burns' 90th Birthday: A Very Special Special*
Jan. 17, 1986, CBS Friday 8-9 p.m.

George Burns. Guests: Ann-Margret, Diahann Carroll, Billy Crystal, John Denver, John Forsythe, Walter Matthau. Cameos in order of appearance: Bill Cosby, Phylicia Rashad, Kenny Rogers, Bob Hope, Don Rickles, Frank Sinatra, Joe Piscopo, Johnny Carson, Steve Allen, Cary Grant, Red Buttons, James Stewart, Chevy Chase, Carol Channing, Milton Berle, Jack Lemmon, Brooke Shields, Danny Thomas, Rich Little, President Ronald Reagan. P: Irving Fein, Walter C. Miller. D: Walter C. Miller. W: Hal Goldman. Music: Peter Matz.

With a plethora of rarely seen and genuinely funny clips of George's movie and TV appearances, plus mini-tributes from A-list guests and long, warm, heartfelt ones from those in the main cast, this is a wonderful celebration to behold. Bob's bit, taped during his latest special, is quick but lands fine: "Hey George, you're amazing. You can still do it all. And on the stage you're not bad either!" George outshines them all at the end with a little dancing and a strong monologue. "I'm going to stay in show business until I'm the only one left ... I never let my hair down. I'm lucky if I can keep it on ... I don't want to get serious here. I'll see when I'm 100." Indeed, like Bob, he too became a centenarian.

Bob and Show: \*\*\*\*


## *Comic Relief*
March 29, 1986, HBO Saturday 9 p.m.-1 a.m.

Hosts: Billy Crystal, Robin Williams, Whoopi Goldberg. Performers: Steve Allen, Harry Anderson, Phil Austin, Richard Belzer, Peter Bergman, Anne Bloom, Danny Breen, Sid Caesar, John Candy, George Carlin, Michael Davis, Michael J. Fox, Bobcat Goldthwait, Mary Gross, Pee-Wee Herman (Paul Reubens), Madeline Kahn, Michael Keaton, Mitchell Laurance, Eugene Levy, Jerry Lewis, Jon Lovitz, Howie Mandel, Dennis Miller, Laraine Newman, Catherine O'Hara, Stuart Pankin, Minnie Pearl, Joe Piscopo, Phil Proctor, Gilda Radner, Harold Ramis, Carl Reiner, Paul Rodriguez, Garry Shandling, Martin Short, Lucy Webb, George Wendt, Weird Al Yankovic, Henny Youngman. Guests: Tom Bradley, Tony Danza, Richard Dreyfuss, Chris Elliott, Estelle Getty, Dick Gregory, Robert Guillaume, Bob Hope, David Letterman, Penny Marshall, Walter Matthau, Rob Reiner, Paul Shaffer, Dick Van Dyke, Bob Zmuda. Music: Doc Severinsen. EP: John Moffitt, Pat Tourk Lee, Bob Zmuda. Co-P: Jacques Fiorentino. D: Walter C. Miller. W: Buz Kohan, Steve Barker, Anne Beatts, Matt Neuman, Tom Perew, Lane Sarasohn, Stu Silver, Alan Zweibel, Gilda Radner. Special Musical Material: Tom Rizzo, Marc Shaiman, Jimmie

Haskell, Earl Brown. Choreographer: Lester Wilson.

Many of America's top comedians join forces to combat homelessness with a live comedy concert crossed with fundraiser emanating from Los Angeles at the Universal Amphitheater. It's a worthy effort with many classic routines being recreated and new material being presented as well, broken up by bits on film, mostly the "guests" urging home viewers to contribute to the cause. One of those is Bob Hope, and while he would seem like a natural for this sort of thing, it's not one of his better appearances. The visuals of him in a golf cap on a course imply he is a rich guy who would rather spend his time on the links than hang out with his fellow humorists and give more of his time to a good cause. Even worse, Bob decides to use the occasion to compare the homelessness problem in America with that in Russia, not a smart move here, and his other gags are nothing to celebrate either. Bob does pitch sincerely for people to pledge their monetary support for the campaign, but with his appearance's brevity and context, one is left with the opinion that Bob's position as a leading comedian is fading fast while many others in this show are raising theirs.

Bob: ** Show: ****

## NBC 60th Anniversary Celebration
May 12, 1986, Monday 8-11 p.m.

Steve Allen, Fran Allison, Harry Anderson, Bea Arthur, Gene Barry, Milton Berle, Tempest Bledsoe, Tom Brokaw, Pierce Brosnan, Raymond Burr, Red Buttons, Sid Caesar, Macdonald Carey, Johnny Carson, Nell Carter, Connie Chung, Dick Clark, Robert Conrad, Robert Culp, Ted Danson, Don DeFore, Angie Dickinson, Hugh Downs, Barbara Eden, Ralph Edwards, Nanette Fabray, Kim Fields, Michael J. Fox, Arlene Francis, Soleil Moon Frye, Estelle Getty, Marla Gibbs, Melissa Gilbert, George Gobel, Lorne Greene, Deidre Hall, Valerie Harper, Julie Harris, David Hasselhoff, Ed Herlihy, Bob Hope, Don Johnson, Perry King, Jack Klugman, Hope Lange, Sabrina La Boeuf, Jerry Lester, Shari Lewis and Lamb Chop, Hal Linden, Norman Lloyd, Shelley Long, Gloria Loring, Peter Marshall, Dick Martin, Rue McClanahan, Ed McMahon, Mitch Miller, Edwin Newman, Merlin Olsen, Jack Paar, Patti Page, Bert Parks, George Peppard, Rhea Perlman, Keshia Knight Pulliam, Sarah Purcell, Charlotte Rae, John Ratzenberger, Gene Rayburn, Martha Raye, Carl

Reiner, Alfonso Ribiero, Joan Rivers, Doris Roberts, Dan Rowan, Pat Sajak, Ricky Schroder, Doc Severinsen, Dinah Shore, Buffalo Bob Smith and Howdy Doody, Robert Stack, Craig Stevens, Mary Stuart, Phillip Michael Thomas, Daniel J. Travanti, Robert Vaughn, Malcolm Jamal Warner, Betty White, Jonathan Winters, Jane Wyatt, Robert Young. EP: Alexander H. Cohen. P/W: Hildy Parks. D: Clark Jones. Music: Elliott Lawrence.

Bob introduces the celebration by saying he's taking the tour of NBC's New York City studios, then vanishes amid an overdone, six-minute-long production number involving female dancers dressed as peacocks and seven peppy tapping tour guides involving Keshia Knight Pulliam and Malcolm Jamal Warner, stars of *The Cosby Show*. The tour serves as a basis for a good but not great summation of the network's history hampered by the phoniness of the setup. Bob shows up a half hour later to introduce and narrate the story of NBC's radio series, which segues into his own program and clips of his overseas shows for radio and TV. He clearly enjoys reminiscing about them and singing "Be a Clown" to Michael J. Fox later in the special, although that is hurt by a fake circus appearing around them for another too-glitzy number. In addition, he hosts another segment on variety specials, TV-movies and miniseries; Dinah Shore presents a mini-tribute to him; and clips of guest shots with him outside his specials appear as well.

Bob: ***** Show: ***

## *All-Star Tribute to General Jimmy Doolittle*
Aug. 18, 1986, Syndicated Two hours

Host: Glen Campbell. Guests: Phyllis Diller, Jimmy Doolittle, Andy Gibb, Scott Grimes, Bob Hope, Delores Hope, Rich Little, Jack Jones, Shirley Jones, Don Knotts, Audrey Landers, The Lennon Sisters, Brooke Shields, James Stewart. Taped Tributes: George Burns, Johnny Carson, President Gerald Ford, Sen. Barry Goldwater, Charlton Heston, Loretta Lynn, Lee Marvin, President Ronald Reagan, Alan Shepard. EP: Bob Hope. D: Bob Wynn. W: Fred S. Fox, Gig Henry, Seaman Jacobs, Robert L. Mills, Gene Perret. Music: Bob Alberti.

A Hope Enterprises special airing on individual stations in late summer rather than NBC (a distinction leading to its inclusion here despite not being viewed), this celebrates an event that actually will happen four months later. Gen. Jimmy Doolittle won the Congressional Medal of Honor for his efforts in aviation combat in World War II, and a host of singers and stars in person and previously recorded come out to pay tribute to him. The taping occurs near the general's residence at San Diego's Miramar Naval Air Station.

### *All Star Party for Clint Eastwood*
Nov. 30, 1986, CBS Sunday 8-9 p.m.

Host: Lucille Ball. Guests: Sammy Davis Jr., Clint Eastwood, Roberta Flack, Cary Grant, Merv Griffin, Monty Hall, Bob Hope, Marsha Mason, Don Rickles, Don Siegel, James Stewart. Music: Nick Perito. P: Paul W. Keyes. D/W: Dick McDonough.

A star-studded audience comes out in force to honor one of their own. Bob appears after Roberta sings her hit "The First Time Ever I Saw Your Face" from Clint's first movie he directed, *Play Misty for Me*, and he falters with a few inside jokes and questionable bits like "How about Clint's hair? I didn't know Stevie Wonder still had the barbershop!" He does score in saying that as mayor of Carmel, California, Clint sends out a SWAT team to collect overdue library books. Regarding Clint's movie *Paint Your Wagon*, the honoree cracked up when Bob cracks, "When Clint sings, that's violence!" Frankly, Don Rickles is much funnier following him. Contributions by Cary Grant, Sammy Davis Jr., and James Stewart make it a winner overall.

Bob: *** Show: ****

### *Emmanuel Lewis: My Very Own Show*
Feb. 13, 1987, ABC Friday 8:30-9:30 p.m.

Host: Emmanuel Lewis. Guests: Bob Hope, Sammy Davis Jr., Debbie Allen, The Los Angeles Raiders, Siegfried and Roy, Paul Rodriguez, Rene Auberjonois, Victoria Jackson, Shelley Berman. P/W: George Schlatter. D: Paul Miller. W: Bob Arnott.

The diminutive star of the sitcom *Webster* meets with network executives (played by those listed after Paul Rodriguez) to plan his special. The cuteness and cheesiness factor here is off the charts and tedious, with Emmanuel doing a long medley of rock tunes with Debbie Allen and a bunch of tweens, acting as a circus ringleader, making a music video with the L.A. Raiders and more. His time with Bob is its liveliest part along with a song-and-dance routine with Sammy Davis Jr. Bob loses to the host in a game of golf, pays him a dollar for the bet, then takes back the cash when Emmanuel asks him for advice. Bob: "In show business, if you got talent, charm and good looks, you don't need anything else." Emmanuel: "Is that why you have so many writers?" This has good interplay, ending with a shuffle by the two on a bench.

Bob: **** Show: **


## *Happy Birthday Hollywood*
May 18, 1987, ABC Monday 8-11 p.m.

Debbie Allen, June Allyson, Ed Asner, Drew Barrymore, Hinton Battle, Sandahl Bergman, Tom Bosley, Morgan Brittany, Charles Bronson, Gregg Burge, Carol Burnett, Dean Butler, Sid Caesar, Lynda Carter, Cyd Charisse, James Coburn, Dabney Coleman, Mike Connors, Don Correia, Arlene Dahl, Sammy Davis Jr., Angie Dickinson, Nancy Dussault, Clint Eastwood, Barbara Eden, Morgan Fairchild, Alice Faye, Bonnie Franklin, Mary Frann, Gil Gerard, Lillian Gish, Whoopi Goldberg, Louis Gossett Jr., Gregory Harrison, Mary Hart, Florence Henderson, Katharine Hepburn, Charlton Heston, Bob Hope, Jill Ireland, Van Johnson, Shirley Jones, Ruby Keeler, Jayne Kennedy-Overton, Stepfanie Kramer, Patti LaBelle, Dorothy Lamour, Burt Lancaster, Michele Lee, Janet Leigh, Shari Lewis, Lorna Luft, Marlee Matlin, Marilyn McCoo, Ann Miller, Donna Mills, Liza Minnelli, Roger Moore, Steve Morris, Donald O'Connor, Maureen O'Sullivan, Gregory Peck, Nia Peeples, Bernadette Peters, Ali Porter, Jane Powell, Stefanie Powers, Luise Rainer, Sheryl Lee Ralph, Lee Roy Reams, Burt Reynolds, Debbie Reynolds, John Ritter, Jason Robards, Ginger Rogers, Jill St. John, Eva Marie Saint, Tracy Scoggins, William Shatner, Ally Sheedy, Jaclyn Smith, James Stewart, Susan Sullivan, Loretta Swit, Lana Turner, Joan Van Ark, Robert Wagner, Dee Wallace Stone, Betty White, Esther Williams, Treat Williams, Henry Winkler, Loretta Young. EP: Jack Haley Jr., Alexander H. Cohen. P/D: Jeff Margolis. P/W: Hildy Parks.

This overlong, overstuffed special is like an endless musical number from an Oscars ceremony, with awkward transitions, corny repartee, and an overextended and jumbled mix of on-stage and previously filmed content. The mixture of A-listers with obscurities like Ali Porter doesn't help either, and there's dozens of others who appear briefly that aren't listed in the main credits to boot. At least Bob comes out well in warmly and confidently saying how much enjoyed working in Hollywood as he introduces a salute to dancers on the silver screen, one of the few moments that really shines.

Bob: \*\*\*\* Show: \*\*


## *That's What Friends Are For: AIDS Concert*
1988, Showtime 90 minutes

Bob Hope, Dionne Warwick, Burt Bacharach, Expose, Howard Hewett, Lena Horne, Elton John, George Kirby, Gladys Knight, Barry Manilow, Yakov Smirnoff, Leslie Uggams, Blair Underwood, Luther Vandross, Mary Wilson, Stevie Wonder. Special Appearances: Sugar Ray Leonard, Kelly McGillis, Catherine Oxenberg, Dustin Nguyen, Robert Townsend, Holly Robinson. D: Don Weiner.

Bob addresses the attendees at the start of the event by saying, "Right now, there's a big need to let all the people of America know about the facts of AIDS. That's why we're here. This is a different kind of battle ... and whatever it takes, we're going to win this one." It is an impassioned concert for a good cause, and Bob does his part admirably.

Bob and Show: \*\*\*\*


## *Dolly*
April 9, 1988, ABC Saturday 8-9 p.m.

Dolly Parton. Guests: The Desert Rose Band, Bob Hope, Jerry Lee Lewis, Miss Piggy, Loretta Swit (Lawanda Novack), Ritch Brinkley (Charlie Boil). EP: Sandy Gallin. P: Don Mischer. Co-P/W: Jack Burns. D: Louis J. Horvitz. W: Phil Hahn, Ann Elder, Brett Butler, Rhea Kohan, Tom Perew, Buddy Sheffield.

The country superstar sings an upbeat opening number before having a joke session with her audience that slogs along. Her talk with Miss Piggy is better, followed by Bob as a city slicker trying to make a sale to a cowgirl (Dolly). "I'm showing my wares, but not as well as you are," he says, looking at her figure. He maximizes all the comic lines, which are pretty good. When Dolly complains, "I don't want to wear all those frilly things with buttons and bows," Bob says, "There's a song cue if I ever heard one. Hit it, boys!" When the music doesn't come in, he adds, "Boy, you can sure tell when it's not your show, can't you?" Dolly finally does have the band do "Buttons and Bows" with new lyrics. She thanks him afterward, and he clearly adores being with her. That's all for Bob, but the rest with Miss Piggy "going country," the Desert Rose Band and Jerry Lee Lewis singing, and Loretta Swit playing an old friend of Dixie the waitress (Dolly) who meets patron Charlie Boil in a dramatic skit is easy to take. Unfortunately, this series already is on its way to being cancelled in its first season by the time this airs.

Bob: **** Show: ***

## *Irving Berlin's 100th Birthday Celebration*
May 27, 1988, CBS Friday 9-11 p.m.

Beatrice Arthur, Tony Bennett, Barry Bostwick, Nell Carter, Ray Charles, Rosemary Clooney, Natalie Cole, Walter Cronkite, Billy Eckstine, Michael Feinstein, ASCAP President Morton Gould, Bob Hope, Marilyn Horne, Madeline Kahn, Garrison Keillor, Shirley MacLaine, Maureen McGovern, Willie Nelson, Jerry Orbach, Maryann Plunkett, Diane Schuur, Frank Sinatra, Isaac Stern, Tommy Tune, Joe Williams, The Boy Scouts of America, The Girl Scouts of America, The U.S. Army Chorus, The U.S. Army Training Center. Music: Elliot Lawrence. EP: Don Mischer. P: Jan Cornell, David J. Goldberg. D: Walter C. Miller.

Broadway's best comes to Carnegie Hall to honor a legend in this classy special with only a few weak moments when some singers are not quite up to snuff in doing justice to the lyrics and music. Bob appears in a pretaped bit that follows a clip when Berlin did a radio show with him. He recalls how he first met the great songwriter in the 1930s and humorously recounts some of the wilder tune titles Berlin created before sincerely wishing him a happy birthday.

Bob and Show: ****

## *Sammy Davis Jr.'s 60th Anniversary Celebration*
Feb. 4, 1990, ABC Sunday 8:30-11 p.m.

Host: Eddie Murphy. Guests: Debbie Allen, Anita Baker, Diahann Carroll, Nell Carter, Bill Cosby, Tony Danza, Clint Eastwood, Lola Falana,

Ella Fitzgerald, Goldie Hawn, Gregory Hines, Bob Hope, Whitney Houston, Michael Jackson, Quincy Jones, Shirley MacLaine, Dean Martin, Gregory Peck, Richard Pryor, Frank Sinatra, Mike Tyson, Dionne Warwick, Stevie Wonder. P: George Schlatter. D: Jeff Margolis. Music: Glen Roven.

The stars come out for this tribute that is as electric and eclectic as the talent they honor. Plenty of rare vintage clips enhance the segments introduced by the guests, all of whom shine. Eddie Murphy is at his most gracious and very funny as well. Bob comes out following bloopers from his 1984 special with Sammy and scores by opening with "I'm here to talk about Sammy Davis the saint. Good night." He mentioned his charity work before saying they were things like for the "Zsa Zsa Gabor Driving School Foundation," and some other lines. However, his delivery is slowing, and the show goes to clips apparently without Bob finishing his monologue.

Bob: \*\*\*\* Show: \*\*\*\*\*

*America's All-Star Tribute to Oprah Winfrey*
Sept. 18, 1990, ABC Tuesday 10-11 p.m.

Host: Bob Hope. Honoree: Oprah Winfrey. Guest: Whoopi Goldberg.

A celebration of the popular talk show hostess receiving the third annual America's Hope Award, this is held again at the Bob Hope Cultural Center in Palm Desert. Bob plays down the title of the facility, noting that "This is like naming a monastery after Madonna!" He does a few jokes about Gerald Ford's golfing and Sonny Bono's tenure as mayor before introducing the first presenter with "They named a cushion after her—Whoopi!" That leads into a virtual lovefest of Oprah's professional accomplishments by presenters along with clips, and it's pretty enjoyable as these sorts of shows go. Bob shows up at the celebratory closing as well.

Bob: \*\*\* Show: \*\*\*\*

*A Salute to America's Pets*
June 13, 1991, ABC Thursday 8-9 p.m.

Hosts: Rick Dees, Mary Frann, Marla Gibbs, Alex Trebek. Guests: Nina Blackwood, Dick Clark, Angie Dickinson, Bob Hope, Lily Tomlin, Betty White. EP: Bob Hope. P: Linda Hope, Loreen Arbus, Helaine

Swerdloff-Ross. D: Sid Smith. W: Jeffrey Barron, Steven Kunes.

Included here despite being unseen because it is a rare program from Bob's Hope Enterprises not to appear on NBC, this celebration of animals, their celebrity owners, and their tricks contains special tributes to Lassie and Dreyfuss, the St. Bernard on the sitcom *Empty Nest*. This somehow merited an Emmy nomination for Outstanding Individual Achievement in Music and Lyrics for Carol Connors and Jimmie Haskell's composition "Love Without Strings."

*Rosemary Clooney's Demi-Centennial: A Girl Singer's Golden Anniversary*
Nov. 11, 1995, A&E Saturday 9-10:30 p.m.

Star: Rosemary Clooney. Host/Narrator: Nick Clooney. Guest Artists: Lily Tomlin, Michael Feinstein, Debby Boone, Kathy Campbell. Special Cameo Appearances: Tony Bennett, George Clooney, Merv Griffin, Bob Hope, Bette Midler, Diane Sawyer, Joanne Woodward. EP: Terry A. Botwick, Allen Sviridoff. P: Victoria Lang, Scott H. Mauro. D: Richie Namm. W: Nick Clooney. Music: John Oddo.

Rosemary sounds beautiful singing alone with a five-piece band along with Lily Tomlin, Michael Feinstein, Debby Boone (her daughter-in-law) and Kathy Campbell (her niece), while her brother Nick helps recount her life story to viewers between numbers. Bob just provides a brief recollection. "I'll never forget when I was in Cincinnati fifty years ago, and I saw Rosemary and Betty [Clooney, Rosemary's sister, who had a solo career in the 1950s] and reported to NBC how good they were. Let me tell you, they didn't become great, they started out great." Expertly edited, Bob comes across well here, and his reminiscing about a woman he admired personally and professionally is a nice way for him to make his last major variety special appearance.

Bob: *** Show: ****

# 11 Guest Shots – Sitcoms, Dramas, One TV-Movie and One Cartoon

**APART FROM PAYING BACK FAVORS** with other entertainers, Bob's TV acting career is rather strange and unimpressive, with no rhyme or reason as to how or why they occurred. He acted on less than forty shows total, and nearly a quarter of those times can be described as cameos. Indeed, that was the case with his first two guest shots, *The Christophers: "You Can Change the World"* in 1949 (which ostensibly was meant to appear primarily in movie theaters, but its running time made it perfect to fill a half hour slot on any TV station), and a gag appearance at the end of an episode of *The Jack Benny Program* in March 1954. He played a full-fledged acting role on the same show two months later.

A couple of other shows featured Bob over the next six years, but none starred him for more than a minute or two until he made a memorable guest shot as himself being harassed comically by Lucille Ball on TV's number one series, *I Love Lucy*, in 1956, After that, Bob's TV acting appearances were almost all on *The Jack Benny Program* and *The Danny Thomas Show* until 1963, when he decided he wanted to host an hour-long anthology series which would allow him to act in a couple of shows as well.

Bob told NBC President Tom Sarnoff and Vice President in Charge of Business Affairs Herb Schlosser that he and his sponsor, Chrysler, wanted to solicit bids and choose which production company would be in charge of handling the package of new programs. Word went out in Hollywood, and Universal studio head Lew Wasserman told Dick Berg, his head of television production, that he wanted him to pitch the studio for the project.

For the live and hilarious "Hope and Benny in Agent's Office" episode of *The Jack Benny Program* on Feb. 24, 1957, Bob guest stars as himself opposite Jack Benny playing themselves during their days of struggle in vaudeville. Courtesy of Getty Images.

Berg crafted a filmed presentation explaining to Hope and executives at Chrysler and NBC why Universal deserved to do the series, stressing how the studio emphasized quality production and held the rights to remake for television its old movies plus those of Paramount from the 1930s that they owned too. "We came up with a half-hour montage with my introduction begging their acquiescence, and a couple of days later, Wasserman called to tell me we not only got the *Chrysler Theatre* but also *Kraft Suspense Theatre*," Berg told the Archive of American Television. Berg would be responsible for up to fifteen shows each season, while Bob Hope's production company would supply nine comedy hours and a few comedies with the comedian.

Incidentally, *Sponsor* magazine reported that *Bob Hope Presents the Chrysler Theatre* was the highest-priced weekly series on network TV, with an average budget of $230,000. That figure would be the equivalent of more than $1.8 million with inflation factored into it by 2017.

When *Bob Hope Presents the Chrysler Theatre* began on Sept. 27, 1963, it bore a rather pretentious opening, with Bob sitting on a moving camera crane to give the appearance he was somehow directing what followed, even though his attire of a pork pie hat and sweater was more appropriate for him to be on the links. Chrysler would flash a variety of its division names and logos before "Thanks for the Memory" would play, and Bob would enter through the curtains with the sponsor's primary symbol, the "pentastar," appearing behind him as he set up each week's offering.

The odd beginning segments were not as much as a disaster as were Bob's introductions, which often tried to be funny and failed. Consider how he described Walter Matthau on the March 3, 1964 episode "White Snow—Red Ice": "A great actor who plays the heavy with a light touch. You don't know whether to kiss him or hiss him."

Bob would appear at the end of every show to promote the next presentation, sometimes with its star, like Eva Marie Saint when they did the coming attraction routine for their episode "Her School for Bachelors." Without any response, this all came across as flat, so by the second season, Bob's portions had heavily dubbed applause for his entrance and laughter for his jokes. They even faked the clapping when Bob noted on the April 2, 1964 show of "Memorandum for a Spy" that co-star Albert Paulsen won an Emmy for his guest work on the series a year earlier!

What really made it bad was Bob's attempts to be a serious host that produced unintentional comedy. Imagine his face looking straight in the camera for the Dec. 20, 1963 Emmy-nominated production of "It's Mental Work" (a John O'Hara story adapted by Rod Serling), saying this: "This isn't one of the patent leather and chromium bistros. This is a sewer. The kind of place that's off limits for longshoremen." Actually, the way Bob did it, it was camp. To top it off, the handful of comedies in which Bob starred for the series were almost always dreadful and hurt his reputation as an actor.

Despite such problems, *Bob Hope Presents the Chrysler Theatre* was a mild hit in its first season, reaching Number Thirty in the ratings tied with *The Danny Kaye Show*, although given its weak competition (*Burke's Law* on ABC and *Route 66* in its last season on CBS), one could argue it should have done better. However, in its second season (1964-1965), *The*

*Addams Family* on ABC often out-rated the series when it did not show a Bob Hope special, and the series fell slightly to Number Thirty-Five.

That same season, Bob entered into an unusual three-way swap deal whereby he, Lucille Ball, and Jack Benny would all appear on each other's shows over the next year. It failed to save Jack's program, which had moved from CBS to NBC after fourteen years on TV but flopped opposite *Gomer Pyle, U.S.M.C.* on CBS. Jack was also the only one to have Bob and Lucy appear in separate episodes of his series, as all three turned up together on both *The Lucy Show* and *Bob Hope Presents the Chrysler Theatre*.

In the fall of 1965, *Bob Hope Presents the Chrysler Theatre* shifted from Fridays to Wednesdays opposite the sitcoms *Green Acres* and *The Dick Van Dyke Show* on CBS. Both were top twenty hits, and they drove down the average ratings for Bob's series to Number Fifty for the 1965-1966 season. When *Gomer Pyle* took over the slot for *The Dick Van Dyke Show* in the 1966-1967 season, *Bob Hope Presents the Chrysler Theatre* now had to grab viewers opposite two top ten hits.

Even given all this, *Bob Hope Presents the Chrysler Theatre* won lots of Emmy nominations (see the 1960s section for a full listing) and gave Bob additional prestige, including his third Peabody Award. It finished at Number Twenty-Six in the ratings when Chrysler canned the series in 1967. While Hope's comedy specials scored high ratings, the shows without him often struggled to finish last in their time slot, and the anthology format was on the wane on TV (*Kraft Suspense Theatre*, the other anthology Dick Berg secured for Universal to produce for NBC, went off in 1965 after two years).

*Bob Hope Presents the Chrysler Theatre* then had an interesting afterlife. NBC collected an assortment of its humorous episodes and reran them as *NBC Comedy Playhouse* in the summer of 1968, with Monty Hall replacing the introductions originally done by Bob Hope. The series reappeared in 1970, this time with Jack Kelly as host. Kelly reappeared when the series came back in the summers of 1971 and 1972 retitled as *NBC Comedy Theatre*. During those two summers, the network also reran *Bob Hope Presents the Chrysler Theatre* shows that fell under the genre indicated by their titles, *NBC Adventure Theatre* hosted by Art Fleming in 1971 and Ed McMahon in 1972, and *NBC Action Playhouse* hosted both years by Peter Marshall (apparently, action needed a playhouse rather than a theatre). This meant that for two seasons, NBC devoted three hours to reruns of shows at least four years old, which is either an impressive testament to the show's quality or NBC's cheapness in trying to fill nighttime programming in this period.

In any case, the *Bob Hope Presents the Chrysler Theatre* presentations then went into reruns in syndication under the titles *Theater of Stars* and *Universal Star Time*. For the latter, Bob's openings were replaced by a montage of shots backstage at the studio with a peppy instrumental version of the Petula Clark hit "A Sign of the Times" leading into the title, a rather odd introduction indeed.

Getting back to Bob's TV acting career, his roles became sparse and pretty much limited to playing himself thereafter, possibly because Bob's middling work on TV and movies by the late 1960s showed him unable to do much beyond that. Additionally, his star power was not enough to save shows like *The Phyllis Diller Show*, *Make Room for Granddaddy*, and *Julia* from being canceled at the end of their seasons with him on them.

Amid those factors, Bob basically spent fifteen years not acting on TV until a slight renaissance from 1986-1992 allowed him a handful of broader acting opportunities, though he often was not as good as one would hope he would be here either. Still, with a resume that includes guest spots on *I Love Lucy*, *Get Smart!*, *The Odd Couple*, *The Golden Girls*, *Roseanne*, and *The Simpsons*, Bob at least displayed having good taste in general on what shows to act on TV, even if the results could have and should have been better in both quality and quantity.

**The Christophers: "You Can Change the World"**
1949, Syndicated 30 minutes

Eddie "Rochester" Anderson, Jack Benny, Ann Blyth, Bing Crosby, Paul Douglas, Irene Dunne, William Holden, Bob Hope, Loretta Young. P: William Perlberg. D: Leo McCarey.

A contrived Cold War relic, this promotional film has Jack inviting Loretta, Irene, Paul, Ann and William to meet Father James Keller, founder of the Christophers, a nondenominational, right-leaning religious group. He thinks a picture with these actors will help get its message out more effectively. What follows is artificial and unconvincing. Paul recites the preamble of the Declaration of Independence and discusses its mention of God with Fr. Keller. William asks Fr. Keller point blank if the Christophers is an anti-Communist movement. He says they're more concerned about getting good people in government than hunting bad ones down, claiming that's why Germany fell to the Nazis. There's more stilted dialogue until songwriters Johnny Burke and Jimmy Van

Heusen show up with Bing Crosby, who sings a song to endorse Fr. Keller, "Early American." Bob fits into all this by summoning Fr. Keller to call him on the set of his latest film. He says he can hardly hear Fr. Keller with the cattle mooing around him ("Will you wait till I turn this Crosby record off?"), then adds it is good to focus on the Declaration of Independence, as most people today only speak of the Constitution and the Bill of Rights, adding, "But let's not forget for a moment that they don't add up to much if you pass up the Declaration." That's about it for his minute-long appearance. The film ends shortly after that, making it now a dated piece of propaganda and not good entertainment. Bob and his wife Delores later did a 1953 episode of *The Christophers* being interviewed by Father Keller.

Bob and Show: **

*The Jack Benny Program*: "Goldie, Fields and Glide"
March 21, 1954, CBS Sunday 7:30-8 p.m.

Jack Benny, Eddie "Rochester" Anderson, Don Wilson. Guests: George Burns, Bing Crosby, Bob Hope (cameo). EP/D: Ralph Levy. P: Hilliard Marks. W: Sam Perrin, George Balzer, Milt Josefsberg, John Tackaberry, Al Gordon, Hal Goldman.

It's apparent from the start that this is a filmed show with canned laughter, with Jack's monologue bombarded with inauthentic reaction. In the main skit, Rochester multitasks while rocking Jack on a hammock and spins him so fast when being overworked that Jack rockets into a tree, to fake applause. Don Wilson sits on the hammock and it collapses to loud laughter. The phoniness continues as Jack recalls his days touring with George Burns and Bing Crosby as "Goldie, Fields and Glide." Their song, dance and comedy routines get wildly zealous reactions from their fake audience, as do their "real" selves when Bing and George visit Jack's place. Later, when Bing wants $10,000 to do Jack's show, Jack puts him in his hammock and flings him into a tree. Bing refuses to come down for less, but Bob interjects from another tree that "You better do what he says, Bing. I've been up here for four months" and mugs a little. That's the big finish. Six writers came up with this fluff?

Bob: *** Show: **

***The Jack Benny Program*: "Road to Nairobi"**
May 23, 1954, CBS Sunday 7:30-8 p.m.

Jack Benny, Eddie "Rochester" Anderson, Don Wilson. Guests: Bob Hope, Dean Martin and Jerry Lewis (cameo). EP/D: Ralph Levy. P: Hilliard Marks. W: Sam Perrin, George Balzer, Milt Josefsberg, John Tackaberry, Al Gordon, Hal Goldman.

Jack, Rochester and Don prepare for this live show when Bob steals Jack's pants so he can do a monologue while Jack looks for them backstage. Bob sees coins tied together on a string in Jack's pants plus his age is removed from his driver's license. Jack comes out in Don's oversized pants held up by suspenders and banters a little with Bob before the latter leaves to get dressed for his sketch. Don comes out in Jack's undersized pants and introduces the skit before the pants supposedly rip. "The Road to Nairobi" has cannibals do a production number before Bob and Jack arrive in pith helmets as hunters. They've bagged a creature that's half lion and half leopard. "He must've gone to a veterinarian in Denmark," says Jack to applause, referring to the country doing sex change operations. "I wondered why he had his hand on his hip when I shot him," ad libs Bob to more laughter, and Jack slaps him playfully. They open the plastic carcass for drinks, then Bob cracks up constantly at the delivery of the cannibals and lines he has to say while he and Jack are put in a cauldron to boil. When the cannibals lack matches to cook them, Dean Martin and Jerry Lewis bolt down one aisle onto the stage to start a fire instead. Jack thanks them both along with Hope at the end for a choppy show that Bob nevertheless energizes as much as he can.

Bob: ***** Show: ***


***Lux Video Theatre*: "Forever Female"**
June 23, 1955, Thursday 10-11 p.m.

Host: Otto Kruger. Theatre Guest: Bob Hope. Cast: Anne Bancroft (Sally Carver), Fred Clark (Harry Phillips), Anita Louise (Beatrice Page), Jeanette Miller (Patty), Maidie Norman (Maid), Richard Shannon (Stanley Crown). Announcer: Ken Carpenter. P: Cal Kuhl. D: Buzz Kulik. W: S.H. Barnett (adaptation of play by J.M. Barrie and screenplay by Julius Epstein and Philip Epstein).

*Forever Female* was a theatrical film released in 1954 with a different cast. Bob appears on an adaptation of it on this playhouse series to promote his new movie, *The Seven Little Foys*, which Paramount Pictures releases as it did with the original *Forever Female*.

### *Screen Directors Playhouse*: "The Silent Partner"
Dec. 21, 1955, Wednesday 8-8:30 p.m.

Buster Keaton (Kelsey Dutton), ZaSu Pitts (Selma), Joe E. Brown (Arthur Vail), Evelyn Ankers (Miss Loving), Jack Kruschen (Ernie), Jack Elam (Mr. Shanks), Percy Helton (Barney), Joseph Corey (Arnold), Lyle Latell (Ernie's friend), Charles Horvath (barber). Uncredited: Bob Hope (Himself), Heinie Conklin (saloon waiter in film shoot), Charles Ferguson (Academy Awards Attendee/ Film Shoot Onlooker), Hank Mann (cameraman), Spec O`Donnell (film shoot onlooker), Snub Pollard (special effects man), Jeffrey Sayre (Academy Awards Attendee/ Film Shoot Onlooker). D/W: George Marshall. W: Barbara Hammer.

Bob plays himself at the Oscars ceremony and quips that any awards not claimed after thirty days go to Walt Disney. He presents a special Academy Award to director Arthur Vail, mugs a little, and sighs about having to give the statuette away before leaving. From there, Arthur mentions how his pal, Kelsey Dutton, had to film silent pictures in 1916 with the bare essentials, leading to a flashback of that period. Kelsey overhears the dialogue about a woman saying she needs help from her burning apartment and assumes it's real, wrecking the shoot until the crew starts laughing at Kelsey's wild actions to intervene. Kelsey becomes a star until the talkies arrive and he languishes in obscurity. Watching the speech in a bar, Kelsey doesn't acknowledge who he is to his fellow rowdy patrons. However, as one of his vintage comedies plays on the Oscar ceremony, Selma recognizes who Kelsey is and informs the bar. Kelsey gets appreciated by all excepted loudmouthed Ernie, who he hits with food to subdue when Arthur arrives from the ceremony. He brings his old friend over to the theater hosting the Oscars to be honored by the industry. This odd mix of slapstick and sentimentality succeeds overall thanks to the comic talent on display by Buster Keaton in a story that resembles what happened to his career for a time. It's interesting that Bob's reference of Walt Disney went unedited, as *Disneyland* opposite this series on ABC beat it handily.

Bob and Show: ***

***The Charlie Farrell Show*: "Secrets"**
July 2, 1956, CBS Monday 9-9:30 p.m.

Charlie Farrell (himself), Charles Winninger (Charlie's father), Richard Deacon (Sherman Hull, club manager), Leon Askin (Pierre the chef), Ann Lee (Doris Mayfield, Charlie's girlfriend), Kathryn Card (Mrs. Papernow, the housekeeper). Guest: Bob Hope (himself). EP: Hal Roach Jr. P: Gordon Hughes. D: Rodney Amateau. W: Gordon Hughes, Lee Karson, Phil Shuken.

Set at the Palm Springs Racquet Club actor Charlie Farrell founded and operated in real life, this has Bob appear briefly as a guest of the hotel. Why he agreed to appear as himself on the debut of a summer sitcom on a rival network is a real mystery, other than he lived in Palm Springs too. This will be rerun on CBS in the summers of 1957 and 1960 before vanishing from public view.


***I Love Lucy*: "Lucy and Bob Hope"**
Oct. 1, 1956, CBS Monday 9-9:30 p.m.

Lucille Ball (Lucy Ricardo), Desi Arnaz (Ricky Ricardo), Vivian Vance (Ethel Mertz), William Frawley (Fred Mertz), Keith Thibodeaux (Little Ricky Ricardo). Guest: Bob Hope (Himself). P: Desi Arnaz. D: James V. Kern. W: Madelyn Martin, Bob Carroll Jr., Bob Schiller, Bob Weiskopf. Special Lyrics: Larry Orenstein. Music: Elliot Daniel. Choreography: Jack Baker.

Bandleader Ricky has booked Bob Hope for the opening of his Club Babalu but tells his wife, Lucy, that she won't appear because of her crazy behavior. Dejected, Lucy sees Bob at a baseball game she's attending with her son, Little Ricky, and her friends the Mertzes. She dresses as a hot dog vendor to meet him, but her activities get him beaned by a ball. Ricky arrives in the locker room to comfort Bob as Lucy appears as a rising player. After she ends her charade, a sympathetic Bob lets Lucy join him and Ricky in Club Babalu as three singing umpires ending with a special version of "Thanks for the Memory" and saying "I may never go back to NBC!" Bob acts as wonderfully and lively as everyone else plus plugs for his new film, *The Iron Petticoat,* and the Cleveland Indians baseball team he owns in this sprightly edition of a classic TV comedy.

Bob and Show: ****

***The Jack Benny Program*: "Hope and Benny in Agent's Office"**
Feb. 24, 1957, CBS Sunday 7:30-8 p.m.

Jack Benny, The Four Sportsmen. Guest: Bob Hope. EP/D: Ralph Levy. W: Hilliard Marks, Sam Perrin, George Balzer, Hal Goldman, Al Gordon.

Jack notes in his opening monologue that he's been nominated for several Emmys without winning, then Bob strides on stage and cracks up the host. "I can't look at the nose!" Jack chuckles. "You're not Tyrone Power!" Bob snaps back. They have good rapport promoting Bob's new movie *Beau James* (which has a cameo by Jack) followed by a song by the Four Sportsmen. Jack and Bob then play themselves auditioning for Mr. Webster in the 1920s, who also sees Eddie Cantor (played by a juvenile actor). Both have good lines in trying to persuade Webster to hire them before Jack amuses everyone when he mistakenly says, "I'm not getting any older!" He goes off to be a solo star, then joins Bob at the curtain call to do a funny special version of "Thanks for the Memory." This lively live show will be remade in 1962.

Bob: ***** Show: ****


***The Danny Thomas Show*: "The Bob Hope Show"**
Jan. 6, 1958, CBS Monday 9-9:30 p.m.

Danny Thomas (Danny Williams), Marjorie Lord (Kathy Williams), Rusty Hamer (Rusty Williams), Angela Cartwright (Linda Williams). Guests: Bob Hope (himself), Mary Wickes (Liz O'Neill), Joan Tabor (Gloria). P/D: Sheldon Leonard. W: Jack Elinson, Charles Stewart.

Comedian Danny Williams frets when Liz, his press agent, secures Bob Hope for his guest on an upcoming TV comedy special. He fantasizes how he will be upstaged by Hope doing a monologue (wherein the latter plugs his upcoming movie, *Paris Holiday*) and a sketch from Hope's writers wherein Danny plays a butler summoned by Bob with a bell playing "Thanks for the Memory" to clean up an apartment while Bob romances Gloria, a bombshell. Danny's fears make him cancel the show until his son, Rusty, reminds Danny how he inspired him to play right tackle on his football team because you don't always have to be the main guy like the quarterback and should never quit. Bob and Liz further energize Danny's spirits when Bob says he'll play the butler on the special, since it will make it quicker for him to leave the studio. Apart from the clever coda wherein Bob and Danny do switch places in the lovers' skit and a spirited performance from Mary Wickes, this is only intermittently interesting in all aspects.

Bob and Show: ***

**The Jack Benny Program: "Stars' Wives Show"**
Nov. 2, 1958, CBS Sunday 7:30-8 p.m.

Jack Benny. Guest: Bob Hope. EP: Irving Fein. P: Hilliard Marks. D: Seymour Berns. W: Sam Perrin, George Balzer, Hal Goldman, Al Gordon.

The wives of four stars, including Bob's wife Delores, are members of the Committee to Improve Beverly Hills who implore the mayor to get rid of Jack's decrepit Maxwell jalopy. Even though Delores lives in Toluca Lake, she's part of the group because she hates how the car looks parked when Jack visits. The group buys a new car and prints only one dollar raffle ticket to sell to Jack. Unfortunately, when Jack lacks enough money to pay his painter, he gives the latter his ticket, to everyone's dismay. At the curtain call, Bob and David Niven join their wives, and Bob ad libs to Delores, "Did you get the money?" Jack loses it before responding, "They didn't get the money, but Bob will make me do three shows for himself!" Mel Blanc takes a bow and does a few cartoon voices at the end of this breezy live show.

Bob: *** Show: ****

**The Thin Man: "The Long Lost Chapter"**
Nov 14, 1958, Friday 9:30-10 p.m.

Peter Lawford (Nick Charles), Phyllis Kirk (Nora Charles). Guests: Gavin MacLeod (Neil Jackson), Ann McCrea (Billie Benson), Robert Tafur (Victor), John Shay (Pete Corell), Nico Minardos (Rudi), Richard Reeves (Mike). Unbilled Cameos: Bob Hope (himself/Cuddles), Jason Wingreen (bum). EP: Richard Maibaum. P: Bob Welch. D: John Newland. W: Sig Herzig.

The Charleses along with their cute dog Asta try to determine why someone murdered Neil Jackson after he called to say he had finished writing his mystery novel. Bob's shot on the series comes as it is beaten soundly in the ratings opposite *77 Sunset Strip* on ABC and will end in 1959 after just two seasons on the air. Lawford will make a cameo as Nick Charles on Bob's Feb. 10, 1959 special.

**The Danny Thomas Show: "Bob Hope and Danny Become Directors"**
Jan. 26, 1959, CBS Monday 9-9:30 p.m.

Danny Thomas (Danny Williams), Marjorie Lord (Kathy Williams), Rusty Hamer (Rusty Williams), Angela Cartwright (Linda Williams). Guests: Bob Hope (himself), Charlotte Foster (Joan Tompkins), Eric Anderson, Terry Burnham, Veronica Cartwright, Dana Dillaway, Joyce Dew (child performers). EP: Louis Edelman. P/D: Sheldon Leonard. W: Charles Stewart, Jack Elinson.

Bob supplies badly need comic energy when he finally appears nearly fourteen minutes into this show. Until then, it drags as Danny thinks his children, Rusty and Linda, are being wasted in bit parts for a school production of *Alice in Wonderland* overseen by Charlotte Foster. Irked by his interference, Charlotte lets Danny run a rehearsal. However, a supposed nephew of Bob Hope's, Leslie (Bob's real first name), is in the play, and his famous uncle appears to contribute his own ideas. Proud of his nephew's portrayal as a duck in the play ("Crosby taught him how to waddle"), Bob wants to expand the role to include a monologue. Bob spends several minutes making peppy cracks at everything from Walt Disney to Jayne Mansfield, with lines like "You remember Elvis? He went to the Army and was replaced by the hula hoop!" Bob also proposes some dance steps until Charlotte returns and a worn-out Danny apologizes and lets her reassume her duties. She thanks him and Bob, who quips, "It's all right with me, cousin Charlotte!" Guest actress Veronica Cartwright is the older sister of series regular Angela Cartwright.

Bob: **** Show: ***

**The Danny Thomas Show: "Tonoose, the Liar"**
Nov. 21, 1960, CBS Monday 9-9:30 p.m.

Danny Thomas (Danny Williams), Marjorie Lord (Kathy Williams), Rusty Hamer (Rusty Williams), Angela Cartwright (Linda Williams). Guests: Hans Conreid (Uncle Tonoose), Art Aragon (Kid Moore),

Richard Correll (Richie), Bob Hope (himself). EP: Louis F. Edelman. P/D: Sheldon Leonard. W: David Adler.

Opinionated Uncle Tonoose causes friction between Danny's children Rusty and Linda and their friend Richie when the latter claims the hard-to-believe stories Tonoose tells are just outright falsehoods. Their father assures them Tonoose is always telling the truth someway, but when he claims to know the middleweight boxing champ Kid Moore, even Danny doubts him. Bob shows up as Danny tries to get the situation settled.


*The Joey Bishop Show*: "A Young Man's Fancy"
March 21, 1962, Wednesday 8:30-9 p.m.

Joey Bishop (Joey Barnes), Marlo Thomas (Stella Barnes), Warren Berlinger (Larry Barnes), Madge Blake (Mrs. Barnes), Ray Hemphill (Danny), Christine Nelson (Mary), Dawn Wells (Connie), Bob Hope (Mary's Other Boyfriend).

Bob provides the only real laugh in this otherwise lifeless first-season episode of this series. It comes after much tedium with Joey and his younger brother Larry suddenly worrying about how they look when their sister Stella brings home Connie, her pretty friend. Connie is married, however, so she doesn't care about either of them, making Larry brood about how no woman will want him. To perk his sibling up, Joey recounts the time when he was heading off to military service while Mary, his girlfriend at the time, possessively tried to keep him with her and gave him mementos to remember her while he's away. Entranced by her strong entreaties, Joey reluctantly leaves her. When he's gone, Bob Hope pokes his head out from behind Mary's sofa and cries out, "I thought he'd never leave!" In his cameo, Bob provides more energy and timing than almost everything else in this blah outing.

Bob: *** Show: *


*The Danny Thomas Show*: "Danny and Bob Get Away from It All"
April 2, 1962, CBS Monday 9-9:30 p.m.

Danny Thomas (Danny Williams), Marjorie Lord (Clancy Williams), Rusty Hamer (Rusty Williams), Angela Cartwright (Linda Williams).

Guests: Bob Hope (himself), Sam Hearn (Mr. Fergus), Stanley Adams (Walter). EP: Louis F. Edelman. P/D: Sheldon Leonard. W: Charles Stewart, Jack Elinson.

After signing autographs for women (during which Bob calls Bing Crosby, father of a new baby, "the Maharishi of the maternity ward"), Bob and Danny get more requests from Danny's own family. Fed up with their fawning treatment there and at a small café, the men escape to Frisbie Falls, population 178, where a hotel clerk doesn't know who they are, even when Bob sings "Thanks for the Memory." Bob mocks the cramped accommodations ("It's an instant room, you just have to add water!") and the sinking mattress ("Hey, Sophie Tucker slept here!"). Becoming bored, the two compete in an amateur show under assumed names. Bob's monologue mercilessly ribs the town's smallness ("sort of a U-turn with a mayor"), among other topics. Yet he and Danny both lose to the clerk. This is richly and unpredictably funny, and Bob superbly carries off one of his largest TV acting jobs ever.

Bob: ***** Show: ****

**The Jack Benny Program: "Jack and Bob Hope in Vaudeville"**
Dec. 4, 1962, CBS Tuesday 9:30-10 p.m.

Host: Jack Benny. Guest: Bob Hope. EP: Irving Fein. P/D: Fred De Cordova. W: Hilliard Marks, Sam Perrin, George Balzer, Hal Goldman, Al Gordon.

This filmed remake of Jack's 1957 show with Bob has less enjoyment despite having most of the cast repeat their roles. That actually might be part of the problem, as despite all being talented, they are performing largely by rote here with few changes. The major exception is a new juvenile male now playing Jimmy Durante auditioning rather than Eddie Cantor, presumably because the latter died during the interim. Bob does his part to interject unexpected levity, however. Interrupting Jack at the start when the host talks about a recent honor he received from American Tailors, Bob calls him "Rickety Nelson" and floors him with "Jack, I tried to get into your dressing room, but I didn't have a nickel." (This was when pay toilets were making inroads at public facilities.)

Bob: **** Show: ***

***Chrysler Presents a Bob Hope Comedy Special*: "The House Next Door"**
Nov. 13, 1963, Friday 8:30-9:30 p.m.

Bob Hope (George Warren), Jill St. John (Binky Norris), Kathryn Crosby (Ginny Warren), Harold J. Stone (Ernie Santee), Jesse White (Marvin), Jerome Cowan (Mr. Bryant), Doris Singleton (Mrs. Carmen Bryant), Frank Albertson (Mr. Morgan), Leo Gordon (Biggie), Dan Frazer (the detective), Lewis Charles (Mike), Clegg Hoyt (the furniture mover), Jimmy Boyd (Jerry). Cameo: Bing Crosby (himself). P: Harry Tugend. D: Jack Arnold. W: Albert E. Lewin, Burt Styler. Music: Joseph Lilley.

Some good Bing Crosby jokes cannot exonerate a deadly unfunny effort shot in color with a laugh track added. Mr. Bryant sells his house for a pittance to George Warren, who has no idea that next-door gangsters Binky Norris, Ernie Santee and Marvin think the newcomer may be muscling into their territory. Binky gives the unsuspecting Warrens a couch stuffed with laundered money her gang is hiding. That night, George watches a Road movie with Bob and Bing and says, "They're funny, weren't they?" "That's what I like about the late movies. You get to see the real old-timers," shoots back his wife, Ginny (played by Bing's wife in real life). It's about the only laugh until the end, as George indulges in stale slapstick like getting his tie stuck in Binky's dress before Ernie and Marvin force George to report their murder of their foe Biggie to the police. "Do I dial operator or just run out in the lawn and scream?" George responds lamely. Ernie and Marvin then steal George's couch filled with loot. George traces it to an upholsterer where feathers fly into a fan and stun the men, allowing the police to arrest the gang. A repentant Binky turns on Ernie and Marvin to get them jailed. It's as monotonous as it sounds until a new neighbor moves in, played by Bing Crosby. "I better freshen up so I can meet him," Ginny says, while George responds by putting his house up for sale. It's a lot of work for little payoff here.

Bob: ** Show: *


***Chrysler Presents a Bob Hope Comedy Special*: "Her School for Bachelors"**
March 20, 1964, Friday 8:30-9:30 p.m.

Bob Hope (Monte Collins), Eva Marie Saint (Diane Wescott), Louis Nye (Jack Roberts), Cass Daley (Patsy), Jackie Coogan (drunk customer), Doris Singleton (Ellen Daniels), Jack Albertson (Bruce Shannon),

Francine York (Sherry), Peter Leeds (Danny the photographer), Linda Hope (Miss November), Stephen Chase (Dave Henning), Frank Evans (Charlie), Paula Lane (Maggie), Pat Priest (Miss March), Myrna Ross (Joanie), Joy Monroe (Laurette Hart), Beverly Adams (Bachelorette), Amadee Chabot (Bachelorette), Leslie Perkins (Bachelorette). Also: Jack Pepper. EP: Alan J. Miller. P: Mort Lachman. D: David Butler. W: Sam Locke, Joel Rapp.

In his previous comedy special, Bob's character was basically boring. Here he is occasionally that as well as unconvincing as Monte Collins, a swinging bachelor publisher whose girlie magazine is called obscene and pornographic by Diane Wescott, a school teacher running for a congressional seat. Thinking that bad publicity beats none at all, Monte has his right-hand man Jack Roberts write letters in support of Diane's cause. She makes a surprise visit to Jack's apartment when Monte answers the door, and Monte takes advantage of Diane thinking he is Jack by encouraging her to protest more. They begin a romance, but when Monte learns her campaign is going so well that his magazine may be banned by the postmaster general if she wins, he takes another tack. Somehow, Monte convinces Diane to pose as a Bachelorette at his club to learn about the magazine's machinations, while his real plan is to get her picture taken in the outfit to use against her. The latter occurs, but when the photographer and Monte's pal Bruce objectify Diane and a drunk customer at a club harasses her, Monte comes to her defense. Then his charade is exposed, and Diane runs away infuriated until he pleads with her and even proposes marriage, which she accepts after forgiving him. Right. This dopey plot wastes some great comic supporting actors, Eva Marie Saint's character is inconsistently headstrong and meek, and Bob has done much better as a romantic and comic lead in other parts. Forget this.

Bob: ** Show: *

***Bob Hope Presents the Chrysler Theatre*: "A Slow Fade to Black"**
March 27, 1964, Friday 8:30-9:30 p.m.

Rod Steiger (Michael Kirsch), Sally Kellerman (Jenny Kirsch), James Dunn (Russ Landers), Robert Culp (Peter Furgatch), Anna Lee (Paula Kirsch), Simon Scott (Henderson), Dabney Coleman (Stanley Rivkin), Sharon Farrell (Melissa Jensen), Woodrow Parfrey (Kessler), Marian Moses (secretary), Scott Elliott (Grannigan), Dennis McCarthy (the man), Clegg Hoyt (the guard), Leon Belasco (Robbins). Cameo: Bob Hope (himself). P: Dick Berg. D: Ron Winston. W: Rod Serling. Music: Benny Carter.

A week after starring in his own comedy, Bob is the weak link in this otherwise fine drama detailing the business and personal failings of movie studio boss Michael Kirsch, a man facing pressure to step down after millions in losses over the last five years. While his board of directors meet at the studio, Michael orders Stanley Rivkin to do retakes of disastrous footage on his latest picture starring the demanding Melissa Jensen. Michael's assistant Peter Furgatch protests that the real problem is an old-fashioned script, which irks Michael. The board members tell Michael they will ask him to resign when the shareholders meet. Michael responds by firing Peter and going home, but he finds no relief there from his twice-divorced daughter Jennie. Tired of her father focusing on her peccadillos, Jennie says she will use the company stock he gave to her for one of her weddings as a gift to vote him out of power by sending a proxy to vote with the directors. Even worse, Michael learns the board already has appointed Peter as its new studio head before receiving the 1964 Producer of the Year award. At a ceremony hosted by Bob Hope, Michael resigns in public while speaking movingly of how he and other immigrants made Hollywood what it is. Rod Steiger earned an Emmy nomination for his pitch perfect work here, and the cast comes close to matching his professionalism if not his intensity except Bob, who cannot play being sincere well. This still sparkles despite Bob's bobbling on display.

Bob: ** Show: ****


**The Lucille Ball Comedy Hour: "Mr. and Mrs."**
April 26, 1964, CBS Sunday 8-9 p.m.

Cast: Lucille Ball (Herself/Bonnie Blakely), Bob Hope (Himself/Bill Blakely), Jack Weston (Cash), Max Showalter (Walter), John Dehner (the sponsor), Gale Gordon (Mr. Harvey), John Lanteau (Mr. Henderson), John Banner (Guard). EP: Jess Oppenheimer. P: Edward H. Feldman. D: Jack Donohue. W: Richard Powell, Sherwood Schwartz, Arthur Julian.

Lucy plays herself fighting for control of a movie company over Mr. Harvey, a prickly banker in a boardroom dustup. He's upset with $10,000 she wants to give writers for a Bob Hope project without having the star under contract. She assures him he'll sign, but Mr. Harvey snipes that "Mr. Hope's only free time is the week following July the Fourth, 1976, after he emcees the 200th anniversary of our independence!" (a lot of this comedy is somewhat based on the truth). Lucy and Gale track down Bob in the Philippines, where Lucy convinces Bob to play her husband who acts opposite her on a TV show. At this point, this special becomes that proposed project with a studio audience. Bonnie Blakely gets irritated with her husband Bill and calls him a bad actor who likes to hang out with "bleach blonde bit players" (again, comedy based on truth) before revealing to Cash, their agent, that they're really not married. Their sponsor insists they have a baby to boost their ratings, and Bonnie's suitor Walter wants to marry her too, before Bill proposes to Bonnie instead. The show returns to the boardroom, where Lucy gets hosannas from all except Mr. Harvey. This comedy is variable as is Bob, who has some good lines ("I signed mine Ringo" he says of his experience with young girls wanting his autograph) but relies on cue cards too often, which muddles his delivery.

Bob and Show: ***


**The Lucy Show: "Lucy and the Plumber"**
Sept. 28, 1964, CBS Monday 8:30-9 p.m.

Lucille Ball (Lucy Carmichael), Gale Gordon (Theodore J. Mooney), Jimmy Garrett (Jerry Carmichael). Guests: Jack Benny (Harry Tuttle), Willard Waterman (Greg Gregory), Tom G. Linder (Mr. Krause), Bob Hope (Plumber's Assistant). P/D: Jack Donohue. W: Milt Josefsberg, Bob O'Brien.

After a spot on Greg Gregory's talent show goes awry for Lucy Carmichael and her client, Mr. Krause, she needs her banker (Mr. Mooney) to pay for her plumber, Harry Tuttle. A dead ringer in looks and vocals for Jack Benny, Tuttle bemoans to Lucy how everyone thinks he's like Jack, even though he plays the violin beautifully. The latter inspires Lucy to pretend to be a dark-haired Italian and return to the talent show to promote Tuttle, but their segment disintegrates again with her interference. Fitfully amusing largely due to the acting, the tired script wastes Bob in a cameo at the end as Tuttle's co-worker who denies he's really you know who. Bob does okay with a nothing part.

Bob and Show: ***

*Chrysler Presents a Bob Hope Comedy Special*: "Have Girls—Will Travel"
Oct. 16, 1964, Friday 8:30-9:30 p.m.

Bob Hope (Horatio Lovelace), Jill St. John (Faith), Rhonda Fleming (Purity), Marilyn Maxwell (Charity), Aldo Ray (Moose), Rod Cameron (Tiny), Sonny Tufts (Mark), Bruce Cabot (Sheriff), Iris Adrian (Queenie), Peter Leeds (Flint), Milton Frome (hotel keeper), Bob Jellison (bath house attendant). Cameos: Lucille Ball, Jack Benny, Richard Deacon. EP: Harry Tugend. P: Mort Lachman. D: Fred de Cordova. W: Alex Gottlieb, Robert Hamner. Choreography: Miriam Nelson. Music: Joseph J. Lilley. "There's Gold in Them Thar Hills" Writers: Sammy Cahn, James Van Heusen.

Bob's only enjoyable acting appearance on his anthology series is this peppy comedy. Horatio is a cowardly, conniving marriage broker in the Old West who promises Moose, Tiny, and Mark he will find them classy women to marry, and they head out of town satisfied with the guarantee. Faith, Purity and Charity arrive but want to break their wedding contract when they learn the brothers are not rich, but the sheriff informs them the deal is ironclad. Horatio locks up the ladies to prevent them from leaving, so each tries unsuccessfully to seduce him to get out from their hotel. They then invite men up to their room to dance (with Jack Benny as a violinist) while Horatio bathes in a tub. The scene becomes so unruly by the time Horatio discovers what is happening that Faith, Purity and Charity are able to burn their contracts and escape. Horatio tries to do the latter as well, but he gets caught. Meanwhile, the women become local saloon singers and perform "There's Gold in Them Thar Hills" to an adoring crowd. Moose, Tiny, and Mark return and are appalled of what their brides to be are doing and plan to kill Horatio in a showdown in the street, with Richard Deacon playing an expecting undertaker. But the men see the ladies dressed up and willing to reform themselves, so they drop the planned shootout. Horatio then greets the arrival of his own fiancée (a beautiful Lucille Ball), who manhandles him. Good lines, pacing and delivery by Bob make this a smooth outing to watch.

Bob and Show: \*\*\*\*

## The Jack Benny Program: "Jack Makes a Comedy Record"
Oct. 23, 1964, Friday 9:30-10 p.m.

Jack Benny. Guests: Bob Hope (himself), Maudie Prickett (Mrs. Gordon), Mel Blanc (Mel), Robert Bull (Bobby), Robert Leeds (producer), Lois Corbett (maid), Jacque Shelton (engineer), Scott Elliott (butler). EP: Irving Fein. P/D: Norm Abbott. W: Sam Perrin, George Balzer, Hal Goldman, Al Gordon.

Jack gets grief from Mrs. Gordon, his secretary, for failed investments, and his two writers, Mel and Bobby, who forgot to put paper in the typewriter when doing his script. Bob comes to Jack's office and demands that Jack open the window so he can hear Les Brown's orchestra play "Thanks for the Memory" as he walks to his seat. He wants Bob to participate in the one area of show business they haven't tried together. "Well, I'm game, if you have the fans and balloons," Bob quips, referencing strip teasing. Jack says no, he means he wants to record a comedy album with Bob. Bob says fine, since he has a producer and engineer in the den of his house. "They sleep in," he ad libs, to which Benny responds, "This I didn't hear before!" "And this is just the start of the show!" Bob wisecracks, adding that he's trying to avoid the plot. At Bob's house, Jack plays "Thanks for the Memory" on his violin and Bob runs out from the shower clothed in a large towel saying, "Oh, thank you, thank you!" He brings out an entourage to laugh on demand. Bob wants to ad lib their recording and he interrupts Jack's efforts to tell a story with gags about each topic Jack mentions, especially Beverly Hills. This infuriates Jack until he learns that he'll get half the profits from one million pre-sold orders, so he serves as Bob's straight man. It's a fun half hour.

Bob and Show: ****


## Chrysler Presents a Bob Hope Comedy Special: "Russian Roulette"
Nov. 17, 1965, Wednesday 9-10 p.m.

Bob Hope (Les Haines), Jill St. John (Janie Douglas), Victor Buono (Grebb), Don Rickles (Vinny, Les's agent), Harold J. Stone (Borginin), Leon Askin (First Russian), Leon Belasco (Second Russian), Magda Harout (Lady Chauffeur), Charles Walsh (Joe Taylor), Jack Pepper (Harry), Charles Cantor (German Waiter), Bob Harvey (Electrician), Linda Carroll (Dotty Baker), Joy Monroe (Chorus Girl). Unbilled: Gary Owens (reporter). EP/W (story): Harry Tugend. P: Mort Lachman. D: David Butler. W (story): Bob

Hope. W (teleplay): Burt Styler, Albert E. Lewin.

Presenting a comic scenario based on the Francis Gary Powers U-2 incident in 1960 is a dubious premise to start with, and padding it with footage of Bob's 1958 special from Russia shows how flimsy the concept is to fill an hour on TV with commercials, not to mention a cheap way to take up time. The plodding plot has comedian Les Haines going to Russia in exchange for a Soviet comedian coming to America in order to facilitate the release of a captured and imprisoned American pilot. Janie Douglas claims to be the pilot's sister, but she's really a spy who transfers a map of missile bases onto Bob's back when she knocks him out while in Russia. Monitoring their activities are Grebb, who after watching the 1958 clips of Bob, er, Les in performance hijacks a plane with Les and Janie after Janie falls in love with Les. Grebb tells them he is waiting for the highest bid from an enemy in America to sell the map. Unbelievably, Les overpowers Grebb, and he and Janie along with a dog parachute to safety—only it's not all clear, as the U.S. Army starts shooting at them, thinking they are spies. The supposedly cute "surprise" ending and waste of Don Rickles and Victor Buono, among others in the supporting cast, make this mission one tedious ordeal for everyone to endure.

Bob: *** Show: **


*Bob Hope Presents the Chrysler Theatre*: "The Blue-Eyed Horse"
Nov. 23, 1966, Wednesday 9-10 p.m.

Ernest Borgnine (Melvin Freebie), Joan Blondell (Mrs. Freebie), Barbara Heller (Jeannie Haggerty), Joyce Jameson (Mrs. Rassendale), Paul Lynde (Judge), Ann Jillian (the daughter), Bob Hope (Spectator). P: Dick Berg. D: Hal Kanter. W: Michael Fessier.

Bob makes a brief uncredited appearance in this comedy.


*The Phyllis Diller Show*: "Learn to Be a Millionaire"
Jan. 20, 1967, ABC Friday 9:30-10 p.m.

Phyllis Diller (Phyllis Pruitt), John Astin (Rudy Pruitt), Marty Ingels (Norman Krump), Pam Freeman (Steffi), Bob Hope (himself).

Launching a change of format along with a new title in a futile bid to have this series last more than one season (it began in the fall of 1966 as *The Pruitts of Southampton*), the formerly rich Phyllis Pruitt opens her mansion into a boardinghouse to stay financially solvent. Bob makes a cameo as a library patron.

### *Get Smart!*: "99 Loses Control"
Feb. 17, 1968, Saturday 8-8:30 p.m.

Don Adams (Maxwell Smart), Barbara Feldon (Agent 99), Edward Platt (The Chief), Robert Karvelas (Larrabee). Guests: Jacques Bergerac (Victor Royal), Maurice Marsac (Louis), Alfred Dennis (Jacques Montaine), Stephen Hart (croupier), Bob Hope (hotel waiter; uncredited cameo). Creators: Mel Brooks with Buck Henry. EP: Leonard Stern. P: Burt Nodella. D: Bruce Bilson. W: William Raynor, Myles Wilder.

Agent 99 leaves Control, a U.S. secret government agency, to marry Victor Royal. Max, a fellow spy secretly in love with 99, saves Victor from a shooting at the latter's casino and agrees to serve as Victor's bodyguard. Calling herself Susan Hilton, 99 arrives and insists to Max that Victor is a good guy—even though Victor kills gambler Jacques Montaine to get the latter's uranium mines for KAOS, a worldwide terror operation. A hotel waiter (Bob) delivers supper to 99 and Victor and tells Max Victor is a ladies' man ("His little black book, it's in its twenty-fourth edition!") Max interrupts the duo before Louis, Victor's aide, warns his boss what's happening. They confront 99 and Max, who plays a game of rigged poker whereby Max loses and Victor shoots him. "The old bulletproof cummerbund in the tuxedo trick" saves Max as he kills Louis and calls the police for Victor. (Also, 99 denies her real name is Susan, by the way.) In a suspenseful, swift installment of the spy spoof series, Bob contributes some of his best acting on TV ever as he for once plays a character and not himself. He delivers good lines naturally and strongly without winking in the camera and helps maintain the episode's realistic atmosphere. Bob packs more laughs in a minute here than he does in most of his other sitcom appearances, and his work fits well with the sharp acting, directing, writing, and production on display.

Bob and Show: ****

*Make Room for Granddaddy*: "Is This Trip Necessary?"
Oct. 28, 1970, ABC Wednesday 8-8:30 p.m.

Danny Thomas (Danny Williams), Marjorie Lord (Kathy Williams), Angela Cartwright (Linda Williams), Rusty Hamer (Rusty Williams), Sid Melton (Charley Halper), Michael Hughes (Michael Wilson). Guest: Bob Hope (himself).

Bob tries to convince a reluctant Danny to join him on one of his USO tours out of the country in this failed, one-season continuation of *The Danny Thomas Show*.


*Julia*: "Cool Hand Bruce"
Jan. 19, 1971, Tuesday 7:30-8 p.m.

Diahann Carroll (Julia Baker), Lloyd Nolan (Dr. Morton Chegley), Michael Link (Earl J. Waggedorn), Betty Beaird (Marie Waggedorn), Fred Williamson (Steven Bruce), Janear Hines (Roberta). Guests: Stephanie James (Kim Bruce), Benny Baker (Mr. Greenburg), Ingeborg Kjelsen (the patient), Bob Hope (himself; uncredited). EP: Hal Kanter. P: Bernard Wiesen. D: Ezra Stone. W: Harry Winkler, Harry Dean. Musical Supervision: Lionel Newman.

The professionalism of all involved cannot compensate for a stupid script that shoehorns Bob into it apparently to let him promote his work with a pet cause. The pathetic plot has Julia's babysitter, Roberta, upsetting her client by saying she saw Julia's boyfriend, aspiring lawyer Steven Bruce, out at a party while Julia stayed up late typing his notes for the bar exam. This makes her angry to go with him to the Inner City Clinic Charity Ball for which Julia's boss, Dr. Chegley, is acting as chair. Desperate for talent, Morton is saved when Bob Hope calls him out of the blue for a favor. The doctor treated one of Bob's writers in World War II, and Bob needs his help as a board member on the Eisenhower Memorial Hospital in Palm Springs. Chegley agrees if Bob will emcee the ball, which of course he does, and Julia learns that Steven was merely networking with others at the party, ending the stupid misunderstanding before they go to the ball. Bob is obviously reading off cue cards and half-heartedly delivers his lines, although when writers have him say that he thinks Julia is a prettier nurse than the one Chegley had in the war—"A Marine from Oklahoma"—one can hardly blame his approach. At one point during all this, Julia's fellow tenant, Earl J. Waggedorn, comments on what his mother is watching on TV with "It's a pretty dumb show." The same assessment applies here.

Bob and Show: **


## *The Odd Couple*: "The Hollywood Story"
Oct. 3, 1974, ABC Thursday 8-8:30 p.m.

Tony Randall (Felix Unger), Jack Klugman (Oscar Madison), Al Molinaro (Officer Murray Greshler). Guests: George Montgomery (Griff), Bob Hope (himself), Allan Arbus (the director), Leonard Barr (Stickman/Mayor), Alan Dexter (J.B.), Alice James (the script girl), Mickey Fox (Hannah). EP: Garry Marshall, Sheldon Keller. P: Tony Marshall. D: Mel Ferber. W: Al Gordon, Hal Goldman. Based on the play *The Odd Couple* by Neil Simon. Music: Neal Hefti.

A wonderful installment from the series' fifth and final season, this has finicky Felix force his grouchy, slovenly roommate, Oscar, to let him join on the latter's flight to film a bit part in a movie in Hollywood. The duo sightsees and unexpectedly finds Bob Hope putting out his trash. "We just got here from New York!" enthuses Felix as they accost the comedian. "Relatives?" asks a nervous Bob. Felix is excited by seeing a used orange in the waste ("Crosby just squeezed those," Bob adds, a nod to Bing's endorsement of a certain orange juice brand), and Bob willingly gives it to him as a souvenir. As Felix and Oscar leave, Bob mutters, "I've got to get a dog." The show moves into high gear as Felix "goes Hollywood" and makes ridiculous demands during the filming as Oscar's representative that ultimately cost his roommate the role. This is good stuff.

Bob: *** Show: ****


## *NBC Welcomes Joe Namath and the Waverly Wonders*
Sept. 7, 1978, Friday 8-9 p.m.

Joe Namath, Jack Albertson, Dick Clark, Melissa Gilbert, Bob Hope, Bruce Jenner, Dean Martin, O.J. Simpson. Special Appearances: Pat Morita (as a caterer), Scott Baio, Jim Belushi, Charles Bloom, Larry Breeding, Joshua Grenrock, Caren Kaye, Kim Lankford, Tammy Lauren, Tierre Turner. P: Jerry Frank. D: Jeff Margolis. W: Marty Farrell.

From cheesy music to a phony setup of Joe Namath visiting NBC's Burbank studios to promote the debut of his new sitcom, *The Waverly Wonders* (and clips of another bomb sitcom that will follow it, *Who's Watching the Kids*), this stinks. The former quarterback professes excitement about his gig ("I do get Sundays off!") and meets NBC stars who plug their shows and wonder what Joe is doing. Dean Martin thinks he's either Johnny Carson or a guest host on *The Tonight Show*, while Dick Clark believes Joe is leading a new musical group. Amid this mess, Joe sits down with Pat Morita to watch his show when Bob is electronically edited into the foreground in a bit taped at a recent special. Calling himself and Joe "the nose and the knees," Bob jokes the ex-player retired when he had more bandages than King Tut and says he's looking forward to watching Joe's show. That's the biggest lie in a preview filled with fakery.

Bob: ** Show: *


*A Masterpiece of Murder*
Jan. 27, 1986, Monday 9-11 p.m.

Bob Hope (Dan Dolan), Don Ameche (Frank Aherne), Jayne Meadows Allen (Matilda Hussey), Claudia Christian (Julia Forsythe), Yvonne De Carlo (Mrs. Bridget Murphy), Anne Francis (Ruth Beekman), Frank Gorshin (Pierre Rudin), Steven Keats (Lt. Simon Wax), Kevin McCarthy (Jonathan Hires), Anita Morris (Lola Crane), Clive Revill (Vincent Faunce), Stella Stevens (Della Valance/Deborah Potts), Jamie Farr (himself), Penny Baker (Christine Manning), Peter Palmer (Bronson), Eddie Ryder (Jerry Page), Louise Sorel (Louise), Joseph Della Sorte (Ugarti Van Meer), Jason Wingreen (Williams). With: Kent Barrett, Drew Borland, Alex Bruhanski, Gary Chalk, Alex Diakun, Anita Edwards, Francois Najda, Richard Sargent. EP: Andrew J. Fenady. P: Terry Morse. D: Charles S. Dubin. W: Andrew J. Fenady (story and teleplay), Terry Nation (teleplay).

Imagine an episode of *Murder She Wrote* stretched thinly over two hours with bad humor. That's *A Masterpiece of Murder*. Bob is Dan Dolan, a low-class private eye who bets on the horses while his landlady, Bridget Murphy, bugs him for late rent payment. Out of the blue, he is invited to the sixty-fifth birthday of Jonathan Hires at fictional seaside Santa Vista, California, along with Frank Aherne, an ex-con Dan arrested who now is living well. Other guests are gossip reporter Matilda Hussey, corporate raider Pierre Rudin, art dealer Vincent Faunce, Vincent's escort Della

Valance, Jonathan's ex-wife Ruth Beekman, Jonathan's niece Julia Forsythe, and Jonathan's wife Lola, who having an affair with Bronson, Jonathan's aide. Jonathan offers Dan and Frank fifty thousand dollars to return an invaluable painting Pierre stole from him. They locate it, but Jonathan is poisoned to death at his party. Pierre then claims Jonathan actually stole the painting from him and offers Dan and Frank one hundred thousand dollars for its recovery. Della reveals she is really art investigator Deborah Potter, says Pierre has other stolen paintings, and teams with the men to find the truth, as does Lt. Wax as he investigates the murder of Jonathan as well as another suspect. Dan and Frank eventually nab the killer and return the paintings after several yawn-worthy twists and turns.

There is a lot wrong here in this, Bob's only movie for television. Yvonne De Carlo and Anne Francis are wasted with few scenes and even fewer lines. It shows it is filmed in Canada, as Dan's car has the steering wheel on the right side instead of the left. When Frank tells Dan to turn left at one point, he goes right with nothing said. The interiors are as screwy as the exteriors—a table pier restaurant has an obviously painted backdrop of a dock behind it. And one ridiculous car chase has Dan and Frank jumping out of their speeding vehicle before it falls off a cliff, and both emerge with nary a scratch.

What really makes this bad are in-jokes that are simply unfunny. On his way to the party, Dan hears Bob Hope singing "Buttons and Bows" and says, "Ah, they don't make singers like they used to." Surveying the suspects in the murder, Dan says, "Hey, we got the makings of a television series here!" Then there is this exchange:

Frank: "Act your age!"
Dan: "My age? That's somewhere between *Blue Lagoon* and *Cocoon*."
Frank: "Closer to *Cocoon*."
Dan: "I don't break dance." (Frank rolls his eyes, as Don Ameche break danced in *Cocoon*.)

It is all as deadly as it sounds, and though just four years younger, Don Ameche looks a decade younger than Bob in the movie. Bob's delivery is a liability too. On several lines, he breaks into a grin like he is doing a monologue on one of his specials, and it is obvious he is using cue cards too. All told, this ain't a masterpiece, and it feels like murder getting through it.

Bob and Show: **

*Highway to Heaven*: "Heaven Nose, Mr. Smith"
March 30, 1988, Wednesday 9-10 p.m.

    Michael Landon (Jonathan Smith), Victor French (Mark Gordon). Guests: Murphy Cross (Constance), Bob Hope (Sycopomp), Patti Karr (Sarah), Bill Macy (Max), John Pleshette (Stanley), Anna Stuart (Nel). EP: Michael Landon. P: Kent McCray. D: Michael Landon. W: Lan O'Kun.
    Jonathan, an angel on Earth, goes into the clouds for an emergency meeting. Sycopomp tell him that thanks to a computer glitch, Max, an angel, has been assigned incorrectly and is now trying to break up the marriage of his son, Stanley, and Constance, a maid, with the more upscale Nel. A worried Sycopomp wants Jonathan to intervene so he won't have to bring it up with God. "He thought an apple was trouble in the Garden of Eden," Sycopomp quips. Jonathan's efforts fail, so he asks Sycopomp for more help, and the latter enlists Max's dead wife, Sarah, who's now an angel. This artificial, ho-hum story wastes Bob as much as a viewer's time. Typical of the "humor" here is Bob telling Jonathan, "You're an angel. Wing it" as he flaps his own. Bob is marginally better than the material, but that's not saying much.
    Bob: \*\*\* Show: \*\*


*The Golden Girls*: "You Gotta Have Hope"
Feb. 25, 1989, Saturday 9-9:30 p.m.

    Bea Arthur (Dorothy Zbornak), Betty White (Rose Nylund), Rue McClanahan (Blanche Devereaux), Estelle Getty (Sophia Petrillo). Guests: Bob Hope (himself), Douglas Seale (Seymour, "the Great Alphonso"), Eadie, Milly and Elena Del Rubio (the Donatello Triplets), Andre Rosey Brown (guitarist), June Claman (Phyllis), Linda L. Rand (Frieda), Daniel Rosen (Misha), Patrick Stack (man in locker room). EP: Paul Junger Witt, Tony Thomas. D: Terry Hughes. W: Barry Fanaro, Mort Nathan.
    The Ladies Auxiliary has Dorothy leading its charity talent fundraiser, but most acts auditioning are horrible, including "the Great Alphonso," a magician who Dorothy's mother, Sophia, forces Dorothy to take in order to get the singing Donatello Triplets Sophia represents. Worse yet, the planned emcee had to drop out. Then Dorothy's roommate, Rose,

insists that she can get Bob Hope, who she regards as her spiritual father, and she tells the auxiliary members he's a lock even though she hasn't confirmed his appearance. Dorothy and Rose's fellow roommate Blanche suggests meeting Bob at a local golf tournament to plead their case. The trio disguise themselves as men but miss him in the locker room. The next night, the variety show occurs with the programs claiming Bob Hope will appear, so Rose apologizes on stage for the mistake, only to see Bob emerge from the cabinet of the Great Alphonso, as the two were vaudeville partners. After huge applause, he quips, "Hey, I know this show is charity, but that's the smallest dressing room I've ever had in my life!" A horny Blanche makes move on him, and he says, "If you were any closer, there wouldn't be room for my car keys!" Bob then does a miniature monologue while Rose looks on adoringly. This is a typically smart, tight, funny episode of this series, but it's obvious that Bob slurs a few words and has a slower delivery than usual, even though his material is pretty good.

Bob: *** Show: ****

### *The Jim Henson Hour*: "Miss Piggy's Hollywood"
May 14, 1989, Sunday 7-8 p.m.

Frank Oz (Miss Piggy), Dave Goelz (Gonzo). Special Guest Stars: Justine Bateman, Bob Hope, Dudley Moore, George Wendt. Also Appearing: Charles Dougherty, Don Draper, Karl Rumberg, Kathleen Wirt. P: Lawrence S. Mirkin. D: Peter Harris. W: Bill Prady, Jim Lewis.

In the second half hour of this show, Miss Piggy hosts a tour of La La Land often interrupted by Gonzo, with questionable assists by Fozzie Bear. One activity is visiting the home of Bob Hope, but they leave before he answers the door in a golf hat and club. "I came all this way for nothing," he says in a slightly hoarse voice. "Kind of like the Oscars." That's it. The rest is intermittently amusing bits mostly with other guest stars playing themselves. As this was the lowest-rated show on the networks for that week, NBC took off the series after this episode (its fifth) before bringing it back for four final weeks in July 1989.

Bob: * Show: ***

*Roseanne*: "Tolerate Thy Neighbor"
Oct. 15, 1991, ABC Tuesday 9-9:30 p.m.

Roseanne Arnold (Roseanne Conner), John Goodman (Dan Conner), Laurie Metcalf (Jackie Harris), Michael Fishman (D.J. Conner), Sara Gilbert (Darlene Conner), Lecy Goranson (Becky Conner). Guests: Martin Mull (Leon Carp), Michael Des Barres (Steven), Meagan Fay (Kathy Bowman), Danton Stone (Jerry Bowman), Bonnie Sheridan (Bonnie Watkins), Carl Franklin (Officer Gil Robbins), Bob Hope (unbilled cameo). EP: Marcy Carsey, Jay Daniel, Bob Myer, Tom Werner. Co-EP: Roseanne Arnold, Tom Arnold, Chuck Lorre. P: Brad Isaacs, Maxine Lapiduss, Al Lowenstein. D: Andrew D. Weyman. W: Martin Mull, Maxine Lapiduss.

The matriarch of the Conner clan of Lanford, Illinois, Roseanne sees what appears to be movers taking out furniture from the Bowman house next door and goes over to snag one item she wants from their truck. The problem is that the "movers" were actually thieves taking goods while the Bowmans were away, and a livid Kathy Bowman tears into Roseanne for not realizing that and stopping them. Kathy remains vexed as the investigating police officer is an old friend of Roseanne's and Roseanne can only describe the suspect as a mutual old high school friend, but with a difference. "This guy's nose was like, way more scoopier, you know, kind of like Bob Hope's," Roseanne says. During the end credits, a lineup appears, and Roseanne's voice nixes them all until they come to Bob in a baseball cap, glowering and carrying a golf club, and she says, "That's him!" This is all quite fast and funny, as is the subplot involving Roseanne's boss, Leon (played by this episode's co-writer), trying to placate his partner Steven while not allowing him to meet Leon's mom for fear of offending her.

Bob: *** Show: ****


*The Simpsons*: "Lisa the Beauty Queen"
Oct. 15, 1992, Fox Thursday 8-8:30 p.m.

Voices: Dan Castellaneta (Homer Simpson, Grandpa, Krusty the Clown, Barney Gumble), Julie Kavner (Marge Simpson), Nancy Cartwright (Bart Simpson, Ralph Wiggum), Yeardley Smith (Lisa Simpson), Hank Azaria (Moe Szyslak, others), Harry Shearer (Ned Flanders, others). Special Guest: Bob Hope (himself). Guest: Amber

Williams (Lona Dempsey). Creator: Matt Groening. Developers/EP: James L. Brooks, Matt Groening, Sam Simon. P: Al Jean, Mike Reiss. W: Jeff Martin. D: Mark Kirkland.

In his last acting role, albeit on an animated cartoon, Bob plays himself addressing soldiers at Fort Springfield assisted by Lisa Simpson, whose father Homer raised money to enter her into the Little Miss Springfield beauty pageant after his daughter thought she was ugly. Lisa finishes as runner-up to Lona Dempsey, but when the latter gets electrocuted from a lightning bolt, Lisa assumes her duties as queen. Bob introduces her with this monologue: "This is Bob 'What the hell am I doing in Springfield?' Hope. How about that Mayor Quimby? He's some golfer. His golf ball spends more time underwater than Greg Louganis! And now I want to show you what you're fighting for—if there was a war—Little Miss Springfield!" The soldiers revolt, expecting to see a mature female instead, so Lisa and Bob ride a chopper out, with Bob asking if he can be dropped to perform at another location. Conan O'Brien, then one of this series' six producers, went to Bob's home to record his lines and got as strong a performance as he could from the comedian at his age. Bob contributes to a fine show where Lisa ends up being overthrown by the pageant sponsor, a cigarette manufacturer, for not endorsing her project but ending up happy anyway.

Bob: *** Show: ****

# 12. News, Informational, Documentary, Retrospective and Archival Shows

IN HIS 1997 COMPENDIUM *Brain Droppings*, comedian George Carlin moaned as he told readers to "imagine all the crap we'll have to endure on TV when Bob Hope dies. First of all, they'll show clips from all his old Road movies with Bing Crosby, and you can bet that some news anchor asshole will turn to the pile of clothing next to him and say, 'Well, Tami, I imagine Bob's on the Road to Heaven now.'"

The humorous musing had a basis in fact, for in reality television had been paying tribute to Bob Hope in some form more than 35 years before Carlin's book came out. Besides his annual birthday party specials that lasted fifteen years, Bob's life and work had been celebrated in dozens of TV shows, a testament to his impact on American culture in the twentieth century.

This section lists the bulk of national TV programs where Bob participates or is profiled as part of the presentation, generally documentary and informational series and specials. It also encompasses Bob's major appearances on news and public affairs programs apart from regular newscasts. Finally, because this is the most appropriate place to put it, shows where old footage of Bob from the movies and his TV work appear as part of the presentation is here too. This is wider than just retrospective specials—for proof of that, see the listing for the sitcom *M\*A\*S\*H*.

As one will see, what follows is an eclectic list that stands as testimony to Bob's achievements. Because of the nature of the material and the way it is used, the grading system does not apply to this chapter.

Bob gets ready to deliver his portion for the informational special *25 Years of Life Magazine*, which aired March 2, 1961. Courtesy of Getty Images.

By the way, Carlin's prediction that NBC would carry a three-hour, prime time special called "Thanks for the Memory" after Bob's death but sell it to CBS in fears about its demographics was somewhat true. It was CBS who presented a program in tribute to Bob on the day of his death. NBC, to its everlasting shame, just did a quick note of thanks before repeating an episode of *Fear Factor*. The network that Bob helped build gave him a terrible goodbye. Luckily, he had received many other salutes during his lifetime to compensate. In fact, one could make a good argument that Bob is the most celebrated civilian ever—even on television.

## *Republican National Convention*
July 7, 1952, Monday Sometime All Day

Bob delivers five minutes of jokes as a commentator for NBC News as part of its coverage of the selection of Dwight D. Eisenhower as a presidential candidate.

## *Person to Person*
June 10, 1955, CBS Friday 10-10:30 p.m.

Host: Edward R. Murrow. Guests: Bob Hope, Delores Hope, John W. Galbreath. P: Edward R. Murrow, Jesse Zousmer, John A. Aaron. D: Bob Daily.
Bob and his wife Delores speak to Edward R. Murrow from their home in Toluca Lake as the newsman profiles them.

## *Wide Wide World*: "The Sound of Laughter"
May 25, 1958, Sunday 4-5:30 p.m.

Host: Dave Garroway. Guests: Al Capp, Hal Holbrook, Bob Hope, Mort Sahl. P: Barry Wood.
On one of the last episodes of this live documentary/interview/variety series that ran three years, Bob discusses his ideas about humor with other guests.

## Exploring with Hope
Nov. 28, 1958, Saturday 4:30-5:30 p.m.

Host: Bob Hope. Guests: Ben Alexander, Molly Bee, Jack Jones, The Mitchell Boys Choir. Music: Les Brown.
Airing live from Hollywood after the Army-Navy football game, this has Bob promoting the new Boy Scouts of America Explorer program to high school students.

## *The Big Picture*: "USO Wherever They Go"
Circa 1960, Syndicated 30 minutes

Host: Army Master Sgt. Stuart Queen. Produced by Army Pictorial Center. Presented by the Office of the Chief of Information for the U.S. Army. No director or writing credits.
This profile of Bob's favorite service organization starts with Bob's monologue from his January 1960 Christmas special filmed in Alaska.

## *Project Twenty*: "Not So Long Ago"
Feb. 19, 1960, Friday 8:30-9:30 p.m.

Narrator: Bob Hope. P/D: Donald B. Hyatt. W: Richard Hanser. Music: Robert Russell Bennett.
Recapping the major political and social developments in the United States during the post-World War II era, this starts with V-J Day in 1945 and goes through the launch of the Korean War in 1950. Bob also appears clowning on a golf course in newsreel footage.

## *Lincoln Mercury Startime*: "Soldiers in Greasepaint"
April 26, 1960, Tuesday 9:30-10:30 p.m.

Host: Bob Crosby. Guests: Jane Morgan, Don Adams, The Modernaires, Paula Kelly, Harry S. Truman. P: Harry Sosnik, Joe Bigelow. D: Grey Lockwood. W: Joe Bigelow.
This tribute to the USO includes a film segment that mentions Bob's

work on behalf of the organization. The *Lincoln Mercury Startime* series only ran one season.


*See You at the Polls*
Fall 1960, Syndicated 30 minutes

Host: Bob Hope. Guests: Anna Maria Alberghetti, William Bendix, Spring Byington, Rosemary Clooney, Jimmy Durante, Peggy King, Peter Lawford, Groucho Marx, Ethel Merman, Donald O'Connor, Byron Palmer, Jane Russell, Danny Thomas. Unbilled: George Fenneman, Sherry Jackson. Narrator: Ed Reimers. P: Jack Denove.

As a slapdash push for Americans to register to vote in the 1960 presidential election, this sorry special has only William Bendix, Spring Byington, Groucho Marx, Danny Thomas, George Fenneman, and Sherry Jackson filming new material along with Bob. The latter rather flatly and falsely proclaims that the show has "probably the greatest collection of musical numbers someone put together in a half hour." It's more like the greatest rush job ever, as all the performances are clips from TV shows and movies, including Bob doing "Buttons and Bows" from his 1948 film *The Paleface*. Bob humorlessly introduces Bing Crosby and later does the same for John C. Cornelius, president of the American Heritage Foundation, a group that produced this mess. Cornelius is bland in his address too. It's hard to imagine this jumble inspired many to go to the ballot box.


*25 Years of Life Magazine*
March 2, 1961, Thursday 9:30-11 p.m.

Sid Caesar, Bob Hope, C.D. Jackson, Henry Luce.

A review of the first quarter century of the pictorial heavy periodical, this quasi-documentary has Bob and Sid Caesar contributing comedy to it. John E. McMillin posted a blistering takedown of this special in *Sponsor* magazine, calling it the worst TV program of the 1960-1961 season. He described it as "a confused, mindless mish-mosh in which Bob Hope, Sid Caesar, *Life* photographs, corny choreography, a pompous sermon on the horrors of war, a parade of stage and screen beauties, and some less than convincing 'dramatic' sequences with Time-Life officials [Henry] Luce and C.D. Jackson were all jumbled up together in a production that lacked point, purpose, dignity or integrity."

*Project Twenty*: "**The Story of Will Rogers**"
March 28, 1961, Tuesday 9-10 p.m.

Narrator: Bob Hope. P/D: Donald B. Hyatt. W: Richard Hanser, Rod Reed. Music: Robert Russell Bennett.
Bob narrates a biography of the humorist whom he admired.

*The DuPont Show of the Week*: "**Laughter, U.S.A.**"
Sept. 17, 1961, Sunday 10-11 p.m.

Narrator: George Burns. P/D: Donald Hyatt. W: Richard Hanser, Rod Reed.
This review of the history of American comedy includes clips of Bob's Berlin monologue.

*The DuPont Show of the Week*: "**USO: Wherever They Go**"
Oct. 8, 1961, Sunday 10-11 p.m.

P: John A. Aaron, Jesse Zousmer. W: George Foster.
Clips and an interview with Bob appear in this survey of nearly two decades of USO activity entertaining America's troops.

*Project Twenty*: "**The World of Bob Hope**"
Oct. 29, 1961, Sunday 7:30-8:30 p.m.

Narrator: Alexander Scourby. EP: Donald B. Hyatt. P/D: Eugene S. Jones. W: Joseph Liss.
NBC News produces this documentary on Bob that includes interviews with him, Mort Lachman, Peter Leeds, his cue card holder Barney McNulty, advertising executive Tom Greenhau, and friend Monte Brice. Along with clips from *The Bob Hope Christmas Show* of Jan. 11, 1961 (see Chapter 3: Specials—1960s), this also shows the taping of *The*

*Bob Hope Buick Sports Awards Show* (see Chapter 9: Games and Sports) with guests Dean Martin, Jayne Mansfield, Dana Andrews, and Esther Williams waiting backstage. Viewers see rare family photos too, plus Bob entertaining patients at a St. Louis children's hospital ward (when one child gets laughs for his own joke, Bob quips, "How can this be a battle of wits and I'm losing?"), schmoozing with guests at a cocktail party, eagerly anticipating a round of golf in Palm Springs, and visiting his home in Toluca Lake, where a six-inch steel door opens up to show it housing every joke and script Bob has collected in his career. This was rerun on *Summer Special* on July 18, 1963, just three weeks after that series reran *The Bob Hope Moscow Show* from 1958.

### *The DuPont Show of the Week*: "Hollywood: My Home Town"
Jan. 7, 1962, Sunday 10-11 p.m.

Host/Narrator: Ken Murray. D: William Martin. W: Royal Foster.

Ken Murray shows his home movies of stars that include Bob Hope. Murray did a lot of these filling up time on NBC's movies in the 1960s, *The Judy Garland Show* in 1963-1964, and more.

### *The Big Picture*: "The Shape of the Nation"
Circa Fall 1962, Syndicated 30 minutes

Host/Narrator: Bob Hope. Also Appearing: Jerry Colonna, Bud Wilkinson, Bob Richards, Alan B. Shepard Jr. Produced by Army Pictorial Center. Presented by the Office of the Chief of Information for the U.S. Army. No director or writing credits given.

As three out of every five men called for U.S. military service are judged unfit for duty, Bob warns that Americans need to get more physical activity in their lives. To make his point, this film shows how other nations, particularly Communist ones, train their youth to work out in preparation for sports and military activities. He discusses the topic with Jerry Colonna before getting reports from University of Oklahoma football Bud Wilkinson, a special consultant to President John F. Kennedy on physical fitness; three-time decathlete winner Bob Richards; and astronaut Alan B. Shepard Jr. It ends with Jerry working out on the parallel bars and lifting weight, with Bob squeezing Colonna's bicep and quipping, "Now that's nice firm flab!" followed by President Kennedy narrating the need for more exercise in everyone's lives.

## *One for the Money*
1963, Syndicated 30 minutes

Host: Dick Van Dyke. Guests: Bob Hope, Gene Barry, Jack Benny, Gary Crosby, Jimmy Durante, Lorne Greene, Joe and Eddie, Red Nichols, The Sportsmen, Jerry Van Dyke, Nancy Wilson, Jane Wyatt. Announcer: Don Wilson.

Basically a plea by entertainers for viewers to contribute to the March of Dimes, this filmed production apparently has vanished from circulation despite the stars involved. Too bad.

## *Hollywood and the Stars*
Mondays 9:30-10 p.m.
"The Fabulous Musicals" (Dec. 2, 1963)
"The Funny Men, Part II" (Dec. 16, 1963)
"The One and Only Bing" (Dec. 23, 1963)
"Hollywood Goes to War" (Jan. 27, 1964)

Host/Narrator: Joseph Cotten. EP: David Wolper. P/D: Jack Haley, Jr. W/P: Irwin Rosten ("The Funny Men, Part II"), Stan Atkinson ("The One and Only Bing"), Nicholas Noxon ("Hollywood Goes to War").

A documentary series that ran one year on NBC, *Hollywood and the Stars* profiles a different aspect of entertainment history every week. "The Fabulous Musicals" presents "Thanks for the Memory" from *The Big Broadcast of 1938*, while other shows include newsreel footage of Bob joking in D.C., playing golf, performing before soldiers, and doing comedy routines with Crosby (including Road picture clips).

## *The World's Greatest Showman: The Legend of Cecil B. DeMille*
Dec. 1, 1963, Sunday 8:30-10 p.m.

P/W: Stanley Roberts. D: Boris Sagal. Music: Elmer Bernstein.

Recounting the story of the popular filmmaker, Bob serves as one of the interviewees here.

## *The Magic of Broadcasting*
May 1, 1966, CBS Sunday 10-11 p.m.

P/W: Lee Mendelson. D: Ben Hill.

Footage of Bob appears along with many other celebrities in this survey of radio and TV history.

## *Wayne and Shuster Take an Affection Look At ...*
June 17, 1966, CBS Friday 10-11 p.m.

Hosts: Johnny Wayne, Frank Shuster. EP: Gil Rodin. P/D: Norman Campbell. W: Frank Shuster, Johnny Wayne, Arthur Knight.

The Canadian comedy duo reviews the careers of Bing Crosby and Bob Hope on the debut of this series, previously seen on the Canadian Broadcasting Corporation as *Television Show of the Week*.

## *From Cat Whiskers to Peacock: Forty Years of NBC*
Dec. 15, 1966, Thursday 10-11 p.m.

Host: Chet Huntley. Interviewees: Bob Hope, Chet Lauck, Art Linkletter, Groucho Marx, Rudy Vallee, Jim Boles, John Guedel, Marty Halperin, Eden Marx, Bernie Milligan, Rev. Peter O'Sullivan, David Brinkley. P/W: Bernard N. Smith. D: Donald I. Davis.

Supposedly honoring 250,000 hours of radio and 125,000 of TV, this dry recitation of the network's history has plenty of film clips and stills to illustrate mostly rare radio bits weighed down by Chet Huntley's stilted commentary and largely unexceptional interviews. The latter includes comments from Bob, seen on tape on the set of his recent special. Asked how things have changed over the thirty years when he started working for NBC, Bob says people are more aware of their world and comedy is now more sophisticated. He downplays ethnic humor from the old days and adds, "Comedy today to be accepted must be based on truth." Bob isn't particularly funny or insightful beyond that, and he's obviously reading cue cards. Incidentally, the odd title's first part comes from how KFI radio in Los Angeles aired its content through a little wire called a cat whisker.

### *The Big Picture*: "When the Chips Are Down"
1968, Syndicated 30 minutes

Host/Narrator: Bob Hope. Also Appearing: Phyllis Diller. Presented by the Office of the Chief of Information for the U.S. Army. No producer, director or writing credits given.

"Hey, this is Bob 'Ready with Your National Guard' Hope, and I want to tell you that the story of today's Army and Air National Guard is something all Americans can be proud of." The men shoot away the enemy so that Bob can play golf, a dubious start to a profile of combat training guardsmen undergo in America. He leavens it with the inevitable Bing Crosby joke and scatters other gags, sometimes inappropriately, while profiling guardsmen from West Virginia to Hawaii. As with most of his Vietnam specials, viewers are left wondering if Bob just accepted everything told to him by military officials, especially as he praises the guardsmen's work in the Watts riots without giving context to what precipitated the event. Phyllis Diller makes a cameo one assumes probably occurred when she filmed *The Private Navy of Sgt. O'Farrell* with Bob.

### *I Remember Illinois*
Feb. 18, 1968, Sunday 6:30-7:30 p.m.

Host/Music Composer: Steve Allen. Interviewees: Bob Hope, Jack Benny, Dave Garroway, Benny Goodman, Mahalia Jackson, Gene Krupa, Mercedes McCambridge, Win Stracke, Burr Tillstrom, Studs Turkel, Teddy Wilson, Chicago Mayor Richard Daley, Illinois Gov. Otto Kerner. EP: Walter Schwimmer. P/D: Harry Rasky. W: Loring Mandel.

This filmed tribute to the 150th anniversary of the statehood of Illinois includes Bob recalling his early days of performing in Chicago during the 1920s.

### *The Sullivan Years*
Oct. 17, 1971, CBS Sunday 9-10:30 p.m.

Host: Ed Sullivan. EP: Bob Precht. P: Robert Arthur, John Moffitt. D: John Moffitt.

Ed reviews highlights of guests including Bob who appeared on his series, which ended four months earlier after an incredible twenty-three years on CBS.

## *The Great Radio Comedians*
May 11, 1972, PBS Thursday 8:30-9:30 p.m.

Bob is seen performing before the troops in World War II in this documentary.

## *The World at War*: "Morning (June-August 1944)"
Feb. 27, 1974, Syndicated 60 minutes

Narrator: Sir Laurence Olivier. P: Jeremy Isaacs.
Bob appears in footage entertaining Allied forces prior to the launch of the D-Day campaign.

## *CBS News Special*: "A Tribute to Jack Benny"
Dec. 29, 1974, CBS Sunday 8:30-9:30 p.m.

Bob delivers a powerful eulogy at Jack Benny's memorial as part of this documentary about the life of the comedian.

## *CBS News Special*: "1974: A Television Album"
Dec. 29, 1974, CBS Sunday 9:30-10:30 p.m.

This retrospective includes clips of Bob in performance, giving Hope back-to-back appearances on one night of news programs on a rival network. Pretty impressive.

## *M\*A\*S\*H*: "Deluge"
Feb. 17, 1976, CBS Tuesday 9-9:30 p.m.

Cast: Alan Alda (Capt. Benjamin Franklin "Hawkeye" Pierce), Mike Farrell (Capt. B.J. Hunnicutt), Harry Morgan (Col. Sherman T. Potter),

Loretta Swit (Maj. Margaret "Hot Lips" Houlihan), Larry Linville (Maj. Frank Burns), Gary Burghoff (Cpl. Walter "Radar" O'Reilly), Jamie Farr (Cpl. Maxwell Klinger), William Christopher (Father Francis Mulcahy), Kario Salem (the Youngster), Anthony Palmer (the Sergeant), Lois Farker (Nurse Lt. Able), Robert Hall (the Corporal). P: Larry Gelbart, Gene Reynolds. D: William K. Jurgensen. W: Larry Gelbart, Simon Muntner.

As the 4077th deals with an aggravating influx of wounded along with horrible weather, snippets of black-and-white newsreels appear as counterpoint in this episode, including Bob Hope clowning with other celebrities playing golf. Interestingly, producer and co-writer Larry Gelbart worked for Hope from 1948-1952 and toured the Korean War (where *M\*A\*S\*H* is set) at that time. Also, frequent *M\*A\*S\*H* director Hy Averback served as announcer for the Hope specials for the years Gelbart wrote for the comedian and into the 1950s.

### *The Big Event*: "Life Goes to the Movies"
Oct. 31, 1976, Sunday 8-11 p.m.

Hosts: Henry Fonda, Shirley MacLaine, Liza Minnelli. EP: Jack Haley Jr. P/ W: Richard Schickel. P/D: Mel Stuart. P: Malcolm Leo.

This history of American cinema includes a survey of the Road pictures with Bob and Bing.

### *The Big Event*: "NBC The First 50 Years"
Nov. 21, 1976, Sunday 7-11:30 p.m.

Host/Narrator: Orson Welles. Presenters: Jack Albertson, Milton Berle, David Brinkley, Johnny Carson, John Chancellor, Angie Dickinson, Bob Hope, Gene Kelly, Jerry Lewis, Dean Martin, Don Meredith, Gregory Peck, Freddie Prinze, George C. Scott. EP/D: Greg Garrison. P: Lee Hale, Chet Hagan. W: Abby Mann. Additional Material: Jess Oppenheimer, Mike Marmer, Bill Angelos, Orson Welles. Music: Jack Elliott.

Celebrating NBC's half century of radio and TV broadcasting, this has an audio clip of Bob's radio show appearing in the opening montage. Bob disappears for roughly two thirds of the program thereafter until he is heard as a commentator on the 1973 Bob Hope Classic and then gets his own segment. The nice tribute commends his service to the network, with clips from him on *All Star Revue* on April 26, 1952, a 1962 special, his first color show on Dec. 15, 1965, his Sept. 25, 1974 special, and one newly taped joke about President Jimmy Carter. He appears one more time with Humphrey Bogart on the 1955 Oscars ceremony before this retrospective ends.

*When Television Was Young*
April 28, 1977, CBS Thursday 9-11 p.m.

Host/Narrator: Charles Kuralt. EP/W: Perry Wolf. P: Max Wilk. Co-P: Judith Hole.

A retrospective of mostly kinescopes of live 1950s TV shows, this includes a clip of Bob, Frank Sinatra and Bing Crosby from *The Edsel Show* in 1957 where the soundtrack was lost and all appear mute (there have been tapes found with the sound on since this first aired).

*TV: The Fabulous 50s*
March 5, 1978, Sunday 8-9:30 p.m.

Hosts: Red Skelton, Michael Landon, Lucille Ball, David Jannsen, Mary Martin, Dinah Shore. P/W: David Lawrence, Draper Lewis. P: Henry Jaffe. D: Jonathan Lucas.

Despite a few inappropriate clips from 1960s series like *My Three Sons* and *The Andy Griffith Show*, this is a fairly solid remembrance of early television. Bob appears in the comedy variety segment hosted by Red Skelton in a great monologue from his May 23, 1954 appearance on *The Jack Benny Program*. "I'm very happy to be over here at CBS, ladies and gentlemen. This is rather strange for me. I'm on the major network." Bob mouths "N-B-C" before he continues with "I really feel like a stranger. I feel like Zsa Zsa at a PTA meeting over here." He adds, "But I am awfully thrilled to be here at CBS, That's Crosby and Benny's Sandbox, and I wanna tell you. But it's a beautiful place, and Television City is right next to Farmers Market. And it's very convenient. You can lay [eggs] here and sell them there."

*A Tribute to "Mr. Television" Milton Berle*
March 26, 1978, Sunday 9-10 p.m.

Lucille Ball, Milton Berle, Joey Bishop, George Carlin, Johnny Carson, Angie Dickinson, Kirk Douglas, Bob Hope, Gabe Kaplan, Gene Kelly, Kermit the Frog, Donny Osmond, Marie Osmond, Gregory Peck, Carl Reiner, Don Rickles, Frank Sinatra, Marlo Thomas, Flip Wilson. EP: Jerry Frank. P/D: Bill Carruthers. P: Jerry Frank. W: Marty Farrell.

Bob tapes a salute to open this special, which has a lot of rare clips of "Uncle Miltie" in action from his 1950s TV series that are enjoyable but only a few new moments from guest stars here that are funny or distinguished. Unfortunately, Bob falls into the latter. His rather standard introduction includes, "Tonight we're going to see some of the great names in entertainment here to pay tribute to another performer, a pioneer in television, a man who blazed the trail. He had the daring, the courage and the guts to be the first. He took on the dangers of the unknown and opened the doors the rest of us followed after." Bob vanishes after that.

*CBS On the Air*
April 1, 1978, CBS Saturday 8:30-11 p.m.

Hosts: Carol Burnett, Art Carney, Sherman Hemsley, Carroll O'Connor, Tony Randall, Isabel Sanford. EP: Alexander H. Cohen. P: Lee Miller. D: Clark Jones. W: Hildy Parks. Co-P: Roy A. Somlyo. Musical Director: Elliot Lawrence. Choreographer: Alan Johnson. 50th Anniversary Music: Leonard Bernstein. "Members of the Family" Music and Lyrics: Jerry Herman.

Bob has a blink-and-you'll-miss it clip of his appearance on *What's My Line?* in 1956 in a tribute to CBS game shows hosted by Art Linkletter. This is a classy, enjoyable finale of a weeklong celebration by the network recounting highlights of its first half-century.

*Bing Crosby: His Life and Legend*
May 25, 1978, ABC Thursday 9-10 p.m.

Narrator: William Holden. Interviewees: Fred Astaire, Frank Capra, Rosemary Clooney, Gary Crosby, Mary Crosby, Ella Fitzgerald,

Princess Grace of Monaco (Grace Kelly), Bob Hope, Danny Kaye, Fred MacMurray, Dean Martin, Mary Martin, Ethel Merman, Merle Oberon, Donald O'Connor, Norman Panama, Al Renker, Dinah Shore, Twiggy, Jane Wyman. EP: Franklin Konigsberg. W/P/D: Marshall Flaum.

A fond remembrance to Bob's late longtime partner and foil, this has only a couple of moments in it from Bob, probably because he was not as effusive or insightful as some of the others recalling their memories of Crosby. Discussing Bing's Oscar win for Best Actor in *Going My Way*, Bob quips, "How could a man with that many kids play a priest?! You've got to be a fine actor for that!" He later summarizes his contemporary's career with "He was such a master of his craft, a great light comedian, and he loved to do holiday stuff. He loved broad stuff. He got a personal kick out of it, and everybody got a kick out of him doing it." Other than clips of the two in action, that's it for Bob in this special.

**The Big Event: "TV Guide: The First 25 Years"**
Oct. 21, 1979, Sunday 8-10 p.m.

Host: Phil Donahue. Guests: Lucille Ball, Lee Grant, Bob Hope, William S. Paley, Arthur Godfrey, Merrill Pannitt, John Chancellor, Richard Salant, Tom Smothers, Norman Lear, Elton Rule, Neil Hickey, Nicholas Johnson, Fred Silverman, Peggy Charren, Aaron Spelling, Carl Reiner, Rev. Jesse Jackson. Music: Peter Matz. EP: Robert H. Precht, Jay S. Harris (based on his book). W: Jeff Greenfield. D: Russ Petranto.

Recapping the initial quarter century of the publication which has the highest circulation covering American television, this special gets some of Bob's better quotes about his work in the medium. As the first interviewee, he tells Phil Donahue, "I remember my first show. I did it at New Amsterdam Theater in 1950, and we had all the help we could get, a great staff and everything. And I came back [to New York City]—I was nervous—because I came back a month later to do my second show, and I got into a cab to go to NBC in front of the Waldorf. And the cab driver said, 'Uh, Bob Hope, huh?' 'That's right,' I said. 'What, are you going to do, another TV show?' I said, 'That's right.' He said, 'The first one wasn't too good, you know.' And I said, 'Who asked you?' And he said, 'I'm the people.'" Bob later reappears on a discussion of TV variety series of the late 1960s and their censorship problems to say NBC was always cautious about including his political jokes in his specials. "We always fought them on that," he said. The show has some great interviews and films to illustrate its points and would be perfect if it didn't make some stupid choices in its montages, like having the Village People's "Macho Man" serve as the soundtrack behind a selection of western clips.

### *Best of the Dean Martin Roasts*
Feb. 26, 1980, Sunday 9-11 p.m.

This retrospective includes clips from the Bob Hope and Lucille Ball roasts.

### *Where Have All the Children Gone*
December 1980, Syndicated 60 minutes

Michael Landon, Melissa Sue Anderson, Carol Burnett, Johnny Cash, Bill Cosby, Glenn Ford, Bob Hope, Ron Howard, Dennis Weaver. D: Michael Landon.
A documentary on drug abuse, with Michael Landon enlisting top celebrity pals including Bob to add straight commentary.

### *Laughing All the Way: 30 Years of TV's Greatest Hits*
Nov. 25, 1980, Tuesday 8-10 p.m.

Hosts: Bea Arthur, Jane Curtin, Howard Hesseman, Carl Reiner, Dick Van Dyke. EP: Howard Lipstone. W: Buz Kohan.
This special contains clips of Bob entertaining troops overseas.

### *NBC Magazine with David Brinkley*
March 20, 1981, Friday 10-11 p.m.

Host/Reporter: David Brinkley.
David Brinkley interviews Bob and gets a look at his joke vault at home.

## Jackie Gleason Presents the Honeymooners Reunion
May 13, 1985, Monday 8-9 p.m.

Hosts: Jackie Gleason, Audrey Meadows. Special Guest: Bob Hope. Incidental Music: Bob Alberti. P/D/W: Andrew Solt. P: Susan F. Walker. W: Robert Strauss.

Even though he had nothing to do with the show in its original run, Bob kicks off a special honoring one of TV's most beloved creations with the following words: "Tonight, we're going to see some of the funniest shows that ever appeared on television. These Honeymooners were broadcast live back in the 1950s and haven't been seen since. So, for the first time in thirty years, let's share some of the greatest moments from one of the longest, noisiest honeymoons in history. Now your host, the Great One himself, Jackie Gleason." The speech runs only twenty-five seconds, but it does a great job in setting the tone for the show, and Jackie is able to tweak Bob with a little joke in response. Jackie isn't on the same stage as Bob, and his commentary feels a little staged, but otherwise this is a treasure trove of rare moments from a top comedy property that often produce belly laughs.

## Milton Berle: Mr. Television
May 28, 1985, PBS Tuesday 9-10 p.m.

Narrator: Alan King. Interviewer: Robert Batscha. Interviewees: Steve Allen, Buddy Arnold, Irving Brecher, Sid Caesar, Sammy Davis Jr., Greg Garrison, Bob Hope, Hal Kanter, Robert Klein, Arnold Stang, Danny Thomas, Barbara Walters, Sylvester "Pat" Weaver. EP: Madison D. Lacy. P/W: Mark Duffy. D: Gary Kaskel.

"What can you say about Milton that hasn't said before and he won't say tomorrow?" says Bob as the first interviewee shown. "He was the only one, Mr. Television. And in those days, if you had a TV set—there weren't too many around—you had to watch Milton because he started the whole thing." He later adds how Milton walked on his ankles to generate laughs and adds, "He was a smash and gave a lot of people ideas." This includes an interview with Milton by the Paley Center for Media (known then as the Museum of Broadcasting) and lots of clips that have been restored to high quality for this special.

***Great Performances*: "Irving Berlin's America"**
March 7, 1986, PBS Friday 9-10:30 p.m.

A superb remembrance of one of the best songwriters of all time, Bob has surprisingly little of note to say about his time working with Berlin. He recalls touring with the USO during World War and having a classic Berlin tune performed. "I think every time that was done overseas, we were there at Christmas time, and there were tears when they sang 'White Christmas.'" He also notes that "In 1948 he went to the Berlin airlift with us. We had a great time, and of course he thrilled everyone." That's pretty much all Bob has to add here.

***Our World*: "Autumn 1956"**
Oct. 16, 1986, ABC Thursday 8-9 p.m.

Hosts: Linda Ellerbee, Ray Gandolf. P: Avram Westin.
Bob appears early in this roundup of news items from the survey period, first in a clip talking about President Dwight Eisenhower and then in a brief new interview discussing the Chief Executive before a few more clips of Bob discussing Eisenhower and his opponent, Adlai Stevenson.

***Dear America: Letters from Vietnam***
April 3, 1988, HBO Sunday 9-10:30 p.m.

D: Bill Couturie.
This powerful history of the Vietnam War uses the perspective of soldiers writing back home to their loved ones as a backdrop of footage supplied by NBC News and other sources. Bob is seen in a clip based on a letter by the soldier Bob introduced to Miss World Reita Faria on his Jan. 18, 1967 special, where the flustered man can only muster an embarrassing "How!" This receives a theatrical release later in 1988.

*Fifty Years of Television: A Golden Celebration*
Nov. 24, 1989, CBS Friday 9-11 p.m.

Hosts: Walter Cronkite, John Larroquette, Carl Reiner, Jane Seymour, Kermit the Frog, Miss Piggy. EP: John Moffitt, Pat Tourk Lee. P/W: Phil Savenick. Supervising P/W: Harry Arends. D: John Moffitt. W: Richard Rosen. Special Material: Ron Richards, Andrew Olstein.

A snippet of Bob's Sept. 26, 1973 monologue appears at the four-minute mark of this fine special, as well as Bob and Milton in drag roughly fifteen minutes later from *The Kraft 75$^{th}$ Anniversary Show* in 1978. About a half hour later, John Larroquette introduces a special two-minute tribute to Bob encompassing his earliest appearances and his USO tours as part of this excellent, tightly edited retrospective.

*American Masters*: "You're the Top—The Cole Porter Story"
July 23, 1990, PBS Monday 9-10 p.m.

Host: Bobby Short. Interviewees: Richard Adler, Kitty Carlisle, Saul Chaplin, Cyd Charisse, James Omar Cole (Porter's cousin), Douglas Fairbanks Jr., Michael Feinstein, Ted Fetter (Porter's cousin), Brendan Gill (author), Bob Hope, Jean Howard, Garson Kanin, Gene Kelly, Robert Kimball (musical theater historian), Lilo, Tony Martin, Honoria Murphy Donnelly (Porter's goddaughter), Hermes Pan, Linda Ronstadt, Jonathan Schwartz, Ben Sturges, Saint Subber, Dionne Warwick, Maury Yeston. EP: Susan Lacy. P: Kirk D'Amico. W/D: Allan Albert.

Bob calls the esteemed songwriter a genius in this documentary profile as he recalls his work in *Red Hot and Blue!* on Broadway in the 1930s. It includes a clip of Bob and Ethel Merman singing "It's De-Lovely" on one of his specials. Clad in a golf outfit, Bob obviously loves the recollection and recalls it clearly too.

*Frank Sinatra: The Voice of Our Time*
March 5, 1991, PBS Tuesday 5:30-7 p.m.

This includes a clip of Frank's TV debut on Bob's second special in 1950.

***Remember Pearl Harbor***
Dec. 7, 1991, CBS Saturday 8-10 p.m.

Host: Charles Kuralt. Interviewees: President George Bush, Gen. H. Norman Schwarzkopf, Bob Hope, James A. Michener, Eric Sevareid. Narrators: Matthew Broderick, Kevin Costner, Richard Dreyfuss, Dustin Hoffman, Jack Lemmon, Robert Mitchum, Paul Newman, George Takei, Peter Yoshida. P: Peter Schweitzer. W: Charles Kuralt, Peter Schweitzer, Andrew Lack. D: Don Roy King.

Ten minutes into this documentary, Bob recalls the mood of the United States prior to the attack fifty years earlier that launched America's entry into World War II. "The country was in great shape, and everything was working. We started doing the Road pictures and having a ball with Crosby, and you had wonderful baseball and great fans. It was a great setting. Everybody was very, very happy until the war started." Surprisingly, that is about all he has to contribute to this otherwise excellent report.

***Lucy and Desi: A Home Movie***
Feb. 13, 1993, Sunday 9-11 p.m.

Host/P/D: Lucie Arnaz. P/D/W: Laurence Luckenbill. W: Lonny Reed.

Bob recalls selling war bonds with Lucy and Desi in the 1940s as part of this special. It also includes a clip from the March 4, 1976 *The Tonight Show* where Bob was talking to Johnny Carson about his days working with Desi with the latter as a fellow guest.

***The Barbara Walters Special: Happy Hour***
May 23, 1994, ABC Monday 8-9 p.m.

Hostess: Barbara Walters.

A retrospective program, this includes a clip from Barbara's 1977 interview with Bob Hope.

*Frank Sinatra Duets*
Nov. 25, 1994, CBS Friday 10-11 p.m.

A promotional special for Frank's new (and last original) album has footage from the "Life Goes to War" special on *The Big Event* with Bing and Bob as part of its clips in the past.

*Classic Stand-Up Comedy on Television: A Museum of Television and Radio Special*
Sept. 14, 1996, Saturday 8-9:30 p.m.

Bob naturally is one of the comics shown in action at this look back in time documentary.

*ABC Originals: "Inside the Osmonds"*
Feb. 5, 2001, ABC Monday 8-10 p.m.

A clip of Bob appearing on *Donny & Marie* is blended into this fictional TV-movie of the family's life story.

*The 76th Annual Academy Awards*
Feb. 29, 2004, ABC Sunday 8:30 p.m.-12:15 a.m.

Tom Hanks pays tribute to Bob and his contributions to the Oscars after his passing as part of the ceremony's activities.

# Epilogue

**BOB'S WORST NIGHTMARE** is now occurring: He's being forgotten.

The man who responded to Neil Hickey's question in *TV Guide* in 1974 about how he wanted to be remembered was "I don't care—just so they don't say, 'Who was he?'" would be disappointed to learn that many people born during or after the tail end of his TV career in the 1990s have no idea who he is without consulting the Internet. Lacking a show in repeats or a movie series that can be a franchise (sorry, the Road pictures are not *Star Wars*), there is little incentive beyond curiosity for them to find more about him.

Bob is not totally unknown by all younger people. Marie Osmond says that when she recently met children of military families, they were familiar who Bob Hope was thanks to his contributions to the USO. "It made me so happy that they knew who he was," she says. "They knew Bob because he served our country and he lifted the spirits of our troops during war. There will never be another Bob Hope, because he started all that."

Beyond that group, though, Bob is pretty much unknown. He is not helped by few comedians today citing him as an inspiration. Some of them might cite their disdain or indifference to him due to his reliance (some may say overreliance) on his writers coming up with his material, as they prefer to write their own jokes, usually incorporating their own personal experiences, something Bob shied away from doing.

Indeed, while Bob's presentation influenced the basic monologues used by most late night TV comedians to introduce their shows, his content of gently needling his targets is not in vogue anymore. As for the remaining parts of his specials, the jokes in the skits and banter are regarded as corny and passé, the type of stuff *Saturday Night Live* and others of its routinely send up as being "uncool."

"I don't think young people would be interested in him," says Howard Albrecht, one of Bob's former writers. "Young people would look at Bob Hope today and say he's old-fashioned. He did stay too long, and when you think of the shows near the end of his career, they were just not good."

Others just say Bob was overrated and that in retrospect, he was nowhere near as funny as his reputation suggests. These statements rankle his defenders, especially when it comes from fellow comedians.

"I do believe many of them were envious of Bob Hope's success and resented it," says longtime writer Gene Perret of the criticism. "I don't like it when they say, 'He wasn't funny.' So many people owe their comedy careers to pioneers like Bob Hope. [Johnny] Carson, [Jay] Leno, [David] Letterman thrived on the style of comedy that Bob Hope developed.

"What you can say is, 'I don't find him funny.' There's a distinction. It's not logical to say he wasn't funny. You don't get to be one of the richest entertainers and perform seventy years without having something to offer."

If the younger generation consults just the news section to learn about Bob, it is a somewhat depressing read. Plans are underway to change the name of the Bob Hope Airport in Burbank to the Hollywood Burbank Airport, though a plaque honoring Bob will remain in the terminal. Meanwhile Bob's daughter, Linda Hope, has led her family's successful fight to avoid having Bob's home in Toluca Lake, California, designated a historic monument and deprive them from selling it. This follows finally selling the family's six-acre estate in Palm Springs with ten bedrooms in 2016 for $13 million, a far cry from its original $50 million list price.

Bob would hate all this talk of money, just as he did when he was alive. However, there were no other options for his family to take. Serving as head of their efforts, Linda wanted to maximize the profits from selling the property to benefit the Bob & Dolores Hope Foundation, which she chairs. Naming it a historic monument would reduce value of a property that had been dormant since Delores Hope died on Sept. 19, 2011 at 102 years old. (Incidentally, by the time of Bob's death, he and Delores had been wed nearly seventy years, from their marriage on Feb. 19, 1934 through June 2003. Among entertainment celebrities, only Karl Malden and Richard Attenborough have managed to match or beat Bob's achievement.)

Linda's argument mentioned that with so many other streets and buildings named after her father, the landmark designation for his longtime home is unnecessary. She did have a point there, for while the Burbank Airport designation will vanish, plenty of other landmarks sport his name across America, even if his name is unfamiliar to many younger individuals.

The result is now that Bob as a philanthropist has superseded Bob as an entertainer. And if a "typical" millennial investigates the latter, he or she might find that putting $21^{st}$ century standards on a $20^{th}$ century legend results in some uncomfortable reactions.

First, some of Bob's material is quite dated, and not just due to references of events that were current and are now forgotten and seem ancient. There are plenty of jokes considered politically incorrect involving women and just about any type of minority you can name, and his delivery of them with an accent or affected impression makes them only worse.

Then there is the presentation of entertainment on his show, which is no longer in vogue. Younger viewers may ask, "Why are his monologues so long and timid? Why do he and his guests engage in phony, artificial dialogue on stage? Why is the laugh track so obvious and loud? Why are actors who can't sing or dance trying to do so?"

The age issue probably appalls some too. The fact that Bob in the 1980s and 1990s was kissing and acting as the romantic lead opposite one woman who was a quarter of his age (Brooke Shields) and another one that had played a child on his 1960s anthology series (Ann Jillian) can be perturbing when viewed in that perspective.

Most perplexing may be watching Bob's comments on politicians and realizing they come across as weak tea in today's hyper-partisan world of comedy. With many comedians and shows regularly tearing nowadays into President Donald Trump, among other politicians, how would Bob handle the situation? Would Bob be considered cowardly for not taking sides if he were working today? If he cozied up to Trump like he did with other presidents from Franklin Delano Roosevelt to Bill Clinton, would he be so beloved? Could anybody be able to unite most Americans in comedy the way Bob did in today's world either?

While these are valid concerns, they all miss the point. Considering himself an average if blessed American at heart, Bob designed shows that were appealing to him on the belief that if he liked it, so would most viewers. When he gave one hundred percent to producing and performing those specials—heck, even when he gave seventy-five percent to it—it was electrifying. He left behind a lot of love as well as a lot of admirers for what he accomplished on TV and elsewhere.

"He was iconic," says Gloria Loring. "There are people of each generation who stand out above the rest, and when it came to have ambition as a performer and making your dreams come true, he just set out to conquer the world, and he did."

"He changed the face of show business by demonstrating that doing benefits would increase their income rather than deplete it," says Bob Mills." They saw him as an example and followed it. Now, benefits are common. Before Hope came along, they weren't."

"Bob Hope was one of a kind," notes Cathy Lee Crosby. "He was talented, dedicated, funny, big-hearted, loyal, smart, a PR genius, successful, wealthy in so many ways and single focused on making sure his life stood for something worthwhile that would stand the test of time. Entertaining others was his greatest happiness and he shared that joy with millions of people across all generations. What a great legacy, what a great example for us all."

"I began writing for Bob Hope in 1969, and I stayed with him practically without interruption until he retired from show business. The greatest compliment I can give him is that I enjoyed him as much on the day we stopped working together as I did on my first day on the job," says Gene Perret.

Bob at his best does provide joy and laughter for a viewer. The proof is there in his TV work for anyone to check out, online, on DVDs or in research collections. The assessments in this book is just one man's opinion, but they do provide anyone with a broad range of possibilities to review what Bob produced and recognize the generally high quality of his efforts.

Research Bob, and see how his mouth breaks into a smile when a joke from a monologue goes over well with an audience. Watch his face light up as he croons everything from "I Love a Rainy Night" with Eddie Rabbitt to "Silver Bells" with everyone from Gale Storm to Delores Hope. Look at the ease and grace he has in wearing a tuxedo and casually joking with leaders from across the world from the White House to Buckingham Palace and beyond.

It's all authentic and all too rare in show business at present, where many entertainers are more concerned with their images on social media than giving us their true selves on stage or through public service. It probably will be the last time our civilization ever witness such a phenomenon, which is a shame, but also a testament to what Bob Hope accomplished.

Thanks for the video memories, Bob. You gave TV some great moments and left us all richer from the experience, and your best work will survive as long as anyone enjoys a good laugh and a good time.

# Bibliography

Allen, Steve. *More Funny People*. Briarcliff Manor, NY: Stein and Day, 1982.

Brooks, Tim and Earle Marsh. *The Complete Directory to Prime Time Network and Cable TV Shows 1946-Present*, 9th ed. New York: Ballantine, 2007.

Carlin, George. *Braindroppings*. New York: Hyperion, 1997.

Einstein, Daniel. *Special Edition: A Guide to Network Television Documentary Series and Special News Reports, 1955-1979*. Metuchen, NJ: Scarecrow, 1987.

Faith, William Robert. *Bob Hope, a Life in Comedy*. New York: Putnam, 1982.

Gelbart, Larry. *Laughing Matters*. New York: Random House, 1998.

Goldberg, Lee. *Unsold Television Pilots*. Jefferson, NC: McFarland, 1990.

Graham, Jefferson. "Paying Homage to Bob Hope," *USA Today*. May 13, 2993, page 3D.

Hyatt, Wesley. *The Encyclopedia of Daytime Television*. New York: Billboard, 1997.

Hyatt, Wesley. *Television's Top 100: The Most-Watched American Broadcasts, 1960-2010*. Jefferson, NC: McFarland, 2012.

Hyatt, Wesley. *The Carol Burnett Show Companion: So Glad We Had This Time.* Albany, GA: Bear Manor Media, 2016.

Kisseloff, Jeff. *The Box: An Oral History of Television, 1920-1961.* New York: Penguin, 1995.

Marx, Arthur. *The Secret Life of Bob Hope.* New York: Barricade, 1993.

Metz, Robert. *The Tonight Show.* New York: Playboy, 1980.

Mills, Robert L., J.D. *The Laugh Makers: A Behind-the-Scenes Tribute to Bob Hope's Incredible Gag Writers.* Albany, GA: Bear Manor Media, 2009.

Murphy, Mary. "Hail to the Chief of Comedy," *TV Guide*, Aug. 10-16, 1996, pp. 33-34.

"NBC's King for 50 Years," *USA Today*, May 16, 1988, page 6D.

Rensin, David and Bill Zehme. *The Bob Book: A Celebration of the Ultimate Okay Guy.* New York: Dell, 1991.

Schafer, Kermit. *Kermit Schafer's Blunderful World of Bloopers.* New York: Crown, 1978.

Stempel, Tom. *Storytellers to the Nation: A History of American Television Writing.* Syracuse University Press, 1996.

Wallace, Irving, David Wallechinsnky, Amy Wallace and Sylvia Wallace. *The Book of Lists #2.* New York: Bantam, 1980.

Wiley, Mason and Damien Bona. *Inside Oscar: The Unofficial History of the Academy Awards*, 10th anniversary ed. New York: Ballantine, 1993.

Young, Jordan R. *The Laugh Crafters: Comedy Writing in Radio and TV's Golden Age.* Beverly Hills, CA: Past Times Publishing Co., 1999.

Zoglin, Richard. *Hope: Entertainer of the Century.* New York: Simon & Schuster, 2014.

## Periodicals

*Broadcasting* (assorted issues 1950-1963)

*Sponsor* (assorted issues 1958-1963)

*USA Today* (assorted Nielsen ratings 1987-1996)

*Variety* and *Daily Variety* (assorted reviews 1948-1992)

## Websites

Eyes of a Generation

Internet Movie Database

TV Tango

TV.com

Ultimate70s.com

# Index

Aames, Willie, 216
Aaron, Henry, 177
Aaron, John A., 457, 460
Abbott, Bud, 48, 285
Abbott, Michael, 355, 358
Abbott, Norman, 219, 380, 385, 409, 444
Abbott and Costello—See Abbott, Bud, and Costello, Lou
*ABC Comedy Hour, The* (TV series), 337
*ABC Originals*: "Inside the Osmonds" (TV movie), 475
Abdul, Paula, 275
Abdul-Jabbar, Kareem, 234
Academy Awards, The, xvii, xix-xx, 3, 37, 48, 50, 53, 59, 63, 70, 75, 79-80, 93, 98, 101-102, 105-106, 111, 116, 120, 123, 130-131, 136, 141, 158, 162, 167-168, 177, 179, 187-188, 206, 219-220, 225-226, 229-231, 236, 238-239, 251, 255, 266, 276, 282-293, 295-301, 331, 333, 355, 387, 420, 432, 452, 467, 469, 475
Ace, Goodman, 351, 357,
*A.D.* (TV miniseries), 240
Adair, Tom, 403
Adams, Beverly, 440
Adams, Don, 122, 127, 129, 182-183, 250, 290, 365, 446, 458
Adams, Edie, 105-106, 159, 163, 359-360, 365
Adams, Neile, 16, 91-92, 95-96
Adams, Richard, 228
Adams, Stanley, 438
Adams, Steven, 403

*Addams Family, The* (TV series), 428
Adelman, Barry, 394
Adler, David, 437
Adler, Richard, 473
Adrian, Iris, 443
Agnew, Spiro, xv, 138, 140, 142, 147, 159, 164, 382-383
Aidem, Monty, 404
Ailey, Alvin, American Dance Theater, The, 249
Air Force Academy Band, The, 95
Air Force Academy Choir, The, 215
Akin, Miss America Susan, 243, 245-246
Akins, Claude, 216
Alabama (band), 246-247
*Alamo, The* (movie), 288
Alan, Ray, 241
Alaway, Robin, 390
Alberghetti, Anna Maria, 45, 76, 114, 459
Alberoni, Sherry, xvii
Albers, Dick, 136
Albert, Allan, 473
Alberti, Bob, 25-27, 145, 209, 213, 226, 257, 332, 418, 471,
Albertson, Frank, 439
Albertson, Jack, 182, 187-188, 390, 405, 439, 448, 466
Albin, Andy, 182
Albrecht, Howard, 7-8, 150-151, 185-187, 189-190, 257, 393, 414, 478
Albrecht, Richard, 151, 199-200
Alda, Alan, 465
Alda, Robert, 48
Alexander, Ben, 458
Alexander, Larry, 370

Alexander, Max, 273
Alexander, Rod, 348, 365
Alexander, Van, 377
ALF (character), 250
ALF (TV series), 212
*Alfie* (movie), 124, 291
*Alfred Hitchcock Presents* (TV series), 72
Ali, Muhammad, 163, 186-187, 333, 393, 409-410
*Alias Jesse James* (movie), 37, 79-81, 230, 354
*All Hands on Deck for Bob Hope's All Star Birthday Party at Annapolis* (1982 special), 226
*All in the Family* (TV series), 164
*All Star Birthday Party for Bob Hope* (1979 special), 198
*All Star Golf* (TV series), 81
*All Star Inaugural Gala* (special), 408
*All Star Party for Clint Eastwood* (special), 419
*All Star Revue* (TV series), 33, 45, 69, 342-344, 467
*All-Star Salute to Mother's Day* (special), 340
*All-Star Tribute to Elizabeth Taylor* (special), 400
*All-Star Tribute to General Jimmy Doolittle* (special), 418
*All-Star Tribute to John Wayne* (special), 395
*All the President's Men* (movie), 184
Allen, Byron, 411
Allen, Clifford, 172
Allen, David, 352
Allen, Dayton, 348-349
Allen, Debbie, 398, 419-420, 422
Allen, Fred, 32, 48, 324, 344-345
Allen, George, 223-224
Allen, Gracie, 137, 160, 236, 230, 269, 285
Allen, Marcus, 224
Allen, Marty, 139-140, 171-172, 182-183, 294, 390
Allen, Patrick, 241

Allen, Peter, 298
Allen, Steve, 7, 36, 66, 68, 70, 101, 127, 139-140, 152, 171, 182, 184, 250-251, 290, 302, 304-305, 326, 332-333, 348-349, 352, 380, 390, 413, 416-417, 464, 471
Allen, Sue, 344
Allen, Woody, 308, 380
Allison, Fran, 417
Allman, Elvia, 50, 53, 55, 65, 159, 268-269
Allyson, June, 400, 420
Alpert, Herb, 290
Amateau, Rodney, 433
*Amazing Dunninger, The* (TV series), 336
Ameche, Don, 299, 449-450
America (band), 154, 179-180
*America is 200 Years Old ... And There's Still Hope!* (comedy album), 85
*America Salutes the Queen* (special), 339
*America's All-Star Tribute to Elizabeth Taylor* (special), 340
*America's All-Star Tribute to Oprah Winfrey* (special), 423
*America's Tribute to Bob Hope* (1988 special), 205, 249
*American Film Institute Presents a Salute to John Ford, The* (special), 339
*American Film Institute Salutes Frank Capra* (special), 411
*American Film Institute Salutes James Cagney* (special), 386
*American Graffiti* (movie), 177
*American Masters: "You're the Top—The Cole Porter Story"* (special), 473
Ames, Florenz, 66
Ames, Nancy, 135
*Amos and Andy* (radio and TV series), 77
Amsterdam, Morey, 371
*Amy* (TV pilot), 91
*... And Debbie Makes Six* (special), 367
Anders, Karen, 170, 172

Anderson, Bobby, 384
Anderson, Eddie "Rochester," 378, 429-431
Anderson, Eric, 436
Anderson, Harry, 416-417
Anderson, Dame Judith, 293
Anderson, Loni, 215-221, 224, 228-229, 235, 256, 269, 276, 278
Anderson, Lynn, 183, 192
Anderson, Marian, 345
Anderson, Melissa Sue, 470
Anderson, Ronald, 240
Andress, Ursula, 161
Andrews, Dana, 328, 461
Andrews, Julie, 116, 228, 367, 383
Andrews, Norman, 172
Andrews, Patti, 244
Andrews, Tige, 390
Andrews Sisters, The, 365
*Andy Griffith Show, The* (TV series), 108, 152, 467
*Andy Williams Show, The* (TV series), 336, 359, 361
Angelos, Bill, 370, 373, 466
*Animal House* (movie), 200
*Anita Bryant Spectacular, The* (special), 340
Anka, Paul, 294, 339, 397
Ankers, Evelyn, 432
Ann-Margret, xvii, 136, 158, 173, 177, 180, 186-187, 218, 249-250, 280, 294, 370, 378-379, 382, 385-386, 398-400, 410, 412, 415
*Ann-Margret: Rhinestone Cowgirl* (special), 398
*Ann-Margret Show, The* (special), 370
*Ann-Margret—When You're Smiling* (special), 385
*Annie* (musical), 198
Anthony, Ray, 352
Anton, Susan, 223
AP All America Football Team, The, 165, 170, 175, 178, 181, 185, 189, 195-196, 200, 210, 217-218, 224, 228-229, 234, 238, 242, 244, 248, 252, 255, 269, 272, 275-278

Apaka, Alfred, 45
*Apartment, The* (movie), 98
Aragon, Art, 436
Arbuckle, Roscoe "Fatty," 2
Arbus, Allan, 448
Arbus, Loreen, 423
Archerd, Army, 247-248, 411
Arden, Eve, 366
Arden, Toni, 43
Arends, Harry, 473
Arlett, Dick, 243, 245,
Arliss, George, 76
Armstrong, Gen. Frank A., 69
Armstrong, Louis, 350, 357
Armstrong, Neil, xiv, 14, 156, 233, 388
Arnaz, Desi, 23, 67, 78, 81, 154, 182, 312, 389, 395, 433, 474
Arnaz, Lucie, 275-276
Arness, James, 293-294
Arnett, Jon, 77, 356
Arnold, Bill, 78-79, 102
Arnold, Buddy, 169, 471
Arnold, Jack, 439
Arnold, Phil, 103, 116, 119, 121, 129, 131
Arnold, Roseanne—See Barr, Roseanne
Arnold, Tom, 266, 271-272, 275-276, 453
Arnott, Bob, 192, 196, 394, 419,
Arquette, Cliff, 356
*Art Linkletter's House Party* (game show), 323
Arthur, Bea/Beatrice, 213, 253-254, 277, 415, 417, 422, 451, 470
Arthur, Maureen, 138-139
Arthur, Robert, 464
*Arthur Murray Party, The* (TV series), 356
Arvan, Jan, 379
Askin, Leon, 433, 444
Asner, Ed, 387, 390, 403, 405, 420
Astaire, Fred, 96, 188, 287, 295, 391-392, 468
Astin, John, 445
*At This Very Moment!* (special), 358
*A-Team, The* (TV series), 212, 240

Atkins, Charlotte, 65-66
Atkins, Chet, 399
Atkinson, Rowan, 241
Atkinson, Stan, 462
*Atlantic City* (movie), 225
Attenborough, Richard, 478
Auberjonois, Rene, 419
Audley, Eleanor, 64, 71, 123
Auger, Claudine, 364
Austin, Butch, 343
Austin, Phil, 416
Austin, Tracey, 218
Avalon, Frankie, 88, 116
Avera, Tom, 39
Averback, Hy, 31, 34, 43, 53-54, 56, 60, 62, 65-66, 70-71, 79, 466
Avery, Linda, 158
Axlerod, David, 414
Aylesworth, John, 357, 394
Ayres, Mitchell, 345, 351, 363, 365
Azaria, Hank, 453

Babilonia, Tai, 215
Bach, Catherine, 234, 414
Bacharach, Burt, 384, 413, 421
*Bachelor Father* (TV series), 152
*Bachelor in Paradise* (movie), 98-99, 231, 284, 329
*Backstreet Dreams* (movie), 268
Bacon, James, 277
Badami II, Frank, 199
Baer, Atra, 77
Bailey, Joseph A., 402
Bailey, Pearl, 34, 65-66, 130-131, 155-156, 192, 222, 235, 346, 367, 383, 397
Bain, Conrad, 411
Baio, Scott, 448
Baker, Anita, 422
Baker, Benny, 447
Baker, Bruce, 67, 73
Baker, Carroll, 90, 115, 119, 132
Baker, Herbert, 353, 374
Baker, Jack, 66, 68-71, 74, 85, 124, 136, 161, 165, 171, 179, 183, 187, 194, 433

Baker, Penny, 449
Baker Hall, Philip—See Hall, Philip Baker
Bakker, Jim and Tammy Faye, 246
Baldwin, Bill, 362
Ball, Lucille, 16, 22, 36, 39, 67, 78, 97, 103, 121, 159-160, 175, 185, 187-188, 192-193, 195, 202, 205, 208, 218, 225, 230-232, 236, 238, 242, 246, 249-250, 276-277, 293-294, 300, 310, 314, 328, 355, 366, 372, 378, 380, 384, 389, 395, 404, 407, 419, 425, 428, 433, 441-443, 467-470
Ballard, Kaye, 159
Ballet Folklorico de Acapulco, 123
Ballet Montmartre, 63
Balzer, George, 354, 362, 430-431, 434-435, 438, 444
*Bambi* (movie), 291
*Bananas* (movie), 308
Bancroft, Anne, 110, 131-132, 405, 431
*Band Wagon, The* (movie), 96
Banner, Bob, 345
Banner, John, 441
Barasch, Norman, 383
*Barbara Mandrell and The Mandrell Sisters* (TV series), 221, 407-408
*Barbara McNair Show, The* (TV series), 374
*Barbara Walters Special, The* (special), 313-314
*Barbara Walters Special, The: "Happy Hour"* (special), 474
Bardot, Brigitte, 357
Bargy, Roy, 343, 357
Barker, Cecil, 326
Barker, Steve, 416
Barkley, Alben W., 306
Barnes, Billy, 361, 367
Barnett, S.H., 431
Barnouw, Erik, 130
Barnstable, Cyb and Trish, 171
Barnum, Pet, 342
Baron, Lita, 43
Barr, Leonard, 448

Barr, Roseanne (Roseanne Arnold), 266, 271-272, 275-276, 453
Barra, Vanda, 187
Barrett, Ken, 449
Barrett, Rona, 182
Barrie, J.M., 431
Barris, Alex, 374
Barron, Jeffrey, 145, 187, 203, 209, 221, 247, 257, 261, 379, 393, 404, 424
Barry, Gene, 353, 417, 462
Barrymore, Drew, 420
Barstow, Dick, 342
Bart, Lionel, 379
Barton, Earl, 345
Barton, Frank, 31, 85, 95, 145
Barton, Steve, 249-250
Barty, Billy, 135, 182, 227
Baryshnikov, Mikhail, 198-199
Basie, Count, 298
*Bat Masterson* (TV series), 79, 81, 353, 357
Batchelor, Ruth, 182
Bateman, Justine, 452
Batscha, Robert, 471
Battle, Hinton, 226, 420
Batts, Miss USA Dianna Lynn, 119
Bauchens, Anne, 355
Baxter, Billy, 377
*Bay City Blues* (TV series), 411
Baylos, Gene, 371
Beach Boys, The, 113-114, 362
Beaird, Betty, 447
Bean, Jack, 390
Bearde, Chris, 150, 181, 191, 369
Beatles, The, 87-88, 110-111, 117, 167, 361
Beatts, Anne, 416
Beattys, The, 399
*Beau James* (movie), 72, 75, 230, 434
*Beautiful Phyllis Diller Show, The* (TV series), 132
Beck, Mary Ann, 159
Bee, Molly, 77-78, 458
Begley Jr., Ed, 411
Belafonte, Harry, 358
Belasco, Leon, 441, 444

Belfer, Hal, 50
Bell, Bob, 165
Bell, Cynthia, 15
Bell, Kay, 15
Bell Sisters, The, 15, 30, 45, 48-49
Bellamy, Ralph, 64
Bellino, Joe, 328
*Bells of St. Mary's, The* (movie), 168
Belushi, Jim, 448
Belzer, Richard, 416
Bence, Bob, 53
Bench, Johnny, 161, 191, 270, 388
Bendix, William, 43, 459
Benham, Miss America Dorothy Kathleen, 185
Bennett, Julie, 98, 139, 165, 169
Bennett, Linda, 136
Bennett, Robert Russell, 458, 460
Bennett, Tony, 6, 125, 278, 290, 319, 346, 356, 422, 424
Bennion, Nicholas Harvey, 405
Benny, Jack, 7, 13, 32, 53-55, 80, 96, 104, 109, 112, 118, 131-132, 149, 160-161, 164, 171-172, 179-180, 238, 277, 279, 287, 307, 354, 362, 366, 370, 378, 380-382, 385, 387-389, 409, 426, 428-431, 434-435, 438, 442-444, 462, 464-465, 467
*Benson* (TV series), 211
Bentine, Michael, 387
Berg, Dick, 425, 428, 441, 445
Bergen, Candice, 275
Bergen, Edgar, 401, 405
Bergen, Jerry, 41
Bergen, Polly, 96, 336, 346, 365
Berger, Harvey, 223, 414
Bergerac, Jacques, 446
Bergman, Ingrid, 168, 180
Bergman, Peter, 416
Bergman, Sandahl, 420
Bergmann, Ted, 290
Berle, Milton, 1, 6, 22, 32-34, 38-39, 42, 48, 51-52, 68, 80, 84, 112, 122, 150, 166, 172-173, 180, 182, 190, 218, 225, 227, 238, 242, 247-248,

250-251, 258, 265, 268-269, 273, 275-276, 285, 293, 301, 335, 339, 341, 343, 353, 364, 380-381, 388, 401, 405-406, 412, 416-417, 466, 468, 471
Berlin, Irving, 187, 297, 368, 422, 472
Berlinger, Warren, 437
Berman, Shelley, 139, 140, 419
Bernard, Alan, 393
Bernard, Crystal, 274, 277
Bernard Brothers, The, 63, 76-77
Bernards, John, 30
Berner, Sara, 344
Bernie, Al, 335
Berns, Seymour, 326, 350, 435
Bernstein, Elmer, 462
Bernstein, Leonard, 468
Berry, Ken, 339, 366, 390, 405
Bertinelli, Valerie, 403
*Best of the Dean Martin Roasts* (special), 470
*Best on Record, The* (awards special), 290
Bettin, Sandra Gale, 105
Betz, Carl, 390
*Beverly Hillbillies, The* (TV series), 23, 86, 107, 174
*Bewitched* (TV series), xiii
Big Bird, 185-186, 198-199, 403
*Big Broadcast of 1938, The* (movie), 3, 60, 75, 214, 230, 462
*Big Event, The* (TV series), 203, 466, 469, 475
*Big Payoff, The* (TV series), 46, 50
*Big Picture, The* (TV series), 458, 461, 464
*Big Record, The* (TV series), 336
*Big Red One, The* (movie), 409
Bigelow, Joe, 363, 365, 458
*Billboard* (publication), 85
Bilson, Bruce, 446
Binder, Steve, 360
*Bing! A 50th Anniversary Special* (special), 397
*Bing Crosby and His Friends* (sports special), 326

*Bing Crosby and His Friends* (1972 special), 339, 383
*Bing Crosby and His Friends* (1974 special), 339
*Bing Crosby Celebrity Golf Tournament, The* (sports special), 329
*Bing Crosby: His Life and Legend* (special), 468
*Bing Crosby Show, The* (1961 special), 338
*Bing Crosby Show, The* (1962 special), 359
*Bing Crosby Show, The* (1964 special), 361
*Bing Crosby Show, The* (1968 special), 369
*Bing Crosby's Sun Valley Christmas Show* (special), 175
*Birds and the Bees, The* (movie), 65
*Birth of a Nation* (movie), 130
Bishop, Joey, 330, 361-362, 376, 393, 437, 468
Bisset, Jacqueline, 405
Bixby, Bill, 390, 403
*B.J. and the Bear* (TV series), 214
Black, Clint, 267, 271, 275
*Black Theater of Prague, The*, 363
Blackburn, Bryan, 214
Blackburn, Norman, 327
Blackburn Twins, The, 47-48
Blackwood, Nina, 423
Blaine, Vivian, 59, 64, 336
Blair, Wally, 43
Blake, Larry, 367
Blake, Madge, 437
Blake, Patricia, 65
Blake, Robert, 400
Blake, Timothy, 159, 165
Blanc, Mel, 177, 435, 444
Blanda, George, 223
Bledsoe, Tempest, 417
Bloch, Ray, 60, 346, 357
Blocker, Dan, 359-360, 378
Blondell, Joan, 445
Bloom, Anne, 416
Bloom, Charles, 448

Bloom, Claire, 282
Bloom, George, 377, 389
Blue, Ben, 366-367
Blue, Vida, 165-166
*Blue Lagoon, The* (movie), 450
*Blue Skies* (movie), 392
Blue Streaks, The, 165
*Bluffers, The* (special), 154, 311, 387
Bluford, Guion, xiv, 18, 233
*Blunderful World of Bloopers* (book), 11
Blyth, Ann, 429
*Bob Goulet Show, The* (special), 376
*Bob Hope All Star Christmas Special, The* (1978 special), 195
*Bob Hope All Star Comedy Special from Australia, The* (1978 special), 191
*Bob Hope American Youth Awards* (1979 sports special), 333
*Bob Hope An Evening at the Palladium, A Lifetime of Laughter* (1979 special), 197
*Bob Hope & Friends ... Making New Memories* (1991 special), 271
*Bob Hope and Other Young Comedians*: "The World Laughs, Young and Old," (1992 special), 259, 273
*Bob Hope Buick Christmas Show, The* (1960 special), 91
*Bob Hope Buick Show, The* (1958-61 series of specials), 74, 76, 80-81, 91-96, 98, 288
*Bob Hope Buick Sports Awards Show, The* (1961 special), 9, 328, 461
*Bob Hope Buys NBC?* (1985 special), 242
*Bob Hope Cavalcade of Comedy, The* (1979 special), 196
*Bob Hope Celebration, A* (1981 special), 222
*Bob Hope Chevy Show, The* (1955-57 series of specials), 34, 62-65, 67-71
*Bob Hope Christmas Show, The* (1961 special), 97, 460
*Bob Hope Christmas Show, The* (1962 special), 100

*Bob Hope Christmas Show, The* (1963 special), 104, 106
*Bob Hope Christmas Show, The* (1985 special), 242
*Bob Hope Christmas Show, The* (1987 special), 248
*Bob Hope Christmas Special, The* (1970 special), xiii, 156
*Bob Hope Christmas Special*: "Around the Globe with the USO," *The* (1971 special), 2, 4, 161
*Bob Hope Christmas Special*: "Around the Globe with the USO," *The* (1972 special), 165
*Bob Hope Christmas Special, The* (1973 special), 171
*Bob Hope Classic Comedy Special from Palm Springs, The* (1978 special), 191
*Bob Hope Goes to College* (1983 special), 211, 234
*Bob Hope in the Starmakers* (1980 special), 209, 214
*Bob Hope Lampoons Show Business* (1990 special), 266
*Bob Hope Lampoons Television 1985* (1985 special), 209, 239
*Bob Hope Lampoons the New TV Scene* (1986 special), 244
*Bob Hope ... Laughing with the Presidents* (1996 special), 265, 280
*Bob Hope Laughs with the Movie Awards* (1982 special), 225
*Bob Hope Moscow Show, The* (1958 special), 75-76, 461
*Bob Hope Olympic Benefit Special, The* (1983 special), 183
*Bob Hope on Campus* (1975 special), 179
*Bob Hope on Campus* (1979 special), 199
*Bob Hope on the Road to China* (1979 special), 198-199
*Bob Hope Presents Ladies of Laughter* (1992 special), 260, 274
*Bob Hope Presents the Hilarious Unrehearsed Antics of the Stars* (1984 special), 238

*Bob Hope Presents the Cavalcade of Champions* (1973-1975 sports specials), 331-333
*Bob Hope Presents The Chrysler Theatre* (TV series), 86-87, 91, 109, 113, 115, 117, 122, 124, 427-429, 440, 445
*Bob Hope Salutes NASA: "25 Years of Reaching for the Stars"* (1983 special), 18, 233
*Bob Hope Salutes the Ohio Jubilee* (1978 special), 195
*Bob Hope Show, The* (1953-55 series and 1957-63 specials), 33, 50-60, 66, 71-82, 91-107
*Bob Hope Show, The* (1971-75 specials), 163, 173-174
*Bob Hope Sings the Best of Radio* (album), 350
*Bob Hope Special, The* (1971-74 specials), 148, 164-172, 175-179
*Bob Hope Special, The: "Hope, Women and Song"* (1980 special), 213
*Bob Hope Stars Over Texas* (1982 special), 226
*Bob Hope Super Bowl Party* (1989 special), 252
*Bob Hope: Don't Shoot, It's Only Me* (1990 special), 268-269, 320
*Bob Hope: Memories of World War II* (1995 special), 269
*Bob Hope: The First 90 Years* (1993 special), 262, 264, 275
*Bob Hope with His Easter Bunnies and Other Friends* (1987 special), 246
*Bob Hope's All Star Comedy Birthday Party: "A USO Salute"* (1980 special), 215
*Bob Hope's All-Star Comedy Birthday Party at West Point* (1981 special), 220
*Bob Hope's All Star Comedy Christmas Special* (1980 special), 217
*Bob Hope's All-Star Comedy Look at the New Season* (1981 special), 221-222
*Bob Hope's All-Star Comedy Salute to the 75$^{th}$ Anniversary of the World Series* (1978 special), 151, 194
*Bob Hope's All Star Comedy Spectacular* (1977 special), 186, 313
*Bob Hope's All Star Comedy Tribute to Vaudeville* (1977 special), 187
*Bob Hope's All Star Look at TV's Prime Time Wars* (1980 special), 216
*Bob Hope's All-Star Super Bowl Party* (1983 special), 229
*Bob Hope's All Star Super Bowl Party* (1986 special), 243
*Bob Hope's America: "Red, White and Beautiful—The Swimsuit Edition,"* 261, 273
*Bob Hope's Bag Full of Christmas Memories* (1993 special), 256, 264, 276-277
*Bob Hope's Bagful of Christmas Cheer* (1986 special), 244
*Bob Hope's Bicentennial Star-Spangled Spectacular* (1976 special), 22, 184
*Bob Hope's Birthday Memories* (1994 special), 264, 277
*Bob Hope's Birthday Spectacular in Paris* (1989 special), 253
*Bob Hope's Christmas Cheer in Saudi Arabia* (1991 special), 259, 170
*Bob Hope's Christmas Show from Bermuda* (1990 special), 269
*Bob Hope's Christmas Show from Waikoloa, Hawaii* (1989 special), 255
*Bob Hope's Christmas Show: "Hopes For The Holidays"* (1994 special), 278
*Bob Hope's Christmas Special* (1981 special), 221
*Bob Hope's Comedy Christmas Special* (1976 special), 185
*Bob Hope's Comedy Salute to the Soaps* (1985 special), 209, 240
*Bob Hope's Cross-Country Christmas Special* (1991 special), 272

Index • 493

*Bob Hope's Easter Vacation in the Bahamas* (1989 special), 253
*Bob Hope's Four-Star Christmas Fiesta from San Antonio* (1992 special), 275
*Bob Hope's Funny Valentine* (1981 special), 219
*Bob Hope's Hilarious Unrehearsed Antics of the Stars* (1984 special), 211, 238
*Bob Hope's High-Flying Birthday Extravaganza* (1986 special), 244
*Bob Hope's High-Flying Birthday Extravaganza* (1987 special), 246
*Bob Hope's Jolly Christmas Show with the All-America Champs* (1988 special), 252
*Bob Hope's Love Affair with Lucy* (1989 special), 254-255
*Bob Hope's Merry All Star Christmas Special* (1979 special), 200
*Bob Hope's Merry Christmas Show* (1983 special), 234
*Bob Hope's NBC Christmas Party* (1975 special), 181
*Bob Hope's Overseas Christmas Tours Parts One and Two* (1980 specials), 203, 210, 213
*Bob Hope's Pink Panther Thanksgiving Gala* (1982 special), 228
*Bob Hope's Road to Hollywood* (1983 special), 230
*Bob Hope's Royal Command Performance from Sweden* (1986 special), 243
*Bob Hope's Spring Break* (1981 special), 219
*Bob Hope's Spring Fling of Comedy and Music from Acapulco* (1990 special), 267
*Bob Hope's Stand up and Cheer National Football League's 60th Year* (1981 special), 223
*Bob Hope's 30th Anniversary Television Special* (1981 special), 218
*Bob Hope's USO Christmas in Beirut* (1984 special), 208, 211, 235
*Bob Hope's USO Christmas Show from the Persian Gulf* (1988 special), 210, 248-249
*Bob Hope's USO Road to the Berlin Wall and Moscow* (1990 special), 268
*Bob Hope's Who Makes the World Laugh? Volume Two* (1984 special), 236—for Volume One, see *Texaco Star Theatre*: "Bob Hope in 'Who Makes the World Laugh … At Itself'"
*Bob Hope's Wicky-Wacky Special in Waikiki* (1984 special), 235
*Bob Hope's Women I Love Beautiful But Funny* (1982 special), 202, 225
*Bob Hope's World of Comedy* (1976 special), 185, 313
*Bob Hope's Yellow Ribbon Celebration* (1991 special), 271
*Bob Hope's Young Comedians Making America Laugh* (1994 special), 277
*Bob Hope's Young Comedians: "A New Generation of Laughs"* (1995 special), 27
*Bobby Darin and Friends* (special), 356
Bobrick, Sam, 376
Bogart, Humphrey, 286, 467
Boles, Jim, 463
Bolger, Ray, 156-157
Bollinger, Russ, 243
Bolton, Martha, 203, 209, 257, 261, 264, 275-276
Bombeck, Erma, 231
*Bonanza* (TV series), 90, 103, 159, 178, 189, 294, 360
Bonet, Lisa, 415
Boni, John, 394
Bono, Sonny, 394, 423
*Book of Lists #2, The* (book), 303
*Boone* (TV series), 411
Boone, Debby, 196-197, 213, 222, 340, 400, 406, 408, 424

Boone, Pat, 196-197, 213, 225, 305, 339, 365, 406
Borge, Victor, 346
Borgnine, Ernest, 129, 365, 377-378, 387, 445
Borland, Drew, 449
Bosley, Tom, 390, 420
Bostwick, Barry, 422
Bosworth, Brian, 242, 245
Botwick, Terry A., 424
Bowab, John, 271
Box, Bill, 373, 414
*Box, The: An Oral History of Television, 1920-1961* (book), 33
Boy George, 243
*Boy, Have I Got a Wrong Number!* (movie), 124
Boy Scouts of America, The, 356, 397, 422, 458
Boyd, Jimmy, 439
Boyd, Stephen, 355
Boyle, Hal, 345
Boyne, Sunny, 69, 70
Boyz II Men, 273
Bracken, Eddie, 43
Bradley, Bart, 65
Bradley, Gen. Omar, 131, 323, 388-389, 408
Bradley, Tom, 416
Bradshaw, Joan, 79-80
*Brady Bunch, The* (TV series), 170
*Brain Droppings* (book), 455
Brando, Marlon, 59, 92, 169, 345
Brandow, Jerry, 39
Brandt, Hank, 80
*Brannigan* (movie), 180
Braun, Bob, 357
Bray, Thom, 415
Breaux, Marc, 357, 361
Brecher, Irving, 471
Breeding, Larry, 448
Breen, Danny, 416
Brennan, Walter, 235, 379
Brice, Fanny, 190, 274
Brice, Monte, 460
Brickhouse, Jack, 343

Brightman, Sarah, 249-250
Brill, Charlie, 369
Bring, Lou, 342
Brinkley, Christie, 226-227, 232
Brinkley, David, 139-140, 463, 466, 470
Brinkley, Ritch, 421
Britt, Jimmy, 343
Britt, May, 82
Brittany, Morgan, 240, 245, 420
Britton, Barbara, 99-100
Broadbent, Aida, 343
Brock, Lou, 333
Broderick, Malcolm, 345
Broderick, Matthew, 474
Brokaw, Tom, 417
*Broken Record* (book), 290
Bronson, Charles, 340, 395, 420
Brooke, Edward, 181
Brooke, Hillary, 52, 76
Brooks, Albert, 404
Brooks, Carol, 72
Brooks, Foster, 182, 222, 250, 388-389, 393
Brooks, Garth, 271-272, 275
Brooks, James L., 454
Brooks, Mel, 405, 446
Brosnan, Pierce, 411, 417
Brothers, Dr. Joyce, 163, 219, 414
Brower, Millicent, 23, 50
Brown, Andre Rosey, 451
Brown, Chelsea, 368-369
Brown, Earl, 361, 366, 370, 401, 403, 417
Brown, Ellen, 254, 268
Brown, Joe E., 432
Brown, Larry, 331
Brown, Les, and His Band of Renown, 23-27, 31, 45, 51, 54, 60, 64, 66, 75, 78-79, 85, 105, 115, 145, 192-193, 257, 275-276, 281, 290, 294, 331, 333, 368, 377, 381, 386, 388, 444, 458
Brown, Olivia, 415
Brown, R.G., 359, 382
Brown, Stumpy, 107
Brown Jr., Les (son of Les Brown), 73

Browne, Roscoe Lee, 378
Browning, Kirk, 345, 350
Bruce, Betty, 41
Bruhanski, Alex, 449
Brumley, Bob, 324
Bryan, Arthur Q., 62
Bryant, Anita, 88, 97, 100, 104, 109-110, 114, 119, 124, 189, 314, 340, 384, 386
Bryant, Paul "Bear," 199-200, 384
Bryant, John, 66
Brynner, Yul, 227
Bubbles, John, 90, 109-110, 114
*Bubbling Brown Sugar* (musical revue), 21-22, 188
Buchanan, Jack, 47, 96
Buchwald, Art, 231
Buckley, William F., 375
Buffano, Jules, 343
*Buick-Berle Show, The*—See *Milton Berle Show, The*
Bull, Robert, 444
Bumbry, Grace, 408
Buono, Victor, 444-445
Burdette, Lou, 352
Burgan, Jerry, 16
Burge, Gregg, 226, 420
Burgundy Street Singers, The, 379
Burghoff, Gary, 466
Burke, Delta, 271
Burke, Johnny, 429
*Burke's Law* (TV series), 427
Burnett, Carol, 132-133, 334, 339, 370, 373, 383, 395, 398, 405, 409, 413, 420, 468, 470
Burnham, Terry, 436
Burnier, Jeannine, 374, 394
Burns, David, 38-39
Burns, George, 137, 156, 159-160, 182, 190, 192, 218, 225, 230, 232, 236, 238-240, 242, 244, 247, 249-252, 254-255, 268-269, 275, 285, 333, 366-367, 378, 380, 385, 400, 405-406, 408-410, 412, 414-415, 418, 430, 460
Burns, Jack, 421

Burns, Ronnie, 352
Burns, Stan, 348-349, 352, 370, 373, 389, 393, 414
Burns, Terry, 223
Burr, Fritzi, 223
Burr, Raymond, 127-128, 338, 417
Burrell, Maryedith, 405-406
Burton, Earl, 360
Burton, Jay, 351, 357, 363, 365, 377, 414
Burton, LeVar, 405
Burton, Richard, 110-111, 120-121, 197, 227, 289, 388, 395
Bush, Barbara, 273-274, 280-281
Bush, George H.W., 221-222, 228, 271, 275
Bushkin, Joe, 391-392, 397
Bushman, Francis X., 73, 355
Butch and Stumpy—See Brown, Stumpy and Stone, Harold "Butch"
Butera, Sam and the Witnesses, 115
Butkus, Dick, 223
Butler, David, 440, 444
Butler, Brett, 421
Butler, Dean, 420
Buttons, Red, 122, 139-140, 171-172, 182, 186-187, 237, 250, 405, 412-414, 416-417
Buttram, Pat, 182
Buzzi, Ruth, 159, 184, 261, 368, 372, 389, 393, 399, 405
Byers, Bill, 390
Byington, Spring, 459
Byner, John, 182, 395
Byrd, Tom, 411
Byrne, George, 2
Byrne, Martha, 271

*Cabaret* (musical), 128, 134
Cabot, Bruce, 443
*Caddyshack* (movie), 246
Caesar, Sid, 42-43, 139-140, 253-254, 265, 293, 301, 343, 345, 353-354, 416-417, 420, 459, 471
Cagney, James, 67, 386-387

Cahn, Sammy, 95, 182-184, 443
Caine, Michael, 123-124, 241, 291, 372
*Caine Mutiny, The* (play), 60
Calabrese, Peter, 411, 415
*Call Me Bwana* (movie), 104, 107, 360
Callas, Charlie, 393
Camarata, 350
Cambridge, Godfrey, 290, 376
Cambridge University Glee Club, The, 396
*Camel News Caravan* (TV series), 343
*Camelot* (musical), 376
Cameron, Joanna, 164
Cameron, Kirk, 246-247, 250, 254-255, 267, 275-276
Cameron, Rod, 127, 443
Campbell, Earl, 189
Campbell, Glen, 17, 135-136, 166, 168-169, 172-173, 178, 182, 194, 218, 220, 222, 243, 246, 378, 382-383, 395, 418
Campbell, Kathy, 424
Campbell, Norman, 463
Campbell, Pat, 379
*Cancel My Reservation* (movie), 153, 169
Candido, Candy, 343
Candy, John, 416
Caniff, Milton, 345
Cannon, Dyan, 167, 175-176, 178-179, 185-186, 278, 312, 332-333, 405
Cantinflas, 123, 405
Cantor, Charles, 444
Cantor, Eddie, 42, 48, 188, 285, 434, 438
Capote, Truman, 358, 381
Capp, Al, 457
Capra, Frank, 411, 468
*Captain & Tennille* (TV series), 393
Captain and Tennille, The, 22, 184, 187-188, 393, 400
*Captain Kangaroo* (TV series), 373
Capstaff, Al, 31
Cara, Irene, 234
Card, Kathryn, 433
Cardenas, Randy, 55

Cardenas, Rudy, 171
Carey, MacDonald, 365, 417
Carey, Philip, 127-128
Carleton, Kyra, 376
Carlin, George, 231, 416, 455, 457, 468
Carlisle, Kevin, 19-20, 117, 135
Carlisle, Kitty, 473
Carlson, Jim, 161, 369, 372
Carlton, Sam, 344
Carlton, Steve, 331
Carmichael, Ralph, 367
*Carnal Knowledge* (movie), 164
Carne, Judy, 307, 368, 372
Carney, Art, 468
*Carol Burnett Show, The* (TV series), 10, 148, 151, 207, 226, 334, 340, 370, 373, 396
Carpenter, Ken, 353, 431
Carpenters, The, 16, 169, 174, 180, 382, 392, 405
Carr, Allen, 385
Carr, Rocky, 73
Carr, Vikki, 132-133
Carroll, Diahann, 198, 213, 240, 243, 249-251, 290, 363, 378, 414-414, 422-423, 447
Carroll, Linda, 444
Carroll, Pat, 345
Carroll, Victoria, 138
Carroll Jr., Bob, 433
Carruthers, Bill, 468
Carsey, John, 372
Carsey, Marcy, 453
Carson, Dick, 371
Carson, Johnny, 8, 115, 117, 122, 139-140, 156-157, 169, 181-183, 190, 216-217, 242, 245, 249-250, 257, 262, 273, 275, 305-308, 310-320, 356, 366, 385, 387, 395, 398, 405-406, 408-409, 411-413, 416-418, 449, 466, 468, 474, 478
Carson, Robert, 65
Carter, Benny, 441
Carter, Billy, 186, 198, 401
Carter, Dixie, 269, 278
Carter, Chris, 141

Carter, Cris, 245
Carter, Jack, xix, 122, 127, 139-140, 171-172, 182, 246-248, 380, 412
Carter, Jimmy, 155, 184, 186-189, 192, 218, 251, 275, 394, 399, 401-402, 404, 467
Carter, Lynda, 232, 242, 246, 420
Carter, Nell, 409, 411, 414-414, 417, 422
Carter, Rosalyn, 155
Carter Cash, June, 237, 375
Carter Family, The, 375
Cartwright, Angela, 434, 436-437, 447
Cartwright, Nancy, 453
Cartwright, Veronica, 102, 436
Caruso, Dee, 367, 379
*Casablanca* (movie), 220, 253
*Casanova's Big Night* (movie), 34
Case, Nelson, 40-41
Case, Stephen, 103
Casey, Harry Wayne, 21
Cash, Johnny, 156-157, 237, 375, 378, 405, 470
Casper, Billy, 157
Cass, Ronnie, 376
Cassavettes, John, 355
Cassidy, David, 169
Cassini, Joseph, 374
Cassini, Oleg, 156-157
Castellaneta, Dan, 453
Castellaw, Chet, 56-57, 59-60, 65
Castle, Nick, 47, 53, 56-58, 61-62, 65, 81, 99-100, 345, 361
Castro, Fidel, 81, 97
Castro Sisters, The, 49
*Cat Ballou* (movie), 117, 120, 238
*Cat on a Hot Tin Roof* (movie), 102
Cates, Joseph/Joe, 385, 406
Caughey, Miss Texas Lu Ann, 226
Caulfield, Joan, 73, 93, 121
*Cavalcade of Sports* (TV series), 343
Cavett, Dick, 237, 242, 307, 309, 317, 380
*CBS News Special*: "1974: A Television Album" (special), 465
*CBS News Special*: "A Tribute to Jack Benny" (special), 465

*CBS On the Air* (special), 468
*CBS Salutes Lucy: The First 25 Years* (special), 395-396
Ceballos, Larry, 43
*Celebrity Golf* (series), 94, 327
Cerf, Bennett, 324-326, 329-330
Cernan, Capt. Eugene U.S.N., 381
Cesario, Jeff, 273
Chabot, Miss USA Amedee, 104, 440
Chaffee, Suzy, 390
Chakiris, George, 293
Chalk, Gary, 449
Chamberlain, Richard, 112
Chamberlain, Wilt, 328
Chambers, Ernest, 382, 403
Chan, Michael, 251
Chancellor, John, 466, 469
Chandler, Chick, 342
Chandler, Guy, 82
Chandler, Jeff, 351
Channing, Carol, 17, 178, 294, 332, 351, 412-413, 416
Chaplin, Charlie, 190
Chaplin, Saul, 473
Charisse, Cyd, 132, 138, 420, 473
Charles, Lewis, 439
Charles, Ray, 138, 403, 422
Charles, Ray (orchestrator and choir leader), 68, 191, 196, 222-223, 233, 263, 275, 347-348, 374, 383
*Charlie Farrell Show, The* (TV series), 433
*Charlie's Angels* (TV series), 193, 216
Charmoli, Tony, 125, 222, 228-229, 390, 394, 396
Charny, Suzanne, 165
Charo, 154, 182, 186-187, 191-192, 194, 198, 294, 389, 405
Charren, Peggy, 469
Chase, Chaz, 187-188
Chase, Chevy, 241, 275-276, 299, 416
Chase, Stephen, 68, 78, 93-95, 110, 440
Chauvin, Lilyan, 121
Checker, Chubby, 99
*Cheers* (TV series), 212, 240, 412
Cheney, Dick, 275

Cher, 190, 290, 336, 394-395
Cherry, Don, 47
*Chesterfield Presents* (TV series), 32
*Chesterfield Sound Off Time* (TV series), 32, 42-44
Chevalier, Maurice, 13, 56-57
*Chevy Show, The* (1955-1956 TV series), 33-34, 61-65, 335
*Chico and the Man* (TV series), 389
Chin, Glenn, 251
*CHiPs* (TV series), 200, 410
Cho, Henry, 277
Cho, Margaret, 274
Choir of the Catholic Church of St. John the Devine, The, 41
*Chorus Line, A* (musical), 249, 398
Chotzinoff, Samuel, 345
Christian, Claudia, 449
Christianis, The, 347
*Christine Jorgensen Story, The* (movie), 308
Christman, Paul, 330
Christopher, William, 466
*Christophers, The* (special and TV series), 425, 429-430
Christy, Ken, 64
*Chrysler Presents a Bob Hope Comedy Special* (1963-1969 specials), 107, 110-113, 115-123, 125, 132, 439, 443-445
*Chrysler Presents The Bob Hope Christmas Special* (specials), xiii, 109-110, 114, 119, 124, 130, 136, 149, 156
Chung, Connie, 417
Churchill, Winston, 60
Cincinnati Reds, The, 325
Claman, June, 451
Clark, Bryan, 168
Clark, Dane, 348
Clark, Dick, 336, 340, 405, 413, 417, 423, 448-449
Clark, Dwight, 229
Clark, Fred, 48-49, 431
Clark, Petula, 162, 166, 180, 290, 429
Clark, Ron, 376

Clark, Roy, 191, 294, 378, 401
Clark, Shari, 65
Clark, Susan, 405
Clark Brothers, The, 46
*Clash By Night* (movie), 46
*Classic Stand-Up Comedy on Television: A Museum of Television and Radio Special* (special), 475
Clements, Curley, 65
*Cleopatra* (movie), 111, 289
Cleveland Indians, The, 194, 232, 323, 325, 433
Cliburn, Van, 205, 249
Clingers, The, 142
Clinton, Bill, 266, 275, 280, 479
Clinton, First Lady Hilary Rodham, 280
Clooney, Betty, 424
Clooney, George, 424
Clooney, Nick, 424
Clooney, Rosemary, 47-50, 53-54, 70, 80, 162, 180, 230, 268, 314, 350, 353, 361, 397, 422, 424, 459, 468
*Club Oasis* (TV series), 336
Coburn, Charles, 346
Coburn, James, 226-227, 420
Coca, Imogene, 42, 159, 163, 343
Coco, James, 309
*Cocoon* (movie), 450
Coe, Fred, 345
Cohen, Alexander H., 418, 420, 468
Cohen, Harold D., 373
Colasanto, Nicholas, 411
Colbert, Claudette, 411
Colby, Marian, 47-48
*Cold Turkey* (movie), 293
Cole, Buddy, 326, 350
Cole, Jack, 39
Cole, James Omar, 473
Cole, Nat King, 353
Cole, Natalie, 298, 422
Coleman, Cy, 250
Coleman, Dabney, 420, 440
Coleman, Fritz, 241
Coleman, Gary, 411, 414
Coleman, Nancy, 345-346

Index • 499

*Colgate Comedy Hour, The* (TV series), 28, 33, 43, 45-50, 57, 72, 324, 344, 346, 348
*College Swing* (movie), 230
Collins, Dorothy, 356
Collins, Joan, 80-81, 101, 121, 245
Collins, Kerry, 278
Collins, Pamela, 171
Collins, Roberta, 159
Collins, Ted, 343
Colman, Ronald, 285
Cologne Male Voice Choir, The, 56-57
Colonna, Jerry, 3, 42, 52, 55, 57, 60, 68-69, 73-74, 77-78, 80, 88, 90-92, 97, 100, 104-105, 109-110, 114, 119, 121, 129, 135-136, 139, 158, 162, 164, 171, 182, 214, 335, 355, 461
*Combat* (TV series), 126
*Comedy Hour, The: The Bob Hope Show* (1950-51 specials), 40-42
Comfort, Bob, 403
*Comic Relief* (special), 416
Como, Perry, 37, 65-66, 68, 73, 94, 127-128, 157-158, 180, 187, 189, 290, 327, 336, 345, 347-349, 351-353, 363, 374, 378, 390, 398-399
*Company* (musical), 384
*Concorde—Airport '79, The* (movie), 211
Condino, Gino, 101
Condos, Steve, 39
Conklin, Heinie, 432
Conley, Peggy, 73
Conlon, Jud, 356
Conn, Mr., and Mr. Mann, 350
Connell, Jim, 392
Connelly, Mike, 73
Connors, Carol, 424
Connors, Chuck, 79
Connors, Jimmy, 333
Connors, Mike, 174, 180, 182-183, 390, 420
Conrad, Michael, 223
Conrad, Robert, 403, 417
Conreid, Hans, 59-60, 366, 436
Considine, Bob, 345

*Continental, The* (TV series), 344
Convy, Bert, 192, 250-251
Conway, Tim, 207, 365
Coogan, Jackie, 439
Cooley, Charles, 56-57, 68-73
Cooney, Gerry, 226-227
Cooper, Alice, 404
Cooper, Gary, 355
Coots, J. Fred, 341-342
Copeland, Alan, 293
Copley, Terry, 219-220
Corbett, Lois, 110, 444
Corcoran, Bob, 347
Corcoran, Joanne, 178
Corcoran, Noreen, 99
Corden, Henry, 132, 135, 138-139, 142, 157, 159, 162, 165, 167, 169
Corey, Joseph, 432
Corey, Wendell, 80-81
Cornelius, John C., 459
Cornell, Jan, 422
Correia, Don, 420
Correll, Richard, 437
Corrigan, William, 355
Cortez, Ricardo, 355
Cosby, Bill, 122, 290, 416
*Cosby Show, The* (TV series), 212, 418, 422, 470
Cosell, Howard, 171-173, 186-187, 194, 223, 232, 337, 388-389, 393, 414
Cossette, Pierre, 298
Costa, Don, 396
Costello, Lou, 48, 285
Costner, Kevin, 474
Cothran, Miss America Shirley, 17, 178
Cotten, Joseph, 462
Cotter, Wayne, 279
*Country Girl, The* (movie), 61, 63, 286
Cowan, Jerome, 113-114, 439
Coward, Noel, 241
Cowles, Fleur, 345
Cowles, Gardner, 343
Cox, Dave, 469
Cox, Wally, 61, 70, 74, 77, 92, 122, 127, 129, 135-136, 139-140, 158, 162-163, 180, 348

*CPO Sharkey* (TV series), 185
Craig, Yvonne, 73
Crain, Jeanne, 62
Crane, Bob, 371, 390
Crane, Harry, 359, 361, 363, 377, 383, 389, 393, 396, 414
Crawford, Joan, 76-77, 94, 317
Crawford, Michael, 250, 266-267
Crew Chiefs, The, 57
Crichton, Don, 138, 217, 219, 263, 275
Crippen, Robert, 18, 233
Cristal, Linda, 163-164
*Critic's Choice* (movie), 103, 310, 330
*Crocodile Dundee* (movie), 245
Crompton, Nancy, 63
Cronkite, Walter, 275-276, 299, 422, 473
Crosby, Bing, 3, 12-13, 15, 17-18, 39, 42, 44, 47, 59-61, 66, 68, 75, 81, 99, 101, 103, 105, 109, 118, 120, 123, 130, 133, 136-137, 142, 153, 156-157, 162, 168, 170, 175-176, 180-181, 183, 188, 196, 213, 231, 270, 285, 289-291, 298, 302, 304, 307, 312-314, 324-326, 329, 334, 338-340, 347, 350-353, 357-365, 368-369, 373, 378-379, 381, 383, 385, 391-392, 397, 401, 429-430, 438-439, 455, 459, 463-464, 467-469
Crosby, Bob, 39-40, 43-44, 401, 458
Crosby, Cathy, 61
Crosby, Cathy Lee, 18, 20, 206, 216, 219, 221, 235, 409, 480
Crosby, Gary, 72, 231, 359, 371, 462, 468
Crosby, Harry, 391, 397
Crosby, Joan, 224, 240
Crosby, Kathryn, 113, 192-193, 196-197, 200-201, 213, 232, 326, 361, 391, 397, 439
Crosby, Lindsay, 350
Crosby, Mary (Frances), 298, 391, 397, 468
Crosby, Nathaniel, 391, 397
Crosby, Norm, 266-267

Crosby, Phillip, 109-110
Crosby Brothers (Gary, Dennis, Phillip and Lindsay), The, 81
Cross, Murphy, 451
Cross, Perry, 379
Crothers, Scatman, 182, 403
Crouch, Andrae, 410
Crystal, Billy, 301, 415-416
Culkin, Macaulay, 258, 272, 278, 300
Cullum, Kaitlin, 278
Culp, Robert, 417, 440
Culture Club, 243
Cummings, Robert/Bob, 41, 352, 355
Cunningham, Merce, 299
Cunningham, Walt, 134, 233
Curb, Mike, Congregation, The, 388
Curry, Mark, 278
Curtice, Harlow, 337
Curtin, Jane, 470
Curtis, Billy, 65, 73, 115, 137, 139
Curtis, Tony, 157-158, 332

Dahl, Arlene, 121, 420
Daily, Bob, 457
*Daily Show, The* (TV series), 266
*Daily Variety* (publication), 47, 264, 337
Daley, Bill, 393
Daley, Cass, 52-53, 55
Daley, Jan, 165-166, 371, 439
Daley, Richard, 484
*Dallas* (TV series), 216, 218, 244, 315, 408
Dallas Cowboy Cheerleaders, The, 402
Dallimore, Maurice, 160
Dalton, Wally, 392
Daly, John (Charles), 324-326, 329-330, 345
D'Ambricourt, Adrienne, 65
D'Amico, Kirk, 473
*Damn Yankees* (movie), 117
Damone, Vic, 65-66, 124, 168-169, 195, 235, 429
Dana, Bill, 122, 127, 139, 171-172, 182, 290, 352, 364, 390, 399
*Dancin'* (musical), 198

Dancing Westchester Wranglerettes, The, 386, 388
Dangerfield, Rodney, 6
*Dangerous Liaisons* (movie), 300
Daniel, Elliot, 433
Daniel, Jay, 453
Daniels, Billy, 43, 48
Daniels, Stan, 377, 385
Daniels, William, 355
*Danny Kaye Show, The* (TV series), 427
*Danny Thomas Hour, The*: "The Royal Follies of 1933" (special), 366
*Danny Thomas Looks at Yesterday, Today and Tomorrow* (special), 338
*Danny Thomas Show, The* (TV series), 78, 91, 425, 434, 436-437, 447
*Danny Thomas Show, The* (1965 special), 336
*Danny Thomas Show, The*: "The Road to Lebanon" (1966 special), 364
*Danny Thomas: Young and Foolish* (special), 339
Danson, Ted, 411, 417
Danza, Tony, 265, 280, 416, 422
DaPron, Louis, 59, 112, 140, 177, 190, 196, 347-348
Dare, Danny, 40-41
Dare Wahl, Walter, 347
Darin, Bobby, 94, 104, 290, 356, 358
Dark, Johnny, 399, 403
Darling, Jennifer, 387
Darren, James, 82, 98
*Date with the Angels, A* (TV series), 255
*Dating Game, The* (TV series), 133
David, Clifford, 141
*David Frost Show, The* (talk show), 309
Davidson, John, 89, 133, 141, 244, 305, 410
Davidson, Mary Anne, 191
Davies, Marion, 355
Davis, Bette, 411
Davis, Clifton, 390
Davis, Don, 162
Davis, Donald I., 463
Davis, Gail, 79

Davis, Hugh, 4
Davis, Joan, 68
Davis, Lisa, 94
Davis, Mac, 186-187, 192, 228-229, 244, 337
Davis, Meryl, 108-109
Davis, Michael, 416
Davis, Tommy, 108
Davis Jr., Sammy, 22, 156, 162-163, 166, 181, 184, 186-187, 190, 192, 196, 216-218, 222, 226-227, 244, 250, 252, 294, 339, 348, 395, 419-420, 422-423, 471
Davison, Gen. Michael, 193
Dawn, Doreen, 56
Dawson, Louis, 307
Day, Dennis, 378
Day, Doris, 24, 132, 159, 355, 386
Dayde, Liane, 56-57
De Mattiattzes, The, 342
Deacon, Richard, 127, 139-140, 433, 443
Dean, Harry, 447
Dean, Maj. Gen. William F., 51
*Dean Martin Celebrity Roast of Dean Martin, The* (special), 393
*Dean Martin Celebrity Roast of Mr. T, The* (special), 414
*Dean Martin Show, The* (TV series), 337, 363, 365-366, 377, 389
*Dean Martin's Celebrity Roast of Bob Hope* (special), 14, 388-389
*Dean Martin's Celebrity Roast of Lucille Ball* (special), 389
*Dear America: Letters from Vietnam* (documentary), 472
*Debby Boone: The Same Brand Old New Me* (special), 340
De Cordova, Fred, 367, 409, 438, 443
De Carlo, Yvonne, 348-349, 449
*Deep Throat* (movie), 331
Dees, Rick, 423
*Defenders, The* (TV series), 106
DeFinizio, Miss Venus USA Bonnie, 235
DeFore, Don, 417

DeGaulle, Gen. Charles, 126, 138, 368
DeHaven, Gloria, 49-50, 52, 356
Dehner, John, 441
Del Rubio Triplets, The—See Rubio, Del
Della Cioppa, Guy, 379
Della Sorte, Joseph, 449
Delmar, Vina, 64
DeLuise, Dom, 365
Demaret, Jimmy, 92-93, 324, 329, 356
Dempsey, Jack, 42-53, 130-131
Dempster, Hugh, 141
Dennis, Alfred, 446
Denoff, Sam, 359
Denove, Jack, 459
Denton, Donna, 123
Denton, Judy and Vicki, 392
Denver, Bob, 376
Denver, John, 173-174, 180, 233, 245-246, 275, 296, 400, 415
*Deputy, The* (TV series), 98
Derek, John, 345-346
DeRogatis, Al, 330
Derringer, Glenn, 348-349
Des Barres, Michael, 353
Descher, Sandra, 105
Desert Rose Band, The, 421-422
Desmond, Jerry, 51, 56
Desmond and Marks, 363
*Desperate Hours, The* (movie), 61, 346
Detmer, Ty, 270, 272
Deutsch, Patti, 376
Devon, Marilyn, 123
Devore, Carolyn, xvii
Dew, Joyce, 436
Dexter, Alan, 448
Diakun, Alex, 449
Diamond, Selma, 357
*Dick Cavett Show, The* (talk show), 309-310
*Dick Clark Show, The* (TV series), 336
*Dick Clark's Live Wednesday* (TV series), 340
*Dick Van Dyke Show, The* (TV series), 428
Dickerson, Eric, 229

Dickinson, Angie, 132-133, 154, 163-164, 181-184, 200, 216-217, 238, 250-251, 277-278, 313, 387, 393, 395, 417, 420, 423, 466, 468
Dickson, Brenda, xvii
Dillaway, Dana, 436
Diller, Phyllis, xviii, 6, 22, 84, 112, 117, 120-122, 124-127, 132, 153, 158-159, 163, 166, 170, 180, 182, 184, 190-191, 206, 208, 219, 228-229, 232, 238, 241-242, 246-252, 258, 261, 267, 273-274, 277, 279, 296, 303, 371, 378, 380, 388-389, 405, 410, 412, 418, 429, 445, 464
DiMaggio, Joe, 54, 56
*Dinah!* (talk show), 151, 303, 305, 314
*Dinah Shore Chevy Show, The* (TV series), 341
*Dinah Shore Special, The:* "How to Handle a Woman" (special), 339
*Dinah's Place* (talk show), 305
*Ding Dong School* (TV series), 85
Ding-a-Lings, The, 161
DiPaolo, Dante, 80, 92
Dirksen, Sen. Everett, 365
Disney, Walt, 355, 362, 383, 403, 432, 436
*Disneyland* (TV series), 60, 432
Dixon, Donna, 219-220
Dixon, Jeanne, 138
Dixon, Paul, 305
*Do Re Mi* (musical), 358
*Dr. Quinn Medicine Woman* (TV series), 265
*Dolly* (TV series), 421-422
Domingo, Placido, 237
*Don Rickles Show, The* (TV series), 371
*Donahue* (talk show), 305
Donahue, Phil, 242, 247, 305, 469
Donahue, Troy, 93
*Donny & Marie* (TV series), 21, 340, 391-392, 399, 403, 409, 475
Donohue, Jack, 441-442
Donovan, Susan, 276
Doodletown Pipers, The, 378-379
Doolittle, Jimmy, 418-419

Dorfman, Sid, 361
Dorov, Yuri, 75
Dors, Diana, 63, 67
Dorsey, John, 290
Dotrice, Alex, 271
Double Daters, The, 345
Dougherty, Charles, 452
Douglas, Buster, 266
Douglas, Donna, 23, 174
Douglas, Jack, 31, 372
Douglas, Kirk, 219, 387, 468
Douglas, Mike, 303, 336
Douglas, Paul, 46, 429
Dowling, Chet, 392
*Down Beat* (magazine), 51, 54
Downes, Barry, 386, 388
Downs, Hugh, 309, 364, 417
Dozer, David, 406
*Dragnet* (TV series), 32, 54, 337
Dragon, Daryl—See Captain and Tennille, The
Drake, Tom, 400
Draper, Don, 452
Dreben, Stan, 161
Dreyfuss, Richard, 416, 474
Drury, James, 127
Drysdale, Don, 108, 366
Dubin, Charles S., 449
Duff, Howard, 216
Duffy, Mark, 471
Dugger, Wayne, 141
Duke of Bedford, 329
Dulles, John Foster, 76, 353
Dulo, Jane, 115, 271
Dumont, Margaret, 53, 64
Dunaway, Faye, 295
Duncan, Arthur, 73, 74
Duncan, Betsy, 92
Duncan, Sandy, 181, 339, 387, 397
Dungy, Tony, 175
Dunham, Jeff, 273
Dunham, William, 267
Dunhills, The, 341-342, 353
Dunn, Elaine, 77-78, 130
Dunn, James, 440
Dunne, Irene, 64, 299, 429

Dunninger, Joseph, 336
Dunsmuir, Tom, 394
*DuPont Show of the Week, The* (TV series), 460-461
DuPre, Toni, 159
Dupree, Roland, 104, 157
Duran Duran, 241
Duran, Roberto, 232
Durante, Jimmy, 33, 42, 59, 73, 89, 96, 122, 126, 138, 140, 181, 293, 315, 335-336, 343-344, 357-358, 365, 372-373, 376, 438, 459, 462
Durbin, Lloyd "Lefty," 2
Dussault, Nancy, 357-358, 420
*Dynasty* (TV series), 230, 240, 242

Earl Twins (Jane and Ruth Earl), The, 109-10
Eason, Tony, 243
*Easter Parade* (movie), 188
Easton, Sheena, 232
Eastwood, Clint, 320, 419-420, 422
Eaton, Shirley, 56, 125
Ebb, Fred, 385
Ebsen, Buddy, 403
Eckstine, Billy, 422
*Ed Sullivan Show, The*, 1, 75, 126, 191, 335, 337, 346, 357, 368
*Eddie Fisher Show, The* (TV series), 336
Eddy, Nelson, 47-48, 52
*Eddy Duchin Story, The* (movie), 65
Edelman, Louis F., 436-438
Eden, Barbara, 130-131, 134, 157, 165, 191, 216, 221, 242-243, 248-249, 255, 276, 278, 331, 365, 417, 420
Edison, Thomas, 231, 404
Edmiston, Walker, 79, 157
*Edsel Show, The* (special), 350, 467
Edwards, Anita, 449
Edwards, Louise, 165
Edwards, Ralph, 60, 325, 327, 345-346, 352, 417
*Eight on the Lam* (movie), 125, 231
*8th Annual Kennedy Center Honors, The* (awards show), 299
Eisele, Donn F., 134, 233

Eisenhower, David, 157, 280
Eisenhower, Dwight, xix, 53, 58, 62, 65, 69, 139, 157-158, 193, 280, 328, 447, 457, 472
Eisenhower, Mamie, 157, 193
Ekberg, Anita, 57-58, 74-75, 360
Elam, Jack, 432
*Eleanor Roosevelt's Diamond Jubilee Plus One* (special), 338
Elder, Ann, 421
Eldridge, Roy, 348
Elias, Michael, 406
Elinson, Jack, 343, 434, 436, 438
Ellerbee, Linda, 472
Ellington, Duke, 290, 349
Elliot, Cass, 163-164, 375, 388
Elliot, Dick, 62
Elliott, Chris, 416
Elliott, Jack, 293, 361, 367, 370, 385, 400, 403, 410, 466
Elliott, Scott, 440, 444
Ellison, Bob, 383
Elvira, 239-240, 242
Elway, John, 229
Emerson, Faye, 42, 71
*Emmanuel Lewis: My Very Own Show* (special), 419
Emmy Awards, The, 12, 37, 70, 81, 91, 98, 116, 149, 152-153, 204, 206, 210-211, 263-266, 269, 287-288, 292, 300-301, 350, 413, 424, 427-428, 434, 441
*Empty Nest* (sitcom), 424
Engel, Georgia, 393
Ennis, Skinnay, 23-24, 91, 104
*Entertainment 1955* (special), 345
Epstein, Julius, 431
Epstein, Philip, 431
Ervin, Sam, 147
Erving, Julius, 409
*Escape from Alcatraz* (movie), 211
Esiason, Boomer, 252
Esposito, Phil, 332
Esquire Calendar Girls, The, 47
Estancia Marching High School Band, The, 392

Estrada, Erik, 199-200, 216
Evanko, Ed, 271
Evans, Dale, 58, 405
Evans, Denny, 399
Evans, Frank, 440
Evans, Harve, 126
Evans, Linda, 221, 227, 253-254
Evans, Ray, 136, 242, 251
Evans, Rex, 64
Evans, Robert (Bob), 19, 410
Evans, Stephanie, 162
*Evening with Fred Astaire, An* (special), 287
Everett, Thomas, 242
Everly Brothers, The, 377
Evert, Chris, 333
*Everything You Always Wanted to Know About Jack Benny But Were Afraid to Ask* (special), 380
Ewbank, Weeb, 223
*Exorcist, The* (movie), 175
*Exploring with Hope* (special), 458
Expose, 421
Eyerman, Patricia, 279

Fabares, Shelley, 94
Fabian, 98, 101-102
Fabray, Nanette, 96, 146, 159, 163, 417
*Face in the Crowd, A* (movie), 35
*Facts of Life, The* (movie), 96-97, 231, 255, 284, 309
Fadiman, Clifton, 326
Fairbanks Jr., Douglas, 38, 63-64, 116-117, 218, 233, 473
Fairchild, Morgan, 220, 226, 234, 239, 248, 251-252, 266-267, 420
Faith, Delores, 113
Falana, Lola, 161, 171, 185-186, 229-230, 422
Falk, Peter, 109, 411
Falkenburg, Jinx, 42
*Fall Guy, The* (TV series), 211
Fanaro, Barry, 451
*Fancy Pants* (movie), 231, 255
*Fantastic Journey* (movie), 123
Farentino, James, 390

Fargo, Donna, 399
Faria, Miss World Reita, 124, 472
Farker, Lois, 466
Farley, Morgan, 162
Farmer, Gene, 372
Farmer, Mimsy, 105
Farr, Jamie, 182, 250, 449, 466
Farrell, Charlie, 51, 433
Farrell, Eileen, 370
Farrell, Marty, 194, 298, 383, 401, 448, 468
Farrell, Mike, 465
Farrell, Sharon, 91, 440
Farrow, Mia, 117
Fascinato, Jack, 38
Fates, Gil, 324-326, 329
Faulk, Marshall, 272
Fawcett, Farrah, 296
Fay, Meagan, 453
Faye, Alice, 420
Faylen, Frank, 43
*Fear Factor* (TV series), 266, 457
Fein, Irving, 362, 367, 380, 385, 400, 408-410, 412, 414, 416, 438, 444
Feinstein, Michael, 273, 422, 424, 435, 473
Felder, Lou, 414
Feldman, Edward H., 441
Feldon, Barbara, 368, 446
Feliciano, Jose, 369
Feller, Bob, 388
Fells, Shirley, 71
Felton, Norman, 345
Felton, Verna, 53-55, 107-108
Fenady, Andrew J., 449
Fenneman, George, 459
Fera, Greg V., 267
Ferber, Mel, 448
Ferguson, Allyn, 241, 293, 361, 367, 385, 396, 400, 403
Ferguson, Charles, 432
Fernandel, 63, 76-77
Ferrer, José, 54
Ferrier, Garry, 392
Ferrigno, Lou, 216
Fessier, Michael, 445

*Festival at Ford's* (special), 338
Fetter, Ted, 473
*Fibber McGee and Molly* (radio series), 36
*Fiddler on the Roof* (musical), 165
Fiedler, Arthur, 383
Field, Ron, 176, 237, 401
Field, Sally, 405
*Field of Dreams* (movie), 266
Fielding, Jerry, 360, 367
Fields, Dorothy, 76, 141
Fields, Kim, 415, 417
Fields, Sid, 367
Fields, Totie, 159, 389
Fields, W.C., 214
*Fifty Years of Television: A Golden Celebration* (special), 473
Finkel, Bob, 293, 351, 353, 359, 361, 383
Finnigan, Tom, 414
Fiorentino, Jacques, 416
*First Annual American Comedy Awards, The* (special), 397
Firstman, Steve, 65
Fischer, Bobby, 169, 170
Fisher, Art, 385, 392, 399, 402-403
Fisher, Bob, 342
Fisher, Eddie, 61, 69, 72, 90, 97, 134-135, 160, 336, 345-346, 353-354
Fisher, Joely, 248
Fisher, Marvin, 31
Fisher, Tricia Leigh, 248
Fishman, Michael, 453
Fitzell, Roy, 126
Fitzgerald, Ella, 21, 298, 373, 423, 468
Fitzsimmons, Bob, 232
*Five Pennies, The* (movie), 284
*Five Women I Love* (book), 90, 123, 125
Flack, Roberta, 419
Flatt, Ernie, 370, 373
Flaum, Marshall, 231, 236, 469
Fleming, Art, 428
Fleming, Rhonda, 73, 82, 121, 230, 314, 443
Flick, Pat, 43
*Flintstones, The* (TV series), 103, 108

*Flip Wilson Comedy Special, The* (special), 339
*Flip Wilson Show, The* (special), 341
Florence, Bob, 361, 370
Flutie, Doug, 239
*Flying Nun, The* (TV series), 126, 132, 157
Flynn, Errol, 345
Flynn, Joe, 171-172
Fockler, Terry, 77
Foley, Ellen, 398
Fonda, Henry, 389, 400, 404, 466
Fontaine, Joan, 121
*Footlights! (The 32nd Annual Tony Awards)* (awards show), 297
*For Love and Honor* (TV series), 411
Foran, Dick, 64
Ford, Betty, 195, 222, 271, 280
Ford, Constance, 35
Ford, Gerald, 155, 191, 195, 216-217, 222, 242, 247, 251, 271, 275, 280, 296, 317, 394, 405, 418, 423
Ford, Glenn, 123, 227, 250, 387, 470
Ford, Tennessee Ernie, 386, 388
*Foreign Intrigue* (TV series), 64
Foreman, George, 14, 171-172, 177
*Forever Female* (movie), 431-432
Forrest, William, 81
Forsythe, John, 234, 249-251, 253-246, 266-267, 277, 412, 414
*48 Hours* (TV series), 266
*42nd Street* (musical), 220-221
Fosse, Bob, 133
Foster, Charlotte, 436
Foster, George, 351, 460
Foster, Jodie, 405
Foster, Royal, 461
Foulk, Robert, 123
Fountain, Pete, 116, 120-121, 172, 359, 363
Four Kinsmen, The, 191
Four Preps, The, 350
Four Sportsmen, The, 434
Four Step Brothers, The, 47
Fowler, Jim, 313
Fox, Fred S., 145, 152, 203, 257, 400, 406, 410, 412, 414, 418

Fox, Michael J., 242, 416-418
Fox, Mickey, 448
Foxe, Fanne, 182
Foxworthy, Jeff, 273
Foxx, Redd, 23, 150, 170-171, 180-181, 192, 272, 313, 393-394
*Frances Langford Presents* (special), 337
Franchi, Sergio, 110-111
Francis, Anne, 449
Francis, Arlene, 306, 324-326, 329, 417
Francis, Connie, 358
Francis, Russ, 243
Frank, Jerry, 448, 468
Frank, Melvin, 358
Frank, Norman, 347
*Frank Sinatra Duets* (special), 475
*Frank Sinatra Show, The* (series), 350
*Frank Sinatra: The Voice of Our Time* (special), 473
Frankland, Miss World Rosemarie, 100
Franklin, Aretha, 154, 179-180, 376
Franklin, Bonnie, 200, 420
Franklin, Carl, 453
Frann, Mary, 420, 423
Fraser, Ian, 249, 391, 401
Frawley, William, 67, 433
Frazer, Dan, 239
Frazier, Joe, 14, 162-163
Frazier, Walt, 332
Freed, Arthur, 290
Freeman, Joan, 105
Freeman, Kathleen, 135
Freeman, Pam, 445
French, Victor, 451
Frey, Glenn, 415
Frome, Milton, 68, 95, 103-104, 125, 138, 170, 182, 443
*From Cat Whiskers to Peacock: "Forty Years of NBC"* (special), 463
*From Tahiti, Bob Hope's Tropical Comedy Special* (1987 special), 243, 245
Frye, David, 380
Frye, Soleil Moon, 417
*Fugitive, The* (TV series), 121, 126
Fuller, Sam, 48, 344

Funicello, Annette, 112, 405
*Funny Girl*, PRE

Gabel, Martin, 329
Gabor, Eva, 167, 332-333, 405
Gabor, Zsa Zsa, 52, 55, 74, 82, 97, 132-133, 146, 159, 163-164, 184, 294, 313, 356, 369, 387-388, 398, 423
Gabriel, Roman, 171
Galbreath, John W., 457
Gallagher, 214
Gallaudet, John, 53, 95
Gallay, Peter, 389
Gallin, Sandy, 421
Gallop, Frank, 341, 347-348, 351
Gamble, Doug, 208, 257-258
*Gandhi* (movie), 231
Gandolf, Ray, 472
Garcia, Hark, 392
Gardner, Ava, 21
Gardner, Gerald, 367, 379
Gardner, Hy, 336
Gardner, Randy, 215
Gardner, Raquel, 271
Gargiulo, Mike, 220
Garland, Judy, 96, 188
Garner, James, 93, 98-100, 107-108, 113, 117, 134-135, 194
Garrett, Bob, 362
Garrett, Jimmy, 442
Garrett, Joy, 406
Garrett, Leif, 197, 407
Garrett, Mike, 365
Garrison, Greg, 363, 377, 389, 393, 414, 466, 471
Garroway, Dave, 457, 464
Garson, Greer, 64, 358,
Garth, Jeannie, 271
Garvey, Steve, 405
Gatlin, Larry and the Gatlin Brothers Band, 217-218, 226, 412
Gavin, John, 124
Gaye, Marvin, 413
Gayle, Crystal, 198-199, 241, 244-245, 402-403
Gaynor, Janet, 285, 355

Gaynor, Mitzi, 133, 140-141, 294, 331, 354, 390
Geary, Tony, 227
Gelbart, Larry, 7, 11, 31, 466
*General Electric's All-Star Anniversary* (special), 404
*General Hospital* (TV series), 227
*Genius of Ray Charles, The* (album), 138
Gennaro, Peter, 392
Gentry, Bobbie, 127-128, 294
George, Christopher, 390
George, Phyllis, 381
George, Susan, 197
*George Burns Celebrates 80 Years in Show Business* (special), 412
*George Burns' Early, Early, Early Christmas Special* (special), 410
*George Burns How to Live to Be 100* (special), 414
*George Burns' 90th Birthday: A Very Special Special* (special), 415
*George Burns' 100th Birthday Party* (special), 406
*George Burns One-Man Show, The* (special), 152, 400
Gerard, Gil, 216, 420
Gerber, Jay, 406
Gerson, Betty Lou, 76
*Get Smart!* (TV series), 429, 446
Getty, Estelle, 244, 415-417, 451
Gibb, Andy, 195-196, 215, 298, 402-403, 406, 410, 418
Gibbs, Marla, 417, 423
Gibson, Bob, 133
Gibson, Henry, 137, 368, 372
Gifford, Alan, 73-74
*Gigi* (movie), 254, 287
Gilbert, Melissa, 403, 417, 448
Gilbert, Sara, 453
Gill, Brendan, 473
Gillard, Stuart, 394
Gilliam, Byron, 368-369, 372
*Gimme a Break!* (TV series), 209
Gipsy Kings, The, 253-254
Girl Scouts of America, The, 422

Giroux, Jackie, 159
Giroux, Lee, 122, 126, 132-133, 138, 157
Gish, Lillian, 420
Gist, Rod, 399
Givens, Robin, 266
Gleason, Jackie, 100, 121, 123, 140, 144, 153, 157, 178, 180, 185, 328, 357, 471
*Glen Campbell Goodtime Hour, The* (TV series), 382
Glenn, John, 101, 111, 195
*Global Affair, A* (movie), 361
*Gloria* (TV series), 211
Glucksman, Ernest D., 43, 48, 371
*GM Motorama* (special), 337
Gobel, George, 65, 139, 182, 223, 307, 336, 352, 417
*Godfather, The* (movie), 165, 308
Godfrey, Arthur, 39, 54-55, 60, 469
Godkin, Paul, 362
Godwin, Earl, 306
Goelz, Dave, 189, 402, 452
*Going My Own Way* (book), 231
*Going My Way* (movie), 469
Goldberg, David J., 422
Goldberg, Lee, 36
Goldberg, Whoopi, 275, 416, 420, 423
Golddiggers, The, 136-137, 161, 377,
*Golden Girls, The* (TV series), 212, 244, 253, 429, 451
*Golden Rainbow* (musical), 127
Goldenberg, Billy, 370
Goldman, Hal, 354, 362, 367, 380, 385, 406, 409-410, 412, 414, 416, 430-431, 434-435, 438, 444, 448
Goldthwait, Bobcat, 416
Goldwater, Sen. Barry, 112, 393. 418
Golonka, Arlene, 387
*Gomer Pyle U.S.M.C.* (TV series), 120, 137, 375, 428
*Gone with the Wind* (movie), xix, xx, 68, 121, 238
Gonzalez, Pancho, 328
*Good Morning Vietnam* (movie), 318
Goodman, Al, 39, 43, 344

Goodman, Benny, 464
Goodman, Hal, 342, 350, 352-353, 370, 373
Goodman, John, 453
Goodpaster, Lt. Gen. Andrew J., 221
Goodtime Singers, The, 361
Goodwin, Bill, 47, 51
Goodwin, Karenjo, 271
Goodwin, Laurel, 105
Goranson, Lecy, 453
Gorbachev, Mikhail, 252, 267
Gordon, Al, 354, 362, 367, 370, 373, 380, 385, 430-431, 434-435, 438, 444, 448
Gordon, Gale, 310, 366, 389, 395, 441-442
Gordon, Lance, 225
Gordon, Leo, 439
Gordon, Marianne, 17-18, 123
Gordon, Michael, 93
Gorme, Eydie, 126, 142, 218, 396
Gorshin, Frank, 387, 400, 449
Gossett Jr., Louis, 420
Gottlieb, Alex, 443
Gottlieb, Richard, 327
Gould, Dana, 277
Gould, Elliott, 192, 405
Gould, Jack, 4
Gould, Morton, 422
Gould, Sandra, 93, 162
Gould, Sid, 187, 190, 213
Gould, Walter, 329
Goulet, Robert, 105, 117-118, 135-136, 165, 169, 176, 180, 226-227, 290, 294, 360, 368, 376
Gowdy, Curt, 330
Grable, Betty, 62, 66, 69-70, 77
Grace, Carrie, 95
Gradishar, Randy, 170, 229
Graham, B.A., 345-346
Graham, The Rev. Billy, xvii, 125, 309, 383, 388-389, 405, 412
Graham, Irvin, 38
Graham, Ronny, 387
Graham, Virginia, 145, 159
*Grammy Hall of Fame, The* (awards show), 298

Grammys, The—See *Best on Record, The*
Grant, Cary, 64, 313, 370, 416, 419
Grant, Johnny, xvii, 90, 125, 132, 166, 177, 248, 270, 327
Grant, Kathryn—See Crosby, Kathryn
Grant, Lee, 469
Grantham, Tom, 228
Grauer, Ben, 50-51, 345
Graves, Teresa, xiv, 4, 156, 159, 162, 372
Gray, Beverly, 98
Gray, Erin, 411
Gray, Linda, 214-215, 410
Grayson, Kathryn, 13, 65
Graziano, Rocky, 356
*Grease* (movie), 223
*Great Performances:* "Irving Berlin's America" (special), 472
*Great Radio Comedians, The* (special), 465
*Greatest Show on Earth, The* (movie), 286
Greaza, Walter, 39
Greco, Buddy, 158
Greco, Jose, 56
Green, Miss World Belinda, 171
Green, Katherine, 145
Green, Mort, 351, 359, 379, 390
Green, Tim, 242
*Green Acres* (TV series), 163, 428
Greene, Mean Joe, 388
Greene, Lorne, 293-294, 359, 378, 417, 462
Greene, Shecky, 139-140, 171-172, 294, 412-413
Greenfield, Jeff, 469
Greenhau, Tom, 460
Greenwood, Lee, 248
Gregory, Dick, 416
Grenrock, Joshua, 448
Grey, Joel, 363
Grier, Rosey, 136, 223, 305, 410
Griffin, Archie, 181, 333
Griffin, Merv, 171, 303, 310, 387, 419, 424

Griffith, Andy, 108, 152, 377, 390, 467
Griffith, Anthony, 277
Griffith-Joyner, Florence, 252
Grimes, Scott, 243, 246, 418
Grizzard, George, 345
Groat, Dick, 328
Groening, Matt, 454
Gross, Mary, 416
Grossman, Larry, 249, 391, 396, 398, 413
Grudt, Miss Universe Mona, 268
Gruenberg, Axel, 327
Grusin, Dave, 361-362, 370
Guardino, Jerome, 414
Guillaume, Robert, 214, 416
Guedel, John, 463
Gueden, Hilde, 344
Guercio, Joe, 376
*Gunsmoke* (TV series), 9, 100, 158, 294, 369, 377
Guzman, Freddie, 123
*Gypsy* (musical), 82

Hackett, Buddy, 127, 139, 329-330, 345, 380, 383, 412
Hagan, Chet, 466
Haggerty, Dan, 403
Hagler, Marvelous Marvin, 232, 237, 241
Hahn, Jess, 72
Hahn, Phil, 369, 394, 403, 421
Haig, Alexander, 226-227
Haig, Sid, 135, 162
Haig, Tony, 80
Haines, Connie, 46, 108-109
Hairston, Happy, 384
Haje, Khrystyne, 270
Hale, Chanin, 142, 182, 379
Hale, Lee, 136-137, 161, 377, 414, 466
Haley, Alex, 404
Haley Jr., Jack, 185, 420, 462, 466
Hall, Gov. David, 384
Hall, Deidre, 240, 417
Hall, Michael, 56
Hall, Monty, 194, 390, 395, 400, 419, 428

Hall, Philip Baker, 406
Hall, Robert, 466
Halloran, Jack, 377
Halloran, Ursula, 77
Halop, Florence, 159
Halperin, Marty, 463
Hamer, Rusty, 434, 436-437, 447
Hamill, Dorothy, 410
Hamill, Mark, 189
Hamilton, Joe, 370, 373
Hamilton IV, George, 349
Hamilton Trio, The, 343
Hamlin, John, 192
Hamlisch, Marvin, 385
Hammer, Barbara, 432
Hamner, Robert, 443
Hampton, Dan, 229
Hampton, Lionel, 360
Handey, Jack, 406
Handley, Alan, 345, 366
Haney, Carol, 78
Haney, Fred, 352
Hanks, Tom, 475
Hanold, Marilyn, 65
Hanrahan, Jack, 369
Hansen, Tom, 102
Hanser, Richard, 458, 460
*Happy Birthday Bob* (1978 special), 3, 192-193
*Happy Birthday Bob* (1983 special), 232
*Happy Birthday Bob*: "50 Stars Salute Your 50 Years With NBC" (1988 special), 250
*Happy Birthday Hollywood* (special), 420
Harbach, Otto, 76, 141
Harbach, William O., 222, 228, 352, 361, 364-365, 378
Hargrove, Dean, 132
Harlan, John, 145, 171, 223, 257, 278
Harlem Globetrotters, The, 392-393
Harmon, Tom, 326
Harout, Magda, 444
Harper, Toni, 341
Harper, Valerie, 417
Harrah, Walter, 240

Harrington Jr., Pat, 116, 132, 387
Harris, Eleanor, 77
Harris, Jay S., 469
Harris, Jeff, 373
Harris, Julie, 417
Harris, Peter, 402, 452
Harris, Phil, 49-50, 172, 285, 380, 403
Harris, Richard, 311
Harris, Stan, 129, 131, 233, 378, 400, 406
Harrison, Gregory, 420
Harrison, Rex, 41-42, 98, 338
Hart, Chris, 217
Hart, Delores, 73
Hart, Mary, 420
Hart, Stan, 217
Hart, Stephen, 446
Hart, Susan, 105
Hart, Terry, 184, 393
Hartman, Don, 60
Hartman, Phil, 275-276
Hartog-Bel, Miss World Madeline, 130
Harvey, Bob, 92, 101, 107, 444
Harwood, Dick, 223
Haskell, Jimmie, 416-417, 424
Hasselhoff, David, 411, 417
Hasso, Signe, 121
Hatcher, Mary, 341
Hausner, Jerry, 54
*Have Tux, Will Travel* (book), 57, 60, 325
Havlicek, John, 333
*Hawaii Five-O* (TV series), 235
Hawkins, Coleman, 348
Hawkins Family, The, 410
Hawn, Goldie, 368, 372, 405-406, 423
Hayek, Miss USA Julie, 235
Hayes, Gabby, 72, 97
Hayes, Helen, 345, 405
Hayes, Isaac, 385
Hayes, Joseph, 345
Haymer, Johnny, 352
Haynes, Mike, 243
Haynie, Sandra, 333
*He and She* (TV series), 126
Head, Edith, 53

Index • 511

Hearn, Sam, 438
Heath, Ted, 63
Heatherton, Joey, 90, 119, 124, 172-174, 365, 385
*Hedda Hopper's Hollywood* (special), 355
Hedren, Tippi, 125
*Hee Haw*, xix, 375, 377
Hefner, Hugh, 369
Hefti, Neal, 448
Helfgott, Daniel, 280
Heller, Barbara, 445
Heller, Franklin, 324-326, 329
*Hello Dolly!* (musical), 21, 113, 155, 176, 192
Helton, Percy, 432
Hemion, Dwight, 241, 249, 348-349, 352, 391, 396, 398, 401, 413
Hemphill, Ray, 437
Hemsley, Sherman, 468
Henderson, Florence, 191, 275-276, 293, 398, 420
Henderson, Pete—See Skiles and Henderson
Henderson, Skitch, 352
Hendra and Ullett, 363
Hendricks, Ted, 229
Henning, Anne, 384
Henry, Bob, 77, 24, 353, 361, 374, 407
Henry, Buck, 446
Henry, Gig, xv, 31, 36, 56-57, 72, 75, 85, 145, 148, 151-152, 203, 209, 294, 328, 331-333, 418
Henry, Stephen, 244
Henson, Jim, 189, 192, 194, 232, 241, 402, 405, 452
Henton, John, 273
Hepburn, Audrey, 116, 291
Hepburn, Katharine, 63, 70, 231, 420
*Here Come the Girls* (movie), 54, 230
*Here Come the Stars* (TV series), 371
*Here's Boomer* (TV series), 216
*Here's Dick Cavett* (talk show special), 307
*Here's Edie* (TV series), 239, 360
*Here's Lucy* (TV series), 152, 372

*Here's Television Entertainment* (special), 413
Herlihy, Ed, 417
Herman, Jerry, 468
Herman, Pee Wee (Paul Reubens), 271, 416
Hershiser, Orel, 252
Hersholt, Jean, 93, 284-285, 288, 292, 298-299
Hervey, Irene, 141
Herzig, Sig, 435
Hesseman, Howard, 470
Heston, Charlton, 127, 226-227, 241, 295, 358, 386, 408, 418, 420
Hewett, Howard, 421
Hi Hatters, The, 34, 40
Hickey, Neil, 469, 477
Hider, Ed, 394, 399, 403
Higgins, Joel, 411
*Highlights of a Quarter Century of Bob Hope on Television* (1975 special), 145, 149, 180
*Highway to Heaven* (TV series), 212, 451
Hill, Ben, 463
Hill, J., 25, 390
*Hill Street Blues* (TV series), 165
Hillis, Janet, 414
Hines, Gregory, 423
Hines, Janear, 447
Hines, Patrick, 178
Hingle, Pat, 404
Hinkley, Don, 348-349, 352, 361, 370, 373, 389, 402
Hirt, Al, 172, 382
Hobin, Bill, 195, 199, 290
Hobson, Dick, 257
Hoff, Carl, 347
Hoffman, Bern, 379
Hoffman, Dustin, 230, 474
Hoffman, Howard, 64
Holbrook, Hal, 457
Holden, William, 57-58, 332, 429, 468
Holdridge, Cheryl, 99
Hole, Judith, 467
Holliday, Judy, 345

Holloway, Sterling, 405
*Hollywood and the Stars* (TV series), 462
Hollywood Deb Stars, 17, 61, 67, 73, 77, 82, 94, 99, 105-106, 165, 271-272
*Hollywood Palace, The* (TV series), 25, 133, 136, 340, 363, 365
*Hollywood Squares, The* (TV series), 180, 323
Hollywood Swimsuit Models, The, 267
Holm, Celeste, 298, 378
Holmes, Clint, 371
Holmes, Larry, 226-227
Holmes, Tom, 345
*Home* (talk show), 306
*Honor America Day* (special), 338
*Hootenanny* (TV series), 108
Hooven, Marilyn, 267
Hope, Delores (Bob's wife), xvii, 171, 192-193, 195-196, 198-199, 202, 215, 220-221, 225-226, 232, 237, 241-242, 244, 246-247, 249-251, 254, 265, 268-274, 276-280, 306, 318, 338, 389, 418, 430, 435, 457, 478, 480
Hope, George (Bob's brother), xvi, 2, 85, 87
Hope, Jack (Bob's brother), 2, 31, 36, 50, 66, 85, 87, 327-328
Hope, Kelly (Bob's son), xvii
Hope, Linda (Bob's daughter), 27, 145-146, 149-150, 198-200, 203, 210, 214-218, 257, 259, 262-263, 266, 325, 423, 440, 478
Hope, Tony (Bob's son), 72-73, 114
*Hope for President* (1980 special), 216-217, 316
Hopper, Hedda, 57-58, 64, 68-69, 73-74, 76-78, 355
Hopper, Jerry, 76
Horne, Lena, 358, 365, 421
Horne, Marilyn, 370, 422
Horne, Pat, 51-52
Horvath, Charles, 432
Horvitz, Louis J., 421

Hosten, Miss World Jennifer, 161
Houston, Whitney, 423
*How to Commit Marriage*, xviii, 139, 185
*How to Succeed in Business Without Really Trying* (musical), 121, 361
Howard, Bob, 400, 404
Howard, Jean, 473
Howard, Ron, 184, 333, 395, 403, 470
Howard, Trustin, 136
Howard, Willie, 1
Hoyt, Clegg, 439, 441
Hoyt, John, 120
Hudson, Rock, 126, 358, 400
Hughes, Gordon, 433
Hughes, Howard, 46, 71, 138
Hughes, Michael, 447
Hughes, Terry, 451
Humperdinck, Engelbert, 160
Humphrey, Hubert, 93, 122, 133, 165, 393
Hunt, Richard, 189, 402
Hunter, Fred, 247
Hunter, Jeffrey, 113, 124
Hunter, Ross, 93, 390
Hunter, Tab, 71
Huntley, Chet, 139-140, 463
Hurley, Fred, 2
Husing, Ted, 93
Hussein, Saddam, 269-272, 320
Hussey, Robert D., 225
*Hustler, The* (movie), 100
Hutton, Betty, 62, 103, 335
Hutton, Jim, 182-183
Hutton, June, 46
Hyatt, Donald B., 458, 460
Hyde-White, Wilfred, 377
Hyer, Martha, 230-231
Hyman, Phyllis, 226

*I Love Lucy* (TV series), 23, 67, 140, 180, 254-255, 324, 396, 425, 429, 433
*I Owe Russia $1,200* (book), 105, 107, 330, 360
*I Remember Illinois* (special), 464
Iacocca, Lee, 242

Index • 513

Ice Capades, The, 399
Ice Follies, The, 391
Iglesias, Julio, 232, 241
*I'll Take Sweden* (movie), 115-116, 231
*Image Empire, The* (book) 130
Impellitteri, Mayor Vincent R., 41
Ingels, Marty, 445
International Children's Choir, The, 129, 238-239
Ireland, Jill, 420
*Iron Petticoat, The* (movie), 35, 63, 69-70, 231, 349, 433
*Ironside* (TV series), 128, 168, 331, 385
*Irving Berlin's 100th Birthday Celebration* (special), 422
Isaacs, Brad, 453
Isaacs, Charles/Charlie, 220, 343
Iscove, Rob, 398
Isley, Don, 171
*It Could Be You* (game show), 323
*It's Ho-Ho Hope's Jolly Christmas Hour* (1984 special), 238
*I've Got a Secret* (game show), 323
Ives, Burl, 346

Jablonski, Carl, 192, 199, 214, 220, 226, 232
*Jack Benny Hour, The* (1959 special), 354
*Jack Benny Hour, The* (1965 special), 362
*Jack Benny Program, The* (TV series), 81, 425-426, 430-431, 434-435, 438, 444, 467
*Jack Benny 20th Anniversary TV Special, The* (special), 378
*Jack Benny's Carnival Nights* (special), 366
*Jack Benny's First Farewell Special* (special), 395
*Jackie Gleason Presents the Honeymooners Reunion* (special), 471
*Jackie Gleason Show, The* (TV series), 33, 157
Jackson, Bo, 242
Jackson, C.D., 459-460
Jackson, Eddie, 335, 343
Jackson, Henry "Scoop," 216-217
Jackson, Rev. Jesse, 469
Jackson, Kate, 185-186
Jackson, La Toya, 253, 268
Jackson, Mahalia, 464
Jackson, Michael, 174, 236, 413, 423
Jackson, Reggie, 332
Jackson, Sherry, 459
Jackson, Victoria, 419
Jackson Five/Jacksons, The, 173-174, 394-395
Jacobs, Seaman, 145, 152, 203, 257, 400, 406, 410, 412, 414, 418
Jaffe, Henry, 467
James, Alice, 448
James, Craig, 234
James, Dennis, 39
James, Harry, 69-70, 353, 368
James, Sheila, 105
James, Sonny, 71-72
James, Stephanie, 447
Jameson, Joyce, 129, 445
*Jane Ahoy* (TV pilot), 36
Janis, Conrad, 214
Janssen, David, 128, 134, 182, 332-333
Jarreau, Al, 410
Jarvis, Carol, 73-74
*Jaws* (movie), 154, 391
Jay, Peter, 192-193
Jean, Al, 454
Jefferson, John, 229
*Jeffersons, The* (TV series), 211
Jeffries, Fran, 171
Jellison, Bob, 53-54, 62, 78, 103, 106, 116, 119, 121, 129, 132-133, 138-139, 142, 159, 165, 167-168, 172, 443
Jenkins, Gordon, 70
Jenner, Bruce, 221, 403, 405, 448
*Jennifer Slept Here* (TV series), 411
*Jeopardy!* (TV series), 279
Jergens, Diane, 73
*Jerry Lewis Show, The* (TV series), 363
Jessel, George, 48, 71-72, 285, 344, 371, 406

Jewison, Norman, 357
Jillian, Ann, 225, 229, 232, 235, 244, 250-251, 253-254, 258, 267-268, 270-271, 411, 414, 445, 479
*Jim Henson Hour, The* (TV series), 452
*Jim Nabors Hour, The* (TV series), xiii, 139
*Jimmy Demaret Show, The* (sports show), 324
*Jimmy Durante Presents the Lennon Sisters Hour* (TV series), 372
*Jimmy Durante Show, The* (TV series), 335
*Jimmy Durante Show, The* (special), 357
*Jo Stafford Show, The* (special), 338
Joe and Eddie, 462
*Joe and Valerie* (TV series), 155
*Joey Bishop Show, The* (TV series), 437
John, Elton, 391, 399, 405, 421
*John Davidson Show, The* (talk show), 305
*Johnny Cash Show, The* (TV series), 375
*Johnny Concho* (movie), 351
Johnson, Alan, 396, 468
Johnson, Arte, 171-172, 182-183, 368-369, 372, 414
Johnson, Chic—See Olsen and Johnson
Johnson, Coslough, 369, 372, 394
Johnson, Don, 244, 246-247, 252, 280, 415, 417
Johnson, Duke, 70
Johnson, Earvin "Magic," 410
Johnson, Lady Bird, 222
Johnson, Lynda Bird, 129
Johnson, Lyndon, 95, 111-112, 115, 117, 120, 122-123, 157, 358, 364, 368
Johnson, Nicholas, 469
Johnson, Rafer, 328
Johnson, Tor, 65
Johnson, Van, 420
Johnson (Howe), Melodie, 17,
Johnstone, Bill, 54
*Joker is Wild, The* (movie), 71
Joli, Frances, 200
Jolson, Al, 188

*Jonathan Winters Show, The* (TV series), 150
Jones, Clark, 418, 468
Jones, Dean, 390, 405
Jones, Eugene S., 460
Jones, Jack, 111, 115, 119, 126, 128, 250-251, 418, 458
Jones, Quincy, 423
Jones, Shirley, 147, 162-163, 168, 175, 180, 183, 213, 225, 238-239, 243, 366, 405, 418, 420
Jones, Tom, 88, 140-141, 159-160, 187, 337, 376, 381
Jordan, Barbara, 216-217
Jordan, Jim, 31, 36, 74
Jordan, Louis, 253-254
Jordan, Marian, 36
Jordan, Will, 346
Josefowicz, Leila, 15-16, 249
Josefsberg, Milt, 353, 367, 430-431, 442
Joseph, Jackie, 366
Joyce, Elaine, 214
Joyce Singers, The James, 365
*Joys!* (1976 special), 154, 182
Judd, Ashley and Wynonna, 255, 276
Judd, Naomi, 280
*Judgment at Nuremberg* (movie), 102
*Judy Garland Show, The* (TV series), 461
Juhl, Jerry, 402
*Julia* (movie), 297
Julia (TV series), 429, 447-448
Julian, Arthur, 441
Junger Witt, Paul, 451
Jurgensen, William K., 466

Kagan, Michael, 402
Kahn, Madeline, 416, 422
Kallen, Lucille, 38
Kaltenborn, H.V., 345
Kamahl, 191
Kanin, Garson, 473
Kanter, Hal, 182, 353, 403, 445, 447, 471
Kaplan, Gabe, 393, 468
Kaprall, Bo, 150, 181

Karr, Patti, 451
Karras, Alex, 405
Karson, Lee, 433
Kartun, Allan, 275
Karvelas, Robert, 446
Kaskel, Gary, 471
Kasznar, Kurt, 366
*Kate & Allie* (TV series), 208
*Kate Smith Evening Hour, The* (TV series), 343
Katleman, Harris, 371
Katz, Raymond, 392, 399, 403
Kavner, Julie, 453
*Kay Kyser's Kollege of Musical Knowledge* (game show), 324
Kaye, Danny, 48, 194, 279, 339, 387, 395, 469
Kaye, Delores, 97
Kaye, Caren, 448
KC and the Sunshine Band, 21, 192, 403-404
Keane, Bob, 184, 219
Keane, Dick, 64
Kearns, Joseph, 66, 80
Keaton, Buster, 342, 432
Keaton, Michael, 416
Keats, Steven, 449
Keel, Howard, 76, 245-246
Keeler, Christine, 108
Keeler, Ruby, 420
Keillor, Garrison, 422
Keith, Hal, 38-39, 42
Kellard, Rick, 403
Keller, Casey, 151, 199-200
Keller, Father James, 429-430
Keller, Sheldon, 150-151, 183, 185-187, 189-190, 214, 366, 395, 448
Kellerman, Sally, 440
Kellogg, Ray, 51, 54, 110, 121, 129, 131, 138-139, 157, 162-163, 165, 168
Kelly, Gene, 357, 393, 405, 466, 468, 473
Kelly, Grace, 63, 65, 469
Kelly, Jack, 127-128, 428
Kelly, Judy, 40
Kelly, Patrick, 254

Kelly, Paula, 458
*Ken Berry Wow Show, The* (TV series), 339
*Ken Berry's Wow: "A Wacky Look at Yesterday"* (special), 339
Kennedy, Bobby, 112, 131
Kennedy, Jacqueline, 101, 134, 140
Kennedy(-Overton), Jayne, 216-217, 340, 420
Kennedy, John F., xiii, 93, 98, 102, 104-105, 111, 135, 280, 328, 358, 360, 461-462
Kennedy, Mimi, 398
Kennedy, Tom, 390
*Kennedy Center Honors, The*—See *8th Annual Kennedy Center Honors, The*
Kern, James V., 433
Kern, Jerome, 76, 141
Kerner, Otto, 464
Kerr, Anita, 290
Kert, Larry, 398
Kessler, Zale, 406
Kessler Twins, The, 363
Keyes, Paul W., 180, 184, 369, 372, 378, 395, 400, 404, 419
Khan, Chaka and Rufus, 154, 178
Khrushchev, Nikita, 81, 107-108, 113, 160, 358
Kidd, Michael, 39
Kids Next Door, The, 128
Kiley, Tim, 203, 257, 357, 394
Kilgallen, Dorothy, 324-326, 329
Kilgariff, Karen, 279
Kimball, Robert, 473
King, Alan, 188, 192, 249-250, 294, 332-333, 356, 401, 471
King, Miss America Becky, 388
King, Billie Jean, 146, 173, 331-332, 390
King, Don, 226-227
King, Don Roy, 474
King, Peggy, 68-69, 459
King, Perry, 415, 417
King Carl Gustav, 243
King Jr., Martin Luther, 291

Kingsley, Ben, 241
Kingston Trio, The, 358
Kirby, George, 182-183, 235, 421
Kirk, Phyllis, 435
Kirkland, Mark, 454
Kirkwood, Jack, 69-71, 80
Kirschbaum, Bruce, 403
Kirtland, Louis, 39
*Kiss Me Kate* (musical), 348
Kisselhoff, Jeff, 33
Kissinger, Henry, 186, 198, 268-269, 311, 389, 394
Kitt, Eartha, 346
Kjelsen, Ingeborg, 447
Klein, Larry, 45, 350, 352-353
Klein, Marty, 406
Klein, Robert, 231, 471
Klingman, Mark, 181
Klosterman, Don, 381
Klugman, Jack, 417, 448
Knight, Arthur, 463
Knight, Gladys, 340, 400, 421
Knight, Ted, 390, 392-393
*Knots Landing* (TV series), 261
Knotts, Don, 125, 140, 154, 159, 182, 184, 198, 223, 348-349, 352, 418
Knudsen Brothers, The, 402
Koch, Howard W., 188
Kogen, Arnie, 399
Kohan, Buz, 196, 205, 249, 263, 275, 301, 370, 373, 391, 396-398, 401, 413, 416, 470
Kohan, Rhea, 421
Kolinsky, Sue, 279
Konigsberg, Frank(lin), 397, 469
Korbut, Olga, 33
Korean Kittens, The, 124
Korman, Harvey, 216, 370, 373
Koufax, Sandy, 108
Kovacs, Ernie, 82
Kozak, Elliott, 13, 203, 210, 233-235, 237, 240, 243, 245, 257
*Kraft Music Hall, The* (TV series), 87, 336, 353, 401
*Kraft 75th Anniversary Show, The* (special), 401, 473

*Kraft Suspense Theatre* (TV series), 426, 428
*Kraft Television Theatre* (TV series), 401
Kramer, Stepfanie, 246-247, 250-251, 415, 420
Kranz, Emily, 123-124
Krauch, Herb, 73
Kreiner, Kathy, 183
Krinski, Sandy, 392
Kristien, Dale, 266-267
Krofft, Sid and Marty, 392, 407
Kronick, William, 380
Krope, Miss Australia Gloria, 191
Kruger, Otto, 431
Krupa, Gene, 464
Kruschen, Jack, 432
Kuhl, Cal, 431
Kukoff, Bernie, 373
Kulik, Buzz, 431
Kunes, Steven, 424
*Kup's Show* (talk show), 305
Kupcinet, Irving, 73, 305
Kupcinet, Karyn, 103
Kuralt, Charles, 467, 474
Kwan, Nancy, 99-100
Kyne, Terry, 379
Kyser, Kay, 324

LaBelle, Patti, 271, 415, 420
Lachman, Mort, xv, 8-10, 25, 31, 36, 48, 66, 72-73, 75, 77, 85, 87, 124, 130, 136, 145, 148, 150, 152, 156, 161, 165, 171, 209, 275-276, 294, 328, 331-333, 360-361, 440, 443-444, 460
Lack, Andrew, 474
Lacy, Madison D., 471
Lacy, Susan, 473
Ladd, Cheryl, 399, 404-405
Ladizinsky, Ivan, 223
Laine, Frankie, 49-50, 285
Lake, Florence, 128-129, 179
Lamarr, Hedy, 121
Lamas, Fernando, 132
Lambert, Hugh, 78

Index • 517

Lamour, Dorothy, xiv, xvi, 3, 39, 54-55, 66, 102, 121, 160-161, 168-169, 181, 192-193, 230-231, 250-251, 271, 275-276, 278, 332, 342, 356, 369, 373, 385, 392, 412, 420
Lamouret, Robert, 348
Lancaster, Burt, 358, 420
Land, Jana, 73
Landa, Dennis, 403
Landers, Audrey, 229-230, 418
Landers, Muriel, 68
Landon, Michael, 239, 242, 247, 250-251, 378, 390, 404, 413, 451, 467, 470
Landry, Greg, 384, 386
Lane, Ken, 365, 377
Lane, Paula, 108, 440
Lang, Victoria, 424
Lange, Hope, 355, 417
Lange, Kelly, 221
Langford, Frances, 47, 91-92, 268-269, 279-280, 337
Lankford, Kim, 448
Lansbury, Angela, 271, 275
Lansing, Joi, 93, 101
Lanteau, John, 441
Lapiduss, Maxine, 453
Largent, Steve, 229
Larkin, Bill, xv, 31, 36, 48, 53-54, 66, 85, 145, 328, 361, 392
LaRosa, Julius, 346
Larroquette, John, 473
*Larry King Live* (talk show), 306
Larsen, Don, 67
*Lassie* (dog and TV series), 60, 62, 163, 225, 403, 424
*Last Christmas Show, The* (book), 179, 312
*Last of the Red Hot Lovers* (Broadway play), 309
*Late Night With David Letterman* (talk show), 317, 319
Latell, Lyle, 432
Lauck, Chet, 463
*Laugh Crafters: Comedy Writing in Radio and TV's Golden Age* (book), 7, 11
*Laugh Makers, The* (book), 244

*Laugh-In*—See *Rowan and Martin's Laugh-In*
*Laughing All the Way: 30 Years of TV's Greatest Hits* (special), 470
*Laughing Matters* (book), 7
Laurance, Mitchell, 416
Lauren, Rod, 82
Lauren, Tammy, 448
Laurie, Piper, 101-102
Lausche, Ohio Gov. Frank, 50
Lawford, Peter, 79, 352, 435-436, 459
Lawrence, Carol, 16, 19, 88, 117, 125, 135, 168-169, 190, 192, 376
Lawrence, David, 467
Lawrence, Elliott, 418, 422, 468
Lawrence, Gail, 217
Lawrence, Joel, 393
Lawrence, Joey, 238-239, 276
Lawrence, Steve, 126-127, 142, 190, 218, 396
Lawrence, Vicki, 306, 370, 373, 411
Lawson, Louise, 138, 140
Layton, Joe, 367
Le Boeuf, Sabrina, 417
Lear, Norman, 185, 356, 359, 469
Leary, Timothy, 165
Lee, Ann, 433
Lee, Anna, 440
Lee, Brenda, 105
Lee, Charles/Charlie, xv, 31, 36, 53-54, 85, 145, 148, 151-152, 209, 224, 294, 328, 331-333
Lee, Christopher, 405
Lee, Johnine, 120-121, 131
Lee, Melinda, 63
Lee, Michele, 141, 420
Lee, Peggy, 39, 285, 350
Lee, Pinky, 61
Lee, Ruta, 73
Leeds, Howard, 361
Leeds, Peter, 23, 53-59, 62, 64-66, 68-69, 71, 73, 77, 79-83, 88, 91-97, 99-100, 102, 104, 106-110, 113-115, 118-119, 121, 123, 125, 167, 169, 175, 238-239, 247-248, 266, 271-272, 440, 443, 460

Leeds, Robert, 444
*Leif Garrett Special, The* (special), 407
Leifer, Carol, 273
Leigh, Janet, 110-111, 118, 132, 135, 400, 420
Lemmon, Jack, 226, 283, 287-288, 290, 367, 387, 411, 416, 474
*Lemon Drop Kid, The* (movie), 42
Lennon Sisters, The, 372-373, 418
Leno, Jay, 250, 263, 275, 301, 305, 478
Leo, Malcolm, 203, 213, 466
Leonard, Jack E., 139-140
Leonard, Sheldon, 54-55, 91, 364, 434, 436-438
Leonard, Sugar Ray, 220, 237, 277, 421
Leopold, Tom, 411
Lerner, Alan Jay, 299
LeRoy, Hal, 38
Les Ballet Trockadero de Monte Carlo, 396-397
Lester, Jerry, 32, 417
Letterman, David, 191, 212, 237, 317, 319-320, 411, 416, 478
Levene, Sam, 341, 353
Levy, Eugene, 416
Levy, Ralph, 362, 430-431, 434
Lewin, Albert E., 439, 445
Lewis, Draper, 467
Lewis, Emmanuel, 194, 242-243, 246-247, 252, 278, 419
Lewis, Frank, 347
Lewis, Jerry, 33, 48, 149, 190, 285, 308, 348, 363, 416, 431, 466
Lewis, Jerry Lee, 421-422
Lewis, Jim, 452
Lewis, Melvin, 253
Lewis, Shari, and Lamb Chop, 417, 420
Leyden, Bill, 325
Liberace, 166, 326, 391, 399
Liberto, Don, 38
Liebman, Max, 38-39, 343
Liebman, Wendy, 260-261, 274
Liebmann, Norm, 377
*Lights Out* (TV series), 341
Lillard, Tom, 406
Lilley, Joe/Joseph J., 66, 439, 443

Lillie, Beatrice, 38-39, 56-57, 116-117, 274
Lilly, Bob, 223
Lilo, 473
*Lincoln Mercury Startime* (TV series), 458-459
Linden, Hal, 239, 250, 417
Linder, Tom G., 442
Lindsay, New York Mayor John V., 130, 180
Lindsay, Mark, 382
Linhart, Buzzy, 181
Link, Michael, 162, 447
Linkletter, Art, 323, 463, 468
Linville, Larry, 466
Lipstone, Howard, 470
Lipton, James, 155, 192, 198-199, 204-205, 215, 220, 226, 232, 237, 241, 244, 246, 250, 253
Lisi, Virna, 142
Liss, Joseph, 460
Lister, Moira, 56-57
Little, Rich, 294, 318, 337, 389-390, 393, 405, 408, 414, 416, 418
Littlefield, Warren, 212
*Live with Regis and Kathie Lee* (talk show), 305
Lively Set, The, 363
Livingston, Jay, 136, 228, 242, 251
Lloyd, Harold, 355
Lloyd, Jeremy, 372
Lloyd, Michael, 407
Lloyd, Norman, 417
Locke, Sam, 440
Locke Elliott, Sumner, 355
Lockwood, Grey, 344, 347, 351, 353, 363, 365, 458
Loewe, Frederick, 299
Logan, Brad, 159, 379
Lollobrigida, Gina, 77, 116, 202, 225
Lombardo, Tony, 410
London, Damian, 120, 138
London, Julie, 68, 79, 98, 110-111, 328
London, Marc, 369, 372, 380, 395, 400
*Lone Ranger, The* (TV series), 353
Long, Howie, 243

Long, Shelley, 250-252, 411, 417
*Long Hot Summer, The* (TV series), 362
Look All-America Football Team, The, 99, 128, 160
Look Magazine Cover Girls, The, 38
Lopez, Trini, 21, 112
Lord, Jack, 235
Lord, Janet, 80
Lord, Marjorie, 434, 436-437, 447
Loren, Sophia, 289
Loring, Eugene, 138, 350
Loring, Gloria, xvi, 2, 4, 15, 161, 170, 246, 265, 268-269, 417, 479
Lorre, Chuck, 453
Lorre, Peter, 102
*Los Angeles* (magazine), 257
Los Angeles Raiders, The, 419-420
Los Angeles Rams Cheerleaders, The, 414
Los Angels du Inferno, 335
*Lost Weekend, The* (movie), 468
Loucks, Susie, 277
Louganis, Greg, 454
Louise, Anita, 431
Louise, Tina, 138-139
*Love American Style* (TV series), 139
*Love Connection* (TV series), 267
*Love Letter to Jack Benny, A* (special), 409
*Love Story* (movie), 163, 253, 293
Lovitz, Jon, 416
Lowenstein, Al, 453
Luana, Miss Tahiti Bohi, 245-246
Luboff, Norman, 350
Lucas, Jerry, 328
Lucas, Jonathan, 161, 377, 467
Luce, Henry, 459
Lucien Bob and Esther, 63-64
*Lucille Ball Comedy Hour, The:* "Mr. and Mrs." (special), 441
Luckenbill, Laurence, 474
*Lucy and Desi: A Home Movie* (special), 474
*Lucy Moves to NBC* (special), 340
*Lucy Show, The* (TV series), 428, 442
Ludden, Allen, 390

Luft, Lorna, 420
Lukas, Paul, 109
Lund, Dave, 101
Lundgren, Dolph, 243
Lung, Charlie, 94
*Lux Video Theatre* (TV series), 431
Lydon, Jimmy, 400
Lynde, Paul, 121, 127-129, 131-132, 181, 278, 391, 393, 445
Lynn, Bambi, 348
Lynn, Loretta, 232, 418
Lynn, Mara, 57
Lyon, Sue, 163
Lyons, Ruth, 305

*Mac Davis Show, The* (TV series), 337
MacArthur, Douglas, 58
MacDonald, Marie, 72
*MacGyver* (TV series), 258
Mack, Johnny, 46
Mackay, Barry, 328
Mackay, Harper, 364
MacLaine, Shirley, 58, 180, 387, 396-397, 422-423, 466
MacLeod, Gavin, 227, 390, 403, 414, 435
MacMurray, Fred, 13, 45-46, 50-51, 107, 182, 191-193, 298, 326, 331, 403, 469
MacPherson, Elle, 273
MacRae, Gordon, 222
MacRae, Sheila, 159
Macy, Bill, 451
Madden, Dave, 368
Madigan, Kathleen, 274
Madison, Guy, 326
Madonna, 423
Maen, Norman, 376, 396
*Magnificent Seven, The* (movie), 227
*Magnum P.I.* (TV series), 236
Maharis, George, 124
Mahesh, Maharishi, 88
Maibaum, Richard, 435
Main, Marjorie, 48
Maize, Joe, and His Chordsmen, 347
*Major Dad* (TV series), 258

*Majority of One, A* (movie), 102
Majors, Lee, 391
*Make Room for Granddaddy* (TV series), 429, 447
*Make Your Own Kind of Music* (TV series), 382
Malden, Karl, 332, 345-346, 478
Maldonado, Larry, 134
Malone, Dorothy, 74
Malone, Gia, 115
Malone, Nancy, 146, 275, 278
Malvin, Artie, 370, 373, 396
*Mame* (musical), 365, 407
*Man from U.N.C.L.E., The* (TV series), 115
Manchester, Melissa, 199, 219-220, 253-254
Mancini, Henry, 290
Mandel, Howie, 416
Mandel, Loring, 464
Mandrell, Barbara, 215, 219, 223, 232, 244, 246, 249-250, 253, 407-408
Mandrell, Irlene, 407-408
Mandrell, Louise, 407-408
Manheim, Mannie, 344
Manilow, Barry, 421
*Manimal* (TV series), 411
Manings, Allan, 369, 372
Mann, Abby, 466
Mann, Hank, 432
Mann, Johnny, 384
Mann, Mabel, 54
Manna, Charlie, 363
Mansfield, Jayne, 73-74, 91-92, 100-101, 123-124, 218, 326-328, 356, 358, 436, 461
Mantle, Mickey, 68-69, 356, 381, 384, 386, 388
Manville, Tommy, 344
*Many Moods of Perry Como, The* (special), 374
Marakova, Natalie, 396
Marciano, Rocky, 49, 130-131
Maren, Jerry, 135
Margolis, Jeff, 420, 423, 448
*Marie* (TV series), 409

Marie, Rose—See Rose Marie
Marinaro, Ed, 165, 276
Maris, Roger, 328
Markes, Larry, 393
Markham, Monte, 390
Markham, Pigmeat, 368
Markman, Pacy, 199-200, 217
Marks, Dennis, 381, 384
Marks, Guy, 365
Marks, Hilliard, 367, 380, 385, 430-431, 434-435, 438
Marks, Larry, 7, 31, 53, 66
Marmer, Mike, 348-349, 352, 370, 373, 389, 393, 466
Marr, Eddie, 53, 64, 94, 103, 107, 113, 116, 121, 126, 129, 131, 138, 142, 157, 159, 162, 165-170, 175, 178, 186, 224, 226
Mars, Kenneth, 215
Marsac, Maurice, 446
Marshall, Brenda, 57
Marshall, Garry, 448
Marshall, George, 432
Marshall, Penny, 416
Marshall, Peter, 390, 404, 417, 428
Marshall, Tony, 448
Marshall, Wilber, 229
Martin, Billy, 194
Martin, Bobbi, 4, 161
Martin, Dean, 33, 37, 48, 81-82, 102, 106-108, 112, 132-134, 142-143, 149, 151, 178, 181-182, 186, 190, 195, 228, 236, 242, 285, 307-308, 328, 332-333, 337, 352, 361, 363, 365-366, 377-378, 385, 388-389, 393, 395, 406, 408, 414, 423, 431, 448-449, 461, 466, 469-470
Martin, Dick, 69, 122, 126-127, 131, 137, 139-140, 181, 184, 290, 336-337, 368, 372-373, 393, 395, 400, 417
Martin, Jeff, 454
Martin, Lori, 105
Martin, Madelyn, 433
Martin, Mary, 220-221, 467, 469
Martin, Pete, 52
Martin, Ross, 365, 390

Martin, Steve, 194, 270, 405-406, 411
Martin, Strother, 390, 405
Martin, Tony, 47, 52, 353, 473
Martin, William, 461
Martinelli, Elsa, 63
Marvin, Lee, 120, 162-163, 165, 180, 225, 238, 277, 352, 395, 418
Marx, Eden, 463
Marx, Groucho, 154, 182, 459, 463
*Mary Hartman, Mary Hartman* (TV series), 184
*Mary Poppins* (movie), 362, 402
*Mary Tyler Moore Show, The* (TV series), 146
Masekela, Hugh, 336
*M\*A\*S\*H* (TV series), 211, 218, 455, 465-466
Mason, James, 62
Mason, Marsha, 419
*Masterpiece of Murder, A* (TV movie), 449
Masters, Larry, 54
Mastin, Will, Trio, The, 348
Mathers, Jerry, 66
Mathews, George, 345
Matlin, Marlee, 420
*Matt Houston* (TV series), 211
Matthau, Walter, 300, 415-416, 427
Matz, Peter, 412, 414, 416, 469
Mauldin, Bill, 115
Mauro, Scott H., 424
*Maverick* (TV series), 93
Maxwell, Edward, 41
Maxwell, Elsa, 345
Maxwell, Marilyn, 27, 34, 40, 43, 47-49, 55-56, 66-67, 110, 121, 443
Maxwell, Robert, 41
May, Billy, 353, 356, 361
May, Phil, 405
Mayehoff, Eddie, 132, 382
Mayer, Jerry, 390
Mayo, Virginia, 121, 230-231
Mays, Willie, 352, 363
McBain, Diane, 125
McCain, Adm. James S., xvii
McCain, John, xvii

McCall, Mitzi, 369
McCambridge, Mercedes, 464
McCann, Chuck, 387
McCarey, Leo, 429
McCarthy, Dennis, 440
McCarthy, Sen. Eugene, 129
McCarthy, Sen. Joseph, 42, 53-55
McCarthy, Kevin, 449
McCartney, Paul, 176, 214
McClanahan, Rue, 274, 415, 417, 451
McCloskey, Isobel, 187
McClure, Doug, 127
McConnell, Lulu, 1
McCoo, Marilyn, 420
McCormack, Patty, 105
McCormick, Pat, 154, 371, 379
McCrary, Tex, 42
McCray, Kent, 451
McCrea, Ann, 435
McCrea, Jody, 355
McDonough, Dick, 76, 85, 91, 145, 152, 294, 331-333, 395, 400, 404, 419
McDowall, Roddy, 400
McEntire, Reba, 248, 250, 272
McEuen, John, 406
McGavin, Darren, 331
McGee, Frank, 163
McGibbon, Scott, 403
McGillis, Kelly, 421
McGovern, George, 310, 408
McGovern, Maureen, 422
McGuire Sisters, The, 357
McKay, Allison, 164
McKay, Coach John, 134-135
McKechnie, Donna, 401
McKinley, J. Edward, 94, 99, 101, 110, 116, 118, 132, 160, 195
McKrell, Jim, 390
McKuen, Rod, 375
McLain, Denny, 133
McLaren, John, 141-142, 157
McLeod, Norman, 327
McLeod, Victor, 327
McMahon, Ed, 115, 184, 242, 271, 310-311, 337, 340, 378, 384, 387, 417, 428

McMahon, Jim, 224, 243
McManus, Michael, 406
McMillin, John E., 459
McNair, Barbara, 130, 134-135, 140-141, 163, 168, 374
McNeill, Don, 49
McNulty, Barney, 152-153, 460
McPeak, U.S. Air Force Chief of Staff Merrill A., 275
McQueen, Steve, 16, 91-92, 95-96, 180
McRaney, Gerald, 271
McVeagh, Eve, 141
Meade, Julia, 357-358
Meadows, Audrey, 471
Meadows, Jayne, 449
Meany, Kevin, 279
*Medic* (TV series), 56
*Meet the Veep* (talk show), 306
Melton, Sid, 58-59, 62, 447
Mendelson, Jack, 369
Mendelson, Lee, 463
Mendes, Sergio, xviii, 88, 138-139
Mendez, Rafael, 343
Menteer, Gary, 82
Mercer, Marian, 359
Meredith, Don, 466
Merithew, Ruth, 394
Merlino, Gene, Choir, 247
Merman, Ethel, 101-102, 104, 323, 356, 368, 396, 408, 459, 469, 473
*Merriest of the Merry, The: Bob Hope's Christmas Show* (1982 special), 228-229
Merrill, Dina, 121, 230
Merrill, Robert, 341-342
Merritt, Larry, 195
Merriman, Randy, 46, 49-50
*Merry Christmas, Fred, from the Crosbys* (special), 391-392
*Merv Griffin Show, The* (talk show), 303, 310
Metcalf, Laurie, 453
Metrinko, Miss USA Michelle, 109-110
Metter, Alan, 406
Metz, Robert, 304
Mexico City Boys Choir, The, 38

Michener, James A., 474
Middlecoff, Cary, 71-72
Midler, Bette, 182, 397, 424
Mike Curb Congregation, The—see Curb, Mike, Congregation
*Mike Douglas Show, The* (talk show), 303
Miles, Sylvia, 39
Miles, Vera, 121
Milland, Ray, 168
Miller, Alan J., 440
Miller, Ann, 72, 420
Miller, Dennis, 416
Miller, Jeanette, 431
Miller, Jody, 290
Miller, Johnny, 333
Miller, Laura, 141
Miller, Lee, 468
Miller, Lisa, 137, 159-160
Miller, Mitch, 86, 417
Miller, Paul, 419
Miller, Roger, 290, 361, 405
Miller, Ron, 383, 405
Miller, Walter C., 196, 242, 245, 251, 298, 367, 410, 412, 414, 416, 422
Milli Vanilli, 269, 272
Milligan, Bernie, 463
Milligan, Spike, 241
Mills, Donna, 239, 243-245, 420
Mills, Robert L. "Bob," 8, 14, 145, 151-152, 203, 207, 209-211, 244-245, 257, 261, 382, 418, 480
Mills Brothers, The, 397
*Milton Berle: Mr. Television* (documentary), 471
*Milton Berle Show, The* (TV series), 364—See also *Texaco Star Theatre*
*Milton Berle Starring in the Kraft Music Hall* (TV series), 353
Minardos, Nico, 435
Minnelli, Liza, 294, 355, 420, 466
Minner, Katherine, 119
Minor, Worthington, 343
Mirkin, Lawrence S., 452
Mischer, Don, 204-205, 232, 262-263, 275, 313, 411, 415, 421-422

Mislove, Michael, 376
Miss Malta and Company Dog Revue, 59-60
Miss Universe—See Morris, Carol
Miss World—See Rueber-Staier, Eva
*Mission Impossible* (TV series), 131-132, 172
*Mr. Smith* (TV series), 411
Mr. T—See T, Mr.
Mitchell, Belle, 168
Mitchell, Cameron, 127
Mitchell, George, 63
Mitchell, Gordon, 159
Mitchell, Guy, 79, 347
Mitchell, John, 147
Mitchell, Martha, 146-147, 163, 386
Mitchell, Roy, 138
Mitchell, Shirley, 118
Mitchell Boys Choir, The, 458
Mitchum, Robert, 474
*Mitzi ... and 100 Guys* (special), 390
*Mitzi's 2nd Special* (special), 141
*Mod Squad, The* (TV series), 158
Modernaires, The, 458
Moffett, Miss America Debra Sue, 229-230
Moffitt, John, 368, 416, 464, 473
Mole, Joe, 43
Molinaro, Al, 448
Monica, Corbett, 171
Monroe, Joy, 440, 444
Monroe, Marilyn, 46, 54, 56, 58, 65-66
*Monsieur Beaucaire* (movie), 60, 199
Montalban, Ricardo, 365, 403
Montana, Joe, 234, 252
Montana, Monte, 47
Montgomery, Elizabeth, 345
Montgomery, George, 448
Montgomery, Ralph, 54
*Moonlighting* (TV series), 244
Moore, Carroll, 383
Moore, Constance, 44, 48
Moore, Dudley, 228, 232, 452
Moore, Garry, 357
Moore, Mary Tyler, 177, 361
Moore, Roger, 420

Moraine, Lyle, 93, 95
Mordente, Tony, 398
*More Funny People* (book), 7, 36, 152, 305
Morgan, Harry, 465
Morgan, Jane, 458
Morgan, Lee, 39
Morita, Pat, 448-449
Mormon Tabernacle Choir, The, 240
Morrell, Les, 163
Morris, Anita, 449
Morris, Miss Universe Carol, 68-69
Morris, Greg, 378, 390
Morris, Steve, 420
Morrison, Michael, 239
Morrow, Bill, 350, 361
Morse, Terry, 449
Morton, Gary, 175, 300, 372, 389, 395
Moses, Marian, 440
Moss, Gene, 85, 141, 156-157
*Mothers-in-Law, The* (TV series), 126
*Movie Game, The* (game show), 323
Mull, Martin, 453
Mulligan, Jim, 369, 372
Mumford, Thad, 394
Mumy, Billy, 98
Munoz, Anthony, 229
Munsel, Patrice, 305, 352
*Munsters, The* (TV series), 21
Muntner, Simon, 466
*Muppet Show, The* (TV series), 402
Muppets, The, 189, 192, 194, 402
*Murder She Wrote* (TV series), 449
Murphy, Eddie, 231, 422-423
Murphy, George, 113
Murphy, Mary, 265
Murphy, Maureen, 414
Murphy Donnelly, Honoria, 473
Murray, Anne, 390, 405
Murray, Arthur, 356
Murray, Don, 355
Murray, James, 359
Murray, Jan, 171, 182
Murray, Kathryn, 356
Murray, Ken, 42, 65-66, 121, 127, 171-172, 461

Murrow, Edward R., 65, 457
*Music Man, The* (musical), 194
*Mutiny on the Bounty* (movie), 246
*My Eyes Are in My Heart* (book), 93
*My Fair Lady* (musical), 116
*My Favorite Blonde* (movie), 61
*My Little Margie* (TV series), 51
*My Mother the Car* (TV series), 116
*My One and Only* (musical), 232, 237
*My Three Sons* (TV series), 467
Myerson, Beth, 46, 49-50
*Myra Breckenridge* (movie), 308, 373, 375

Nabors, Jim, 165, 171, 367, 371, 390
Nader, George, 352
Nader, Ralph, 381
Nagel, Conrad, 283, 285
Naish, J. Carrol, 132
Najda, Francois, 449
*Naked City* (TV series), 115
Namath, Joe, 9, 199, 223, 393, 405, 448-449
Namm, Richie, 424
Nash, Clarence, 324
Nathan, Mort, 451
Nation, Terry, 449
*National Enquirer* (publication), 394
Navarro, Ramon, 355
*NBC Action Playhouse* (TV series), 428
*NBC Adventure Theatre* (TV series), 428
*NBC All Star Hour* (1983 special), 411—See also *Third Annual NBC All Star Hour, The*
*NBC Comedy Playhouse* (TV series), 428
*NBC Comedy Theatre* (TV series), 428
*NBC Family Christmas, An* (special), 340
*NBC Investigates Bob Hope* (1987 special), 209, 247
*NBC Magazine with David Brinkley* (TV series), 470
*NBC Monday Night at the Movies* (TV series), 87

*NBC Salutes the 25th Anniversary of the Wonderful World of Disney* (special), 403
*NBC 60th Anniversary Celebration* (special), 417
*NBC Star Salute to 1980* (special), 340
*NBC Star Salute to 1981* (special), 340
*NBC Welcomes Joe Namath and the Waverly Wonders* (special), 448
Neil, Warden, 264
Nelson, Christine, 437
Nelson, David, 378-379
Nelson, Gene, 51-52, 349
Nelson, Jerry, 189, 402
Nelson, Lori, 61
Nelson, Miriam, 128, 130, 443
Nelson, Rick, 378-379
Nelson, Willie, 228, 405, 422
Nero, Peter, 357
Neuman, Alfred E. (fictional character), 96, 163
Neuman, Matt, 416
*Never Say Die* (movie), 230
New Christy Minstrels, The, 359, 381
*New Faces of Hollywood, The*, 17, 123
*New York Times, The* (newspaper), 4
Newbury, Mickey, 384
Newhart, Bob, 177, 180, 365
Newland, John, 435
Newley, Anthony, 142-143
Newman, Edwin, 417
Newman, Laraine, 416
Newman, Lionel, 447
Newman, Paul, 239, 345-346, 357-358, 387, 400, 410, 474
Newman, Phyllis, 163
Newman, Tracy, 178
Newsome, Ozzie, 189, 229
*Newsweek* (magazine), 1
Newton, Wayne, 182, 294
Newton-John, Olivia, 178-179, 189, 223, 228-229, 403
Nguyen, Dustin, 421
Nicholas, Fayard, 162
Nicholas Brothers, The, 44, 119, 342
Nichols, Nichelle, 23, 181

Nichols, Red, 462
Nickerson, Ira, 181
Nicklaus, Jack, 138-139, 316, 331-332
Nielsen, Leslie, 226-227, 277
*Night Court* (TV series), 244
Niles, Ken, 132
Niles, Wendell, 38-39, 325
Nilsson, 169
Nimoy, Leonard, 390
*9 to 5* (movie), 200
*1974 Las Vegas Entertainment Awards, The* (1974 special), 5, 178, 294
Niven, David, 53, 56, 59, 79-80, 180, 311, 387, 435
Nixon, Richard, xiv, xvi-xvii, 133-135, 137-138, 146-148, 157, 159, 162, 164-165, 170, 175, 251, 275, 293, 338, 369, 384, 388
Nixon, Tricia, 381
Nixon (Eisenhower), Julie, 157, 280
Nizer, Louis, 124
Nizer, Mark, 259-260, 273
Nodella, Burt, 446
Noel, Chris, 123, 125
Nolan, Lloyd, 59-60, 447
Norfleet, Susan, 277
Norman, Maidie, 431
Norris, Chuck, 391
North, Sheree, 73
Norton, Cliff, 106, 116
Norton, Ken, 14
Novak, Kim, 65, 348, 350
Noxon, Nicholas, 462
Nugent, Ted, 410
Nye, Louis, 138-139, 171, 216-217, 247-248, 348-349, 352, 390, 439

Oakland, Ben, 41
Oberon, Merle, 123, 469
O'Brian, Hugh, 378
O'Brien, Bob, 442
O'Brien, Conan, 454
O'Brien, Edmond, 35, 54-55
O'Brien, Erin, 73-74, 349
O'Brien, Margaret, 400
O'Brien, Pat, 53

O'Connor, Carroll, 400, 468
O'Connor, Donald, 48, 112, 140, 249-251, 285, 397, 420, 459, 469
*Odd Couple, The* (TV series), 126, 429, 448
Oddo, John, 424
O'Donnell, Gen. Emmett "Rosie," 35, 131,
O'Donnell, Spec, 432
O'Dwyer, William, 38-40
*Off Limits* (movie), 48-49
*Officer and a Gentleman, An* (movie), 244
O'Flaherty, Terence, 73
O'Hara, Catherine, 416
O'Hara, John, 427
O'Hara, Maureen, 78, 395
O'Hara, Quinn, 107
Ohlmeyer, Don, 194
Oistrakh, David, 75
O'Kun, Lan, 451
Oldfield, Emmet, 347
Olivier, Laurence, 311, 465
Olsen, [Ole] and Johnson, [Chic], 33, 349
Olsen, Johnny, 388
Olsen, Merlin, 221, 229, 417
Olstein, Andrew, 473
*On the Road to Vietnam* (album), 115
Onassis, Aristotle, 134-135
Onassis, Jackie—See Kennedy, Jacqueline
*One for the Money* (special), 462
*100 Years of Hope and Humor* (2003 special), 266
O'Neal, Tatum, 177, 183
O'Neill, Eileen, 123
O'Neill, Jennifer, 333
Oppenheimer, Jess, 132, 441, 466
Orbach, Jerry, 422
Orenstein, Bernie, 365
Orenstein, Larry, 433
Orich, Steven, 280
Orlando, Tony, 192, 222, 296, 393-394
Ormes, Miss United Kingdom Yvonne, 161

Orr, Bobby, 331, 333
Ortega, Kenny, 223
*Oscar, The* (movie), 284
Oscars, The—See Academy Awards, The
Osmond, Alan, 245
Osmond, Donny and Marie, 22, 156, 181, 184, 190, 192, 195, 340, 360, 391-392, 394, 399, 402-404, 408, 468
Osmond, Jimmy, 409
Osmond, Marie, 20, 22, 156, 175, 181, 184, 190, 192, 195, 202, 218, 220, 225, 233, 250, 259, 270-271, 278, 340, 391-392, 399, 402-404, 407-409, 413, 468, 477
Osmond Boys Second Generation, The, 244-245, 278
Osmond Brothers/Osmonds, The, 164, 245, 359, 361, 372-373, 391, 399, 402-403, 475
*Osmond Brothers Special, The* (special), 402
O'Sullivan, Maureen, 420
O'Sullivan, Rev. Peter, 463
*Our World* (TV series), 472
Owen, Lt. Col. Jim, 386, 388
Owens, Gary, 216-217, 239-240, 247-248, 368, 372, 405, 444
Owens, Jesse, 183
Owens, Steve, 381, 384
*Owl and the Pussycat, The* (movie), 293
Oxenberg, Catherine, 421
Oz, Frank, 189, 192, 194, 241, 402, 452

Paar, Jack, 79, 92, 101, 302, 304-306, 358, 417
Packard, Elon, 400
Page, Patti, xviii, 82, 93-94, 98, 107, 138-139, 336, 347, 413, 417
Paige, George, 280
Paige, Janis, 41-42, 50-51, 53, 61, 71, 76, 82, 90, 97, 102, 104-105, 114, 121, 141, 180, 230-231
*Paint Your Wagon* (movie), 419
Painter, Walter, 136, 250, 415

Palance, Jack, 127
*Paleface, The* (movie), 60, 230, 309, 399, 459
Paley, William S./Bill, 396, 469
Palme, Olaf, 243
Palmer, Arnold, 107, 131-132, 328-329
Palmer, Anthony, 466
Palmer, Byron, 459
Palmer, Lilli, 41
Palmer, Peter, 449
Palmer, Sandra, 390
Pan, Hermes, 72, 473
Panama, Norman, 358, 469
Panich, David, 369, 372, 380
Pankin, Stuart, 416
Pannitt, Merrill, 469
*Paper Moon* (movie), 176
*Papillon* (movie), 176
Paramount Studios, 1, 52, 60, 75, 108, 308, 346-347, 361, 373, 426, 432
Pardo, Don, 347
Parent, Gail, 370, 398
Parfrey, Woodrow, 440
*Paris Holiday* (movie), 74-75, 231, 326-327, 351-352, 434
Parker, Fess, 79, 135, 403
Parker, James, 402
Parker, Larry, 145, 164, 194
Parker, Ray, 145, 164
Parker, Sarah Jessica, 198, 278
Parks, Bert, 417
Parks, Hildy, 418, 420, 468
Parnell, Jack, 396
Parseghian, Ara, 176
Parsons, Louella, 285
Parton, Dolly, 152, 225, 247, 252, 273, 399, 421
Pasetta, Marty, 293, 376, 383, 397, 408
*Pat Boone and Family Thanksgiving Special* (special), 339
*Pat Boone in Hollywood* (talk show), 305
*Pat Boone Show, The* (talk show), 305
Patchett, Tom, 382
Patrice, Gloria, 38

Index • 527

Patterson, Dick, 371
Patterson, Floyd, 328
Patterson, Lee, 362
*Patti Page Show, The* (TV series), 347
*Patton* (movie), 220
Paul, Norman, 343
*Paul Anka: Music My Way* (special), 339
Paulsen, Albert, 91, 427
Paulsen, Pat, 139
Payant, Leroy, 72
Peaches & Herb, 198-199, 410
Peardon, Patricia, 345
Pearl, Minnie, 146, 159, 398, 416
Peary, Hal, 401
Peck, Gregory, 405-406, 420, 423, 466, 468
Peel, K.D., 249
Peeples, Nia, 420
Peking Opera, 198
Peking Opera School, 198
Penn, Arthur, 33
Penny, Don, 415
Pensacola Naval Aviation Station Training Command Choir, The, 244
*People's Choice Awards, The* (awards show), 295-296, 298
Peppard, George, 414-415, 417
Pepper, Cynthia, 99
Pepper, Jack, 51, 56, 70, 82, 129, 138-139, 141, 168, 440, 444
Peppiatt, Frank, 357, 394
*Pepsodent Show, The* (radio series), 3
Peralta, Louis, 135
Perani, Stephen, 199-200, 217
Perenchio, Jerry, 16
Perew, Tom, 416, 421
Perito, Nick, 27, 257, 275, 374, 383, 419
Perkins, Anthony, 329, 355
Perkins, Carl, 375
Perkins, Leslie, 440
Perkins, Marlin, 343
Perkins, Millie, 93
Perlberg, William, 429
Perlman, Rhea, 411, 417

Perret, Gene, xv, 8, 151, 203, 208-209, 211, 257-258, 261, 264, 275-276, 418, 478, 480
Perret, Linda, 275
Perrin, Sam, 354, 362, 430-431, 434-435, 438, 444
Perry, Ty, 68
Perry, William "Refrigerator," 242-243
*Perry Como Show, The/Perry Como's Kraft Music Hall* (TV series), 68, 86, 327, 336, 347-348, 351
*Perry Como's Lake Tahoe Holiday* (special), 390
*Perry Mason* (TV series), 80, 106
Persky, Bill, 359
*Person to Person* (TV series), 54, 65, 457
Perzigian, Jerry, 401
*Peter Loves Mary* (TV series), 98
Peters, Bernadette, 187, 214, 226-228, 241, 412, 420
Peters, Johnny, 69
Peterson, Monica, xvii
Petranto, Russ, 469
Petruzzi, Jack, 65
Peyser, Arnold, 358
Peyser, Lois, 358
*Peyton Place* (TV series), 113, 132, 140
*Phantom of the Opera, The* (musical), 250, 267
*Phil Donahue Show, The*—See *Donahue*
Philadelphia Boys Choir and Men's Chorale, The, 198-199
Phillips, Nancie, 157
*Phyllis Diller Kitchen Kween* (TV pilot), 303
*Phyllis Diller Show, The* (TV series), 429, 445
Pickford, Mary, 285, 362
Pidgeon, Walter, 285
Piero Brothers, The, xiv, 156
*Pillow Talk* (movie), 93
Pink Lady, 407
*Pink Lady and Jeff* (TV series), 407
Pinkard, Fred, 181
Piper, Laura, 271

Piscopo, Joe, 416
Pitta, Mark, 279
Pitts, ZaSu, 432
*Planet of the Apes* (movie), 163
Platt, Edward, 446
*Play Misty for Me* (movie), 419
*Playboy* (magazine), 124, 135, 159, 253, 366
Playboy Playmates, The, 410
*Playhouse 90* (TV series), 35-36
Pleshette, John, 451
Plimpton, George, 380
*Plimpton: Did You Hear the One About?* (special), 380
Plummer, Miss World Penny, 136
Plunkett, Maryann, 422
Pogostin, S. Lee, 91
Pointer Sisters, The, 270
Poitier, Sidney, 357
*Police Hall of Fame, The* (TV pilot), 36
*Police Woman* (TV series), 181, 238
Pollack, Sydney, 91
Pollard, Snub, 432
*Polly Bergen Show, The* (TV series), 336
Pons, Lily, 41
Popov the Clown, 75
Porter, Ali, 420
Porter, Cole, 228, 389, 396, 473
Porter, Rod, 377
Poston, Tom, 348-349, 352
"Potomac Madness" (1960 special), 94-95
Powell, Gen. Colin, 271
Powell, Jane, 420
Powell, Richard, 441
Powell, Miss America Susan, 216-217
Power, Tyrone, 434
Powers, Dave, 370, 373
Powers, Jimmy, 343
Powers, Stefanie, 216-217, 420
Prady, Bill, 452
Precht, Robert H./Bob, 357, 368, 464, 469
Prentiss, Paula, 94
Presley, Elvis, 6, 68-71, 77-78, 87, 347, 349, 436

Preston, Robert, 228
Price, Georgie, 43
Price, Leontyne, 345-346
Price, Vincent, 182, 348
Prickett, Maudie, 4
Pride, Charley, 165, 176, 404, 408
Priest, Pat, 21, 112, 440
Prima, Louis, 115
Prince Phillip, 241
*Prince Valiant* (TV pilot), 36
*Princess and the Pirate, The* (movie), 231
Principal, Victoria, 410
Prinze, Freddie, 182-183, 466
*Private Navy of Sgt. O'Farrell, The* (movie), 464
Proctor, Phil, 416
*Producers' Showcase*: "Dateline," 325, 345
Proft, Pat, 181
*Project Twenty* (series of specials), 8, 12, 458, 460
Prohaska, Janos, 163
Provine, Dorothy, 100
Prowse, Juliet, 98-99, 103, 109, 134-135, 166-167, 176, 294, 363
*Pruitts of Southampton, The*—see *Phyllis Diller Show, The*
Pryor, Richard, 231, 315, 423
*Psycho* (movie), 99
Puleo, Johnny, 351
Pulliam, Keshia Knight, 415, 417-418
Pully, B.S., 41
Pumpian, Paul, 182, 184, 399, 403
Purcell, Sarah, 411, 417
Purdue University Glee Club, The, 68

Quayle, Dan, 251
Queen, Army Master Sgt. Stuart, 458
Queen Elizabeth, 193, 338
*Queen for a Day* (TV series), 55, 133
Quinlan, Bob, 326
Quinlan, Jack, 326
Quintetto Allegro, 59
Quirk, James T., 106, 111

Rabbitt, Eddie, 234, 480
Radner, Gilda, 416
Rae, Charlotte, 216, 415, 417
Rae, Jimmy, 343
Rafshoon, Gerald, 155-156, 192
Raft, George, 308
Ragaway, Martin, 56-57, 59-60
Raikin, David, 75
Rainer, Iris, 394
Rainer, Luise, 420
*Rainmaker, The* (movie), 70
Raitt, John, 298
Ralph, Sheryl Lee, 420
Ramis, Harold, 416
Ramsen, Bobby, 190
Rand, Linda L., 451
Randall, Tony, 93, 111, 171-172, 199-200, 216-217, 244, 247-248, 250-253, 332-333, 448, 468
Randolph, Isobel, 64
Rapp, Joel, 440
Rapp, John, xv, 31, 36, 66, 85, 87, 328
Rappaport, John, 372
*Raquel* (special), 338
Rashad, Phylicia, 244, 246, 275, 416
Raskin, Carolyn, 29, 151, 230, 235, 369, 372
Rasky, Harry, 464
*Rat Patrol* (TV series), 291
Ratzenberger, John, 411, 417
*Rawhide* (TV series), 115
Rawls, Lou, 131-132, 386
Ray, Aldo, 443
Ray, Johnny, 46, 346
Ray, Marc B., 370
Rayburn, Gene, 348-349, 352, 417
Raye, Martha, 22, 90, 106, 108-109, 111, 113, 119-120, 129, 137, 159, 163-164, 166, 230, 292, 345, 397, 417
Rayfiel, David, 91
Raymond, Verna, 341
Raynor, William, 446
*Readers Digest* (magazine), 107
Reagan, Nancy, xvii, 205, 221-222, 230, 232, 250

Reagan, Ronald, xvii, 16, 123, 218-219, 222, 225, 228, 232, 239, 246-247, 249-251, 267, 275, 296, 328, 385-386, 389, 408, 411, 416, 418
Reams, Lee Roy, 420
Reasoner, Harry, 293
Reckell, Peter, 240
*Red Hot and Blue* (musical), 296, 396, 473
*Red Skelton Show/Hour, The* (TV series), 152, 335, 379
Reddle, Bill, 376
Reddy, Helen, 312, 405-406
*Reds* (movie), 225
Reed, Alan, 50
Reed, Donna, 411
Reed, Janet, 39
Reed, Lonny, 474
Reed, Rod, 460
Reed, Vivien, 21-22, 187-188
Reeves, Richard, 435
Regas, Jack, 367, 373-374
Reid, Miss Teenage America Rebecca Ann, 185, 339
Reilly, Charles Nelson, 192
Reimers, Ed, 459
Reiner, Carl, 38, 345, 387, 417-418, 468-470, 473
Reiner, Rob, 416
Reiser, Paul, 275-276
Reisner, Col. Robinson, 386
Reiss, Mike, 454
*Remember Pearl Harbor* (special), 474
Renaud, Line, 58-60, 63
René, Henri, 345
Renker, Al, 469
Renzi, Eva, 123-124
Reo, Don, 373
*Republican National Convention* (special), 457
Retton, Mary Lou, 238-239
Reuben, Dr. David, 380
Reubens, Paul—See Herman, Pee Wee
Revere, Paul and the Raiders, 367-368
Revill, Clive, 449
Reynolds, Allie, 384

Reynolds, Burt, 168, 175-176, 229, 271-272, 393, 405, 410, 420
Reynolds, Debbie, 22, 61, 72-73, 126-127, 164, 176, 181, 184, 196-197, 241, 355, 367, 397, 420
Reynolds, Gene, 466
Rhine, Larry, xv, 85, 87
Rhoades, Barbara, 387
Rhodes, Billy, 73
Rhodes, Erik, 41
Rhodes, Joan, 62-63, 278
Ribiero, Alfonso, 418
Rich, Adam, 200, 278, 405
Rich, Buddy, 307
Rich, Charlie, 177
Rich, Pete T., 217
*Rich Little Show, The* (TV series), 337
Richard, Timothy, 253
Richards, Bob, 461
Richards, Michael, 275-276
Richards, Ron, 473
Richards Jr., Danny, 65
Richardson, Cheryl, 271
Richman, Arthur, 64
Rickles, Don, 122, 127-128, 171-172, 174-175, 182, 185, 229, 238, 243, 250-251, 312, 365-366, 371, 378, 389, 393, 396, 406, 412-414, 416, 419, 444-445, 468,
Rickles, Donald (announcer), 236-238
Riddle, Nelson, 350, 395, 400
Ride, Sally, 18
Ridgely, Bob, 387
Riding, Miss Universe 1984 Yvonne, 243
Riggs, Bobby, 146, 173-174, 387
Rietti, Victor, 56
Righteous Brothers, The, 119-120, 190
Riley, Jeannie C., 133
Ringrowe, Denis, 63
Rinsler, Dennis, 411
Rio Brothers, The, 43
*Rippling Rhythm Revue, The* (radio series), 3
*Riptide* (TV series), 415
Ritter, John, 237, 277, 404, 420

Ritter, Thelma, 286
Ritz, Harry, 182-183
Ritz Brothers, The, 285
Rivera, Geraldo, 270
Rivers, Joan, 208, 418
Rizzo, Tom, 416
Roach Jr., Hal, 433
*Road to Bali, The* (movie), 47, 66
*Road to Hong Kong, The* (movie), 99, 101, 103, 188, 358-359
*Road to Morocco, The* (movie), 342, 395
*Road to Singapore, The* (movie), 3
*Roaring Twenties, The* (TV series), 100
Robards, Jason, 420
Robbins, Gale, 45
Robbins, Marty, 407, 408
*Robe, The* (movie), 107
*Roberta* (musical), 3, 45, 76-77, 141, 273, 298, 310
Roberts, Doris, 227, 418
Roberts, John, 174
Roberts, Sandy, 157
Roberts, Stanley, 462
Roberts, Tony, 353
Robertson, Cliff, 91
Robertson, Dale, 127, 381
*Robin and the Seven Hoods* (movie), 361
Robinson, Edward G., 358
Robinson, Eric, 56
Robinson, Frank "Sugar Chile," 41-42, 278
Robinson, Holly, 421
Robinson, Jerry, 189
Robinson, Smokey & The Miracles, 165
Robinson, Sugar Ray, 168-169, 377
Rocco, Maurice, 34, 38
Rockefeller, Gov. Nelson, 157, 181
Rockwell, Norman, 52
Rodell, Gregg, 277
Rodgers, Bob, 361, 367
Rodgers, Danny, 224
Rodgers, Pamela, 372
Rodgers, Richard, 345
Rodin, Gil, 463
Rodriguez, Paul, 236, 416, 419

Rodzianko, Anna, 406
Rogers, Brian, 241
Rogers, Charles "Buddy," 299
Rogers, Doug, 40
Rogers, Ginger, 68-70, 80, 92, 94-95, 181, 195, 328, 389, 392, 420
Rogers, Jaime, 164, 293
Rogers, Kenny, 375, 384, 405, 412, 416
Rogers, Roy, 58, 61, 405
Rogers, Will, 404, 460
*Rolling Stone* (magazine), 317
Rolling Stones, The, 88, 161
Romaine, Lyle, 98
Romaniak, Bob, 172
Romano, Tony, 91-92
*Romeo and Juliet* (movie), 292
Romero, Cesar, 326, 345
Romey, Linda, 43
Romney, George, 367
Romoff, Colin, 359
Ronstadt, Linda, 473
Rooney, Mickey, 48, 123, 220-221, 231, 236, 298, 328, 343-344, 365, 371, 405, 407
Rooney, Teddy, 355
Roosevelt, Eleanor, 41, 338, 358
Roosevelt, Franklin Delano, 193, 269, 280, 479
Rose, David, 78, 80-81, 92-96, 98-99, 101-102, 106-107, 328, 354, 359
Rose, Norman, 192
Rose, Si, 31
Rose Marie, 163, 365
Rose Queen and Her Court, The, 181, 185, 195-196, 200-201, 210, 217-218, 224, 228-229, 234, 238-239, 242-243, 248, 252, 255, 269-270, 272, 275, 278
*Roseanne* (TV series), 429, 453
*Rosemary Clooney's Demi-Centennial: A Girl Singer's Golden Anniversary* (special), 424
Rosemont, Norman, 376
Rosen, Arnie, 370, 373
Rosen, Burt, 370, 374
Rosen, Daniel, 451

Rosen, Milt, 367, 389, 393
Rosen, Richard, 473
*Rosey Grier Show, The* (talk show), 305
Ross, Diana, xvii, 137, 215, 372
Ross, Dick, 371
Ross, Donald, 376
Ross, Mike, 65, 79, 96, 98, 108, 116, 118-119, 121, 126, 129, 133, 138, 157, 159-160, 162, 175
Ross, Myrna, 440
Ross, Shirley, 3, 60
Rosten, Irwin, 462
Roth, Jack, 343
Rote, Kyle, 330
Rothenberg, Marvin, 324
Rothman, Bernie, 377
*Rousters, The* (TV series), 411
*Route 66* (TV series), 427
Roven, Glen, 423
Rowan, Dan, 69, 122, 126-127, 131, 137, 139-140, 181, 184, 290, 336-337, 368-369, 372-373, 378, 389, 393, 395, 400, 418
Rowan and Martin—See Martin, Dick and Rowan, Dan
*Rowan and Martin's Laugh-In*, xiv, xvii, xix, 29, 131, 134, 139, 150, 162, 173, 207, 216, 307, 336-337, 368-369, 372, 374, 379, 397, 414
*Royal Gala, A* (special), 338
*Royal London Gala for Bob Hope's Happy Birthday Homecoming, The* (1985 special), 241
Royer, Miss USA Michelle, 248
Rozario, Bob, 415
Rubin, Benny, 96, 157, 168, 367
Rubio, Del, Triplets, The (Eadie, Milly and Elena Del Rubio), 68-69, 451
Rudner, Rita, 273-275
Rueber-Staier, Eva, xiv, 156
Rufus—See Khan, Chaka and Rufus
Rule, Janice, 357
Rumberg, Karl, 452
*Run Buddy Run* (TV series), 121
*Run for Your Life* (TV series), 116

Russell, Harry, 46
Russell, Jack, 39
Russell, Jane, 30, 46, 50, 60, 61, 66-67, 108-109, 230, 271, 314, 328, 356, 399, 459
Russel, Ken, 250
Russell, Mark, 222, 389, 393
Russell, Nipsey, 139-140, 171-172
Ryan, Irene, 146, 159
Ryan, Marian, 76-77
Ryder, Eddie, 449

Sagal, Boris, 462
Sager, Carol Bayer, 413
Sahl, Mort, 457
Saint, Eva Marie, 420, 427, 439-440
St. James, Susan, 123
St. John, Jill, 11, 90, 114, 119-120, 125, 129, 131-132, 163, 165-166, 219-220, 230-231, 420, 439, 443-444
Sajak, Pat, 250, 418
Salant, Richard, 469
Salatich, Bill, 331
Salem, Kario, 466
Sales, Soupy, xix, 103, 122, 139
*Sally* (TV series), 73
Salmon, Scott, 406-407
Saltzman, Harry, 313
Saluga, Bill, 376
*Salute to America's Pets, A* (special), 423-424
*Salute!: "Gladys Knight and the Pips"* (special), 340
Salzburg, J. Milton, 324
*Sammy Davis Jr.'s 60th Anniversary Celebration* (special), 422-423
Sand, Arlene, 411
Sand, Bob, 411
Sandburg, Carl, 345, 358
Sanders, George, 65-66
Sands, Billy, 129, 139, 162
Sanford, Charles, 38-39, 41
Sanford, Isabel, 468
Sanford, Ralph, 65
*Sanford and Son* (TV series), 170
Santiago, Saundra, 415

Santley, Joseph, 343-344
Saphier, Jimmy, 13
Sapp, Miss America Suzanne, 272
Sapp, Warren, 278
Sarasohn, Lane, 416
Sargent, Herbert, 348-349, 352
Sargent, Richard, 449
Sarnoff, Bob/Robert, 307, 345-346
Sarnoff, "Gen." David, 56
Sarnoff, Tom, 13, 425
Saroyan, William, 306
Sassoon, Vidal, 216
*Saturday Evening Post, The* (magazine), 52-53
*Saturday Night Fever* (movie), 191
*Saturday Night Live* (TV series), 341, 477
*Saturday Night Live with Howard Cosell* (TV series), 337
Saunders, Audrey, 82
Saunders, Mary Jane, 99
Savalas, Telly, 182, 191-192, 388, 411
Sawyer, Diane, 424
Savenick, Phil, 233, 473
*Say One for Me* (movie), 81
Sayre, Jeffrey, 432
Scandore, Joseph, 371
*Scent of Mystery* (movie), 82
Schafer, Kermit, 11
Scharfman, Mort, 399
Scharlach, Ed, 136
Scheerer, Robert, 359, 383
Schell, Maximilian, 101
Schell, Ronnie, 405
Schickel, Richard, 466
Schiller, Bob, 433
Schipper, Henry, 290
Schirra, Walter, 134, 233
Schlatter, George, 290, 369, 372, 396-397, 419, 423
Schlosser, Herbert, 13, 425
Schmidtmer, Christianne, 160
Schnarre, Monika, 271
Schneider, Bert, 295
Schneider, Dick, 106, 111, 358, 381, 384, 386, 388

Schneider, Romy, xiv, 156
Schroder, Ricky, 227, 242, 278, 414, 418
Schurlach, Ed, 377
Schuur, Diane, 422
Schwartz, Al, 7, 31
Schwartz, Alan, 341
Schwartz, Jonathan, 473
Schwartz, Sherwood, 7, 275-276, 441
Schwarzkopf, Gen. Norman, 270-271, 474
Schweitzer, Peter, 474
Schwimmer, Walter, 464
Scoffield, Jon, 376
Scofield, Mark, 101
Scoggins, Tracy, 420
Scott, George C., 3, 168, 192, 220, 232, 289, 296, 466
Scott, Rita, 228
Scott, Simon, 440
Scotti, Tony, 407
Scourby, Alexander, 460
*Screen Directors Playhouse* (TV series), 432
Seale, Douglas, 451
Searles, Bucky, 380
*Second City TV* (TV series), 209
*Secret of Santa Vittoria, The* (movie), 142
Sedaka, Neil, 185-186
Sedawic, Norman, 294
*See You at the Polls* (special), 459
Segal, Alex, 343
Segal, George, 387
Segall, Ricky, 388
Seigel, Don, 401
*Seinfeld* (TV series), 212
Seinfeld, Jerry, 212
Selden, Maj. Gen. John, 55
Self, William, 350
Seligman, Michael, 408
Selleck, Tom, 227, 232, 235-236, 242, 247, 275-276, 280
Sellers, Peter, 176, 228, 405
Serling, Rod, 35, 91, 293-294, 427, 441
*Sermonette* (TV series), 313
Sessions, Almira, 62, 367

Sevareid, Eric, 474
*Seven Little Foys, The* (movie), 60-61, 230, 284, 286, 309, 346, 387, 432
*77 Sunset Strip* (TV series), 78, 436
Severinsen, Doc, 184, 386, 405, 416, 418
Sevilla, Carmen, 165
Seymour, Dan, 168, 172
Seymour, Jane, 473
Sha Na Na, 404
Shaffer, Paul, 416
*Shaft* (movie), 382
Shaiman, Marc, 416
Shandling, Garry, 416
Shane, Sara, 56
Shannon, Richard, 431
Shapiro, Danny, 48
Sharif, Omar, 243
Sharpe, Karen, 61
Sharper, Al, 73
Shatner, William, 378, 390, 429
*Shaughnessy* (TV pilot), 154
Shavelson, Mel(ville), 268, 275-276
Shaw, Artie, 347
Shaw, Reta, 115, 138-139, 162
Shaw, Sonia, 73
Shawlee, Joan, 51
Shawn, Dick, 122, 414
Shay, John, 435
Shea, Jack, 31, 36, 54, 66, 85, 91, 328
Shearer, Harry, 453
Sheedy, Ally, 420
Sheffield, Buddy, 421
Sheldon, Diane, 124
Shelton, Jacque, 444
Shelton, James, 347
Shepard, Alan, 165-166, 215, 233, 416, 461
Sheridan, Bonnie, 453
Sherman, Bobby, 374
Sherwood, Robert, 345
Shields, Brooke, 10, 22, 216, 218-220, 224, 226-227, 232, 234-235, 237-238, 241-242, 244-246, 248, 250-254, 258, 268, 270-271, 273, 275-276, 278, 407, 416, 418, 479

Shields and Yarnell, 192-193, 198-199, 405
*Shining, The* (movie), 409
*Ship of Fools* (movie), 120
*Shirley MacLaine: Where Do We Go From Here?* (special), 396-397
Shoemaker, Ann, 141
Shor, Toots, 42, 344
Shore, Dinah, 38-40, 42, 116-117, 151, 180, 249-251, 290, 293, 314, 331, 333, 339, 341, 345, 353-354, 358, 378, 413, 418, 467, 469
Shore, Roberta, 105
Short, Bobby, 473
Short, Martin, 416
Short, U.S. Navy Admiral Wallace B., 275
*Show Business Salute to Milton Berle, A* (special), 339
Showalter, Max, 441
Shuken, Phil, 433
Shulman, Arthur A., 106, 11
Shuster, Frank, 463
*Sidewalks of New York* (musical), 2, 297
Sidney, Bob (Robert), 124, 126, 141, 383
Sidney, George, 354
Siegel, Don, 419
Siegfried and Roy, 419
Signoret, Simone, 91
Siller, Raymond, 145, 331, 332
Silver, Barry, 394
Silver, Franelle, 403
Silver, Stu, 416
Silverman, Fred, 200, 203, 218, 469
Silverman, Treva, 374
Silvers, Phil, 34, 129, 139-140, 182, 307, 346, 357-358, 380
Simard, René, 183
Simmons, Richard, 236
Simon, Neil, 185, 448
Simon, Sam, 454
Simpson, Jim, 330
Simpson, O.J., 128, 135, 223, 249-250, 332, 405, 448
*Simpsons, The* (TV series), 429, 453-454

Sims, Billy, 196, 200
Sinatra, Frank, 6, 13, 39, 42, 71, 73, 99, 102-105, 117, 120, 162, 180-181, 222, 283, 285, 295, 350, 353-354, 358, 361, 386, 395, 408, 416, 422-423, 467-468, 473, 475
Sinatra, Nancy, 138, 374-375
Sincere, Jean, 271
Sinclair, Diane, 334
*Sing Along with Mitch* (TV series), 86
Singing Angels youth choir, The, 178-179
Singing Super Sportsmen, The, 388
Singleton, Doris, 74, 78, 175, 343, 439
Siskind, Carol, 260, 274
*16th Annual Miss Teenage America Pageant, The* (special), 339
6th Fleet Show Band, The, 235
*60 Minutes* (TV series), 403
Skelton, Red, 43, 149, 166, 195-196, 277, 300, 326, 335, 378-379, 404, 467
Skiles and Henderson (Bill Skiles and Pete Henderson), 234
Skylarks, The, 43, 345
Slavin, Millie, 175
Smirnoff, Yakov, 251-252, 268, 421
Smith, Alexis, 169, 332
Smith, Bernard N., 463
Smith, Bruce, 239
Smith, Buffalo Bob and Howdy Doody, 418
Smith, Miss World USA Karen Brucene, 165, 384
Smith, Charles, 108
Smith, Gary, 249, 266, 391, 396, 398, 401, 413
Smith, Jaclyn, 420
Smith, Kate, 310, 343, 391
Smith, Lee Allan, 381, 384, 386, 388
Smith, Margaret, 279
Smith, Sen. Margaret Chase, 110
Smith, Roger, xvi-xvii, 385
Smith, Sid, 152, 178, 194, 200, 214, 217, 225, 228, 231, 234-235, 237-238, 243-244, 252, 255, 269, 272, 275-276, 343, 424
Smith, Yeardley, 453

Smith and Dale, 346
Smothers, Dick, xix, 139, 359, 366-367, 382
Smothers, Tom, xix, 139, 359, 366-367, 378, 382, 469
*Smothers Brothers Comedy Hour, The* (TV series), 9, 139
*Snap Judgment* (game show), 323
Snead, Sam, 80-81, 327, 382
Snider, Duke, 352
Snyder, Tom, 12, 316
Solms, Kenny, 370, 398
Soloff, Fred, 247
Solomon, Leo, 342
Solt, Andrew, 203-204, 213, 471
*Some of Manie's Friends* (special), 353-354
Somers, Suzanne, 403-404
Somlyo, Roy A., 468
Sommer, Elke, 123-124, 128, 142, 160, 167, 170, 362
Sommers, Joanie, 101, 356, 374
*Son of Paleface* (movie), 46, 60
Songe, Cynthia, 414
Sonny and Cher—See Bono, Sonny, and Cher
*Sonny and Cher Comedy Hour, The* (TV series), 339
*Sonny Comedy Revue, The* (TV series), 148
Sons of the Pioneers, The, 58-59
*Sophisticated Ladies* (musical), 226
Sorel, Louise, 449
Sorenson, Paul, 165
*Sorrowful Jones* (movie), 61, 255
Sosnik, Harry, 345, 458
Sothern, Ann, 359-360
Soul, David, 192
*South Pacific* (musical), 354
Sparks, Randy, 77-78
Spaulding, Ken, 344
Spears, Stephen, 372, 394, 407
Spellbinders, The, 347
Spelling, Aaron, 469
Spellman, Cardinal, 125
Spence, Johnnie, 376

Spitz, Mark, 14, 153-154, 169-170, 331, 389
Spivak, Lawrence, 345
*Sponsor* (magazine), 427, 459
*Sport* (magazine), 67
Sportsmen, The, 462
Sprigg, Sondra, 271
Spurrlows, The, 158
Stabile, Dick, 81
Stabler, Ken, 186-187, 333
*Staccato* (TV series), 81
Stack, Lenny, 384, 394
Stack, Patrick, 451
Stack, Robert, 135, 418
Stafford, Jo, 338
*Stalag 17* (movie), 58
*Stand By for the HNN ... The Hope News Network* (1988 special), 251
Stang, Arnold, 39, 471
Stanley, Don, 238
*Star Search* (TV series), 337
*Star Trek* (TV series), 23
*Star Wars* (movie), 233, 405, 477
Starbuck, James, 38, 41
Starr, Ben, 182
Starr, Kay, 95, 353-354, 381
Starr, Ringo, 88, 117
*Stars and Stripes Show, The* (1971-1974 series of specials), 381, 384, 386, 388
Statler Brothers, The, 375
Staubach, Roger, 223-224, 226-227, 384
Stauffer, Teddy, 123
Steckler, Doug, 415
Steel, Richard, 411
*Steel Magnolias* (movie), 255, 277
Steiger, Rod, 91, 282, 296, 440-441
Steinbeck, John, 90
Stempel, Tom, xv, 10
Stephenson, Skip, 231, 411
Sterling, Linda, 76
Stern, Isaac, 422
Stern, Leonard, 352, 446
*Steve Allen Show, The* (TV series), 70, 336, 348-349, 352-353

*Steve Allen Show, The* (talk show), 305
*Steve Lawrence and Eydie Gorme: From This Moment On ... Cole Porter* (special), 396
*Steve Martin: A Wild and Crazy Guy* (special), 405-406
Stevens, Connie, xiv, xvi, 156, 159, 167, 248-249, 268-269
Stevens, Craig, 418
Stevens, Dodie, 15, 80
Stevens, Kaye, 90, 119, 126
Stevens, Naomi, 362
Stevens, Stella, 112, 216, 250, 369, 449
Stevenson, Adlai, 101, 472
Stevenson, McLean, 369
Stevenson, Venetia, 355
Stewart, Charles, 434, 436, 438
Stewart, Gloria, 406
Stewart, James, 250, 271, 355, 389, 393, 395-396, 404-406, 408, 411, 416, 418-420
Stewart, Martha, 45
Stewart, Michael (We Five), 16
Stewart, Mike, 41
Stiles, Norman, 394
Stokowski, Leopold, 24
Stone, Danton, 453
Stone, Ezra, 447
Stone, Harold J., 439, 444
Stone, Henry "Butch," 26, 107
Stone, Pam, 273
Stone, Tim, 228
Storch, Larry, 127, 182, 364
Stordahl, Axel, 345, 353, 355
Storey, Roy, 326
Storm, Gale, 51, 277, 480
*Storytellers to the Nation: A History of American Television Writing* (book), xv, 10
Stracke, Win, 464
Stram, Hank, 223, 365
Strategic Air Command Band, The, 386
Strauss, Peter, 405
Strauss, Robert (actor), 58, 76-77
Strauss, Robert (writer), 471
Street, Bob, 141

Streisand, Barbra, xvii-xviii, 107-108, 187, 190, 367
*Strike It Rich* (TV series), 56
Strut, 187
Struthers, Sally, 163
Stuart, Anna, 451
Stuart, Mary, 418
Stuart, Mel, 466
*Studio One* (TV series), 52, 343
Sturges, Ben, 473
Styler, Burt, 439, 445
Subber, Saint, 473
Sues, Alan, 368, 372, 377
Sullivan, Ed, 1, 13, 60, 66, 75, 130-131, 139, 149, 162, 191, 293-294, 308, 335, 337, 346, 354, 357, 368, 464
Sullivan, Norman, xv, 31, 36, 64, 85, 94, 145, 148, 151, 207, 209, 294, 328, 331-333
Sullivan, Susan, 420
*Sullivan Years, The* (special), 464
Sumac, Yma, 110
*Summer Special* (TV series), 461
*Sunday Spectacular Presents the Road to Hollywood, The* (1956 special), 66
Sunday's Child, 165-166
*Super Birthday: "A World's Fair Salute to Bob Hope,"* 237
*Super Bowl* (sports special), 170, 229, 243, 252, 323, 330
Super Bowl Dancers, The, 248-249
*Superman* (movie), 196
*Superman II* (movie), 221
Supremes, The, xvii, 137, 172-173, 368-369, 372
*Survivors, The* (TV series), 139
Susann, Jacqueline, 163
Susman, Todd, 247, 414
*Suspense* (TV series), 285
Sutton, Frank, 371
Sutton, Grady, 357
Sviridoff, Allen, 424
Swann, Lynn, 175, 276
Swanson, Gloria, 77, 355
Swanson, Maureen, 63
Swayze, John Cameron, 68, 343

Sweeney, Bob, 47, 49
Sweet, Dolph, 411
Swerdloff-Ross, Helaine, 424
*Swing Out Sweet Land* (special), 378-379
Swingle Singers II, 396
Swit, Loretta, 217-218, 250, 273-274, 420-422, 466
Swordsmen of the Lido, 365
Sydney, Miss World Ann, 114
Symington, Stuart, 181, 193

T, Mr., 235-237, 239-240, 242, 414
Tabor, Joan, 73, 80, 95, 434
Tackaberry, John, 430-431
Taco, 234
Tadman, Audrey, 392
Taft, Sarah, 123
Tafur, Robert/Bob, 69, 435
*Take Two* (game show), 323
Takei, George, 474
Talbot, Gloria, 61
Talbott, Harold, 58
*Tall Man, The* (TV series), 98
*Tall Men, The* (movie), 61
Tapps, Georgie, 45
Tarkenton, Fran, 186-187
Tarses, Jay, 382
Tartikoff, Brandon, 242, 247, 250-251
Tate, David, 410
*Taxi* (TV series), 154
Taylor, Elizabeth, 97, 105-106, 108, 110-111, 156, 160, 186, 192-193, 223, 227, 244, 289, 340, 371, 388, 400-401, 404
Taylor, Henry, 43
Taylor, June, Dancers, The, 346, 357
Taylor, Lawrence, 218, 229-230
Taylor, Meshach, 217
Taylor Maids, The, 40
Tebet, Dave, 311
*10* (movie), 228
*Ten Commandments, The* (movie), 68
Tennessee Three, The, 375
Tennille, Toni, 22, 184, 187-188, 216-217, 303, 393-394, 400,

Tenowich, Tom, 377, 385, 389
Terry, George, 376
Testaverde, Vinnie, 245
*Texaco Presents Bob Hope in a Very Special Special: On the Road with Bing* (1977 special), 153, 188
*Texaco Presents the Bob Hope All Star Christmas Comedy Special* (1977 special), 189
*Texaco Presents the Bob Hope Show All Star Comedy Tribute to the Palace Theatre* (1978 special), 190
*Texaco Star Theatre* (TV series), 32, 342; See also *Milton Berle Show, The*
*Texaco Star Theatre:* "Bob Hope in 'Who Makes the World Laugh ... At Itself'" (1983 special), 231
*Texaco Star Theatre:* "Opening Night" (1982 special), 28
Texas Boys Choir, The, 388
"Thanks for the Memory" (song), 3, 17, 20, 25, 42-43, 53, 55-56, 69-70, 72, 80, 93, 96, 98, 104, 122, 129, 167, 172, 180, 193-194, 205, 215, 223-224, 233, 237, 239, 250-251, 254, 267, 275, 279, 294, 299, 318, 344, 357, 378, 387, 395, 413, 427, 433-434, 438, 444, 457, 462
*That Certain Feeling* (movie), 65-67, 325, 336, 347-348
*That's Incredible* (TV series), 18, 216, 219
*That's What Friends Are For: AIDS Concert* (special), 421
*Theater of Stars* (TV series), 429
Thibodeaux, Keith, 433
Thicke, Alan, 279
*Thin Man, The* (TV series), 79, 435
*Third Annual NBC All Star Hour, The* (special), 415
*This is Tom Jones* (TV series), 337, 376
*This is Your Life* (TV series), 60, 323, 327

Thomas, Bob, 129
Thomas, Danny, 22, 33, 73, 78, 91, 99-100, 109, 119-120, 127, 139, 142, 149, 159-160, 167, 171-172, 180-181, 192, 192, 216, 218, 222, 242, 244, 247-250, 254-255, 268-269, 315, 331, 336-339, 353-354, 358, 364-366, 370, 377, 392, 395, 412, 416, 425, 434, 436-438, 447, 459, 471
Thomas, Dave, 275-277
Thomas, Marlo, 437, 468
Thomas, Patty, 57, 91-92, 279-280
Thomas, Philip Michael, 415, 418
Thomas, Tony, 451
Thompson, Bob, 394
Thompson, Claude, 376
Thrash, Bill, 381, 384, 386, 388
*Three Faces of Eve, The* (movie), 74
*3 Girls 3* (TV series), 398
*Three's Company* (TV series), 207
Thurman, James, 85, 141, 156-157
Tiegs, Cheryl, 194, 221-222, 232, 410
Tiffany, 252
Tillis, Mel, 408
Tillstrom, Burr, 343, 464
Tilton, Charlene, 219
*Time* (magazine), 1, 107, 142, 147, 368-369
Tiny Tim, 132, 142, 157-158, 369-370
Tippin, Aaron, 270
*To Tell the Truth* (TV series), 96
*Toast of the Town*—See *Ed Sullivan Show, The*
*Tobacco Road* (movie), 158
*Today* (talk show), 307, 309, 364
*Today's Children*, 386
Todd, Nick, 74
Tolkin, Mel, xv, 38, 85, 87, 145, 148, 294, 331-333, 345
*Tom Jones* (movie), 11
Tomack, Sid, 65
Tomlin, Jeff, 56
Tomlin, Lily, 162, 423-425
*Tomorrow Coast to Coast* (talk show), 12, 316

*Toni Tennille Show, The* (talk show), 303
*Tonight Show* (Jack Paar), *The* (talk show), 92, 101, 304, 306
*Tonight Show Starring Johnny Carson, The* (talk show), 8, 26, 115, 140, 154, 183-184, 238, 257, 260, 262, 275, 303-320, 402, 406, 449, 474
*Tonight Show with Jay Leno, The* (talk show), 306
Tony Awards, The—See *Footlights! (The 32nd Annual Tony Awards)*
*Tony Orlando and Dawn Rainbow Hour, The* (TV series), 149
*Tootsie* (movie), 229-230
Toppel, Leona, 145, 149
*Tora! Tora! Tora!* (movie), 225
Touber, Selwyn, 353
Tourk Lee, Pat, 416, 473
*Tournament of Roses Parade* (special), 338
*Towering Inferno, The* (movie), 295, 332
Townsend, Robert, 421
Tozere, Fred, 68
*Trail of the Pink Panther* (movie), 228
*Trapper John, M.D.* (TV series), 211
Travalena, Fred, 192, 412
Travanti, Daniel J., 418
Travis, Randy, 253-254
Travolta, John, 191, 297, 393-394
Treacher, Arthur, 41-42
Trebek, Alex, 423
Trefethen, Tina, 390
Trenner, Donn, 155, 192, 374, 397
Trevino, Lee, 385
Trevor, Claire, 395
*Tribute to "Mr. Television" Milton Berle, A* (special), 468
Trinder, Tommy, 63-64
Tro, Rob, 240
Trotter, John Scott, 361
*True Grit* (movie), 292
Truman, Harry, 157, 280, 306, 458
Truman, Margaret, 65
Trump, Donald, 267, 319, 479
*Truth or Consequences* (TV series), 57

Tucker, Forrest, 127, 364
Tucker, Sophie, 188, 438
Tucker, Tanya, 199-200, 218
Tufts, Sonny, 369, 443
Tugend, Harry, 439, 443-444
Tune, Tommy, 232, 377, 422
Tunney, Gene, 130
Turkel, Studs, 464
*Turn On* (TV series), 307
Turner, Alan, 56
Turner, Lana, 13, 70, 99, 104, 420
Turner, Lloyd, 159
Turner, Ted, 242, 251
Turner, Tierre, 448
*TV Guide* (magazine), 81, 86, 106, 111, 265, 469, 477, 482
*TV: The Fabulous 50s* (special), 467
Twain, Mark, 231, 404
*25 Years of Life Magazine* (special), 456, 459
Twiggy, 128, 130, 232, 237, 469
*227* (TV series), 212
*Two Women* (movie), 289
Tyler, Bonnie, 234
Tyson, Mike, 266, 423

UCLA Fife and Drums Corps, The, 216-217
Uggams, Leslie, 197, 250, 378, 401, 421
Ukraine State Dancers, The, 75
Ulanova, Galena, 75
Ullman, Liv, 243
*Underwater* (movie), 61
Underwood, Blair, 421
Unitas, Johnny, 381, 384
United Nations Children's Choir, The, 360
United States Organizations—see USO
*Universal Star Time* (TV series), 429
*Unsinkable Molly Brown, The* (musical), 126
*Unsold Television Pilots* (book), 36
Up with People, 128, 338
*Up with People* (special), 338
Upton Bell, Jane, 223
Urbisci, Rocco, 403

Urich, Robert, 214, 218, 220-221
U.S. Air Force and the Singing Sergeants, The, 192
U.S. Air Force Presidential Drill Team, The, 222
U.S. Army, Navy, Air Force and Marines Bands, The, 232
U.S. Army Band, The, 192, 381
U.S. Army Chorus, The, 222, 381, 386, 422
U.S. Army Training Center, The, 422
U.S. Coast Guard Band, The, 192
U.S. Marine Band, The, 192
U.S. Marine Drum and Bugle Corps, The, 192, 198
U.S. Navy Band and Sea Chanters, The, 192
University of Michigan Marching Band, The, 222
*USA Today* (newspaper), 7
USO, xiii-xiv, 2, 4, 14, 15, 27, 50, 69, 74, 78, 85-86, 90, 100, 109, 115, 120, 125, 131, 155-156, 161, 165-166, 192-193, 206, 210-211, 213, 215, 220, 232, 235, 248, 251, 259, 268-269, 276-277, 293, 330, 369, 405, 447, 458, 460, 472-473, 477

Valachi, Joe, 108
Valente, Caterina, 365
Valenti, Jack, 124
Valentine, Karen, 387
Vallee, Rudy, 126, 410, 463
Van Ark, Joan, 240, 269, 420
Van Brocklin, Norman, 328
Van Dyke, Dick, 395, 416, 462, 470
Van Dyke, Jerry, 462
Van Heusen, James, 95, 443
Van Patten, Dick, 403, 405
Van Sickle, Dale, 81
Vance, Vivian, 67, 389, 395, 433
Vandross, Luther, 421
Vanocur, Sander, 163
Vanoff, Nick, 348-349, 352, 361, 363-365, 378, 394
Vaughn, Robert, 418

Verdon, Gwen, 133, 180
Vereen, Ben, 408, 413
Vernon, Jackie, 377
*Vicki!* (talk show), 306
*Victor/Victoria* (movie), 228
Vidor, King, 355
Vigoda, Abe, 182
Vigran, Herb, 94, 157, 367
Vilanch, Bruce, 399
Village People, The, 198-200, 470
Vincent, Jan-Michael, 405
Vincent, Louise, 82
Vinnedge, Syd, 407
Von Essen, Desiree, 390
Von Zell, Harry, 327
Vrba, John, 329

Waggoner, Lyle, 370, 373, 390
Wagner, Jack, 240
Wagner, Lindsay, 278
Wagner, Mike, 138
Wagner, Robert, 74-75, 228, 420
*Wagon Train* (TV series), 85, 98, 102
*Wait Until Dark* (movie), 291
Wakely, Jimmy, 402
Waldman, Frank, 376
Waldman, Tom, 376
Walker, Betty, 349
Walker, Bill, 398
Walker, Herschel, 218, 224, 229
Walker, Jimmie, 181-182, 184, 187-188, 190, 295, 396, 402
Walker, Nancy, 159
Walker, Ray, 64
Walker, Susan F., 471
Wallace, Gov. George, 128, 369
Wallace, Jean, 63-64
Wallace Stone, Dee, 420
Wallis, Shani, 371
Walsh, Bill, 383
Walsh, Charles, 444
Walston, Ray, 345
Walt, Marine Gen. Lew, 125
Walters, Barbara, 185, 313, 332-333, 405, 471, 474
Walton, Bill, 332
Walton, Kip, 215, 217-218, 221, 224-225, 230, 244
*Wanted Dead or Alive* (TV series), 16
Ward, Bill, 76
Ward, Clara, Singers, The, 376
Ward, Wayne, 414
Waring, Fred, 368
Warner, John, 156, 401
Warner, Malcolm Jamal, 418
Warnick, Clay, 38
Warren, Bob, 327
Warren, Marc, 411
Warren, Mark, 372
Warren, Michael, 411
Warren, Rod, 399, 407
Warwick(e), Dionne, 175-176, 195-196, 199, 234, 278, 380, 382, 388, 412-413, 421, 423, 473
Wasserman, Lew, 425-426
Waterman, Willard, 442
Watkins, Pierre, 64
Wattis, Richard, 63-64
Watts 103rd Street Rhythm Band, The, 374
Watson, Honey Boy, 49-50
*Waverly Wonders, The* (TV series), 448-449
Wayne, Frank, 371
Wayne, Fredd, 239, 244, 247
Wayne, John, 134-135, 156, 164, 179-180, 185-186, 192, 229, 255, 277, 292, 312, 331, 369, 378-380, 386, 389, 393, 395, 400, 403-404
Wayne, Johnny, 463
*Wayne and Shuster Take an Affection Look At ...* (TV series), 463
We Five, The, 16, 117
*We Got It Made* (TV series), 411
Weaver, Dennis, 378, 470
Weaver, Doodles, 172
Weaver, Sylvester "Pat," 345-346, 471
Webb, Jack, 353
Webb, Lucy, 414, 416
Webber, Andrew Lloyd, 249
*Webster* (TV series), 211, 419
Wedlock Jr., Hugh, 369, 373, 380, 385, 409

Weinberger, Ed., 165-168
Weiner, Don, 421
Weinstein, Sol, 150-151, 185-187, 189-190, 393, 414
Weis, Gary, 406
Weiskopf, Bob, 433
Weissmuller, Johnny, 154
Weitzman, Harvey, 182, 184, 399
Welch, Bob, 435
Welch, Ken, 216-217, 415
Welch, Mitzie, 217, 415
Welch, Raquel, 130, 146, 156-157, 181, 191, 197, 275-276, 338, 375, 382, 397, 405
*Welcome Back, Kotter* (TV series), 207
Weld, Tuesday, 107-109, 328
Welk, Lawrence, 81, 137, 405
Welles, Orson, 153, 393, 396, 466
Wellingtons, The, 112
Wells, Dawn, 437
Wells, Robert, 370
Wences, Senor, 354
Wendt, George, 411, 416, 452
Werber, Frank, 16
Werner, Tom, 453
West, Dottie, 226
West, Jerry, 331
West, Randy, 153
West Point Glee Club, The, 130-131, 156-157
*West Side Story* (movie), 292, 359
Westin, Avram, 472
Westmore Brothers, The, 355
Westmoreland, Gen. William, 90, 114, 166, 275,
Weston, Jack, 441
Weyman, Andrew D., 453
*What's My Line?* (game show), 324-326, 329, 468
Wheaton, Glen, 31, 42
Wheeler, Josh, 345-346
*When Television Was Young* (special), 467
*Where Have All the Children Gone* (special), 470

White, Betty, 223, 250-251, 254-255, 273, 275, 277, 403, 411, 415, 418, 420, 423, 451
White, Charles, 200
White, David, 345
White, Jesse, 107-108, 132, 439
White, Lester, xv, 31, 36, 66, 85, 87, 145, 148, 284, 328, 331-333
White, Slappy, 377, 414
White, Steve, 145, 294, 333
White, Vanna, 246, 273
*White Christmas* (movie), 392
White Jr., Al, 54
Whiting, Margaret, 47-48, 57-58
Whitmore, James, 404
Whittington, "Sweet Brother" Dick, 368
*Who's Afraid of Virginia Woolf* (movie), 291
*Who's Watching the Kids* (TV series), 449
Wickes, Mary, 39, 434-435
*Wide Wide World* (TV series), 457
Wiesen, Bernard, 447
Wilcox, Larry, 216, 410
Wilde, Cornel, 63-64
Wilder, Myles, 446
Wiles, Gordon, 369
Wilk, Max, 467
Wilkerson, Doug, 229-230
Wilkinson, Bud, 461
Willard, Fred, 376
Willenborg, Gregory J., 249
Williams, Amber, 453-454
Williams, Andy, 20, 97, 116-117, 142, 181, 191, 224, 253, 298, 336, 359-362, 372
Williams, Anson, 397
Williams, Billy, Quartet, The, 343
Williams, Cindy, 404
Williams, Doug, 189
Williams, Edy, 163
Williams, Esther, 328, 420, 461
Williams, Fred, 40
Williams, Joe, 298, 422
Williams, Mason, 415

Williams, Paul, 194, 200
Williams, Robin, 318-319, 416
Williams, Treat, 420
Williams, Vanessa, 234
Williamson, Fred, 447
Willis, Victor, 198
Wills, Chill, 381, 384
Wilson, Daniel, 313
Wilson, Don, 378, 430-431, 462
Wilson, Earl, 130, 165, 356
Wilson, Flip, 139-140, 168, 179-180, 182, 191, 232, 339, 374-375, 385, 389, 407, 468
Wilson, Lester, 416
Wilson, Gen. Louis H., 275
Wilson, Mary, 421
Wilson, Nancy, 113-114, 116, 384, 462
Wilson, Teddy, 464
Wimoness, Teddy, 72
Winchell, Paul, 325
Winfrey, Oprah, 423
Wingreen, Jason, 435, 449
*Wings* (movie), 226
Winkler, Harry, 447
Winkler, Henry, 395, 404-405, 410, 420
Winninger, Charles, 433
Winston, Ron, 441
Winters, David, 370, 374
Winters, Gloria, 73
Winters, Jonathan, 120-122, 125, 180, 216-217, 231, 244-246, 250-251, 277, 380, 383, 405, 418
Winters, Shelley, 71, 91, 216,
Winther, Jorn, 374
Wintour, George, 167
Wirt, Kathleen, 452
Wise, Anita, 274
Witnesses, The—See Butera, Sam and the Witnesses
*Wiz, The* (musical), 222
*Wizard of Oz, The* (movie), 279
Wohl, Jack, 377
Wolf, Benita, 123
Wolf, Perry, 467
Wolfe, Digby, 396
Wolper, David, 462

Wonder, Stevie, 419, 421, 423
*Wonderful World of Disney, The* (TV series), 383, 403, 405
Wood, Barry, 457
Wood, Dee Dee, 357, 361
Wood, Lana, 105
Wood, Natalie, 71, 74-75, 81, 181
Wooden, John, 179, 332
Woods, Tiger, 303
Woodward, Joanne, 358, 424
*World at War, The* (TV series), 465
"World of Bob Hope, The" (documentary), 8, 12, 21, 460
World's Fair Aquacade, The, 237
*The World's Greatest Showman: The Legend of Cecil B. DeMille* (special), 462
Worley, Jo Anne, 20, 33, 137, 157, 159, 162-163, 171, 368, 372, 376, 404
Wyatt, Jane, 418, 462
Wyle, George, 359, 361, 373
Wyman, Jane, 138-139, 328, 353-354, 469
Wynn, Bob, 183, 192, 198-199, 418
Wynn, Ed, 33, 42, 342

Xiaoping, Chinese Vice Premier Deng, 196

Yana, 63
Yankovic, Weird Al, 416
Yarwood, Mike, 241
Yeager, Chuck, 125, 254
Yeager, Steve, 152
*Yellow Rose, The* (TV series), 411
Yen, Miss Vietnam Bach, 123
Yepremian, Garo, 223
Yeston, Maury, 473
York, Francine, 440
Yorkin, Bud, 354, 356, 359
Yorty, Sam, 161
Yoshida, Peter, 474
*You'll Never Get Rich* (TV series), 34
Young, Jordan R., 7, 11
Young, Loretta, 53, 420, 429
Young, Robert, 293-294, 418

Young, Steve, 236
Young, Victor, 337
Young Americans, The, 391-392
Youngman, Henny, 6, 184, 405, 416
*Your Hit Parade* (TV series), 294
*Your Hollywood Parade* (radio series), 3
*Your Show of Shows* (TV series), 10, 343
*You're In the Picture* (game show), 328
Youth Band Council of Southern California, The, 354

Zellman, Shelly, 392
*Zenith Presents a Salute to Television's 25th Anniversary* (special), 293
*Ziegfeld Follies of 1936* (Broadway revue), 3
Ziegler, Ted, 394
Zimbalist, Stephanie, 411
Zimmerman, Harry, 370, 373
Zmuda, Bob, 416
*Zoo Parade* (TV series), 343, 398
Zousmer, Jesse, 457, 460
Zuckert, Bill, 163, 178
Zuckert, Secretary of the Air Force Eugene, 100
Zukor, Adolph, 291, 345-346
Zweibel, Alan, 416

www.ingramcontent.com/pod-product-compliance
Lightning Source LLC
Chambersburg PA
CBHW060310230426
43663CB00009B/1657